Lecture Notes in Computer Science   14498

The series Lecture Notes in Computer Science (LNCS), including its subseries Lecture Notes in Artificial Intelligence (LNAI) and Lecture Notes in Bioinformatics (LNBI), has established itself as a medium for the publication of new developments in computer science and information technology research, teaching, and education.

LNCS enjoys close cooperation with the computer science R & D community, the series counts many renowned academics among its volume editors and paper authors, and collaborates with prestigious societies. Its mission is to serve this international community by providing an invaluable service, mainly focused on the publication of conference and workshop proceedings and postproceedings. LNCS commenced publication in 1973.

Bin Sheng · Lei Bi · Jinman Kim ·
Nadia Magnenat-Thalmann · Daniel Thalmann
Editors

Advances in
Computer Graphics

40th Computer Graphics International Conference, CGI 2023
Shanghai, China, August 28 – September 1, 2023
Proceedings, Part IV

Springer

Editors
Bin Sheng ⓘ
Shanghai Jiao Tong University
Shanghai, China

Jinman Kim ⓘ
University of Sydney
Sydney, NSW, Australia

Daniel Thalmann
Swiss Federal Institute of Technology
Lausanne, Switzerland

Lei Bi ⓘ
Shanghai Jiao Tong University
Shanghai, China

Nadia Magnenat-Thalmann ⓘ
MIRALab-CUI
University of Geneve
Carouge, Geneve, Switzerland

ISSN 0302-9743   ISSN 1611-3349 (electronic)
Lecture Notes in Computer Science
ISBN 978-3-031-50077-0   ISBN 978-3-031-50078-7 (eBook)
https://doi.org/10.1007/978-3-031-50078-7

This Springer imprint is published by the registered company Springer Nature Switzerland AG
The registered company address is: Gewerbestrasse 11, 6330 Cham, Switzerland

Paper in this product is recyclable.

Preface Lecture Notes in Computer Science (14498)

CGI is one of the oldest annual international conferences on Computer Graphics in the world. Researchers are invited to share their experiences and novel achievements in various fields of Computer Graphics and Virtual Reality. Previous recent CGI conferences have been held in Sydney, Australia (2014), Strasbourg, France (2015), Heraklion, Greece (2016), Yokohama, Japan (2017), Bintan, Indonesia (2018), and Calgary in Canada (2019). CGI was virtual between 2020 and 2022 due to the COVID pandemic. This year, CGI 2023 was organized by the Shanghai Jiao Tong University, with the assistance of the University of Sydney and Wuhan Textile University, and supported by the Computer Graphics Society (CGS). The conference was held during August 28 to September 1, 2023.

These CGI 2023 LNCS proceedings are composed of 149 papers from a total of 385 submissions. This includes 51 papers that were reviewed highly and were recommended to be published in the CGI Visual Computer Journal track. To ensure the high quality of the publications, each paper was reviewed by at least two experts in the field and authors of accepted papers were asked to revise their paper according to the review comments prior to publication.

The CGI 2023 LNCS proceedings also include papers from the ENGAGE (Empowering Novel Geometric Algebra for Graphics & Engineering) 2023 Workshop (11 full papers), focused specifically on important aspects of geometric algebra including surface construction, robotics, encryption, qubits and expression optimization. The workshop has been part of the CGI conferences since 2016.

We would like to express our deepest gratitude to all the PC members and external reviewers who provided timely high-quality reviews. We would also like to thank all the authors for contributing to the conference by submitting their work.

September 2023

Bin Sheng
Lei Bi
Jinman Kim
Nadia Magnenat-Thalmann
Daniel Thalmann

Organization

Honorary Conference Chairs

Enhua Wu — Chinese Academy of Sciences/University of Macau, China

Dagan Feng — University of Sydney, Australia

Conference Chairs

Nadia Magnenat Thalmann — University of Geneva, Switzerland

Bin Sheng — Shanghai Jiao Tong University, China

Jinman Kim — University of Sydney, Australia

Program Chairs

Daniel Thalmann — École Polytechnique Fédérale de Lausanne, Switzerland

Stephen Lin — Microsoft Research Asia, China

Lizhuang Ma — Shanghai Jiao Tong University, China

Ping Li — Hong Kong Polytechnic University, China

Contents – Part IV

Image Analysis and Visualization in Advanced Medical Imaging Technology

Empowering Novel Geometric Algebra for Graphics and Engineering Workshop

Theoretical Analysis

An Efficient Algorithm for Degree Reduction of MD-Splines

Zushang Xiao and Wanqiang Shen[✉]

School of Science, Jiangnan University, Wuxi 214122, Jiangsu, China
wq_shen@163.com

Abstract. This paper analyzes the computational time complexity of the previously proposed methods for constructing dual basis functions. It presents a method that employs discrete numerical summation for computing the integral of a polynomial, enabling rapid calculation of the inner product of two polynomial functions. Building on this approach, an algorithm is obtained to address the degree reduction problem for MD-spline curves. It efficiently computes the control points after degree reduction, ensuring the least square approximation.

Keywords: B-splines · MD-splines · Degree reduction · Dual bases · Least square approximation

1 Introduction

Curve and surface degree reduction is crucial for product data exchange and compression, leading to cost reduction in data storage and transmission [1–3]. An algorithm for B-spline curve degree reduction is proposed in [4], using a constrained optimization approach to minimize the distance between high-degree and reduced-degree B-spline curves [5,6]. Reference [7] introduces a simpler and more intuitive method based on NURBS curves' local control property.

The dual basis of spline functions is essential in least square approximation, and several studies have explored the dual Bernstein polynomials [8–10], dual polynomial bases [11], and dual B-spline functional [12]. Dual Wang-Bézier and Bézier-Said-Wang type generalized Ball polynomials are investigated in [13–15], while [16] presents the study of the dual NS power basis. Space extension methods, introduced in [17], are employed for constructing the dual basis. These methods, particularly emphasized in [18] for their improved computational efficiency, are subsequently applied to the dual basis for generalized B-splines in [19].

MD-splines, allowing different degrees within intervals, extend B-splines [20]. Various studies propose polynomial functions with variable degrees for shape-preserving interpolation [21,22]. The concept of MD-splines is introduced in [23], and two types of MD-splines with different continuities are defined in [20,24]. [25]

Supported by the National Natural Science Foundation of China (Grant No. 61772013).

provides an explicit expression for MD-splines, and [26] explores the property of degree elevation. The definition of MD-splines is improved in [27] for creating MD-splines with arbitrary continuity.

Numerical algorithms are proposed for MD-splines due to inefficiency in integration-based definitions. They use simpler basis functions to compute the representation matrix [28]. Chebyshev extension of this construction is presented in [30], and the algorithm in [31] computes the transition matrix through reverse knot insertion (RKI). Various improved algorithm versions are outlined in [32], and recursive methods are provided in [33,34] to compute the representation matrix between MD-spline basis functions and Bernstein basis functions.

Degree reduction for B-splines requires each segment to maintain the same degree after reduction [1]. In contrast, MD-splines to MD-splines degree reduction allows local segment degree reduction and greater flexibility. The dual basis of MD-spline functions can be used for least square approximation of MD-spline curves in a lower-dimensional space. However, existing methods for constructing the dual basis involve computing integrals, which lack efficiency [35]. In this paper, we propose to optimize the degree reduction algorithm by directly discretely calculating the integral of the product of basis functions using the linear representation coefficients of MD-spline's Bernstein basis functions [36], leveraging the integral properties of Bernstein basis functions.

2 Review

Given a breakpoint sequence $\boldsymbol{Y} := \{x_i\}_{i=1}^{q}$ on $[a, b]$, a degree vector $\boldsymbol{D} := (d_0, d_1, \cdots, d_q)$, and a continuity vector $\boldsymbol{K} := (k_1, k_2, \cdots, k_q)$ with $a \equiv x_0 < x_1 < \cdots < x_q < x_{q+1} \equiv b$ and $0 \le k_i \le \min(d_{i-1}, d_i)$, $i = 1, \cdots, q$., two knot sequences $\boldsymbol{\mu}$ and $\boldsymbol{\lambda}$ are $\boldsymbol{\mu} := \{\mu_j\}_{j=1}^{V} = \{\underbrace{a, \cdots, a}_{d_0+1 \text{ times}}, \underbrace{x_1, \cdots, x_1}_{d_1-k_1 \text{ times}}, \cdots, \underbrace{x_q, \cdots, x_q}_{d_q-k_q \text{ times}}\}$,

and $\boldsymbol{\lambda} := \{\lambda_j\}_{j=1}^{V} = \{\underbrace{x_1, \cdots, x_1}_{d_0-k_1 \text{ times}}, \cdots, \underbrace{x_q, \cdots, x_q}_{d_{q-1}-k_q \text{ times}}, \underbrace{b, \cdots, b}_{d_q+1 \text{ times}}\}$, where $V := d_0 + 1 + \sum_{i=1}^{q}(d_i - k_i)$ is the dimension of the MD-spline space, denoted as $\mathcal{S}(\boldsymbol{Y}, \boldsymbol{D}, \boldsymbol{K})$ [23,27]. Let $m := \max\{d_0, \cdots, d_q\}$. The MD-spline basis functions $\{N_{i,m}(x)\}_{i=1}^{V}$ are recursively generated from the function sequence $N_{i,n}(x)$ on each non-empty interval $[x_j, x_{j+1}) \subseteq [\mu_i, \lambda_{i-m+n})$ with $n = 0, 1, \cdots, m$ by

$$N_{i,n}(x) := \begin{cases} 1, & n = m - d_j, \\ \dfrac{\int_{-\infty}^{x} N_{i,n-1}(u)du}{\int_{-\infty}^{+\infty} N_{i,n-1}(x)dx} - \dfrac{\int_{-\infty}^{x} N_{i+1,n-1}(u)du}{\int_{-\infty}^{+\infty} N_{i+1,n-1}(x)dx}, & n > m - d_j, \\ 0, & \text{otherwise.} \end{cases} \quad (1)$$

If the function $N_{i,n}(x)$ is zero, then $\int_{-\infty}^{x} \delta_{i,n} N_{i,n}(u)du := \begin{cases} 0, & x < \mu_i, \\ 1, & x \ge \mu_i. \end{cases}$

Like the B-splines, $\{N_{i,m}(x)\}_{i=1}^{V}$ have the following properties [27].

(i) Positivity and local support: Each $N_{i,m}(x) = \begin{cases} > 0, & \text{for } x \in (\mu_i, \lambda_i), \\ = 0, & \text{for } x \notin [\mu_i, \lambda_i]; \end{cases}$

(ii) End point: Each $N_{i,m}(x)$ vanishes exactly $d_{p\mu_i} - \max\{j \geq 0 | \mu_i = \mu_{i+j}\}$ times at μ_i and $d_{p\lambda_i - 1} - \max\{j \geq 0 | \lambda_{i-j} = \lambda_i\}$ times at λ_i, where $p\mu_i$ and $p\lambda_i$ are s.t. $x_{p\mu_i} = \mu_i$ and $x_{p\lambda_i} = \lambda_i$;

(iii) Degree and continuity: Each $N_{i,m}$ is d_j-degree polynomial on $x \in [x_j, x_{j+1})$ and is C^{k_h} continuity at x_h for $h = \max\{p\mu_i, 1\}, \cdots, \min\{p\lambda_i, q\}$;

(iv) Partition of unity : $\sum_{i=1}^{V} N_{i,m}(x) \equiv 1, \forall x \in [a, b]$;

(v) B-spline subcase : If $d_0 = \cdots = d_q$, then $\{N_{i,m}(x)\}_{i=1}^{V}$ is the B-spline basis.

The MD-spline curve defined is given by $\boldsymbol{P}(x) = \sum_{i=1}^{V} N_{i,m}(x)\boldsymbol{P}_i, x \in [a, b]$, where $\boldsymbol{P}_1, \boldsymbol{P}_2, \cdots, \boldsymbol{P}_V$ are control points. MD-spline curves and B-spline curves share many similar properties, including convex hull property, geometric invariance property, degree property, and local control property.

Let $l_j := \begin{cases} 1, & j = 0, \\ 1 + \sum_{t=1}^{j}(d_{t-1} - k_t), & 1 \leq j \leq q. \end{cases}$ Then the curve on $[x_j, x_{j+1})$ is $\boldsymbol{P}(x) = \sum_{h=0}^{d_j} N_{l_j+h,m}(x)\boldsymbol{P}_{l_j+h}$. Every $N_{i,m}(x)$ on each interval $[x_j, x_{j+1}) \subseteq [\mu_i, \lambda_i)$ can be linearly represented by Bernstein basis of degree d_j as $N_{i,m}(x) = \sum_{k=0}^{d_j} B_{k,d_j,j}(x)\boldsymbol{M}_{i,j}(k)$, $B_{k,d_j,j}(x) = \binom{d_j}{k}\left(\frac{x_{j+1}-x}{x_{j+1}-x_j}\right)^{d_j-k}\left(\frac{x-x_j}{x_{j+1}-x_j}\right)^k$. where $\boldsymbol{M}_{i,j}$ is the coefficient vector. The vector $\boldsymbol{M}_{i,j}$ is associated with the right derivatives of $N_{i,m}(x)$ at x_j as $N_{i,m}^{(k)}(x_j+) = \frac{d_j!}{(d_j-k)!(x_{j+1}-x_j)^k}\sum_{p=0}^{k}(-1)^p\binom{k}{p}\boldsymbol{M}_{i,j}(p)$. The Bernstein basis functions have integral properties $\int_{x_j}^{x_{j+1}} B_{k,d_j,j}(x)dx = \frac{x_{j+1}-x_j}{d_j+1}$, $k = 0, 1, \cdots, d_j$.

Let $\mathcal{N}_V := \{N_1, \cdots, N_V\}$ be a set consisting of V linearly independent functions [17,18]. Let the linear space $\Gamma_V := \text{span } \mathcal{N}_V$ with an inner product $\langle \cdot, \cdot \rangle : \Gamma_V \times \Gamma_V \to \mathbb{C}$. The dual basis of $\mathcal{N}_V$ with respect to $\langle \cdot, \cdot \rangle$, noted as $\mathcal{D}_V := \{D_1, \cdots, D_V\}$, satisfies $\text{span } \mathcal{D}_V = \Gamma_V, \langle N_i, D_j \rangle = \delta_{ij}$ $(1 \leq i, j \leq V)$, where δ_{ij} is the Kronecker symbol, which is equal to 1 when $i = j$ and 0 otherwise. Additionally, given any function f, its least square approximation in Γ_V can be expressed as $g^* := \sum_{i=1}^{V} p_i N_i$, where $p_i := \langle f, D_i \rangle$. That is, $\|f - g^*\| = \min_{g \in \Gamma_V} \|f - g\|$, where $\|\cdot\| := \sqrt{\langle \cdot, \cdot \rangle}$.

3 Degree Reduction of Multi-degree Splines

3.1 Construction of the Dual Basis

Let $N_j = \sum_{i=1}^{V} h_{ij}D_i$. From the properties of dual basis, we have $h_{ij} = \langle N_i, N_j \rangle$. Assuming that $\boldsymbol{H}(\mathcal{N}_V, \langle \cdot, \cdot \rangle) := (h_{ij})_{V \times V}$, there exists

$$[D_1, D_2, \cdots, D_V]^{\text{T}} = \boldsymbol{H}(\mathcal{N}_V, \langle \cdot, \cdot \rangle)^{-1}[N_1, N_2, \cdots, N_V]^{\text{T}}, \quad (2)$$

In Table 1, the number of computational operations required for computing the algorithm in [18] and the dual basis using (2) is tabulated separately. The table indicates that while the algorithm in [18] for constructing dual bases reduce the number of arithmetic operations, it increases the number of inner product computations. Moreover, the actual number of arithmetic operations for a single inner product computation will not be less than V. In fact, consider the commonly used discrete inner product $\langle N_i(x), N_j(x) \rangle_G := \sum_{h=0}^{G} N_i \left(a + \frac{b-a}{G} h \right) N_j \left(a + \frac{b-a}{G} h \right)$ on $[a, b]$ and $G \geq V - 1$. Here, G cannot be smaller than $V - 1$, because even if we use a vector over a field to describe a basis function of a V-dimensional space, if it is not a vector of dimension greater than V, it cannot form a V-dimensional linear space. Therefore, the actual number of arithmetic operations for the algorithm in [18] will not be less than $3V^3 - V^2$, while computing the inner product using Eq. (2) will not be less than $2V^3 + \frac{V^2}{2}$. It is evident that the number of arithmetic operations for constructing the dual basis of basis functions primarily depends on the complexity of inner product calculations. The more inner product computations, the more arithmetic operations are required.

Table 1. Comparison of Operation Count for the Dual Basis Construction Algorithms.

Operations	In [18]	In This Paper
Arithmetic Operations	$(3V^2 - V)/2$	V^3
Function Inner Product	$(3V^2 - V)/2$	$(V^2 + V)/2$
Function Scalar Multiplication	V^2	V^2
Function Addition	$V^2 - V$	$V^2 - V$

Therefore, in terms of computation, using Eq. (2) takes an advantage of constructing the dual basis.

Theorem 1. *The least square approximation of f in the space Γ_V is given by*

$$g^* = \begin{bmatrix} N_1 & N_2 & \cdots & N_V \end{bmatrix} \boldsymbol{H}(\mathcal{N}_V, \langle \cdot, \cdot \rangle)^{-1} \left[\langle N_1, f \rangle, \langle N_2, f \rangle, \cdots, \langle N_V, f \rangle \right]^T.$$

Proof. Based on the property of least square approximation by the dual basis and relationship (2), the result are obtained.

3.2   Degree Reduction Algorithm for MD-Splines

After degree reduction, note that the degree and continuity vectors are $\widehat{\boldsymbol{D}}$ and $\widehat{\boldsymbol{K}}$ with each $\widehat{d}_i \leq d_i$ and each $\widehat{k}_i := \begin{cases} k_i, & k_i \leq \min\{\widehat{d}_{i-1}, \widehat{d}_i\}, \\ \min\{\widehat{d}_{i-1}, \widehat{d}_i\}, & k_i > \min\{\widehat{d}_{i-1}, \widehat{d}_i\}. \end{cases}$ The breakpoint sequence $\widehat{\boldsymbol{Y}} := \boldsymbol{Y}$, the space $\widehat{\mathcal{S}}(\widehat{\boldsymbol{Y}}, \widehat{\boldsymbol{D}}, \widehat{\boldsymbol{K}})$ with dimension $\widehat{V} := \widehat{d}_0 + 1 + \sum_{i=1}^{q} (\widehat{d}_i - \widehat{k}_i)$, the maximum degree $\widehat{m} := \max\{\widehat{d}_0, \widehat{d}_1, \cdots, \widehat{d}_q\}$, the MD-spline basis is $\{\widehat{N}_{i,\widehat{m}}(x)\}_{i=1}^{\widehat{V}}$, and the curve $\widehat{\boldsymbol{P}}(x) = \sum_{i=1}^{\widehat{V}} \widehat{N}_{i,\widehat{m}}(x) \widehat{\boldsymbol{P}}_i, x \in [a, b]$,

---

Algorithm 1. Degree reduction for MD-splines

Input: $Y, D, K, \widehat{D}, P_i, i = 1, 2, \cdots, V.$ **Output:** $\widehat{K}, \widehat{P}_i, i = 1, 2, \cdots, \widehat{V}.$

1: **for** $i \leftarrow 1$ to q **do**
2:     **if** $k_i \leq \min\{\widehat{d}_{i-1}, \widehat{d}_i\}$ **then** $\widehat{k}_i = k_i$;
3:     **else** $\widehat{k}_i = \min\{\widehat{d}_{i-1}, \widehat{d}_i\}$;
4:     **end if**
5: **end for**
6: **for** $i \leftarrow 1$ to $\widehat{V}$ **do**
7:     **for** $k \leftarrow i$ to $\widehat{V}$ **do** $T_{i,k} \leftarrow \langle \widehat{N}_{i,\widehat{m}}, \widehat{N}_{k,\widehat{m}} \rangle$;
8:         **if** $k \neq i$ **then** $T_{k,i} \leftarrow T_{i,k}$;
9:         **end if**
10:     **end for**
11: **end for**
12: **for** $i \leftarrow 1$ to $\widehat{V}$ **do** $F_i \leftarrow \langle \widehat{N}_{i,\widehat{m}}(x), P(x) \rangle$;
13: **end for**
14: **for** $i \leftarrow 1$ to $\widehat{V}$ **do** $\widehat{P}_i \leftarrow \sum_{j=1}^{\widehat{V}} T_{i,j}^{-1} F_j$;
15: **end for**

---

where $\widehat{P}_1, \cdots, \widehat{P}_{\widehat{V}}$ are the control points. To find the curve $\widehat{P}(x)$, which is the least square approximation of $P(x)$, we design Algorithm 1 to calculate $\widehat{K}$ and $\{\widehat{P}\}_{i=0}^{\widehat{V}}$.

According to Algorithm 1, the degree reduction of MD-spline curves can be performed using $\langle \cdot, \cdot \rangle_G$. The advantage of this method is its high efficiency. But the issue with $\langle \cdot, \cdot \rangle_G$ is that it cannot accurately characterize the basis functions. In other words, using the discrete inner product may not yield the least square approximation. Without considering computational errors, increasing the value of G will bring the results closer to the desired outcome. However, considering both computational errors and costs, a larger value of G may lead to increased errors and computational costs. Determining the appropriate value of G to achieve the desired results is a complex problem.

The integral inner product is defined as $\langle N_i(x), N_j(x) \rangle_T := \int_a^b N_i(x) N_j(x) dx$. It accurately characterizes the basis functions to obtain the desired least square approximation, but its integral computation very challenging.

3.3   Simple Method to Compute Inner Product $\langle \cdot, \cdot \rangle_T$ of Polynomials

Let $f(x) := \sum_{i=0}^{d_f} M_f(i) B_{i,d_f,j}(x), g(x) := \sum_{k=0}^{d_g} M_g(k) B_{k,d_g,j}(x)$, where d_f and d_g represent the degree of $f(x)$ and $g(x)$, respectively, and $B_{i,d,j}(x)$ denotes the $(i+1)$th Bernstein basis function of degree d over the interval $[x_j, x_{j+1})$, and $M_f(i)$ and $M_g(k)$ are the $i + 1$th and $k + 1$th values of the coefficient vectors representing $f(x)$ and $g(x)$, respectively.

Theorem 2. *On the interval* $[x_j, x_{j+1})$, *there exists*

$$\int_{x_j}^{x_{j+1}} fg = \frac{x_{j+1} - x_j}{d_f + d_g + 1} \sum_{h=0}^{d_f+d_g} \binom{d_f+d_g}{h}^{-1} \sum_{i=\max\{h-d_g, 0\}}^{\min\{d_f, h\}} M_f(i) M_g(h-i) \binom{d_f}{i} \binom{d_g}{h-i}.$$

Proof. $\int_{x_j}^{x_{j+1}} fg = \int_{x_j}^{x_{j+1}} \sum_{i=0}^{d_f} M_f(i) B_{i,d_f,j}(x) \sum_{k=0}^{d_g} M_g(k) B_{k,d_g,j}(x) dx$

$= \int_{x_j}^{x_{j+1}} \sum_{i=0}^{d_f} \sum_{k=0}^{d_g} M_f(i) M_g(k) \binom{d_f}{i}\binom{d_g}{k} \left(\frac{x_{j+1}-x}{x_{j+1}-x_j}\right)^{d_f+d_g-(i+k)} \left(\frac{x-x_j}{x_{j+1}-x_j}\right)^{i+k}$

$= \int_{x_j}^{x_{j+1}} \sum_{h=0}^{d_f+d_g} \sum_{i=max\{h-d_g,0\}}^{min\{d_f,h\}} M_f(i) M_g(h-i) \frac{\binom{d_f}{i}\binom{d_g}{h-i}}{\binom{d_f+d_g}{h}} B_{h,d_f+d_g,j}(x) dx$

$=$

$\sum_{h=0}^{d_f+d_g} \binom{d_f+d_g}{h}^{-1} \sum_{i=max\{h-d_g,0\}}^{min\{d_f,h\}} M_f(i) M_g(h-i) \binom{d_f}{i}\binom{d_g}{h-i} \int_{x_j}^{x_{j+1}} B_{h,d_f+d_g,j}.$

To facilitate the computation of inner products, we store the binomial coefficients in a matrix C such that $C_{k,i} := \binom{k}{i}$. We store the integrals of Bernstein basis functions in a matrix L such that $\forall i = 0, \cdots, k, L_j := \int_{x_j}^{x_{j+1}} B_{i,d_f+d_g,j}(x) dx = \frac{x_{j+1}-x_j}{d_f + d_g + 1}$. Algorithm 2 can compute the integration of the product of two polynomials over the interval $[x_j, x_{j+1})$. Consider the inner products between the basis functions after degree reduction and the inner products between the basis functions and the original curve.

Algorithm 2. Integrating the product of two polynomials on $[x_j, x_{j+1})$

Input: C, L_j, M_f, M_g. **Output:** $I := \int_{x_j}^{x_{j+1}} f(x)g(x)dx.$

1: **function** CALCULATEBERNSTEININT(M_f, M_g, C, L_j)
2:     $I \leftarrow 0$;
3:     **for** $h \leftarrow 0$ to $d_f + d_g$ **do** $I_1 \leftarrow 0$;
4:         **for** $s \leftarrow max\{h - d_g, 0\}$ to $min\{d_f, h\}$ **do**
5:             $I_1 \leftarrow I_1 + M_f(s)M_g(h-s)C_{d_f,s}C_{d_g,h-s}$;
6:         **end for**
7:         $I \leftarrow I + I_1/C_{d_f+d_g,h}$;
8:     **end for**
9:     $I \leftarrow L_j I$;
10:    **return** I;

According to the properties of the inner product, let's assume $i \leq k$. Based on the local support property of MD-splines, we can obtain the inner product as follows $\langle \widehat{N}_{i,\widehat{m}}(x), \widehat{N}_{k,\widehat{m}}(x) \rangle_T = \int_{\widehat{\mu}_k}^{\widehat{\lambda}_i} \widehat{N}_{i,\widehat{m}}(x) \widehat{N}_{k,\widehat{m}}(x) dx$. If $\widehat{\lambda}_i \leq \widehat{\mu}_k$, then $\langle \widehat{N}_{i,\widehat{m}}(x), \widehat{N}_{k,\widehat{m}}(x) \rangle_T = 0$. Otherwise, according to Theorem 2, we have

$\langle \widehat{N}_{i,\widehat{m}}(x), \widehat{N}_{k,\widehat{m}}(x) \rangle_T = \sum_{j=p\widehat{\mu}_k}^{p\widehat{\lambda}_i-1} \int_{x_j}^{x_{j+1}} \widehat{N}_{i,\widehat{m}}(x) \widehat{N}_{k,\widehat{m}}(x) dx$

$= \sum_{j=p\widehat{\mu}_k}^{p\widehat{\lambda}_i-1} \frac{x_{j+1}-x_j}{2\widehat{d}_j+1} \sum_{h=0}^{2\widehat{d}_j} \binom{2\widehat{d}_j}{h}^{-1} \sum_{s=max\{h-\widehat{d}_j,0\}}^{min\{\widehat{d}_j,h\}} \widehat{M}_{i,j}(s) \widehat{M}_{k,j}(h-s) \binom{\widehat{d}_j}{s}\binom{\widehat{d}_j}{h-s}$,

where $p\widehat{\mu}_i$ and $p\widehat{\lambda}_i$ are such that $x_{p\widehat{\mu}_i} = \widehat{\mu}_i$ and $x_{p\widehat{\lambda}_i} = \widehat{\lambda}_i$, $\widehat{M}_{i,j}$ and $\widehat{M}_{k,j}$ represent column vectors formed by the Bernstein basis representation coefficients of the basis functions $\widehat{N}_{i,\widehat{m}}(x)$ and $\widehat{N}_{k,\widehat{m}}(x)$, respectively, on $[x_j, x_{j+1})$. Assume

$\boldsymbol{P}(x) = \begin{bmatrix} N_{l_j,m}(x) \cdots N_{l_j+d_j,m}(x) \end{bmatrix} \begin{bmatrix} \boldsymbol{P}_{l_j}, \cdots, \boldsymbol{P}_{l_j+d_j} \end{bmatrix}^T$

$= \begin{bmatrix} B_{0,d_j,j}(x) \cdots B_{d_j,d_j,j}(x) \end{bmatrix} \begin{bmatrix} \boldsymbol{M}_{l_j,j}, \cdots, \boldsymbol{M}_{l_j+d_j,j} \end{bmatrix} \begin{bmatrix} \boldsymbol{P}_{l_j}, \cdots, \boldsymbol{P}_{l_j+d_j} \end{bmatrix}^T.$

$$\langle \widehat{N}_{i,\widehat{m}}(x), \boldsymbol{P}(x)\rangle_T = \int_{\widehat{\mu}_i}^{\widehat{\lambda}_i} \widehat{N}_{i,\widehat{m}}(x)\boldsymbol{P}(x)dx = \sum_{j=p\widehat{\mu}_i}^{p\widehat{\lambda}_i-1}\int_{x_j}^{x_{j+1}} \widehat{N}_{i,\widehat{m}}(x)\boldsymbol{P}(x)dx$$

$$= \sum_{j=p\widehat{\mu}_i}^{p\widehat{\lambda}_i-1} \frac{x_{j+1}-x_j}{\widehat{d}_j+d_j+1} \sum_{h=0}^{\widehat{d}_j+d_j} \frac{1}{\binom{\widehat{d}_j+d_j}{h}} \sum_{k=max\{h-d_j,0\}}^{min\{\widehat{d}_j,h\}} \binom{\widehat{d}_j}{k}\binom{d_j}{h-k}\widehat{\boldsymbol{M}}_{i,j}(k)$$

$$\times \sum_{t=0}^{d_j} \boldsymbol{M}_{l_j+t,j}(h-k)\boldsymbol{P}_{l_j+t}.$$

We can obtain the Algorithm 3 based on Theorem 1.

Algorithm 3. Degree Reduction of MD-Spline the Inner Product $\langle\cdot,\cdot\rangle_T$:

Input: $\boldsymbol{Y},\boldsymbol{D},\boldsymbol{K},\widehat{\boldsymbol{D}},\boldsymbol{P}_i, i=1,2,\cdots,V$. **Output:** $\widehat{\boldsymbol{K}},\widehat{\boldsymbol{P}}_i, i=1,2,\cdots,\widehat{V}$.
1: Perform $1-5$ Row of the Algorithm 1;
2: $\boldsymbol{M} \leftarrow$ BernsteinRepresentationCalculate$(\boldsymbol{Y},\boldsymbol{D},\boldsymbol{K})$;
3: $\widehat{\boldsymbol{M}} \leftarrow$ BernsteinRepresentationCalculate$(\widehat{\boldsymbol{Y}},\widehat{\boldsymbol{D}},\widehat{\boldsymbol{K}})$;
4: **for** $j\leftarrow 0$ to q **do** $\boldsymbol{U}_j \leftarrow \sum_{i=0}^{d_j}\boldsymbol{M}_{l_j+i,j}\boldsymbol{P}_{l_j+i}$;
5: **end for**
6: $m \leftarrow$max$\{\boldsymbol{D}\}, C \leftarrow \boldsymbol{0}_{2m\times(2m+1)}, L \leftarrow \boldsymbol{0}_{2\times(q+1)}$;
7: **for** $j\leftarrow 0$ to q **do**
8:     **for** k in $\{d_j,\widehat{d}_j,2\widehat{d}_j,\widehat{d}_j+d_j\}$ **do**
9:         **if** $C_{k,0}=0$ **then**
10:             **for** $i\leftarrow 0$ to $[k/2]$ **do** $C_{k,i} \leftarrow \binom{k}{i}$; $C_{k,k-i} \leftarrow C_{k,i}$;
11:             **end for**
12:         **end if**
13:     **end for**
14: **end for**
15: **for** $j\leftarrow 0$ to q **do** $L_{0,j} \leftarrow (x_{j+1}-x_j)/(2\widehat{d}_j+1)$; $L_{1,j} \leftarrow (x_{j+1}-x_j)/(\widehat{d}_j+d_j+1)$;
16: **end for**
17: $T \leftarrow \boldsymbol{0}_{\widehat{V}\times\widehat{V}}$;
18: **for** $i\leftarrow 1$ to $\widehat{V}$ **do**
19:     **for** $k\leftarrow i$ to $\widehat{V}$ **do**
20:         **if** $\widehat{\lambda}_i > \widehat{\mu}_k$ **then**
21:             **for** $j\leftarrow p\widehat{\mu}_k$ to $p\widehat{\lambda}_i-1$ **do**
22:                 $T_{i,k} \leftarrow T_{i,k}+$ CalculateBernsteinInt$(\widehat{\boldsymbol{M}}_{i,j}, \widehat{\boldsymbol{M}}_{k,j}, C, L_{0,j})$;
23:             **end for**
24:             **if** $k\neq i$ **then** $T_{k,i} \leftarrow T_{i,k}$;
25:         **end if**
26:     **end if**
27:     **end for**
28: **end for**
29: **for** $i\leftarrow 1$ to $\widehat{V}$ **do**
30:     **for** $j\leftarrow p\widehat{\mu}_i$ to $p\widehat{\lambda}_i-1$ **do** $F_i \leftarrow F_i+$CalculateBernsteinInt $(\widehat{\boldsymbol{M}}_{i,j}, \boldsymbol{U}_j, C, L_{1,j})$;
31:     **end for**
32: **end for**
33: Perform $14-15$ Row of the Algorithm 1;

---

4   Other Applications

When $d_0 = d_1 = \cdots = d_q$, the MD-splines degenerate into traditional B-splines. Therefore, the algorithm proposed in this paper can be used to reduce the degree of traditional B-splines. Based on the idea of progressive iteration approxima- tion [38, 39], using MD-splines to approximate a set of discrete points can help us quickly achieve curve modeling with MD-splines, which is a common modeling technique. For any given ordered sequence of points $Q := \{q_i\}_{i=1}^s$, we consider using MD-splines in the space $\mathcal{S}(Y, D, K)$ to perform a least square approxima- tion. Our approach is to discretize the basis functions in the space $\mathcal{S}(Y, D, K)$ into s-dimensional vectors in the number field. As mentioned before, the dimen- sion of the discretized basis function vectors should not be smaller than the total dimension V of the original space, i.e., $s \geq V$. First, each point q_i in Q is assigned a parameter value t_i, such that $a = t_1 < t_2 < \cdots < t_{s-1} < t_s = b$. Then, the inner product is defined as $\langle N_{k,m}(x), Q \rangle_S := \sum_{i=1}^s N_{k,m}(t_i) q_i, (1 \leq k, j \leq V), \langle N_{k,m}(x), N_{j,m}(x) \rangle_S := \sum_{i=1}^s N_{k,m}(t_i) N_{j,m}(t_i)$. Finally, according to Theorem 1, the control vertices of the MD-spline curve that provides the least square approximation are given by

$$[P_1, \cdots, P_V]^T = H(\mathcal{N}_V, \langle \cdot, \cdot \rangle_S)^{-1} [\langle N_{1,m}(x), Q \rangle_S, \cdots, \langle N_{V,m}(x), Q \rangle_S]^T.$$

5   Examples and Numerical Experiments

5.1   Degree Reduction Examples

Using the cumulative arc length parameterization method, assign correspond- ing parameters $\{t_i\}_{i=1}^s$ to a given ordered set of points $Q := \{q_i\}_{i=1}^s$, which $t_1 = a$, $t_s = b$, for $i = 2, 3, \cdots, s - 1, t_i = t_{i-1} + \frac{\|q_i - q_{i-1}\|}{\sum_{j=2}^s \|q_j - q_{j-1}\|}$. The values of the discrete points are shown in Fig. 1(a). Setting the MD-spline space as $Y = \{0, 3, 9, 14, 19, 23, 25, 27, 31, 36, 41, 47, 50\}$, $D = (4, 4, 5, 6, 6, 4, 4, 6, 6, 5, 4, 4)$, $K = (0, 2, 1, 3, 0, 1, 0, 3, 1, 2, 0)$, the shaped MD- spline curve is shown in Fig. 1(b).

Using Algorithm 3, the tree curve is reduced in degree. The vector represent- ing the reduced degree is set as $\widehat{D} = (4, 4, 4, 4, 4, 4, 4, 4, 4, 4, 4)$. The result of the degree reduction is shown in Fig. 1(c). The curve becomes a traditional B- spline curve. Considering further reducing the traditional B-spline, the reduced degree is $\widetilde{D} := (3, 3, 3, 3, 3, 3, 3, 3, 3, 3, 3, 3)$. Using Algorithm 3, the result of the degree reduction is shown in Fig. 1(d). This completes the degree reduction of the traditional B-spline curve.

5.2   Comparison of Our Algorithm with Other Methods

The MD-spline spaces for four degree reduction test experiments and the target degrees to which they need to be reduced are shown in Table 2.

The experimental environment used for these computations is Matlab 2016a. Algorithm 3 is used to perform degree reduction on these four experiments, as

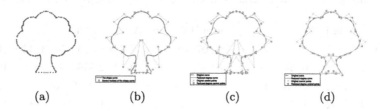

Fig. 1. Degree reduction of fitted MD-spline. (a) Data point. (b) Fitted MD-spline. (c) Degree reduction to B-spline of degree 4. (d) Degree reduction to B-spline of degree 3.

Table 2. Test Experiment Setup.

	Y	D	K	$\widehat{D}$
Test1	$\{0, 2, 4, 7, 9, 11\}$	$(7, 4, 7, 6, 5)$	$(1, 2, 3, 1)$	$(4, 4, 3, 5, 3)$
Test2	$\{0, 2, 5, 10\}$	$(15, 3, 15)$	$(3, 1)$	$(5, 3, 7)$
Test3	$\{-10^2, -10^2 + 1, 0, 10^2 - 1, 10^2\}$	$(7, 8, 8, 7)$	$(3, 2, 4)$	$(6, 5, 4, 5)$
Test4	$\{4^0, 4^1, 4^2, 4^3, 4^4, 4^5\}$	$(6, 7, 8, 9, 10)$	$(1, 2, 3, 4)$	$(3, 4, 5, 6, 7)$

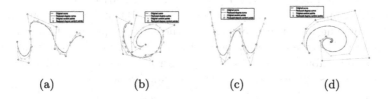

Fig. 2. Degree reduction by Alg. 3. (a) Test 1. (b) Test 2. (c) Test 3. (d) Test 4.

Table 3. Efficiency Comparison between Alg. in [18] Using $\langle \cdot, \cdot \rangle_T$ and Alg. 3(s).

	Alg in [18]	Alg in [18] Using Alg 2	Alg 3
Test1	2.231×10^1	7.708×10^{-3}	6.273×10^{-3}
Test2	5.411×10^1	9.166×10^{-3}	9.051×10^{-3}
Test3	1.783×10^2	7.571×10^{-3}	6.915×10^{-3}
Test4	3.302×10^3	1.401×10^{-2}	1.210×10^{-2}

Table 4. Efficiency Comparison between Alg. in [18] Using $\langle \cdot, \cdot \rangle_G$ and Alg. 1(s).

	[18] Using $\langle \cdot, \cdot \rangle_{G_1}$	[18] Using $\langle \cdot, \cdot \rangle_{G_2}$	Alg 1 Using $\langle \cdot, \cdot \rangle_{G_1}$	Alg 1 Using $\langle \cdot, \cdot \rangle_{G_2}$
Test1	6.804×10^{-3}	8.232×10^{-3}	5.914×10^{-3}	6.624×10^{-3}
Test2	8.806×10^{-3}	1.177×10^{-2}	7.390×10^{-3}	1.007×10^{-2}
Test3	1.086×10^{-2}	1.504×10^{-2}	9.723×10^{-3}	1.148×10^{-2}
Test4	1.398×10^{-2}	1.856×10^{-2}	1.095×10^{-2}	1.300×10^{-2}

Table 5. Error Comparison between Alg. in [18] Using $\langle \cdot, \cdot \rangle_T$ and Alg. 3.

	Alg in [18]	Alg in [18] Using Alg 2	Alg 3
Test1	$1.316075193832 \times 10^{-2}$	$1.316075193832 \times 10^{-2}$	$1.316075193832 \times 10^{-2}$
Test2	$2.830374396924 \times 10^{-1}$	$2.830374396924 \times 10^{-1}$	$2.830374396924 \times 10^{-1}$
Test3	$2.249658336903 \times 10^{-3}$	$2.249658336903 \times 10^{-3}$	$2.249658336903 \times 10^{-3}$
Test4	$1.579026131912 \times 10^{-2}$	$1.579026131912 \times 10^{-2}$	$1.579026131912 \times 10^{-2}$

Table 6. Error Comparison between Alg. in [18] Using $\langle \cdot, \cdot \rangle_G$ and Alg. 1. ($\times 10^{-3}$)

	[18] Using $\langle \cdot, \cdot \rangle_{G_1}$	[18] Using $\langle \cdot, \cdot \rangle_{G_2}$	Alg 1 Using $\langle \cdot, \cdot \rangle_{G_1}$	Alg 1 Using $\langle \cdot, \cdot \rangle_{G_2}$
Test1	13.24404151245	13.16517325301	13.24404151245	13.16517325301
Test2	289.2057517905	283.4126629867	289.2057517905	283.4126629867
Test3	6.159172771991	2.903327500803	6.159172771991	2.903327500803
Test4	16.34737870912	15.79453479166	16.34737870910	15.79453479166

shown in Figs. 2(a), (b), (c) and (d). When computing the algorithm in [18] using $\langle \cdot, \cdot \rangle_T$, we use the integral formula (1) for generating MD-splines.

The algorithm used to compute the value of MD-spline at a point is based on [28], while the algorithm to compute the linear representation coefficients of MD-spline's Bernstein basis is derived from [36]. The final results are shown in Table 3 and Table 4. We computed the errors of each method after degree reduction. The results are shown in Tables 5 and Tables 6.

6   Conclusions

This paper introduces a novel and efficient method for computing least square approximations using dual basis properties. The method is applied to address the degree reduction problem of MD-spline curves. Various degree-reducing algorithms, utilizing different inner products, are proposed. An integration algorithm for computing the product of polynomials represented by Bernstein bases is presented, crucial for the degree-reducing process. The algorithm enables direct least square approximation after degree reduction, providing a practical and fast modeling approach for MD-spline curves. Notably, this method can be used for degree reduction of B-splines. The method's limitation lies in its applicability only to degree reduction of polynomial splines. While extensions to handle the integration of more than two polynomials are possible, it cannot handle the inner product of rational polynomial splines or other non-polynomial spline basis functions. Consequently, special attention should be given to the inner product calculation of the spline basis functions that require reduction.

Acknowledgements. We are very grateful to the referees for their helpful suggestions and comments.

References

1. Piegl, L., Tiller, W.: Algorithm for degree reduction of B-spline curves. Comput. Aided Des. **27**(2), 101–110 (1995)
2. Alhasson, H.F., Willcocks, C.G., Alharbi, S.S., et al.: The relationship between curvilinear structure enhancement and ridge detection methods. Vis. Comput. **37**, 2263–2283 (2021)
3. Lin, X., Sun, S., Huang, W., et al.: EAPT: efficient attention pyramid transformer for image processing. IEEE Trans. Multimed. **25**, 50–61 (2023)
4. Yong, J., Hu, S., Sun, J., et al.: Degree reduction of B-spline curves. Comput. Aided Geom. Des. **18**(2), 117–127 (2001)
5. Li, Z., Guo, B., Meng, F., et al.: Fast shape recognition via a bi-level restraint reduction of contour coding. Vis. Comput. (2023)
6. Xu, R., Jin, Y., Zhang, H., et al.: A variational approach for feature-aware B-spline curve design on surface meshes. Vis. Comput. **39**, 3767–3781 (2023)
7. Lai, Y., Wu, J.S.S., Hung, J., et al.: Degree reduction of NURBS curves. Int. J. Adv. Manuf. Technol. **27**, 1124–1131 (2006)
8. Lewanowicz, S., Woźny, P.: Connections between two-variable Bernstein and Jacobi polynomials on the triangle. J. Comput. Appl. Math. **197**, 520–533 (2006)
9. Lewanowicz, S., Woźny, P.: Dual generalized Bernstein basis. J. Approx. Theory **138**, 129–150 (2006)
10. Lewanowicz, S., Woźny, P.: Bézier representation of the constrained dual Bernstein polynomials. Appl. Math. Comput. **218**, 4580–4586 (2011)
11. Goldman, R.N.: Dual polynomial bases. J. Approx. Theory **79**, 311–346 (1994)
12. Zhao, G., Liu, X., Su, Z.: A dual functional to the univariate B-spline. J. Comput. Appl. Math. **195**, 292–299 (2006)
13. Zhang, L., Tan, J., Dong, Z.: The dual bases for the Bézier-Said-Wang type generalized Ball polynomial bases and their applications. Appl. Math. Comput. **217**, 3088–3101 (2010)
14. Zhang, L., Tan, J., Wu, H., et al.: The weighted dual functions for Wang-Bézier type generalized Ball bases and their applications. Appl. Math. Comput. **215**, 22–36 (2009)
15. Zhang, L., Wu, H., Tan, J.: Dual bases for Wang-Bézier basis and their applications. Appl. Math. Comput. **214**, 218–227 (2009)
16. Zhang, L., Wu, H., Tan, J.: Dual basis functions for the NS power and their applications. Appl. Math. Comput. **207**, 434–441 (2009)
17. Woźny, P.: Construction of dual bases. J. Comput. Appl. Math. **245**, 75–85 (2013)
18. Woźny, P.: Construction of dual B-spline functions. J. Comput. Appl. Math. **260**, 301–311 (2014)
19. Zhang, L., Wang, H., Ge, X., et al.: Dual generalized B-spline functions and their applications in several approximation problems. J. Adv. Mech. Des. Syst. Manuf. **9**(4), 1–12 (2015)
20. Shen, W., Wang, G.: A basis of multi-degree splines. Comput. Aided Geom. Des. **27**, 23–35 (2010)
21. Costantini, P.: Variable degree polynomial splines. In: Curves and Surfaces with Applications in CAGD, pp. 85–94. Vanderbilt University Press, Nashville (1997)
22. Costantini, P.: Curve and surface construction using variable degree polynomial splines. Comput. Aided Geom. Des. **17**, 419–446 (2000)
23. Sederberg, T.W., Zheng, J., Song, X.: Knot intervals and multi-degree splines. Comput. Aided Geom. Des. **20**(7), 455–468 (2003)

24. Shen, W., Wang, G.: Changeable degree spline basis functions. J. Comput. Appl. Math. **234**, 2516–2529 (2010)
25. Shen, W., Wang, G., Yin, P.: Explicit representations of changeable degree spline basis functions. J. Comput. Appl. Math. **238**, 39–50 (2013)
26. Shen, W., Yin, P., Tang, C.: Degree elevation of changeable degree spline. J. Comput. Appl. Math. **300**, 56–67 (2016)
27. Beccari, C.V., Casciola, G., Morigim, S.: On multi-degree splines. Comput. Aided Geom. Des. **58**, 8–23 (2017)
28. Speleers, H.: Algorithm 999: computation of multi-degree B-splines. ACM Trans. Math. Softw. **45**(4), 1–15 (2019)
29. Toshniwal, D., Speleers, H., Hiemstra, R.R., et al.: Multi-degree B-splines: algorithmic computation and properties. Comput. Aided Geom. Des. **76**, 101792 (2020)
30. Hiemstra, R.R., Hughes, T.J., Manni, C., et al.: A Tchebycheffian extension of multi-degree B-splines: algorithmic computation and properties. SIAM J. Numer. Anal. **2**, 1138–1163 (2020)
31. Beccari, C.V., Casciola, G.: Matrix representations for multi-degree B-splines. J. Comput. Appl. Math. **381**, 113007 (2021)
32. Beccari, C.V., Casciola, G.: Stable numerical evaluation of multi-degree B-splines. J. Comput. Appl. Math. **400**, 113743 (2022)
33. Li, X., Huang, Z., Liu, Z.: A geometric approach for multi-degree spline. J. Comput. Sci. Technol. **27**(4), 841–850 (2012)
34. Beccari, C.V., Casciola, G.: A Cox-de Boor-type recurrence relation for C^1 multi-degree splines. Comput. Aided Geom. Des. **75**, 10784 (2019)
35. Wang, Z., Li, Y., Xu, H., et al.: P-spline curves. Vis. Comput. (2022)
36. Ma, X., Shen, W.: Generalized de Boor-Cox formulas and pyramids for multi-degree spline basis functions. Mathematics **11**(2), 367 (2023)
37. Farouki, R.T.: The Bernstein polynomial basis: a centennial retrospective. Comput. Aided Geom. Des. **29**, 379–419 (2012)
38. Lin, H., Bao, H., Wang, G.: Totally positive bases and progressive iteration approximation. Comput. Math. Appl. **50**(3), 575–586 (2005)
39. Jiang, Y., Lin, H., Huang, W.: Fairing-PIA: progressive-iterative approximation for fairing curve and surface generation. Vis. Comput. (2023)

Dynamic Ball B-Spline Curves

Ciyang Zhou, Yu Zhang, Xingce Wang, and Zhongke Wu[✉]

Beijing Normal University, Beijing, China
zwu@bnu.edu.cn

Abstract. A ball B-spline curve (BBSC) is a skeleton-based 3D geometric representation, which can represent 3D tubular objects with varying radius, such as trunks, plants, and blood vessels. To enhance the ability of BBSC, we propose a physics-based generalization of BBSC called dynamic BBSC (D-BBSC), which can describe the deformation behavior of a BBSC over time. We provide the mathematical expression of D-BBSC and prove its several mathematical properties. We derive the equations of motion of D-BBSC based on Lagrangian mechanics and investigate the equations of motion when it is under linear geometric constraints. Additionally, a D-BBSC physical simulation system based on the finite difference method (FDM) is implemented and several experimental results are demonstrated. The D-BBSC can be applied to simulate the elastic behavior of 3D tubular objects with varying radius in entertainment applications.

Keywords: Dynamics · Physics-based model · Ball B-spline curves

1 Introduction

A ball B-spline curve (BBSC) is an extension of the B-spline curve that was first proposed by [19]. It is widely used to represent 3D tubular objects with varying radius, such as trunks, plants, and blood vessels [26, 34]. However, all of those studies focused on the static form of BBSC with limited capabilities and flexibility, and several drawbacks remain to be improved:

1. It is difficult to adjust a BBSC to the expected shape in geometric modeling. To adjust the shape of a BBSC to the expected result, users have to manipulate the control balls of the BBSC. This method is time-consuming and relies on the skill of the designer.
2. It is cumbersome to generate physics-based computer animations using BBSC. Users have to compute the instantaneous state of BBSC at each frame and adjust the shape of the BBSC frame-by-frame, which requires a large amount of work.

To overcome these drawbacks, in this paper, we propose a physics-based generalization of a BBSC called dynamic BBSC (D-BBSC). A D-BBSC is an extension of a BBSC in the time domain that can describe the deformation behavior of BBSC over time. We employ Lagrangian mechanics to describe the

© The Author(s), under exclusive license to Springer Nature Switzerland AG 2024
B. Sheng et al. (Eds.): CGI 2023, LNCS 14498, pp. 15–27, 2024.
https://doi.org/10.1007/978-3-031-50078-7_2

motion of a BBSC and incorporate several physical quantities into it, such as mass, tension, rigidity, and external force distribution. We propose the D-BBSC model for the fast simulation of 3D tubular objects with varying radius. Our model can be applied in computer animation for entertainment applications

The physics-based D-BBSC model has the following important advantages:

1. D-BBSC is suitable for interactive geometric design. By applying a external force or force field on a BBSC, users can manipulate the shape of the BBSC directly to obtain the expected shape.
2. Generating physics-based animations using D-BBSC is convenient. Since D-BBSC is physics-based, users can create physics-based animations automatically by choosing proper initial physical parameters.

In this paper, we propose the D-BBSC concept and provide a mathematical expression of D-BBSC. Based on Lagrangian mechanics, we derive equations of motion of D-BBSC. Finally, we implement a D-BBSC physical simulation system using the finite difference method and present several experimental results. Our study makes the following contributions:

1. We propose the concept of D-BBSC and build the dynamics model of BBSC based on Lagrangian mechanics. D-BBSC expands the BBSC modeling method in time domain, can describe D-DBSC's deformation under physical laws over time.
2. We derive the motion equations of D-BBSC, and give the simplified and discretized version of motion equations, which provides a foundation for future research related to D-BBSC.
3. We give a numerical implementation of D-BBSC using a finite difference method. This method is easy to implement in computer for entertainment applications.

2   Related Work

Modeling a 3D tubular object with a varying radius is a classical problem in computer graphics. Over the past few decades, several geometric modeling methods for 3D tubular objects have been proposed. [15,16] proposed canal surfaces to represent 3D tubular objects. Subsequently, they further used a curve in R^4 to represent the 3D rational canal surface and investigated its mathematical properties [14]. [11] investigated a similar problem, where they proposed a G^1 continuous surface to represent the skin of an ordered set of discrete circles. Researchers proposed ball Bézier curves [12], interval Bézier curve [20], and interval B-spline curve [25], which are skeleton based models. Our work is based on the BBSC theory, which was proposed by [19]. Different from researches mentioned a bove, BBSC uses a B-spline curve to represent the skeleton curve. Thus, nice mathematical properties of B-spline curve can be adopted into BBSC.

Since the BBSC theory was proposed, several important studies of BBSC have been performed. Researchers propose several models based on BBSC, such as 3D trees [1,19,29], 3D plant models [34], real-time animation of 3D trees [1], a 3D human modeling method [30], and cerebral blood vessels model [26]. Some researchers improve BBSC's properties [8,27] and employ it in fitting [28].

Until now, there have been no related studies on a physics-based model similar to D-BBSC. Since the D-BBSC is an extension of a B-spline curve, we will review related studies of physics-based models of B-spline curves. [23] proposed an elastically deformable model that uses the elasticity theory to simulate the deformation behavior of nonrigid solids. Based on his work, [3] developed a free-form design system, and [2] developed similar physics-based models based on B-splines. [4] investigated physics-based models of B-splines with linear geometric constraints. [17,18,24] proposed a physics-based model of nonuniform rational B-splines(NURBS) curves and surfaces called dynamic NURBS (D-NURBS). Deformable B-spline curve are used in arbitrary shape text detection [33] and fairing curve generation [9]. In deep learning, researchers proposed deformable feature extraction framework [32] and Deformable Attention [13]. However, all these models are not designed specifically for BBSC, nor they cannot utilize the properties of BBSC. The D-NURBS focuses on the spline surfaces, while the D-BBSC simulates 3D tubular objects's deformation. Our model focuses on the surface of the BBSC for the fast simulation of 3D tubular objects with varying radius.

Compared with physics-based models of B-spline and NURBS curves, developing a physics-based model of BBSC is more challenging. The BBSC has a more complicated geometric expression than B-spline and NURBS, which make deriving explicit expressions of partial derivative in the equations of motion difficult.

3   Fundamentals

In this section, we describe several mathematical and physical concept that are relevant to our model and derive corresponding expressions and equations.

3.1   Lagrangian Mechanics

In the Lagrangian mechanics, a physical system is described by a finite set of parameters, and that group of parameters is called generalized coordinates. Using $p_i(t)$ to represent the i-th generalized coordinates of a physical system, we can denote generalized coordinates of that physical system by $\mathbf{p}$ and their derivatives with respect to time t by $\dot{\mathbf{p}}$; then, we have

$$\mathbf{p} = \begin{bmatrix} \cdots p_i(t) \cdots \end{bmatrix}^T, \qquad \dot{\mathbf{p}} = \begin{bmatrix} \cdots \dot{p}_i(t) \cdots \end{bmatrix}^T$$

In this paper, we adopt the work-energy version of Lagrangian equations [6,7]. We use T, U, and D to represent the kinetic energy, potential energy and Raleigh dissipation energy, respectively, of a physical system. Then, we can express the Lagrangian equations in matrix form:

$$\frac{d}{dt}\frac{\partial T}{\partial \dot{\mathbf{p}}} - \frac{\partial T}{\partial \mathbf{p}} + \frac{\partial D}{\partial \dot{\mathbf{p}}} + \frac{\partial U}{\partial \mathbf{p}} = \mathbf{f}_p \tag{1}$$

where $\frac{\partial T}{\partial \mathbf{p}} = \begin{bmatrix} \cdots \frac{\partial T}{\partial p_i} \cdots \end{bmatrix}^T$, $\mathbf{f}_p = \begin{bmatrix} \cdots f_i \cdots \end{bmatrix}^T$, and the other terms are similar.

3.2   Jacobian Matrix

The Jacobian matrix is a matrix-valued function, and every element of a Jacobian matrix is the first-order derivative of a vector-valued function with respect to its every parameter.

We use $\mathbf{p}$ to represent the generalized coordinates of a D-BBSC in vector form. If there are N control balls, then $\mathbf{p}$ will be a vector of size $4N \times 1$:

$$\mathbf{p}(t) = \begin{bmatrix} \cdots & x_i(t) & y_i(t) & z_i(t) & r_i(t) & \cdots \end{bmatrix}^T \tag{2}$$

An arbitrary point $\mathbf{s}(u, v, \mathbf{p})$ on the D-BBSC is determined by three variables u, v, and $\mathbf{p}$. However, we only pay attention to the Jacobian matrix with respect to the generalized coordinates $\mathbf{p}$. The Jacobian matrix $\mathbf{J}(u, v, t)$ of a D-BBSC with respect to the generalized coordinates $\mathbf{p}$ is a $3 \times 4N$ matrix that can be written as

$$\mathbf{J} = \left(\frac{\partial \mathbf{s}}{\partial \mathbf{p}}\right)^T = \begin{bmatrix} \cdots & \frac{\partial \mathbf{s}_x}{\partial x_i} & \frac{\partial \mathbf{s}_x}{\partial y_i} & \frac{\partial \mathbf{s}_x}{\partial z_i} & \frac{\partial \mathbf{s}_x}{\partial r_i} & \cdots \\ \cdots & \frac{\partial \mathbf{s}_y}{\partial x_i} & \frac{\partial \mathbf{s}_y}{\partial y_i} & \frac{\partial \mathbf{s}_y}{\partial z_i} & \frac{\partial \mathbf{s}_y}{\partial r_i} & \cdots \\ \cdots & \frac{\partial \mathbf{s}_z}{\partial x_i} & \frac{\partial \mathbf{s}_z}{\partial y_i} & \frac{\partial \mathbf{s}_z}{\partial z_i} & \frac{\partial \mathbf{s}_z}{\partial r_i} & \cdots \end{bmatrix} \tag{3}$$

where $\mathbf{s}_x, \mathbf{s}_y, \mathbf{s}_z$ are components of vector $\mathbf{s}$, namely, $\mathbf{s} = \begin{bmatrix} \mathbf{s}_x & \mathbf{s}_y & \mathbf{s}_z \end{bmatrix}^T$. Additionally $\frac{\partial \mathbf{s}}{\partial \mathbf{p}}$ is an abbreviation of

$$\begin{bmatrix} \cdots & \frac{\partial \mathbf{s}}{\partial x_i} & \frac{\partial \mathbf{s}}{\partial y_i} & \frac{\partial \mathbf{s}}{\partial z_i} & \frac{\partial \mathbf{s}}{\partial r_i} & \cdots \end{bmatrix}^T$$

For convenience, all parameters of functions are omitted. Note that we will use similar notation in the subsequent sections.

4   Formulation of D-BBSC

In the first, we provide a geometric expression of BBSC. In the second, we propose the D-BBSC concept and corresponding expressions. Then, We discuss several important properties of the D-BBSC.

4.1   BBSC Representation

A BBSC is a skeleton-based 3D solid with varying radius and can be regarded as an extension of a B-spline curve (see Fig. 1). A BBSC is controlled by a group of control balls instead of control points. Its the skeleton curve and radius function share the same B-spline basis functions

A ball $\langle \mathbf{P}; R \rangle$ is a spherical solid in 3D space with center $\mathbf{P}$ and radius R. we define a ball $\langle \mathbf{P}; R \rangle$ specifically as $\left\{ \mathbf{x} \in \mathbb{R}^3 \mid \|\mathbf{x} - \mathbf{P}\| \leq R, \ \mathbf{P} \in \mathbb{R}^3, R \in \mathbb{R}^+ \right\}$. and a BBSC can be represented as $\mathbf{s}(u) = \left\{ \sum_{i=0}^{n} N_{i,p}(u)\mathbf{P}_i; \sum_{i=0}^{n} N_{i,p}(u)R_i \right\}$.

(a) Surface of a BBSC(b) The skeleton of a
BBSC

Fig. 1. Demonstration of a BBSC. Part (a) shows the surface of a BBSC. Part (b) shows the sectional view of a BBSC. The blue balls are control balls, and the green curve is the skeleton curve of the BBSC. (Color figure online)

where $N_{i,p}(u)$ is i-th B-spline basis function of degree p. $\langle \mathbf{P}_i; R_i \rangle$ is the i-th control balls of the BBSC, and $n+1$ is the number of control balls of the BBSC.

The expression above provides the geometric expression of BBSC. Since the expression is not an explicit expression of BBSC, it cannot be employed directly for mathematical analysis.

For convenience of analyzing the mathematical properties of BBSC, we use an alternative geometric expression of BBSC in this paper later. We use a vector form $\mathbf{p}_i = \begin{bmatrix} x_i & y_i & z_i & r_i \end{bmatrix}^T$ to represent the i-th control ball $\langle \mathbf{P}_i; R_i \rangle >$, use $\mathbf{p}_i^* = \begin{bmatrix} x_i & y_i & z_i \end{bmatrix}^T$ to represent the position of center $\mathbf{P}_i$ of i-th control ball, and r_i is the radius R_i of i-th control ball. We use $\mathbf{c}(u)$ and $r(u)$ to represent the parametric expression of the skeleton curve and varying radii along that curve, respectively. Additionally, we define the Frenet frame along the skeleton curve of the BBSC as $\mathbf{T}(u)$, $\mathbf{B}(u)$, and $\mathbf{N}(u)$. As a result, we have the following symbols:

$$\mathbf{c}(u) = \sum N_{i,p}(u)\mathbf{p}_i^* \quad r(u) = \sum N_{i,p}(u)r_i \quad \mathbf{T}(u) = \frac{\mathbf{c}'(u)}{\|\mathbf{c}'(u)\|}$$

$$\mathbf{B}(u) = \frac{\mathbf{c}'(u) \times \mathbf{c}''(u)}{\|\mathbf{c}'(u) \times \mathbf{c}''(u)\|} \quad \mathbf{N}(u) = \frac{\mathbf{c}'(u) \times (\mathbf{c}''(u) \times \mathbf{c}'(u))}{\|\mathbf{c}'(u)\|\|\mathbf{c}''(u) \times \mathbf{c}'(u)\|} \tag{4}$$

Then, the geometric expression of the surface of a BBSC can be defined in an explicit form (see [5]):

$$\mathbf{s}(u,v) = \mathbf{c}(u) - \frac{r(u)r'(u)}{\|\mathbf{c}'(u)\|}\mathbf{T}(u)$$

$$+ r(u)\sqrt{1 - \left(\frac{r'(u)}{\|\mathbf{c}'(u)\|}\right)^2} \ [\cos(v)\mathbf{B}(u) + \sin(v)\mathbf{N}(u)] \quad v \in [0, 2\pi] \tag{5}$$

According to the explicit form of a BBSC, we can modify its' shape by adjusting control points. Compared to rational parametric form, the explicit form is more convenient to the shape control.

4.2   D-BBSC Model

In this paper, we only focus on the changes of control balls of the D-BBSC, while the numbers of control balls and the knot vector remains unchanged.

Under this hypothesis, a D-BBSC is fully determined by its control balls. If we denote by t the time parameter, we can use $\mathbf{p}_i(t) = \begin{bmatrix} x_i(t) & y_i(t) & z_i(t) & r_i(t) \end{bmatrix}^T$ to represent the i-th control ball of the D-BBSC over time during the deformation. We can also represent all control balls in vector form denoted by $\mathbf{p}(t)$, which is introduced in the Eq. 2.

In Lagrangian mechanics, we call $\mathbf{p}(t)$ generalized coordinates. If there are N control balls, the vector $\mathbf{p}(t)$ will has $4N$ components.

A D-BBSC is a physics-based generalization of a BBSC in the time domain. Thus, symbols in Eq. (4) all are influenced by the time parameter t.

Based on the geometric expression of the BBSC and the above hypothesis, a D-BBSC is fully determined by its generalized coordinates $\mathbf{p}(t)$.

4.3   Mathematical Properties of D-BBSC

In this section, we will investigate the mathematical properties of D-BBSC. The important properties that will be used in subsequent sections are listed as follows:

$$\mathbf{s} = \mathbf{J}\mathbf{p} \quad \dot{\mathbf{s}} = \mathbf{J}\dot{\mathbf{p}} \quad \dot{\mathbf{J}}\mathbf{p} = 0 \tag{6}$$

where $\mathbf{s}$ is the position of an arbitrary point on the surface of a D-BBSC, $\mathbf{J}$ is the Jacobian matrix that is introduced in the expression Eq. (3), and $\mathbf{p}$ are the generalized coordinates.

For the property $\mathbf{s} = \mathbf{J}\mathbf{p}$, we can employ Euler's theorem on homogeneous function. First we prove $\mathbf{s}(\mathbf{p})$ is a homogeneous function: A function $\mathbf{f} : \mathbb{R}^n \to \mathbb{R}^m$ is said to be homogeneous of degree k if $\mathbf{f}(\lambda\mathbf{x}) = \lambda^k \mathbf{f}(\mathbf{x})$ for any scalar λ.

From Eq. (4), we have

$$\mathbf{s}(\lambda\mathbf{p}) = \lambda\, \mathbf{s}(\mathbf{p}) \tag{7}$$

Since $\mathbf{s}(\mathbf{p})$ is a homogeneous function of degree 1, we have $\mathbf{J}\mathbf{p} = \mathbf{s}$.

The proof of the other properties refer to paper [21]. They are important mathematical properties of D-BBSC that are used in Subsect. 6.2.

5   D-BBSC Dynamics

In this section, we will derive equations of motion of D-BBSC. Afterward, we will consider a D-BBSC under linear geometric constraints and provide the corresponding equations of motion. The derivation of the equations of motion is similar to [31].

5.1   Equations of Motion of D-BBSC

The D-BBSC system is defined in the Sect. 4.2. We apply the Lagrangian equations (1) to describe the motion of the D-BBSC system, and the definition of control points is defined in the Eq. 2. Because of the existence of control radii, D-BBSC is a nonlinear physical system, and several physical quantities such as the mass and the damping matrix should be recalculated at every frame during simulation.

For a D-BBSC system, we use $\mu(u, v)$ and $\mathbf{M}(\mathbf{p})$ to represent the mass density distribution and the mass matrix; therefore, kinetic energy T can be expressed as

$$T = \frac{1}{2} \iint \mu \dot{\mathbf{s}}^T \dot{\mathbf{s}} \, du dv = \frac{1}{2} \dot{\mathbf{p}}^T \mathbf{M} \dot{\mathbf{p}} \quad \mathbf{M} = \iint \mu \mathbf{J}^T \mathbf{J} du dv \qquad (8)$$

Similarly, we denote by $\gamma(u, v)$ and $\mathbf{D}(\mathbf{p})$ the damping density distribution and the damping matrix; therefore, dissipation energy D can be expressed as

$$D = \frac{1}{2} \iint \gamma \dot{\mathbf{s}}^T \dot{\mathbf{s}} \, du dv = \frac{1}{2} \dot{\mathbf{p}}^T \mathbf{D} \dot{\mathbf{p}} \quad \mathbf{D} = \iint \gamma \mathbf{J}^T \mathbf{J} du dv \qquad (9)$$

To calculate the potential energy of a D-BBSC, we use the energy model proposed in [22]. We denote by $\alpha(u, u)$, $\beta(u, v)$ and $\mathbf{K}(\mathbf{p})$ the local tension function, rigidity function and stiffness matrix, respectively; the potential energy of the D-BBSC can be expressed as

$$U = \frac{1}{2} \mathbf{p}^T \mathbf{K} \mathbf{p} \qquad (10)$$

Using Eq. (6) leads to the following expression for the stiffness matrix $\mathbf{K}(\mathbf{p})$:

$$\mathbf{K}(\mathbf{p}) = \iint (\alpha_{1,1} \mathbf{J}_u^T \mathbf{J}_u + \alpha_{2,2} \mathbf{J}_v^T \mathbf{J}_v + \beta_{1,1} \mathbf{J}_{uu}^T \mathbf{J}_{uu}$$
$$+ \beta_{1,2} \mathbf{J}_{uv}^T \mathbf{J}_{uv} + \beta_{2,2} \mathbf{J}_{vv}^T \mathbf{J}_{vv}) du dv \qquad (11)$$

where subscripts of $\mathbf{J}$ indicate partial derivatives.

The generalized external force $\mathbf{f}_p$ can be obtained based on the principle of virtual work [7]. We denote the external distribution force by $\mathbf{f}(u, v, t)$; the generalized external force of the D-BBSC can be expressed as

$$\mathbf{f}_p = \iint \mathbf{J}^T \mathbf{f}(u, v, t) du dv \qquad (12)$$

Therefore, in a D-BBSC system, according to the mathematical properties of D-BBSC [24] Eq. (1) can be transformed to:

$$\mathbf{M} \ddot{\mathbf{p}} + \mathbf{D} \dot{\mathbf{p}} + \mathbf{K} \mathbf{p} = \mathbf{f}_p - \mathbf{I} \dot{\mathbf{p}} \quad \mathbf{I} = \iint \mu \mathbf{J}^T \mathbf{J} du dv \qquad (13)$$

5.2 Linear Geometric Constraints

A D-BBSC with geometric constraints is pretty useful in many applications. For example, users may rely on the two ends of the D-BBSC being fixed during the deformation. Because linear geometric constraints can meet the needs of most users, in this paper, we only investigate such constraints.

In general, linear geometric constraints can be mathematically expressed as

$$\mathbf{C}(\mathbf{p}) = \mathbf{A}\mathbf{p} + \mathbf{b} = 0 \tag{14}$$

If there are M independent linear constraints, then $\mathbf{A}$ will be an $M \times N$ coefficient matrix. Moreover, we can express generalized coordinates $\mathbf{p}$ as

$$\mathbf{p} = \mathbf{G}\mathbf{q} + \mathbf{q}_0 \tag{15}$$

where $\mathbf{G}$ is an $N \times (N - M)$ matrix, $\mathbf{q}_0$ is a constant vector, and $\mathbf{q}$ represents the new lower-dimensional generalized coordinates that can be computed by the Gaussian elimination method.

Using new generalized coordinates $\mathbf{q}$, we can express the equations of motion of a D-BBSC with linear geometric constraints as

$$\mathbf{M}_q\ddot{\mathbf{q}} + \mathbf{D}_q\dot{\mathbf{q}} + \mathbf{K}_q\mathbf{q} = \mathbf{f}_q + \mathbf{g}_q - \mathbf{I}_q\dot{\mathbf{q}} \tag{16}$$

where

$$\mathbf{M}_q = \mathbf{G}^T\mathbf{M}\mathbf{G}, \quad \mathbf{D}_q = \mathbf{G}^T\mathbf{D}\mathbf{G}, \quad \mathbf{K}_q = \mathbf{G}^T\mathbf{K}\mathbf{G}$$
$$\mathbf{f}_q = \iint \mathbf{L}^T\mathbf{f}(u,v,t)dudv, \quad \mathbf{g}_q = -\mathbf{G}^T\mathbf{K}\mathbf{q}_0, \quad \mathbf{I}_q = \mathbf{G}^T\mathbf{I}\mathbf{G} \tag{17}$$

and $\mathbf{L} = \mathbf{J}\mathbf{G}$ is the new Jacobian matrix of $\mathbf{s}$ with respect to $\mathbf{q}$. The detailed proof of Eq. (16) can be found in [24].

6   Numerical Implementation

In this section, we will introduce the use of the finite difference method (FDM) in our implementation and provide the discretized equations of motion of D-BBSC.

6.1   Finite Difference Method

Since the mathematical expression of D-BBSC is complicated, it is difficult to derive an explicit expression for some terms. To solve this problem, we use FDM to approximate the terms that are not easily derived. FDM is a traditional numerical approximation method, in which a continuous parameter field is approximated by a finite set of nodes, and the derivatives of a function at one node can be approximated by the finite difference of the values of that function at adjacent nodes.

For the derivatives in the Eq. 13, we use FDM to approximate them. For examples, the stiffness matrix $\mathbf{K}$ has the derivative $\mathbf{J}_u, \mathbf{J}_v, \mathbf{J}_{uv}, \mathbf{J}_{uu}$, and $\mathbf{J}_{vv}$. They can be derived by the finite difference of the values at adjacent nodes.

6.2   Time Integration

Equation (13) is a second-order partial difference equation. In general, Eq. (13) has no analytical solution; to solve this difference equation in our implementation, we discretize time t and approximate $\dot{\mathbf{p}}$ and $\ddot{\mathbf{p}}$ using the finite difference method in Eq. (13) to obtain a numerical solution. Given some specific physical parameters, Eq. (13) will be a stiff physical system. In this case, explicit time integration can lead to an unstable result. Therefore, in our implementation an implicit Euler method is used to ensure stability:

$$\ddot{\mathbf{p}} = \frac{\mathbf{p}^{(t+\Delta t)} - 2\mathbf{p}^{(t)} + \mathbf{p}^{(t-\Delta t)}}{\Delta t^2}, \qquad \dot{\mathbf{p}} = \frac{\mathbf{p}^{(t+\Delta t)} - \mathbf{p}^{(t-\Delta t)}}{2\Delta t} \qquad (18)$$

We substitute the equations above into the Eqs. 13. For all matrices without superscripts should be evaluated at time $t + \Delta t$. According to [10], we can use the following approximation: $\mathbf{M}^{(t+\Delta t)} = \mathbf{M}^{(t)}$

Then, we can similarly write the corresponding discretized equation of motion:

$$\left(4\mathbf{M}_q + 2\Delta t \mathbf{D}_q + 4\left(\Delta t\right)^2 \mathbf{K}_q\right) \mathbf{q}^{(t+\Delta t)} = 4(\Delta t)^2(\mathbf{f}_q + \mathbf{g}_q)$$
$$+ 8\mathbf{M}_q \mathbf{q}^{(t)} - (3\mathbf{M}_q - 2\Delta t \mathbf{D}_q)\mathbf{q}^{(t-\Delta t)} - \mathbf{G}^T \mathbf{M}\mathbf{q}_0 - \iint \mu \mathbf{L}^T \mathbf{s}^{(t-\Delta t)} du dv \qquad (19)$$

7   Experimental Results and Analysis

In this section, we demonstrate and analyze several experimental results for D-BBSC. Our model aims at simulating the deformation of the surface of BBSCs, and the experiments in this section focus on the behavior of surfaces of tubular objects.

7.1   Comparion Experiment

In this subsection, we design an experiment that compares the simulation results of our model and D-NURBS model. We make a program to realize the D-NURBS model, which refers to [24]. The material parameter of the tubular object is: $\mu = 30$, $\gamma = 10$, $\alpha_{1,1} = 40$, $\alpha_{2,2} = 5$, $\beta_{1,1} = \beta_{1,2} = \beta_{2,2} = 10$. The constant radii constraint is applied to the D-BBSC model, and the constrained weight vector evolution is applied to the D-NURBS model. For each model, we set different force field to make sure that the two models' deformation is not too large. The original states of two models are shown in Fig. 2(a), 2(b). The states of two models after deformation are shown in Fig. 2(c), 2(d). From the figures, we find that the D-NURBS model is more likely to encounter the self-intersection problem. As our model employs control balls to control tubular objects' shapes, our model is easier to avoid the problem above. Therefore, our model is more suitable for simulating tubular objects' deformation than the D-NURBS model.

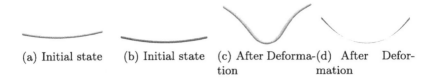

(a) Initial state   (b) Initial state   (c) After Deforma-(d) After Defor-
                                             tion   mation

Fig. 2. The figures 2(a) 2(b) show the original state of a BBSC model a NURBS model. The figures 2(c) and 2(d) show their states after deformation.

7.2   Demonstration of D-BBSC Application

In this subsection, we present several experimental results of our D-BBSC physical simulation system.

Figure 3 shows a metal pipe that is stretched by an external force. The material parameter of the object is: $\mu = 30$, $\gamma = 10$, $\alpha_{1,1} = 10$, $\alpha_{2,2} = 5$, $\beta_{1,1} = 0.037$ $\beta_{1,2} = \beta_{2,2} = 10$. Figure 3(c) shows a group of cerebral blood vessels that are fitted by BBSCs.

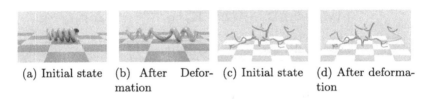

(a) Initial state   (b) After   Defor- (c) Initial state   (d) After deforma-
                    mation   tion

Fig. 3. Figures 3(a) and 3(b) shows that a metal pipe is stretched when a horizontal outward force is applied to it. Figures 3(c) and 3(d) shows the cerebral blood vessels fitted by BBSCs. One of the blood vessels (orange) is stretched by an external force. (Color figure online)

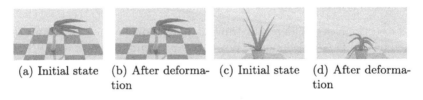

(a) Initial state   (b) After deforma- (c) Initial state   (d) After deforma-
                    tion   tion

Fig. 4. Figures 4(a) and 4(b) show that leaves of a palm tree are blown by the wind. Figures 4(c) and 4(d) show that a potted plant bent by a downward force.

Figure 4(a) shows a scenario simulated using D-BBSCs. In this simulated scenario, wind blows on a palm tree.

Figure 4(c) shows a potted plant bent by an external force. The material parameter of the object is: $\mu = 30$, $\gamma = 10$, $\alpha_{1,1} = 10$, $\alpha_{2,2} = 5$, $\beta_{1,1} = 0.0$, $\beta_{1,2} = \beta_{2,2} = 10$.

Since we use an FDM as our numerical method, the time cost of our implementation mainly depends on the grid resolution in FDM. When the Grid resolution $u \times v$ is $200 \times 20, 1000 \times 20$, and$1000 \times 50$, the corresponding time cost of one frame is 0.76 s, 4.23 s, and 9.12 s.

8 Conclusion

In this paper, we propose a physics-based generalization of BBSC called D-BBSC, which combines BBSC's geometric expression with a time parameter to describe the deformation behavior of a BBSC over time. We propose the concept of D-BBSC and corresponding mathematical expression. Then, we derive and prove several mathematical properties of D-BBSC. We derive the equations of motion of D-BBSC based on Lagrangian mechanics and analyze the equation under linear geometric constraints. Finally, we implement a D-BBSC physical simulation system using the finite difference method, and demonstrate several experimental results. The experimental results show that D-BBSC can reliably describe the deformation behavior of a BBSC. We believe that D-BBSC will be a useful tool in the domains of computer-aided design and 3D physics-based animation.

Acknowledgements. The authors want to thank the anonymous reviewers for their constructive comments. This research was partially supported by the Beijing Municipal Science and Technology Commission and Zhongguancun Science Park Management Committee (No. Z221100002722020), National Key R & D Program of China (No. 2020YFC1523300), National Nature Science Foundation of China (No.61972041, No. 62072045), Innovation & Transfer Fund of Peking University Third Hospital (No. BYSYZHKC2021110).

References

1. Ao, X., Wu, Z., Zhou, M.: Real time animation of trees based on BBSC in computer games. Int. J. Comput. Games Technol. **2009**, 5 (2009)
2. Bloor, M.I., Wilson, M.J.: Representing PDE surfaces in terms of B-splines. Comput. Aided Des. **22**(6), 324–331 (1990)
3. Celniker, G., Gossard, D.: Deformable curve and surface finite-elements for free-form shape design. ACM SIGGRAPH Comput. Graph. **25**(4), 257–266 (1991)
4. Celniker, G., Welch, W.: Linear constraints for deformable non-uniform B-spline surfaces. In: Proceedings of the 1992 Symposium on Interactive 3D Graphics, pp. 165–170. ACM (1992)
5. Fu, Q., Wu, Z., Wang, X., Zhou, M., Zheng, J.: An algorithm for finding intersection between ball B-spline curves. J. Comput. Appl. Math. **327**, 260–273 (2018)
6. Goldstein, H., Poole, C., Safko, J.: Classical mechanics (2002)
7. Gossick, B.R.: Hamilton's Principle and Physical Systems. Academic Press (1967)
8. Jiang, Q., Wu, Z., Zhang, T., Wang, X., Zhou, M.: G2-continuity extension algorithm of ball B-spline curves. IEICE Trans. Inf. Syst. **97**(8), 2030–2037 (2014)
9. Jiang, Y., Lin, H., Huang, W.: Fairing-pia: progressive-iterative approximation for fairing curve and surface generation. Vis. Comput. 1–18 (2023)

10. Kardestuncer, H., Norrie, D.H.: Finite Element Handbook. McGraw-Hill, Inc. (1987)
11. Kunkli, R., Hoffmann, M.: Skinning of circles and spheres. Comput. Aided Geom. Des. **27**(8), 611–621 (2010)
12. Lin, Q., Rokne, J.G.: Disk Bézier curves. Comput. Aided Geom. Des. **15**(7), 721–737 (1998)
13. Lin, X., Sun, S., Huang, W., Sheng, B., Li, P., Feng, D.D.: EAPT: efficient attention pyramid transformer for image processing. IEEE Trans. Multimed. (2021)
14. Peternell, M.: Rational two-parameter families of spheres and rational offset surfaces. J. Symb. Comput. **45**(1), 1–18 (2010)
15. Peternell, M., Pottmann, H.: Computing rational parametrizations of canal surfaces. J. Symb. Comput. **23**(2–3), 255–266 (1997)
16. Pottmann, H., Peternell, M.: Applications of Laguerre geometry in CAGD. Comput. Aided Geom. Des. **15**(2), 165–186 (1998)
17. Qin, H.: Dynamic non-uniform rational B-splines. Ph.D. thesis, University of Toronto (1995)
18. Qin, H., Terzopoulos, D.: D-NURBS: a physics-based framework for geometric design. IEEE Trans. Vis. Comput. Graph. **2**(1), 85–96 (1996)
19. Seah, H.S., Wu, Z.: Ball B-spline based geometric models in distributed virtual environments. In: Proceedings of the Workshop towards Semantic Virtual Environments (SVE 2005), pp. 1–8 (2005)
20. Sederberg, T.W., Farouki, R.T.: Approximation by interval Bézier curves. IEEE Comput. Graph. Appl. **12**(5), 87–95 (1992)
21. Pereira da Silva, J., Lopes Apolinário Júnior, A., Giraldi, G.A.: A review of dynamic NURBS approach. arXiv e-prints, pp. arXiv-1303 (2013)
22. Terzopoulos, D.: Regularization of inverse visual problems involving discontinuities. IEEE Trans. Pattern Anal. Mach. Intell. **4**, 413–424 (1986)
23. Terzopoulos, D., Platt, J., Barr, A., Fleischer, K.: Elastically deformable models. ACM SIGGRAPH Comput. Graph. **21**(4), 205–214 (1987)
24. Terzopoulos, D., Qin, H.: Dynamic NURBS with geometric constraints for interactive sculpting. ACM Trans. Graph. (TOG) **13**(2), 103–136 (1994)
25. Tuohy, S.T., Maekawa, T., Shen, G., Patrikalakis, N.M.: Approximation of measured data with interval B-splines. Comput. Aided Des. **29**(11), 791–799 (1997)
26. Wang, X., Wu, Z., Shen, J., Zhang, T., Mou, X., Zhou, M.: Repairing the cerebral vascular through blending ball B-spline curves with G2 continuity. Neurocomputing **173**, 768–777 (2016)
27. Wu, Z., Seah, H.S., Zhou, M.: Skeleton based parametric solid models: ball B-spline curves. In: 2007 10th IEEE International Conference on Computer-Aided Design and Computer Graphics, pp. 421–424. IEEE (2007)
28. Wu, Z., et al.: Fitting scattered data points with ball B-spline curves using particle swarm optimization. Comput. Graph. **72**, 1–11 (2018)
29. Wu, Z., Zhou, M., Wang, X., Ao, X., Song, R.: An interactive system of modeling 3D trees with ball B-spline curves. In: 2006 Second International Symposium on Plant Growth Modeling and Applications, pp. 259–265. IEEE (2006)
30. Xu, X., Leng, C., Wu, Z.: Rapid 3D human modeling and animation based on sketch and motion database. In: 2011 Workshop on Digital Media and Digital Content Management, pp. 121–124. IEEE (2011)
31. Zhang, Y., Wu, Z., Wang, X.: Dynamic disk B-spline curves. Comput. Animation Virtual Worlds **31**(4–5), e1955 (2020)

32. Zhao, Y., Zhang, H., Lu, P., Li, P., Wu, E., Sheng, B.: DSD-MatchingNet: deformable sparse-to-dense feature matching for learning accurate correspondences. Virtual Reality Intell. Hardw. **4**(5), 432–443 (2022)
33. Zhu, C., Yi, B., Luo, L.: CNBCC: cubic non-uniform b-spline closed curve for arbitrary shape text detection. Vis. Comput. 1–10 (2023)
34. Zhu, T., Tian, F., Zhou, Y., Seah, H.S., Yan, X.: Plant modeling based on 3D reconstruction and its application in digital museum. Int. J. Virtual Reality **7**(1), 81–88 (2008)

Schatten Capped p Regularization for Robust Principle Component Analysis

Lan Yang[1], Bin Zhang[2], Qingrong Feng[3], Xinling Liu[3], and Jianjun Wang[3(⊠)]

[1] College of Computer and Information Science College of Software,
Southwest University, Chongqing 400715, China
[2] Department of Neurosurgery, General Hospital of Ningxia Medical University,
Yinchuan 750001, Ningxia, China
[3] School of Mathematics and Statistics, Southwest University,
Chongqing 400715, China
`wjj@swu.edu.cn`

Abstract. Robust Principal Component Analysis (RPCA) is widely used for low-rank matrix recovery, which restores low-rank structures in damaged data through matrix decomposition. Existing approaches adopt the nuclear norm as a convex approximation of rank function. However, the nuclear norm treats the different singular values equally, leading to suboptimal matrix representation. To better depict the low-rank part, in this paper, we adopt a better surrogate of rank function, namely Schatten Capped p regularization. Further, the Schatten Capped p regularization-based RPCA model is proposed. And then we propose an efficient Alternating Direction Method of Multiplier (ADMM) algorithm to solve for the resulting optimization model. Experimentally, our algorithm is compared to state-of-the-art methods in practical applications such as image denoising, video background and foreground separation, and face de-shadowing. Especially, our algorithm can separate the noise better than other algorithms in the case of low noise levels in image denoising.

Keywords: RPCA · schatten capped p regularization · ADMM · background subtraction · image denoising

1 Introduction

Robust Principal Component Analysis (RPCA) has gained significant attention since Candès et al.'s seminal work [6]. The core idea of RPCA is to decompose a data matrix into low-rank and sparse components [16]. This technique has been extensively utilized in various research fields, including image denoising [1,3,18,23,25], video surveillance [4,20], and face recognition [9,21].

Specifically, suppose that a matrix $D \in \mathbb{R}^{m \times n}$ can be expressed by $D = X + E$, where $E \in \mathbb{R}^{m \times n}$ is sparse component (outliers) and $X \in \mathbb{R}^{m \times n}$ is low-rank component (clean data). And it can be mathematically described as the

B. Sheng et al. (Eds.): CGI 2023, LNCS 14498, pp. 28–40, 2024.
https://doi.org/10.1007/978-3-031-50078-7_3

following optimization problem:

$$\min_{E,X} \lambda \|E\|_0 + \text{rank}(X) \quad \text{s.t. } D = E + X, \tag{1}$$

where $\text{rank}(X)$ is the rank of the matrix X, $\|E\|_0$ denotes the number of nonzero entries in E, and λ is a parameter balancing the two components. However, problem (1) is nonconvex and discontinuous, solving this problem is NP-hard. A common strategy is to relax the rank of matrix to the nuclear norm $\|\cdot\|_*$, and the $\|\cdot\|_0$ to the ℓ_1 norm, respectively. Hence, problem (1) can be reformulated as:

$$\min_{E,X} \lambda \|E\|_1 + \|X\|_* , \quad \text{s.t. } D = E + X, \tag{2}$$

where $\|X\|_* = \sum_r \sigma_r(X)$ denotes the nuclear norm of X, $\sigma_r(X)(r = 1, 2, ..., \min(m, n))$ is the r_{th} singular value of X, $\|E\|_1 = \sum_{ij} |e_{ij}|$ denotes the ℓ_1 norm of E and e_{ij} is the element in the i_{th} row and j_{th} colunm of E. Although the algorithm has strong theoretical guarantees and has been successfully used to solve low-rank minimization problems, the nuclear norm can only obtain sub-optimal solutions in practice due to its inability to accurately approximate the rank of the matrix, which treats all non-zero singular values equally.

To alleviate the problems, some researchers have proposed non-convex alternatives to the relevant work. Hu et al. [13] proposed a new norm, named Truncation Nuclear Norm (TNN), which removes large singular values and adds smaller ones to reduce the impact of large singular values on low-rank. The authors of [19] proposed Capped Norm (CN) that minimizes insignificant singular values less than a threshold. Both TNN and CN aim to suppress significant singular values and penalize insignificant ones. The relationship between the two norms has been derived from literature [24]. Gu et al. [12] introduced a weighted nuclear norm to balance the contribution of different singular values to the rank function and demonstrated its better approximation effect. However, these methods have limitations in approximating the rank function and separating complex scenes. For better approximation, Wang et al. [22] proposed a flexible model with a novel nonconvex regularizer to overcome the rank function approximation. Nie et al. [17] introduced a non-convex minimal optimal method, called Schatten p Norm (SPN), to replace the nuclear norm. As p is a variable, it better approximates the rank of the matrix. However, like the nuclear norm, the SPN cannot handle different singular values flexibly. Therefore, this has raised the question of how to improve the accuracy of matrix rank approximation and provide the flexibility to handle diverse singular values. Recently, Li et al. [14] proposed a novel non-convex norm named the Schatten Capped p norm (SCP) to address this issue. The SCP is defined as:

$$\|X\|_{sp,\tau} = \left(\sum_{i=1}^{\min(m,n)} \min(\sigma_i, \tau)^p \right)^{\frac{1}{p}}, \tag{3}$$

where σ_i is i_{th} largest singular value of X, $\tau > 0$ is a threshold value to limit the upper bound of σ_i, and $p \in (0, 1]$. The SCP combines the benefits of CN and SPN. It balances rank function, treating large/small singular values differently for better accuracy. Experimental results have shown that the SCP has superior image restoration performance.

To address the problem of matrix rank approximation and flexible handling of different singular values for sparse and low-rank solutions simultaneously. This paper introduces a new RPCA model, which uses the SCP to replace nuclear norm, called Schatten Capped p minimization (SC2P).

However, the convexity property of the optimization problem cannot be preserved due to the truncation and capping in nuclear norm [13,24]. Therefore, the non-convex relaxation brought by the SCP makes the problem much more challenging. To obtain the optimal solution for our proposed model, we employ the Alternating Direction Method of Multiplier (ADMM) [5] for solving. To the best of our knowledge, our approach is the first to leverage SCP to approximate the rank function in the RPCA model.

The main contributions of this study are summarized as follows:

- We propose a new RPCA method based on the SCP, which is called SC2P. Due to the flexibility of parameter p and τ, this method achieves a closer approximation to the rank function, while also flexibly handling different singular values. Then, based on the ADMM framework, we have designed an effective algorithm to solve the model.
- Experimental results demonstrate the superiority of our proposed method over state-of-the-art algorithms in tasks such as image recovery, background separation, and face de-shadowing. Especially in image denoising, our method can restore the image structure more accurately, and the visual effect is better.

The structure of this paper is arranged as follows. In Sect. 2, our model and the corresponding algorithm is proposed. In Sect. 3, we will present some experimental results in order to demonstrate the effectiveness of our algorithm. Finally we conclude the paper in Sect. 4, and discuss our future research.

2 The SC2P Model for Robust Principal Component Analysis

2.1 The SC2P Model

The SCP improves low-rank matrix recovery performance compared to other non-convex regularizers when $0 \leq p < 1$ and $\tau > 0$, by approximating rank function and flexibly handling singular values. SCP and ℓ_1-norm together provide an interesting approach to non-convex RPCA:

$$\min_{E,X} \lambda \|E\|_1 + \|X\|_{sp,\tau}^p \quad \text{s.t. } D = E + X. \tag{4}$$

Theoretically, if τ is sufficiently large (e.g., $>$ all singular values), the SCP raised to the power of p becomes equivalent to the Schatten p-norm. Setting $p = 1$ as nuclear norm and large τ reduce SC2P model (4) to problem (2).

2.2   Optimization Algorithm of SC2P Model

We employ ADMM to solve the above problem (4). And its augmented Lagrangian function is as follows.:

$$L(X, E, Y, \mu) = \lambda \|E\|_1 + \|X\|_{sp,\tau}^p + \langle Y, D - X - E \rangle + \frac{\mu}{2} \|D - X - E\|_F^2, \quad (5)$$

where $Y \in \mathbb{R}^{m \times n}$ is the Lagrangian multiplier, and $\mu > 0$ is the regularization parameter. By following the framework of ADMM, we can solve the original problem through optimizing its subproblems iteratively.

(I) Updating X_{k+1}: when we fix E_k and minimize $L(X, E, Y, \mu, \lambda)$ for X_{k+1}:

$$X_{k+1} = \arg \min_X \|X\|_{sp,\tau}^p + \langle Y_k, D - X - E_k \rangle + \frac{\mu_k}{2} \|D - X - E_k\|_F^2, \quad (6)$$

then, X_{k+1} can be computed as follows:

$$X_{k+1} = \arg \min_X \frac{1}{2} \|X - G\|_F^2 + \psi \|X\|_{sp,\tau}^p, \quad (7)$$

where $G = D - E_k + \frac{1}{\mu_k} Y_k$ and $\psi = \frac{1}{\mu_k}$. For the subproblem (7), owing to the fact that it is nonconvex, and it seems hard to solve. To achieve an effective solution, we present the following lemma.

Lemma 1. *[14] Let the SVD of matrix G be $Q\Delta R^T$ with Q and R are the left and right singular vector matrices of G, respectively. The optimal solution of X is $U\Sigma V^T$, where U and V are the left and right singular vector matrices of X, respectively. Additionally, $\Delta = \text{diag}(\delta_1, \ldots, \delta_r)$ and $\Sigma = \text{diag}(\sigma_1, \ldots, \sigma_r)$ are a diagonal matrix. The i-th diagonal element σ_i of Σ is given by the problem below:*

$$\min_{\sigma_i \geq 0} \frac{1}{2}(\sigma_i - \delta_i)^2 + \psi \min(\sigma_i, \tau)^p. \quad (8)$$

In order to solve the subproblem (8), the above equality can define:

$$\sigma = \begin{cases} \frac{1}{2}(\sigma - \delta)^2 + \psi \sigma^p, & if \sigma \in [0, \tau] \\ \frac{1}{2}(\sigma - \delta)^2 + \psi \tau^p, & if \sigma \in [\tau, \infty] \end{cases}. \quad (9)$$

Lemma 2. *[14] For given parameters $p \in (0, 1]$ and $\psi \in \left(0, \frac{\tau^{2-p}}{p(1-p)}\right)$, the minimum solution of (9) is*

$$\hat{\sigma} = \begin{cases} \delta, & \text{if } \tau \in [0, \tau^*] \\ \hat{x}, & \text{if } \tau \in (\tau^*, \infty) \end{cases}, \qquad \hat{x} = \begin{cases} 0, & \text{if } \delta \in [0, \upsilon'] \\ x^*, & \text{if } \delta \in (\upsilon', \infty) \end{cases}, \quad (10)$$

where $\tau^* = \left(\frac{1}{2\psi}(\hat{x} - \delta)^2 + (\hat{x})^p\right)^{\frac{1}{p}}$, $\upsilon' = \upsilon + \psi p \upsilon^{p-1}$ *and* $\upsilon = (2\psi(1-p))^{\frac{1}{2-p}}$.

For the proofs of Lemma 1 and Lemma 2, please refer to the paper [14]. To get $\hat{x}$ when $\delta > v'$, it can use the classical gradient descent method. Empirically, this method yields satisfactory results with only a few iterations($i > 0$): $x_{i+1} = \delta - \psi p x_i^{p-1}$. According to Lemma 1 and Lemma 2. The solution of subproblem (7) can be constructed as follows:

$$X_{k+1} = U \text{diag}(\hat{\sigma}_1, \hat{\sigma}_2, \ldots, \hat{\sigma}_r) V^T. \tag{11}$$

(II) Updating E_{k+1}: fix X_k and Y_k to calculate E_{k+1} as follows:

$$E_{k+1} = \arg\min_E \lambda \|E\|_1 + \langle Y_k, D - X_{k+1} - E \rangle + \frac{\mu_k}{2} \|D - X_{k+1} - E\|_F^2, \tag{12}$$

this can be rewritten as:

$$E_{k+1} = \arg\min_E \frac{1}{2} \|E - Z_k\|_F^2 + \frac{\lambda}{\mu_k} \|E\|_1, \tag{13}$$

where $Z_k = D - X_{k+1} + \frac{1}{\mu_k} Y_k$. By the proximity operator [10], we can solve the above subproblem (13) as:

$$E_{k+1} = \mathcal{S}_{\lambda/\mu_k}(Z_k), \tag{14}$$

the $\mathcal{S}_{\lambda/\mu_k}(\cdot) = \text{sign}(\cdot) \max\{|\cdot| - \lambda/\mu_k, 0\}$ is the well-known soft-thresholding operator.

(III) Updating Y_{k+1}: fix X_k and E_k, calculate Y_{k+1} as follows:

$$Y_{k+1} = Y_k + \mu_k(D - X_{k+1} - E_{k+1}). \tag{15}$$

The $\mu_{k+1} = \min(\rho\mu_k, \mu_{\max})$, where $\rho > 1$ is a constant. The whole corresponding procedure is summarized in Algorithm 1.

Algorithm 1. SC2P for RPCA

Input: observation data D.
Output: Matrix E and X.
 1: Initialize $\mu_0 > 0, \rho > 1, \tau > 0, 0 < P \leq 1, k = 0, Iter, X_0 = D, Y = 0$.
 2: **while** $k > Iter$ and not convergence **do**
 3:     Update X_{k+1} based on Eq. (7).
 4:     Update E_{k+1} based on Eq. (13).
 5:     Update Y_{k+1} based on Eq. (15).
 6:     $\mu_{k+1} = min(\rho\mu_k, \mu_{max})$;
 7:     $k = k + 1$.
 8: **end while**
 9: **return** $E = E_{k+1}$ and $X = X_{k+1}$.

---

3   Experiment Results

In this section, we assess the performance of our proposed method on image and video datasets via three experiments. We compare it with ohter state-of-the-art algorithms and set several parameters in the proposed algorithm. According to the analysis of power p (discussed below), we tune p in the range of (0.1,10] for noise level $\Phi = 0.1$, 0.2 and 0.3 in the proposed SC2P and choose $\tau = 6$. Other parameters remain consistent with those used in NNM.

All experiments were conducted on a PC equipped with a 2.5 GHz CPU and 16G RAM using Matlab R2021b. Specifically, we take the Peak Signal-to-Noise Ratio (RSNR) and the Structural Similarity Index Measure (SSIM) as the metrics:

$$\text{PSNR} = 10 \cdot \log_{10} \frac{\text{MAX}^2}{\text{MSE}}, \quad \text{SSIM}(x,y) = \frac{(2\mu_x\mu_y + c_1)(\sigma_{xy} + c_2)}{\mu_x^2 + \mu_y^2 + c_1(\sigma_x^2 + \sigma_y^2 + c_2)},$$

where the MAX represents the maximum gray value in an image. And μ_x and μ_y represent the average values of x and y, and the σ_x and σ_y represent the standard deviation of x and y, respectively. And c is constant.

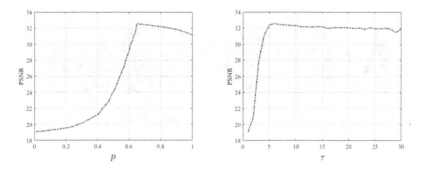

Fig. 1. The PSNR of SC2P under different values of p and τ is displayed in the fig-peppers image.

We evaluate the effect of the parameters p and τ on the low-rank matrices decomposition. The parameter p is vital in regulating the non-convexity of the objective function in problem (4). To investigate further, we added $\Phi = 0.1$ random noise to a grayscale image of figpeppers (see Fig. 3). Figure 1 illustrates PSNR accuracy variation of our proposed method across different p values. It can be seen that the accuracy of our proposed method shows an initial rise as p increases, followed by a gradual descent and the optimal recovery matrix corresponds to a value of p between 0.6 and 0.7. Clearly, neither the recovery matrix with the lowest rank nor the one obtained with the nuclear norm corresponds to our intended optimal solution.

Our proposed method also utilizes the τ parameter for minimizing insignificant singular values in the SC2P definition. In the experiment with a grayscale figpeppers image, we added noise $\Phi = 0.1$ and set $p = 0.6$. The PSNR was depicted at different τ values in Fig. 1. It is evident that the PSNR of the image increases rapidly with increasing τ, followed by a slight decrease, and then stabilizes. Consequently, increasing τ keeps important information while improving the validity of this decomposition. When τ exceeds the largest singular value, the accuracy remains the same regardless of its value. Thus, the proposed method of treating larger and smaller singular values differently offers higher precision in matrix decomposition.

3.1 Image Denoising

We first assess the effectiveness of the proposed SC2P algorithm for image denoising, and benchmark it against seven representative RPCA algorithms. These include NNM [6], CPNM [19], NSA [2], TNNR [7], SPNM [8], WNNM [12], and WSNM [23]. In total, we tested 20 common images that encompass both medical and natural categories, as shown in Fig. 2. To generate noisy observations, we introduced random noise to the images. All methods are generated from the source codes or executables provided by their authors respectively.

Fig. 2. The 20 test images for image denoising.

Table 1. The mean SSIM of all images after denoising with different methods

$\Phi = 0.1$								
AVG.	NOISE	CPNM	NAS	NNM	TNNR	SPNM	WNNM	WSNM	**OURS**
	0.3162	0.8791	0.9009	0.8872	0.8963	0.8573	0.8593	0.8116	**0.9102**
$\Phi = 0.2$								
AVG.	NOISE	CPNM	NAS	NNM	TNNR	SPNM	WNNM	WSNM	**OURS**
	0.1847	0.8226	0.8309	0.8241	0.8003	0.8129	0.6237	0.7645	**0.8290**
$\Phi = 0.3$								
AVG.	NOISE	CPNM	NAS	NNM	TNNR	SPNM	WNNM	WSNM	**OURS**
	0.1275	0.6888	0.6917	0.6666	0.5674	0.7022	0.6459	0.6372	**0.7482**

Table 1 and Table 2 report the SSIM and PSNR performance of seven competing denoising algorithms (the highest values are marked in bold). As shown in Table 2, the proposed SC2P method achieves the highest PSNR across almost all cases, improving upon the NNM method by 3.95 dB on average, and surpassing the benchmark SPNM and CPNM methods by 3.89 dB and 4.32 dB, respectively. To sum up, the SC2P method outperforms all other competitors in

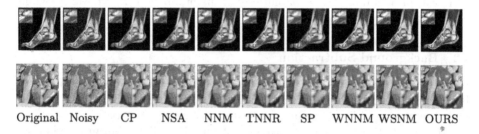

Original Noisy CP NSA NNM TNNR SP WNNM WSNM OURS

Fig. 3. Denoising results of medical image (noise level $\Phi = 0.1$) and peppers image (noise level $\Phi = 0.3$) for different models

Table 2. Denoising result PSNR by different methods (noise level $\Phi = 0.1$)

	NOISE	CPNM	NAS	NNM	TNNR	SPNM	WNNM	WSNM	**OURS**
camera	18.27	23.13	23.29	22.96	24.71	23.60	25.00	22.45	**26.80**
castle	18.16	27.11	27.24	26.92	28.87	27.50	28.24	25.35	**30.74**
elephant	18.31	28.44	28.75	28.56	30.02	28.81	28.69	26.64	**31.45**
formula1	18.37	24.30	24.50	24.31	26.57	24.98	26.26	23.55	**28.29**
Glass	17.96	24.61	24.88	25.23	25.94	25.58	25.23	23.64	**26.62**
house	18.86	26.52	26.65	26.31	29.59	27.54	29.50	26.17	**32.63**
kiln	19.02	29.41	29.70	29.61	30.87	29.52	29.16	27.54	**32.42**
mushroom	17.58	26.69	27.05	27.00	28.37	27.60	27.18	25.22	**29.67**
penguin	17.60	30.84	31.03	30.91	32.31	31.17	30.29	28.42	**34.22**
pine	17.77	23.90	24.00	23.67	25.41	24.31	25.29	23.09	**27.38**
slope	17.21	27.62	27.62	27.40	29.01	27.87	27.23	27.32	**29.37**
tower	17.98	26.89	27.08	26.83	28.87	27.48	27.48	27.13	**30.51**
papers	18.67	28.42	29.45	28.17	29.05	26.51	29.27	32.26	**33.33**
plane	18.01	25.19	25.42	25.02	28.71	24.22	28.09	30.10	**31.78**
Barbara	18.59	25.24	26.96	25.37	26.05	22.73	26.93	23.97	**28.22**
boat	18.71	26.92	27.92	26.84	27.64	24.56	28.17	24.84	**30.36**
dolphin	19.56	32.25	33.11	32.12	33.88	30.36	32.02	29.94	**36.21**
foot	15.75	23.98	25.26	23.20	26.00	21.83	27.94	24.54	**33.10**
goldhill	18.79	28.88	30.31	29.21	29.89	26.64	29.01	26.68	**31.25**
livingroom	19.46	28.04	29.17	27.90	28.66	25.92	28.23	25.80	**32.29**
AVG.	18.23	26.89	27.42	26.83	28.59	26.46	28.00	26.26	**30.84**

terms of average performance at all noise levels, particularly at low noise, where the improvement is most significant. In terms of visual quality, our proposed method is also superior to other RPCA methods, as shown in Fig. 3 (the visual effect can be better seen through the enlarged area). SC2P accurately reconstructs the ankle structure, while CPNM and SPNM produce more artefacts. Furthermore, at higher noise levels (0.3), SC2P effectively suppresses artifacts and reconstructs pepper surface brightness. In conclusion, the SC2P method offers exceptional denoising capabilities and maintains high PSNR values while exhibiting strong visual quality.

3.2 Background Subtraction

Surveillance video data is typically low-rank, as it exhibits temporal continuity. The stationary background of the video can be represented as a low-rank matrix, while the moving objects can be represented as a sparse matrix.

We validate the superior performance of the SC2P algorithm in video background separation and compare it with state-of-the-art methods, including the Mixture of Gaussians (MoG) [26], RegL1A, NNM, WNNM, WSNM, and TNNR. We set the parameters as suggested in the original paper and analyzed various standard video sequences from the I2R dataset [15], which include airport, curtain, escalator, fountain, lobby, shopping center, and tree sequences. We converted the original color videos to grayscale images, transformed each frame into a long column vector, and combined all columns to form a data matrix. The resulting data matrix, $X \in \mathbb{R}^{25344 \times 200}$, contains 200 grayscale frames of size 144×176 pixels.

To quantitatively compare the effectiveness of various methods, we use the Area Under ROC Curve (AUC) measurement. The larger AUC, the more outstanding the performance. AUC is calculated as follows:

$$\text{AUC} = \frac{\sum_{\text{positive}} \text{rank}_i - \frac{M(1+M)}{2}}{M * N},$$

where $\sum_{\text{positive}} \text{rank}_i$ is a rank summation for positive class samples, M and N are the number of positive and negative samples, respectively, where positive class samples represent video foreground. When we compared the background separation results of multiple algorithms (as shown in Fig. 4), we found that all algorithms were able to distinguish foreground from background, but our algorithm was able to capture more complex details, such as a person holding a suitcase in the airport background, that were not as apparent in the results produced by other algorithms. For a more comprehensive comparison, Table 3 displays the AUC values, which indicate that our algorithm has higher accuracy in extracting clear backgrounds and accurately separating foregrounds. In summary, our algorithm performs better in restoring backgrounds and eliminating most shadows.

Table 3. AUC of all methods on the I2R dataset.

method	data							avg.
	airport	curtain	escalator	fountain	lobby	shoppingMall	tree	
MoG	0.7937	0.8761	0.8038	0.9468	0.8736	0.9027	0.8923	0.8699
RegL1	0.8967	0.8460	0.9108	0.9538	0.9244	0.9083	0.8867	0.9038
RPCA	0.8721	0.8823	0.9112	0.9461	0.9222	0.9030	0.8943	0.9045
WNNM	0.8869	0.9049	0.9139	0.9260	0.8878	0.9100	0.8872	0.9024
WSNM	0.8721	0.8736	0.9021	0.9409	0.8804	0.9012	0.8867	0.8939
SC2P	**0.9083**	**0.9061**	**0.9217**	**0.9545**	**0.9412**	**0.9115**	**0.8953**	**0.9198**

3.3 Face Shadowing

The quality of face recognition is strongly influenced by lighting factors such as shadows and brightness. By regarding shadows and light as sparse and facial structure as low-ranking, removing these elements from facial images becomes a low-rank and sparse decomposition challenge.

We employ our proposed algorithm to address the issue of removing shadows from facial images, and compare its efficacy with MoG, RegL1, NNM, WNNM, and WSNM. We conduct the experiment using the Extended YaleB dataset [11].

Figure 5 shows the visual quality of facial images for different algorithms. The results indicate that our method outperforms MoG and RegL1 algorithms in terms of shadow removal. Additionally, our approach skillfully maintains the low-rank structure and sparse element information of the original image, while

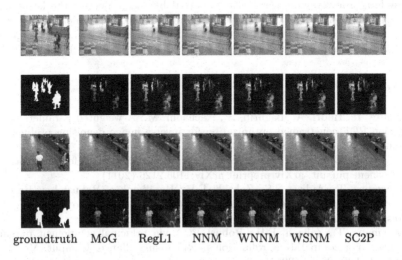

groundtruth   MoG   RegL1   NNM   WNNM   WSNM   SC2P

Fig. 4. This figure shows the results of all methods in separating foreground and background before and after separation. From top to bottom is Airport and shoppingMall video sequences.

other methods suffer from either shadow artifacts or loss of fine details. This observation clearly suggests that our proposed algorithm is better suited for complex lighting conditions and significantly augments the accuracy and efficiency of image processing.

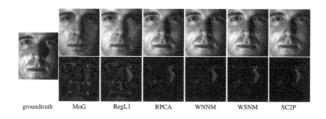

groundtruth   MoG   RegL1   RPCA   WNNM   WSNM   SC2P

Fig. 5. The figure showcasing the performance of various methods on processing facial images in the extended Yale B dataset.

4 Conclusion and Future Work

This article studies a new RPCA model based on SCP. We further proposed an effective ADMM algorithm to solve the new RPCA model. The obtained E and X are optimal for the linearized sub-problem. We present extensive experiments on real-world data to demonstrate the effectiveness of our method. Interesting future work will be applying SC2P in the field of video denoising and color image denoising.

Acknowledgements. Our work was supported by the project of the key research and development ecological conservation and highquality development of the Yellow River Basin Science and Technology of NingXia (No. 2022BEG03165), National Natural Science Foundation of China (Grant Numbers 12071380, 11971374, 12201505).

References

1. Afraites, L., Hadri, A., Laghrib, A., Nachaoui, M.: A weighted parameter identification PDE-constrained optimization for inverse image denoising problem. Vis. Comput. **38**(8), 2883–2898 (2022)
2. Aybat, N.S., Goldfarb, D., Iyengar, G.: Fast first-order methods for stable principal component pursuit. arXiv preprint arXiv:1105.2126 (2011)
3. Bouwmans, T., Aybat, N.S., Zahzah, E.H.: Handbook of Robust Low-Rank and Sparse Matrix Decomposition: Applications in Image and Video Processing. CRC Press, Boca Raton (2016)
4. Bouwmans, T., Zahzah, E.H.: Robust PCA via principal component pursuit: a review for a comparative evaluation in video surveillance. Comput. Vis. Image Underst. **122**, 22–34 (2014)
5. Boyd, S., Parikh, N., Chu, E., Peleato, B., Eckstein, J., et al.: Distributed optimization and statistical learning via the alternating direction method of multipliers. Found. Trends Mach. Learn. **3**(1), 1–122 (2011)

6. Candès, E.J., Li, X., Ma, Y., Wright, J.: Robust principal component analysis? J. ACM (JACM) **58**(3), 1–37 (2011)
7. Cao, F., Chen, J., Ye, H., Zhao, J., Zhou, Z.: Recovering low-rank and sparse matrix based on the truncated nuclear norm. Neural Netw. **85**, 10–20 (2017)
8. Chang, H., Luo, L., Yang, J., Yang, M.: Schatten p-norm based principal component analysis. Neurocomputing **207**, 754–762 (2016)
9. Chang, K.I., Bowyer, K.W., Flynn, P.J.: Face recognition using 2D and 3D facial data. In: Workshop in Multidimonal User Authentication, pp 25–32. Citeseer (2003)
10. Donoho, D.L.: De-noising by soft-thresholding. IEEE Trans. Inf. Theory **41**(3), 613–627 (1995)
11. Georghiades, A., Belhumeur, P., Kriegman, D.: From few to many: illumination cone models for face recognition under variable lighting and pose. IEEE Trans. Pattern Anal. Mach. Intell. **23**(6), 643–660 (2001). https://doi.org/10.1109/34.927464
12. Gu, S., Xie, Q., Meng, D., Zuo, W., Feng, X., Zhang, L.: Weighted nuclear norm minimization and its applications to low level vision. Int. J. Comput. Vis. **121**(2), 183–208 (2017)
13. Hu, Y., Zhang, D., Ye, J., Li, X., He, X.: Fast and accurate matrix completion via truncated nuclear norm regularization. IEEE Trans. Pattern Anal. Mach. Intell. **35**(9), 2117–2130 (2012)
14. Li, G., et al.: Matrix completion via schatten capped p norm. IEEE Trans. Knowl. Data Eng. **34**(1), 394–404 (2020)
15. Li, L., Huang, W., Gu, I.Y.H., Tian, Q.: Statistical modeling of complex backgrounds for foreground object detection. Trans. Image Process. **13**(11), 1459–1472 (2004)
16. Luo, Q., Liu, B., Zhang, Y., Han, Z., Tang, Y.: Low-rank decomposition on transformed feature maps domain for image denoising. Vis. Comput. **37**, 1899–1915 (2021)
17. Nie, F., Wang, H., Cai, X., Huang, H., Ding, C.: Robust matrix completion via joint schatten p-norm and lp-norm minimization. In: 2012 IEEE 12th International Conference on Data Mining, pp. 566–574 (2012). https://doi.org/10.1109/ICDM.2012.160
18. Qin, N., Gong, Z.: Color image denoising by means of three-dimensional discrete fuzzy numbers. Vis. Comput. **39**(5), 2051–2063 (2023)
19. Sun, Q., Xiang, S., Ye, J.: Robust principal component analysis via capped norms. In: Proceedings of the 19th ACM SIGKDD International Conference on Knowledge Discovery and Data Mining, pp. 311–319 (2013)
20. Tan, H., Wang, J., Kong, W.: Deep plug-and-play for tensor robust principal component analysis. In: ICASSP 2023-2023 IEEE International Conference on Acoustics, Speech and Signal Processing (ICASSP), pp. 1–5. IEEE (2023)
21. Tolba, A., El-Baz, A., El-Harby, A.: Face recognition: a literature review. Int. J. Signal Process. **2**(2), 88–103 (2006)
22. Wang, Z., et al.: Large-scale affine matrix rank minimization with a novel nonconvex regularizer. IEEE Trans. Neural Netw. Learn. Syst. **33**(9), 4661–4675 (2022). https://doi.org/10.1109/TNNLS.2021.3059711
23. Xie, Y., Gu, S., Liu, Y., Zuo, W., Zhang, W., Zhang, L.: Weighted schatten p-norm minimization for image denoising and background subtraction. IEEE Trans. Image Process. **25**(10), 4842–4857 (2016)
24. Zhang, F., Yang, Z., Chen, Y., Yang, J., Yang, G.: Matrix completion via capped nuclear norm. IET Image Process. **12**(6), 959–966 (2018)

25. Zhang, J., Wang, F., Zhang, H., Shi, X.: Compressive sensing spatially adaptive total variation method for high-noise astronomical image denoising. Vis. Comput. 1–13 (2023)
26. Zhao, Q., Meng, D., Xu, Z., Zuo, W., Zhang, L.: Robust principal component analysis with complex noise. In: International Conference on Machine Learning, pp. 55–63. PMLR (2014)

Sparse Graph Hashing with Spectral Regression

Zhihao He[1], Jianyang Qin[2], Lunke Fei[1(✉)], Shuping Zhao[1], Jie Wen[2],
and Banghai Wang[1]

[1] Guangdong University of Technology, Guangzhou, China
flksxm@126.com
[2] Harbin Institute of Technology, Shenzhen, China

Abstract. Learning-based hashing has received increasing research attention due to its promising efficiency for large-scale similarity search. However, most existing manifold-based hashing methods cannot capture the intrinsic structure and discriminative information of image samples. In this paper, we propose a new learning-based hashing method, namely, Sparse Graph Hashing with Spectral Regression (SGHSR), for approximate nearest neighbor search. We first propose a sparse graph model to learn the real-valued codes which can not only preserves the manifold structure of the data, but also adaptively selects sparse and discriminative features. Then, we use a spectral regression to convert the real-valued codes into high-quality binary codes such that the information loss between the original space and the Hamming space can be well minimized. Extensive experimental results on three widely used image databases demonstrate that our SGHSR method outperforms the state-of-the-art unsupervised manifold-based hashing methods.

Keywords: Learning to hash · sparse graph hashing · spectral regression

1 Introduction

Large-scale similarity search has become a challenging problem due to the rapid growth of the scale and dimensions of internet data such as images, videos and text. Thus, Approximate Nearest Neighbor (ANN) search, which can match the most similar items from datasets, is proposed. As a promising solution to the Approximate Nearest Neighbor (ANN) problem, hashing method aims to map the original data into a low-dimensional Hamming space while preserving the original similarity. The advantages of hashing make it more efficient and powerful for practical search problems, such as image retrieval [1,2] and object recognition [3]. In recent years, there have been a number of hashing methods proposed in the literature, which can are roughly classified into: supervised, semi-supervised and unsupervised based methods. Supervised-learning-based hashing methods [4–9] generally generate efficient binary codes by analyzing the semantic relevance of class labels, and the representative methods include Supervised Discrete Hashing (SDH) [4] and Robust Supervised Discrete Hashing (RSDH)

© The Author(s), under exclusive license to Springer Nature Switzerland AG 2024
B. Sheng et al. (Eds.): CGI 2023, LNCS 14498, pp. 41–53, 2024.
https://doi.org/10.1007/978-3-031-50078-7_4

[5]. By contrast, semi-supervised-based hashing methods [10,11] aim to capture the semantic relevance of unlabeled data by a few labeled data, and the typical methods include Semi-Supervised Hashing (SSH) [10] and Semi-Supervised Metric Learning-based Anchor Graph Hashing (MLAGH) [11].

In recent years, unsupervised-learning-based hashing methods [12–18], which can learn a binary representation without semantic labels, are the mainstream of hash learning. For example, manifold-based methods, such as Spectral Hashing(SH) [12], Anchor Graph Hashing (AGH) [13] and Large Graph Hashing with Spectral Rotation (LGHSR) [14], learns a binary representation through the graph Laplacian. Iterative Quantization (ITQ) [15] minimizes the quantization loss by finding an orthogonal rotation matrix to rotate the PCA projection into a more suitable space. Simultaneous Compression and Quantization (SCQ) [16] is an ITQ-based method that combines dimensionality reduction and rotation operations for hash code learning. Discrete Spectral Hashing (DSH) [17] aim to transform the graph hashing problem into a discrete optimization framework to learn discrete hash codes. Unsupervised Discrete Hashing (UDH) [18] utilizes a balanced graph semantic loss to capture the semantic information of data, thereby exploring the similarity and dissimilarity relations in the original space. However, most unsupervised hashing methods focus only on preserving the similarity of neighbor data and cannot capture the intrinsic structures of data.

To address this, there have been some studies that uses the sparse feature selection [19–24] to extract and preserve the sparse manifold structures in data. For example, Hu et al. [19] proposed a sparse graph method to learn the manifold information using sparsity and spectral embedding. Lai et al. [20] proposed a Joint Sparse Hashing (JSH) to learn an optimal joint sparse projection matrix via an $\ell_{2,1}$-norm regularization for binary codes learning. Wang et al. [21] proposed a Jointly Personalized Sparse Hashing (JPSH) to adaptively project different clusters into corresponding personalized subspace. Wang et al. [22] proposed a sparse graph based self-supervised hashing (SGSH) to use a new type of sparse nearest neighbor graph to preserve neighborhood information. Wang et al. [23] proposed a "Set and Rebase" mechanism to learn a sparse graph structure to preserve the similarity information for hash code learning. While the afore-mentioned sparse-based hashing methods have achieved encouraging performance in image retrieval, they cannot assign different weights among the different instances to select discriminative information. In addition, most existing sparse based hashing methods are sensitive to the noise and outlier due to the quadratic forms of graph embedding.

In this paper, we propose a two-step hashing method, namely, Sparse Graph Hashing with Spectral Regression (SGHSR), to adaptively select sparse and discriminative features for generating hash codes and hash functions. First, we introduce a sparse graph model, which combines the graph Laplacian with re-weighted ℓ_1- norm, to learn the real-valued hash codes. The proposed sparse graph model can not only enhance the sparsity of hash codes to extract intrinsic structure, but also adaptively choose parameters among the hash codes to select discriminative information. Then, we utilize a spectral regression model with ℓ_2-regularization for alternately learning a projection matrix and encoding binary codes, such that the information loss of discrete hash codes and hash functions can be minimized. Extensive experimental results clearly show the effectiveness and efficiency of the proposed method.

The remainder of this paper is organized as follows: Section 2 describes our proposed SGHSR method. Section 3 presents the experimental results. Section 4 offers the conclusion of this paper.

2   SGHSR

In this section, we elaborate the Sparse Graph Hashing with Spectral Regression method for robust image retrieval.

2.1   Notations and Definitions

In this paper, the matrix $X = [x_1, x_2, \cdots, x_n]^T$ represents the training sample set, where $x_i \in R^{1 \times d}$ represents the i-th training sample. The solutions in continuous space are denoted by $Y \in R^{k \times n} = [y_1, y_2, \cdots, y_n]^T$. The solutions in Hamming space are denoted by $B = [b_1, b_2, \cdots, b_n]^T$, where $b_i \in R^{1 \times k}$ ($k \ll d$) is the number of bits. I represents the identity matrix. 1^T represents a column vector in which all elements are 1. tr() denotes the matrix trace norm and sgn() denotes the sign function, which equals to $+1$ if $x > 0$ and -1 otherwise. The $\ell_{p,q}$-norm is defined as follows:

$$\|x\|_{p,q} = \left(\sum_{i=1}^{n} \left(\sum_{j=1}^{m} |x_{ij}|^p \right)^{\frac{q}{p}} \right)^{\frac{1}{q}}. \tag{1}$$

2.2   Learning Real-Valued Codes Using a Sparse Graph Model

Most manifold-based hashing methods focus most on preserving the data similarity, which usually cannot well extract the intrinsic structure in data and learn discriminative information. In this study, due to the fact that the similar hash codes should be as close as possible in the Euclidean space, we aim to learn more effective and efficient hash codes by making the hash codes sparse. Moreover, since different instances have different total amounts of information, we adaptively learn the hash codes to enhance the discriminative power of the hash codes. To achieve this, we formulate a sparse graph model by imposing the re-weighted ℓ_1-norm on manifold learning as follows:

$$\min_{Y^T Y = I} \frac{\sum\limits_{i,j=1}^{n} A_{ij} \|y_i - y_j\|_2}{\sum\limits_{i,j} \|y_i - y_j\|_2}, \tag{2}$$

where y_i is the column of real-valued codes Y. A is an approximate adjacency matrix for preserving local discriminative information [13]. In addition, the re-weighted ℓ_1-norm is defined as $\omega\|Y\|_1$, and ω is defined as follows:

$$\omega_i = \frac{1}{|y_i| + \varepsilon},\tag{3}$$

where $\varepsilon = 0.01$ is a parameter for adaptive weight estimation. ω_i represents inverse of the magnitude of y_i for avoiding inconsistency of the ℓ_1-norm. Obviously, if we use p_{ij} to denote the element $\|y_i - y_j\|_2$, the $\min\limits_{Y^T Y=1} \sum\limits_{i,j=1} \|y_i - y_j\|_2$ can be presented as $\min\limits_{Y^T Y=1} \|p\|_1$. If we regard $\tilde{A}_{ij} = A_{ij}/\|y_i - y_j\|_2$ as a re-weighted coefficient, the sparse graph model can be rewritten as a common manifold learning problem (i.e., $\min\limits_{Y^T Y=I} \sum\limits_{i,j=1}^{n} \tilde{A}_{ij} \|y_i - y_j\|_2$), which is equivalent to a re-weighted ℓ_1-norm problem (i.e., $\min\limits_{Y^T Y=I} \tilde{A}\|p\|_1$). It can be seen that the proposed sparse graph model combines the graph Laplacian with the re-weighted ℓ_1-norm. Therefore, in comparison with SH, it can well alleviate the sensitivity to outliers by using the residual $\|y_i - y_j\|_2$, and reduces the computational complexity by using a sparse adjacency matrix A instead of a dense affinity matrix.

2.3 Learning Binary Codes and Projection Matrix via Spectral Regression

As real-valued codes were learned by the graph Laplacian, we must convert the real-valued codes into binary codes. For this, we still need to capture the projection matrix since cannot be generalized to unseen data. To solve this problem, motivated by the fact that the local feature contains local discriminative information for retrieval, in this study, we compute binary codes and projection matrix by using spectral regression [25] as follows:

$$\min_P \|ZP - B\|_2^2, \\ s.t. b_i \in \{-1,1\}^k, B1^T = 0, B^T B = nI, \tag{4}$$

where $b_i \in \{-1,1\}^k$ represents the duality of the codes. $B1^T = 0$ represents a balanced probability for each bit to be zero or one. $B^T B = nI$ is added to make binary bits irrelevant. Moreover, we impose ℓ_2-regularization on the projection matrix P for discriminative information capture [26]. Therefore, this Problem (4) can be formulated as follows:

$$\min_P \|ZP - B\|_2^2 + \alpha\|P\|_2^2, \\ s.t. b_i \in \{-1,1\}^k, B1^T = 0, B^T B = nI, \tag{5}$$

where P can be initialized by solving problem $\min\limits_{P} \|ZP - Y\|_2^2 + \alpha\|P\|_2^2$. $\alpha \geq 0$ is a weighting parameter that is used to control the amounts of shrinkage. In

---

Algorithm 1 SGHSR

Input: The original affinity matrix $A \in R^{n \times n}$.

1: Use the k-means clustering algorithm to generate m anchors.

2: Construct anchor graph Z based on AGAH.

3: Construct approximate adjacency matrix $A = Z^T \Lambda Z$, where $\Lambda = \text{diag}\left(Z^T 1\right)$.

4: Initialize real-valued codes Y as a random orthogonal matrix and set $t = 1$.

5: **while** not converge **do**

6:     Calculate $\tilde{L}_t = \tilde{D}_t - \tilde{A}_t$, where $\tilde{A}_{ij} =$
   $A_{ij}/2 \left\| y_t^i - y_t^j \right\|_2$ and $\tilde{D}_t = \text{diag}\left(\tilde{A}_t 1^T\right)$;

7:     Calculate $Y_{t+1} = \left[\left(y_t^1\right)^T, \left(y_t^2\right)^T, \cdots, \left(y_t^n\right)^T \right]^T$,
   where the columns of Y_{t+1} are the first eigenvectors
   of k, which correspond to the first $\tilde{L}$ smallest eigenvalues (excluding trivial eigenvalues that are smaller
   than 1e-3);

8:     $t = t + 1$;

9: **end while**

10: Initialize the projection matrix P via solving $\min_P \|ZP - Y\|_2^2 + \alpha \|P\|_2^2$.

11: **while** not converge **do**

12:     Update B by solving Eq.(8);

13:     Update P by solving Eq.(5);

14: **end while**

Output: The real-valued codes $Y \in R^{n \times k}$, binary codes
   $B \in R^{n \times k}$ and projection matrix $P \in R^{d \times k}$.

---

general, the Problem (5) can learn the discrete hash codes, while captures robust local discriminative information and simultaneously minimizes the information loss during projection.

2.4   Optimization

In this section, we iteratively optimize Problem (2) and Problem (5) to obtain the solutions of real-valued codes Y, the projection matrix P and binary codes B.

Solution of Y. The augmented Lagrangian function of Problem (2) is:

$$L(Y) = \sum_{i,j=1}^{n} \tilde{A}_{ij} \|y_i - y_j\|_2 + \text{tr}\left(\Lambda\left(Y^T Y - I\right)\right), \qquad (6)$$

where $\tilde{A}_{ij} = A_{ij} / \|y_i - y_j\|_2$ is a re-weighted affinity matrix, $\tilde{L} = \tilde{D} - \tilde{W}$ is a re-weighted graph Laplacian and $D = \text{diag}\left(\tilde{A} 1^T\right)$ is a diagonal matrix. Since the re-weighted coefficients form a symmetric matrix, re-weighted matrix $\tilde{A}$ is non-negative, sparse, low-rank and doubly stochastic, like the original affinity matrix A. Taking the derivative of $L(Y)$ w.r.t Y and setting the derivative to zero yields:

$$\frac{\partial L(Y)}{\partial Y} = \tilde{L}Y - Y\Lambda = 0, \tag{7}$$

which indicates that the solution of Y is the top k eigenvectors of the re-weighted graph Laplacian $\tilde{L}$. Since $\tilde{L}$ is a sparse Hermitian matrix, the solution of Y satisfies the orthogonality constraint $Y^T Y = I$ and can be efficiently calculated by Lanczos algorithms [27].

Solution of P. When B is fixed, Problem (5) w.r.t B is a regularized least-square problem, which is also called ridge regression. Ridge regression is comprehensively utilized to interpret data due to its homogeneity, graduality, and robustness. Many existing iterative algorithms can effectively deal with a very-large-scale least-square problem [28] to obtain the solution of P.

Solution of B. When P is fixed, the optimal method of solving for b_j is to assign the first half of descending-ordered w_j to $+1$ and the second half to -1, where w_j is the column of projection result $W = XP$. This is formulated as:

$$b_{ij} = \begin{cases} 1, & q\left(w_{ij}\right) \leq n/2, \\ -1, & otherwise, \end{cases} \tag{8}$$

where $q(w_{ij})$ denotes the order of w_{ij} after sorting and the assigned vector b_j represents the binary codes B as a column vector. With this approach, all columns of binary codes B have equal numbers of $+1$ and -1 entries.

To obtain the final solution, we repeatedly calculate the real-valued codes of Y corresponding to the eigenvector of the re-weighted graph Laplacian $\tilde{L}$, until convergence. Then, we alternately update the projection matrix P and binary codes B until B is unchanged. The details of the proposed algorithm are presented in Algorithm 1.

2.5   Computational Complexity Analysis

For each iteration, the memory cost of constructing $\tilde{L}$ is $o\left(n^2\right)$, and the time cost is $o\left(n^2\right)$. Constructing $\tilde{L}$ requires a huge amount of memory when the samples are of large scale. To address this, we can solve this problem by using block operation, which divides a large-scale samples into several blocks, such that a small space is required for each block. For calculating the top k eigenvectors Y, it requires a memory cost of $o(nk)$ and a time cost of $o(n(r+8))$. For updating P, it requires a memory cost of $o(dk)$ and a time cost of $o(2dn)$ for each iteration. Therefore, the total memory cost of SGHSR is approximately $o\left(n^2 + nk + dk\right)$ and the total time cost is $o\left(\left(n^2 + n(r+8)T_2\right)T_1 + 2dnT_3\right)$, where T_i is the number of iterations.

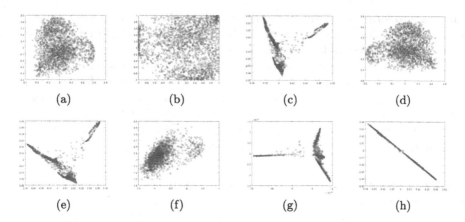

Fig. 1. (a) The original distributions of the training samples on the MNIST database in two-dimensional space. The real values of the training samples that are learned by the (b) SH, (c) AGH, (d) ITQ, (e) LGHSR, (f) JSH, (g) our proposed SGHSR method without spectral regression and (h) the SGHSR method on the MNIST database with 2-bit length. The Euclidean-distance-based information losses are 2.468, 0.195, 0.422, 0.195, 0.700, 0.194 and 0.188, respectively, corresponding to (b) to (h). It can be seen that the proposed SGHSR method performs the best in reducing the information loss and preserving the manifold structure in binary codes.

3   Experiments

In this section, we evaluate the proposed method on three widely used image databases: MNIST[1], CIFAR-10[2] and SUN-397[3] Five state-of-the-art unsupervised manifold-based hashing methods, namely, SH [12], AGH [13], ITQ [15], JSH [20] and LGHSR [14], are selected for comparison with our method. In the experiment, we used a computer with Intel Core i5 13600KF processor, 32 GB memory and 1 TB solid state, and installed Windows 10 Professional 64-bit operating system on it. In addition, we used the MATLAB R2021b development environment to realize the relevant functions of the experiment.

3.1   Databases

The MNSIST database contains 70,000 images of handwritten digits from 0 to 9 in 10 categories. In the experiments, we randomly select 6900 images from each class as training samples, and the rest compose the testing samples. In addition, all samples are converted into 784-dimensional vectors.

The CIFAR-10 database contains 60,000 tiny images of 10 objects, each of which provides 6,000 samples. Similarly, we randomly select 5,900 images from

---

[1] http://yann.lecun.com/exdb/mnist/.

[2] https://www.cs.toronto.edu/~kriz/cifar.html.

[3] https://groups.csail.mit.edu/vision/SUN/.

each class to form the training sample set and use the remaining samples as the test samples. In the experiment, we extract the 512-dimensional GIST features for each image as the data descriptors.

The SUN397 database contains 108,753 images of 397 scene categories, with more than 100 samples for each category. In our experiment, we form a sample set by selecting 10,756 samples from 7 common categories, where each category contains at least 1,000 samples. Then, we randomly select 50 images per class as the test samples and employ the remaining samples as the training samples. All samples are converted into 1,600-dimensional vectors.

Table 1. MAP values of six methods with various code lengths on the MNIST, CIFAR-10 and SUN397 databases

Method	MNIST						CIFAR-10						SUM397					
	12bits	16bits	32bits	64bits	96bits	128bits	12bits	16bits	32bits	64bits	96bits	128bits	12bits	16bits	32bits	64bits	96bits	128bits
SH	0.2943	0.2828	0.2636	0.2446	0.2368	0.2361	0.1314	0.1326	0.1303	0.1299	0.1289	0.1282	0.4146	0.3620	0.3095	0.2906	0.2815	0.2919
AGH	0.5526	0.5222	0.4301	0.3509	0.3201	0.3005	0.1534	0.1529	0.1509	0.1463	0.1418	0.1387	0.4307	0.4073	0.3559	0.3200	0.3085	0.2982
ITQ	0.3969	0.4267	0.4288	0.4263	0.4489	0.4516	0.1539	0.1557	0.1553	0.1554	0.1575	0.1616	0.5919	0.5732	0.5505	0.5443	0.5444	0.5440
JSH	0.3704	0.4264	0.5477	0.5485	0.5388	0.5591	**0.2080**	0.1781	0.1883	0.1693	0.1666	0.1714	**0.5972**	0.5750	**0.6246**	0.6336	0.6357	0.6401
LGHSR	0.6349	0.5724	0.5074	0.4167	0.3658	0.3386	0.1656	0.1638	0.1629	0.1573	0.1541	0.1503	0.5456	0.5254	0.4555	0.4428	0.4289	0.4225
SGHSR	**0.6628**	**0.6720**	**0.6684**	**0.7188**	**0.7238**	**0.7224**	0.2007	**0.1987**	**0.1967**	**0.1966**	**0.1809**	**0.1854**	0.5486	**0.6480**	0.6124	**0.6355**	**0.6363**	**0.6447**

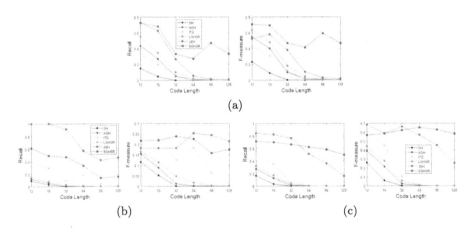

Fig. 2. The Recall and F-measure curves of different methods on the (a) MNIST, (b) CIFAR-10 and (c) SUN397 databases.

3.2   Experimental Results on MNIST

To illustrate the effects of our methods, we explore distributions of real-valued samples that are learned by different methods in the MNIST database, as shown in Fig. 1. The proposed method outperforms the compared methods. This is because the proposed method can better capture the intrinsic structures in data. Moreover, the proposed method can use spectral regression to further fit the binary codes to the original data.

In addition, we use three widely used metrics, including the Mean Average Precision (MAP), Recall and F-measure, for consistent evaluation. In the experiments, we set the repeat number of k-means clustering as 5 and choose the common parameter settings of $m = 300$, $s = 3$ and $\alpha = 20$ on the MNIST database. The bits of binary codes are selected from the candidate set [12,16] to evaluate the performances of the different methods.

The Hamming ranking performance (in MAP) of different methods on the MNIST database is shown in Table 1 (left part). It can be seen that the proposed SGHSR method outperforms most existing methods. This is because the proposed method can better extract sparse and discriminative features using the sparse graph model and can learn a valid projection matrix via spectral regression. Moreover, the proposed method avoids the degradation of the performance as the length of the hash codes increase. A possible reason is that the proposed method imposes the sparsity on manifold learning to extract complicated latent structures of the data, which are insensitive to the dimension of hash codes. In addition, the SGHSR achieves a higher accuracy than the JSH method. This is because the proposed method can adaptively learn the optimal parameters among the different instances to capture the most discriminative information.

The hash lookup results in terms of Recall and F-measure on the MNIST database are plotted in Fig. 2(a). The performances of all the methods are gradually degraded with increasing code lengths due to the accumulation of quantization error and the enlarged Hamming distance. In this scenario, our method shows remarkable improvement on the hash lookup results and the best performance among the methods. This is because, in the proposed method, the sparse graph model can minimize the distance of similar hash codes and spectral regression can make the hash codes consistent with original data.

3.3 Experimental Results on CIFAR-10

The experimental settings on the CIFAR-10 database are the same as those on the MNIST database. Table 1 (middle part) tabulates the Hamming ranking performances (in MAP), and Fig. 2(b) shows the corresponding Recall and F-measure results of different method on the CIFAR-10 database. It can be seen our proposed method outperforms most compared methods, demonstrating the promising effectiveness of the proposed method. In addition, it is worth noting that all methods shows lower MAP on the CIFAR-10 database than that on the MNIST database. A possible reason is that there exist large semantic gaps between the samples of CIFAR-10 database.

3.4 Experimental Results on SUN397

For the complex images in the SUN397 database, we choose similar experimental settings to those on the two databases above, except the number of repeats of

k-means clustering is 15 and s = 5. The Hamming ranking performances (in MAP) of different methods on the SUN397 database are presented in Table 1 (right part), and Recall and F-measure results are shown in Fig. 2(c). We can see that our proposed SGHSR achieves better or comparable performance than the state-of-the-art methods. Particularly, Fig. 2(c) shows that our method yields much better recall and F-measure results than the state-of-the-art methods. It demonstrates that the proposed SGHSR can efficiently obtain the most similar items corresponding to the query items since neighbor data falls into the same hashing balls as much as possible.

3.5 Convergence Analysis

The convergence curves of our method on the MNIST, CIFAR-10 and SUN397 databases are shown in Fig. 3. It can be seen that our proposed method can converge in less than 10 iterations, which demonstrate that the SGHSR method has a fast convergence speed. The convergence speed on real image databases such as CIFAR-10 and SUN397 is faster than on digital databases such as MNIST, which demonstrates the feasibility of practical application.

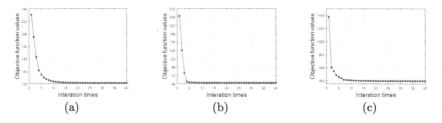

Fig. 3. The convergence lines of the SGHSR method with 32 bits on the (a) MNIST, (b) CIFAR-10 and (c) SUN397 databases.

Table 2. Comparison between with/without using the re-weighted ℓ_1-norm and spectral regression on the MNIST and CIFAR-10 databases

Database	Code Length	12bits		16bits		32bits		64bits	
	Results	MAP	Recall	MAP	Recall	MAP	Recall	MAP	Recall
MNIST	SGHSR-WRL	0.5874	0.4775	0.5623	0.3548	0.5651	0.1991	0.6625	0.1365
	SGHSR-WSR	0.6364	0.6910	0.5274	0.6316	0.5885	0.2382	0.6609	0.1509
	SGHSR	**0.6628**	**0.7280**	**0.6720**	**0.6830**	**0.6684**	**0.3327**	**0.7188**	**0.2823**
CIFAR-10	SGHSR-WRL	0.1738	0.2436	0.1798	0.1826	0.1831	0.0914	0.1858	0.0567
	SGHSR-WSR	0.1743	**0.8917**	0.1687	**0.8425**	0.1405	**0.5920**	0.1288	0.1778
	SGHSR	**0.2007**	0.6125	**0.1987**	0.4935	**0.1967**	0.4740	**0.1966**	**0.3334**

3.6   Ablation Analysis

Effectiveness of the Re-Weighted ℓ_1-Norm. To investigate the effectiveness of the re-weighted ℓ_1-norm on improving the manifold learning, we compare the proposed model with that without using the re-weighted ℓ_1-norm (referred to as SGHSR-WRL). Table 2 presents the MAP and recall results of SGHSR and SGHSR-WRL on the MNIST and CIFAR-10 databases with various code lengths. The results demonstrate the re-weight ℓ_1-norm of the SGHSR can facilitate the learning of sparse and discriminative features to obtain a superior performance.

Effectiveness of Spectral Regression. To investigate the performance of spectral regression on reducing the information loss between the original data and the binary data, we compare the proposed model with that without using the spectral regression (referred to as SGHSR-WSR), as tabulated in Table 2. It can be seen that the spectral regression can effectively improve the overall performance, especially in sparse Hamming space with long code lengths.

4   Conclusion

In this paper, we propose a Sparse Graph Hashing with Spectral Regression method for efficient hash code learning. To make the learned binary code sparse and discriminative, we enforce two important criteria, namely, re-weighted ℓ_1-norm and spectral regression, on the manifold learning for hash codes. The experimental results on three benchmark databases demonstrate that our SGHSR method outperforms or performs competitively with the state-of-the-art hashing methods. However, this method also has some limitations, such as quantization loss and space cost are still too high. In future work, it could be an interesting direction to improve the proposed method by integrating mapping with quantization to simultaneously learn more discrete codes and to improve the computational efficiency.

Acknowledgement. This work was supported in part by the National Natural Science Foundation of China under Grants 62176066, 62106052 and 62006059, and in part by the Natural Science Foundation of Guangdong Province under Grant 2023A1515012717.

References

1. Andoni, A., Indyk, P.: Near-optimal hashing algorithms for approximate nearest neighbor in high dimensions. Commun. ACM **51**(1), 117–122 (2008)
2. Shuai, C., Wang, X., He, M., Ouyang, X., Yang, J.: A presentation and retrieval hash scheme of images based on principal component analysis. Vis. Comput. **37**, 2113–2126 (2021)

3. Dean, T., Ruzon, M.A., Segal, M., Shlens, J., Vijayanarasimhan, S., Yagnik, J.: Fast, accurate detection of 100,000 object classes on a single machine. In: Proceedings of the IEEE Conference on Computer Vision and Pattern Recognition, pp. 1814–1821 (2013)

4. Shen, F., Shen, C., Liu, W., Tao Shen, H.: Supervised discrete hashing. In: Proceedings of the IEEE Conference on Computer Vision and Pattern Recognition, pp. 37–45 (2015)

5. Xiao, Y., Zhang, W., Dai, X., Dai, X., Zhang, N.: Robust supervised discrete hashing. Neurocomputing **483**, 398–410 (2022)

6. Qin, J., Fei, L., Zhang, Z., Wen, J., Xu, Y., Zhang, D.: Joint specifics and consistency hash learning for large-scale cross-modal retrieval. IEEE Trans. Image Process. **31**, 5343–5358 (2022)

7. Su, H., Han, M., Liang, J., Liang, J., Yu, S.: Deep supervised hashing with hard example pairs optimization for image retrieval. Vis. Comput. **39**, 1–16 (2022)

8. Liu, J., et al.: Discrete semantic embedding hashing for scalable cross-modal retrieval. In: 2021 IEEE International Conference on Systems, Man, and Cybernetics (SMC), pp. 1461–1467. IEEE (2021)

9. Qin, J., et al.: Discrete semantic matrix factorization hashing for cross-modal retrieval. In: 2020 25th International Conference on Pattern Recognition (ICPR), pp. 1550–1557. IEEE (2021)

10. Wang, J., Kumar, S., Chang, S.F.: Semi-supervised hashing for scalable image retrieval. In: 2010 IEEE Computer Society Conference on Computer Vision and Pattern Recognition, pp. 3424–3431. IEEE (2010)

11. Hu, H., Wang, K., Lv, C., Wu, J., Yang, Z.: Semi-supervised metric learning-based anchor graph hashing for large-scale image retrieval. IEEE Trans. Image Process. **28**(2), 739–754 (2018)

12. Weiss, Y., Torralba, A., Fergus, R.: Spectral hashing. In: Advances in Neural Information Processing Systems, vol. 21 (2008)

13. Liu, W., Wang, J., Kumar, S., Chang, S.F.: Hashing with graphs. In: ICML (2011)

14. Li, X., Hu, D., Nie, F.: Large graph hashing with spectral rotation. In: Thirty-First AAAI Conference on Artificial Intelligence (2017)

15. Gong, Y., Lazebnik, S., Gordo, A., Perronnin, F.: Iterative quantization: a procrustean approach to learning binary codes for large-scale image retrieval. IEEE Trans. Pattern Anal. Mach. Intell. **35**(12), 2916–2929 (2012)

16. Hoang, T., Do, T.T., Le, H., Le-Tan, D.K., Cheung, N.M.: Simultaneous compression and quantization: a joint approach for efficient unsupervised hashing. Comput. Vis. Image Underst. **191**, 102852 (2020)

17. Hu, D., Nie, F., Li, X.: Discrete spectral hashing for efficient similarity retrieval. IEEE Trans. Image Process. **28**(3), 1080–1091 (2018)

18. Jin, S., Yao, H., Zhou, Q., Liu, Y., Huang, J., Hua, X.: Unsupervised discrete hashing with affinity similarity. IEEE Trans. Image Process. **30**, 6130–6141 (2021)

19. Hu, Z., Nie, F., Chang, W., Hao, S., Wang, R., Li, X.: Multi-view spectral clustering via sparse graph learning. Neurocomputing **384**, 1–10 (2020)

20. Lai, Z., Chen, Y., Wu, J., Wong, W.K., Shen, F.: Jointly sparse hashing for image retrieval. IEEE Trans. Image Process. **27**(12), 6147–6158 (2018)

21. X, W., et al.: Binary representation via jointly personalized sparse hashing. ACM Trans. Multimed. Comput. Commun. Appl. **18**(3s), 1–20 (2022)

22. Wang, W., Zhang, H., Zhang, Z., Liu, L., Shao, L.: Sparse graph based self-supervised hashing for scalable image retrieval. Inf. Sci. **547**, 622–640 (2021)

23. Wang, W., Shen, Y., Zhang, H., Yao, Y., Liu, L.: Set and rebase: determining the semantic graph connectivity for unsupervised cross-modal hashing. In: Proceedings of the Twenty-Ninth International Conference on International Joint Conferences on Artificial Intelligence, pp. 853–859 (2021)

24. Panda, M.R., Kar, S.S., Nanda, A.K., Priyadarshini, R., Panda, S., Bisoy, S.K.: Feedback through emotion extraction using logistic regression and CNN. Vis. Comput. **38**(6), 1975–1987 (2022)

25. Cai, D., He, X., Han, J.: Spectral regression: a unified subspace learning framework for content-based image retrieval. In: Proceedings of the 15th ACM International Conference on Multimedia, pp. 403–412 (2007)

26. Zhang, L., Yang, M., Feng, X.: Sparse representation or collaborative representation: Which helps face recognition? In: 2011 International Conference on Computer Vision, pp. 471–478. IEEE (2011)

27. Stewart, G.W.: Matrix Algorithms: Volume II: Eigensystems. In: SIAM (2001)

28. Cou, C., Guennebaud, G.: Depth from focus using windowed linear least squares regressions. Vis. Comput. 1–10 (2023)

A Crowd Behavior Analysis Method for Large-Scale Performances

Qian Zhang, Tianyu Huang, Yihao Li, and Peng Li[(✉)]

Beijing Institute of Technology, Beijing 100081, China
pengl@bit.edu.cn

Abstract. This study combines visual and athletic information to analyze crowd performance, using performance density entropy and performance consistency as visual descriptors and group collectivity as an athletic descriptor. We used these descriptors to develop a crowd performance behavior classification algorithm that can distinguish between different behaviors in large-scale performances. The study found that the descriptors were weakly correlated, indicating that they capture different dimensions of performance. The crowd behavior classification experiments showed that the descriptors were valid for qualitative analysis and consistent with human perception. The proposed algorithm successfully differentiated and described performance behavior in the dataset of a large-scale crowd performance and was demonstrated to be effective.

Keywords: Crowd Behavior analysis · Large-scale crowd performances · Crowd descriptors

1 Introduction

Large-scale crowd performances are commonly used in athletic celebrations and national ceremonies. Crowd performance analysis and evaluation are critical aspects for crowd performance design, and computer technology plays a significant role in this field. The analysis of artistic works such as crowd performance is beneficial for summarizing and understanding the design standards [1].

Crowd performance behavior analysis currently relies on manual evaluation and group behavior motion analysis. Human-centered qualitative evaluation, using artistic experiences from audiences and artists, is a mainstream approach for manual evaluation [1]. Analyzing group motion behavior involves extracting information on group trajectories, summarizing motion flow [2], and constructing group motion models [3] to segment groups and reduce behavioral analysis time. Feedback evaluation from audiences and artists remains the primary performance analysis method, but generic evaluation metrics can improve automatic analysis and reduce costs.

In summary, the purpose of our study is to define the evaluation metrics for crowd performance and quantify crowd description information. The main contributions are as follows.

B. Sheng et al. (Eds.): CGI 2023, LNCS 14498, pp. 54–66, 2024.
https://doi.org/10.1007/978-3-031-50078-7_5

- Design descriptors for crowd performance behavior. We proposed descriptors focusing on visual information to describe performances in spatial and temporal dimensions, respectively.
- Analyze and understand crowd performances. Visual information descriptors can help us understand crowd performances by analyzing variations in these descriptors. Our study has shown that combining visual and motion information descriptors is better than using only aspect descriptors for detecting performance behavior.
- Propose a qualitative and quantitative evaluation algorithm for crowd performances. Through behavioral classification experiments, it is verified that the proposed algorithm is effective in identifying different types of performance. In addition, the performance scores represent formation-change degree levels.

This paper is organized as follows. Section 2 provides an overview of previous work related to this paper. Section 3 focuses on the performance behavior descriptors, the design of these descriptors and the analysis algorithm used. Section 4 reports our experimental methodology and analysis of the results. Section 5 shows the application results of these descriptors in a large-scale crowd performance. Section 6 summarizes the current experimental results and describes future directions of this work.

2   Related Work

Refer to value-based approach [4], researchers in related fields shifted their focus towards developing quantitative and qualitative evaluation methods with the continuous improvement of digital art and CG technology [5]. The current dominant evaluation method involves collecting questionnaires from audiences, performers, and artists [6] and providing evaluation results based on post-hoc feedback.

In the last two decades, large-scale crowd performance simulation has rapidly grown [7]. In 2008, multidimensional layered crowd performance parallel simulation was used at the Beijing Olympics to assist in choreography realization [8]. Higher-order dynamic information was utilized by Pierre A. et al. [9] to optimize group editing and their framework has been borrowed by subsequent population crowd behavior simulation methods. Lv L. et al. [7] proposed a method for generating large-scale population motion from a tiny population to address complex simulation and tedious manual planning. And Li Y. et al. [10] proposed a strategy based on time-slicing and spatially hierarchical layering to achieve dense group automated editing to some extent in 2020. While crowd performance editing methods continue to evolve, there is still no convincing solution for understanding crowd behavior.

Group analysis can be divided into two branches: group counting and group behavior analysis [11]. Researchers typically approach group behavior analysis from two perspectives: micro and macro, which represent the interpretation of group behavior from individual and overall perspectives, respectively. The micro approach, based on social forces of target agents proposed by Helbing D. et al. [12] has been widely used by researchers for group behavior analysis. For instance, Ramin M. et al. [13] utilized a social forces model to locate abnormal crowd behavior in video surveillance. Moreover, it is also used in target tracking [14] and crowd simulation. Macro-level applications, such as dynamic target agents and the utilization of spatial and temporal features [15] are popular methods for understanding and analyzing crowd behavior.

Researchers are focusing on the attributes of groups themselves for behavior analysis in recent years. They extract descriptions like dispersion, collectivity, and stability for dense crowd analysis and study normative definitions of group attributes [16]. Zhou B. et al. [17] proposed a group collectiveness descriptor based on the observation that groups self-organize into collective movements. Shao J. et al. [18] designed scenario-independent descriptors by extracting basic attributes like collectivity and conflict. Zou Y. et al. [19] proposed a new framework measuring crowd collectivity using macroscopic and microscopic motion consistency. While progress has been made, achieving a fine-grained group description in all scenarios remains challenging.

In contrast to previous studies on group behavior, we propose a novel method to describe crowd performance behavior. Our method includes:

- Interpreting performance behavior from two aspects, visual information and motion information.
- Focusing on behavioral changes that occur during performances and evaluating crowd performance both qualitatively and quantitatively.

3   Method

3.1   Expression Approach of Crowd Performance

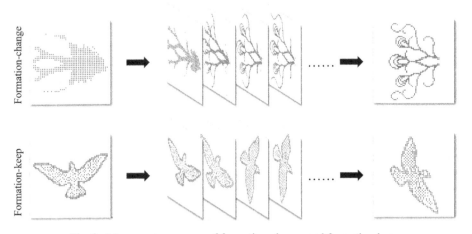

Fig. 1. Movement processes of formation-change and formation-keep.

Group formation and transformation are one of the focuses of crowd behavior researchers [20]. Based on the effect of formation changes, the crowd behavior can be divided into categorized formation-change performances and formation-keep performances. As illustrated in Fig. 1, the formation-change performance represents a transition from one formation pattern to another. During this transition process, group members have their own target positions, and the group can be subdivided into small groups based on their targets. In the formation-keep performance, collective crowd maintain a stable formation structure [21], the spatial arrangement around each member and the k-nearest neighbor (KNN) distance between them remaining steady. It results in a visually stable group profile, with the crowd moving consistently in a same direction.

The expression of crowd performance state at moment t is shown in Eq. 1.

$$P_t = \{D_1, D_2, \ldots D_i\} \tag{1}$$

The crowd performance state is divided into several aspects based on the information changes: visual information D_1, motion information D_2, and auditory information et al D_i. We focus on visual and motion information in this study.

3.2 Visual Information Analysis

The spatial and temporal locations of the members in the performance crowd together compose the information such as group shape or density. Thus, location information of crowd members is stored in the array $F\{f_1, f_2, f_3, \ldots, f_t\}$. The array F can be seen as keyframe information in formation transformation [22]. Here, f_t indicates the location of all members in the crowd at moment t.

$$A = \begin{bmatrix} a_{00} & \cdots & a_{0n} \\ \vdots & \ddots & \vdots \\ a_{m0} & \cdots & a_{mn} \end{bmatrix} \tag{2}$$

$$a_{ij} = 2 * \frac{\left(g'_{ij} * d'_{ij}\right)}{\left(g'_{ij} + d'_{ij}\right)} \tag{3}$$

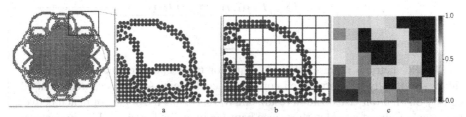

Fig. 2. Visual information visualization process. Fig. a shows the membership distribution. Fig. b illustrates the rasterized schematic representation. Fig. c shows the visualization results, with redder colors indicating more persons and greater density in the corresponding raster space. (Color figure online)

The process of visualizing visual information in crowd performance is shown in Fig. 2. We use matrix G to store the number of people inside each raster grid g_{ij} and matrix D to store the average KNN distance d_{ij}. Then, the elements in matrix D will be updated using d_{max}/d_{ij}. To avoid d'_{ij} quantity becomes infinite, we set the minimum value of d_{ij} equals $d_{max} * 0.01$. Visual information for crowd performances is stored in matrix A with m rows and n columns. The numerical values of m and n depend on the size of the performing crowd. The a_{ij} is the harmonic average of the elements in the normalized matrix of G and the normalized matrix of D.

Performance Density Entropy
In this section, a Performance Density Entropy (*PDE*) metric is proposed to quantify the process of group density distribution uniformity changes within a performance clip, with the calculation equations shown as follows. And *PDE* is represented as Ψ.

$$\psi_t = \frac{1}{M} \sum_{a_{ij}>0} (a_{ij} - \bar{a})^2 \tag{4}$$

$$\Psi = \frac{1}{T} \sum_{t=1} |\psi_t - \psi_{t-1}| \tag{5}$$

The element in Eq. 4 can only be calculated when $a_{ij} > 0$. M is the number of elements greater than zero. ψ_t represents the degree of uniformity in group distribution at time t. A smaller value of ψ_t indicates a more average density distribution of crowd. Thus, the value of ψ_t will be minimum only when all elements in matrix A are the same. The value range of ψ_t and Ψ is [0,0.25).

Performance Consistency
In reality, a group formation's most salient visual feature is generally its contour shape [23]. And the motion-shape [24] of a crowd is a crucial factor in behavior detection. Therefore, we proposed Performance Consistency (*PC*) to measures consistency in the formation of the performing crowd between adjacent moments in crowd performance. Since crowd performance has been visualized, we can use image processing methods to calculate the *PC* metric.

$$R_t = \frac{\sum_{i,j} |I_{t-1}(i,j) \cdot I_t(i,j)|}{\sqrt{\sum_{i,j} I_{t-1}(i,j)^2 \cdot \sum_{i,j} I_t(i,j)^2}} \tag{6}$$

$$\Upsilon = \frac{1}{T} \sum_{t=1} R_t \tag{7}$$

The *PC* metric is represented as Υ. Equation 6 presents a template matching algorithm, specifically the normalized correlation coefficient. At time t, I_t represents the density distribution visualization result, and R_t represents the degree of match between the visual results of crowd performance between time t and time $t - 1$. Υ indicates the average consistencies of group formations in the segment. A smaller value of Υ indicates a better retention effect of the group formation pattern. Same to the range of R_t, the value range of Υ is [0,1].

3.3 Motion Information Analysis

Collective crowd movements are significant motion information in crowd performance behavior [21]. The average velocity similarity of all individuals within a group does not provide clear feedback on individual collectivity. Therefore, *MCC* (Measuring Crowd Collectiveness) [17] proposed a method deriving the global consistency among individuals through path consistency, and integrating the group to derive the overall collective consistency. As a general algorithm for measuring collective consistency, *MCC* and its deformation algorithms are widely used in both group behavior analysis and group segmentation. We also use *MCC* to calculate collective consistency result and the metric is represented as Φ.

$$\Phi = \frac{1}{|T|} \sum_{t=0} \widehat{\Phi}(t) \tag{8}$$

$$\widehat{\Phi}(t) = \frac{1}{|C|} \sum_{i \in C} \Phi(i) = \frac{1}{|C|} e^T Z e \tag{9}$$

$\widehat{\Phi}(t)$ denotes the quantitative value of the collectiveness of performance at moment t. In Eq. 9, C is the set of all the members in the group, and a matrix e is used, where all the elements are equal to 1. The quantified collectiveness value of member i is $\Phi(i)$, and Z is the matrix containing information about path consistency of the individuals in the group. In MCC [17], it is proved that $\widehat{\Phi}(t)$ has the value range [0, 1], and our metric Φ is the same.

3.4 Behavior Analysis Method for Crowd Performances

We propose an algorithm to qualitatively and quantitatively analyze the group performance based on the definitions of *PDE*, *PC*, and *MCC*, as shown in Algorithm 1.

$$P_\psi = \begin{cases} 3, \psi \geq k_1 \cdot \xi_1 \\ 1, \psi \geq \xi_1 \, and \, \psi < k_1 \cdot \xi_1 \\ -1, \psi < \xi_1 \end{cases} \tag{10}$$

$$P_\Upsilon = \begin{cases} 3, \Upsilon \leq k_2 \cdot \xi_2 \\ 1, \Upsilon < \xi_2 \, and \, \Upsilon > k_2 \cdot \xi_2 \\ -1, \Upsilon \geq \xi_2 \end{cases} \tag{11}$$

$$P_\Phi = \begin{cases} 3, \Phi \leq k_3 \cdot \xi_3 \, \Phi \\ 1, \Phi < \xi_3 \, and \, \Phi > k_3 \cdot \xi_3 \\ -1, \Phi \geq \xi_3 \end{cases} \tag{12}$$

$$P_t = \begin{cases} 0, P_\psi + P_\Upsilon + P_\Phi < 0 \\ 1, P_\psi + P_\Upsilon + P_\Phi \geq 0 \end{cases} \tag{13}$$

The current crowd behavior is represented by either a formation-change state or a formation-keep state, with 1 and -1 indicating a high probability for each state, respectively. The threshold value for distinguishing between two states is denoted by ξ_1. During performance behavior detection, if $\Psi \geq k_1 \cdot \xi_1$, it indicating an extremely high probability of formation-change state. To ensure that the final P_t is equals to 1, a weight value of 3 is assigned at that moment. Similarly, ξ_2, ξ_3, k_2, and k_3 are used in the same way. In Eq. 13, a weighted analysis approach is employed to combine the three descriptors, resulting in a binary performance state output with 1 indicating formation-change and 0 indicating formation-keep. In experiments, the numerical values of various empirical parameters are as follows: $\xi_1 = 0.004$, $\xi_2 = 0.6$, $\xi_3 = 0.6$, $k_1 = 1.333$, $k_2 = 0.667$, $k_3 = 0.667$.

Algorithm 1: Crowd Performance Behavior Analysis

Input:
    Set of frames about individuals' location F.
Output:
    Crowd performance behavior classification $\{P_1,...P_n\}$.
Procedure:
    1: Initialize sliding window size $num=3$, $t=1$, separate F into $\{F_1,...F_n\}$ using num.
    2: rasterize crowd location of F_t as $\{A_1,...A_{num}\}$ by Eq.3.
    3: Compute Ψ by Eq. 5, Compute Y by Eq. 7, Compute Φ from F_t by Eq. 8.
    4: Compute P_t by Eq. 13
    5: Update $t = t + 1$.
    6: Repeat 2~5, until $t = n+1$.

---

4 Experiment and Analysis

4.1 Analysis for Descriptors

In this section, we explored the practical implications of visual information descriptors to better analyze the change process of *PDE* and *PC* within a crowd performance. We design a case with the same start formation and end formation with different performance processes as shown in Fig. 3a. In this case, we set the rasterization parameters $m = n = 8$, and set the sliding window size $num = 3$. Visually, the formation changes of Per1 are more pronounced than in Per2. And in Fig. 3b, *PDE* value is larger in Per 1, which means that the *PDE* is proportional to the degree of formation change.

In Fig. 3c, a case of consistent initial state and different final states is presented. Per 1 and Per 2 have the same movement trend and similar velocity directions, while Per 2 has obvious deformation. In this case, we set the rasterization parameters $m = n = 5$, and set the sliding window size $num = 3$. In Fig. 3d, a smaller value of *PC* is observed in adjacent moments for Per 2. It is the same as human visual perception.

4.2 Dataset Analysis

The data are from a large-scale crowd performance simulation dataset [10], which contains more than 3,000 people performing. It can be divided into three chapters based on the content. We use 1_0, 2_0, 3_0 to represent the three chapters.

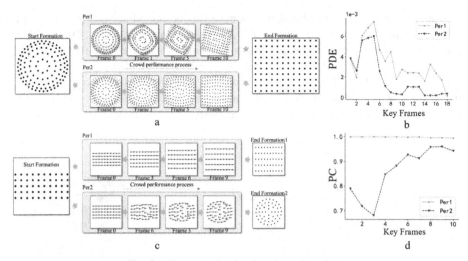

Fig. 3. The examples for descriptors' analysis

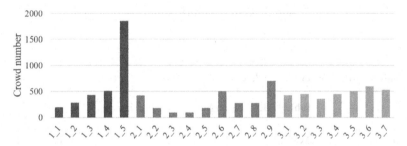

Fig. 4. The detailed information for the items in our dataset.

Based on the manual classification, the members within a chapter are grouped, and different groups are labeled as formation-change grouping and formation-keep grouping based on their behavior, and these groups form the items of our dataset. The final dataset has 14 formation-change performances and 10 formation-keep performances. The details of the dataset are shown in Fig. 4. It shows the composition of the dataset in the group performances and the number of people in performance segments. The naming convention for the dataset is X_X. The first X represents which performance chapter the current performance segment belongs, and the second X represents the number of the current performance group in this corresponding chapter. In subsequent experiments, we adjusted the rasterization parameters for each item based on the group size. Specifically, we used three different $m = n = 8$ values of 25, 35, and 45.

4.3 Correlation Between Descriptors

In this section, we examined the correlation among different descriptors and demonstrated their significance in describing crowd performance scenes while complementing each other. In the following experiments, the k-nearest neighbor number is 5.

From Fig. 5d, it is evident that there is a negative correlation between *PC* and both *PDE* (correlation factor of –0.12) and *MCC* (correlation factor of –0.44). On the other hand, *PDE* and *MCC* exhibit weak positive correlation with a correlation factor of 0.21. The metric *PDE* reflects the level of uniformity in the distribution of group density during the performance, while *PC* represents the change in performance formations over time. *MCC*, on the other hand, characterizes the overall movement consistency exhibited by the group. The correlation result shows these metrics capture different aspects of the group performance process.

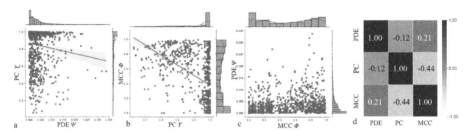

Fig. 5. Correlation analysis results

4.4 Evaluation of Descriptor Classification Results

Table 1. Evaluation Metrics for descriptors

Descriptor	ACC	P	R	F1
PDE	0.750	0.900	0.643	0.750
PC	0.583	0.667	0.571	0.616
MCC	0.750	0.833	0.714	0.769
PDE + PC	0.792	1.000	0.643	**0.783**
PC + MCC	0.750	1.000	0.571	**0.727**
PDE + MCC	0.792	0.846	0.786	**0.815**
All	**0.875**	0.867	0.929	**0.897**

Experiments using *PDE*, *PC*, and *MCC* descriptors separately, as well as their combinations, were performed to classify crowd performance behavior. The results of the comparisons are obtained and presented in Table 1. Descriptors' combination has a better classification result in F1 value than considering these descriptors separately. Moreover, the combination of all the three descriptors improved the recall *R* and *F1* values for crowd behavior classification.

5   Crowd Performance Evaluation

Our performance behavior evaluation method was conducted on the using dataset of large-scale square performance choreography. The results are presented in Fig. 6. This data consisted of 60 keyframes of group member information, with each step comprising 5 keyframes (step = 1, 2,..., 12). The corresponding descriptor values at each step indicate that the more intense the visual formation change process between adjacent steps, the greater the change in *PDE* and the lower the *PC* value.

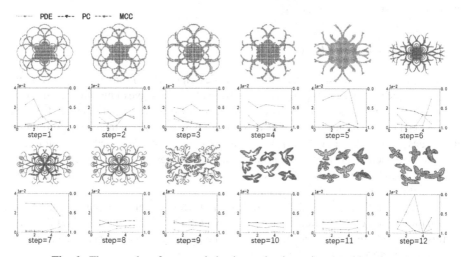

Fig. 6. The crowd performance behavior evaluation using three descriptors.

In Fig. 7a, the score represents the possibility of formation-change performance. It shows the compare results between the MCC [17] method and ours. In most steps, the results were consistent with ground truth. According to the scores, our method is more sensitive to the degree levels of formation-change. Based on the visual effect, the performance fragments can be divided into four stages, 1 to 5, 6 to 8, 8 to 10, 11 to 12. Among them, the average score in the 1–5 steps is higher. Observing the changes between these performance clips, formation changes are more drastic in 1–5 steps.

We test the effectiveness of the proposed method in quantitative analysis of performance behavior in the dataset. Choreographer artist have already divided the intensity of formation-change for each performance chapter when designing the crowd performances in the dataset. As a result, this section classifies the dataset into three levels of formation-change behaviors based on the crowd performance chapters: weak formation-change (or formation-keep), medium formation-change, and strong formation-change. It can be observed from Fig. 7b that as the intensity of formation-change behavior increases, the average weight score also increases.

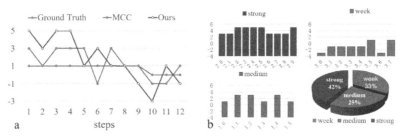

Fig. 7. Fig. a shows calculation score for formation-change behavior. Fig. b Score analysis about different levels of formation-change performances.

6   Summary and Future Work

In this paper we propose two visual information descriptors: *PDE* and *PC*. Moreover, the generic collective descriptor *MCC* is applied from the perspective of motion information. The correlation analysis experiment demonstrate that the descriptors belong to different dimensional information features. The classification results also indicate that combining all the descriptors is better than using them separately. The designed descriptors can quantitatively detect different performance stages during the performance evaluation experiment, and the intensity of formation-change can be quantitatively described by the formation-change weights using Algorithm 1.

As the method proposed in this article mainly focuses on studying overall visual information based on formation patterns, it may not be well-suited for analyzing group performances where member actions serve as the primary visual effects, such as large-scale dance performances.

In the future, we will continue to design descriptors for crowd performance behavior in different features such as music and rhythm. And we will conduct an in-depth performance behavior analysis based on more crowd performance data.

Acknowledgements. This research was supported by the National Key Research and Development Program of China funded by the Ministry of Science and Technology (No2020YFC2007200 and No. 2020YFF0305200).

References

1. Candy, L.: Evaluation and Experience in Art, pp. 25–48. Springer, Cham (2014). https://doi.org/10.1007/978-3-319-04510-8_3
2. Tripathi, G., Singh, K., Vishwakarma, D.K.: Convolutional neural networks for crowd behaviour analysis: a survey. Vis. Comput. **35**, 753–776 (2019). https://doi.org/10.1007/s00371-018-1499-5
3. Liu, P., Chao, Q., Huang, H., et al.: Velocity-based dynamic crowd simulation by data-driven optimization. Vis. Comput. **38**, 3499–3512 (2022). https://doi.org/10.1007/s00371-022-02556-5
4. Cockton, G.: Revisiting usability's three key principles. In: CHI '08 Extended Abstracts on Human Factors in Computing Systems, pp. 2473–2484. Association for Computing Machinery, New York, NY, USA (2008). https://doi.org/10.1145/1358628.1358704

5. England, D., Fantauzzacoffin, J., Bryan-Kinns, N., et al.: Digital art: evaluation, appreciation, critique (invited SIG). In: CHI 2012 Extended Abstracts on Human Factors in Computing Systems, Austin, Texas, USA, pp. 1213–1216. Association for Computing Machinery, New York, NY, USA (2012). https://doi.org/10.1145/2212776.2212426

6. Wang, Y., Liu, Y.: Evaluation system of CG art communication platform based on user experience. IEEE Access. **10**, 128742–128753 (2022). https://doi.org/10.1109/ACCESS.2022.322 7931

7. Lv, L., Mao, T., Liu, X., et al.: Optimization-based group performance deducing. Comput. Anim. Virtual Worlds **25**, 171–184 (2014). https://doi.org/10.1002/cav.1544

8. Yang, J., Huang, T., Ding, G., et al.: Parallel live performance simulation based on a multidimensional hierarchy and application. J. Syst. Simul. **34**, 1750–1761 (2022). https://doi.org/10.16182/j.issn1004731x.joss.21-0271E

9. Pierre, A., Nicolas, C., Thomas, C.: Optimal crowd editing. Graph. Models. **76**(1), 1–16 (2014). https://doi.org/10.1016/j.gmod.2013.09.001

10. Li, Y., Huang, T., Ding, G., et al.: Research on performance modeling and simulation method based on dense crowd. J. Syst. Simul. **33**(7), 1617–1625 (2021). https://doi.org/10.16182/j.issn1004731x.joss

11. Mounir, B., Jonathan, W., Germain, F., et al.: Recent trends in crowd analysis: a review. Mach. Learn. Appl. **4**, 100023 (2021). https://doi.org/10.1016/j.mlwa.2021.100023

12. Helbing, D., Molnár, P.: Social force model for pedestrian dynamics. Phys. Rev. E **51**(5), 4282–4286 (1995). https://doi.org/10.1103/physreve.51.4282

13. Ramin, M., Alexis O., Mubarak S.: Abnormal crowd behavior detection using social force model. In: 2009 IEEE Conference on Computer Vision and Pattern Recognition, pp. 935–942 (2009). https://doi.org/10.1109/CVPR.2009.5206641

14. Patel, A.S., Vyas, R., Vyas, O.P., et al.: Motion-compensated online object tracking for activity detection and crowd behavior analysis. Vis. Comput. **39**, 2127–2147 (2023). https://doi.org/10.1007/s00371-022-02469-3

15. Zaharescu, A., Wildes, R.: Anomalous behaviour detection using spatiotemporal oriented energies, subset inclusion histogram comparison and event-driven processing. In: Daniilidis, K., Maragos, P., Paragios, N. (eds.) ECCV 2010. LNCS, vol. 6311, pp. 563–576. Springer, Heidelberg (2010). https://doi.org/10.1007/978-3-642-15549-9_41

16. Voon, W.P., Mustapha, N., Affendey, L.S., et al.: Crowd behavior classification based on generic descriptors. In: 2019 International Symposium on Intelligent Signal Processing and Communication Systems (ISPACS), pp.1–2 (2019). https://doi.org/10.1109/ISPACS48206.2019.8986333

17. Zhou, B., Tang, X., Wang, X.: Measuring crowd collectiveness. IEEE Trans. Pattern Anal. Mach. Intell. **36**, 1586–1599 (2013). https://doi.org/10.1109/CVPR.2013.392

18. Shao, J., Loy, C.C., Wang, X.: Learning scene-independent group descriptors for crowd understanding. IEEE Trans. Circ. Syst. Video Technol. **27**, 1290–1303 (2016). https://doi.org/10.1109/TCSVT.2016.2539878

19. Zou, Y., Zhao, X., Liu, Y.: Measuring crowd collectiveness by macroscopic and microscopic motion consistencies. IEEE Trans. Multimedia **20**, 3311–3323 (2018). https://doi.org/10.1109/TMM.2018.2832601

20. Wang, X., Zhou, L., Deng, Z., et al.: Flock morphing animation. Comput. Anim. Virtual Worlds **25**, 351–360 (2014). https://doi.org/10.1002/cav.1580

21. Xu, M., Wu, Y., Ye, Y., et al.: Collective crowd formation transform with mutual information–based runtime feedback. Comput. Graph. Forum. **34**(1), 60–73 (2015). https://doi.org/10.1111/cgf.12459

22. Gu, Q., Deng, Z.: Formation sketching: an approach to stylize groups in crowd simulation. In: Graphics Interface 2011, pp. 1–8, GI '11, Canadian Human-Computer Communications Society, Waterloo (2011). https://doi.org/10.5555/1992917.1992919

23. Gu, Q., Deng, Z.: Generating freestyle group formations in agent-based crowd simulations. IEEE Comput. Graphics Appl. **33**(1), 20–31 (2011). https://doi.org/10.1109/MCG.2011.87
24. Farooq, M.U., Saad, M.N.M., Khan, S.D.: Motion-shape-based deep learning approach for divergence behavior detection in high-density crowd. Vis. Comput. **38**, 1553–1577 (2022). https://doi.org/10.1007/s00371-021-02088-4

PPI-NET: End-to-End Parametric Primitive Inference

Liang Wang and Xiaogang Wang[(✉)]

College of Computer and Information Science, Southwest University, Chongqing,
China
wangxiaogang@swu.edu.cn

Abstract. In engineering applications, line, circle, arc, and point are collectively referred to as primitives, and they play a crucial role in path planning, simulation analysis, and manufacturing. When designing CAD models, engineers typically start by sketching the model's orthographic view on paper or a whiteboard and then translate the design intent into a CAD program. Although this design method is powerful, it often involves challenging and repetitive tasks, requiring engineers to perform numerous similar operations in each design. To address this conversion process, we propose an efficient and accurate end-to-end method that avoids the inefficiency and error accumulation issues associated with using autoregressive models to infer parametric primitives from hand-drawn sketch images. Since our model samples match the representation format of standard CAD software, they can be imported into CAD software for solving, editing, and applied to downstream design tasks.

Keywords: Parametric primitive · End-to-end · Hand-drawn sketch image · CAD software

1 Introduction

Parametric CAD starts with a 2D sketch containing geometric primitives such as lines, circles, arcs, and points which is a widely used method in mechanical engineering and aerospace. Engineers then import these primitives into CAD software, which can be edited with constraints and position adjustments. Additional CAD operations, like extrusion, result in the creation of a 3D model. Figure 1 illustrates a functionality achieved through our method. The process is robust but repetitive, prompting the need for accurate pattern prediction to reduce manual tasks and increase work efficiency. Converting hand-drawn sketches or noisy inputs into editable models is a desired feature.

Object detection in computer vision, particularly the DETR [1] algorithm, a transformer-based approach that eliminates the need for hand-designed components and achieves good performance. However, DETR [1] has issues with slow convergence during training and unclear interpretation of queries. To address these, various approaches have been proposed, such as deformable attention [3] and denoising techniques [12,26].

B. Sheng et al. (Eds.): CGI 2023, LNCS 14498, pp. 67–78, 2024.
https://doi.org/10.1007/978-3-031-50078-7_6

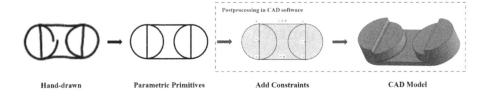

Fig. 1. CAD model generation. Hand-drawn sketch images as input, we feed them into image primitive network to generate parametric primitives. By adding constraints, adjust the positions of primitives to create a coherent sketch, final extrusion the sketch to generate a 3D model in CAD software.

All previous detection methods detect the object category associated with fixed four parameters (x, y, w, h) of the box. In our task, as shown in Table 1, the parameter length of the primitive varies dynamically according to its type, which is unsuitable for the anchor-based DETR [1] method described above.

Table 1. Parameter representation for different primitives.

Line	x_1	y_1	x_2	y_2	0	0
Circle	x	y	r	0	0	0
Arc	x_1	y_1	x_{mid}	y_{mid}	x_2	y_2
Point	x	y	0	0	0	0

In this work, we introduce the PPI-NET network, a detection network that, after training, detects geometric primitives to synthesize coherent CAD sketches. The image primitive model uses the original Transformer and a denoising module in DN-DETR [12] to infer the parameters of primitives end-to-end. We make the following contributions:

1. We convert real hand-drawn sketches into editable forms within CAD software, enabling designers to communicate and collaborate more efficiently with team members, clients, and suppliers.
2. We can bind different parameters to various types of primitives by employing primitives' dynamic parametric inference.
3. We propose an end-to-end network called PPI-Net for inferring parametric primitives from hand-drawn sketch images, which provides users with a more flexible and manipulable data representation.
4. Our method has achieved better results compared with Vitruvion [21] in both qualitative and quantitative aspects.

2 Related Work

2.1 Parametric Primitive Inference

Parameterized primitive fitting is a long-standing problem in the field of geometric processing. Researchers have explored methods for detecting or fitting parameterized feature curves, such as Bézier and B-spline, often using least squares representation [6, 11]. These methods [9, 22–25] share the common characteristic of taking three-dimensional point cloud data as input. In contrast, Vitruvion [21] extracts parameterized primitives from real hand-drawn sketches.

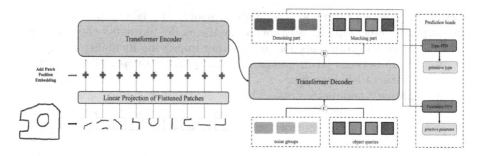

Fig. 2. Image Primitive Model Pipeline. Input a hand-drawn sketch image, and the network predicts the type and parameters of the primitive. "C" means cat the noise groups and object queries. "D" means decoupling the noise groups and object queries.

2.2 CAD Sketch Generation

The SketchGraphs dataset [20] was recently introduced to target the underlying relational structure and construction operations found in mechanical design software. [7,18,21,27] all utilize auto-regressive models to model the primitives and the constraint relationships between them. However, this approach cannot directly output results end-to-end and is easily influenced by the previous time steps' outputs. Vitruvion [21] is similar to our method, this input approach allows for better reconstructing primitives from hand-drawn sketches.

2.3 Vector Graphics Generation

Vector graphics are used in commercial software to enable the resolution independent design of fonts, logos, animations, and illustrations. In recent years, generative models [2,5,8,10,15,17,19] have been successfully applied to the field of vector graphics. [13] infers sketches from facial images. Conversely, our method is similar to the image-conditional version of Vitruvion [21], which takes hand-drawn raster images as input and generates vector graphics.

3   Method

The pipeline of PPI-Net network is illustrated in Fig. 2. Given an input image, a detection module detects the four types of primitives implicitly embedded in the image and extracts their parameterized information as object queries.

3.1   Denoising

We collect all ground-truth (GT) objects for each image and add random noises to their parameter and class labels. We use multiple noised versions for each GT object to maximize the utility of denoising learning. For label noise, we use label flipping, which means we randomly flip some GT labels to other labels. The purpose of label flipping is to encourage the model to predict the GT labels based on the noised primitives' parameter, thus improving its ability to capture the relationship between labels and primitives. We have a hyper-parameter γ to control the ratio of labels to flip.

For primitives' parameter noise, which is obtained by adding noise of standard normal distribution to the corresponding GT primitive parameters of each GT primitive type, λ to control the ratio of noise to add, as $q_{parameter} = (GT_{parameter} + \lambda * noise) * mask_{GT_{type}}$.

The losses of the denoising part are $l1$ loss and Chamfer Distance (CD) loss for primitive of parameters and focal loss [14] for class labels as in DAB-DETR [16]. In our method, we employ a function $\delta(\cdot)$ to represent the noised GT objects. Thus, each query in the denoising part can be expressed as $q_m = \delta(GT_m)$, where GT_m corresponds to the m-th GT object.

3.2   Attention Mask

The inclusion of an attention mask is vital in our model. It has been observed from the results presented in Table 5, that the absence of an attention mask during denoising training hinders performance rather than enhancing it. To introduce attention mask, we need to first divide the noised GT objects into groups. Each group is a noised version of all GT objects. The denoising part becomes where g_p is defined as the p-th noise group. Each noise groups contains N queries where N is set to be significantly larger than the typical number of primitives in an image. So we have where $q_p^n = \delta(GT_n)$.

The purpose of the attention mask is to prevent information leakage. There are two types of potential information leakage. One is that the matching part may see the noised GT objects and easily predict GT objects. The other is that one noised version of a GT object may see another version. Therefore, our attention mask is to make sure the matching part cannot see the denoising part and the denoising groups cannot see each other.

We use $A = [a_{ij}]_{W \times W}$ to denote the attention mask where $W = P \times N$, P is the numbers of groups. We let the first $P \times N$ rows and columns to represent the denoising part and the latter to represent the matching part. $a_{ij} = 1$ means the i-th query cannot see the j-th query and $a_{ij} = 0$ otherwise.

$$a_{ij} = \begin{cases} 0, & \text{if } P * N \leq (i,j) \leq (P+1) * N, \\ 1, & otherwise. \end{cases} \tag{1}$$

3.3   Embedding

The decoder embedding is specified as label embedding in our model to support both primitive parameter denoising and label denoising. We embed the noise label as a content query. We denote $P_i = (p_1, p_2, p_3, p_4, p_5, p_6)$ as the noise parameter information of the i-th primitive, $p_1, p_2, p_3, p_4, p_5, p_6 \in [0, 1]$. D is the dimension of decoder embeddings and positional queries. Given a primitive parameter P_i, its positional query V_i is generated by: $V_i = MLP(PE(P_i))$, where PE means positional encoding to generate sinusoidal embeddings from float numbers and the parameters of MLP are shared across all layers. In our implementations, the positional encoding function PE maps a float to a vector with $D/2$ dimensions as: $R \rightarrow R^{D/2}$. Hence the function MLP projects a $3D$ dimensional vector into D dimensions: MLP: $R^{3D} \rightarrow R^D$. The MLP module has two submodules, each composed of a linear layer and a ReLU activation, and the feature reduction is conducted at the first linear layer.

3.4 Image Primitive Model

The image primitive model is inspired by DETR [1] and applies the denoising part of DN-DETR [12] to accelerate the convergence of DETR [1]. We hope it can accurately recover parameterized primitives from hand-drawn sketches.

Architecture. The model is based on an image encoder using a visual converter [4], which uses 128×128 size image as input. Extract size 16 from input image 16×16 non-overlapping square blocks are flattened to produce a sequence of 64 flattened blocks. Then, before entering the standard converter encoder, each one undergoes a linear transformation of the embedding dimension of the model (256 in this case), and adds corresponding position encoding to each image sequence. For the decoder, which is the same as DETR [1], we use learnable position encoding as object queries and use it as input for each attention layer. Object queries will be converted into outputs in each Decoder layer. Ultimately, they will all independently pass the Type-FFN and Parameter-FFN, predicting the corresponding primitive types and primitive parameters separately.

Denoising and Matching Part. The matching part uses the same method as the DETR [1], which obtains the corresponding relationship to perform loss calculations. Denoising part: since we know the primitive type and primitive parameters that each query should correspond to when building the noise groups, we can directly calculate the loss without bipartite matching. Please note that the denoising part is only considered during training, removing the denoising part during the inference process and leaving only the matching part.

Cost Matrix. Like DETR [1], each image contains different primitive types and parameters, so we use bipartite matching to determine the corresponding relationship between prediction and ground truth. The cost matrix for classification is the same as DAB-DETR [16]. Treating a parameter with a length of six as the parameter to be used and directly comparing the parameter to be used with the ground truth parameter for L1 loss as $cost_p$. The parameters to be used are sampled according to four types: line, circle, arc, and point. The CD between the sampling point of ground truth and prediction is calculated, and the type with the smallest distance is taken for the cost matrix as $cost_{CD}$.

$$Cost\ Matrix = \omega_c * cost_c + \omega_p * cost_p + \omega_{cd} * cost_{CD}, \qquad (2)$$

This optimal assignment is computed efficiently with the Hungarian algorithm.

Loss. With the bipartite matching result, the one-to-one correspondence between prediction and ground truth, we can calculate the classified loss as focal loss for primitives type, as $Loss_c$. Calculate the loss of primitive parameters,

$$Loss_p = \frac{1}{K} \sum_{i=1}^{K} ||\hat{y} - y|| * mask_{T_y}, \tag{3}$$

K is the actual number of primitives in the image, T_y is the corresponding GT primitive type, $\hat{y}$ is the predicted primitive parameter, and y is the ground truth primitive parameter. Because different types of parameters use different positions, so use the binary mask to calculate the actual loss.

Using the $\hat{y}$ and y, we perform point sampling based on T_y, and calculate the CD between the sampled points, which bind different parameters to various types of primitives,

$$Loss_{CD} = \frac{1}{K} \sum_{i=1}^{K} CD(\hat{y}, y, T_y), \tag{4}$$

$Loss_{CD}$ represents the sum of CD for all types of primitives. The final loss is the weighted sum of the above loss,

$$Loss = \omega_c * Loss_c + \omega_p * Loss_p + \omega_{cd} * Loss_{CD}. \tag{5}$$

4   Experiments

4.1   Training Dataset

Our model is trained on a filtered version of the SketchGraphs dataset [20] by Vitruvion [21], which has a collection of 1.7 million unique sketches. As shown in the Fig. 4, we demonstrate the relative proportion of each primitives type in the dataset. However, unlike Vitruvion [21], we do not consider the *isConstruction* boolean of the parametric primitive in Table 1, which clarifies differences through rendering as shown in Fig. 3. We randomly divided the filtered sketch set into 92.5% training, 2.5% validation, and 5% testing partitions. Before training the image primitive model, we generate samples using the mathplotlib to simulate sketches of hand-drawn style. The model selects one random image from the five generated samples during each training epoch. Random affine transformations are applied to the images to further augment the data during training. These transformations include translation (up to 8 pixels), rotation (up to 10°), shear (up to 10°), and scaling (up to 20%).

4.2   Evaluation Metrics

We implemented four metrics to measure the performance of the image primitive model: (1) type accuracy, which measures the primitive type classification performance, (2) The Chamfer Distance (CD), (3) precision, (4) recall.

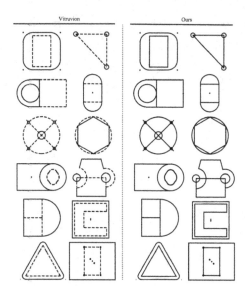

Fig. 3. Each primitive has an attribute isConstruction, and when isConstruction = *True*, Vitruvion renders the primitive with a dashed line (*left*). In contrast, our method disregards attribute isConstruction and directly renders all primitives with solid lines (*right*).

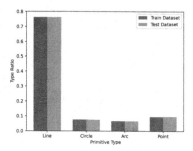

Fig. 4. The proportion of each primitives type in the dataset.

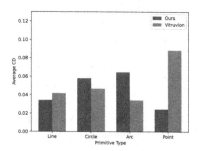

Fig. 5. Comparison of the average CD for each primitives type.

The type accuracy is calculated as: $Type\_acc = \frac{1}{K}\sum_{i=1}^{K} \mathbb{1}(t_i = \hat{t}_i)$, where K is the actual number of primitives contained in the image, $\hat{t}_i$ is the predicted primitive type, and t_i is the ground truth primitive type. $Precision = \frac{TP}{TP+FP}$, $Recall = \frac{TP}{TP+FN}$, We use the probabilities of the primitive types as the confidence scores and the CD as one of the evaluation metrics.

$$TP = score_{confidence} > \tau_{con} \ \& \ CD < \tau_{CD}, \tag{6}$$

$$FP = score_{confidence} > \tau_{con} \ \& \ CD > \tau_{CD}, \tag{7}$$

$$FN = score_{confidence} < \tau_{con} \ \& \ CD > \tau_{CD}, \tag{8}$$

In this case, we use $\tau_{con} = 0.50$ and $\tau_{CD} = 0.40$ as the threshold values.

4.3 Parameter Setting

The training was conducted on a server with four Nvidia 3090 GPUs, and our model was trained for 250 epochs, which took 72 h. Our model is configured with standard Transformer encoder and decoder components, with six layers each. We set $\gamma = 0.4$ to control the label flipping and $\lambda = 0.3$ to control the noise parameter in the denoising part. We have also incorporated three sets of

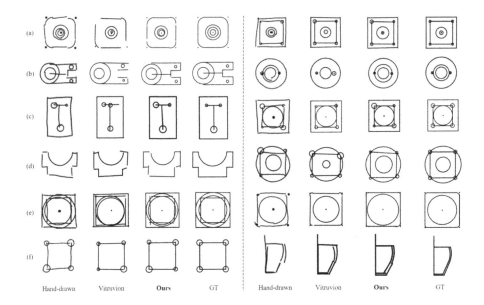

Hand-drawn   Vitruvion   **Ours**   GT   Hand-drawn   Vitruvion   **Ours**   GT

Fig. 6. Compare with Vitruvion [21]. Raster images of real hand-drawn sketches are input to the image primitive model.

denoising groups and the weight parameters for loss are set to $\omega_c = 2$, $\omega_p = 2$, and $\omega_{cd} = 5$. All models were trained with $N = 20$ decoder query slots. The initial learning rate was set to 3e-5 (at reference batch size 128, scaled linearly with the total batch size). The batch size was set 256 / GPU for the model.

4.4   Comparisons to the State-of-the-Art

Currently, there is relatively limited research on the task of inference parametric primitives from real hand-drawn images. To the best of our knowledge, in 2021, the Vitruvion [21] introduced this task for the *first* time and employed an auto-regressive model to address it.

As seen in Fig. 5, compared with Vitruvion [21], the average CD between primitives of the same type. The better support of Vitruvion's [21] auto-regressive model for the primitives' types represented in long sequential lists is reflected in the Fig. 5, where it can be observed that *Point* has the largest CD, while *Arc* has the smallest CD. Each primitive in PPI-Net is treated as an independent object, and there is a certain correlation between the number of parameters and the average CD of the primitives.

Under the same input conditions, Fig. 6 showcases our model's ability to detect primitives, in Table 2 has been evaluated through quantitative comparisons with the image to primitive model of Vitruvion [21]. Our model demonstrates outstanding performance in these aspects.

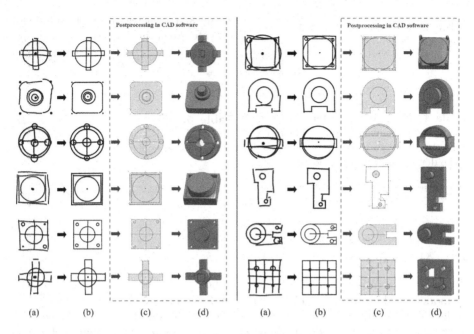

Fig. 7. Editing infer primitives in CAD software. Hand-drawn sketch images (*a*), infer parametric primitives (*b*), import the parametric primitives, add constraints in Onshape Gui (*c*), adjust primitives' positions, and use CAD operations to make the sketch to generate a 3D model (*d*).

4.5 Import into CAD Software

As shown in the Fig. 7, the hand-drawn sketch is first input into the image primitive network to extract primitives. These extracted primitives are then imported into professional CAD software. Within the CAD software, tools and commands are used to add constraint relationships (e.g., coincident, parallel) and adjust positions and sizes, ensuring a coherent sketch. Once the sketch meets the desired geometric criteria, CAD operations like extrusion, hole-cutting, and rotation create the final CAD model.

4.6 Test Strategy

Table 3 presents the evaluation of the image primitive model on a dataset of 128×128-pixel human-drawn sketch images, as described in Sect. 4.2. We conduct tests on the model using different types of rendering: precise renderings, renderings from the hand-drawn simulator, and renderings with random affine augmentations from the hand-drawn simulator. The results show that both the hand-drawn simulation and augmentations significantly enhance the model's performance.

Table 2. Compare metrics with Vitruvion [21].

Metric	Type_acc↑	CD↓	Precision↑	Recall↑	GFLOPs	Params
Vitruvion [21]	91.0%	0.0428	66.9%	65.3%	230	172
Ours	**93.2%**	**0.0368**	**73.9%**	**71.1%**	93	61

Table 3. The metrics highlighted in bold indicate the optimal values.

Training regimen	Type_acc↑	CD↓	Precision↑	Recall↑
Precise rendering	82.5%	0.0597	58.6%	51.5%
Hand-drawn augmentation	92.6%	0.0383	71.2%	67.4%
Hand-drawn + affine	**93.2%**	**0.0368**	**73.9%**	**71.1%**

Table 4. Ablation results for comparing the effects of denoising groups. The model does not converge within the 250 epochs if the denoising groups are not used.

Denoise Groups	Type_acc↑	CD↓	Precision↑	Recall↑	GFLOPs	Params
No Group	80.2%	0.0581	58.9%	54.1%	93	61
1 Group	92.3%	0.0388	67.9%	66.1%	93	61
3 Groups	**93.2%**	**0.0368**	**73.9%**	**71.1%**	93	61

Table 5. Ablation results for denoising part. All models use 1 denoising group under the same default settings.

Parameter Denoise	Label Denoise	Attention Mask	Type_acc↑	CD↓	Precision↑	Recall↑
✓	✓	✓	92.3%	0.0388	67.9%	66.1%
✓		✓	91.9%	0.0397	66.8%	65.3%
		✓	91.7%	0.0403	66.5%	65.1%
✓	✓		57.2%	0.0730	31.2%	26.7%

4.7 Ablation Study

We employ denoising groups to accelerate the convergence speed of the DETR [1] model and improve the metric scores. In Table 4, we demonstrate the effects of denoising groups and varying the number of denoising groups on the results under the same conditions. The findings in Table 5 demonstrate that each component utilized in the denoising training contributes to enhancing performance. It is worth highlighting that the absence of an attention mask, which prevents information leakage, leads to a significant decline in performance.

5   Conclusion

We propose PPI-Net, an end-to-end network for inferring parametric primitives from hand-drawn sketches, providing a flexible data representation. This approach optimizes primitive representation and facilitates efficient communication and collaboration among engineers, team members, clients, and suppliers.

Limitation. As shown in Fig. 8(a), due to the method being derived from object detection, its inference capability for small primitives is not strong. As shown in Fig. 8(b, c), there is a deviation between the extracted circles and arcs compared to the ground truth (GT). Therefore, we hope further to enhance the inference capability of the image primitive model.

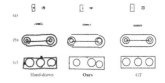

Fig. 8. Failure cases.

Future Work. Currently, the main method involves inferring primitives from hand-drawn sketch images, but it overlooks the constraints between primitives, which are pivotal for constructing continuous sketches. Therefore, in future work, we aim to achieve end-to-end inference primitives and the constraint relationships between them from hand-drawn sketch images to improve the quality and coherence of the generated sketches.

Acknowledgements.. We thank the anonymous reviewers for their valuable comments. This work was supported in part by Natural Science Foundation of China (No. 62102328), in part by the Fundamental Research Funds for the Central Universities (No. SWU120076) and in part by the Open Project Program of State Key Laboratory of Virtual Reality Technology and Systems, Beihang University (No.VRLAB2023C01).

References

1. Carion, N., Massa, F., Synnaeve, G., Usunier, N., Kirillov, A., Zagoruyko, S.: End-to-end object detection with transformers. In: Vedaldi, A., Bischof, H., Brox, T., Frahm, J.-M. (eds.) ECCV 2020. LNCS, vol. 12346, pp. 213–229. Springer, Cham (2020). https://doi.org/10.1007/978-3-030-58452-8_13

2. Chakrabarty, S., Johnson, R.F., Rashmi, M., Raha, R.: Generating abstract art from hand-drawn sketches using GAN models. In: Uddin, M.S., Bansal, J.C. (ed.) Proceedings of International Joint Conference on Advances in Computational Intelligence. IJCAI 2022. Algorithms for Intelligent Systems, pp. 539–552. Springer, Singapore (2022). https://doi.org/10.1007/978-981-99-1435-7_45

3. Dai, X., et al.: Dynamic head: unifying object detection heads with attentions. In: Proceedings of the IEEE/CVF Conference on Computer Vision and Pattern Recognition, pp. 7373–7382 (2021)

4. Dosovitskiy, A., et al. An image is worth 16x16 words: transformers for image recognition at scale. arXiv preprint arXiv:2010.11929 (2020)

5. Egiazarian, V.: Deep vectorization of technical drawings. arXiv preprint arXiv:2003.05471 (2020)

6. Flöry, S., Hofer, M.: Constrained curve fitting on manifolds. Comput. Aided Des. **40**(1), 25–34 (2008)

7. Ganin, Y., Bartunov, S., Li, Y., Keller, E., Saliceti, S.: Computer-aided design as language. In: Advance in Neural Information Processing System, vol. 34, pp. 5885–5897 (2021)

8. Goodfellow, I., et al.: Generative adversarial networks. Commun. ACM **63**(11), 139–144 (2020)

9. Guo, H., Liu, S., Pan, H., Liu, Y., Tong, X., Guo, B.: Complexgen: CAD reconstruction by b-rep chain complex generation. bACM Trans. Graph. (TOG) **41**(4), 1–18 (2022)

10. Ha, D., Eck, D.: A neural representation of sketch drawings. arXiv preprint arXiv:1704.03477 (2017)

11. Li, C.-Y., Wang, R.-H., Zhu, C.-G.: Design and G1 connection of developable surfaces through bézier geodesics. Appl. Math. Comput. **218**(7), 3199–3208 (2011)

12. Li, F., Zhang, H., Liu, S., Guo, J., Ni, L. M., Zhang, L.: DN-DETR: accelerate DETR training by introducing query denoising. In: Proceedings of the IEEE/CVF Conference on Computer Vision and Pattern Recognition, pp. 13619–13627 (2022)

13. Li, P., Sheng, B., Chen, C.P.: Face sketch synthesis using regularized broad learning system. IEEE Trans. Neural Netw. Learn. Syst. **33**(10), 5346–5360 (2021)

14. Lin, T. Y., Goyal, P., Girshick, R., He, K., Dollár, P.: Focal loss for dense object detection. In Proceedings of the IEEE International Conference on Computer Vision, pp. 2980–2988 (2017)

15. Lin, X., Sun, S., Huang, W., Sheng, B., Li, P., Feng, D.D.: EAPT: efficient attention pyramid transformer for image processing. IEEE Trans. Multimedia **25**, 50–61 (2021)

16. Liu, S., et al.: DAB-DETR: dynamic anchor boxes are better queries for DETR. arXiv preprint arXiv:2201.12329 (2022)

17. Lopes, R.G., Ha, D., Eck, D., Shlens, J.: A learned representation for scalable vector graphics. In Proceedings of the IEEE/CVF International Conference on Computer Vision, pp. 7930–7939 (2019)

18. Para, W., et al.: Sketchgen: generating constrained CAD sketches. In: Advances in Neural Information Processing Systems, vol. 34, pp. 5077–5088 (2021)

19. Reddy, P., Gharbi, M., Lukac, M., Mitra, N.J.: Im2vec: synthesizing vector graphics without vector supervision. In: Proceedings of the IEEE/CVF Conference on Computer Vision and Pattern Recognition, pp. 7342–7351 (2021)

20. Seff, A., Ovadia, Y., Zhou, W., Adams, R.P.: Sketchgraphs: a large-scale dataset for modeling relational geometry in computer-aided design. arXiv preprint arXiv:2007.08506 (2020)

21. Seff, A., Zhou, W., Richardson, N., Adams, R.P.: Vitruvion: a generative model of parametric cad sketches. arXiv preprint arXiv:2109.14124 (2021)

22. Sharma, G., Liu, D., Maji, S., Kalogerakis, E., Chaudhuri, S., Měch, R.: PARSENET: a parametric surface fitting network for 3D point clouds. In: Vedaldi, A., Bischof, H., Brox, T., Frahm, J.-M. (eds.) ECCV 2020. LNCS, vol. 12352, pp. 261–276. Springer, Cham (2020). https://doi.org/10.1007/978-3-030-58571-6_16

23. Uy, M. A., et al.: Point2cyl: reverse engineering 3D objects from point clouds to extrusion cylinders. In: Proceedings of the IEEE/CVF Conference on Computer Vision and Pattern Recognition, pp. 11850–11860 (2022)

24. Wang, X., Yuelang, X., Kai, X., Tagliasacchi, A., Zhou, B., Mahdavi-Amiri, A., Zhang, H.: Pie-net: Parametric inference of point cloud edges. In: Advance in Neural Information Processing System, vol. 33, pp. 20167–20178 (2020)

25. Ying, W., Dong, T., Ding, Z., Zhang, X.: PointCNN-based individual tree detection using LiDAR point clouds. In: Magnenat-Thalmann, N., et al. (eds.) CGI 2021. LNCS, vol. 13002, pp. 89–100. Springer, Cham (2021). https://doi.org/10.1007/978-3-030-89029-2_7

26. Zhang, H., et al.: Dino: DETR with improved denoising anchor boxes for end-to-end object detection. arXiv preprint arXiv:2203.03605 (2022)

27. Zhang, L.: Hand-drawn sketch recognition with a double-channel convolutional neural network. EURASIP J. Adv. Signal Process. **2021**(1), 1–12 (2021)

A ReSTIR GI Method Using the Sample-Space Filtering

Jie Jiang[1], Xiang Xu[2(✉)], and Beibei Wang[1]

[1] Nanjing University of Science and Technology, Nanjing, Jiangsu, China
[2] Shandong Key Laboratory of Blockchain Finance, Shandong University of Finance and Economics, Jinan, Shandong, China
xuxiang@sdufe.edu.cn

Abstract. In real-time ray tracing applications, only a small number of samples per pixel can be traced, limited by the computational power of the hardware. Maximizing the rendering quality with a low sampling rate is an important problem for real-time ray tracing. Reservoir-based spatiotemporal importance resampling with multi-bounce global illumination (ReSTIR GI) improves the rendering quality of a low sampling rate. However, the noise introduced by Monte Carlo sampling still exists. We propose a lightweight and efficient sample-space filtering method applied to ReSTIR GI that filters the sample distribution before resampling, thus reducing the noise in the final rendering result. Compared to the original ReSTIR GI, our method achieves a smaller mean squared error (MSE) of $1.1\times$ to $5.6\times$ and a higher peak signal-to-noise ratio (PSNR) of $1.1\times$ at the cost of an average increase in rendering time of 12%.

Keywords: Real-time rendering · Filtering · Resampling

1 Introduction

The widespread use of real-time rendering places higher demands on both rendering speed and quality. Even with the support of hardware-accelerated ray tracing [11,16], achieving real-time path tracing with a high sampling rate is still difficult. Moreover, restricting the number of samples per pixel (spp) results in significant variance and noise. Therefore, some neural denoising methods [15] or resampling methods have been raised to enhance the quality of low-sampling rendered images.

Resampled importance sampling (RIS) [20] reuses existing sample sequences and optimizes them iteratively to obtain samples that approximate the optimal distribution. Based on RIS, Reservoir-based Spatiotemporal Importance Resampling (ReSTIR) [3] was proposed to address the direct illumination sampling. Then, the ReSTIR GI [17] extended the ReSTIR method to global illumination by resampling indirect lighting paths obtained by path tracing.

Introducing such resampling methods to path tracing can reduce certain noise by resampling and sharing important paths across frames and pixels. Nevertheless, the resampling process cannot eliminate the noise from Monte Carlo

B. Sheng et al. (Eds.): CGI 2023, LNCS 14498, pp. 79–92, 2024.
https://doi.org/10.1007/978-3-031-50078-7_7

estimation sampling, especially under a low sampling rate. Therefore, we propose a lightweight and efficient sample-space filtering method of ReSTIR GI that reduces sample distribution noise by smoothing the radiance contribution in the sample space. We apply the path space filtering [10] to the sample distribution generated by ReSTIR GI and then use the smoothed distribution in the sample space for further reuse. The results show that our method can reduce the MSE of ReSTIR GI with a small additional overhead. Moreover, compared with post-processing denoising methods such as Bilateral filtering and Optix denoiser [5], our method can avoid over blur as it doesn't directly filter the final shading results.

2   Previous Work

Real-time rendering imposes a strict constraint on the frame time budget, which makes it infeasible to use more than one sample per pixel (spp) per frame. However, such a low sampling rate inevitably leads to noisy results. Therefore, various methods have been developed to reduce the variance and noise of real-time path tracing.

2.1   Resampling-Based Method

Talbot et al. [20] proposed the RIS method that extends the importance sampling technique by resampling the initial samples to obtain candidate samples more consistent with the target distribution. This method enhances the rendering quality in complex scenes with multiple light sources and specular reflections.

Based on the RIS method, many studies have been explored to improve rendering quality and efficiency. Bitterli et al. [3] presented the ReSTIR method, which shares light samples in temporal and pixel space to improve the rendering quality of dynamic direct lighting. Ouyang et al. [17] introduced ReSTIR GI, which applies ReSTIR to sample indirect light transport in global illumination. This method generates new paths by connecting resampled candidates with existing path-traced samples. Lin et al. proposed Volume ReSTIR [13] that uses ReSTIR in real-time volume rendering to achieve the fast and accurate performance of volumetric data. Then, considering that the original ReSTIR GI only resample the first indirect bounced samples of path tracing, Boissé et al. [4] extended the sample reuse to the world space and allowed further light transport bounces. Lin et al. [12] introduced a new theoretical generalized resampled importance sampling (GRIS) in their ReSTIR PT, which selects samples from independent samples in different domains. Moreover, they combined GRIS with shift mapping to evaluate the final result to transform the different domains into a unified integral field.

2.2   Path Space Filtering

Keller et al. [10] introduced the path space filtering method, which can enhance the quality and efficiency of real-time path tracing in complex scenes. It smooths the radiance distribution by using the weighted average contribution of adjacent samples within a specific range before image generation. Gautron et al. [8] proposed a progressive real-time path space filtering method. They applied the Fourier histogram descriptors to encode the statistical distribution of paths in the frequency domain and used these descriptors to compare and match the similarity of paths. However, storing and querying data in the path space is expensive. Binder et al. [1] optimized the original path space filtering technique by using a jittered spatial hashing data structure [21] to speed up the filtering step and reduce computation costs. To efficiently map the path space filtering process on the GPU, Binder et al. [2] proposed a massively parallel path space filtering technique that splits the paths into smaller groups and allocates them to multiple GPU cores. Each core then filters the paths independently and efficiently using multi-resolution filtering techniques. The separate paths are then combined using a parallel reduction method to generate the final image. Deng et al. [7] proposed an iterative path space filtering method to identify and extract relevant paths from a given graph based on certain criteria or constraints. The process involves iteratively exploring the graph and filtering out less important paths. This method helps to reduce noise and focus on the most important connections in the graph.

Also, there are many other image restoration [18, 23] and visual related methods. [14, 24]

Our work filters the reservoir buffers generated by resampling in ReSTIR GI in the sample space, instead of directly filtering the final radiance in the image result. Our method can improve the quality of ReSTIR GI rendering and avoid the over blur associated with directly filtering the final radiance in the screen space.

3   Background

3.1   ReSTIR and ReSTIR GI

RIS is an effective method to approximate complex distributions that are difficult to sample directly. It resamples the initial samples in order to obtain candidate samples that are more consistent with the target distribution. Firstly RIS uses a source distribution p to generate M candidate samples $x = \{x_1, \cdots, x_M\}$ with proposal weight $w(x)$. Then, it resamples N new samples $y_i \equiv x_z, z \in \{1, \cdots, M\}$ from the candidate pool by a target distribution $\hat{p}$, where the probability $p(z \mid x)$ is proportional to $w(x)$. The unbiased estimate of f given by RIS:

$$\langle L_r \rangle_{ris}^{N,M} = \frac{1}{N} \sum_{i=1}^{N} \left(\frac{f(y_i)}{\hat{p}(y_i)} \cdot \left(\frac{1}{M} \sum_{j=1}^{M} w(x_{ij}) \right) \right), \tag{1}$$

where

$$p(z \mid x) = \frac{w(x_z)}{\sum_{i=1}^{M} w(x_i)} \quad with \quad w(x) = \frac{\hat{p}(x)}{p(x)}. \tag{2}$$

Weighted reservoir sampling (WRS) [6] is a stream-based method that can obtain a uniform random sample of all the items from a large population without storing them in memory. The method only needs to store the selected samples in the reservoir, making it very memory efficient.

ReSTIR enables RIS to be implemented on GPU through WRS. The method employs chained reservoir resampling to share light samples between frames and pixels. It repeatedly resamples the light sample candidate and applies further spatial and temporal reuse to share information with relevant samples. This reduces the cost of initializing new samples and improves the rendering quality.

ReSTIR GI is an extension of the ReSTIR method for global illumination by using reservoirs to store and reuse the paths generated by path tracing. Moreover, to exploit the temporal and spatial coherence, ReSTIR GI stores the temporal and spatial coherence samples in temporal and spatial reservoir buffers separately and shares them with existing samples in the initial sample buffer. This allows us to share the radiance of important paths between samples in the temporal or spatial reservoir buffer to update the final shading result.

In each frame, ReSTIR GI performs the following steps for each pixel. The first step is to trace a ray from each visible point and record both the visible point and the closest intersection as a sample point in the initial sample buffer, along with their positions and face normals. The next step is to apply temporal resampling. The sample in the temporal reservoir buffer of the current frame is updated by selecting one candidate sample with a resampling weight from the temporal reservoir of the previous frame. And the reprojection is applied to find the corresponding sample in the last frame according to the motion vector. Then, in the spatial reuse stage, the sample in the spatial reservoir is updated by iterative choosing a sample of neighbor pixels with a resampling weight from the temporal reservoir saved in the last frame. The final step is to shade the pixel by combining the sampled path.

3.2   Path Space Filtering

The path space filtering approach uses a low discrepancy sequence to generate path segments and computes the average radiance contribution. This approach first selects a suitable vertex of the light transport path and replaces its radiance contribution with the weighted averaging contributions of vertices inside the filtering range.

Filtering with adjacent samples takes advantage of spatial coherence to smooth the final rendering, although it introduces bias.

4   Our Method

4.1   Overview of Our Method

Resampling methods make a significant contribution to sample reuse, which can build a new sample distribution that is more consistent with the integrand function. However, the noise introduced by rendering with a low sampling rate still exists.

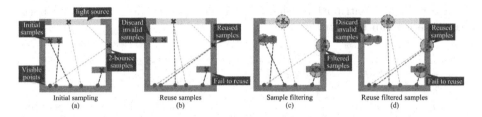

Initial sampling   Reuse samples   Sample filtering   Reuse filtered samples
(a)   (b)   (c)   (d)

Fig. 1. Original ReSTIR GI and our method. (a) The original ReSTIR GI generates initial samples by tracing ray paths to find the closest intersection in the scene. The blue crosses represent the original initial samples. (b) ReSTIR GI performs spatiotemporal reuse for samples, selecting one sample at a time from adjacent frames and pixels for reuse. (c) Our method filters the initial samples to obtain the smoothed radiance values of samples. The pink crosses represent the filtered samples, and the pink circles represent the filtering range. (d) Our method applies the same sample reuse process as ReSTIR GI. This allows more sample contributions to participate in the same reuse process, thus reducing noise when only one single sample is reused. (Color figure online)

Figure 1(a)(b) shows the resampling process of ReSTIR GI. As we mentioned in Sect. 3.2, ReSTIR GI only selects one sample to be reused for path reconnection for each time each pixel by temporal or spatial reuse. However, the samples generated by 1 spp path tracing have high variance, and ReSTIR GI directly performs reuse without filtering them. The reuse process can reduce noise to some extent by sharing paths from existing samples, but the noise brought by the original samples still exists in the reuse process.

We proposed a method that applies the sample-space filtering to ReSTIR GI to reduce the noise of the initial sample buffer, as shown in ·Fig. 1(c)(d). We use the weighted average radiance of neighboring samples to represent the radiance of a single sample. Then, we apply spatial and temporal resampling on the smoothed samples. Compared with ReSTIR GI, reusing the filtered sample in this way can be seen as reusing a group of nearby samples at the same time. However, the final shading result is optimized by reusing only one sample and sharing one path for each pixel on each frame. This shared path is less noisy than ReSTIR GI because it is smoothed by all the valid nearby paths around the filtered sample.

To apply the sample-space filtering to smooth radiance contribution from the reservoir buffer in ReSTIR GI, we assume that samples adjacent in the screen space are also adjacent in the path space. Moreover, since ReSTIR GI only resamples indirect illumination and then accumulates the portion of direct illumination, our filtering is only used for indirect illumination.

4.2 Sample Filtering

Based on our analysis in Sect. 3.2, both the temporal reservoir and spatial reservoir of ReSTIR GI store samples from the initial sample buffer generated by path tracing. So we choose to filter the samples in the initial sample buffer, and the average radiance contribution calculated in the sample space inspired by path space filtering can be rewritten as:

$$\overline{(L_o)}_i = \frac{\sum_{j=0}^{x_{i+j} \in \mathcal{B}(n)} \chi_{\mathcal{B}(n)}(x_{i+j} - x_i) \cdot w_{i+j} \cdot c_{i+j}}{\sum_{j=0}^{x_{i+j} \in \mathcal{B}(n)} \chi_{\mathcal{B}(n)}(x_{i+j} - x_i) \cdot w_{i+j}}, \tag{3}$$

where L_o is the outgoing radiance of the sample point, i and $i+j$ is the sample index, x_i is the selected sample point in the initial sample buffer, x_{i+j} is the surrounding neighbor sample point within a circular range $\mathcal{B}(n)$. c_{i+j} is the radiance contribution of the sample point. To ensure the filtering performance without reducing rendering speed, the filter range is not going to be set too large. w_{i+j} is the weight of the neighbor sample point. Due to the fact that we will control the filter radius r_n not to be set too large, it is usually within the size of ten pixels. Inspired by original path space filtering, it is reasonable to directly set $w_{i+j} \equiv 1$ while limiting the filter radius to a small range, and doing so will not cause over blur. So some complex methods for determining weights based on distance, such as Gaussian filter, Bilateral filter, and irradiance interpolation are not considered. $\chi_{\mathcal{B}(n)}$ is a characteristic function to determine whether the neighbor sample is within the circle $\mathcal{B}(n)$ with the radius of r_n, which is computed as follows:

$$\chi_{\mathcal{B}(n)}(x_{i+j} - x_i) := \begin{cases} 1 & ||x_{i+j} - x_i||_2 < r_n \\ 0 & \text{otherwise} \end{cases}. \tag{4}$$

where

$$r_n = \frac{r_0}{n^\alpha} \; for \; \alpha \in (0, 1). \tag{5}$$

where r_0 is the initial search radius. It should be noted that the radius we discussed is measured in pixels in the screen space. n is the total number of available samples within the range determined by the initial radius r_0, and when $\alpha = \frac{1}{4}$ turns out to be a robustly working choice.

It is also important to note that the data stored during path generation can also be used to evaluate the validity of adjacent samples. And since our method focuses on diffuse reflective materials, we compute the angle between the normals of x_{i+j} and x_i. If the angle is below a threshold ($||n_{i+j} \cdot n_i||_2 < 0.05$), the contribution of x_{i+j} will be treat as a valid neighboring sample.

The original path space filtering selects the initial radius proportional to the length of the distance from the selected sample to the camera. Inspired by that, we set the initial radius r_0 according to the distance between the selected sample point and the camera, which is computed as follows

$$r_0 = \frac{\sqrt{\mathcal{S}}}{f} d. \tag{6}$$

We take the distance between the sample points in the reservoir and the camera as the value of d, where $d = ||x_s, x_c||_2$, x_c is the position of the camera in the scene. For simplicity, we set $k = \frac{\sqrt{\mathcal{S}}}{f}$, $\mathcal{S}$ is the footprint size and f is the focal length. The value of footprint size is based on selected constants. Choosing the footprint and focal length to define the parameters allows the filtering kernel size to be adjusted with the zoom of the camera. The longer the focal length, the smaller the field of view angle, the less footprint size and content presented on the screen, and the results in more details of objects. Therefore, we can control the initial radius by the footprint size, so that the initial radius can adapt to different sizes of focal lengths.

Applying path space filtering to the sample space requires two range queries. The first query searches the n valid samples within the circular area with initial radius r_0, while the second query searches for all neighbor samples within the circular with the optimized radius r_n. Then, we use the neighbor samples searched in the second query to filter the radiance values of the target sample. The computation of the first query is complicated, especially for a large r_0. Therefore, to reduce the time cost in real-time applications, we designed an empirical formula to obtain n by the r_0 determined fixed range in the sample space as:

$$n = n_{calculated} = \lceil \pi r_0{}^2 \rceil. \tag{7}$$

For some complex scenes, the value of r_0 can be very large. Even with an approximate estimation of n, the search range may contain hundreds of pixels. Moreover, as the r_0 increases, the search range will be closer to the real circle (See Fig. 2). Therefore, we estimate the value of n using r_0 through Eq. 7, but still use Eq. 5 to calculate r_n. The power calculation of the Eq. 5 can help us reduce the error between our approximation of n to the actual value. Therefore, this approximation of n can preserve the filtering algorithm's denoising effect and save the traversal cost in the first query.

5   Implementation

We implemented our algorithm in NVIDIA *Falcor* [9] ray tracer. Our filtering and resampling process is performed after the original ReSTIR GI method stores the corresponding sample information.

For efficiency, we treat samples adjacent in screen space as if they are also adjacent in path space. This assumption is reasonable in general, except for edge regions of objects and other specific cases.

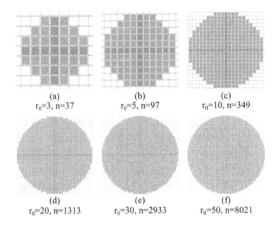

Fig. 2. Search range defined by r_0. The gray and pink parts show the search range with x_i as the center and r_0 as the radius, while the gray part represents the two central axes of the circular area. In practice, r_0 is usually very large reaching hundreds of pixels in complex scenes. (Color figure online)

There are three reservoir buffers used in the ReSTIR GI. In order to balance the filtering overhead with the rendering quality, we chose to filter the initial sample buffer based on our experience and analysis.

For the search radius r_n, we test the rendering performance for different scenes and different r_n. We find that filtering does not visually optimize the original distribution when r_n is too small (less than three pixels). Therefore, we can adjust r_n by the footprint size to avoid it being too small to achieve good filtering results. However, it is still important to note that the value of r_n should not be too large (larger than ten pixels), as an excessively large filter range not only affects rendering speed but may also lead to over blur.

6 Results

We evaluated our method in various scenes using an NVIDIA RTX 3070 GPU. All the scenes were rendered at a resolution of 1920×1080 without applying any post-processing effects.

We used a standard path tracer with next-event estimation for comparison. Reference images are computed using the path tracer with high spp. Errors are reported as the MSE and the PSNR. The rendering time that we report includes the cost of sample generation, path tracing, ReSTIR GI, sample-space filtering, and final shading.

6.1 Performance

In Fig. 3, we compared the rendering results of our method with those of path tracing and ReSTIR GI for similar rendering times in different scenes. It can be seen that our method can smooth the noise caused by Monte Carlo sampling.

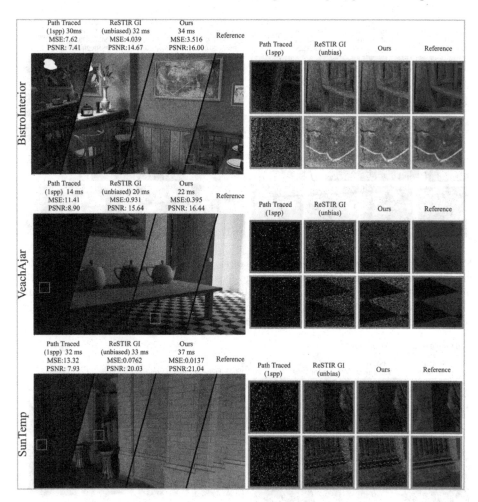

Fig. 3. Rendering results of standard path tracing, ReSTIR GI, and our method with roughly equal rendering time. Two bouncing indirect lightings were rendered in each scene. Our method exhibits a 1.1× to 5.6× improvement in MSE and a 1.1× improvement in PSNR compared to ReSTIR GI.

We take the third scene as an example to demonstrate the time occupation of the rendering pipeline, where 17.2 ms for trace rays and storing initial samples of the direct and indirect illumination, 14 ms for the spatial resampling and temporal resampling of the ReSTIR GI, 2.6 ms for our filter pass and the rest of time for final shading. To summarize, our method outperforms ReSTIR GI, delivering a smaller MSE ranging from 1.1× to 5.6× and a higher PSNR of about 1.1×, with only a slight increase in time consumption of approximately 12%.

The parameter setting of r_0 significantly impacts the rendering results. Using a small r_0 cannot achieve good filtering effects, while a large value may give

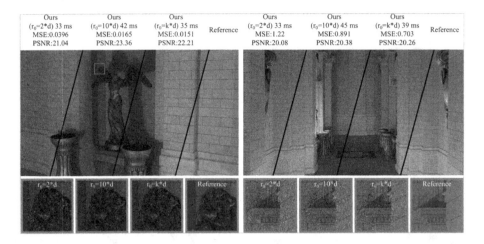

Fig. 4. Rendering results in different values of r_0. Setting r_0 to a small fixed parameter (2*d) results in a large MSE, while a large fixed parameter (10*d) can significantly increase the rendering time. Compared to the 2*d case, our method shows a significant MSE improvement of 1.7× and 2.6× for focal lengths of 45 and 50, respectively. While, compared to the 10*d case, our method can achieve a 1.17× average speed up.

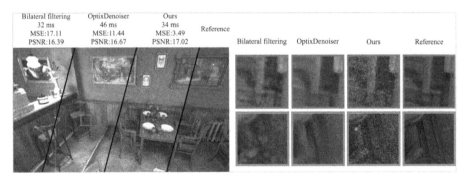

Fig. 5. Comparison of our method, Bilateral filtering method, and OptixDenoiser. We unify the filter radius of both to a relatively small value. The results show that our method is 4.9× better than the Bilateral filtering method and 3.28× better than Optix denoiser in MSE.

better results, but costs more time. In Fig. 4, we compared the rendering results obtained using Eq. 6 with using two fixed parameters. It can be found that using Eq. 6 reduces the MSE by 1.7× to 2.6× compared to the two fixed values. Using flexible parameters in Eq. 6 also shows a PSNR of 1.1× higher than using a small fixed parameter, and is significantly rendering faster than using the large fixed value r_0.

Fig. 6. Comparison of convergence results. (Left) The result of the convergence of our method. (Right) The reference result. Our method shows the MSE of $1.16e^{-3}$ compared to the reference.

Simultaneously, we also compare our method with post-processing denoising methods, as shown in Fig. 5. We consider two existing denoising methods, Bilateral filtering and the OptixDenoiser in Falcor. The Bilateral filtering method directly filters the final shading radiance resulting in pixel space generated by ReSTIR GI so it inevitably leads to obvious over blur and brings great bias. The OptixDenoiser is a model trained by a neural network using tens of thousands of images rendered from one thousand 3D scenes. However, from the result, it can be seen that its noise reduction effect blurs the geometric shape and material of the model and still has a high MSE loss. Our method can effectively avoid these unfavorable situations.

Figure 6 shows the bias between the convergence result of our method and the reference. Our method can effectively converge and ensure a smaller bias compared with the reference.

6.2 Limitations

Storing samples in reservoirs in screen space is easy to query and update. However, the drawback is that we mainly focus on the filtering effect of the diffuse material scene, so the reused samples may not be suitable for specular or glossy objects in the scene. Figure 7 shows the performance of our method in the glossy scene. Even though the result of using filtering shows a smaller MSE than 1 spp path tracing and ReSTIR GI. However, in terms of visual effects, filtering tends to smooth out the results, making glossy objects lose high-frequency reflection information.

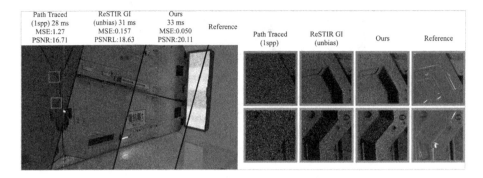

Fig. 7. Performance of our method in the glossy scene. Although our method shows a smaller MSE of 3.13× compared with ReSTIR GI and 25.5× compared with 1 spp path tracing. However, our result has a significant difference from the reference. Visually, the result obtained by our method tends to be smoother and loses the glossy properties of the material itself.

7   Conclusion and Future Work

We proposed a lightweight and efficient sample-space filtering method of ReSTIR GI that filters the sample distribution before reusing them. Our method substantially reduced the noise problem that cannot be solved by resampling in path tracing. In our test scenes, our method outperformed ReSTIR GI with 1.1× to 5.6× MSE reduction and 1.1× PSNR improvement with only 12% rendering time increasing. Compared with path tracing, our method can achieve 972.3× MSE reduction and 2.7× PSNR improvement.

However, in this paper, we only consider the diffuse reflective materials in the scene. Therefore, important future work is to design an adaptive filter kernel for different materials in the scene to make the method more robust for complex scenes. Moreover, extending our method to further bounces is also worth researching since our method currently only filters the global illumination of two bounces limited by ReSTIR GI. Another interesting direction is to try to combine our method with image space denoising methods such as SVGF [19] or some supersampling methods like neural supersampling [22].

Acknowledgments. This work is supported by the National Natural Science Foundation of China under Grant No. 62172220, and the Shandong Provincial Natural Science Foundation of China under Grant NO. ZR202211110175.

References

1. Binder, N., Fricke, S., Keller, A.: Fast path space filtering by jittered spatial hashing. In: ACM SIGGRAPH 2018 Talks, pp. 1–2 (2018)
2. Binder, N., Fricke, S., Keller, A.: Massively parallel path space filtering. In: Keller, A. (ed.) MCQMC 2020. Springer Proceedings in Mathematics & Statistics, vol. 387, pp. 149–168. Springer, Cham (2022). https://doi.org/10.1007/978-3-030-98319-2_7

3. Bitterli, B., Wyman, C., Pharr, M., Shirley, P., Lefohn, A., Jarosz, W.: Spatiotemporal reservoir resampling for real-time ray tracing with dynamic direct lighting. ACM Trans. Graph. (TOG) **39**(4), 148–151 (2020)
4. Boissé, G.: World-space spatiotemporal reservoir reuse for ray-traced global illumination. In: SIGGRAPH Asia 2021 Technical Communications, pp. 1–4 (2021)
5. Chaitanya, C.R.A., et al.: Interactive reconstruction of Monte Carlo image sequences using a recurrent denoising autoencoder. ACM Trans. Graph. (TOG) **36**(4), 1–12 (2017)
6. Chao, M.T.: A general purpose unequal probability sampling plan. Biometrika **69**(3), 653–656 (1982)
7. Deng, X., Hašan, M., Carr, N., Xu, Z., Marschner, S.: Path graphs: iterative path space filtering. ACM Trans. Graph. (TOG) **40**(6), 1–15 (2021)
8. Gautron, P., et al.: Path space similarity determined by Fourier histogram descriptors. In: ACM SIGGRAPH 2014 Talks (2014)
9. Kallweit, S., et al.: The Falcor rendering framework (2022). https://github.com/NVIDIAGameWorks/Falcor
10. Keller, A., Dahm, K., Binder, N.: Path space filtering. In: Cools, R., Nuyens, D. (eds.) Monte Carlo and Quasi-Monte Carlo Methods. SPMS, vol. 163, pp. 423–436. Springer, Cham (2016). https://doi.org/10.1007/978-3-319-33507-0_21
11. Kopta, D., Shkurko, K., Spjut, J., Brunvand, E., Davis, A.: Memory considerations for low energy ray tracing. In: Computer Graphics Forum, vol. 34, pp. 47–59. Wiley Online Library (2015)
12. Lin, D., Kettunen, M., Bitterli, B., Pantaleoni, J., Yuksel, C., Wyman, C.: Generalized resampled importance sampling: foundations of ReSTIR. ACM Trans. Graph. (TOG) **41**(4), 1–23 (2022)
13. Lin, D., Wyman, C., Yuksel, C.: Fast volume rendering with spatiotemporal reservoir resampling. ACM Trans. Graph. (TOG) **40**(6), 1–18 (2021)
14. Ma, J., Lv, Q., Yan, H., Ye, T., Shen, Y., Sun, H.: Color-saliency-aware correlation filters with approximate affine transform for visual tracking. Vis. Comput. **39**, 1–22 (2022)
15. Munkberg, J., Hasselgren, J.: Neural denoising with layer embeddings. In: Computer Graphics Forum, vol. 39, pp. 1–12. Wiley Online Library (2020)
16. NVIDIA: Nvidia Turing GPU architecture. In: ACM SIGGRAPH 2014 Talks (2018)
17. Ouyang, Y., Liu, S., Kettunen, M., Pharr, M., Pantaleoni, J.: ReSTIR GI: path resampling for real-time path tracing. In: Computer Graphics Forum, vol. 40, pp. 17–29. Wiley Online Library (2021)
18. Ruhela, R., Gupta, B., Singh Lamba, S.: An efficient approach for texture smoothing by adaptive joint bilateral filtering. Vis. Comput. **39**(5), 2035–2049 (2023)
19. Schied, C., et al.: Spatiotemporal variance-guided filtering: real-time reconstruction for path-traced global illumination. In: Proceedings of High Performance Graphics, pp. 1–12 (2017)
20. Talbot, J.F.: Importance resampling for global illumination (2005)
21. Teschner, M., Heidelberger, B., Müller, M., Pomerantes, D., Gross, M.H.: Optimized spatial hashing for collision detection of deformable objects. In: Vmv, vol. 3, pp. 47–54 (2003)
22. Xiao, L., Nouri, S., Chapman, M., Fix, A., Lanman, D., Kaplanyan, A.: Neural supersampling for real-time rendering. ACM Trans. Graph. (TOG) **39**(4), 142–151 (2020)

23. Yang, H., Zhou, D., Li, M., Zhao, Q.: A two-stage network with wavelet transformation for single-image deraining. Vis. Comput. **39**, 1–17 (2022)
24. Zhao, Y., Zhang, H., Lu, P., Li, P., Wu, E., Sheng, B.: DSD-MatchingNet: deformable sparse-to-dense feature matching for learning accurate correspondences. Virtual Reality Intell. Hardware **4**(5), 432–443 (2022)

Group Perception Based Self-adaptive Fusion Tracking

Yiyang Xing[1,2(✉)], Shuai Wang[1,2], Yang Zhang[3], Shuangye Zhao[1,2], Yubin Wu[1,2], Jiahao Shen[1,2], and Hao Sheng[1,2]

[1] State Key Laboratory of Virtual Reality Technology and Systems, School of Computer Science and Engineering, Beihang University, Beijing 100191, China
xingyiyang@buaa.edu.cn

[2] Zhongfa Aviation Institute, Beihang University, Hangzhou 311115, China

[3] College of Information Science and Technology, Beijing University of Chemical Technology, Beijing 100029, China

Abstract. Multi-object tracking (MOT) is an important and representative task in the field of computer vision, while tracking-by-detection is the most mainstream paradigm for MOT, so that target detection quality, feature representation ability, and association algorithm greatly affect tracking performance. On the one hand, multiple pedestrians moving together in the same group maintain similar motion pattern, so that they can indicate each other's moving state. We extract groups from detections and maintain the group relationship of trajectories in tracking. We propose a state transition mechanism to smooth detection bias, recover missing detection and confront false detection. We also build a two-level group-detection association algorithm, which improves the accuracy of association. On the other hand, different areas of the tracking scene have diverse and varying impact on the detections' appearance feature, which weakens the appearance feature's representation ability. We propose a self-adaptive feature fusion strategy based on the tracking scene and the group structure, which can help us to get fusion feature with stronger representative ability to use in the trajectory-detection association to improve tracking performance. To summary, in this paper, we propose a novel Group Perception based Self-adaptive Fusion Tracking (GST) framework, including Group concept and Group Exploration Net, Group Perception based State Transition Mechanism, and Self-adaptive Feature Fusion Strategy. Experiments on the MOT17 dataset demonstrate the effectiveness of our method. The method achieves competitive results compared to the state-of-the-art methods.

Keywords: Multi-object tracking (MOT) · Group perception · Self-adaptive · Feature fusion

1 Introduction

Multi-object tracking (MOT) is an important and representative task in the field of computer vision [1], which is widely used in security and safety, video understanding, autonomous driving and many other fields. Thanks to the significant

B. Sheng et al. (Eds.): CGI 2023, LNCS 14498, pp. 93–105, 2024.
https://doi.org/10.1007/978-3-031-50078-7_8

improvement in object detection methods, such as DPM [2], SDP [3] and FRCNN [5], nowadays, tracking-by-detection is the most mainstream MOT paradigm, which transforms tracking into data association [6], so that target detection quality, feature representation ability, and association algorithm greatly affect tracking performance [8]. When attempting to further improve tracking performance, it is a feasible idea to start from these three aspects.

As shown in Fig. 1(a), there are multiple pedestrians moving together with the same path in the tracking scene, which we called a tracking group [13]. The targets in the same group maintain a very similar motion pattern, so that when one target disappears, other remained targets can help to indicate whether the target is temporarily lost (like target 16 and 17) or permanently left from the tracking scene (like target 18). This inspires us to improve tracking performance through both target detection quality and association algorithm. We extract groups from detections and maintain the group relationship of trajectories in tracking. Based on groups among detections, we can smooth detection bias, recover missing detection and confront false detection, which can further improve tracking performance through target detection quality. Based on groups among trajectories, we can build a two-level group-detection association algorithm, which achieves matching from collective to individual, from group to detection. With this association algorithm, we can further improve the accuracy of association, and improve tracking performance through association algorithm.

In previous methods, most of them use motion feature and appearance feature to describe detection. As shown in Fig. 1(b), different areas of the tracking scene, due to various factors such as scene background and lighting intensity, have diverse and varying impact on the detections' appearance feature, which weakens the feature representation ability. When targets pass through such different areas in sequence, their appearance features often show significant difference and are hard to be associated with each other. This inspires us to improve tracking performance through feature representation ability. We propose a self-adaptive feature fusion strategy based on the tracking scene and the group structure. Based on the group structure and the association status of group members in the pre-tracking, we determine whether appearance features in current association are reliable. We further balance appearance information and motion information by a self-adaptive strategy, which can help us get fusion feature with stronger representative ability to use in the trajectory-detection association to improve tracking performance.

In this paper, we propose a novel Group Perception based Self-adaptive Fusion Tracking (GST) framework.

- Based on the similarity of motion patterns, we define the concept of Group in tracking. We design a special graph convolutional network called Group Exploration Net to extract groups from detections.
- Based on the extracted groups, we propose a State Transition Mechanism to maintain group structure, smooth detection bias, recover missing detection and confront false detection.

Fig. 1. Our main innovation points: (a) We extract groups from detections and maintain the group relationship of trajectories in tracking. (b) We propose a self-adaptive feature fusion strategy based on the tracking scene and the group structure.

- We also design a Self-adaptive Feature Fusion Strategy to obtain a better fusion of detection's appearance and motion information for stronger representation capability and better tracking performance.

2   Proposed Method

2.1   Overview

Some excellent previous works introduce advanced graph neural network or graph fusion network to improve tracking accuracy, such as [9–11] and [12]. These works prove the meaning of introducing graph neural network and multi-feature fusion in tracking and provide a foundation for constructing our method. Our tracking-by-detection paradigm is the mainstream paradigm in the field of MOT, which regards the tracking problem as the association problem between detections. Different detections are linked to build track proposals frame-by-frame, and the trackers finally link the best proposals as trajectories to represent objects.

In this paper, we propose a novel Group Perception based Self-adaptive Fusion Tracking (GST) framework, which also follows the tracking-by-detecting paradigm as well. Different from the previous works, our GST framework introduces the concept of group in tracking, correcting detection errors through groups, and design self-adaptive feature fusion strategy in association.

As shown in Fig. 2, each node represents a detection in a frame, and the links between nodes form trajectories of different objects. Firstly, we use a detector to obtain the detections in the frame fr^t, such as detection d_1 to d_7. Then, the Group Exploration Net is used to extract groups from detections (in step 1), such as Group G_1 composed of d_2 to d_4, and Group G_2 composed of d_5 and d_6. Based on the group relationship between detections, the State Transition Mechanism could smooth detection bias, recovers missing detection and confronts false detection (in step 2), as d_8 added in G_2. Since trajectories are composed of detections frame-by-frame, they can obtain and maintain group relationship from their detections. Considering group structure of trajectories, finally, we performs the Self-adaptive Feature Fusion Strategy (in step 3). Based on the trajectories' internal information including group relationship, we decide whether to use appearance feature in the data association of frame fr^t, as well as the proportion of appearance feature and motion feature.

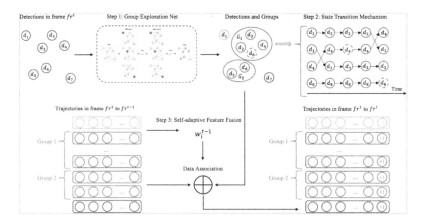

Fig. 2. The general overview of our GST framework.

2.2   Group Concept and Group Exploration Net

It has been proved by [21] that the relation between objects is a core clues for MOT. Inspired by them, we introduce the group concept into the tracking field, and build a social relationship graph G in tracking scene, using detections as the nodes of the graph. We define the group in tracking scene as a collection of multiple targets with similar motion patterns and stable relative positions. Nodes corresponding to targets in the same group are connected by edges in G. In real world, moving objects and scene background change smoothly in adjacent frames, indicating that the motion features of the same object in consecutive frames can represent its motion pattern. Considering the complexity of possible target-target interaction and target-background interaction, we use both appearance feature and motion feature. Before learning group relationship, an adjacency matrix of graph G, consisting of 1/0, is used to indicate whether two targets are related to each other, which means whether they are in the same group.

In this paper, we design our Group Exploration Net (GEN) based on graph convolutional network and exploit its ability to process graph structure data by aggregating high-level social relationship information from adjacent nodes to integrate information in the tracking social relationship graph. $\mathbb{N}$ targets in tracking scene are regarded as $\mathbb{N}$ nodes in graph G, and each target has an M-dimensional feature, so the graph G has a feature matrix $F^{\mathbb{N} \times M}$, and their group relations are represented by an adjacency matrix $A^{\mathbb{N} \times \mathbb{N}}$. The feature matrix $F^{\mathbb{N} \times M}$ and the adjacency matrix $A^{\mathbb{N} \times \mathbb{N}}$ are the inputs to the GEN model, and the propagation pattern between the intermediate layers is shown in Eq. 1.

$$
\begin{aligned}
F^{(l+1)} &= \sigma \left(\tilde{D}^{-\frac{1}{2}} \tilde{A} \tilde{D}^{-\frac{1}{2}} F^{(l)} W^{(l)} \right) \\
&= ReLU \left(\tilde{D}^{-\frac{1}{2}} (A + I) \tilde{D}^{-\frac{1}{2}} F^{(l)} W^{(l)} \right)
\end{aligned}
\tag{1}
$$

In Eq. 1, $\tilde{A}$ is the sum of adjacency matrix A and identity matrix I, $\tilde{D}$ is the degree matrix of $\tilde{A}$, $F^{(l)}$ and $F^{(l+1)}$ respectively represent the feature matrix of the l and $l+1$ layers of GEN model. In this paper, we design and train the two-layer GEN model to propagate interaction information, which means that $l = 1$ in Eq. 1, and use ReLU as the activation function.

$$
f_i^l = \frac{\sum_{j \in [0,N), j \in \mathbb{N}} v_j^{l-1} e_{ij}}{\sum_{j \in [0,N), j \in \mathbb{N}} e_{ij}}
\tag{2}
$$

Equation 2 shows that social interactions pass along edges in the graph, giving rise to the intermediate feature f_i^l of node d_i. We adopt a common practice in group network that the aggregated feature from adjacent nodes of d_i is adjusted by weights of all its adjacent nodes, to avoid bias due to the different adjacent number owned by different nodes. $l \in \{0,1\}$ indicates the depth of the GEN network we use.

$$
v_j^{l-1} = ReLU(f_C(f_j^{l-1}))
\tag{3}
$$

Equation 3 shows the method for accumulating information to update the state of node d_i. We use a fully connection layer f_C for mapping with ReLU activation, which can take any differentiable mapping function from tensor to tensor together. $l \in \{0,1\}$ indicates the depth of the GEN network we use.

2.3   Group Perception Based State Transition Mechanism

The group maintains a stable structure and similar motion pattern over a short period of time, which allows us to infer the state of target in the group through its peer members, e.g. whether it is still in the tracking scene but just invisible, or has left. We define five different tracking states for a single object, and then obtain our state transition mechanism by analysing the interaction of the group members' states and the transfer relationships between the different states.

Table 1 shows the states defined and used in our state transition mechanism. For each object in the tracking scene, its state varies between these five states. We use d_0 as the leading role to give the definition of these states. d_0, d_1, and d_2 together form group G.

Table 1. The states in state transition mechanism.

State	Symbol	Description
No-group	S_0	d_0 appears without group members.
Activated	S_1	d_0 appears with group members.
Obscured	S_2	d_0 disappears, but at least one group member remains.
Slumbering	S_3	d_0 and all group members disappear temporarily.
Disappearing	S_4	d_0 and all group members keep disappearing.

Table 2 shows the four types of object changes defined and used in our state transition mechanism. These changes are possible for each object in the tracking scene. For the purpose of scientific description, we evaluate the entropy level of these four changes. Change with higher level is more active and represents more group relationship. $C_i = n$ in Tab. 2 indicates that the level of change C_i is n.

Table 2. The changes in state transition mechanism.

Change	Symbol	Description
Appear	$C_0 = 2$	d_0 appears in the scene.
Group Founded	$C_1 = 3$	Find the group relationship between d_0 and other objects.
Group Cancelled	$C_2 = 1$	Group relationship between d_0 and other objects disappears.
Disappear	$C_3 = 0$	d_0 disappears from the scene.

In order to obtain more general conclusions, we introduce the concept of peer members' change with symbol ch_p. For d_0, its change is represented by ch_0, and its peer members are d_1 and d_2, whose changes are ch_1 and ch_2. As shown in Eq. 4, peer members' change ch_p is determined by ch_1 and ch_2.

$$ch_p = \{ch_i \mid d_i \in G \text{ and } \forall d_j \in G, d_j \neq d_i, ch_i \geq ch_j\}$$
$$= max\{ch_1, ch_2\} \tag{4}$$

The process of transferring from state S_i to state S_j is regarded as a basic state transition action, donated as a_{ij}. The state transition action is determined by object change ch_0 and peer members change ch_p, as expressed in Eq. 5.

$$a_{ij} : S_i \xrightarrow{<ch_0, ch_p>} S_j \tag{5}$$

The relationship between S_i, a_{ij} and S_j is shown in Table 3. The two states connected by the arrow are S_i and S_j respectively, and the arrow points from S_i to S_j. The event on the arrow represents $a_{ij} = \{ch_0, ch_p\}$. N means no change happens for a fixed short period of time T_{wait}.

Table 3. The complete state transition mechanism.

S_i	a_{ij}		.5	S_j	S_i	a_{ij}		.5	S_j
	ch_0	ch_p				ch_0	ch_p		
-	C_0	-		S_0	S_2	C_0	-		S_1
S_0	C_1	-		S_1	S_2	-	C_3		S_4
S_0	C_3	-		S_4	S_2	N	N		S_4
S_1	C_2	-		S_0	S_3	-	C_0		S_1
S_1	C_3	-		S_2	S_3	C_3	-		S_2
S_1	-	C_3		S_3	S_3	N	N		S_0

2.4 Self-adaptive Feature Fusion Strategy

In the tracking-by-detection framework, the problem of assigning ID labels to detections is transformed into the problem of data association between trajectories and detections, meaning that the similarity measurement between trajectories and detections is very important. We use sm_{ij}^t to denote the result of similarity measurement for trajectory T_i^{t-1} and detection d_j^t. Trajectory $T_i^{t-1} = \{d^1, d^2, \cdots, d^{t-1}\}$ consists of a sequence of detections from frame fr^1 to frame fr^{t-1}, where d^i denotes the detection of T_i^{t-1} in frame fr^i. Detection d^{t-1} also belongs to a group G^{t-1} in frame fr^{t-1}. Detection d_j^t is one of the detections in frame fr^t. In the previous methods, sm_{ij}^t typically integrated appearance and motion information using subjective weight setting w, as shown in Eq. 6.

$$sm_{ij}^t = w * f_{app}(T_i^{t-1}, d_j^t) + (1 - w) * f_{mov}(T_i^{t-1}, d_j^t) \tag{6}$$

In Eq. 6, $f_{app}(T_i^{t-1}, d_j^t)$ and $f_{mov}(T_i^{t-1}, d_j^t)$ represent the appearance measurement and the motion measurement between trajectory T_i^{t-1} and detection d_j^t respectively. As shown in Eq. 7, the appearance measurement $f_{app}(T_i^{t-1}, d_j^t)$ between trajectory T_i^{t-1} and detection d_j^t is defined as

$$f_{app}(T_i^{t-1}, d_j^t) = \frac{F_{app}^i \cdot F_{app}^j}{||F_{app}^i|| \cdot ||F_{app}^j||} \tag{7}$$

F_{app}^i means the appearance feature of trajectory T_i^{t-1} in frame fr^{t-1}, and F_{app}^j means the appearance feature of detection d_j^t in frame fr^t.

As shown in Eq. 8, the motion measurement $f_{mov}(T_i^{t-1}, d_j^t)$ between trajectory T_i^{t-1} and detection d_j^t is defined as

$$f_{mov}(T_i^{t-1}, d_j^t) = p(F_{mov}^j | f_p(F_{mov}^i)) \tag{8}$$

F_{mov}^i is the motion feature of trajectory T_i^{t-1} in frame fr^{t-1}, $f_p(F_{mov}^i)$ is the position prediction of this trajectory in frame fr^t, and F_{mov}^j is the motion feature of detection d_j^t in frame fr^t. Equation 8 is the probability that trajectory T_i^{t-1} will be at the position represented by detection d_j^t in frame fr^t.

In our method, we take advantage of the stable group structure to replace subjective weight settings with self-adaptive feature fusion strategy for better fusion of appearance and motion, as shown in Eq. 9.

$$
\begin{aligned}
new\_sm_{ij}^t =& w_i^{t-1} * f_{app}(T_i^{t-1}, d_j^t)+ \\
& (1 - w_i^{t-1}) * f_{mov}(T_i^{t-1}, d_j^t)
\end{aligned}
\tag{9}
$$

w_i^{t-1} is the appearance-motion ratio of trajectory T_i^{t-1} for data association in frame fr^t, determined by the nature of the trajectory itself. Due to the fact that trajectory T_i^{t-1} is only composed of detection from frame fr^1 to frame fr^{t-1} before data association in frame fr^t, w_i^{t-1} is only determined by the state of the trajectory after completing data association in frame fr^{t-1}, or more precisely, by the group structure of the trajectory at this time.

$$
w_i^{t-1} = \begin{cases} sin\,(coupling) & f_{app}(T_u^{t-2}, d_v^{t-1}) \geq \delta \\ 0 & f_{app}(T_u^{t-2} f d_v^{t-1}) < \delta \end{cases}
\tag{10}
$$

$$
coupling = \frac{\pi}{2} - \frac{\pi}{4} * \frac{\sum_{T_k^{t-1} \in G^{t-1}} f_{mov}(T_m^{t-2}, d_n^{t-1})}{\sum_{T_k^{t-1} \in G^{t-1}}}
\tag{11}
$$

In frame fr^{t-1}, trajectory T_i^{t-1} belongs to a group, denoted as G^{t-1}. We split trajectory T_i^{t-1} in frame fr^{t-1} into a combination of trajectory T_u^{t-2} in frame fr^{t-2} and detection d_v^{t-1} in frame fr^{t-1}, where $T_i^{t-1} = T_u^{t-2} + d_v^{t-1}$. For other trajectories T_k^{t-1} in group G^{t-1}, there is a similar relationship $T_k^{t-1} = T_m^{t-2} + d_n^{t-1}$.

As described above, in the case of $f_{app}(T_u^{t-2}, d_v^{t-1}) < \delta$, the trajectory-detection association in frame fr^t is performed based on motion information only, without considering appearance information. In the case when $f_{app}(T_u^{t-2}, d_v^{t-1}) \geq \delta$, the association needs to consider both appearance and motion aspects. δ is the association threshold. As shown in Eq. 11, when the peer members of trajectory T_i^{t-1} in group G^{t-1}, like T_k^{t-1} in G^{t-1}, have high motion matching degrees in their historical tracking process, which means high $f_{mov}(T_m^{t-2}, d_n^{t-1})$ for any T_m^{t-2} and d_n^{t-1}, T_i^{t-1} will increase the ratio of motion feature in the association.

3   Experiments

3.1   Implementation Details

Dataset and Metrics: In our experiments, we test baseline and our method using MOT17 dataset [18], which is the most widely used datasets in the MOT field. We evaluate and compare our method with TrackEval, the official evaluation tool provided by MOT Challenge, focusing on metrics such as MOTA↑

(multi-object tracking accuracy) [19], IDF1↑ (IDF1 score) [19], HOTA↑ (higher order tracking accuracy) [23] and IDs↓ (identity switches) [19]. MOTA mainly reflects the most tracks are tracked or not, which is easily affected by the total number of detections. IDF1 concerns whether a target is labeled with a correct ID. HOTA incorporates measuring the localisation accuracy of tracking results which isn't present in either MOTA or IDF1. IDs pays attention to the total number of identity switching. To ensure the reliability of evaluation results and the fairness of comparison results, all methods are tested using the public detections provided by the dataset.

Training: We further divided MOT17 training set into training set and validation set, the model is trained with MOT17 training set, and the ablation experiment is conducted with validation set. When the change of relative distance is less than 50% of the average target speed between the adjacent frames, detections are divided into the same group. We randomly shifting bounding boxes, randomly delete vertices and interpolate between tracklets (trajectory fragments) to simulate the deviation and missing detection. We obtain positive samples through the heuristic algorithm and set the ratio of positive and negative samples to 1:3. We train for 6000 iterations with a learning rate $5 \cdot 10^{-4}$, and weight decay term is 10^{-4}. By searching and comparing the parameters in training set, we obtained the optimal parameters.

Parameters: By searching and comparing the parameters in training set, we obtained the optimal parameters. We use various excellent tracking algorithms as our baseline, among which the experiment results in this chapter are based on StrongSORT [24], a novel and powerful MOT algorithm and is built on Deep-SORT [25]. In the tracking framework, we set the state transition waiting time to 5 frames, the association threshold to 0.8, and all other parameters remain the same as the baseline.

3.2 Ablation Study

Verification of each component in our method on MOT17 training set is shown in Table 4. Since Group concept and Group Exploration Net are the most fundamental design in our tracking framework, using this design alone could not affect the results, we don't test the result of using this design only. In Table 4, S denotes the Group Perception based State Transition Mechanism, and W denotes the Self-adaptive Feature Fusion Strategy.

Table 4. Ablation study results on MOT17 training set.

Method	MOTA↑	IDF1↑	HOTA↑	FP↓	FN↓	IDs↓
Baseline	75.0	79.5	64.6	469	**27319**	202
$+S$	75.1	80.8	65.1	443	27349	204
$+S+W$	**75.2**	**81.7**	**65.8**	**437**	27327	**170**

As shown in row 3 in Table 4, the increase of IDF1↑ (from 79.5 to 80.8) and HOTA↑ (from 64.6 to 65.1) proves the effectiveness of our state transition mechanism. It proves that by maintaining the group structure and inferring the status of its members based on the group structure, we can smooth detection bias, recover missing detection and confront false detection, which means improving tracking performance through target detection quality; we can also build a two-level group-detection association algorithm, which means improved association strategy, thereby improving the tracking accuracy. Figure 3(a) shows the tracking results of baseline and method $+S$. It can be seen that using our method can maintain the stability of the group during the tracking process, thereby increasing association accuracy and reducing ID Switch.

As shown in row 4, by using the self-adaptive feature fusion strategy simultaneously, FP and IDs are significantly reduced, while MOTA, IDF1 and HOTA increase. It proves that by adaptively fusing multiple target features in tracking, the representation ability of target feature can be enhanced, thereby improving the adaptability of our tracking model to complex and changing scenes, and improving the tracker's robustness and accuracy. Compared with baseline, in the final result as shown in the fourth row, it is obvious that MOTA, IDF1 and HOTA raise by 0.2, 2.2 and 1.2 respectively, while FP and IDs reduce by 32/469 and 32/202 respectively. Figure 3(b) shows the tracking results of baseline and our tracking framework $+S + W$. It can be seen that using our tracking framework can achieve more stable tracking and obtain more complete trajectory.

Fig. 3. The tracking results of baseline and our tracking framework.

3.3   Benchmark Evaluation

We compare our method with state-of-the-art methods on MOT17 benchmark. In order to make a fair comparison and better evaluate the effect of our tracking framework, all selected and listed methods use the public detections provided by the benchmark. As shown in Table 5, We choose five state-of-the-art methods (as shown in row 2 to 6) from MOT Challenge website to compare with our whole method (as shown in row 7, equals to method $+S + W$ in Table 4). The results show that our method conducts state-of-the-art performance among other methods. We achieve the highest MOTA, IDF1 and HOTA by 81.7, 81.8

and 66.1, 0.7, 1.8 and 2.1 higher than the second result given by GGDA respectively. Although the FN of our method is not the best, but our methods have the best (lowest) FN+FP by 102165. It proves that the group based data association strategy is conducive to achieve higher tracking accuracy. Our method and GGDA have achieved the best IDs, with a gap of only 33/1335, which shows our method's ability in recovering missing detection, confronting false detection and reducing ID switches. The results can be found on the official website of the MOTChallenge.

Table 5. Comparison with state-of-the-art methods on MOT17 benchmark.

Method	MOTA↑	IDF1↑	HOTA↑	FP↓	FN↓	IDs↓
STC [26]	75.8	70.8	59.5	33833	99074	3787
VAI [27]	77.0	74.4	61.0	31648	94966	3315
ppb [28]	79.4	76.7	62.9	31716	82257	2316
BoT [29]	79.6	77.3	63.1	26709	86424	1998
GGDA [21]	81.0	80.0	64.0	**25786**	79882	**1335**
Ours	**81.7**	**81.8**	**66.1**	30789	**71376**	1368

4   Conclusion

This paper aims to solve the difficulties in MOT in complex scenes with graph network based method. In this paper, we propose a novel Group Perception based Self-adaptive Fusion Tracking (GST) framework, including Group concept and Group Exploration Net, Group Perception based State Transition Mechanism, and the Self-adaptive Feature Fusion Strategy. Experiments on the MOT17 dataset verify the effectiveness of different components of our method. On the premise of fully respecting of previous state-of-the-art works, our method achieves better results in benchmarks over other methods. The proposed method has applications in the fields of security and safety, video understanding, autonomous driving and so on.

Acknowledgements. This study is partially supported by the National Key R&D Program of China (No.2022YFB3306500), the National Natural Science Foundation of China (No.61872025). Thanks for the support from HAWKEYE Group.

References

1. Xiong, Z., Sheng, H., Rong, W., Cooper, D.E.: Intelligent transportation systems for smart cities: a progress review. Sci. Chin. Inf. Sci. **55**, 2908–2914 (2012)
2. Forsyth, D.: Object detection with discriminatively trained part-based models. Computer **47**(02), 6–7 (2014)

3. Yang, F., Choi, W., Lin, Y.: Exploit all the layers: Fast and accurate CNN object detector with scale dependent pooling and cascaded rejection classifiers. In: Proceedings of the IEEE Conference on Computer Vision and Pattern Recognition, pp. 2129–2137 (2016)

4. Wang, S., Sheng, H., Zhang, Y., Wu, Y., Xiong, Z.: A general recurrent tracking framework without real data. In: Proceedings of the IEEE/CVF International Conference on Computer Vision, pp. 13219–13228 (2021)

5. Ren, S., He, K., Girshick, R., Sun, J.: Faster R-CNN: towards real-time object detection with region proposal networks. In: Advances in Neural Information Processing Systems, vol. 28 (2015)

6. Luo, W., Xing, J., Milan, A., Zhang, X., Liu, W., Kim, T.K.: Multiple object tracking: a literature review. Artif. Intell. **293**, 103448 (2021)

7. Zhang, Y., et al.: Long-term tracking with deep tracklet association. IEEE Trans. Image Process. **29**, 6694–6706 (2020)

8. Meyer, F., Win, M.Z.: Scalable data association for extended object tracking. In: IEEE Transactions on Signal and Information Processing Over Networks, vol. 6. pp. 491–507. IEEE (2020)

9. Xie, Z., Zhang, W., Sheng, B., Li, P., Chen, C.P.: BaGFN: broad attentive graph fusion network for high-order feature interactions. IEEE Transactions on Neural Networks and Learning Systems (2021)

10. Liu, R., et al.: NHBS-Net: a feature fusion attention network for ultrasound neonatal hip bone segmentation. IEEE Trans. Med. Imaging **40**(12), 3446–3458 (2021)

11. Wang, X., Wang, J., Kang, M., Feng, Z., Zhou, X., Liu, B.: LDGC-Net: learnable descriptor graph convolutional network for image retrieval. Vis. Comput. 1–15 (2022)

12. Yang, Y., Qi, Y., Qi, S.: Relation-consistency graph convolutional network for image super-resolution. Vis. Comput. 1–17 (2023)

13. Minoura, H., Hirakawa, T., Sugano, Y., Yamashita, T., Fujiyoshi, H.: Utilizing human social norms for multimodal trajectory forecasting via group-based forecasting module. IEEE Trans. Intell. Veh. 8, 836–850 (2022)

14. Wang, S., Sheng, H., Zhang, Y., Yang, D., Shen, J., Chen, R.: Blockchain-empowered distributed multi-camera multi-target tracking in edge computing. IEEE Transactions on Industrial Informatics (2023)

15. Sun, Z., Chen, J., Chao, L., Ruan, W., Mukherjee, M.: A survey of multiple pedestrian tracking based on tracking-by-detection framework. In: IEEE Transactions on Circuits and Systems for Video Technology, vol. 31, pp. 1819–1833. IEEE (2020)

16. Zhang, P., Zhao, J., Bo, C., Wang, D., Lu, H., Yang, X.: Jointly modeling motion and appearance cues for robust RGB-T tracking. In: IEEE Transactions on Image Processing, vol. 30, pp. 3335–3347. IEEE (2021)

17. Sheng, H., Chen, J., Zhang, Y., Ke, W., Xiong, Z., Yu, J.: Iterative multiple hypothesis tracking with Tracklet-level association. IEEE Trans. Circ. Syst. Video Technol. **29**(12), 3660–3672 (2018)

18. Milan, A., Leal-Taixé, L., Reid, I., Roth, S., Schindler, K.: MOT16: a benchmark for multi-object tracking. arXiv preprint arXiv:1603.00831 (2016)

19. Bernardin, K., Stiefelhagen, R.: Evaluating multiple object tracking performance: the clear mot metrics. EURASIP J. Image Video Process. **2008**, 1–10 (2008)

20. Sheng, H., et al.: Hypothesis testing based tracking with spatio-temporal joint interaction modeling. IEEE Trans. Circ. Syst. Video Technol. **30**(9), 2971–2983 (2020)

21. Wu, Y., Sheng, H., Wang, S., Liu, Y., Xiong, Z., Ke, W.: Group guided data association for multiple object tracking. In: Proceedings of the Asian Conference on Computer Vision, pp. 520–535 (2022)
22. Wang, L., Yu, Z., Yang, D., Ma, H., Sheng, H.: Efficiently targeted billboard advertising using crowdsensing vehicle trajectory data. IEEE Trans. Industr. Inf. **16**(2), 1058–1066 (2019)
23. Luiten, J., et al.: HOTA: a higher order metric for evaluating multi-object tracking. Int. J. Comput. Vision **129**, 548–578 (2021)
24. Du, Y., et al.: StrongSORT: make DeepSORT great again. IEEE Trans. Multimedia (2023)
25. Veeramani, B., Raymond, J.W., Chanda, P.: DeepSORT: deep convolutional networks for sorting haploid maize seeds. BMC Bioinform. **19**, 1–9 (2018)
26. Galor, A., Orfaig, R., Bobrovsky, B.Z.: Strong-TransCenter: improved multi-object tracking based on transformers with dense representations. arXiv preprint arXiv:2210.13570 (2022)
27. Quach, K.G., et al.: DyGLIP: a dynamic graph model with link prediction for accurate multi-camera multiple object tracking. In: Proceedings of the IEEE/CVF Conference on Computer Vision and Pattern Recognition, pp. 13784–13793 (2021)
28. Cao, J., Pang, J., Weng, X., Khirodkar, R., Kitani, K.: Observation-centric SORT: rethinking SORT for robust multi-object tracking. arXiv preprint arXiv:2203.14360, 2022
29. Aharon, N., Orfaig, R., Bobrovsky, B.-Z.: BoT-SORT: robust associations multi-pedestrian tracking. arXiv preprint arXiv:2206.14651 (2022)

Cross-Modal Information Aggregation and Distribution Method for Crowd Counting

Yin Chen⬤, Yuhao Zhou⬤, and Tianyang Dong(✉)

College of Computer Science and Technology, Zhejiang University of Technology,
Hangzhou, Zhejiang, China
dty@zjut.edu.cn

Abstract. Crowd counting is a fundamental and challenging task in computer vision. However, existing methods are relatively limited in dealing with scale and illumination changes simultaneously. To improve the accuracy of crowd counting and address the challenges of illumination and scale changes, we adopt the concept of crowding degree information. Due to the fact that a count map can accurately obtain the population in an image and solve the occlusion problem, we use the count map as a specific form of crowding degree information and propose a new cross-modal information aggregation and distribution model for crowd counting. We first input the crowding degree information into LibraNet and modify it with Information Aggregation Transfer (IAT) and Information Distribution Transfer (IDT) modules to obtain a count map. Then, light information, thermal information and crowding degree information are respectively input into the network through RGB image, themal image, and count map. A more accurate density map can be obtained through multiple convolution operations and IADM processing to improve counting accuracy. Finally, the density map is integrated to obtain the number of people. Experiments demonstrate that our methods provide superior quality and higher parallelism. Therefore, we can obtain higher-accuracy density maps by using light information, thermal information, and crowding degree information.

Keywords: Crowd counting · Cross-Modal · Density Map · Crowding Degree Information

1 Introduction

Crowd counting is a highly important task that has received widespread attention in recent years due to its significant potential applications in traffic management, video surveillance, social distance detection, and other fields with high application demand. As a method of crowd scene analysis, crowd counting has rapidly evolved from simple pedestrian counting to crowd density map [1]. A density map displays people's spatial distribution and quantity information in

Supported by the National Key R&D Program of China under Grant No. 2021ZD0200403 and 2018YFB1404102.

a picture, allowing for the total number of people by integrating the density map. The rapid development of crowd counting can be attributed to novel convolutional neural networks [2–4] and challenging datasets [5–7]. However, crowd counting still faces challenges related to illumination and scale changes.

(a) RGB   (b) Smaller σ (c) Larger σ (d) Geometry-adaptive σ

Fig. 1. The choice of Gaussian kernel σ, where (a) is the original image; (b) shows that the smaller Gaussian kernel σ only contains parts; (c) depicts that the larger Gaussian kernel σ contains the background; (d) shows that the geometry-adaptive kernel σ [7] could not cover all heads precisely.

The problem of illumination change in crowd counting is a practical issue in real-world application scenarios. To address this problem, Liu et al. [8] proposed a method that leverages RGB image and thermal image to capture the complementary aspects of multimodal data, which helps to overcome the effects of illumination change, and proposed the RGBT-CC dataset [8]. In addition to illumination change, scale change is another challenge in crowd counting. Due to the irregular distribution of the crowd, differences between individuals and the camera angle, people in an image are not equal, and the same person in a picture from different angles or at different times may exhibit variation. This inconsistency can cause issues when selecting the Gaussian kernel σ for the density map, as an inappropriate kernel may only cover part of the target (mainly the person's head) or even the background, resulting in a degradation of the model's generalization performance, as shown in Fig. 1.

To address the aforementioned problems, we adopt a concept called "crowding degree information [9]". This information shows the approximate number of people in each patch with the same number of pixels in a given image. We find that patches with the same number of pixels have the same crowding degree and the same scale level. Furthermore, we adopt the count map as a specific form of the manifestation of crowding degree information. The count map is more robust against Gaussian kernel variations within a certain interval [10]. Finally, we develop a deep reinforcement learning model [11] for crowd counting using LibraNet [12] to build count maps. While our methods do not require highly accurate count maps, it still enables the approximate count of each patch to be reflected, which allows for the identification of crowded or sparse patches (i.e., those with the same number of pixels). This is precisely what we need for obtaining crowding degree information. By using count maps, we can determine each patch's relative change of scale and obtain crowding degree information.

To tackle the issues of illumination and scale changes simultaneously, we propose a new cross-modal information aggregation and distribution model for crowd counting. This model can accept RGB image, thermal image, and count map as a set of input models to obtain a more accurate density map. In summary, the major contributions of the paper are shown as follows:

1. We adopt the concept of crowding degree information to handle the problems of illumination and scale changes [9]. To obtain an accurate count of the population in an image, we adopt the count map as its concrete representation, which can reflect the approximate count of each patch and the crowding degree information.
2. Based on the crowding degree information obtained from the count map, we develop a cross-modal information aggregation and distribution (IADM [8]) model for crowd counting. This model is composed of Information Aggregation Transfer (IAT) and Information Distribution Transfer (IDT) modules [8], inputting RGB image, thermal image and count map, generating a detailed density map.
3. Our IADM model boasts superior quality, higher parallelism, and shorter training time. Compared to existing crowd-counting methods, our model outperforms all others on the RGBT-CC dataset. Moreover, our methods still exhibit the best performance on other crowd-counting datasets.

2   Related Work

Crowd counting methods can be broadly categorized into three types: detection-based, regression-based [13], and CNN-based methods. Of these, the CNN-based method has emerged as the predominant approach in recent years, thanks to its high accuracy and robustness.

CNN-based crowd-counting methods typically employ a multi-task framework [14] and multi-level context feature fusion [15–18] to achieve high accuracy. To further improve the precision, some researchers have incorporated perspective mechanism [19], Bayesian loss [20], the combination of attention map and density map [21–23], and count map [10,12] into crowd counting.

Perspective was initially used to standardize the features extracted from foreground objects [24]. In CNN-based crowd-counting methods, perspective information is typically utilized as a preprocessing step to generate density maps [7,25], but it is rarely encoded directly into the network architecture. Yan et al. [19]. employed automatic coding to learn the perspective of an image, realizing a more accurate estimation under the perspective mechanism. However, calculation errors may occur due to the precision of the perspective transformation being affected by image quality.

Ma et al. [20] proposed Bayesian loss (BL) for crowd counting. Their approach involved constructing a probability model of density contribution from point annotations and applying it to crowd counting. However, BL may struggle to cope with false positives in the background.

Miao et al. [26] introduced the panoramic attention convolutional neural network (PACNN), based on multi-column architecture with discrete scale. PACNN produces two predicted density maps from two backbone networks. The two predicted density maps are given weights generated from perspective and then combined as final estimates. In contrast, Liu et al. [21] used a multiple extended convolution structure [22] to generate an attention map, and then utilized deformable convolution [23] to generate the estimated density map. However, the size of the two-dimensional Gaussian kernel used to represent the estimated human size in the density map directly impacts the final counting results, resulting in a significant error between the estimates and ground truth in crowded scenes, which cannot be fully eliminated.

Due to the significant estimation error that density maps can incur in dense scenes, some researchers have shifted their focus to count maps. This relatively new approach was first introduced by Liu et al. [10]. However, the error caused by the size of the Gaussian kernel in the count map is considerably smaller than those in the density map. Subsequently, Liu et al. [12] designed a more precise model by using deep reinforcement learning methods after generating a count map.

While count maps can be more robust to the Gaussian kernel, there are still some limitations. One significant drawback is that the size of the count map is much smaller than that of a density map. No matter how much the size of the count map can be enlarged by post-processing, the spatial information at the pixel level is not as detailed as that of a density map. This is a critical disadvantage of a count map. Therefore, their effectiveness in practical applications is not ideal.

In our work, we utilize LibraNet [12] to produce a count map, which is then combined with the RGB image and thermal image and inputted into the CNN. By employing multiple convolution operations and IADM processing, we obtain a more accurate density map that significantly reduces estimation errors. Experiments demonstrate that our methods exhibit stronger robustness when counting in dense scenes.

3   Methods

In this section, we present the main body of our research and propose a novel network architecture.

3.1   Overview

In this work, we propose a new cross-modal information aggregation and distribution model. Light information, thermal information, and crowding degree information are three-dimensional indicators for crowd counting, and they are captured by the RGB image, thermal image, and count map, respectively. We first train the LibraNet [12] model and modify it with Information Distribution Transfer (IDT) to obtain the count map. Then three kinds of images are input into the network as a set of input modes, and a more accurate density map can be obtained through multiple convolution operations and IADM [8] processing. Finally, we integrate the density map [1] to estimate the number of people in the scene. As shown in Fig. 2, the thermal image is consistent with the annotation of the RGBT-CC dataset, so we take a thermal image as a training sample instead of an RGB image.

(a) fused with RGB image   (b) fused with thermal image

Fig. 2. The annotation point map is formed by the fusion of (a) RGB image and (b) thermal image. The annotation points are consistent with the thermal image.

3.2 Network Structure

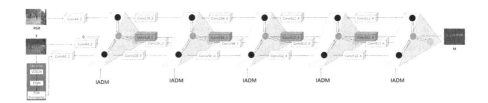

Fig. 3. The proposed architecture with BL as a backbone. $Convi\_j$ indicates j convolution layers with i channels in each layer. The count map is generated by LibraNet [12]. IADM is composed of Information Aggregation Transfer (IAT) and Information Distribution Transfer (IDT). Different from CMCRL [8], our IADM inputs features from the branches of RGB image, thermal image, count map, and modality-shared branch. The final output is the modality-shared feature.

Our framework is shown in Fig. 3, each layer is composed of four parallel backbone networks and a module called Information Aggregation-Distribution Module (IADM). The vertex backbones are designed for modality-specific representation learning of the RGB image, thermal image, and count map, while the middle backbone is used for learning modality-shared representation. To exploit multi-modal information hierarchically, the IADM is embedded after different

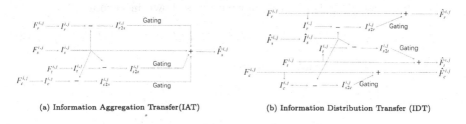

(a) Information Aggregation Transfer(IAT)   (b) Information Distribution Transfer (IDT)

Fig. 4. Structure of IAT and IDT. [8]

layers. As illustrated in Fig. 2, the RGB image is not completely consistent with the thermal image due to the different types of electronic sensors. Despite the short interval, these differences can be compensated for by leveraging contextual information [8]. Following the method of context information extraction in the literature [8], at the lth level ($l = 1, \ldots, L$), we apply a $2^{l-1} \times 2^{l-1}$ max-pooling layer to generate $\frac{h}{2^{l-1}} \times \frac{w}{2^{l-1}}$ feature $F^{i,j,l}$, which is then upsampled to $h \times w$ by nearest neighbor interpolation. Finally, the context information $I^{i,j} \in R^{h \times w \times c}$ of feature $F^{i,j}$ is given by the following expression:

$$I^{i,j} = Conv_{1\times1}(F^{i,j,1} \oplus F^{i,j,2} \oplus \cdots \oplus F^{i,j,L}), \tag{1}$$

where $\oplus$ denotes feature concatenation and $Conv_{1\times1}$ is a 1×1 convolutional layer.

Information Aggregation Transfer(IAT). We input the branch of RGB image, thermal image, and count map in IAT. The formula is as follows:

$$I_{r2s}^{i,j} = I_r^{i,j} - I_s^{i,j}, \omega_{r2s}^{i,j} = Conv_{1\times1}(I_{r2s}^{i,j}),$$
$$I_{t2s}^{i,j} = I_t^{i,j} - I_s^{i,j}, \omega_{t2s}^{i,j} = Conv_{1\times1}(I_{t2s}^{i,j}),$$
$$I_{c2s}^{i,j} = I_c^{i,j} - I_s^{i,j}, \omega_{c2s}^{i,j} = Conv_{1\times1}(I_{c2s}^{i,j}),$$
$$\hat{F}_s^{i,j} = F_s^{i,j} + I_{r2s}^{i,j} \odot \omega_{r2s}^{i,j} + I_{t2s}^{i,j} \odot \omega_{t2s}^{i,j} + I_{c2s}^{i,j} \odot \omega_{c2s}^{i,j}, \tag{2}$$

where $I_r^{i,j}, I_t^{i,j}$ and $I_c^{i,j}$ are the features corresponding to the RGB image, thermal image, and count map, respectively, calculated by Formula 1; $\omega_{r2s}^{i,j}, \omega_{t2s}^{i,j}, \omega_{c2s}^{i,j}$ are the gating weights, implemented by 1×1 convolutional layers, and $\odot$ is element-wise multiplication. Through this mechanism, the modality-shared feature $\hat{F}_s^{i,j}$ can learn complementary information from each of RGB image, thermal image, and count map.

Information Distribution Transfer (IDT). IDT is used to refine the features of RGB, thermal image, and count map. The structure of IAT and IDT is shown in Fig. 4.

The refinement of RGB feature information is shown in Formula 3:

$$I_{s2r}^{i,j} = I_s^{i,j} - I_r^{i,j}, \quad \omega_{s2r}^{i,j} = Conv_{1\times1}(I_{s2r}^{i,j}), \quad \hat{F}_r^{i,j} = F_r^{i,j} + I_{s2r}^{i,j} \odot \omega_{s2r}^{i,j}. \quad (3)$$

The refinement of thermal feature information is shown in Formula 4:

$$I_{s2t}^{i,j} = I_s^{i,j} - I_t^{i,j}, \quad \omega_{s2t}^{i,j} = Conv_{1\times1}(I_{s2t}^{i,j}), \quad \hat{F}_t^{i,j} = F_t^{i,j} + I_{s2t}^{i,j} \odot \omega_{s2t}^{i,j}. \quad (4)$$

The refinement of count map feature information is shown in Formula 5:

$$I_{s2c}^{i,j} = I_s^{i,j} - I_c^{i,j}, \quad \omega_{s2c}^{i,j} = Conv_{1\times1}(I_{s2c}^{i,j}), \quad \hat{F}_c^{i,j} = F_c^{i,j} + I_{s2c}^{i,j} \odot \omega_{s2c}^{i,j}. \quad (5)$$

We use Formula 1 to transform modality-shared features $\hat{F}_s^{i,j}$ into contextual information $I_s^{i,j}$, and then input the three feature information to the next layer of the corresponding branch.

3.3   Implementation Process

We select the RGBT-CC dataset [8], which contains 2,030 pairs of RGB thermal images, along with 138,389 annotated pedestrians. The dataset also includes 1,013 pairs of images captured in bright scenes and 1,017 pairs of images captured in dark scenes.

To implement our methods, we use PyTorch and employ MCNN [7], SANet [27], CSRNet [28], and BL [20] as backbone networks. Due to the large number of parameters in CSRNet and BL, we reduce the number of channels in these two networks to 70% and 60% of their original values, respectively. We initialize the kernel parameters using a Gaussian distribution with a mean of 0 and a standard deviation of 1e−2.

4   Results

4.1   Ground Truth Generation

We use geometry-adaptive Gaussian kernel [7] to generate ground truth density maps. The specific formula is as follows:

$$F(x) = \sum_{i=1}^{N} \delta(x - x_i) * G_{\sigma_i}(x), with \sigma_i = \beta \overline{d_i}, \quad (6)$$

where x represents the position of the pixel in an image, $G_{\sigma_i}(x)$ is a Gaussian kernel with parameter σ_i (standard deviation), $\overline{d_i}$ indicates the average distance of k nearest neighbors, $*$ indicates convolution operations, and δ is the ground truth dot annotation. According to the literature [7], we set $k = 3, and \beta = 0.03$.

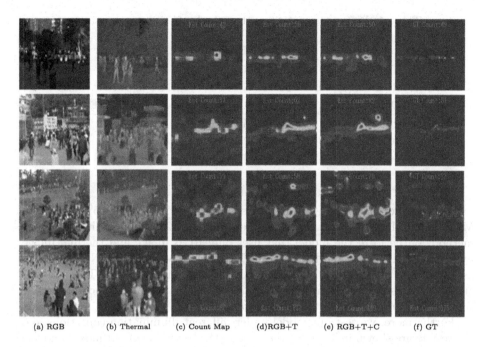

(a) RGB   (b) Thermal   (c) Count Map   (d)RGB+T   (e) RGB+T+C   (f) GT

Fig. 5. Visualization of the density map.(a), (b) and (c) are RGB image, thermal image, and count map, respectively; (d) is the estimated density map of RGB and thermal image; (e) is the estimated density map of RGB, thermal image, and count map; (f) is the ground-truth density map; From top to bottom, the number of people increases.

4.2 Experimental Results and Evaluation

The counting results are shown in Fig. 5. Although the count map may not produce completely accurate results, it can reduce the influence of the choice of Gaussian kernel σ on the density map. By allowing the model to learn this ability, we are able to reduce the impact of inaccurate Gaussian kernel σ on our experimental results. Therefore, we find that the model, which inputs RGB image, thermal image, and count map as three models, yields counting results that are closer to the ground truth, as compared to the model that inputs only RGB image and thermal image as two models.

Model Performance. Table 1 indicates that our methods with different backbones perform better than the original methods. We select MCNN [7], SANet [27], CSRNet [28], and BL [20] as different backbones for comparison, which are typical networks with good results in crowd counting in recent years. Specifically, for the CSRNet model, our methods achieve 22.5% and 25.7% improvement on MAE and RMSE, respectively, compared to the original CSRNet model. In addition, our methods yield 11.9% and 15.2% improvement on MAE and RMSE, respectively, compared to the model that uses only RGB image and thermal

Table 1. Performance of different methods after post-processing.

Backbone	MAE	RMSE	Backbone	MAE	RMSE
MCNN [7]	21.89	37.44	CSRNet [28]	20.40	35.26
MCNN+RGB+T [8]	19.77	30.34	CSRNet+RGB+T [8]	17.94	30.91
MCNN+Ours	17.16	27.03	CSRNet+Ours	15.81	26.20
SANet [27]	21.99	37.44	BL [20]	18.70	32.67
SANet+RGB+T [8]	18.18	33.72	BL+RGB+T [8]	15.61	28.18
SANet+Ours	17.76	28.40	BL+Ours	15.34	24.68

image. For the BL model, our methods perform 18.0% and 24.5% better on MAE and RMSE, respectively, than the original BL model. Additionally, our methods outperform the model that uses only RGB image and thermal image by 1.7% and 12.4% on MAE and RMSE, respectively. Using MCNN or SANet as a backbone also shows a significant performance improvement. These results clearly demonstrate that with the help of a count map, our methods have been significantly improved over the original ones.

Furthermore, we test our model under different illumination conditions and the results are shown in Table 2. In this case, the backbone of our model and the original model [8] are BL [20]. Under bright conditions, our methods perform 0.82% and 13.2% better on MAE and RMSE, respectively, than the original method. Under dark conditions, our methods achieve 2.46% and 8.32% improvement on MAE and RMSE, respectively, compared to the original method. These results suggest that our methods perform better under both bright and dark illumination conditions, highlighting the significance of our count map modality.

Post Processing. Given that the size of the count map output is only $\frac{1}{32}$nd of the original, it is necessary to apply upsampling or sliding window to match their size. Previous research [10] has shown that sliding window is a post-processing method. When evaluating an image, we input a series of offset images into the network to obtain more accurate evaluation results. These offset $S(Image)$ can be defined as follows:

$$S(Image) = \{S_{i,j}|S_{i,j} = Image(x + X_{off\_i}, y + Y_{off\_j})\}, \tag{7}$$

where X_{off_i} and Y_{off_j} respectively represent the corresponding offsets. We set $Offset \in as(-16, -8, -4, 0, 4, 8, 16)$. To combine a series of results, we divide the 32×32 count results into each pixel equally and calculate the density map C_m:

$$C_m(x,y) = \frac{\sum_{i,j} C(x,y,i,j)}{N(x,y)}, \tag{8}$$

where $C(x,y,i,j)$ indicates the image with offsets X_{off_i} and Y_{off_j}, and $N(x,y)$ denotes the frequency of pixels calculated in the sequence.

Table 2. Performance in different illumination conditions. The RGBT and RGBTC input data are fed into CMCRL [8] and our network respectively, and both backbones are BL [20].

Illumination	Method	Input Data	MAE	RMSE
Brightness	CMCRL	RGBT	15.82	28.17
	Ours	RGBTC	15.69	24.46
Darkness	CMCRL	RGBT	15.86	28.58
	Ours	RGBTC	15.47	24.79

Table 3. Performance of post-processing methods.

Method	MAE	RMSE
LibraNet(No post-processing metod)	23.48	41.42
Nearest neighbor	16.86	26.76
Nearest neighbor & divided by 32	15.23	24.89
Nearest neighbor & divided by 32 × 32	15.32	25.35
Bilinear Interpolation	14.73	25.22
Sliding Window	15.34	24.68

Table 3 presents the results of different post-processing methods. We observe that bilinear interpolation performs the best in MAE, while it has average performance in RMSE. On the other hand, sliding window yields the best performance in RMSE, but not in MAE. The nearest neighbor method divides each pixel value by 32, and its performance is slightly inferior to sliding window in RMSE and second only to bilinear interpolation in MAE.

4.3 Ablation Studies

In this subsection, to verify the effectiveness of each component in our framework, we adopt BL [20] as the backbone network to perform extensive ablation studies.

Count Map or Class Map? A class map is the quantitative form of a count map. We compare the performance of the count map and class map. As shown in Table 4, we find that the count map outperforms the class map, regardless of the post-processing method used. This may be because the count map is more intuitive and better suited to reflect the changes in the number of people between pixels, while the class map undergoes a discretization process that is not suitable for our models.

Table 4. Performance of count map and class map with different post-processing methods.

Method	Kind	MAE	RMSE
Bilinear Interpolation	Class map	15.92	27.57
	Count map	14.73	25.22
Sliding Window	Class map	17.12	26.92
	Count map	15.34	24.68
Nearest neighbor & divided by 32	Class map	16.04	27.09
	Count map	15.23	24.89
Nearest neighbor & divided by 32 × 32	Class map	16.20	28.46
	Count map	15.32	25.35

Table 5. Different Input Modals.

Method	MAE	RMSE
Early Fusion	17.59	31.30
Late Fusion	16.94	30.69
W/O Gating	16.93	29.79
W/O Modality-Shared Feature	16.91	28.72
W/O IDT	16.50	27.36
Ours	15.34	24.68

Different Fusion Methods. As our model's core component is the cross-modal fusion module, we have enhanced the original IADM [8] module by adapting it to the input of three models: RGB image, thermal image, and count map. We perform ablation studies to compare the performance of different fusion methods and demonstrate that the network with the IADM module performs the best. The results are shown in Table 5, where all post-processing methods are sliding windows.

"Early Fusion" refers to a serial input of RGB image, thermal image, and count map into BL [20]. In contrast, "Late Fusion" uses three branches, each dedicated to one modality, to extract features from the RGB image, thermal image, and count map, and then combine their features to generate a density map. "W/O Gating" means that information is directly transmitted between different features without information filtering. "W/O Modality-Shared Feature" means that the modal sharing branch is removed, and each modality's specific characteristics are directly refined. Finally, the features from the three branches are connected to generate the density map. "W/O IDT" refers to using modal sharing branches but only aggregating multi-modal information and refining the features of the modal sharing branches without refining the features of RGB image, thermal image, and count map.

Table 5 shows that the "Early Fusion" has an MAE of 17.59 and RMSE of 31.30; "Late Fusion" has an MAE of 16.94 and RMSE of 30.69; "W/O Gating" has an MAE of 16.93 and RMSE of 29.79; "W/O Modality-Shared Feature" has an MAE of 16.91 and RMSE of 28.72; and "W/O IDT" has an MAE of 16.50 and RMSE of 27.36. "W/O IDT" performs the best out of the five methods, with a 7.03% decrease in MAE and a 27.35% decrease in RMSE. These results demonstrate that our proposed module has the most significant effect, achieving the lowest MAE of 15.34 and the lowest RMSE of 24.68.

Different Input Modals. We further perform ablation studies using different input models with the count map, including RGB image and count map, thermal image and count map, and all three models. The results are shown in Table 6, where all post-processing methods are sliding windows.

Table 6. Performance of different input models.

Input Modals	MAE	RMSE
RGB + Count map	24.64	45.34
Thermal + Count map	17.72	30.98
RGB + Thermal + Count map	15.34	24.68

We can make the discovery that the MAE and RMSE for the input data of RGB image and count map are 24.64 and 45.34, respectively, indicating the poorest performance among the tested combinations because it is based on thermal image. In contrast, the combination of thermal image and count map shows better performance with an MAE of 17.72 and RMSE of 30.98. The best performance is achieved when using all three RGB image, thermal image, and count map: for the input data of thermal image and count map, the MAE decreased by 13.4% and the RMSE decreased by 20.3%, while for the input data of RGB image and count map, the MAE decreased by 37.7% and the RMSE decreased by 45.6%. Based on these results, we conclude that the model compose of RGB image, thermal image, and count map has the best performance.

Table 7. Estimation errors on ShanghaiTechA [7].

Methods	MAE	RMSE
BL [20]	62.8	101.8
LibraNet [12]	55.9	97.1
ADCrowdNet [21]	63.2	98.9
AMRNet [29]	61.6	98.4
DM-Count [30]	59.7	95.7
Ours	55.1	93.1

4.4 Other Datasets

We test the dataset ShanghaiTechA [7] without thermal images. We use the pre-training model provided by [12] to generate a count map and input the RGB image and the count map into the network to generate a density map. Results are shown in Table 7. It can be concluded that whether it is compared with the backbone BL [20] or the model LibraNet [12] that generates the count map, our methods have practical improvements.

5 Conclusions

In this work, to deal with scale and illumination changes simultaneously, we propose a new cross-modal information aggregation and distribution model to capture the complementary information of light information, thermal information, and crowding degree information, so that the model can better deal with the scale change and illumination change of image, and higher-accuracy density maps are output to improve the counting accuracy. We also evaluate the performance of various post-processing methods and demonstrate the effectiveness of our proposed models. In the future, we aim to explore alternative models to replace the crowding degree information modal and further enhance the performance of our model.

Acknowledgements. This research was supported by STI 2030-Major Projects 2021ZD0200400 and the National Key R&D Program of China under Grant No. 2018YFB1404102.

References

1. Lempitsky, V., Zisserman, A.: Learning to count objects in images. In: Advances in Neural Information Processing Systems, vol. 23 (2010)
2. Chen, X., Yu, X., Di, H., Wang, S.: SA-InterNet: scale-aware interaction network for joint crowd counting and localization. In: Ma, H., et al. (eds.) PRCV 2021. LNCS, vol. 13019, pp. 203–215. Springer, Cham (2021). https://doi.org/10.1007/978-3-030-88004-0_17
3. Senthilkumar, R., Ritika, S., Manikandan, M., Shyam, B.: Crowd counting using federated learning and domain adaptation. In: Badica, C., Paprzycki, M., Kharb, L., Chahal, D. (eds.) ICICCT 2022. Communications in Computer and Information Science, pp. 97–111. Springer, Cham (2022). https://doi.org/10.1007/978-3-031-20977-2_8
4. Ilyas, N., Ahmad, Z., Lee, B., Kim, K.: An effective modular approach for crowd counting in an image using convolutional neural networks. Sci. Rep. **12**(1), 5795 (2022)
5. Wang, Q., Gao, J., Lin, W., Li, X.: NWPU-crowd: a large-scale benchmark for crowd counting and localization. IEEE Trans. Pattern Anal. Mach. Intell. **43**(6), 2141–2149 (2020)
6. Zhang, C., Li, H., Wang, X., Yang, X.: Cross-scene crowd counting via deep convolutional neural networks. In: Proceedings of the IEEE Conference on Computer Vision and Pattern Recognition, pp. 833–841 (2015)
7. Zhang, Y., Zhou, D., Chen, S., Gao, S., Ma, Y.: Single-image crowd counting via multi-column convolutional neural network. In: Proceedings of the IEEE Conference on Computer Vision and Pattern Recognition, pp. 589–597 (2016)
8. Liu, L., Chen, J., Wu, H., Li, G., Li, C., Lin, L.: Cross-modal collaborative representation learning and a large-scale RGBT benchmark for crowd counting. In Proceedings of the IEEE/CVF Conference on Computer Vision and Pattern Recognition, pp. 4823–4833 (2021)
9. Babu Sam, D., Surya, S., Venkatesh Babu, R.: Switching convolutional neural network for crowd counting. In: Proceedings of the IEEE Conference on Computer Vision and Pattern Recognition (CVPR) (2017)
10. Liu, L., Hao, L., Xiong, H., Xian, K., Cao, Z., Shen, C.: Counting objects by blockwise classification. IEEE Trans. Circ. Syst. Video Technol. **30**(10), 3513–3527 (2019)
11. Mnih, V., et al.: Human-level control through deep reinforcement learning. Nature **518**(7540), 529–533 (2015)
12. Mnih, V., et al.: Human-level control through deep reinforcement learning. Nature **518**(7540), 529–533 (2015)
13. Idrees, H., Saleemi, I., Seibert, C., Shah, M.: Multi-source multi-scale counting in extremely dense crowd images. In: Proceedings of the IEEE Conference on Computer Vision and Pattern Recognition, pp. 2547–2554 (2013)
14. Zhao, M., Zhang, J., Zhang, C., Zhang, W.: Leveraging heterogeneous auxiliary tasks to assist crowd counting. In: Proceedings of the IEEE/CVF Conference on Computer Vision and Pattern Recognition, pp. 12736–12745 (2019)

15. Khan, S.D., Salih, Y., Zafar, B., Noorwali, A.: A deep-fusion network for crowd counting in high-density crowded scenes. Int. J. Comput. Intell. Syst. **14**(1), 168 (2021)
16. Sindagi, V.A., Patel, V.M.: Multi-level bottom-top and top-bottom feature fusion for crowd counting. In: Proceedings of the IEEE/CVF International Conference on Computer Vision, pp. 1002–1012 (2019)
17. Sindagi, V.A., Yasarla, R., Patel, V.M.: Pushing the frontiers of unconstrained crowd counting: new dataset and benchmark method. In: Proceedings of the IEEE/CVF International Conference on Computer Vision, pp. 1221–1231 (2019)
18. Fang, Y., Gao, S., Li, J., Luo, W., He, L., Bo, H.: Multi-level feature fusion based locality-constrained spatial transformer network for video crowd counting. Neurocomputing **392**, 98–107 (2020)
19. Yan, Z., et al.: Perspective-guided convolution networks for crowd counting. In: Proceedings of the IEEE/CVF International Conference on Computer Vision, pp. 952–961 (2019)
20. Ma, Z., Wei, X., Hong, X., Gong, Y.: Bayesian loss for crowd count estimation with point supervision. In: Proceedings of the IEEE/CVF International Conference on Computer Vision, pp. 6142–6151 (2019)
21. Liu, N., Long, Y., Zou, C., Niu, Q., Pan, L., Wu, H.: Adcrowdnet: an attention-injective deformable convolutional network for crowd understanding. In: Proceedings of the IEEE/CVF Conference on Computer Vision and Pattern Recognition, pp. 3225–3234 (2019)
22. Szegedy, C., et al.: Going deeper with convolutions. In: Proceedings of the IEEE Conference on Computer Vision and Pattern Recognition, pp. 1–9 (2015)
23. Dai, J., et al.: Deformable convolutional networks. In: Proceedings of the IEEE International Conference on Computer Vision, pp. 764–773 (2017)
24. Chan, A.B., Liang, Z.S.J., Vasconcelos, N.: Privacy preserving crowd monitoring: counting people without people models or tracking. In: 2008 IEEE Conference on Computer Vision and Pattern Recognition, pp. 1–7. IEEE (2008)
25. Huang, S., et al.: Body structure aware deep crowd counting. IEEE Trans. Image Process. **27**(3), 1049–1059 (2017)
26. Shi, M., Yang, Z., Xu, C., Chen, Q.: Perspective-aware CNN for crowd counting. PhD thesis, Inria Rennes-Bretagne Atlantique (2018)
27. Cao, X., Wang, Z., Zhao, Y., Su, F.: Scale aggregation network for accurate and efficient crowd counting. In: Proceedings of the European Conference on Computer Vision (ECCV), pp. 734–750 (2018)
28. Li, Y., Zhang, X., Chen, D.: CSRNet: dilated convolutional neural networks for understanding the highly congested scenes. In: Proceedings of the IEEE Conference on Computer Vision and Pattern Recognition, pp. 1091–1100 (2018)
29. Liu, X., Yang, J., Ding, W., Wang, T., Wang, Z., Xiong, J.: Adaptive mixture regression network with local counting map for crowd counting. In: Vedaldi, A., Bischof, H., Brox, T., Frahm, J.-M. (eds.) ECCV 2020. LNCS, vol. 12369, pp. 241–257. Springer, Cham (2020). https://doi.org/10.1007/978-3-030-58586-0_15
30. Wang, B., Liu, H., Samaras, D., Nguyen, M.H.: Distribution matching for crowd counting. In: Advances in Neural Information Processing Systems, vol. 33, pp. 1595–1607 (2020)

Lightweight Separable Convolutional Dehazing Network to Mobile FPGA

Xinrui Ju[1], Wei Wang[1,2(✉)] [ID], and Xin Xu[1,2]

[1] School of Computer Science and Technology, Wuhan University of Science and Technology, Wuhan 430081, China
wangwei8@wust.edu.cn
[2] Hubei Province Key Laboratory of Intelligent Information Processing and Real-Time Industrial System, Wuhan University of Science and Technology, Wuhan 430081, China

Abstract. The advancement of deep learning has significantly increased the efficiency of picture dehazing techniques. Convolutional neural networks can't, however, be implemented on portable FPGA devices because to their high computing, storage, and energy needs. In this paper, we propose a generic solution for image dehazing from CNN models to mobile FPGAs. The proposed solution designs lightweight network using depthwise separable convolution and channel attention mechanism, and uses an accelerator to increase the system's processing efficiency. We implemented the entire system on a custom and low-cost FPGA SOC platform (Xilinx Inc. ZYNQ^{TM} XC7Z035). Experiments can conclude that our approach has compatible performance to GPU-based methods with much lower resource usage.

Keywords: FPGA-based · Dehazing · Lightweight Network · Accelerator

1 Introduction

Images captured by cameras can have poor visibility due to the loss of saturation and contrast caused by the presence of cloudy media such as water vapour, mist, dust and smoke in the atmosphere. With these hazy images as input, autonomous systems such as self-driving cars, intelligent traffic surveillance and unmanned aerial vehicles face degraded performance or severe failures. In addition these systems are used in scenarios where efficiency and low power consumption are sought. Therefore, a dedicated dehazing hardware solution is required to meet these limitations.

Early hardware systems for image dehazing were only designed to speed up software algorithms. Lu et al. [18] combines dark channel prior algorithm to implement an improved fast image dehazing system on a DSP embedded platform. In particular, the system's computing effort is drastically lowered while yet maintaining the highest possible image quality. However, as camera technology continues to evolve and the resolution of images becomes higher and higher,

B. Sheng et al. (Eds.): CGI 2023, LNCS 14498, pp. 120–131, 2024.
https://doi.org/10.1007/978-3-031-50078-7_10

DSP-based hardware systems struggle to keep up with the speed of image processing. To enhance the apparent size of various objects in a depth picture, Kasauka [14] installs a multi-scale retinex approach using an FPGA. However, when the haze concentration is not uniformly distributed, the image dehazing effect will be unsatisfactory. With the low-power flexibility of FPGAs, Ju et al. [13] successfully dehaze photos using the dark channel prior approach, but processes low-resolution images and still lacks the ability to process high-definition images.

In all, FPGA-based image dehazing system promises for a universal solution to FPGAs with high image definition. The hardware implementation of deep learning based image dehazing algorithms is constrained by the on-chip memory. Both the image frames and the hardware resources required to implement the dehazing logic need to be stored in on-chip memory. When implementing image dehazing algorithms in hardware, it is a challenging task to perform complex mathematical operations with minimal logic resources without compromising the quality of the output image. In this study, we implemented a convolutional accelerator and a lightweight end-to-end neural network for the FPGA. The processing speed of the system is increased while ensuring the dehazing effect. Lightweight networks can utilise fewer hardware resources. It also requires less consideration when deploying on hardware and enables faster deployment on the hardware side.

2   Related Work

The primary available approaches may be roughly categorized as **prior-based and deep learning-based methods**, with the goal of single picture dehazing being to restore a hazy image to a clear one.

The prior-based technique uses a physical scattering model to produce crisp pictures, but it also needs a natural prior to calculate the transmission map and atmospheric light. He et al. [10] discovered that the majority of partially clear pictures included at least one color channel with multiple extremely low intensity pixels and suggested the Dark Channel Prior (DCP) technique of dehazing.

A non-local prior dehazing technique was suggested by Berman et al. [5] when they noticed that the colors of a clear image can closely resemble hundreds of other colors that group together in small groups in the RGB color space. In order to perform picture dehazing, Zhu et al. [28] suggest using a color attenuation prior approach to learn the scene depth of a hazy image using supervised learning. This method then calculates the transmission and recovers the scene radiance. Prior-based methods only work well when the assumed prior is appropriate, and results are often poor when the prior is not satisfied.

Researchers have started to recognize deep learning-based picture dehazing solutions more and more recently. Although some methods [8,20,24,27] have been proposed with high dehazing effect, these models have high model complexity, complex computation and huge storage requirements, which make them difficult to deploy in resource-limited platforms. Ren et al. [21] learn to anticipate the scene transmission map using a coarse-scale neural network, then learn local information that used a fine-scale neural network, and lastly recover a clean picture that use the output of both scales of the network. By learning to derive the confidence map of the input, Ren et al. [22] developed a multi-scale gated fusion network based on an encoder decoder network to tackle the single-image dehazing problem. A generative adversarial network (GAN) and an enhancer make up the image dehazing network (DCPDN) that Zhang et al. [25] suggested. The enhancer creates high-quality images after the discriminator directs the generator to create images at a coarse scale.

Although the above mentioned methods are effective in image dehazing, their high number of parameters and high computational effort hinder their deployment on resource-limited platforms. Cai et al. [6] propose the DehazeNet deep learning neural network for estimating media transmission map. The network receives a bad photo as input and then waits for the image to be recovered using its transmission map and atmospheric light. By integrating an atmospheric scattering model into the network and fusing the two variables in the model into a single K parameter, Li et al. [16] design a lightweight trainable end-to-end image dehazing network (AOD-Net) in order to minimize errors. However, the quality of these lightweight networks is not high enough for high resolution image recovery while few people deploy them to hardware platforms, such as FPGAs.

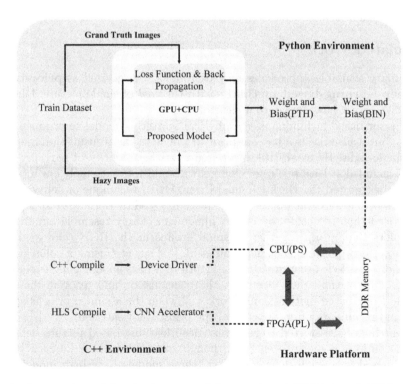

Fig. 1. An overview of the development of the mentioned FPGA-based CNN accelerator for image dehazing.

3   Approach

Figure 1 shows the process of implementing an FPGA-based image dehazing system. First, an embedded-friendly lightweight dehazing deep learning network is designed and trained. Then, a CNN accelerator is designed using the HLS compiler. Finally, a device driver is created using a standard C++ compiler. The designed and developed accelerator and device driver will control and accelerate the model inference on the hardware platform.

3.1   Network Structure

In this research, we build an encoder-decoder structure-based residual attention-based picture dehazing system. The multi-scale feature extraction blocks, gated fusion sub-network, channel attention block, and encoder-decoder block are the four modules that make up this algorithm's network model. The overall network structure proposed in this paper is shown in Fig. 2. We apply depthwise separable convolution to decrease the total amount of parameters and constructed a lightweight network framework to enable deployment on devices with restricted resources.

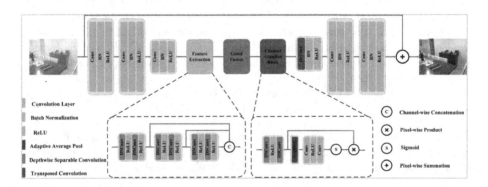

Fig. 2. The overall of our proposed encoder-decoder network. The network contains a feature extraction block, a gated fusion sub-network and a channel attention unit.

Encoder-Decoder Block. The input hazy image is first put into the encoder module as a feature map, and the encoder part uses three convolutional layers to learn the haze image, with the last convolutional layer downsampling the feature map by a factor of $1/2$. On the contrary, the decoder module contains a transpose convolution to upsample the feature map to it's own original resolution. The next two convolutional layers then nonlinearly map the upsampled feature to produce the desired final hazy residual map.

Feature Extraction Block. Spatially separable convolution was used to improve computational efficiency as early as 2012 [19]. Sooner or later, a depthwise version of AlexNet [15] has been added in order to increase accuracy, speed up convergence, and compact the model. Recently, several light-weight network architectures with accuracy, MobileNet [11] and ShuffleNet [26], have been developed for edge devices. Due to the limited computational resources of the FPGA platform, it was found from these research concepts that depth-wise separable convolution could be less complex in terms of computational resources and we introduced it as the base module for feature extraction. Although minimal parameters are used, the quality of image dehairing is still guaranteed. Each feature extraction block (FEB_i, i = 1, 2, 3) contains two depth-wise separable convolution (DSConv) and two relu layers(ReLU). The feature extraction module $FEB_i(x)$ is represented as

$$FEB_i(x) = ReLU_{i2}(DSC_{i2}(ReLU_{i1}(DSC_{i1}(F_{i-1}(x))))) \tag{1}$$

where $F_{i-1}(x)$ denotes the current input feature and $DSC_i(x)$ denotes the depth-wise separable convolution.

Gated Fusion Sub-Network. Based on Chen's [7] research, we fuse the characteristics among several layers using a gated fusion sub-network. In order to fuse the feature maps, F_0, F_1 and F_2 are first extracted from the feature extraction block and then linked in series by channel. The fused feature maps are then sent into the gated fusion sub-network. The weights of the preceding three related feature maps (W_0, W_1 and W_2) are the output of the gated fusion sub-network. The last step is to multiply the three relevant feature maps F_0, F_1 and F_2 by the appropriate weight layers. As shown, the gated fusion sub-network is as follows:

$$\begin{aligned} (W_0, W_1, W_2) &= Gat\,(F_0, F_1, F_2) \\ F_o &= W_0 \otimes F_0 + W_1 \otimes F_1 + W_2 \otimes F_2 \end{aligned} \tag{2}$$

The CAU receives additional input from the combined feature map F_o. The gated fusion sub-network in this study has three output channels and one kernel size 3×3 convolutional layer with a cascade of F_0, F_1 and F_2 inputs.

Channel Attention Unit. Inspired by PCNet [12] with high effective channel attention units, we use the CAU as our basic block in the proposed network. Depth-wise separable convolution, which performs similarly to regular convolution while being more computationally more efficient, is employed to design CAU in order to further minimize the number of parameters. The depth-wise separable convolution is immediately followed by a global average pooling without changing the dimensionality. Then two convolutional layers of 1×1 size for cross-channel information interaction. The weights are then used to adjust the input feature map to produce the output feature map after the feature map has been through the Sigmoid function to obtain the weight values. By weighing and filtering out the prominent characteristics at the present scale instead of the original features for backward propagation, an efficient channel attention is employed to increase the network's efficiency and performance. The efficient channel attention mechanism $CAU_i(x)$ is expressed as

$$DSC_i(x) = DSConv_{2i}(ReLU(DSConv_{1i}(F_{i-1}))$$
$$CAU_i(x) = \sigma(Conv_{2i}(Conv_{1i}(g(DSC_i(x))))) \otimes DSC_i(x)$$

(3)

where $DSConv(x)$ denotes the depth-wise separable convolution, σ denotes the Sigmoid function and $g(x)$ denotes the global average pooling function. By dynamically adjusting the feature map channel weights to reduce redundancy and learning rich contextual information to enhance the network's ability to extract haze density images, the effective Channel Attention Unit (CAU), when used after the gated fusion sub-network, enables a more detailed dehazing.

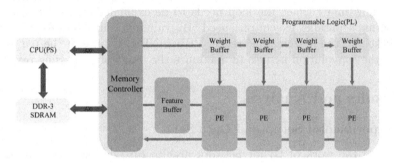

Fig. 3. Hardware architecture of the proposed CNN accelerator for image dehazing.

3.2   Hardware Optimizations

The most frequent and largest operation in the network is convolution operation, because convolution operation requires a lot of multiplication and addition operations, and a large number of access operations on parameters during the operation also consumes a lot of time. The hardware architecture of the dehazing network is designed around the convolution operations and access features in the network layer, so we need to design a convolution accelerator to ensure the speed of convolutional operations while balancing the relationship between hardware resources and memory bandwidth.

Huge data must be stored on off-chip resources due to the FPGA's restricted on-chip capacity. Nevertheless, data from the off-chip memory must first be transmitted through AXI to the on-chip memory within the FPGA before the device can run a parallel on-chip program. Every time the FPGA runs a task, it will have to read data from off-chip memory, which will take a lot of time and cause performance to suffer. We store as much data as we can in FPGA on-chip memory on our limited on-chip resources to prevent constantly reading and writing data from off-chip memory. In designing the memory access section, we used a cyclic partitioning approach. Suppose the size of input feature map In is $N \times H_{in} \times W_{in}$, the weight is $M \times N \times K \times K$, the size of output feature map Out is $M \times H_{out} \times W_{out}$, and the input channel, output channel and output feature map height and width of the partitioning factor are Tn, Tm, Tr and Tc respectively. During each calculation, we load $Tn \times (Tr + K - P) \times (Tc + K - P)$

size of the input feature block, $Tm \times Tn \times K \times K$ weights, and then perform a convolution calculation to obtain an output feature block of size $Tm \times Tr \times Tc$. Once the computation is complete, we will read the input features and weights for the next block and continue the computation until the convolution is complete. As shown in the Fig. 3, we store the intermediate output of each operation on a feature buffer in on-chip memory. This saves a lot of time by reading the data directly from the on-chip each time a new convolution calculation is performed.

The computation of the convolutional layers is that of a multi-layer loop nested, which means that the computation of the convolution is very slow. The PIPELINE command, which defines the loop to be enlarged and informs the compiler how many times the loop needs to be expanded, is used to optimize the program's parallel execution speed. By running computations in parallel and quickening the system's inference, PIPELINE takes use of the parallelism between the convolution kernels to maximize the usage of processing resources.

4   Results and Analysis

4.1   Experimental Setup and Data Set

We refer to the work of [7] for network architecture design and training. An Intel(R) Xeon(R) Processor E5-2620 v3 @ 2.40 GHz processor, 16.0 GB of Memory, and two NVIDIA Titan Xp graphics cards made up the experimental setup. The network was created using the Pytorch framework, with a training batch size of 16. The learning rate started out at 0.01 and declined to 0.1 times every 40 iterations for a total of 100. We used the Indoor Training Set (ITS), a subset of the publicly accessible image dehazing RESIDE [17] dataset, as the training dataset. Using a special development board made by Xillinx Inc., the suggested image dehazing technology is put into practice. It was made up of an XC7Z035 FPGA and a dual-core ARM Cortex-A9 CPU. Prior to deployment, we performed a tuning optimization of the network. There are a large number of convolutional and batch normalisation layer structures in the network. Due to their computational properties, we can reduce the model inference time by merging the batch normalization layers into the convolutional layers.

4.2   Comparisons with State-of-Arts

Compare with Other GPU-Based Methods. Table 1 gives the results of this experiment tested on synthetic datasets and compared quantitatively and qualitatively with recent methods, including AODNet [16], DehazeNet [6], DCPDN [25] and GCANet [7]. Peak Signal to Noise Ratio (PSNR) and Structural Similarity (SSIM) index measurements were also used for quantitative evaluation, with higher values indicating greater dehazing. Our approach gives a competitive performance to GPU-based methods with a relative small parameter size, which is around 0.1 million. For visual comparisons on the SOTS test set, hazy pictures of various intensities were also chosen for the evaluation of subjective quality. Figure 4 displays the dehazing impacts of each approach together with the related peak signal-to-noise ratios. The photos that were recovered using AODNet techniques had dark colors and insufficient dehazing. Nevertheless, when eliminating intense haze, the pictures recovered by DehazeNet and DCPDN approaches are prone to insufficient dehazing. Our approach shows a better dehazing effect, no obvious color distortion, more complete dehazing of dense hazy images, and the recovered image details and colors are closer to the original clear image. Although the dehazing effect of GCANet is slightly better than the method in this paper, the model size of GCANet is about 7 times larger than ours. And when processing some photographs with sections of sky, GCANet warps the colors. By contrast, our method does a good job of restoring the original colours.

Fig. 4. Qualitative comparison of different image dehazing methods on the SOTS dataset.

Compare with Other Traditional Methods. As for the evaluation dataset, as deep learning based methods are mostly trained on the RESIDE dataset,

Table 1. Quantitative comparisons of image dehazing on the SOTS indoor dataset from RESIDE.

Methods	PSNR	SSIM	Par. (Million)
AODNet [16]	19.06	0.85	0.002
DehazeNet [6]	21.14	0.84	0.0802
DCPDN [25]	15.85	0.82	66.89
GCANET [7]	30.06	0.96	0.7028
Ours	27.26	0.93	0.1297

Table 2. Scores for structural similarity, peak signal to noise ratio (PSNR), and mean squared error (MSE) on various datasets. The best result is shown in red.

DATASET	He et al. [10]		Zhu et al. [28]		Berman et al. [5]		Cho et al. [9]		Our	
	MSE	SSIM	MSE	SSIM	MSE	SSIM	MSE	SSIM	MSE	SSIM
FRIDA2	0.0744	0.5969	0.0744	0.5473	0.0705	0.6603	0.1559	0.5517	0.0642	0.6687
D-HAZY	0.0309	0.8348	0.0483	0.7984	0.0492	0.7473	0.0606	0.7212	0.0458	0.7629
O-HAZE	0.0200	0.7709	0.0226	0.6647	0.0255	0.8024	0.0196	0.7745	0.0197	0.6319
I-HAZE	0.0535	0.6580	0.0362	0.6864	0.0275	0.7959	0.0344	0.7693	0.0308	0.7169
Dense-Haze	0.0549	0.4662	0.0646	0.4171	0.0597	0.5225	0.0549	0.5254	0.0613	0.4174
Total	0.0467	0.6653	0.0492	0.6227	0.0464	0.7056	0.0650	0.6684	0.0444	0.6396

their performance on this dataset is better than other datasets. For the sake of fairness, when comparing with traditional methods, we employ FRIDA2 [23], D-HAZY [3], O-HAZE [2], I-HAZE [4], and Dense-Haze [1]. Moreover, we employ Mean Square Error (MSE) and Structural Similarity (SSIM), two full-reference criteria, to quantitatively assess the dehazing performance. The results of this experiment tested on the five datasets mentioned previously and compared with conventional FPGA-based dehazing methods, those proposed by He et al. [10], Zhu et al. [28], Berman et al. [5], and Cho et al. [9], are given in the Table 2. The traditional methods cannot effectively handle the sky region leading to their poor performance on FRIDA2. On the contrary, our approach ranks first in the overall SSIM evaluation, which is the primary indicator for visible edges, on five databases from different conditions.

Table 3. Ablation study on SOTS dataset.

Depth-Wise Convolution		✓			✓
Gated Fusion			✓		✓
CAU				✓	✓
PSNR	22.93	24.24	23.43	26.44	27.26
Par. (Million)	0.1288	0.1250	0.1309	0.1336	0.1297

4.3 Ablation Study

We combine the depth-wise separable convolution, channel attention unit, and gated fusion sub-networks into our suggested model, as was already indicated. To confirm the contribution of each component to the final dehazing performance, we conduct ablation experiments on the SOTS dataset. Instead of using depth-wise separable convolution, we use conventional convolution instead, and we change the number of convolutions to roughly equalize the size of the network overall. As demonstrated in the Table 3, the introduction of the channel attention module significantly improves the model's performance, demonstrating the efficacy of CAU. Subsequently, the performance of the model is somewhat improved by the addition of deep separable convolution and gated sub-networks. Eventually, including all three modules into the model yields the optimal outcome.

Table 4. Convolutional Accelerator Resource utilization.

Resource	DSP48E	BRAM_18K	LUT	FF
Used	213	161	60803	58930
Available	900	1000	171900	343800
Utilization	23	16	35	17

Table 5. Comparison with other platforms.

Platform	GPU	CPU	FPGA
Device	Titan Xp	i7-8700	XC7Z035
Power (Watt)	250	85	4.2
Performance (FPS)	394	1.5	8.3
Energy efficiency (FPS/W)	1.57	0.017	1.97

4.4 Hardware Evaluation

In this subsection, we first provide the resource utilization rate. Then, we compared the software implementation (on CPU and GPU) with our accelerator on FPGA. Placement and wiring are done through the Vivado toolset. After the collection is completed, the resource utilization rate we achieved is reported, as shown in the Table 4. We can see that our CNN accelerator requires very little FPGA hardware resources. We compared our method on FPGA with other platforms. We selected NVIDIA Titan-Xp GPU and Intel i7-8700 CPU for comparison. We tested the power consumption of the FPGA end, and the power consumption of the GPU and CPU came from the user manual. From the Table 5, it can be concluded that our method is suitable for edge platforms with low power consumption and few resources.

5   Conclusion

In this research, we provide a lightweight FPGA-based deep learning-based approach for image dehazing. A CNN network based on depth-wise separable convolution and channel attention to limit the network size is suggested in order to lower the storage and computing requirements. Then, using our suggested accelerated design strategy, we deploy the entire algorithm on a low-cost custom FPGA development board from Xilinx Inc. Therefore, our method is an universal solution to image dehazing on FPGAs.

Acknowledgments. This work was supported by the Natural Science Foundation of China (62202347) and the Natural Science Foundation of Hubei Province (2022CFB578).

References

1. Ancuti, C.O., Ancuti, C., Sbert, M., Timofte, R.: Dense-haze: a benchmark for image dehazing with dense-haze and haze-free images. In: 2019 IEEE International Conference on Image Processing (ICIP), pp. 1014–1018. IEEE (2019)
2. Ancuti, C.O., Ancuti, C., Timofte, R., De Vleeschouwer, C.: O-HAZE: a dehazing benchmark with real hazy and haze-free outdoor images. In: Proceedings of the IEEE Conference on Computer Vision and Pattern Recognition Workshops, pp. 754–762 (2018)
3. Ancuti, C., Ancuti, C.O., De Vleeschouwer, C.: D-HAZY: a dataset to evaluate quantitatively dehazing algorithms. In: 2016 IEEE International Conference on Image Processing (ICIP), pp. 2226–2230. IEEE (2016)
4. Ancuti, C., Ancuti, C.O., Timofte, R., De Vleeschouwer, C.: I-HAZE: a dehazing benchmark with real hazy and haze-free indoor images. In: Blanc-Talon, J., Helbert, D., Philips, W., Popescu, D., Scheunders, P. (eds.) ACIVS 2018. LNCS, vol. 11182, pp. 620–631. Springer, Cham (2018). https://doi.org/10.1007/978-3-030-01449-0_52
5. Berman, D., Avidan, S.: Non-local image dehazing. In: Proceedings of the IEEE Conference on Computer Vision and Pattern Recognition, pp. 1674–1682 (2016)
6. Cai, B., Xu, X., Jia, K., Qing, C., Tao, D.: DehazeNet: an end-to-end system for single image haze removal. IEEE Trans. Image Process. **25**(11), 5187–5198 (2016)
7. Chen, D., et al.: Gated context aggregation network for image dehazing and deraining. In: 2019 IEEE Winter Conference on Applications of Computer Vision (WACV), pp. 1375–1383. IEEE (2019)
8. Chen, Z., Zhou, Y., Li, R., Li, P., Sheng, B.: SCPA-NET: self-calibrated pyramid aggregation for image dehazing. Comput. Animation Virtual Worlds **33**(3–4), e2061 (2022)
9. Cho, Y., Jeong, J., Kim, A.: Model-assisted multiband fusion for single image enhancement and applications to robot vision. IEEE Robot. Autom. Lett. **3**(4), 2822–2829 (2018)
10. He, K., Sun, J., Tang, X.: Single image haze removal using dark channel prior. IEEE Trans. Pattern Anal. Mach. Intell. **33**(12), 2341–2353 (2010)
11. Howard, A.G., et al.: MobileNets: efficient convolutional neural networks for mobile vision applications. arXiv preprint arXiv:1704.04861 (2017)

12. Jiang, K., Wang, Z., Yi, P., Chen, C., Lin, C.W.: Rain-free and residue hand-in-hand: a progressive coupled network for real-time image deraining. IEEE Trans. Image Process. **30**, 7404–7418 (2021)
13. Ju, Y.K., Jeon, J.W.: Implementation of a single-image haze removal using the FPGA. In: the 12th International Conference (2018)
14. Kasauka, D., Sugiyama, K., Tsutsui, H., Okuhata, H., Miyanaga, Y.: An architecture for real-time Retinex-based image enhancement and haze removal and its FPGA implementation. IEICE Trans. Fundam. Electron. Commun. Comput. Sci. **102**(6), 775–782 (2019)
15. Krizhevsky, A., Sutskever, I., Hinton, G.E.: ImageNet classification with deep convolutional neural networks. Commun. ACM **60**(6), 84–90 (2017)
16. Li, B., Peng, X., Wang, Z., Xu, J., Feng, D.: AOD-Net: all-in-one dehazing network. In: Proceedings of the IEEE International Conference on Computer Vision, pp. 4770–4778 (2017)
17. Li, B., et al.: Benchmarking single-image dehazing and beyond. IEEE Trans. Image Process. **28**(1), 492–505 (2018)
18. Lu, J., Dong, C.: DSP-based image real-time dehazing optimization for improved dark-channel prior algorithm. J. Real-Time Image Proc. **17**(5), 1675–1684 (2020)
19. Mamalet, F., Garcia, C.: Simplifying ConvNets for Fast Learning. In: Villa, A.E.P., Duch, W., Érdi, P., Masulli, F., Palm, G. (eds.) ICANN 2012. LNCS, vol. 7553, pp. 58–65. Springer, Heidelberg (2012). https://doi.org/10.1007/978-3-642-33266-1_8
20. Manu, C.M., Sreeni, K.: GANID: a novel generative adversarial network for image dehazing. Visual Comput. **39**, 3923–3936 (2022)
21. Ren, W., Liu, S., Zhang, H., Pan, J., Cao, X., Yang, M.-H.: Single image dehazing via multi-scale convolutional neural networks. In: Leibe, B., Matas, J., Sebe, N., Welling, M. (eds.) ECCV 2016. LNCS, vol. 9906, pp. 154–169. Springer, Cham (2016). https://doi.org/10.1007/978-3-319-46475-6_10
22. Ren, W., et al.: Gated fusion network for single image dehazing. In: Proceedings of the IEEE Conference on Computer Vision and Pattern Recognition, pp. 3253–3261 (2018)
23. Tarel, J.P., Hautiere, N., Caraffa, L., Cord, A., Halmaoui, H., Gruyer, D.: Vision enhancement in homogeneous and heterogeneous fog. IEEE Intell. Transp. Syst. Mag. **4**(2), 6–20 (2012)
24. Yi, W., Dong, L., Liu, M., Hui, M., Kong, L., Zhao, Y.: MFAF-net: image dehazing with multi-level features and adaptive fusion. Visual Comput. 1–15 (2023)
25. Zhang, H., Patel, V.M.: Densely connected pyramid dehazing network. In: CVPR (2018)
26. Zhang, X., Zhou, X., Lin, M., Sun, J.: ShuffleNet: an extremely efficient convolutional neural network for mobile devices. In: Proceedings of the IEEE Conference on Computer Vision and Pattern Recognition, pp. 6848–6856 (2018)
27. Zhou, Y., Chen, Z., Sheng, B., Li, P., Kim, J., Wu, E.: AFF-Dehazing: attention-based feature fusion network for low-light image dehazing. Comput. Animation Virtual Worlds **32**(3–4), e2011 (2021)
28. Zhu, Q., Mai, J., Shao, L.: A fast single image haze removal algorithm using color attenuation prior. IEEE Trans. Image Process. **24**(11), 3522–3533 (2015)

Image Analysis and Visualization in Advanced Medical Imaging Technology

Automated Marker-Less Patient-to-Preoperative Medical Image Registration Approach Using RGB-D Images and Facial Landmarks for Potential Use in Computed-Aided Surgical Navigation of the Paranasal Sinus

Suhyeon Kim[1], Haill An[1], Myungji Song[1], Sungmin Lee[1],
Hoijoon Jung[2], Seontae Kim[3], and Younhyun Jung[1]([✉])

[1] School of Computing, Gachon University, Seongnam-si, Republic of Korea
{kih629,xenotic,qqqgina,yugioh1118,younhyun.jung}@gachon.ac.kr
[2] School of Computer Science, University of Sydney, Sydney, Australia
hjun6058@uni.sydnet.edu.au
[3] Department of Otolaryngology-Head and Neck Surgery, College of Medicine,
Gil Medical Center, Seongnam-si, Republic of Korea
kst2383@gilhospital.com

Abstract. Paranasal sinus surgery is an established treatment option for chronic rhinosinusitis. Because this surgery is performed inside the nasal cavity, where critical anatomical structures, such as optic nerves and pituitary glands, exist nearby, surgeons usually rely on computer-aided surgical navigation (CSN) to provide a wide field of view in the surgical site and to allow for precise control of surgical instruments. In the CSNs, it is essential to register the surgical site of the actual patient with the corresponding view from the preoperative computed tomography (CT) images. The traditional registration approaches are performed manually by the user or automatically by attaching fiducial markers on both the patient's surgical site and preoperative CT images for every surgery before use. In this work, we propose an automated approach to register patient-to-preoperative CT image without fiducial markers. The proposed approach detected and extracted facial anatomical landmarks in 2D RGB images through the use of deep learning models. These landmarks were located in 3D facial mesh reconstructed from depth images by using unprojection and ray-marching algorithms. The facial landmark pairs acquired from the patient site and the preoperative CT images are then registered with singular value decomposition and iterative closet point algorithms. We demonstrate the registration capability of our approach using Microsoft HoloLens 2, a mixed reality head-mounted display because it facilitates the acquisition of RGB-depth images and the prototype development of in-situ visualization to illustrate how the CT images are properly registered on the target surgical site. We compared our automated marker-less registration approach to the manual counterpart using a facial phantom with three participants. The results show that our approach produces relatively good registration accuracy, with a marginal target registration error of 4.4 mm when compared to the manual counterpart.

Keywords: Automated marker-less registration · Computer-aided surgical navigation · Paranasal sinus surgery · Facial landmarks

1   Introduction

Chronic rhinosinusitis is a prevalent and persistent condition that occurs in 1% to 5% of the United State population and significantly impacts the quality of daily life [8,21]. This clinical condition occurs when acute sinusitis is not effectively managed or when there is a recurrence of inflammation. In cases where pharmacological interventions fail to alleviate the symptoms, paranasal sinus surgery (PSS) is the commonly available treatment alternative [12]. It is a minimally invasive procedure that uses a nasal endoscope to access the sinus and ease inflammation. The high field of view in the surgical sites and precise control over surgical instruments is fundamental for PSS because the sinus is typically located near critical anatomical structures within the skull, such as the orbit, optic nerve, carotid arteries, and pituitary gland [29]. To enhance the precision of the surgical instrument pathing and thus the outcomes of surgeries, computer-aided surgical navigation (CSN) is commonly employed to guide an operator through the visualization of preoperative medical images such as computer tomography (CT) or magnetic resonance (MR) images. In cases of PSS, CSN relies on CT images to provide timely and precise localization of surgical instruments in terms of the actual inner surgical site of the nasal cavity [23].

CSN essentially requires an easy-to-use, rapid, accurate patient-to-preoperative medical image registration process that correlates the surgical site of the actual patient with the corresponding view from the preoperative medical images. Traditionally, this registration process is performed manually by the user, or automatically by using fiducial markers such as adhesive and implantable ones. In the manual registration approaches, a set of landmarks in the outer surfaces to approximate surgical sites are carefully defined with a pointer tip by a user, which is then registered to the predefined corresponding landmarks in the preoperative images through point-to-point matching algorithms. These approaches have been widely investigated to develop a variety of CSNs [2,7,13]. They, however, are time-consuming, require a high-level of human involvement, and more importantly introduce intra- and inter-observer errors [14]. Furthermore, there is a potential risk of infection due to the unnecessary physical contact with the patient during the registration process. The use of fiducial markers addressed the shortcomings of the manual registration approaches to some extent by using them as landmarks to be tracked and registered in an automated manner [9,16,27,30]. However, none of them was a complete solution.

The marker attachment needed to be done individually for every patient before use. In addition, adhesive markers carried the risk of marker point migration, and implantable markers could cause complications by surgical trauma.

Several studies have been conducted to attempt the patient-to-preoperative medical image registration approach without relying on fiducial markers [1,5, 10,11]. These marker-less approaches extracted relevant image features to the patient's surgical sites from camera feeds and registered them with the corresponding features in the preoperative medical images. These features vary depending on the surgical sites and include surface shapes or anatomical landmarks, acquired with the use of computer vision algorithms. Fan et al. [5] used the point cloud of the patient's surface, obtained through a 3D scanner, and registered with the surface mesh extracted from CT images. This registration was applied in the field of neurosurgery. Long et al. [10] focused on reconstructing facial surfaces from depth images captured using structured light techniques. They applied a registration approach with CT images based on the scale-invariant feature transformations. Additionally, Kang et al. [11] performed registration of a maxillofacial model by leveraging anatomical landmarks such as tooth cusps, bony landmarks, and the anterior wall region of the maxillary sinus.

In this work, we propose a new automated marker-less registration approach for use in PSS-CSN. Our approach is designed to locate facial anatomical landmarks in the vicinity of the sinus from RGB-depth (RGB-D) images using deep learning models. The landmark pairs in the patient site and preoperative CT image are then registered based on a 3D point-to-point matching algorithm. This enhances the registration approach by ensuring that the relevant facial landmarks are acquired and tracked consistently and automatically. We demonstrate our approach using Microsoft HoloLens 2 [18], a mixed reality head-mounted display, due to the capabilities in the easy acquisition of RGB-D images and the fast development of in-situ visualization prototypes to illustrate how the virtual preoperative contents are registered on the target sites. We evaluate the registration accuracy of our approach using a phantom by comparing to a manual registration counterpart. The contributions of our work are summarized as follows: (1) We propose a new automated marker-less registration approach dedicated for the sinus in facial anatomy and potential use in PSS-CSN, and (2) We validate our registration approach under practical environments using a commodity device of Microsoft HoloLens 2.

2   Method

2.1   Overview

We outline an overview of the proposed marker-less registration approach in Fig. 1 using a facial phantom. Our approach consists of four components: (i) 2D facial landmark extraction in patient (phantom) sites; (ii) the corresponding facial landmark extraction in preoperative CT images; (iii) the 3D localization of the extracted 2D landmarks and; (iv) 3D to 3D registration between the landmark pairs (patient-to-CT). For the patient sites, we acquired the RGB-D images

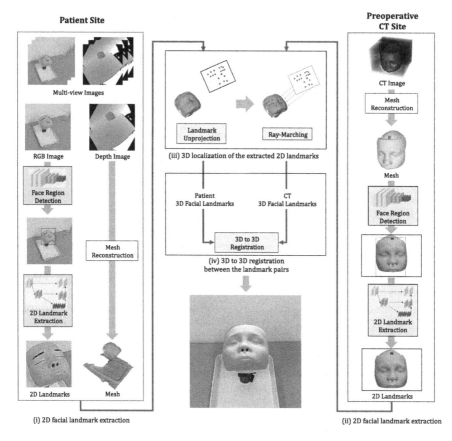

Fig. 1. Overview of our marker-less patient-to-preoperative CT image registration approach.

using HoloLens 2 to extract and locate the facial landmarks. With the acquired RGB images, we detected and cropped the facial region from the background using multi-task cascaded convolutional network (MTCNN) [31] and utilized high-resolution network (HRN) [24,26] to extract 2D eighteen facial landmarks within the bounding box region. We relied on the corresponding depth image to reconstruct the 3D facial mesh with a ball pivot algorithm [3], which was used to locate the positions of the landmarks in 3D space. For the 3D localization, we introduced an unprojection and a ray-marching algorithm. We performed a similar procedure in preoperative CT images to extract and locate facial landmarks. Here, we used the 2D frontal view and the 3D mesh reconstructed by a marching-cube algorithm [28]. Finally, a registration between the 3D landmark pairs was performed to derive a transformation matrix. We adopted a two-stage registration using singular value decomposition (SVD) [25] and iterative closest point (ICP) [4] algorithms.

2.2   Deep Learning Models for 2D Facial Landmark Extraction

We designed a two-stage 2D facial landmark extraction in RGB images: (i) facial bounding box region detection using MTCNN [31] and; (ii) facial landmark extraction based on HRN [24,26]. Our two-stage facial landmark extraction was fully automated and did not require any user involvement.

MTCNN was an established deep learning model for detecting face regions in a RGB image. We chose MTCNN model due to its multi-step architecture being robust to variations in image resolutions, face shapes, and location of viewpoints. MTCNN consisted of two cascaded networks: a proposal network and a refinement network. The proposal network served, as the initial step, generating a set of candidate bounding boxes and their confidence scores, indicating the likelihood of each box containing a face. The subsequent refinement network enhanced the bounding boxes by eliminating redundant detections and raising their accuracy through regression. The final output of the MTCNN was a minimal bounding box that contains the detected face within the RGB image. This stage effectively constrained the region of interest for the subsequent facial landmark extraction stage, thereby mitigating the risk of inaccurate extraction.

We employed the HRN model, which has demonstrated outstanding performance in capturing fine-grained details, such as facial landmarks. HRN was a high-resolution convolutional neural network architecture that excelled in handling tasks that required sophisticated feature descriptions, such as facial landmarks. Instead of downsampling the feature maps at early streams to reduce computational complexity, HRN maintained multiple parallel streams with different resolutions throughout the network. HRN then employed multi-resolution fusion to integrate features derived from various resolutions. It enabled the enhancement of higher resolution representations through the incorporation of information from lower resolution representations, and vice versa. This multi-resolution design enabled HRN to capture both local and global information effectively to extract representative landmarks for human faces.

2.3   3D Localization of 2D Facial Landmarks

Like Zhang et al. [33], we estimated 2D landmarks from RGB and localized 3D landmarks using depth images. We noted that the acquired depth images inherently had missing values (depth holes) due to the physical properties including light reflection, object boundaries, and inaccurate refraction. The direct use of the depth images could produce imprecise 3D localization of 2D facial landmarks. We, instead, reconstructed the 3D mesh using the depth image and it allowed us to fill the missing values by interpolating the neighboring depth values. Our mesh-based 3D landmark localization consisted of (i) unprojection of 2D facial landmarks; (ii) 3D facial mesh reconstruction based on depth images; and (iii) ray-marching of the unprojected landmarks in the 3D facial mesh.

The unprojection of 2D facial landmarks was based on camera calibration parameters and geometric transformation matrix to the camera origin. The unprojection stage lets us know the 3D directional vector of the facial landmarks in 2D image planes to the camera origin. For the 3D facial mesh reconstruction, we employed two distinct algorithms. For patient sites, the ball pivot algorithm [3] was employed. It involved iteratively selecting seed points within the depth images and constructing mesh triangles by pivoting balls around the seeds. It incrementally expands the mesh by effectively filling gaps, resulting in the reconstruction of a complete and accurate 3D mesh representation. The facial mesh reconstruction in CT images was based on a marching-cube algorithm [28] with an intensity threshold range from 0 to -300 that is representative of the facial skin. It partitioned the CT volumetric space into small cubic cells and determined the surface configuration within each cell based on the intensity range threshold. By connecting the vertices of these cells, a triangulated mesh representation of the facial surface was constructed. Finally, ray-marching was performed from the camera origin to the directional vector of the facial landmarks to obtain the intersection points with the facial mesh. We used the intersection points as the 3D location of the facial landmarks. We performed averaging the 3D locations of the same facial landmark from multi-views to compensate for potential errors caused by a single-view depth image.

2.4   3D to 3D Registration

We obtained an initial transformation matrix between the 3D facial landmarks pairs (patient-to-CT) using the SVD algorithm [25], which was then fine-tuned based on the ICP algorithm [4]. The SVD algorithm enabled effective initial matching through data compression and denoising, whereas the ICP algorithm has been shown to produce accurate 3D geometry matching when initial points were well-defined. This enabled our registration approach to be robust to initialization variations in 3D facial landmarks and to produce a precise final transformation matrix.

In the SVD algorithm, we first constructed a covariance matrix using the correspondences between the patient landmark and CT landmark pairs. This covariance matrix captured the statistical relationship between them. By performing SVD decomposition on the covariance matrix, we obtained the singular vectors and singular values. The singular vectors represented the optimal rotation matrix that aligns the landmark pairs, while the singular values indicated the scaling factors along each axis. The registration performance of the ICP algorithm largely relied on the quality of initializations, and only local optimality is guaranteed. We employed the ICP algorithm to iteratively refine the initial transformation matrix from the SVD algorithm. In each iteration, the ICP algorithm estimated an intermediate transformation matrix by minimizing a distance value between point (landmark) pairs. The distance value calculated the discrepancy between a point in the patient site to the closest point in the CT images for all points. This iterative optimization process continued until convergence is achieved, resulting in a highly accurate transformation matrix.

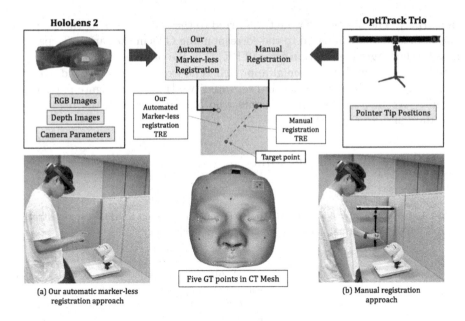

Fig. 2. Overview of performance evaluation and comparison experiment.

3   Experiment

For our experiment, we prepared a facial phantom affixed to a support structure and its CT images. To make the phantom as similar as possible to the human face, masking tape was attached to the eyebrows and eyes of the phantom face. We evaluated the registration capability of our automated marker-less approach by comparing with a manual counterpart based on ground truth (GT) sample points. We employed the HoloLens 2 to acquire RGB-D images with camera parameters, which were transferred through TCP connection for a remote PC to compute the transformation matrix of our marker-less approach. The manual registration approach was based on an optical tracking system, OptiTrack V120 Trio [20], certified for 6 degrees of freedom tracking of marker ball-equipped pointer tips, and 3D Slicer PC software [6].

We illustrate our performance evaluation and comparison experiment procedure in Fig. 2. Our experiment was divided into three phases. Initially, a participant manually performed phantom-to-CT registration in the OptiTrack environment. The participant was required to choose 18 facial landmarks by using the pointer tip tracked by the OptiTrack. The ICP algorithm [4] computed a transformation matrix between the facial landmarks and the corresponding ones in the CT images. As the second phase, the participant conducted our marker-less registration in the HoloLens 2 environment (see Sect. 2.2 and Fig. 1). Lastly, we prepared the predefined five GT points in the phantom and asked the participant to select the corresponding points using the pointer tip. The user-selected five points were applied to both our automated approach and the manual counterpart. The five points were transferred to the CT space using the transformation matrix and compared to the corresponding GTs in the same CT space to measure the target registration error (TRE) [17]. We compared TRE of our automated approach with the manual approach. The experiment was conducted by alternating both the approaches and repeated two times to mitigate participant learning. We invited three participants who are familiar with the registration procedure and averaged their TRE.

4   Results and Discussions

Table 1. Comparison results of TRE between our automated marker-less registration approach and the manual counterpart for three participants.

	TRE (mm)	Participant 1	Participant 2	Participant 3	Total
Our automated marker-less	Mean	11.1016	10.2548	10.8204	10.7257
	Standard deviation	2.1580	1.5812	1.9831	1.8894
Manual	Mean	5.7740	7.6058	5.5344	6.3047
	Standard deviation	2.4294	2.4245	2.6074	2.5790

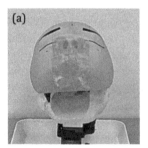 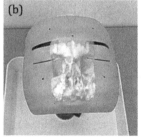 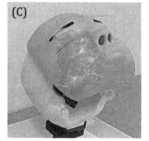

Fig. 3. In-situ visualization results to augment the virtual rendering contents of the CT images on the target phantom using the transformation matrix from our automated marker-less registration approach. The phantom is augmented with the sinus in (a) bottom view; (b) top view; and (c) lateral view.

We present the mean and standard deviation of TRE for three participants, comparing our automated marker-less registration approach to the manual counterpart in Table 1. The results show that our approach was able to obtain relatively good registration accuracy with TRE mean of 10.7 mm. It is also observed that although our approach was inferior to the manual counterpart in terms of TRE mean, the difference was not obvious with a 4.4 mm error. Our approach also produced a lower standard deviation of TRE, indicating that it was more robust to the intra- and inter-observer errors that usually encounter when the manual counterparts are used. These findings suggested that our automated approach could be an alternative as it could produce comparable registration accuracy and minimize the tedious human involvement and the unnecessary physical contact during the manual registration process.

We attempted in-situ visualization, since previous studies [22,32] have shown the benefit of representing it in a 3D model for better comprehension of the anatomy. In-situ visualization results using the transformation matrix from our automated marker-less registration approach were shown in Fig. 3, where the preoperative rendering of the CT images was augmented on the target phantom. In the visualization, the sinus structure was situated within the intracranial space of the skull bone. The augmentation results from all three views show that the internal invisible sinus structures of the phantom seem to be accurately registered with the virtual rendering. It shows the practical applicability of our approach in the context of PSS-CSN, where the precise alignment of the internal structural details of the sinuses is paramount to guide the surgical instrument path routing.

5   Conclusion and Future Work

In this work, we proposed a registration process for use in PSS-CSN by automatically detecting and registering the anatomical landmarks relevant to the sinus. Our results demonstrated that our approach did not require any manual procedures, such as marker attachment or landmark selection, and could be an easy-to-use and intuitive tool, particularly for novice users in CSN. More importantly, our approach produced relatively comparable registration accuracy to the manual counterpart, thus providing users with an effective alternative.

Our current work poses some limitations. Our approach has been only evaluated with the limited experimental environments, not yet clinically. We are currently investigating the integration of our registration approach to the pilot version of the commercial PSS-CSN [15], and this would provide an opportunity to conduct a user study with real patient cases, where we could evaluate the clinical utility of our registration approach. Our results showed our approach was still inferior to the manual counterpart in terms of registration accuracy. The higher TRE from our approach could be partially attributed to the low-quality depth images of Microsoft HoloLens 2 used for data acquisition. The low-quality images (e.g., depth holes) impacted on the 3D localization of the anatomical landmarks being detected. We addressed the issue by complementing the missing depth values with the multi-view images, but the solution was not sufficient enough to address all and outperform the manual approach. We believe that adopting the image restoration algorithms, e.g., neural radiance fields [19], may largely improve the quality of the depth images and thus the registration accuracy. Furthermore, our approach is methodological, meaning that the elements that make up our approach can be modularized and replaced with other state-of-the-art techniques to improve performance. We consider these as interesting future work.

Acknowledgments. This work was supported by the Korea Health Technology R&D Project by the Korea Health Industry Development Institute (Grant Number: HI22C1651), by the National Research Foundation of Korea (NRF) grant funded by the Korea government (Grant Number: 2021R1F1A1059554), and also by the Gachon University research fund of 2023 (Grant Number: GCU-202304220001).

References

1. Ali, S.G., et al.: Cost-effective broad learning-based ultrasound biomicroscopy with 3D reconstruction for ocular anterior segmentation. Multimedia Tools Appl. **80**, 35105–35122 (2021)
2. Bae, D.K., Song, S.J.: Computer assisted navigation in knee arthroplasty. Clin. Orthop. Surg. **3**(4), 259–267 (2011)
3. Bernardini, F., Mittleman, J., Rushmeier, H., Silva, C., Taubin, G.: The ball-pivoting algorithm for surface reconstruction. IEEE Trans. Visual Comput. Graphics **5**(4), 349–359 (1999)
4. Chetverikov, D., Svirko, D., Stepanov, D., Krsek, P.: The trimmed iterative closest point algorithm. In: 2002 International Conference on Pattern Recognition, vol. 3, pp. 545–548. IEEE (2002)
5. Fan, Y., Jiang, D., Wang, M., Song, Z.: A new markerless patient-to-image registration method using a portable 3D scanner. Med. Phys. **41**(10), 101910 (2014)
6. Fedorov, A., et al.: 3D slicer as an image computing platform for the quantitative imaging network. Magn. Reson. Imaging **30**(9), 1323–1341 (2012)
7. Grauvogel, T.D., Engelskirchen, P., Semper-Hogg, W., Grauvogel, J., Laszig, R.: Navigation accuracy after automatic-and hybrid-surface registration in sinus and skull base surgery. PLoS ONE **12**(7), e0180975 (2017)
8. Hamilos, D.L.: Chronic sinusitis. J. Allergy Clin. Immunol. **106**(2), 213–227 (2000)
9. Hong, J., Hashizume, M.: An effective point-based registration tool for surgical navigation. Surg. Endosc. **24**, 944–948 (2010)
10. Jiang, L., Zhang, S., Yang, J., Zhuang, X., Zhang, L., Gu, L.: A robust automated markerless registration framework for neurosurgery navigation. Int. J. Med. Robot. Comput. Assist. Surg. **11**(4), 436–447 (2015)
11. Kang, S., Kim, M., Kim, J., Park, H., Park, W.: Marker-free registration for the accurate integration of CT images and the subject's anatomy during navigation surgery of the maxillary sinus. Dentomaxillofacial Radiol. **41**(8), 679–685 (2012)
12. Khalil, H., Nunez, D.A.: Functional endoscopic sinus surgery for chronic rhinosinusitis. Cochrane Database Syst. Rev. (3) (2006)
13. Kosugi, Y., et al.: An articulated neurosurgical navigation system using MRI and CT images. IEEE Trans. Biomed. Eng. **35**(2), 147–152 (1988)
14. Krueger, S., et al.: Fast and accurate automatic registration for MR-guided procedures using active microcoils. IEEE Trans. Med. Imaging **26**(3), 385–392 (2007)
15. Lee, S., Jung, H., Lee, E., Jung, Y., Kim, S.T.: A preliminary work: mixed reality-integrated computer-aided surgical navigation system for paranasal sinus surgery using Microsoft HoloLens 2. In: Magnenat-Thalmann, N., et al. (eds.) CGI 2021. LNCS, vol. 13002, pp. 633–641. Springer, Cham (2021). https://doi.org/10.1007/978-3-030-89029-2_47
16. Lin, Q., Yang, R., Cai, K., Si, X., Chen, X., Wu, X.: Real-time automatic registration in optical surgical navigation. Infrared Phys. Technol. **76**, 375–385 (2016)

17. Maurer, C.R., Fitzpatrick, J.M., Wang, M.Y., Galloway, R.L., Maciunas, R.J., Allen, G.S.: Registration of head volume images using implantable fiducial markers. IEEE Trans. Med. Imaging **16**(4), 447–462 (1997)

18. Microsoft: Microsoft hololens 2 docs. https://www.microsoft.com/it-it/hololens. Accessed 12 June 2023

19. Mildenhall, B., Srinivasan, P.P., Tancik, M., Barron, J.T., Ramamoorthi, R., Ng, R.: NeRF: representing scenes as neural radiance fields for view synthesis. Commun. ACM **65**(1), 99–106 (2021)

20. OptiTrack: Optitrack v120:trio. https://optitrack.com/cameras/v120-trio/. Accessed 12 June 2023

21. Sedaghat, A.R.: Chronic rhinosinusitis. Am. Fam. Physician **96**(8), 500–506 (2017)

22. Shetty, V., et al.: CT-based 3D reconstruction of lower limb versus X-ray-based 3D reconstruction: a comparative analysis and application for a safe and cost-effective modality in TKA. Indian J. Orthop. **55**, 1150–1157 (2021)

23. Singh, A., Kumar, R., Thakar, A., Sharma, S., Bhalla, A.: Role of image guided navigation in endoscopic surgery of paranasal sinuses: a comparative study. Indian J. Otolaryngol. Head Neck Surg. **72**, 221–227 (2020)

24. Sun, K., Xiao, B., Liu, D., Wang, J.: Deep high-resolution representation learning for human pose estimation. In: Proceedings of the IEEE/CVF Conference on Computer Vision and Pattern Recognition, pp. 5693–5703 (2019)

25. Van Loan, C.F.: Generalizing the singular value decomposition. SIAM J. Numer. Anal. **13**(1), 76–83 (1976)

26. Wang, J., et al.: Deep high-resolution representation learning for visual recognition. IEEE Trans. Pattern Anal. Mach. Intell. **43**(10), 3349–3364 (2020)

27. Wang, M., Song, Z.: Automatic localization of the center of fiducial markers in 3D CT/MRI images for image-guided neurosurgery. Pattern Recogn. Lett. **30**(4), 414–420 (2009)

28. We, L.: Marching cubes: a high resolution 3D surface construction algorithm. Comput. Graph. **21**, 163–169 (1987)

29. Wise, S.K., DelGaudio, J.M.: Computer-aided surgery of the paranasal sinuses and skull base. Expert Rev. Med. Devices **2**(4), 395–408 (2005)

30. Yamamoto, S., Taniike, N., Takenobu, T.: Application of an open position splint integrated with a reference frame and registration markers for mandibular navigation surgery. Int. J. Oral Maxillofac. Surg. **49**(5), 686–690 (2020)

31. Zhang, K., Zhang, Z., Li, Z., Qiao, Y.: Joint face detection and alignment using multitask cascaded convolutional networks. IEEE Signal Process. Lett. **23**(10), 1499–1503 (2016)

32. Zhang, X., et al.: Application of three-dimensional reconstruction and printing as an elective course for undergraduate medical students: an exploratory trial. Surg. Radiol. Anat. **41**, 1193–1204 (2019)

33. Zhang, Z., Lian, D., Gao, S.: RGB-D-based gaze point estimation via multi-column CNNs and facial landmarks global optimization. Vis. Comput. **37**, 1731–1741 (2021)

Challenges and Constraints in Deformation-Based Medical Mesh Representation

Ge Jin[1]([✉]) [iD], Younhyun Jung[2], and Jinman Kim[1]

[1] University of Sydney, Camperdown, NSW 2050, Australia
gjin5774@uni.sydney.edu.au
[2] Gachon University, Seongnam, Gyeonggi 13306, Republic of Korea

Abstract. Mesh representation of medical imaging isosurfaces are essential for medical analysis. These representations are typically obtained using mesh extraction methods to segment 3D volumes. However, the meshes extracted from such methods often suffer from undesired staircase artefacts. In this paper, we evaluate the existing mesh deformation methods that deform a template mesh to desired shapes. We evaluate two variants of such method on three datasets of varying topological complexity. Our objective is to demonstrate that, despite the mesh deformation methods having their limitations, they avoid the generation of staircase artefacts.

Keywords: Medical Imaging Rendering · Mesh Deformation · Deep Learning

1 Introduction

Polygon meshes have seen great advances in the medical imaging community, propelled by modern graphics processing units (GPUs) that are optimized for mesh rasterization. These advances have facilitated the polygon mesh representation to be easily rendered, and the adoption of powerful modern rendering engines, such as Unity, are enabling efficient visualization. Although previous works such as [3] enable directly rendering the polygonised isosurface of binary volumes, the ray casting technique used is much more computational expensive than mesh rasterization. The polygon mesh is a graph-based representation that consists of vertices and their connecting edges to model the isosurfaces of objects in 3D space. The graph-based data structure enables arbitrary vertex placements in continuous 3D space, therefore the isosurface can be stored in varying levels-of-detail and resulting in a highly compact data structure. Moreover, the shape of the mesh can be easily deformed by displacing the vertices, and the spatial topology is preserved by the edges that connect the vertex pairs, making it ideal for medical simulations such as cardiac cycles [4].

However, generation of meshes of segmented isosurfaces from medical images is a complex task involving a pipeline that consists of segmentation of the regions of interest (ROIs) and polygon extraction from volumetric segmentation data. Example ROIs

(a) Marching Cube   (b) Marching Cube with smooth filtering   (c) Voxel2Mesh

Fig. 1. A close-up visual comparison of the mesh surface extracted using (a) MC, (b) MC with TwoStep Smooth filter from Voreen [1], and (c) Voxel2Mesh [2]. The contour of (c) is slight different from (a) and (b) due to the limited deformation ability.

include specific anatomical structures such as the boney structures e.g., skull and ribs, and organs such as the liver structure. The conventional approach to generating polygon mesh is by reconstruction from 3D volumetric data acquired by imaging techniques such as computed tomography (CT) and magnetic resonance imaging (MRI). The acquired 3D volumetric data uses a dense discrete voxelized grid of uniform precision to represent the internal spatial properties. It is subsequently segmented to a volumetric mask of the desired ROI, either by scanning each slice of the input volume, such as U-Net [5], or by processing the entire input volume, as in the case of 3D U-Net [6].

Marching Cubes (MC) [7] is the conventional method to generate 3D polygon meshes from volumetric segmentation masks. The quality of the extracted mesh is determined by the resolution of the 3D volumetric data, where the z-axis resolution is often limited by the medical imaging protocols. The meshes extracted by volumes with low z-axis resolution suffer from the staircase artefacts and the visual quality is degraded. Although smoothing filters can be applied to mitigate the staircase artefacts, they often cause volume shrinkage and losing overall shape [8].

To eliminate the staircase artefacts and create smooth meshes while keeping the volume shape, Wickramasinghe et al. proposed Voxel2Mesh [2], a mesh deformation deep neural network for medical ROI representation. The mesh deformation approach is inspired by the Pixel2Mesh [9] and its following Pixel2Mesh++ [10], which utilized graph convolutional network (GCN) to optimize the vertex displacement of an ellipsoid mesh template from a single image. In Voxel2mesh, the authors adapted the Pixel2Mesh to process 3D volumetric data as input and generate mesh representation of the ROIs.

The staircase artefacts often occur when using the MC process to extract meshes from discrete volumetric data of low resolution, as the low level-of-detail limits the volumetric representation to capture the smooth curvatures of the surfaces. On the other hand, the mesh template is a continuous representation of the shape that allows arbitrary level-of-details that are capable of capturing the details of the curvatures. The deformation network bypasses the MC process and performs deformation on the mesh template in continuous space to produce smooth surfaces, and therefore avoid the staircase artefacts, as shown in Fig. 1.

However, a key limitation is that the graph convolution layers cannot alter the connections of the edges, therefore it cannot change the topological structure, e.g., genus value, which describes the number of handles or "holes" in the surface of a 3D object.

This limitation hinders the ability of Voxel2Mesh to deform the spherical template mesh to complex anatomical structures with higher genus values, such as the pelvis.

In this study, we evaluate the numerical and visual quality of the medical mesh deformation networks, on three anatomical structures of varying degrees of complexity and topological structures, pelvis from CTPelvic1K [11], liver from CHAOS [12], and kidney from CT-ORG [13]. For evaluation and demonstrate the general challenges and constraints of deformation-based medical mesh representation, in addition to Voxel2Mesh, we also used Pixel2Mesh-3D, a variant of Pixel2Mesh with 3D convolution layers instead of 2D convolution layers. The purpose of these experiments is to investigate the unique characters of deformation networks that bypass the MC process and demonstrate their current limitations in optimizing topological structures. The goal is to provide insights for the medical mesh representation community regarding the importance of such networks and the key challenges to be addressed in future research.

2 Related Work

2.1 Medical Imaging Mesh Generation

The medical isosurface mesh generation consists of the volumetric segmentation task and the mesh extraction process. Convolutional neural networks (CNNs) are widely used for medical imaging segmentation tasks, e.g., fully convolutional networks (FCNs) [14], PSPNet [15], and U-Net [5]. Among which, U-Net and its variants [6, 16–18] are the most popular choices for this task. The U-Net utilizes the encoder-decoder architecture with skip connections, which enables direct connections between mirroring layers of the encoder and the decoder. These skip connections help preserve both the coarse information and the fine details in the results. However, both the vanilla U-Net and many of its variants operate on 2D image slices, without utilizing the spatial information of the 3D volume. Both 3D U-Net [6] and V-Net [18] were proposed to directly operate on 3D volume by replacing the 2D operations found in vanilla U-Net to their 3D counterparts. To solve the foreground-background imbalance problem, which becomes exponentially severe in 3D, V-Net also introduced a new loss function based on Dice coefficient. However, due to the hardware limitation and the medical restrictions on radiation dosage, the resolution of the result volume is limited, therefore the extracted mesh would suffer from staircase artefacts. MC is the most prominent method for mesh extraction, it extracts a triangle mesh isosurface from the volumetric data using pre-calculated potential cube configurations to match the ROI's boundary of the volumetric data. However, the MC process is non-differentiable, therefore the extracted mesh cannot be end-to-end trained for mesh optimization. Liao et al. [19] and Chen et al. [20] used deep learning networks to learn the optimal cube configuration instead of using the pre-calculated configuration during the surface extraction process, therefore making the mesh extraction process differentiable, and the output mesh can be directly optimized using deep learning methods. However, their works are limited by hardware constraints and extracted meshes from smaller volumetric data (up to 128^3 volume resolution) [21].

2.2 Mesh Deformation Models

The deformable mesh models was first introduced by Terzopoulos et al. [22, 23], and was quickly adapted for medical image segmentation tasks [24, 25]. By implementing the graph convolutional network (GCN) model [26] that optimize the vertex placement, Wang et al. [9] introduced the first deep learning based mesh deformation model Pixel2Mesh, which generates a 3D mesh from a single image by deforming an ellipsoid mesh template. This model takes a 2D image as input and cannot be used to process the 3D volumetric data. Wickramasinghe et al. then utilized its GCN model and adapted to process 3D volumetric data in Voxel2Mesh [2]. In Voxel2Mesh, an encoder-decoder network with skip connections is used to extract features from the input volume, where these features are then sampled by an adaptive mesh unpooling strategy that maps the spatial features in volume space to the corresponding vertices in mesh space. The sampled features are used to guide the GCN to deform the sphere template to desired shape. The Voxel2Mesh is then extended for various medical mesh generation tasks [4, 27–30] where sophisticated data-driven templates of the target anatomical structures are used, to minimize the required deformation. The quality of the result mesh is heavily dependent on the initialization of the deformable templates [31], as misaligned spatial features in volume space and mesh space would destabilize the deformation. Kong et al. [4] solved this problem by predicting the displacement of a control point grid to align the features in different space. Although there are works [32–34] addressing the topology-dependent problem of using pre-defined templates, the template selection process is non-differentiable and therefore cannot be end-to-end trained, it is hard to address in the deep learning context.

3 Experiments

3.1 Data and Experiment Setup

Three datasets of varying shape complexity are used to evaluate the deformation networks.

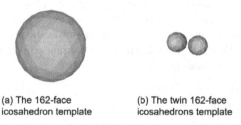

(a) The 162-face   (b) The twin 162-face
icosahedron template   icosahedrons template

Fig. 2. The templates used for deformation networks. The 162-face icosahedron template (a) is used for both the CHAOS and Pelvic1K dataset, and the twin 162-face icosahedrons template (b) is used for CT-ORG dataset.

1) Liver segmentation (simple shape complexity): The CHAOS dataset [12] consists of 20 CTs of human abdomen and their liver segmentation masks.

2) Kidney segmentation (moderate shape complexity): The CT-ORG dataset [13] consists of 40 CTs of the lower human body and their kidney (among other organs) segmentation masks. The two kidneys are selected because of their different topological structures.

3) Pelvis segmentation (high shape complexity): CTPelvic1K dataset [11] consists of 103 CTs and the pelvis segmentation masks. The pelvis is selected for its complex topological structures such as the obturator foramen.

Each dataset is randomly divided into a training set and a testing set with a ratio of 7:3. Each volume is down-sampled using trilinear interpolation to 256^2 in slice resolution, with proportional slice counts for training, while the ground truth isosurface mesh models are generated using MC with step size 1 on the full-resolution segmentation labels to minimize the staircase artefacts.

We evaluate the deformation networks visually and numerically with a traditional pipeline that uses the standard U-Net for ROI segmentation and MC for mesh extraction. As shown in Fig. 2, the deformation models use a 162-face icosahedron as the template for CHAOS and Pelvic1K, and a twin 162-face icosahedron as the template for CT-ORG to accommodate the two kidneys. The U-Net uses RMSprop optimizer, BCE with logits loss, and has a batch size of 8. The U-Net is trained on the same datasets used for Voxel2Mesh until convergence. The step size of MC is 1.

We conducted all our experiments, both training and inference, on a workstation with NVIDIA Tesla V100 GPU with Ubuntu 20.04. All the mesh rendering images were captured using MeshLab [35].

3.2 Metrics

The following 3 metrics were used to evaluate our mesh quality quantitatively:

The average symmetric surface distance [36] (ASSD), measures all the average distance of all points from one mesh to the other's isosurface, and vice versa, hence the name symmetric; the lower the better;

The Hausdorff distance [37] (HD), measures the maximum distance of all the minimum-distance pair of the points between two meshes; the lower the better;

The Chamfer distance [38] (CD), measures the average distance of all the minimum-distance pair of the points between two meshes; the lower the better;

For all point-based metrics (ASSD, HD, CD), we randomly sample 100,000 points on the isosurface for each mesh model.

3.3 Quantitative Result

In Table 1, the U-Net reports best scores of all three metrics in CHAOS dataset. The U-Net also reports best score in ASSD of the Pelvic1K dataset. The Voxel2Mesh reports the best scores of all three metrics in CT-ORG, and best score of HD and CD in Pelvic1K. The Pixel2Mesh-3D reports the worst scores in all experiments.

Table 1. Quantitative comparison of Voxel2Mesh, Pixel2Mesh-3D and 2D U-Net, using three metrics, over three different datasets. The best score of the three is in bold font.

CHAOS	Voxel2Mesh	Pixel2Mesh-3D	U-Net
ASSD↓	0.012034↓	0.047262	**0.005411**
HD↓	0.154371	0.244806	**0.124324**
CD↓	**0.001177**	0.007982	0.003276
CT-ORG	Voxel2Mesh	Pixel2Mesh-3D	U-Net
ASSD↓	**0.008519**	0.089067	0.010392
HD↓	**0.098444**	0.098721	0.165157
CD↓	**0.006342**	0.006593	0.007234
Pelvic1K	Voxel2Mesh	Pixel2Mesh-3D	U-Net
ASSD↓	0.028900·	0.069296	**0.012221**
HD↓	**0.199291**	0.286626	0.383156
CD↓	**0.002640**	0.016262	0.005481

3.4 Qualitative Result

In Fig. 3, the U-Net (a) exhibits high visual similarity with the ground truth mesh (c) in both tasks of liver (first row) and kidney (second row). However, the U-Net fails to reconstruct the lower parts of the pelvis, as indicated by the blue arrow. Moreover, the U-Net also reconstructed parts of the spine and femur that were outside the ROIs (see the red arrow). The visual quality of all three meshes from U-Net, as well as the ground truth images which are extracted using MC, are compromised by the staircase artefacts. The mesh liver generated by both Voxel2Mesh (b), and Pixel2Mesh-3D (c) is unable to preserve the sharp edges of the organ, as indicated by the blue arrows in the first row. We note that in the second row, The lower parts of the kidney pairs are stretched to the opposite kidneys in both deformation networks. In the third row, Both Voxel2Mesh and Pixel2Mesh3D results suffer from the problem of fixed topology and thereby fail to reconstruct the pelvis with the detailed structures such as the obturator foramen, indicated by the red arrows, and resulted in a basin-shaped mesh.

We applied the curvature principal directions from MeshLab to examine the staircase artefacts. We visualize the magnitude of the curvature by encoding the maximum curvature direction with red, the minimum curvature direction with green, and the third principal direction that is perpendicular to both maximum and minimum direction with blue. The intensity of each colour channel indicates the magnitude of each curvature direction, that is, the green regions indicate flat surface, the red and blue regions indicate sharp edges. In Fig. 4, the mesh generated by Pixel2Mesh (a–c) exhibits high strength of curvature in regions corresponding to the overall shape. The mesh extracted from MC (d), however, exhibits distinct steep edges along the shape curves.

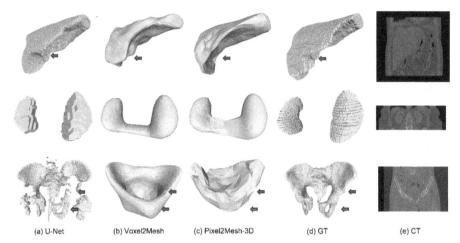

(a) U-Net   (b) Voxel2Mesh   (c) Pixel2Mesh-3D   (d) GT   (e) CT

Fig. 3. Visual comparison of the CHAOS (first row), CT-ORG (second row), and Pelvic1K (third row) meshes between (a) U-Net, (b) Voxel2Mesh, (c) Pixel2Mesh-3D,(d) the ground truth, and (e) a coronal view of the CT used as input.

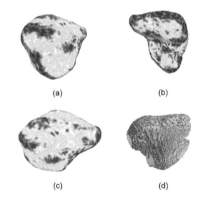

(a)   (b)

(c)   (d)

Fig. 4. The visualization of curvature principal directions where red encodes maximal curvature and green encodes minimal curvature. (a–c) are taken from the mesh generated by Voxel2Mesh from different viewpoints, and (d) is taken from mesh extracted by MC for reference of staircase artefacts.

4   Discussion

We observed several limitations in the performance of the mesh deformation networks when evaluating the reconstructed meshes of various complexity. Specifically, we found that:

The networks are unable to reconstruct the meshes with sharp edges,
The networks are unable to deform templates with multiple objects, and
The networks are unable to reconstruct organs of different topological structures.

As shown in the first row of Fig. 3, both Voxel2Mesh and Pixel2Mesh-3D can deform their icosahedron templates to simple shapes, such as the liver in CHAOS dataset. However, it fails to preserve the fine details such as the sharp edges indicated by the blue arrows in the first row of Fig. 3.

In the second row of Fig. 3, where the deformation networks deform the template of a icosahedron pair, the networks failed to differentiate the vertices from the two icosahedrons, causing the vertices to be misplaced to match the surface of the opposite kidney.

Furthermore, due to its graph convolution network (GCN) structure, it is unable to deform to complex shapes. The GCN consists of graph convolution layers that modify the value of graph vertices but are constrained by the topology of the graph as it cannot change the connectivity of the mesh edges. As shown in the third row, both networks were able to deform the template to the shape of a basin. However, the details of the pelvis and the foramen are all missing from the mesh. This again is due to the limited capacity of the sphere to deform to a complex basin shape with multiple openings.

In comparison to the mesh models extracted from a U-Net segmented volume using MC, which are affected by the staircase artefacts, the meshes deformed from templates remain unaffected. This is because the sphere template with smooth surfaces is directly deformed into the output shape, without using the voxelized grid which causes the artefacts. In the third row of Fig. 3, the U-Net fails to reconstruct thin structures such as indicated by both red and blue arrows, and erroneously reconstructs parts outside the ROIs. Conversely, these issues are not presented in the deformation networks' outputs, as the topology structure is constrained by the pre-defined template.

We further verify the absence of staircase artefacts in meshes generated by deformation-based networks by examining the curvature direction distribution in Fig. 4. The staircase artefacts can be visually identified by the contrastive colour ripples that indicate high strength of curvatures and high homogeneity along the z-axis, as shown in (d). However, such ripples are not presented in (a–c), which are generated from a deformation network.

In future work, we will investigate other medical isosurface representations that can minimize the staircase artefacts and can be used for more complex anatomical structures, such as the signed distance functions (SDF) [38] that uses mathematical functions to represent the 0-level distance isosurfaces of the desired shape. As this representation does not require any template as initial input, it is not restricted by the pre-defined shape and can be used to represent any arbitrary shapes. Moreover, the SDF describes the shape in a continuous space, and therefore it can be sampled at arbitrary high resolution when MC is used for mesh extraction; this potentially can minimize the staircase artefacts that are mainly caused by low z-axis resolution.

5 Conclusion

In this study, we highlighted the existing limitations of utilizing a mesh deformation network for representing medical ROIs, which includes the restricted ability to reconstruct shapes with sharp edges, and the inability to change the topological structures of the template. Although the visual quality is inferior compared to the traditional pipelines that utilize the MC for mesh extraction, deformation networks' benefit to bypass the MC process and avoid the staircase artefacts makes it worthwhile for future research.

Acknowledgments. This research was supported by ARC DP200103748.

References

1. Meyer-Spradow, J., et al.: Voreen: a rapid-prototyping environment for ray-casting-based volume visualizations. IEEE Comput. Graphics Appl. **29**(6), 6–13 (2009)
2. Wickramasinghe, U., Remelli, E., Knott, G., Fua, P.: Voxel2mesh: 3d mesh model generation from volumetric data. In: Martel, A.L., et al. (eds.) Medical Image Computing and Computer Assisted Intervention – MICCAI 2020: 23rd International Conference, Lima, Peru, October 4–8, 2020, Proceedings, Part IV, pp. 299–308. Springer, Cham (2020). https://doi.org/10.1007/978-3-030-59719-1_30
3. Li, W., Hahn, J.K.: Efficient ray casting polygonized isosurface of binary volumes. Vis. Comput. **37**(12), 3139–3149 (2021). https://doi.org/10.1007/s00371-021-02302-3
4. Kong, F., Shadden, S.C.: Whole heart mesh generation for image-based computational simulations by learning free-from deformations. In: de Bruijne, Marleen, et al. (eds.) Medical Image Computing and Computer Assisted Intervention – MICCAI 2021: 24th International Conference, Strasbourg, France, September 27–October 1, 2021, Proceedings, Part IV, pp. 550–559. Springer, Cham (2021). https://doi.org/10.1007/978-3-030-87202-1_53
5. Ronneberger, O., Fischer, P., Brox, T.: U-net: convolutional networks for biomedical image segmentation. In: Navab, N., Hornegger, J., Wells, W.M., Frangi, A.F. (eds.) Medical Image Computing and Computer-Assisted Intervention – MICCAI 2015: 18th International Conference, Munich, Germany, October 5-9, 2015, Proceedings, Part III, pp. 234–241. Springer, Cham (2015). https://doi.org/10.1007/978-3-319-24574-4_28
6. Çiçek, Ö., Abdulkadir, A., Lienkamp, S.S., Brox, T., Ronneberger, O.: 3D U-Net: learning dense volumetric segmentation from sparse annotation. In: Ourselin, S., Joskowicz, L., Sabuncu, M.R., Unal, G., Wells, W. (eds.) Medical Image Computing and Computer-Assisted Intervention – MICCAI 2016: 19th International Conference, Athens, Greece, October 17-21, 2016, Proceedings, Part II, pp. 424–432. Springer, Cham (2016). https://doi.org/10.1007/978-3-319-46723-8_49
7. Lorensen, W.E., Cline, H.E.: Marching cubes: a high resolution 3D surface construction algorithm. ACM siggraph Comput. Graph. **21**(4), 163–169 (1987)
8. Moench, T., et al.: Context-aware mesh smoothing for biomedical applications. Comput. Graph. **35**(4), 755–767 (2011)
9. Wang, N., Zhang, Y., Li, Z., Yanwei, F., Liu, W., Jiang, Y.-G.: Pixel2mesh: generating 3d mesh models from single RGB images. In: Ferrari, V., Hebert, M., Sminchisescu, C., Weiss, Y. (eds.) ECCV 2018. LNCS, vol. 11215, pp. 55–71. Springer, Cham (2018). https://doi.org/10.1007/978-3-030-01252-6_4
10. Wen, C., et al.: Pixel2mesh++: multi-view 3D mesh generation via deformation. In: Proceedings of the IEEE/CVF International Conference on Computer Vision (2019)
11. Liu, P., et al.: Deep learning to segment pelvic bones: large-scale CT datasets and baseline models. Int. J. Comput. Assist. Radiol. Surg. **16**, 749–756 (2021). https://doi.org/10.1007/s11548-021-02363-8
12. Kavur, A.E., et al.: CHAOS challenge-combined (CT-MR) healthy abdominal organ segmentation. Med. Image Anal. **69**, 101950 (2021)

13. Rister, B., et al.: CT-ORG, a new dataset for multiple organ segmentation in computed tomography. Sci. Data **7**(1), 381 (2020)

14. Long, J., Shelhamer, E., Darrell, T.: Fully convolutional networks for semantic segmentation. In: Proceedings of the IEEE Conference on Computer Vision and Pattern Recognition (2015)

15. Zhao, H., et al.: Pyramid scene parsing network. In: Proceedings of the IEEE Conference on Computer Vision and Pattern Recognition (2017)

16. Zhou, Z., Rahman Siddiquee, M.M., Tajbakhsh, N., Liang, J.: Unet++: a nested u-net architecture for medical image segmentation. In: Stoyanov, Danail, et al. (eds.) DLMIA/ML-CDS -2018. LNCS, vol. 11045, pp. 3–11. Springer, Cham (2018). https://doi.org/10.1007/978-3-030-00889-5_1

17. Isensee, F., et al.: NnU-Net: a self-configuring method for deep learning-based biomedical image segmentation. Nat. Methods **18**(2), 203–211 (2021)

18. Milletari, F., Navab, N., Ahmadi, S.-A.: V-net: Fully convolutional neural networks for volumetric medical image segmentation. In: 2016 fourth international conference on 3D vision (3DV). IEEE (2016)

19. Liao, Y., Donne, S., Geiger, A.: Deep marching cubes: Learning explicit surface representations. In: Proceedings of the IEEE Conference on Computer Vision and Pattern Recognition (2018)

20. Chen, Z., Zhang, H.: Neural marching cubes. ACM Trans. Graph. (TOG) **40**(6), 1–15 (2021)

21. Liu, R., et al.: TMM-Nets: transferred multi-to mono-modal generation for lupus retinopathy diagnosis. IEEE Trans. Med. Imaging **42**(4), 1083–1094 (2022)

22. Terzopoulos, D., Fleischer, K.: Deformable models. Vis. Comput. **4**(6), 306–331 (1988). https://doi.org/10.1007/BF01908877

23. Terzopoulos, D., Witkin, A., Kass, M.: Constraints on deformable models: recovering 3D shape and nonrigid motion. Artif. Intell. **36**(1), 91–123 (1988)

24. Kass, M., Witkin, A., Terzopoulos, D.: Snakes: active contour models. Int. J. Comput. Vision **1**(4), 321–331 (1988). https://doi.org/10.1007/BF00133570

25. Berger, M.-O.: Snake growing. In: Faugeras, O. (ed.) ECCV 1990. LNCS, vol. 427, pp. 570–572. Springer, Heidelberg (1990). https://doi.org/10.1007/BFb0014909

26. Scarselli, F., et al.: The graph neural network model. IEEE Trans. Neural Netw. **20**(1), 61–80 (2008)

27. Lebrat, L., et al.: Corticalflow: a diffeomorphic mesh transformer network for cortical surface reconstruction. Adv. Neural. Inf. Process. Syst. **34**, 29491–29505 (2021)

28. Bongratz, F., et al.: Vox2Cortex: fast explicit reconstruction of cortical surfaces from 3D MRI scans with geometric deep neural networks. In: Proceedings of the IEEE/CVF Conference on Computer Vision and Pattern Recognition (2022)

29. Ma, Q., Robinson, E.C., Kainz, B., Rueckert, D., Alansary, A.: PialNN: a fast deep learning framework for cortical pial surface reconstruction. In: Abdulkadir, Ahmed, et al. (eds.) Machine Learning in Clinical Neuroimaging: 4th International Workshop, MLCN 2021, Held in Conjunction with MICCAI 2021, Strasbourg, France, September 27, 2021, Proceedings, pp. 73–81. Springer, Cham (2021). https://doi.org/10.1007/978-3-030-87586-2_8

30. Kong, Fanwei, Shadden, Shawn C.: Learning whole heart mesh generation from patient images for computational simulations. IEEE Trans. Med. Imaging **42**(2), 533–545 (2022)

31. Yang, J., et al.: ImplicitAtlas: learning deformable shape templates in medical imaging. In: Proceedings of the IEEE/CVF Conference on Computer Vision and Pattern Recognition (2022)

32. McInemey, T., Terzopoulos, D.: Topology adaptive deformable surfaces for medical image volume segmentation. IEEE Trans. Med. Imaging **18**(10), 840–850 (1999)

33. Sapiro, G., Kimmel, R., Caselles, V.: Object detection and measurements in medical images via geodesic deformable contours. In: Vision Geometry IV. SPIE (1995)

34. McInerney, T., Terzopoulos, D.: Topologically adaptable snakes. In: Proceedings of IEEE International Conference on Computer Vision. IEEE (1995)
35. Cignoni, P., et al.: Meshlab: an open-source mesh processing tool. In: Eurographics Italian Chapter Conference, Salerno, Italy (2008)
36. Heimann, T., et al.: Comparison and evaluation of methods for liver segmentation from CT datasets. IEEE Trans. Med. Imaging **28**(8), 1251–1265 (2009)
37. Gerig, G., Jomier, M., Chakos, M.: Valmet: a new validation tool for assessing and improving 3D object segmentation. In: Niessen, W.J., Viergever, M.A. (eds.) MICCAI 2001. LNCS, vol. 2208, pp. 516–523. Springer, Heidelberg (2001). https://doi.org/10.1007/3-540-45468-3_62
38. Borgefors, G.: Distance transformations in digital images. Comput. Vision Graph. Image Process. **34**(3), 344–371 (1986)

LS-Net: COVID-19 Lesion Segmentation from CT Image via Diffusion Probabilistic Model

Aiwu Shi, Bei Sheng, Jin Huang$^{(\boxtimes)}$, Jiankai Sun, Gan Luo, Chao Han, He Huang, and Shuran Ma

School of Computer Science and Artificial Intelligence, Wuhan Textile University, Wuhan, China
derick0320@foxmail.com

Abstract. Coronavirus Disease 2019 (COVID-19) ravaged the world in early 2020, causing great harm to human health. However, there are several challenges to segment the infected areas from computed tomography (CT) image, including blurry boundaries between the lesion and normal lung tissues, and uncertain characteristics about lesion's scale, location, and texture. To solve these problems, a COVID-19 lesion segmentation network (LS-Net) based on probabilistic diffusion model is proposed to segment lesion areas from CT images. The feature fusion decoder module is introduced to aggregate high-level features and generate a guidance as the next steps so that the small lesion could not be omitted. In addition, the attention mechanism is set to pay attention to the information about position of lesion's edge. So, the LS-Net framework can improve the precision of lesion segmentation result from CT image slice. Experiments on datasets such as the COVID-19 CT Segmentation dataset shows that LS-Net is advanced than most current segmentation models.

Keywords: COVID-19 · computed tomography · lesion segmentation · feature fusion · diffusion probabilistic

1 Introduction

Causing by severe acute respiratory syndrome coronavirus type 2 (SARSCoV-2), the coronavirus disease 2019 (COVID-19) has exploded around the world, with a massive increase in the number of people who infected with the virus [1]. Updated 8 October, 2022, more than 620 million infections have been recorded, including about 6.55 million deaths (data from the World Health Organization). These cases caused a significant public health concern in the international community [2]. Therefore, in the absence of specific therapeutic drugs or vaccines for COVID-19 [3], it is great important for the treatment of patients and public health safety that accurate and rapid diagnosis of suspected cases at the early stage and immediate isolation of infected people from healthy people.

Reverse transcriptase polymerase chain reaction (RT-PCR) is considered to be the primary standard for COVID-19 screening, according to the Diagnosis

B. Sheng et al. (Eds.): CGI 2023, LNCS 14498, pp. 157–171, 2024.
https://doi.org/10.1007/978-3-031-50078-7_13

and Treatment Protocol for COVID-19 (Trial Version 9) officially issued by the National Health Commission [4]. However, the process could be affected by the course of disease, specimen collection, testing process, testing reagents and other factors, even the time limit of specimen transportation, which can lead to that the sensitivity of RT-PCR for early COVID-19 with a high false-negative rate. The asymptomatic patients do not have clinical symptoms in the early stage, but chest CT images can show lesions [4]. With the use of advanced medical imaging equipment, the sensitivity of chest computed tomography (CT) on early COVID-19 has reached 0.98 [5]. Therefore, in clinical diagnosis, because of being easy to operate and fast to diagnose, chest CT is often preferred to make a comprehensive judgment based on clinical manifestations and underlying diseases [4].

CT images can show different features of patients from infection to recovery [6,7]. In the early stage of COVID-19, the image showed single or multiple ground-glass opacity (GGO) in both lung tissues. At next stage, they were overlaid with consolidation and crazy dotted pattern, which were absorbed over the course of the treatment (usually after 14 days), then the lesion would leaving only the GGO [6–8]. Therefore, GGO is an important criterion for CT-based assessment of COVID-19 severity [6]. However, in the early stage of COVID-19, the location and size of the lesions in CT image slices are not fixed. At the meantime, its shape and texture also have different performance [8]. Moreover, GGO tended to have blurred edges, which was similar to consolidation, and thus showed a small inter-class difference that was difficult to distinguish from other lung tissues. In addition, due to privacy and other reasons [9], manual annotation for dataset segmentation is very limited, which would increase the difficulty of the segmentation task.

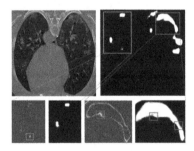

Fig. 1. Comparing to other's result, our result is more precise and complete of lesion's edge and some small lesion. Original CT image is in the left, and the otherside is ground truth. The left circled by orange line is the comparision between our result and other's sgmentation result about lesion's edge, the right circled by red line is the comparision between our result and other's sgmentation result about small lesion. (Color figure online)

In order to solve these problems, we propose a novel CT lesion segmentation network based on diffusion probability model. And we have obvious result, it is shown in Fig. 1. The main contributions of the work are:

- We modify the neural network model in the reverse diffusion process to improve the accuracy of localization and segmentation of infection/non-infection areas. By extracting and aggregating the high-level features of the input image, the information includs global features and local features, then applies to the problem of lesion segmentation in COVID-19 CT images.
- We propose the FFD module to aggregates high-level features without omitting small lesion areas, because it will generate a global map combined with features obtain context information, which will serve as a guidance for the next steps and up-sampling. The attention mechanism is introduced to pay attention to local features such as the edge of the lesion, so that our network can improve the segmentation accuracy of the blurry edge of the lesion.
- We consider the characteristics of both the neural network model and the probability diffusion model, and use the hybrid loss function to improve the robustness of the model. In the experiment process, we explore the influence of hyperparameter T in the network to determine the optimal number of iterations, and then average to improve model performance and generalization ability.

2   Related Work

2.1   COVID-19 CT Lesion Segmentation

Chest CT is currently the main means of screening and diagnosis of COVID-19, and image segmentation is a key step in the study of the disease [8]. Currently, chest CT images usually delineate regions of interest (ROI), such as infected areas or lesions in the lung tissue [8,10]. Segmentation methods based on deep learning have been widely used in lung lesion segmentation, among which the most widely used is the U-net network model and its variants [11–13]. For example, Ferdinandus [11] used the U-Net model for CT image semantic segmentation, while Adnan [12] et al. compared the U-Net model and the SegNet model, and concluded that they are suitable for multi-class lung disease classification and infection/non-infection area segmentation, respectively. After segmenting the ROI, the lesion features are further extracted for the next training network model [14,15]. For example, Zhang [14] et al. used cross-modal feature fusion to learn rich feature representations by transferring knowledge across different modal data and fusing knowledge from different modal data. Cheng [15] combined semantic branch and a detail branch. One focuses on extracting the semantic features from shallow and deep layers, the other one is used to enhance the contour information implied in the shallow layers.

2.2   Deep Learning for COVID-19 Detection

Deep learning is an emerging technology in the field of medical imaging [16, 17] that has made a positive contribution to the fight against COVID-19. The application of deep learning in COVID-19 can solve the problem of insufficient label data and small inter-class variance between itself and other pneumonias [18,19]. For example, Ebenezer [18] et al. used false-positive and false-negative ensemble data to increase the diversity of models and reduce the error rate of detecting diseases. Chen [19] et al. proposed a segmentation model based on unsupervised region adaptation, which uses synthetic data and limited unlabeled data to jointly train the network. In addition, attention mechanisms, combined with convolutional neural networks in medical image segmentation, are widely used to suppress irrelevant information and highlight the ROI [20–23]. Zhao [21] et al. proposed a supervised spatial attention mechanism, which combines the attention of the lesion region with the features extracted by the network, so that the multi-lesion segmentation is decomposed into two simpler stages: coarse and fine. Li [22] et al. added an attention module between every two features of the middle layer feature map of the model to capture global information and place it in the process of feature fusion to enhance the features. These studies coupled with the use of deep learning to segment lesions in CT images, so the quantitative features obtained can be used for COVID-19, which can help clinicians assess the extent of disease and timely treatment.

2.3 Diffusion Drobabilistic Model in Segmentation

Generative models have a long history in traditional machine learning, which focus on using some internal mechanism to characterize the distribution of things that are actually observed. With the rising of deep learning, generative models have formed a new concept by combining with deep neural networks: deep generative models (DGMs). That is, using a neural network with a certain amount of parameters to simulate the process of data generation [24]. In the past two years, DGM has made new developments [25,26], Prafula [26]and others have demonstrated that the diffusion model becomes a new SOTA in DGM, because of solving the problems of slowly sampling speed, maximum likelihood difference and weakly data generalization ability in the original diffusion models [27], which leads to a widely application in many fields and has achieved good performance [28], etc. Recently, there are studies on the application of the diffusion probabilistic model to medical image segmentation with excellent results [29–32]. For example, Kim [31] et al. introduced a diffusion adversarial representation learning (DARL) model, in which the latent features of diffusion module provide vessel information and thus improve the segmentation performance. And the model has a good generalization ability. Wu [32] et al. combined with dynamic coding methods to establish state adaptive conditions for sampling during the denoising process, and used the characteristic frequency analyzer (FF-Parser) to eliminate the interference of high-frequency noise during the segmentation process, then achieved good performance in brain tumor segmentation on MRI images and thyroid nodule segmentation on ultrasound images.

3   Method

We designed our models based on the denoising diffusion probability models. In this section, we explain how to modify the neural network model during the reverse process and show the main equation from the probability diffusion model, which also is the framework of our LS-Net. In addition, we introduce the core network structure and loss function in our model in detail.

3.1   Lesion Segmentation Network (LS-Net)

In short, the diffusion probability model can be roughly divided into two processes. One is the forward diffusion process, which is to add Gaussian noise to the segmentation label X through a series of steps T. Another is the reverse denoising process, which trains the neural network to gradually denoise the noisy in to the picture, until restoring the original picture. Actually, the forward diffusion process P is a Markov chain process that can be expressed as:

$$p\left(X_{1:T} \mid X_0\right) = \prod_{t=1}^{T} \mathcal{N}\left(X_t; \sqrt{1 - \beta_t}X_{t-1}; \beta_t I\right) \tag{1}$$

In each iteration of the forward difussion process, T is the number of steps in the model, $X_1, X_2, \cdots X_T$ is the latent variables, and X_0 is the data sample. β_t is the constant that defines the addition noise schedule, and I is the identity matrix of size of $n \times n$. Since the added noise parameters are determined by β_t and X_{t-1}. It is a fixed value rather than a learnable process. Therefore, in the forward diffusion process, it is not necessary to go from $X_0, X_1, \cdots$ to X_T which could be calculated at any moment. The method is completed through parameter retuning techniques. The variance parameter for the forward diffusion process is a liner function [24] from $\beta_1 = 10^{-4}$ to $\beta_T = 2 \times 10^{-2}$, and the expression is:

$$\beta_t = \frac{10^{-4}\left(T - t\right) + 2 \times 10^{-2}\left(t - 1\right)}{T - 1} \tag{2}$$

In the section of experiment, we will explain the reason of chosing the liner function.

The reverse denoising process is the learning of a neural network to approximate the conditional probability distribution $q\left(X_{t-1} \mid X_t\right)$ that simulates this process:

$$q_\theta\left(X_{0:T}\right) = q\left(X_T\right) \prod_{t=1}^{T} q_\theta\left(X_{t-1} \mid X_t\right)$$

$$q_\theta\left(X_{t-1} \mid X_t\right) = \mathcal{N}\left(X_{t-1}; \mu_\theta\left(X_t, t\right), \textstyle\sum_\theta\left(X_t, t\right)\right) \tag{3}$$

The μ_θ is mean function and the $\sum_\theta$ variance function. This is also the main part of our LS-Net model.

Our neural network structure is based on the denoising diffusion probability models. As can be seen from the previous work, the forward diffusion process is a

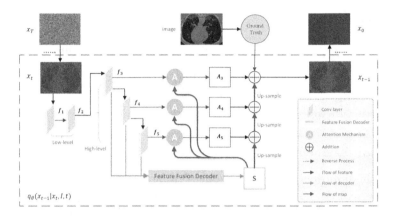

Fig. 2. The architecture of our proposed LS-Net model, which bases of diffusion probability model, and consists of feature fusion decoder (FFD) and attention mechanism and other details.

mathematical process. We add Gaussian noise to the image I, after determining the input image I and the variance parameter β_t, the image X_t which can be calculated at any moment in the process. In the reverse denoising process, the function p_θ is used to approximate the probability of simulated conditions which is obtained by learning a neural network with structural details, as shown in Fig. 2. The diffusion probability model is modified using the function p_θ, which combines the information of the image X_t at the current moment and the information of the input image I. The function p_θ is modified on the basis of the Res2Net network model. As can be seen from the Fig. 2, the CT image X_t at the current moment is first transmitted to two low-level convolutional layers to extract low-level features with high resolution but weak semantic information, and then the obtained low-level features are input to the next three high-level convolutional layers to extract high-level features with low resolution but strong semantic information, and finally we use the feature fusion decoder module (FFD) to aggregate these high-level features. FFD modules are connected in parallel to generate images of coarse localization of lung lesions. Image S works with the higher features to direct the attention mechanism to focus on the edge information of the lesion, and it will feed back directly to the higher features. The output of advanced features is cascaded, i.e. the output of f_4 is determined by f_5 and image S, and the output of f_3 is determined by f_4. The final output f_3 will be used with ground truth as the next output image of the inverse diffusion process. Next we will cover the details of the FFD module and our loss function.

3.2   Feature Fusion Decoder Module

In medical image segmentation networks, it is often the case that the ROI region, such as organs or lesions, is segmented and then aggregated [33,40] from the low/high level features. Generally speaking, low-level features have more fine-grained feature information than high-level features, which will increase the demand for computing resources while contributing less to performance. Based on this principle, we only select the output features of the last three convolution blocks of the encoder, and do not use the first two, because the first two convolution blocks will consume a lot of computing resources. We recommend aggregating high-level features using only parallel partial decoder components, as shown in Fig. 3. Specifically, for the input CT image I, we utilize the first of the five convolutional blocks of Res2Net to extract two sets of low-level features $\{f_i, i = 1, 2\}$ firstly,and utilize the last three groups of high-level features $\{f_i, i = 3, 4, 5\}$. Then, we leverage this decoder component to connect and aggregate three sets of advanced features in parallel. In order to accelerate, each branch uses 1×1 convolution to reduce channel dimension. In particular, the high-level feature f_5 separately uses a combination of 1×1 convolution and 3×3 convolution modules to extract key feature information again. Finally, features aggregated by feature fusion decoder module will generate a rough global map S, which is then used to adjust the three sets of advanced features $\{f_i, i = 3, 4, 5\}$ and serve as a guide for up-sampling.

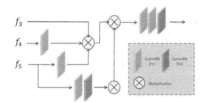

Fig. 3. Feature fusion decoder is utilized to generate the global map.

After rough localization of FFD, we also introduced attention mechanisms in three groups of high-level features $\{f_i, i = 3, 4, 5\}$ for fine segmentation of lesion edges. The attention mechanism will select the edge information of learning attention lesion location from the characteristics of S feedback by refining the features of the three convolution blocks from high-lever and eliminate the abnormal information in the features. Then, we will use the following formula to calculate the weight R_t of the output image X_{t-1},

$$R_i = A_i \oplus f_i + R_{i+1}$$
$$A_i = \mathcal{P}(S) \tag{4}$$

which R_i represents the feature weight output at each step, $i = 3, 4, 5$, and A represents the feature information obtained after the attention mechanism learns S, which P represents the upsampling operation, and $R_i = R_3$ is the final output result.

3.3 Loss Function

When setting the loss function L_{loss}, we also considered the differences between the denoising diffusion probability model and the convolutional neural network model. The loss function L_{loss} will eventually consist of these two parts together, here are the details.

In the reserve denoising process, it is mainly the calculation of the loss function of the convolutional neural network training process. Following the previous work [33, 40], we define L_{IoU} as the loss function of the roughly extracted lesion features, which is the loss L_{IoU} of each inverse diffusion step segmentation supervision, calculated as :

$$L_{IoU} = \sum_{i=1}^{step} \frac{TP\,(y, y_i)}{FP\,(y, y_i) + FN\,(y, y_i) + TP\,(y, y_i)} \tag{5}$$

where TP is the true positive between the ground truth y and output mask y_i, FN is a false negative, and FP is a false positive. And the $step$ is the number of diffusion steps.

For the fine extraction of the loss function of lesion edge features, we set it to L_{am}:

$$L_{am} = \sum_{x=1}^{w} \sum_{y=1}^{h} [G_e log S_e + (1 - G_e)\, log\,(1 - S_e)] \tag{6}$$

where (x, y) are the coordinates of each pixel in the predicted edge map S_e and edge of ground truth map G_e. The G_e is calculated using the gradient of the ground truth map.

Additionally, w and h denote the width and height of corresponding map, respectively. Finally, we pay additional attention to the three high-level feature outputs, setting our loss function to:

$$L_{roi} = L_{IoU}\,(G, S) + L_{am} + \sum_{i=3}^{i=5} L_{IoU}\,(G, S_i) \tag{7}$$

Therefore, L_{roi} provides pixel-level supervision for both the coarse segmentation process and the fine edge segmentation process of lesions.

For the entire denoising diffusion probability model, according to [25], it is found that the diffusion model can be trained better with the simplified objective function ignoring the weighted terms, so we set the loss function for this part as:

$$L_t^s = E_{X_0, Z_t} \left[\left\| Z_t - Z_\theta \left(\sqrt{\bar{\alpha}_t} X_0 + \sqrt{1 - \bar{\alpha}_t} Z_t, t \right) \right\|^2 \right] \tag{8}$$

Therefore, the final simplified objective function is:

$$L_{loss} = L_t^s + L_{roi} \tag{9}$$

4   Experiment

The basis of our LS-Net is denoising diffusion probability model, so the forward diffusion process is a computable mathematical process. X_t can be viewed as a linear combination of the original image X_0 and the noise β_t. This process is important because the next steps will only yield meaningful information if the resulting X_t is completely lost to the original data and reduced to a random noise. As a result, the forward process usually uses a defined variance schedule. In the forward diffusion process, we decide to adopt linear function [25].

4.1   Datasets

According to [33], there are very few datasets applied for image segmentation. So, the dataset we chose was the COVID-19 CT Segmentation dataset, which consists of 100 different axial CT images of COVID-19 patients, all collected by the Italian Society of Medical and Interventional Radiology. Radiologists segmented the images using three labels, ground-glass opacities, consolidation, and pleural effusion, to identify areas of lung lesions. We randomly select 50 images as the training dataset, and the remaining 50 randomly form the test dataset and validation dataset according to the 9:1 ratio.

In addition, we also used another dataset, the COVID-19 infection segmentation dataset (COVID-SemiSeg), to increase the amount of training data. The dataset is from the dataset collected in Inf-net, derived from the COVID-19 CT Collection consisting of 20 CT volumes from different COVID-19 patients, from which 1600 two-dimensional CT axial slides have been labeled with lesion areas.

4.2   Evaluation

The end result of our measurement is the similarity problem between the prediction image and the ground truth [33]. So we use the common metrics of mean intersection over Union (mIoU)as evaluation, which is the average of the ratio of the intersection and union of each CT image.

In addition, we also used three evaluation indicators that are widely used in segmented areas, the Dice similarity coefficient, Sensitivity (Sen.), Specificity (Spec.) as auxiliary evaluation indicators, caculated as:

$$
Dice = \frac{2TP}{FP + 2TP + FN}
$$
$$
Sen = \frac{TP}{TP + FN}
$$
$$
Spec = \frac{TN}{TN + FP}
$$
(10)

where TP is the true positive between the ground truth y and output mask y_i, FN is a false negative, TN is a truth negative, and FP is a false positive (Fig. 4).

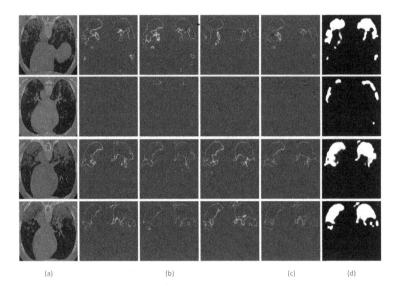

Fig. 4. (a) is input image,(b) is a subset of the obtained results for multiple runs on the same input,(c) is average result, and (d) is ground truth.

4.3   Training Details

The training of our model is implemented in Pytorch, the model is trained on ground truth many times and averaged as the final segmentation result, by the scheme of random sampling and extraction of training images. Following the previous working, although the more diffusions, the more accurate of the model. For example, there are people with a diffusion step of 1000 or even 4000. But in order to segment the immediacy of the lesion, we decided to use 100 diffusion steps, and did a set of comparative experiments to study the effect of the number of diffusion steps on the accuracy and running time of the model.

All of our experiments used the Adam optimizer with a learning setup rate of 1e-5. Before training, we uniformly adjust the image size of all inputs to 256×256, resample the training image, that is, randomly scale within the range of [0.75, 1.25], and rotate horizontally with a probability of 0.5. The resampled image is then used for model training, which can improve the generalization ability of the model.

The process of 1600 images which have been labeled, we trained them by the batch size of 8, and it would take nearly 80 h. We followed the same channels setting as in SegDiff, the network had 15 RRDB blocks and a depth of 6. The number of channels was set [C, C, 2C, 4C, 4C], with C = 128. We returning the 50 CT images that have been labeled by ground truth labels. Our network randomly initializes the weights with every training. In our experiment, when using only one GPU that usually takes like 20 h to train one single model for a dataset. Compared to the previous one single network based denoising method, our method indeed requires much more time for inference.

4.4   Result

As shown in Table 1, we compare the U-Net and SegNet models which perform best in the filed of COVID-19 lesion segmentation with three aspects of Dice, Sen., and Spec.. It can be seen that LS-Net proposed in this paper is superior to U-Net and SegNet [12] in these three aspects, and also has obvious advantages compared with other methods [10,14,33,40,41], and it mainly reflected in the two aspects of Dice. and Sen.. This is due to the improvement of the model based on the diffusion probabilistic model, and the introduction of the feature fusion decoder module and attention mechanism, focusing on the segmentation of lesion edges and small lesion locations. This is at the expense of a decline in Spec., we also referenced [31,32,36] as a comparison, and these are the same uses of the diffusion probabilistic model for image segmentation.

And mIoU as the main evaluation measure of the segmentation model, as shown in Table 2. The diffusion probabilistic model also has some advantages

Table 1. Quantitative results of our's LS-Net compare to others. The upper part of the table compares with other network models, while the lower part compares with the diffusion models.

Method	Backbone	Param.	ELOPs	Dice	Sen.	Spec.
DeCovNet [10]	ResNet50	0.35M	10.6G		0.947	0.786
CMFT [14]	VGG16	19.85M	31.73G	0.843	0.867	
FCF-Dense [40]	DenseNet	24.20M	13.20G		0.956	
CR-Net [41]	ResNet34	21.94M	37.95G	0.901	0.934	
Inf-Net [33]	Res2Net	33.12M	13.92G	0.739	0.725	0.960
U-Net [12]	U-Net	17.2M	80.5G	0.964	0.948	0.733
SegNet [12]	VGG16	9.16M	65.84G	0.956	0.954	0.749
MedSegDiff [32]	SegNet			0.905		
DARL [31]	PatchGAN			0.636		
CS40DB [36]	U-Net				0.910	0.750
LS-Net	Res2Net	34.2M	13.5G	0.967	0.961	0.843

Table 2. Segmentation results evaluates with mIoU by our LS-Net. And other methods include diffusion models and models applied in medical image segmentation.

Method	backbone	mIoU
Axial-Deeplab-L [35]	ResNet	62.49
DTC [37]	V-Net	64.75
MedT [34]	U-Net	66.17
PP-DDPM [38]	AttU-Net	68.90
MGCC [39]	U-Net	68.06
LS-Net	ResNet	69.01

compared to the model [34,35,37–39] and the it's variant. However, compared with other medical image segmentation models [34,37,39], mIoU has no obvious improvement, which we believe is caused by the imaging characteristics of medical image itself, which is jointly affected by the physical equipment and the patient's state at the time of detection.

4.5   Ablation Study

We evaluate our method by following experiments, including the importance of FFD module and the influence of diffusion steps.

The Effect of FFD. In this part, to exploring the importance of the feature fusion decoder module, we performed an ablation experiment, and derived two baselines: No.1 (backbone) and No.3 (backbone + FFD) in table. The result has shown the necessary of the Feature Fusion Decoder module in the network. In addition to, the No.1 and No.2 (backbone + attention mechanism) in Table 3, the result shows the attention mechanism can enable our model to accurately distinguish true infected areas. Finally, we introduced the FFD module and attention mechanism at the same time, it can effectively improve the segmentation performance in our network.

Table 3. Ablation studies of our LS-Net, the results are shown.

Method	Dice	Sen	Spec.	mIoU
backbone	0.648	0.657	0.825	58.25
backbone+attention mechanism	0.724	0.848	0.817	62.12
backbone+FFD	0.819	0.756	0.840	65.86
backbone+attention mechanism+FFD	0.967	0.961	0.843	69.01

Varying the Number of Diffusion Steps T. We explored the influence of the number of diffusion steps T to our network from two aspects: accuracy and runtime. The experiment had two different datasets setting, the one is only COVID-19 CT Segmentation dataset(D1), and another one is adding COVID-19 CT Collection dataset (D1 + D2). The result has shown in Fig. 5.

As shown in Fig. 5(a), the mIoU values of D1 and D2 increase slightly when the diffusion step increases, and decrease when the diffusion step continues to increase, but overall, the segmentation results do not fluctuate significantly.

As shown in Fig. 5(b), the sample generation time is proportional to the diffusion step, and the elapsed time increases faster when the diffusion step increases substantially.

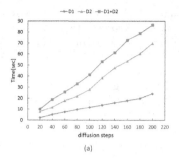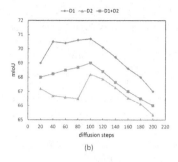

(a)   (b)

Fig. 5. Generation time in seconds and mIou per number of diffusion steps for COVID-19 CT Segmentation datasets and COVID-SemiSeg datasets. (a) Time adds with diffusion step increase, (b) mIoU changes with diffusion step increase.

5   Conclusion

As so far, a large number of studies have been applied to the field of medical image segmentation which has broad development prospects, with U-Net and its variant models being the most widely used. In this work, we propose a COVID-19 CT image lesion segmentation technology based on diffusion probabilistic model, which adopts ResNet architecture. And we introduce feature fusion decoder module and attention mechanism to improve the recognition accuracy of early lesion edges and subtle lesion locations. The COVID-19 CT Segmentation dataset and COVID-SemiSeg showed that our model significantly outperformed other models on a range of different baselines. However, the diffusion probabilistic model is usually slow in the training and inference stage, it cannot be well adapted to clinical medicine. So, finding the way to reduce the time required is the direction of our future research.

References

1. Wang, C., Horby, P.W., Hayden, F.G., Gao, G.F.: A novel coronavirus outbreak of global health concern. Lancet **395**(10223), 470–473 (2020)
2. Statement on the second meeting of the international health regulations (2005) emergency committee regarding the outbreak of novel coronavirus (2019-nCoV). WHO, Geneva, Switzerland (2020)
3. Clinical management of severe acute respiratory infection when novel coronavirus (nCoV) infection is suspected: Interim Guidance 12 January 2020. WTO, nCoV, Clinical (2020)
4. Scheme for Diagnosis and Treatment of 2019 Novel Coronavirus Pneumonia (The 9th Trial Edition). China (2019)
5. Fang, Y., et al.: Sensitivity of chest CT for COVID-19: comparison to RT-PCR. Radiology **296**, 200432 (2020)
6. Ye, Z., Zhang, Y., Wang, Y., Huang, Z., Song, B.: Chest CT manifestations of new coronavirus disease 2019 (COVID-19): a pictorial review. Eur. Radiol. **2019**(37), 1–9 (2020)

7. Pan, F., et al.: Time course of lung changes at chest CT during recovery from coronavirus disease 2019 (COVID-19). Radiology **295**(3), 715–721 (2020)
8. Shi, F., Wang, J., et al.: Review of artificial intelligence techniques in imaging data acquisition, segmentation, and diagnosis for COVID-19. IEEE Rev. Biomed. Eng. **14**, 4–15 (2021)
9. Sharma, P., Shamout, F.E., Clifton, D.A.: Preserving patient privacy while training a predictive model of in-hospital mortality. In: 33rd Conference on Neural Information Processing Systems (NeurIPS 2019), Vancouver, Canada (2019)
10. Wang, X., Deng, X., Fu, Q., et al.: A weakly-supervised framework for COVID-19 classification and lesion localization from chest CT. IEEE Trans. Med. Imaging **39**(8), 2615–2625 (2020)
11. Ferdinandus, F., Yuniarno, E.M., Purnama, I.K.E., Purnomo, M.H.: Covid-19 lung segmentation using U-Net CNN based on computed tomography image. In: 2022 IEEE 9th International Conference on Computational Intelligence and Virtual Environments for Measurement Systems and Applications (CIVEMSA) (2022)
12. Saood, A., Hatem, I.: COVID-19 lung CT image segmentation using deep learning methods: U-Net versus SegNet. BMC Med. Imaging **21**(1), 19 (2021)
13. Xiao, H., Ran, Z., Mabu, S., et al.: SAUNet++: an automatic segmentation model of COVID-19 lesion from CT slices. Vis Comput. **39**, 2291–2304 (2023)
14. Zhang, D., Huang, G., Zhang, Q., et al.: Cross-modality deep feature learning for brain tumor segmentation. Pattern Recogn. **110**, 107562 (2021)
15. Cheng, Z., Qu, A., He, X.: Contour-aware semantic segmentation network with spatial attention mechanism for medical image. Vis. Comput. **38**, 749–762 (2022)
16. Nazir, A., Cheema, M.N., Sheng, B., et al.: ECSU-Net: an embedded clustering sliced U-net coupled with fusing strategy for efficient intervertebral disc segmentation and classification. IEEE Trans. Image Process. **31**, 880–893 (2022)
17. Bhattacharyya, D., Thirupathi Rao, N., Joshua, E.S.N., et al.: A bidirectional deep learning architecture for lung nodule semantic segmentation. Vis. Comput. **39**, 5245–5261 (2022)
18. Jangam, E., Barreto, A.A.D., Annavarapu, C.S.R.: Automatic detection of COVID-19 from chest CT scan and chest X-Rays images using deep learning, transfer learning and stacking. Appl. Intell. **52**(2), 2243–2259 (2022). https://doi.org/10.1007/s10489-021-02393-4
19. Chen, H., Jiang, Y., Loew, M., Ko, H.: Unsupervised domain adaptation based COVID-19 CT infection segmentation network. Appl. Intell. **52**, 6340–6353 (2022). https://doi.org/10.1007/s10489-021-02691-x
20. Karthik, R., Menaka, R., Hariharan, M., Won, D.: Contour-enhanced attention CNN for CT-based COVID-19 segmentation. Pattern Recogn. **125**, 108538 (2022)
21. Zhao, X., Zhang, P., et al.: Prior attention network for multi-lesion segmentation in medical images. IEEE Trans. Med. Image **41**(12), 3812–3823 (2022). https://doi.org/10.1109/TMI.2022.3197180
22. Li, X., Jiang, Y., et al.: Lightweight attention convolutional neural network for retinal vessel image segmentation. IEEE Trans. Ind. Inf. **17**(3), 1958–1967 (2021)
23. Xia, H., Ma, M., Li, H., Song, S.: MC-Net: multi-scale context-attention network for medical CT image segmentation. Appl. Intell. **52**, 1508–1519 (2021)
24. Goodfellow, I., et al.: Generative adversarial nets. In: NIPS, Canada (2014)
25. Ho, J., et al.: Denoising diffusion probabilistic models. In: Advances in Neural Information Processing Systems, vol. 33 (2020)
26. Dhariwal, P., Nichol, A.: Diffusion models beats GANs on image synthesis. In: Advances in Neural Information Processing Systems, vol. 34 (2021)

27. Yang, L., Zhang, Z., Song, Y.: Diffusion models: a comprehensive survey of methods and applications. Comput. Vis. Pattern Recogn. (2022). https://doi.org/10.48550/arXiv.2209.00796

28. Luo, S., Hu, W.: Diffusion probabilistic models for 3d point cloud generation. In: IEEE Conference on Computer Vision and Pattern Recognition, pp. 2836–2844 (2021). https://doi.org/10.1109/CVPR46437.2021.00286

29. Kazerouni, A., Aghdam, E.K., et al.: Diffusion model for medical image analysis: a comprehensive survey. Image Video Process. (2022)

30. Wolleb, J., et al.: Diffusion models for implicit image segmentation ensembles. Comput. Vis. Pattern Recogn. (2023). https://doi.org/10.48550/arXiv.2112.03145

31. Kim, B., Oh, Y., Ye, J.C.: Diffusion adversarial representation learning for self-supervised vessel segmentation. Comput. Vis. Pattern Recogn. (2023). https://doi.org/10.48550/arXiv.2209.14566

32. Wu, J., Fang, H., et al.: MedSegDiff: medical image segmentation with diffusion probabilistic model. Comput. Vis. Pattern Recogn. (2023). https://doi.org/10.48550/arXiv.2211.00611

33. Fan, D.-P., Zhou, T., et al.: Inf-Net: automatic COVID-19 lung infection segmentation from CT images. IEEE Trans. Med. Imaging **39**(8), 2626–2637 (2020)

34. Valanarasu, J.M.J., Oza, P., Hacihaliloglu, I., Patel, V.M.: Medical transformer: gated axial-attention for medical image segmentation. In: de Bruijne, M., et al. (eds.) MICCAI 2021. LNCS, vol. 12901, pp. 36–46. Springer, Cham (2021). https://doi.org/10.1007/978-3-030-87193-2_4

35. Wang, H., Zhu, Y., Green, B., Adam, H., Yuille, A., Chen, L.-C.: Axial-DeepLab: stand-alone axial-attention for panoptic segmentation. In: Vedaldi, A., Bischof, H., Brox, T., Frahm, J.-M. (eds.) ECCV 2020. LNCS, vol. 12349, pp. 108–126. Springer, Cham (2020). https://doi.org/10.1007/978-3-030-58548-8_7

36. Federau, C., Christensen, S., Scherrer, N., Ospel, J.M., Schulze-Zachau, V., Schmidt, N., et al.: Improved segmentation and detection sensitivity of diffusion-weighted stroke lesions with synthetically enhanced deep learning. Radiol.: Artif. Intell. **2**(5), e190217 (2020)

37. Luo, X., Chen, J., Song, T., Wang, G.: Semi-supervised medical image segmentation through dual-task consistency. In: Proceedings of the AAAI Conference on Artificial Intelligence, vol. 35, p. 10 (2021)

38. Guo, X., et al: Accelerating diffusion models via pre-segmentation diffusion sampling for medical image segmentation. Image Video Process. (2022). https://doi.org/10.48550/arXiv.2210.17408

39. Tang, F., et al.: Multi-level global context cross consistency model for semi-supervised ultrasound image segmentation with diffusion model. Comput. Vis. Pattern Recogn. (2023). https://doi.org/10.48550/arXiv.2305.09447

40. Liang, S., Nie, R., Cao, J., et al.: FCF: feature complement fusion network for detecting COVID-19 through CT scan images. Appl. Soft Comput. **125**, 109111 (2022)

41. Huang, Z., Li, L., Zhang, X., et al.: A coarse-refine segmentation network for COVID-19 CT images. IET Image Process. **16**, 333–343 (2022)

Empowering Novel Geometric Algebra for Graphics and Engineering Workshop

Intersection of Conic Sections Using Geometric Algebra

Clément Chomicki[1]($\boxtimes$), Stéphane Breuils[2], Venceslas Biri[1],
and Vincent Nozick[1]

[1] LIGM, Univ Gustave Eiffel, CNRS, Marne-la-Vallée, France
`clement.chomicki@univ-eiffel.fr`
[2] LAMA, Univ Savoie Mont-Blanc, CNRS, Annecy, France

Abstract. Conic sections are extensively encountered in a wide range
of disciplines, including optics, physics, and various other fields. Consequently, the geometric algebra community is actively engaged in developing frameworks that enable efficient support and manipulation of conic
sections. Conic-conic intersection objects are known and supported by
algebras specialized in conic sections representation, but there is yet
no elegant formula to extract the intersection points from them. This
paper proposes a method for point extraction from an conic intersection through the concept of pencils. It will be based on QC2GA, the 2D
version of QCGA (Quadric Conformal Geometric Algebra), that we also
prove to be equivalent to GAC (Geometric Algebra for Conics).

Keywords: Conics · Geometric Algebra · Projective Geometry ·
Clifford Algebra · QCGA (Quadric Conformal Geometric Algebra) ·
GAC (Geometric Algebra for Conics) · Pencil

1 Introduction

Geometric algebras (GA) are a convenient way to represent and manipulate
geometric primitives. They have been used in physics for decades [12,15,16] to
unify and simplify some models.

Presently, GA applications in computer sciences are widespread, used in various domains such as neural networking [4,21] and computer graphics - where
they can be used to manipulate geometric primitives [6]. For an introduction to
geometric algebras, please refer to Perwass' and Dorst's textbooks [7,19].

Because polynomial embedding [19] is done very naturally in geometric algebras, polynomial curves and geometric algebra form a promising marriage. This
is why several GA frameworks have already been proposed for both curves and
surfaces in order to represent, transform and intersect these objects.

Perwass [19] started with a simple blade-based approach in $\mathbb{G}_{5,3}$ to represent
2D conics constructed from 5 points. This algebra also supports translations
and rotations of conics, but is presented as just a proof of concept to be further
developed. Later on, Goldman et al. proposed $\mathbb{R}(4,4)$ [11], an algebra composed

of two projective $\mathbb{R}^4$ basis capable of supporting quadrics (and so conic when one dimension is removed). Similarly, DCGA introduced by Easter et al. [8] is composed of two CGA basis and can represent general Darboux cyclide, which embeds quadrics. The common weakness of those two algebras is that their curves and surfaces are not constructed from control points.

Another algebra supporting quadric surfaces is QCGA (Quadric Conformal Geometric Algebra) [1] from Breuils et al, which is a 3D extension of Perwass' conic algebra that explores intersections and transformations. QCGA can be lowered in dimension (by removing 7 vectors of its basis) to get QC2GA, an algebra for handling conics. Finally, GAC (Geometric Algebra for Conics) [17] is a more recent proposition from Hrdina et al., which unlike the other ones, is fully dedicated to conics. It is very similar to QC2GA, the 2D version of QCGA. These two algebras, just like Perwass', support constructing their object from points, and notable distinction between the two lies in the inclusion of a third spatial dimension within QCGA, while GAC (Geometric Algebra of Conics) offers a broader range of geometric transformations. The common point of these algebras is the lack of way to process conic intersection objects into points, and other things that would be extremely useful such as determining the type of a conic. We also want to be able to tell if a conic is a pair of lines, and if so, we should have a way to extract these two lines. Conic section also have a center and several other relevant lines and foci that would be interesting to extract and manipulate. GAC is actually able to extract points from conic intersection on some very specific and easy cases [5], but what we want is a general method that works on any intersection.

This paper presents a method to extract the points from any conic intersection objects. The paper is organized as follows: Sect. 2 introduces state-of-the-art of conic intersection in both projective geometry and geometric algebra. Section 3 focuses on QC2GA and GAC. Section 4, as a first contribution, demonstrates that they are actually equivalent. Our major contribution is detailed in Sect. 5 that presents an algorithm to find the intersection points of two conics in QC2GA by using an associated cubic polynomial and the naturally-supported pencils of conics.

2   Conics Theoretical Background

This section introduces various ways of representing conics and their properties.

2.1   Conics Representation

Conics' traces can be found as far as 380 BC by Menaechmus in the ancient Greece. In the last couple of centuries, mathematicians linked these planar curves to the quadratic equations of two variables and projective algebra. This is the formalism that this paper uses.

As stated by Faucette [9], conics are planar polynomial curves of degree 2:

$$C : g(x, y) = ax^2 + by^2 + cxy + dx + ey + f = 0 \tag{1}$$

With $(a, b, c, d, e, f) \in \mathbb{K}^6$ and $\mathbb{K} = \mathbb{R}$ or $\mathbb{C}$. When not degenerate and not complex, a conic can be seen as the intersection between a double cone and a plane.

It is common to work in the projective space $\mathbb{P}^2$ to represent points and in $\mathbb{P}^5$ to represent conics. $\mathbb{P}^n$ is the set of all equivalence classes $(a_i)_{i \in [1, n+1]} \in \mathbb{K}^{n+1} \setminus \{0_n\}$ under the equivalence relation $(a_1, \ldots, a_{n+1}) \sim (b_1, \ldots, b_{n+1}) \iff \exists \lambda \in \mathbb{K}, (a_1 \ldots, a_{n+1}) = \lambda(b_0, \ldots, b_{n+1})$. A finite point (x, y) of $\mathbb{K}^2$ is then embedded as $(x, y, 1)$ (or more generally as (wx, wy, w)) in $\mathbb{P}^2$, and infinite points of direction (x, y) is embedded as $(x, y, 0)$. In order to embed $\mathbb{P}^2$ into $\mathbb{P}^5$, we consider the polynomial map $Q : \mathbb{P}^2 \to \mathbb{P}^5$ so that $Q(x, y, w) = (x^2, y^2, xy, xw, yw, w^2)$. Conics are then represented by the vectors of $\mathbb{P}^5$, and the Eq. (1) becomes

$$C : \mathfrak{C}^\top \cdot Q(x, y, w) = 0 \quad \text{with} \quad \mathfrak{C} = [a, b, c, d, e, f]^\top \in \mathbb{P}^5 \qquad (2)$$

Conics are also often represented by their Hessian matrix, which enables to reformulate Eq. (1):

$$C : p^\top \mathcal{H} p = 0 \qquad \text{with} \quad \mathcal{H} = \begin{bmatrix} a & \dfrac{c}{2} & \dfrac{d}{2} \\ \dfrac{c}{2} & b & \dfrac{e}{2} \\ \dfrac{d}{2} & \dfrac{e}{2} & f \end{bmatrix} \qquad (3)$$

Assume five linearly independent points $(p_i)_{i \in [1,5]}$ with coordinates $(x_i, y_i, w_i)_{i \in [1,5]} \in \mathbb{P}^2$ and another point p_0 of coordinate $(x, y, w) \in \mathbb{P}^2$. Let $q_i = Q(p_i), \forall i \in [0, 5]$. The conic equation (C) is often expressed in the form of the vanishing determinant of a matrix $\mathcal{P} = [q_{i,j}]$ [13]:

$$C : \det(\mathcal{P}) = \begin{vmatrix} x^2 & y^2 & xy & xw & yw & w^2 \\ x_1^2 & y_1^2 & x_1 y_1 & x_1 w_1 & y_1 w_1 & w_1^2 \\ x_2^2 & y_2^2 & x_2 y_2 & x_2 w_2 & y_2 w_2 & w_2^2 \\ x_3^2 & y_3^2 & x_3 y_3 & x_3 w_3 & y_3 w_3 & w_3^2 \\ x_4^2 & y_4^2 & x_4 y_4 & x_4 w_4 & y_4 w_4 & w_4^2 \\ x_5^2 & y_5^2 & x_5 y_5 & x_5 w_5 & y_5 w_5 & w_5^2 \end{vmatrix} = 0 \qquad (4)$$

Then, if we denote by $m_i^j(A)$ the respective minor of matrix A, i.e. the determinant of A with its i-th column and j-th line removed. If we drop the superscript for $j = 1$, i.e. $m_i = m_i^1$ we have:

$$\begin{aligned} a = & \ m_1(\mathcal{P}) & b = -m_2(\mathcal{P}) & \quad c = & \ m_3(\mathcal{P}) \\ d = & -m_4(\mathcal{P}) & e = \ m_5(\mathcal{P}) & \quad f = -m_6(\mathcal{P}) \end{aligned} \qquad (5)$$

There is a more general rule to that: the set of conics passing through n non-aligned points is a dimension $(5 - n)$ vector subspace of $\mathbb{P}^5$ [10]. We could then argue that 4 control points would form at most a 1-vector subspace, 3 points a 2-vector subspace, etc. This implies that the n-intersection of two conics C_a and C_b is more than their n common points, as the 3 points of a 3-intersection generates a 2-vector subspace when the two conics only creates a 1-vector subspace.

2.2　Type of a Conic and Degenerate Case

When $\mathbb{K} = \mathbb{R}$, the type of the conic is ruled by these two discriminants [20]:

$$\Delta_2(C) = m_3^3(\mathcal{H}) = ab - \frac{1}{4}c^2 \tag{6}$$

$$\Delta_3(C) = \det(\mathcal{H}) = abf + \frac{ced - c^2f - bd^2 - ae^2}{4} \tag{7}$$

$\Delta_2(C)$	$\Delta_3(C)$	type of C
$+$	$\neq 0$	Ellipse (may be imaginary)
0	$\neq 0$	Parabola
$-$	$\neq 0$	Hyperbola
$+$	0	Point
0	0	Two parallel lines
$-$	0	Two intersecting lines

Whether $\mathbb{K} = \mathbb{R}$ or $\mathbb{C}$, if $\Delta_3(C) = 0$, C is called **degenerate** or **reducible**, meaning that it can be factored into two complex lines.

2.3　Pencils

Let $C_a : g_a(x,y) = 0$ and $C_b : g_b(x,y) = 0$ be two conics and $\lambda \in \mathbb{R}^*$. $C_\lambda : g_\lambda(x,y) = g_a(x,y) + \lambda g_b(x,y) = 0$ is also a conic since g_a and g_b are linear forms of $\mathbb{P}^5$ and

$$C_a \cap C_b = C_a \cap C_\lambda = C_b \cap C_\lambda \tag{8}$$

where $\cap$ is the set theory intersection operator.

This is because $g_\lambda(x,y,w) = g_a(x,y,w) + \lambda g_b(x,y,w)$ then if two of the terms are 0, the third one is also 0, and if one term is not zero, then at least one other is not zero. The 1-vector space generated C_a and C_b is called their **pencil**.

$$\text{Pencil}(C_a, C_b) = \{K(C_a + \lambda C_b) \qquad\qquad K, \lambda \in \mathbb{K}\} \tag{9}$$

$$= \{K(\cos(\theta)C_a + \sin(\theta)C_b) \qquad K, \theta \in \mathbb{K}\} \tag{10}$$

Four non-aligned points also generate a pencil of conics, but the reciprocal is not true: the intersection of two conics might contain less than 4 points (when $\mathbb{K} = \mathbb{R}$) or have one or several multiple points (see Fig. 1).

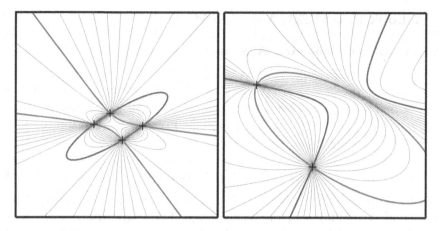

Fig. 1. The pencil (in grey) generated by two conics (in red and yellow) with 4 intersection points (left) and 2 intersection points (right). (Color figure online)

2.4 Intersecting Conics

Finding the intersection between two conic sections is an old problem. Two different conics can have from 0 to 4 points of intersections (the intersection of a conic with itself is of course the whole conic). Gröbner basis [14] can be used to express the conic intersection problem as a quartic polynomial. Also, Faucette [9] describes a method to solve any quartic polynomial by finding the intersection points of two conics. Therefore, finding the intersection points of two conic sections is equivalent to find the root of a quartic polynomial.

The method described by Faucette [9] consists of finding a degenerate conic (i.e. that can be factored into two lines) in the pencil generated by the two intersecting conics. That pair of lines is then separated into two distinct lines, which can be subsequently used to find the intersection points with one of the conics of the pencil. Another method is to directly solve the associated quartic equation of the problem . Richter-Geber [20] reformulates this method in a more complete way and gives a detailed process to find the intersections. Just like [9], they solve the associated cubic equation, find any complex solution using a given formula, split the resulting degenerate complex conic into two complex lines and intersect the two resulting complex lines with one of the intersecting conic. Both of these method heavily relies on complex numbers and lines, but one could choose to only use real lines if they limited themselves to conic-lines intersections.

Now that conic intersections are introduced, the following section will present two algebras that handle conics.

3   A Look into QC2GA and GAC

3.1   Conics and Geometric Algebra

Let's look back at Eqs. (4) and (5), assuming that $\mathbb{K} = \mathbb{R}$. Computing the determinant of the matrix $\mathcal{P}$ can be done by working in $\mathbb{G}_6 = \bigwedge \mathbb{P}^5$ [18,19], where we find that the parameters of the conic (a, b, c, d, e, f) are the coordinates of the blade of grade 5, $\bigwedge_{i \in [1,5]} q_i$. The equation of the conic (4) then becomes.

$$C : q_1 \wedge q_2 \wedge q_3 \wedge q_4 \wedge q_5 \wedge q = 0 \tag{11}$$

Hence five points determines a conic gives us a natural outer product representation of the implicit equation of the conic. This leads directly to Perwass' proposition [19], and then to QC2GA [1] and GAC [17]. In these algebras, points and conics are represented this way with their respective $\mathbb{G}_{5,3}$ bases:

$$p = x^2 e_1 + y^2 e_2 + xy e_3 + x e_4 + y e_5 + e_6 \tag{12}$$

$$C = p_1 \wedge p_2 \wedge p_3 \wedge p_4 \wedge p_5 \wedge e_7 \wedge e_8 \tag{13}$$

$$= a e_1^c + b e_2^c + c e_3^c + d e_4^c + e e_5^c + f e_6^c \tag{14}$$

In (12), $e_1^c, \ldots, e_6^c$ denotes the (right) complement-dual of the multivectors $e_1, \ldots, e_6$, defined through $m \wedge m^c = I$ for all multivector m [3].

3.2   Two-Dimensional Quadric Conformal Algebra (QC2GA)

QC2GA is the 2D-version of the QCGA algebra [1] by Breuils et al. Its signature is $\mathbb{R}^{5,3}$, but we use this more convenient non-diagonal basis:

	e_1	e_2	e_{o_1}	e_{∞_1}	e_{o_2}	e_{∞_2}	e_{o_3}	e_{∞_3}
e_1	1	.	.	.	.	.	.	.
e_2	.	1	.	.	.	.	.	.
e_{o_1}	.	.	0	−1	.	.	.	.
e_{∞_1}	.	.	−1	0	.	.	.	.
e_{o_2}	.	.	.	.	0	−1	.	.
e_{∞_2}	.	.	.	.	−1	0	.	.
e_{o_3}	.	.	.	.	.	.	0	−1
e_{∞_3}	.	.	.	.	.	.	−1	0

QC2GA formalism relies on the following blades:

$$e_o = e_{o_1} + e_{o_2} \tag{15}$$

$$e_\infty = \frac{e_{\infty_1} + e_{\infty_2}}{2} \tag{16}$$

$$I_o^\triangleright = (e_{o_1} - e_{o_2}) \wedge e_{o_2} \tag{17}$$

$$I_\infty^\triangleright = (e_{\infty_1} - e_{\infty_2}) \wedge e_{\infty_2} \tag{18}$$

$$I_o = e_{o_1} \wedge e_{o_2} \wedge e_{o_2} \tag{19}$$

$$I_\infty = e_{\infty_1} \wedge e_{\infty_2} \wedge e_{\infty_3} \tag{20}$$

$$I_\epsilon = e_1 \wedge e_2 \wedge e_3 \tag{21}$$

$$I = I_\epsilon \wedge I_\infty \wedge I_o \tag{22}$$

QC2GA points $\overset{QC2GA}{p}$ and conics $\overset{QC2GA}{C}$ are defined as follows:

$$\overset{QC2GA}{p} = e_o + xe_1 + ye_2 + x^2\frac{e_{\infty_1}}{2} + y^2\frac{e_{\infty_2}}{2} + xye_{\infty_3} \tag{23}$$

$$\overset{QC2GA}{C} = \overset{QC2GA}{p_1} \wedge \overset{QC2GA}{p_2} \wedge \overset{QC2GA}{p_3} \wedge \overset{QC2GA}{p_4} \wedge \overset{QC2GA}{p_5} \wedge I_o^\triangleright \tag{24}$$

$$\overset{QC2GA}{C^*} = a(\frac{e_{\infty_1}}{2})^{-1} + b(\frac{e_{\infty_2}}{2})^{-1} + ce_{\infty_3}^{-1} + de_1^{-1} + ee_2^{-1} + fe_o^{-1} \tag{25}$$

$$= -2ae_{o_1} - 2be_{o_2} - ce_{o_3} + de_1 + ee_2 - fe_\infty \tag{26}$$

With $(a, b, c, d, e, f) \in \mathbb{R}^6$ the parameters of the conic C represented by $\overset{QC2GA}{C}$. QC2GA supports intersections of conics, and evaluating if a point lies on one:

$$\overset{QC2GA}{Inter} = \overset{QC2GA}{C_1} \vee \overset{QC2GA}{C_2} = (\overset{QC2GA}{C_1^*} \wedge \overset{QC2GA}{C_2^*})^* \tag{27}$$

$$\overset{QC2GA}{p} \in \overset{QC2GA}{C} \iff \overset{QC2GA}{p} \wedge \overset{QC2GA}{C} = 0 \iff \overset{QC2GA}{p} \cdot (\overset{QC2GA}{C^*}) = 0 \tag{28}$$

3.3 Geometric Algebra for Conics (GAC)

GAC is another geometric algebra for conics from [17] by J. Hrdina et al. Its basis $(e_1, e_2, \bar{n}_+, n_+, \bar{n}_-, n_-, \bar{n}_\times, n_\times)$ has the same signature as QC2GA.

Points $\overset{GAC}{p}$ and conics $\overset{GAC}{C}$ are constructed this way in GAC:

$$\overset{GAC}{p} = \bar{n}_+ + xe_1 + ye_2 + \frac{x^2 + y^2}{2}n_+ + \frac{x^2 - y^2}{2}n_- + xyn_\times \tag{29}$$

$$\overset{GAC}{C} = \overset{GAC}{p_1} \wedge \overset{GAC}{p_2} \wedge \overset{GAC}{p_3} \wedge \overset{GAC}{p_4} \wedge \overset{GAC}{p_5} \wedge e_{o_2} \wedge e_{o_3} \tag{30}$$

$$\overset{GAC}{C^*} = -(a + b)\bar{n}_+ - (a - b)\bar{n}_- - c\bar{n}_\times + de_1 + ee_2 - fn_+ \tag{31}$$

The usage we have of GAC is the same than QC2GA.

$$\overset{GAC}{Inter} = \overset{GAC}{C_1} \vee \overset{GAC}{C_2} = (\overset{GAC}{C_1^*} \wedge \overset{GAC}{C_2^*})^* \tag{32}$$

$$\overset{GAC}{p} \in \overset{GAC}{C} \iff \overset{GAC}{p} \wedge \overset{GAC}{C} = 0 \iff \overset{GAC}{p} \cdot (\overset{GAC}{C^*}) = 0 \tag{33}$$

4 GAC and QC2GA Are Equivalent

The metric of GAC and QC2GA are identical, and at first sight the objects of these algebras looks very similar. It would make sense to find out that these two algebras are the same thing, which would unify all the work done on these two algebras. We actually can express GAC basis with QC2GA's, which shows a direct equivalence between QCGA and GAC objects:

$$\bar{n}_+ = e_{o_1} + e_{o_2} \quad (34) \quad \bar{n}_- = e_{o_1} - e_{o_2} \quad (35) \quad \bar{n}_\times = e_{o_3} \quad (36)$$

$$n_+ = \frac{e_{\infty_1} + e_{\infty_2}}{2} \quad (37) \quad n_- = \frac{e_{\infty_1} - e_{\infty_2}}{2} \quad (38) \quad n_\times = e_{\infty_3} \quad (39)$$

$$\overset{\text{GAC}}{p} = e_o + xe_1 + ye_2 + \frac{x^2 e_{\infty_1} + y^2 e_{\infty_2}}{2} + xye_{\infty_3} = \overset{\text{QC2GA}}{p} \quad (40)$$

$$\overset{\text{GAC}}{C} = -2ae_{o_1} - 2be_{o_2} - ce_{o_3} + de_1 + ee_2 - fe_\infty = \overset{\text{QC2GA}}{C} \quad (41)$$

Thanks to this reformulation, we establish the equivalence of GAC and QC2GA. GAC possess versors for rotation, translations, dilation and even "general reflection" (which looks similar as a CGA's spherical inversion but with conics [19]). QC2GA also have rotations and translations (inherited directly from Perwass' conformal conic algebra), and its translator is easier to express than GAC's. Due to the equivalence of these two algebras, tools from GAC and QC2GA can be utilized interchangeably. For the rest of this article, we will then omit the "QC2GA" or "GAC" on top of the geometric objects and follow the formalism of QC2GA, and every property relative to QC2GA will also hold for GAC.

5 Extracting Points from QC2GA Conics Intersections

An intersection might contain from 0 to 4 points. However, the grade of that object is always 6. Therefore it is neither trivial to distinguish the type of intersection nor to extract the points, hence our method. By selecting a real degenerate conic from the intersection object's pencil, the conic is factorized into two lines. These lines are then intersected with another conic from the same pencil, resulting in the desired intersection points. Notably, this method exclusively operates on real objects, unlike from Faucette's approach that uses complex lines.

5.1 Pencil of Conics in QC2GA

Let $Inter$ be an intersection of two conics and p a point not in $Inter$, we define $C = Inter \wedge p$ as the conic passing through every point of $Inter$ and through p. Summation of two conics is allowed by QC2GA, hence we can write $\forall \lambda \in \mathbb{R}, C_\lambda = C_a + \lambda C_b$. Summations of points is also supported, which gives the following:

$$Inter = C_a \vee C_b = (C_a^* \wedge C_b^*)^* \quad (42)$$

$$C_a = Inter \wedge p_a \qquad\qquad p_a \in C_a \setminus C_b \quad (43)$$

$$C_b = Inter \wedge p_b \qquad\qquad p_b \in C_b \setminus C_a \quad (44)$$

$$C_\lambda = Inter \wedge (p_a + \lambda p_b) \quad (45)$$

The pencil of C_a and C_b is then generated by their intersection $Inter$.

5.2   Extraction Method

The next step consists in the extraction of the points contained in an intersection.

The two conics will be used to find a new pair of conics with one degenerate, by finding the root of an associated cubic polynomial. The degenerate conic will then be factored into two lines, that will be intersected with the other conic to get the intersection points using a simpler algorithm.

Building Two Conics from Inter. In order to build two conics from *Inter*, one could just pick two random points and use the formulas of (42)–(45), but this would lead to possibilities of p_a and p_b to generate the same conic. In order to avoid that, it is possible to only pick one point p_a randomly, to generate a conic C_a from it and *Inter* and to extract C_b as the normed element in the 2D-vector space *Inter* perpendicular to C_a.

$$C_a = Inter \wedge p_a \qquad (46) \qquad C_b = Inter \wedge C_a{}^c \qquad (47)$$

Finding a Degenerate Conic (Algorithm 1). Now that we have two relevant conics to work with, we would like to find a degenerate conic, because a degenerate conic is either a point (which makes the problem trivial as we just take that point as the eventual solution), or a pair of lines that we will treat as two distinct lines, which reduces the conic-conic intersection to the simpler task of determining conic-line intersections. Finding a degenerate conic in the pencil of C_1 and C_2 can be done by solving the equation $\Delta_3(C_1 + \lambda C_2) = 0$, which can be expanded into Eq. (48).

$$\Delta_3(C_2)\lambda^3 + \left(\frac{\Delta_3(C_1 + C_2) + \Delta_3(C_1 - C_2)}{2} - \Delta_3(C_1) \right)\lambda^2$$
$$+ \left(\frac{\Delta_3(C_1 + C_2) - \Delta_3(C_1 - C_2)}{2} - \Delta_3(C_2) \right)\lambda + \Delta_3(C_1) = 0 \qquad (48)$$

To solve this cubic equation, we use a formula similar than Cardano's, but which allows to do less divisions and which allows us to easily obtain a real root when $k = 0$:

$$\Delta_0 = b^2 - 3ac \qquad\qquad \Delta_1 = 2b^3 - 9abc + 27a^2d \qquad (49)$$

$$\Omega_\pm = \sqrt[3]{\frac{\Delta_1 \pm \sqrt{\Delta_1^2 - 4\Delta_0^3}}{2}} \qquad x_k = -\frac{b + e^{i\frac{2\pi k}{3}}\Omega_+ + e^{i\frac{-2\pi k}{3}}\Omega_-}{3a} \qquad (50)$$

Using this approach, we may write the Algorithm 1 that samples a degenerate conic and another conic significantly different (noticing that $\lambda C_a + \mu C_b$ is a rotation of angle $\arctan(\mu/\lambda)$ in the pencil) from the degenerate one from the pencil of conic of *Inter*. The variables a, b, c, d are not conic parameters, but rather the four parameters of the cubic polynomial.

Algorithm 1: Find a degenerate conic and a different one in the pencil of *Inter*

Function gen_degen_and_other
  Input: *Inter*
  Output: $C_{deg}, C_\perp$

  do $p_a \leftarrow$ random_point() **while** $p_a \wedge Inter = 0$
  $C_a \leftarrow Inter \wedge p_a$ $C_b \leftarrow Inter \wedge (C_a^c)$
  $a \leftarrow \Delta_3(C_b)$ $b \leftarrow \dfrac{\Delta_3(C_a + C_b) + \Delta_3(C_a - C_b)}{2} - \Delta_3(C_a)$
  $d \leftarrow \Delta_3(C_a)$ $c \leftarrow \dfrac{\Delta_3(C_a + C_b) - \Delta_3(C_a - C_b)}{2} - \Delta_3(C_b)$
  $\Delta_0 \leftarrow b^2 - 3ac$ $\Delta_1 \leftarrow 2b^3 - 9abc + 27a^2 d$
  $\Omega_- \leftarrow \sqrt[3]{\dfrac{\Delta_1 - \sqrt{\Delta_1^2 - 4\Delta_0^3}}{2}}$ $\Omega_+ \leftarrow \sqrt[3]{\dfrac{\Delta_1 + \sqrt{\Delta_1^2 - 4\Delta_0^3}}{2}}$
  $\lambda \leftarrow -3a$ $\mu \leftarrow b + \Omega_- + \Omega_+$
  $C_{deg} \leftarrow \lambda C_a + \mu C_b$ $C_\perp \leftarrow -\mu C_a + \lambda C_b$

Factorize Lines Pairs (Algorithm 2). A line pair is of the form:

$$l_1 = \cos(\alpha_1)x + \sin(\alpha_1)y + w_1 \tag{51}$$

$$l_2 = \cos(\alpha_2)x + \sin(\alpha_2)y + w_2 \tag{52}$$

$$C : Kl_1 l_2 = ax^2 + by^2 + cxy + dx + ey + f = 0 \tag{53}$$

where $K \in \mathbb{R}^*$ is a multiplicative constant coming from the projective aspect of the conic (it can be any constant). These two lines can be extracted using the method presented by Richter-Gebert [20]. This method is also used by Byrtus et al. for their specific GAC intersection extraction [5]. Algorithm 2 implements that.

Algorithm 2: Line pair factorization algorithm

Function `factor_line_pair`

   Input: C_{deg}

   Output: $\alpha_1, \alpha_2, w_1, w_2$ // lines angles and offsets

   $H \leftarrow \text{hessian\_matrix}(C_{deg})$ $A \leftarrow \text{adjoint}(H)$ $i \leftarrow \arg\min_{k}\{A_{k,k}\}$

   $D \leftarrow \begin{bmatrix} 0 & -A_{i,2} & +A_{i,1} \\ +A_{i,2} & 0 & -A_{i,0} \\ -A_{i,1} & +A_{i,0} & 0 \end{bmatrix} / \sqrt{-A_{i,i}}$ $N \leftarrow H + D$

   $u_1, v_1, w_1 \leftarrow N\left[*, \arg\max_{j}\{N[1,j]^2 + N[2,j]^2\}\right]$

   $u_2, v_2, w_2 \leftarrow N\left[\arg\max_{j}\{N[j,1]^2 + N[j,2]^2\}, *\right]$

   $\alpha_1 \leftarrow \text{arctan2}(v_1, u_1)$ $\alpha_2 \leftarrow \text{arctan2}(v_2, u_2)$

   return $\{\alpha_1, \alpha_2, w_1/\sqrt{u_1^2 + v_1^2}, w_2/\sqrt{u_2^2 + v_2^2}\}$

Conic-Line Intersection (Algorithm 3). The idea is to rotate the problem to have the line vertical (which means a known x), and we are then left with a trivial quadratic polynomial in y.

Algorithm 3: Conic-Line intersection algorithm

Function `conic_line_inter`

   Input: C, θ, w

   Output: points

   $R \leftarrow \text{qc2ga\_rotor}(-\theta)$ $[a, b, c, d, e, f] \leftarrow RC\tilde{R}$

   $x \leftarrow -w$ $\delta \leftarrow (cx + e)^2 - 4b(ax^2 + dx + f)$ $\gamma \leftarrow \dfrac{cx + e}{2b}$

   $p_0 \leftarrow \begin{pmatrix} \cos(\theta)x - \gamma\sin(\theta) \\ \sin(\theta)x + \gamma\cos(\theta) \end{pmatrix}$ $u \leftarrow \dfrac{1}{2b}\begin{pmatrix} -\sin(\theta) \\ \cos(\theta) \end{pmatrix}$

   switch $sgn(\delta)$ **do**

       case + **do return** $\{p_0 \pm \sqrt{\delta}u\}$

       case 0 **do return** $\{p_0\}$

       case − **do return** $\{\}$

   end

5.3 Full Algorithm

Using the algorithms we just presented, we can write the Algorithm 4 that extracts the points in an intersection object. This algorithm have been implemented in C++ with Garamon [2] (see https://github.com/technolapin/qc2ga-intersection). Figure 2 gives outputs of our code.

Algorithm 4: Point extraction algorithm

Function `extract_pts_from_inter`
> **Input:** *Inter*
> **Output:** a set of points
>
> $C_{deg}, C_\perp \leftarrow$ gen_degen_and_other(*Inter*)
> $\alpha_1, \alpha_2, w_1, w_2 \leftarrow$ factor_line_pair(C_{deg})
> **return** conic_line_inter($C_\perp, \alpha_1, w_1$) $\cup$ conic_line_inter($C_\perp, \alpha_2, w_2$)

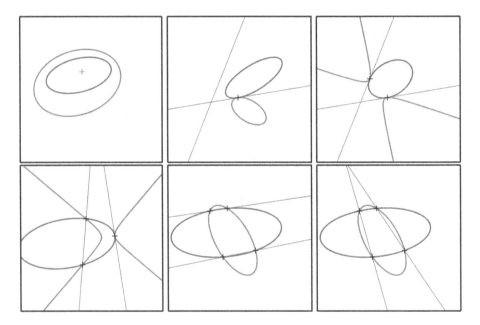

Fig. 2. Extraction of 0,1,2,3 and 4-intersections where the green curve is the degenerate conic, which can be a line pair or a point. The 4-intersection is depicted twice with different line pairs. (Color figure online)

6   Conclusion

This paper established the equivalence of QC2GA and GAC, and presented a geometric-algebra driven method for the decomposition of a conic-conic intersection object into points. Further work is to be done to increase the part of geometric algebra in the process.

References

1. Breuils, S., Fuchs, L., Hitzer, E., Nozick, V., Sugimoto, A.: Three-dimensional quadrics in extended conformal geometric algebras of higher dimensions from control points, implicit equations and axis alignment. Adv. Appl. Clifford Algebras **29**, 1–22 (2019)
2. Breuils, S., Nozick, V., Fuchs, L.: Garamon: a geometric algebra library generator. Adv. Appl. Clifford Algebras **29**(4), 69 (2019)
3. Browne, J.M: Grassmann Algebra Volume 1: Foundations: Exploring Extended Vector Algebra with Mathematica, vol. 1 (2012)
4. Buchholz, S., Tachibana, K., Hitzer, E.M.S.: Optimal learning rates for clifford neurons. In: de Sá, J.M., Alexandre, L.A., Duch, W., Mandic, D. (eds.) ICANN 2007. LNCS, vol. 4668, pp. 864–873. Springer, Heidelberg (2007). https://doi.org/10.1007/978-3-540-74690-4_88
5. Byrtus, R., Derevianko, A., Vašík, P., Hildenbrand, D., Steinmetz, C.: On specific conic intersections in GAC and symbolic calculations in GAALOPWeb. Adv. Appl. Clifford Algebras **32**(1), 2 (2021)
6. Keninck, S.: Non-parametric realtime rendering of subspace objects in arbitrary geometric algebras. In: Gavrilova, M., Chang, J., Thalmann, N.M., Hitzer, E., Ishikawa, H. (eds.) CGI 2019. LNCS, vol. 11542, pp. 549–555. Springer, Cham (2019). https://doi.org/10.1007/978-3-030-22514-8_54
7. Dorst, L.: The inner products of geometric algebra. In: Dorst, L., Doran, C., Lasenby, J. (eds.) Applications of Geometric Algebra in Computer Science and Engineering, pp. 35–46. Springer, Cham (2002). https://doi.org/10.1007/978-1-4612-0089-5_2
8. Easter, R.B., Hitzer, E.: Double conformal geometric algebra. Adv. Appl. Clifford Algebras **27**(3), 2175–2199 (2017)
9. Faucette, W.M.: A geometric interpretation of the solution of the general quartic polynomial. Am. Math. Mon. **103**(1), 51–57 (1996)
10. Fulton, W.: Algebraic Curves, vol. 54. Addison-Wesley, Boston (2008)
11. Goldman, R., Mann, S.: R(4, 4) as a computational framework for 3-dimensional computer graphics. Adv. Appl. Clifford Algebras **25**(1), 113–149 (2015)
12. Gregory, A.L., Lasenby, J., Agarwal, A.: The elastic theory of shells using geometric algebra. Roy. Soc. Open Sci. **4**(3), 170065 (2017)
13. Hartley, R., Zisserman, A.: Multiple View Geometry in Computer Vision. Cambridge University Press, Cambridge (2003)
14. Heck, A.: A Bird's-Eye View of Gröbner Bases, pp. 697–746. Springer, New York (2003)
15. Hestenes, D.: The zitterbewegung interpretation of quantum mechanics. Found. Phys. **20**(10), 1213–1232 (1990)
16. Hestenes, D.: New Foundations for Classical Mechanics, vol. 15. Springer, Cham (2012)
17. Hrdina, J., Návrat, A., Vašík, P.: Geometric algebra for conics. Adv. Appl. Clifford Algebras **28**, 1–21 (2018)
18. Kirillov, A.A.: Elements of the Theory of Representations. Springer, Berlin Heidelberg (1976)
19. Perwass, C.: Geometric Algebra with Applications in Engineering, Geometry and Computing, vol. 4. Springer, Cham (2009)
20. Richter-Gebert, J.: Perspectives on projective geometry (2011)
21. Ruhe, D., Gupta, J.K., Keninck, S.D., Welling, M., Brandstetter, J.: Geometric clifford algebra networks. CoRR abs/2302.06594 (2023)

A Multi-dimensional Unified Concavity and Convexity Detection Method Based on Geometric Algebra

Jiyi Zhang[1,2,3,4], Tianzi Wei[5], Ruitong Liu[1], Fan Yang[1,2,3(✉)], Yingying Wei[1], and Jingyu Wang[1]

[1] School of Geographical Science, Nantong University, Nantong 226019, China
yhlx125@ntu.edu.cn
[2] Key Laboratory of Spatial Information Technology Spatial Information Technology R&D and Application, Nantong 226019, China
[3] Jiangsu Yangtze River Economic Belt Research Institute, Nantong 226019, China
[4] School of Geographic Information and Tourism, Chuzhou University, Chuzhou 239000, China
[5] Business School, Nantong Institute of Technology, Nantong 226002, China

Abstract. The detection of concavity and convexity of vertices and edges of three-dimensional (3D) geometric objects is a classic problem in the field of computer graphics. As the foundation of other related graphics algorithms and operations, scholars have proposed many algorithms for determining the concavity and convexity of vertices and edges. However, existing concavity and convexity detection algorithms mainly focus on vertices and not on concavity and convexity detection methods for edges of 3D geometric objects. Furthermore, existing algorithms often require different detection methods when dealing with two-dimensional (2D) planar geometric objects and 3D spatial geometric objects. This means that the algorithm structure of those algorithms becomes very complex when dealing with concavity and convexity judgments involving both planar polygon vertices and 3D geometric object edges. To solve the above problems, this paper proposes a multi-dimensional unified concave convex detection algorithm framework for geometric objects taking advantage of geometric algebra in multi-dimensional unified expression and calculation. The method proposed in this article can not only achieve concavity and convexity detection of planar polygon vertices and 3D geometric object vertices based on unified rules, but also further achieve concavity and convexity detection of 3D geometric object edges on this basis. By unifying the framework and detection rules of different dimensional geometric object concavity detection algorithms, the complexity of synchronous detection algorithms for planar polygon vertices and 3D geometric object vertices and edges concavity can be effectively simplified.

Keywords: concavity-convexity detection · geometric algebra · outer product · three-dimensional objects · multi-dimensional unified

B. Sheng et al. (Eds.): CGI 2023, LNCS 14498, pp. 188–199, 2024.
https://doi.org/10.1007/978-3-031-50078-7_15

1 Introduction

The detection algorithm of concavity and convexity of 3D space objects is the basis of many computer graphics algorithms [1–9]. Related algorithms for concavity-convexity detection are widely used in fields such as convex hulls method [10], angle method [11], left-right-point method [12], vector area method [13], the cross product method [14], slope method [15] and extremity vertices sequence methods [16]. Among them, the angle method, left and right point method, and vector area method utilize the inherent properties of simple polygons for algorithm design, while the cross product method, ray method, slope method, and pole order method greatly reduce the complexity of the algorithm in determining the convexity of simple polygons at fixed points. The existing research on vertex concavity detection algorithms mainly focuses on the field of two-dimensional polygons, lacking research on methods for detecting vertex concavity and concavity of 3D polyhedron and 3D object edges (Fig. 1). In recent years, the rapid development of virtual simulation reality, real 3D modeling, 3D printing and other technologies has greatly expanded the application scope of 3D modeling and 3D spatial analysis technology. As a fundamental algorithm in 3D spatial graphics, the detection of concavity and convexity of 3D spatial entities plays an extremely important supporting role in improving the performance of algorithms such as 3D spatial modeling, analysis, and visual rendering.

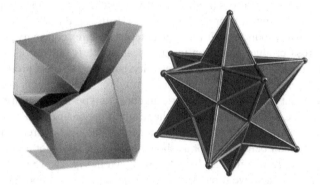

Fig. 1. Concave Convexity of Objects in 3D Space.

Most existing vertex concavity and convexity detection algorithms are based on Euclidean geometry design, which is limited by itself. When dealing with geometric relationships of objects with different dimensions, different calculation methods are often required. When dealing with the detection of concavity and convexity of 3D spatial objects, these methods based on Euclidean geometry can lead to a sharp increase in algorithm complexity. Although optimization methods can improve the efficiency of algorithm operation, the complex algorithm structure causes a lot of invariance in algorithm maintenance.

In recent years, the wide application of geometric algebra in computer graphics [17–23], GIS 3D modeling [24–31], and other fields has fully proved its advantages over traditional linear algebra and Euclidean geometry. The advantages of geometric algebra in performing related algebraic operations based on spatial object representation, handling geometric problems in an algebraic manner, and unifying the expression and operation rules of different dimensional spaces make the geometric calculation process more intuitive and concise. This provides a foundation of mathematics for the unified expression of 3D complex entities and spatial analysis operations.

In previous research explored vertex concavity and convexity detection methods applicable to geometric objects of different dimensions using the properties of outer product operations in geometric algebra. A unified framework for vertex concavity and convexity detection algorithm applicable to geometric objects of different dimensions has been proposed. The above research solves the problems faced by current vertex concavity detection algorithms based on Euclidean geometry, such as the lack of 3D vertex concavity detection and complex algorithm structure.

On the basis of existing research, this article summarizes the previous research results. At the same time, based on the previous research results, a method for detecting the concavity and convexity of 3D spatial object edges was further explored. This study further expands the application of geometric algebra in the field of 3D computer graphics.

2 Basic Idea

Among numerous polygon vertex concavity and convexity detection algorithms based on Euclidean geometry, the cross product algorithm is one of the most commonly used algorithms. The core of the cross product algorithm is to use the directional characteristics contained in the cross product result vector to determine vertex concavity and convexity. However, the cross product operation in Euclidean space is only applicable between vectors. This means that vertex concavity detection based on the cross product method is only applicable to planar polygons and cannot be used for 3D object concavity detection.

The outer product operation in geometric algebra is a type of operation extending the cross product [32]. Like the cross product, the result of the outer product operation also has directionality, which can be used to determine the topological direction. But unlike the cross product result being a vector as shown in Fig. 2a, the outer product operation between two vectors results in a 2D bivector as shown in Fig. 2b. The outer product in geometric algebra can achieve dimensional enhancement. More importantly, the outer product operation in geometric algebra can be applied to all dimensional objects and has a unified and clear geometric meaning. The above characteristics of outer product operation provide an ideal operational tool for conducting multidimensional unified spatial object concavity and convexity judgment.

The characteristic of outer product operation is the main theoretical basis for the multidimensional unified object concavity and convexity judgment algorithm constructed in this article. We constructed a detection method for the inner and outer spaces of objects using the directionality of the outer product operation results. On this basis, the topological relationship features between convex objects and adjacent objects, as well as the topological relationship features between concave objects and adjacent objects, are studied separately. By analyzing the differences between the two topological relationships mentioned above, a detection method suitable for the concavity and convexity of objects with different dimensions has been proposed in this paper.

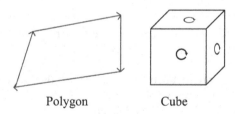

Fig. 2. Schematic diagrams of the cross product (a) and outer product (b) operation results (the blue objects are the results of calculation). (Color figure online)

3 Method for Concavity and Convexity Detection

3.1 Directionality of Spatial Objects

The directionality of a spatial object is reflected by the order of its topological boundary features. This means that the boundary features of a spatial object should have the same topological order. For example, the four edges of the polygon in Fig. 3 should be connected end-to-end to form a closed loop, while meeting the right-hand rule. For 3D objects, the direction of all the bounding surfaces that make up the body should follow the same rule (for example, in Fig. 3, all the bounding surface directions of the cube comply with the right-hand rule).

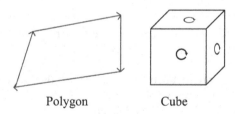

Polygon   Cube

Fig. 3. Schematic diagram of spatial object directionality.

3.2 Internal and External Spatial Detection of Geometric Objects

It is well known from geometric algebra that the outer product operation in geometric algebra has directionality. We can use the property of outer product to determine the internal and external spaces of an object. Taking the polygon in Fig. 4 as an example, the coordinates of points in the figure are expressed in conformal geometric algebra space with five basis vectors knowing as e_1, e_2, e_3, e_0, e_∞. And the coordinates of vertices in the figure are p1(-0.47, -0.50, 1.92, 1.00, 2.08), p2(-0.44, -1.82, -0.22, 1.00, 1.77), p3(0.58, 0.81, -2.07, 1.00, 2.64), p4(0.67, 2.53, -0.07, 1.00, 3.42), p5(0.28, 0.90, -0.25, 1.00, 0.48) and point p6(-1.05, -2.33, 2.31, 1.00, 5.92).

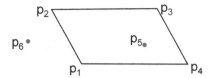

Fig. 4. Schematic diagram of the interior and exterior space of a polygon.

According to the outer product expression of lines in conformal geometric algebra, we can obtain the outer product expression of the four edges of polygon in Fig. 4 as follows.

$$l_{p_1p_2} = p_1{}^\wedge p_2{}^\wedge e_\infty$$
$$= 0.63 * e_1{}^\wedge e_2{}^\wedge e_\infty + 0.94 * e_1{}^\wedge e_3{}^\wedge e_\infty + 3.60 * e_2{}^\wedge e_3{}^\wedge e_\infty$$
$$- 0.03 * e1{}^\wedge e_0{}^\wedge e_\infty + 1.32 * e_2{}^\wedge e_0{}^\wedge e_\infty + 2.14 * e_3{}^\wedge e_0{}^\wedge e_\infty$$

$$l_{p_2p_3} = p_2{}^\wedge p_3{}^\wedge e_\infty$$
$$= 0.69 * e_1{}^\wedge e_2{}^\wedge e_\infty + 1.03 * e_1{}^\wedge e_3{}^\wedge e_\infty + 3.93 * e_2{}^\wedge e_3{}^\wedge e_\infty$$
$$- 1.01 * e1{}^\wedge e_0{}^\wedge e_\infty - 2.62 * e_2{}^\wedge e_0{}^\wedge e_\infty + 1.86 * e_3{}^\wedge e_0{}^\wedge e_\infty$$

$$l_{p_3p_4} = p_3{}^\wedge p_4{}^\wedge e_\infty$$
$$= 0.91 * e_1{}^\wedge e_2{}^\wedge e_\infty + 1.35 * e_1{}^\wedge e_3{}^\wedge e_\infty + 5.18 * e_2{}^\wedge e_3{}^\wedge e_\infty$$
$$- 0.10 * e1{}^\wedge e_0{}^\wedge e_\infty - 1.72 * e_2{}^\wedge e_0{}^\wedge e_\infty - 2.00 * e_3{}^\wedge e_0{}^\wedge e_\infty$$

$$l_{p_4p_1} = p_4{}^\wedge p_1{}^\wedge e_\infty$$
$$= 0.85 * e_1{}^\wedge e_2{}^\wedge e_\infty + 1.26 * e_1{}^\wedge e_3{}^\wedge e_\infty + 4.83 * e_2{}^\wedge e_3{}^\wedge e_\infty$$
$$+ 1.14 * e1{}^\wedge e_0{}^\wedge e_\infty + 3.02 * e_2{}^\wedge e_0{}^\wedge e_\infty - 1.99 * e_3{}^\wedge e_0{}^\wedge e_\infty$$

We calculate the outer product between point p5 and the four edges of the polygon, as well as the outer product between point p6 and the four edges of the polygon in Fig. 4. The following calculation results can be obtained.

$$p_5{}^\wedge l_{p_1p_2} = 1.03 * e_1{}^\wedge e_2{}^\wedge e_0{}^\wedge e_\infty + 1.53 * e_1{}^\wedge e_3{}^\wedge e_0{}^\wedge e_\infty + 5.86 * e_2{}^\wedge e_3{}^\wedge e_0{}^\wedge e_\infty + 0$$
$$* e_1{}^\wedge e_2{}^\wedge e_3{}^\wedge e_\infty$$

$$p_5{}^\wedge l_{p_2p_3} = 0.87 * e_1{}^\wedge e_2{}^\wedge e_0{}^\wedge e_\infty + 1.29 * e_1{}^\wedge e_3{}^\wedge e_0{}^\wedge e_\infty + 4.94 * e_2{}^\wedge e_3{}^\wedge e_0{}^\wedge e_\infty + 0$$
$$* e_1{}^\wedge e_2{}^\wedge e_3{}^\wedge e_\infty$$

$$p_5{}^\wedge l_{p_3p_4} = 0.52 * e_1{}^\wedge e_2{}^\wedge e_0{}^\wedge e_\infty + 0.77 * e_1{}^\wedge e_3{}^\wedge e_0{}^\wedge e_\infty + 2.94 * e_2{}^\wedge e_3{}^\wedge e_0{}^\wedge e_\infty + 0$$
$$* e_1{}^\wedge e_2{}^\wedge e_3{}^\wedge e_\infty$$

$$p_5{}^\wedge l_{p_4p_1} = 0.67 * e_1{}^\wedge e_2{}^\wedge e_0{}^\wedge e_\infty + 0.99 * e_1{}^\wedge e_3{}^\wedge e_0{}^\wedge e_\infty + 3.80 * e_2{}^\wedge e_3{}^\wedge e_0{}^\wedge e_\infty + 0$$
$$* e_1{}^\wedge e_2{}^\wedge e_3{}^\wedge e_\infty$$

$$p_6{}^\wedge l_{p_1p_2} = -0.83 * e_1{}^\wedge e_2{}^\wedge e_0{}^\wedge e_\infty - 1.23 * e_1{}^\wedge e_3{}^\wedge e_0{}^\wedge e_\infty - 4.42 * e_2{}^\wedge e_3{}^\wedge e_0{}^\wedge e_\infty$$
$$- 0.13 * e_1{}^\wedge e_2{}^\wedge e_3{}^\wedge e_\infty$$

$$p_6 \wedge l_{p_1p_2} = 1.09 * e_1 \wedge e_2 \wedge e_0 \wedge e_\infty + 1.41 * e_1 \wedge e_3 \wedge e_0 \wedge e_\infty + 5.66 * e_2 \wedge e_3 \wedge e_0 \wedge e_\infty$$
$$-0.14 * e_1 \wedge e_2 \wedge e_3 \wedge e_\infty$$

$$p_6 \wedge l_{p_3p_4} = 2.50 * e_1 \wedge e_2 \wedge e_0 \wedge e_\infty + 3.67 * e_1 \wedge e_3 \wedge e_0 \wedge e_\infty + 13.81 * e_2 \wedge e_3 \wedge e_0 \wedge e_\infty$$
$$-0.18 * e_1 \wedge e_2 \wedge e_3 \wedge e_\infty$$

$$p_6 \wedge l_{p_4p_1} = 0.33 * e_1 \wedge e_2 \wedge e_0 \wedge e_\infty + 0.72 * e_1 \wedge e_3 \wedge e_0 \wedge e_\infty + 2.49 * e_2 \wedge e_3 \wedge e_0 \wedge e_\infty$$
$$-0.17 * e_1 \wedge e_2 \wedge e_3 \wedge e_\infty$$

Obviously, to determine whether a point is inside a polygon, we only need to calculate the outer product of the modified point and the four edges of the polygon. And then, based on the outer product result, make the following judgment: If the coefficient symbols of the corresponding dimensional blade in the calculation results are completely consistent; then this point is located inside the polygon, otherwise it is located outside the polygon. The method for determining the internal and external spaces of a polyhedron is exactly the same as for polygons. The only difference is calculating the outer product of the fixed point and the faces of the polyhedron.

3.3 Concave-Convexity Detection for Vertices

A vertex concavity convex algorithm based on outer product operation is proposed in this paper. This algorithm can be used to simultaneously determine the vertex concavity and convexity of planar polygons and polyhedron in 3D space. The core idea of the algorithm is to carry out the outer product between the point to be detected and the boundaries of geometric objects. The difference among coefficient symbols in the results of above outer product is used to determine the concavity and convexity of the vertex. The specific framework of the algorithm is shown in Fig. 5. The first part of the algorithm is to determine the coefficient symbol in the result of outer product between the internal points of the geometric object and the boundaries of the same geometric object. And then record all end nodes (such as point p6 and p8 in Fig. 6a, or point p6, p8 and p10 in Fig. 6b) connected to the vertex to be determined (such as point p7 in Fig. 6a, or point p7 in Fig. 6b). The third step is to generate new judgment objects with the same dimensions with current geometric object's boundaries using the outer product of these end nodes (such as the yellow segment p6p8 in Fig. 6a, or the yellow triangle p6p8p10 in Fig. 6b). The fourth step is to calculate the outer product between the vertex to be detected and the newly generated geometric object. Finally, the concavity and convexity of vertices are determined by comparing the same blade coefficient symbols in the two outer product results obtained in the first and fourth steps.

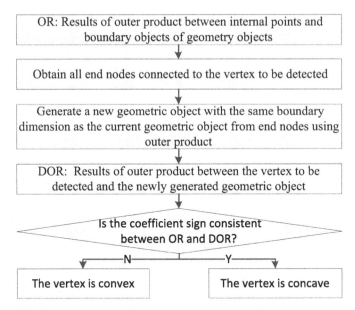

Fig. 5. Algorithm flow for detecting vertex concavity and convexity.

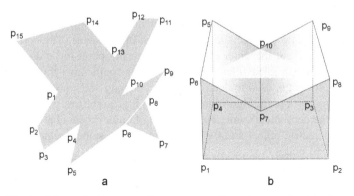

Fig. 6. Schematic diagrams of vertex concavity and convexity detection.

3.4 Concave-Convexity Detection for Edges

The convexity of edges in three-dimensional space is shown in Fig. 6b, the edge p_7p_{10} is concave while the other edges are convex. The detection of concavity and convexity of 3D object's edge is based on the concavity and convexity detection results of vertexes composing the edge. The concavity and convexity detection results of the two vertices that make up the edge is used to determine the concavity and convexity of the edge. The concavity and convexity detection method for edges includes the following two main steps:

(1) Firstly, detect the concavity and convexity of the two vertices that make up the edge to be detected (such as edge p_6p_7 and edge p_7p_{10} in Fig. 6b).

(2) Secondly, Based on the detection results of vertex concavity and convexity, determine the concavity and convexity of edges using the following rules: If both vertices that make up an edge are concave points (such as point p7 and p10 in Fig. 6b, then the edge is concave (like edge p7p10 in Fig. 6b), otherwise, the edge is convex (such as edge p6p7 in Fig. 6b with convex point p6 and concave point p7).

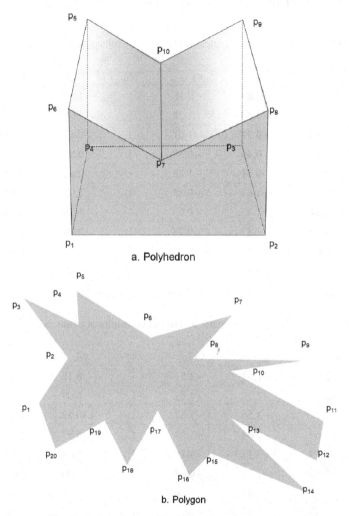

a. Polyhedron

b. Polygon

Fig. 7. Polyhedron and Polygon Case Test Graphics.

4   Case study

This article takes the polyhedron and polygon in Fig. 7 as an example to validate the concavity and convexity detection method for vertices and edges proposed in the article. The vertex conformal coordinates as well as vertex concavity detection results for polyhedron and polygons in Fig. 7 can be found in Tables 1 and 2. And the concavity and convexity detection results of each edge of the polyhedron are shown in Table 3.

Table 1. Conformal coordinates and detection results of points in Fig. 7a.

Point	e_1	e_2	e_3	e_0	e_∞	Result
p_1	1.57	−0.84	−0.18	1	1.61	convex
p_2	0.79	−1.03	1.28	1	1.66	convex
p_3	0.19	0.31	1.01	1	0.57	convex
p_4	1.1	0.46	−0.52	1	0.85	convex
p_5	−0.15	−0.31	−1.23	1	0.82	convex
p_6	0.73	−1.67	−0.85	1	2.02	convex
p_7	0.71	−1.43	0.03	1	1.28	concave
p_8	−0.16	−1.87	0.78	1	2.06	convex
p_9	−1.01	−0.44	0.35	1	0.67	convex
p_{10}	−0.1	−0.11	−0.26	1	0.05	concave

Table 2. Conformal coordinates and detection results of points in Fig. 7b.

Point	e_1	e_2	e_3	e_0	e_∞	Result
p_1	−2.65	−1.73	−2.5	1	8.15	convex
p_2	−2.01	−2.21	−1.81	1	6.09	concave
p_3	−2.2	−3.56	−1.87	1	10.52	convex
p_4	−1.66	−2.64	−1.41	1	5.87	concave
p_5	−1.49	−3.17	−1.19	1	6.84	convex
p_6	−0.8	−1.74	−0.63	1	2.04	concave
p_7	0.43	−1.31	0.56	1	1.11	convex
p_8	−0.35	−0.96	−0.26	1	0.55	concave
p_9	1.16	0.22	1.15	1	1.35	convex

(*continued*)

Table 2. (*continued*)

Point	e_1	e_2	e_3	e_0	e_∞	Result
p_{10}	0.13	−0.35	0.17	1	0.08	concave
P_{11}	1.11	1.52	0.97	1	2.24	convex
p_{12}	0.75	2.18	0.54	1	2.8	convex
p_{13}	−0.18	0.48	−0.23	1	0.16	concave
p_{14}	0.46	2.69	0.2	1	3.75	convex
p_{15}	−0.63	0.92	−0.72	1	0.89	concave
p_{16}	−1.12	1.03	−1.23	1	1.92	convex
p_{17}	−1.15	−0.38	−1.12	1	1.36	concave
p_{18}	−1.88	0.21	−1.92	1	3.63	convex
p_{19}	−1.89	−0.74	−1.83	1	3.75	concave
P_{20}	−2.71	−0.8	−2.65	1	7.49	convex

Table 3. Detection results of edges in figure 7a.

Edge	Result	Edge	Result	Edge	Result
p_1p_2	convex	p_5p_{10}	convex	p_6p_1	convex
p_2p_3	convex	p_7p_6	convex	p_5p_6	convex
p_3p_4	convex	p_8p_7	convex	p_8p_9	convex
p_4p_1	convex	$p_{10}p_9$	convex	p_9p_3	convex
p_4p_5	convex	$p_{10}p_7$	concave	p_2p_8	convex

5   Case study

Based on the directionality of the outer product result of geometric algebra, this paper explores the detection method of topological space of geometric objects based on the outer product result. A multidimensional unified vertex concavity and convexity detection algorithm based on the results of outer product operation is proposed in this paper. Meanwhile, utilizing the concavity and convexity of vertices, a method for detecting the concavity and convexity of polyhedral edges is proposed.

This article summarizes the previous research results on vertex concavity detection and further explores polyhedral edge detection methods based on vertex concavity detection results. Geometric algebra has been introduced into the field of vertex concavity and convexity detection of spatial objects and related topology detection in this paper. The advantages of geometric algebra in calculating geometric relationships of spatial objects can be used for other graphic and topological relationship calculations, including the detection of concave and convex edges of three-dimensional spatial objects. However, this study only utilizes knowledge related to geometric algebra for application research, lacking rigorous mathematical and logical reasoning verification. In the later research, the logical derivation and completeness verification of relevant rules need to be further carried out.

References

1. Zhao, J., Gao, M., Wang, S.: Orientation, convexity-concavity and inclusion test algorithms for polygons. In: International Conference on Information Technology & Computer Science. IEEE Computer Society (2009)
2. Li, W., et al.: A point inclusion test algorithm for simple polygons computational science and its applications. In: Gervasi, O., et al. (eds.) Computational Science and Its Applications. Lecture Notes in Computer Science, pp. 769–775. Springer, Heidelberg (2005). https://doi.org/10.1007/11424758_79
3. Wu, H., et al.: An algebraic algorithm for point inclusion query. Comput. Graph. **24**(4), 517–522 (2000)
4. Li, J., Wang, W., Wu, E.: Point-in-polygon tests by convex decomposition. Comput. Graph. **31**(4), 636–648 (2007)
5. Hormann, K., Agathos, A.: The point in polygon problem for arbitrary polygons. Comput. Geom. Theory Appl. **20**(3), 131–144 (2001)
6. Zhao, J., et al.: An algorithm for determining the orientation and convexity-concavity of simple polygons. In: First International Workshop on Education Technology & Computer Science (2009)
7. Wu, C.: Determining convexo-concave vertices of polygon by topological mapping. J. Comput. Aided Design Comput. Graph. **14**(9), 810–814 (2002)
8. Amato, N.: Approximate convex decomposition of polyhedron. Comput. Aided Geom. Design **25**(7), 503–522 (2008)
9. Lien, J., Amato, N.: Approximate convex decomposition of polygons. Comput. Geom. **35**, 100–123 (2006)
10. Zhou, P.: An algorithm for determining convexo-concave vertices of an arbitrary polygon. J. Softw. **6**(5), 276–279 (1995)
11. Xu, R., Zhang, Z.: An algorithm for rapidly determining the convexity-concavity of the vertices of an arbitrary polygon. J. Huazhong Univ. Sci. Technol. **25**(1), 103–104 (1997)
12. Zhou, P.: Computational Geometry: Algorithm Design and Analysis. Tsinghua University Press, Beijing (2006)
13. Feito, F., et al.: Orientation, simplicity, and inclusion test for planar polygons. Comput. Graph. **19**(4), 55–600 (1995)
14. Jin, W., et al.: A fast algorithm for determining the convexity-concavity of vertices of simple polygon. J. Eng. Graph. **1**, 66–70 (1998)
15. Pang, M., Lu, Z.: An algorithm for rapidly identifying convexo-concave vertices of simple polygon based on comparing the slopes of two adjacent edge vectors. J. Eng. Graph. **3**, 71–77 (2004)
16. Zhao, J., et al.: Orientation and convexity-concavity identification for polygons using extremity vertices sequence. J. Eng. Graph. **1**, 55–59 (2007)
17. Li, H.B.: Invariant Algebras and Geometric Reasoning. World Scientific, Singapore (2008)
18. Li, H., Hestenes, D., Rockwood, A.: Generalized homogeneous coordinates for computational geometry. In: Sommer, G. (ed.) Geometric Computing with Clifford Algebras, pp. 27–59. Springer, Heidelberg (2001). https://doi.org/10.1007/978-3-662-04621-0_2
19. Perwass, C.B.U., Lasenby, J.: A unified description of multiple view geometry. In: Sommer, G. (ed.) Geometric Computing with Clifford Algebras, pp. 337–369. Springer, Heidelberg (2001). https://doi.org/10.1007/978-3-662-04621-0_14

20. Cameron, J., Lasenby, J.: Oriented conformal geometric algebra. In: Proceedings of ICCA7 (2005)
21. Lasenby, J., et al.: A new methodology for computing invariants in computer vision. In: Proceedings of ICPR 96 (1996)
22. Lasenby, J., Fitzgerald, W.J., Lasenby, A., et al.: New geometric methods for computer vision: an application to structure and motion estimation. Int. J. Comput. Vision **3**(26), 191–213 (1998)
23. Penvass, C.: Applications of geometric algebra in computer vision, Ph.D. thesis, Cambridge University (2000)
24. Yuan, L., et al.: A 3D GIS spatial data model based on conformal geometric algebra. Sci. China Ser D-Earth Sci. **54**(1), 101–112 (2011). https://doi.org/10.1007/s11430-010-4130-9
25. Zhang, J., et al.: 3D cadastral data model based on conformal geometry algebra. ISPRS Int. J. Geo-Inf. **5**(2), 20 (2016)
26. Yuan, L.W., et al.: Multidimensional-unified topological relations computation: a hierarchical geometric algebra-based approach. Int. J. Geogr. Inf. Sci. **28**(12), 2435–2455 (2014)
27. Yuan, L., et al.: CAUSTA: Clifford algebra-based unified spatio-temporal analysis. Trans. GIS **14**(s1), 59–83 (2010)
28. Yuan, L., et al.: A Hierarchical tensor-based approach to compressing, updating and querying geospatial data. IEEE Trans. Knowl. Data Eng. **27**(2), 312–325 (2015)
29. Yu, Z., et al.: Change detection for 3D vector data: a CGA-based Delaunay–TIN intersection approach. Int. J. Geogr. Inf. Sci. **29**(12), 1–20 (2015)
30. Luo, W., et al.: A hierarchical representation and computation scheme of arbitrary-dimensional geometrical primitives based on CGA. Adv. Appl. Clifford Algebras **27**(3), 1977–1995 (2017). https://doi.org/10.1007/s00006-016-0697-3
31. Luo, W., et al.: Template-based GIS computation: a geometric algebra approach. Int. J. Geogr. Inf. Sci. **31**(10), 2045–2067 (2017)
32. Yin, P.C., et al.: A vertex concavity-convexity detection method for three-dimensional spatial objects based on geometric algebra. ISPRS Int. J. Geo-Inf. **9**(1), 25 (2020)

Splossoms: Spherical Blossoms

Alyn Rockwood[(⊠)]

Boulder, Boulder County, CO, USA
alyrock@gmail.com

Abstract. This paper provides an overview of *spherical blossoms,* called *splossoms,* and some of its implications.

The *blossom* of a polynomial is a multi-affine function of euclidean space with the same number of variables as the degree of the polynomial. It provides many insights to the polynomial and simplifies methods not otherwise apparent. One example is the de Casteljau algorithm for computing and subdividing a Bezier curve. This report describes a blossom for a parametric de Casteljau-like curve on the sphere, leading to similar insights and simplification of algorithms on the sphere. Two earlier such methods are the well-known SLERP and SQUAD interpolations of points on the sphere. These methods are re-formulated with our new concept, the *splossom,* which plays the role of a blossom in spherical space. Some of its implications are briefly sketched to illustrate its potential.

The splossom itself is neatly described in terms of spinors in Geometric Algebra. This development follows the Geometric Algebra approach and points to considerable further research within its broad vista.

1   Introduction

Position parameters alone are not always adequate to represent object motion. Orientation of the object is often needed, e.g. its heading, pitch, and roll. Representing orientation is central to disciplines such as computer graphics, computer vision, photogrammetry, robotics, CAD/CAM, and extended reality XR, among others. A typical example from computer graphics is the interpolation of keyframe orientations to compute esthetically pleasing results in the motion of an object, not only in terms of position, but also in terms of the changes in its orientation [1,2,4]. In an inverse fashion, 3D computer vision often takes images from an unknown object, captured from unknown positions, then automatically constructs a 3D representation plus camera parameters and their poses [8].

Orientation can be represented succinctly by points on the unit sphere; its motion is typically modeled as interpolating curves on the sphere. Keyframes, for example, are usually given as points on the unit sphere and the path between them is computed as a curve on the sphere that passes through the keyframes.

In euclidean space, interpolation curves are commonly parametric polynomials, e.g., Bezier, B-spline, Hermite, Lagrange, etc. Associated with every polynomial of degree d is a multi-affine function of d variables called the *blossom* [6]. The blossom gives insight and leads to algorithms about the polynomial that

© The Author(s), under exclusive license to Springer Nature Switzerland AG 2024
B. Sheng et al. (Eds.): CGI 2023, LNCS 14498, pp. 200–209, 2024.
https://doi.org/10.1007/978-3-031-50078-7_16

are not nearly as apparent without it. Although a circle cannot be expressed as a polynomial (nor curves on a sphere), there are many analogs to polynomial curves on a sphere. A well known example is the SLERP algorithm for computing curves in the same way the de Casteljau algorithm computes Bezier polynomials [7]. In the Bezier case, iterated linear interpolation is used. In SLERP, one iterates on arcs of great circles. This leads to the question:- does there exist a blossom for curves on the sphere? We answer this in the affirmative, defining the spherical blossom, the *splossom*, and show some of the directions this leads.

We choose Geometric Algebra (GA) as the language of convenience for defining the splossom. In particular, the concepts of *spinor* and *rotor* are foundational. This paper assumes a modicum of familiarity to GA. We recommend [3,5] as background material.

This is a preliminary paper; a more detailed version is planned.

2   The Blossom

For every polynomial P of degree d, there exists a multi-affine function Bl_P with d variables such that

(1) $\text{Bl}_P(u_1, \dots, u_d) = \text{Bl}_P(\pi(u_1, \dots, u_d))$, where π permutates. (permutation)
(2) $\text{Bl}_P(u, \dots, u) = P(u)$ (diagonal)
(3) $\text{Bl}_P(u_1, \dots \alpha u + \beta v \dots, u_d) = \alpha \text{Bl}_P(u_1, \dots u \dots, u_d) + \beta \text{Bl}_P(u_1, \dots v \dots, u_d)$,
    where α, β are constant and $\alpha + \beta = 1$. (affine).

For example, the blossom for $P(x) = x^3 + 6x^2 - 3x + 3$ is
$\text{Bl}_P(u, v, w) = uvw + 2uv + 2vw + 2uw - u - v - w + 3$.

The reader should check that it satisfies the three properties above. Surprisingly, one rarely uses the blossom per se; it is enough to know that the blossom exists for every polynomial. This existence was proven in [6], which also details many of its ramifications. The blossom extends trivially to parametric polynomials in R^d via its component functions.

The sublime idea behind blossoms is that given d samples of the blossom, one can discover a rich set of algorithms that evaluate, transform bases, embed in higher degree, approximate in lower degree, subdivide, induce continuity between abutting polynomials, and so forth. This is done by simply applying the three properties on the sample points. As an example, we show that the points $\text{Bl}_P(0,0)$, $\text{Bl}_P(0,1)$, and $\text{Bl}_P(1, 1)$ are control points for the Bezier form of a quadratic polynomial P. We do this by evaluating the polynomial at u. In other words, according to the diagonal property (2) we seek $\text{Bl}_P(u, u) = P(u)$ in terms of the given three points. The *blossoming technique* works iteratively, replacing arguments of the points with u (see Fig. 1); therefore from the affine property (3), we find $\text{Bl}_P(u, 0) = (1 - u)\text{Bl}_P(0,0) + u\text{Bl}_P(1,0)$, which is a point along the line segment between $\text{Bl}_P(0,0)$ and $\text{Bl}_P(1,0)$. We do this by replacing the 0 and 1 in the terms on the right with u. Similarly, $\text{Bl}_P(u, 1) = (1 - u)\text{Bl}_P(0,1) + u\text{Bl}_P(1,1)$. In the final step we obtain $P(u) = \text{Bl}_P(u, u) = (1 - u)\text{Bl}_P(u,0) + u\text{Bl}_P(u,1)$. Notice we have freely permuted parameters for understanding.

The astute observer will recognize the steps from the de Casteljau algorithm for computing the Bezier curve; thus the given points must be Bezier control points. Using the blossom technique we have not only evaluated the polynomial, but regenerated the de Casteljau algorithm.

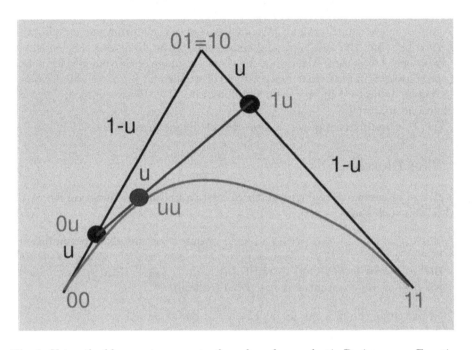

Fig. 1. Using the blossom to compute the value of a quadratic Bezier curve. Function values are abbreviated by just the parameter values

If we had chosen arguments of the points in a shifted sequence, *viz.* $\mathrm{Bl}_P(0, 1)$, $\mathrm{Bl}_P(1, 2)$, and $\mathrm{Bl}_P(2, 3)$, then the method would have yielded the well-known de Boor algorithm for B-splines and evaluated the quadratic B-spline. Extensions to higher degrees are straightforward. There is no longer any need to memorize the sundry algorithms for polynomials, the blossom technique will recreate them!

3   Spinors, Rotors and Spirals

A good basic introduction to the GA that follows can be found in [5, Sec 2.7.1]. For vectors a, b, the geometric product in GA defines a bivector $S = a \wedge b$. The familiar sandwich operation of S and its reverse $S^\sim$

$$v' = SvS^\sim \tag{1}$$

spins a vector v about the vector dual IS of S, which is the normal of the bivector S, where I is the pseudoscalar of the space.

It is often desirable in (1) to preserve the vector length, that is keep $|v'| = |v|$. It is sufficient that vectors a, b are unit length to ensure this. In this case we call S a *rotor*, denote it as $R = ab$, then

$$u' = RvR^{\sim} \tag{2}$$

preserves length. Formula (2) yields a pure rotation, whereas (1) might scale the vector as well as rotate. We derive a rotor by dividing through with the lengths, thus $R = \frac{1}{|a||b|}ab$. Furthermore, we can unitize the bivector part of R

$$R = a \bullet b/|a||b| + \frac{1}{|a||b|\sin\theta}a \wedge b, \tag{3}$$

where θ is the angle between a and b. (It is shown that $(a \wedge b)^2 = -\sin\theta$ in [5, Sec 2.7]).

Therefore, we write

$$R = \cos\theta - B\sin\theta = e^{-B\theta/2}, \tag{4}$$

where $B = \frac{a \wedge b}{|a||b|\sin\theta}$. We rewrite (2) as

$$u' = e^{-B\theta/2}ve^{B\theta/2}. \tag{5}$$

Hestenes [3, pp. 58–60] shows that quaternions (used by SLERP [7]) are a special case of spinors, the even subalgebra of GA over 3D vectors. Hestenes also shows that the spinor can be decomposed into 1) a rotation and 2) a linear function of the angle θ. Case 1) connects SLERP-like interpolation schemes with GA. These routines are analogs to the affine iterative routines for polynomials such as de Casteljau, or de Boor algorithms [4]. In SLERP one iterates with the great circle on the sphere instead of line segments in euclidean space as with de Casteljau. GA has the advantage that it works in any dimension, and being coordinate free, is more succinct and mathematically expressible without the need for extensive translation between other mathematical forms such as Euler angles or Euler matrices [3, pp. 289].

In the second case 2), it is readily apparent that the GA spinor on the bivector plane in polar coordinates is equivalent to the *Archimedean spiral* created by a point moving at constant speed along a line that rotates with constant angular velocity (Fig. 2). In polar coordinates (r, θ) it is described by

$$r = p + q^*\theta \tag{6}$$

with scalars p and q. Changing the parameter p moves the centerpoint outward from the origin (positive p on $\theta = 0$ and negative p on $\theta = \pi$), while q controls the distance between loops. In 3D, the spiral is best represented as a rotation/dilation, i.e., a spinor in geometric algebra:

$$A(\theta) = (1 + \text{off } \theta)e^{-B\theta/2} \text{ a } e^{B\theta/2}, \tag{7}$$

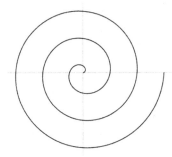

Fig. 2. Archimedean spiral

where $(1 + \textit{off}\ \theta)$ is the dilation which grows linearly with θ for constant *off*. The rest of Formula (7) is the familiar sandwich form of a rotation in the bivector plane B (4). Hence, $A(\theta)$ is an arc of the Archimedean spiral lying in the bivector plane B, starting at a and subtending an angle θ.

The absolute value $|A(\theta)|$ is affine invariant, symmetric and diagonally equivalent. The rotor part of (7) is unitary so it disappears in the norm, leaving only the linear scale function. Formula (7) is the lynchpin; it is our definition for the *splossom*, i.e., the blossom of the spherical curve.

4   The Splossom

As in Fig. 3, a de Casteljau-like iteration for (1) is formed by spinning a point a on the control frame at parameter θ, and then spinning that point with respect to another leg of the control frame by a parameter ϕ. From a blossom/splossom point of view, this is evaluating the multi-affine function at the two parameters. From a formulaic point of view it looks like

$$F(\theta,\ \phi) = (1 + \textit{off}\ \phi)\ (1 + \textit{off}\ \theta)\ e^{-B2\phi/2}(e^{-B01\theta/2}\ a\ e^{B01\theta/2}\ )e^{B2\phi/2}, \qquad (8)$$

where $e^{-B2\phi/2}$ is the spinor from $e^{-B01\theta/2}$ to $e^{-B10\theta/2}$. It is like the SQUAD method [9], except that instead of unit quaternions, we use non-unitary spinors. Think of $e^{-B2\phi/2}$ as the second iterate in the SQUAD algorithm, if we were restricted to 3D and to quaternions. The splossom $|F(\theta,\ \phi)\ |$ satisfies our conditions for a blossom. This is a key point.

The control points for the curve in Fig. 3 are $(1,0,0)$, $(0,1,0)$ and $(-1,0,0)$. The curved edge seen on the left is the curve lying on the sphere. Figure 4 shows two more views of its splossom.

The splossom is a pencil, i.e., a parametrized family of spinor curves. (Archimedean spiral arcs in the corresponding bivector planes). The intersection of the splossom with the unit sphere is the spinor "polynomial." It is the left hand envelope in Fig. 3. We call it the *spolynomial*. It is a designable curve which we propose for our applications.

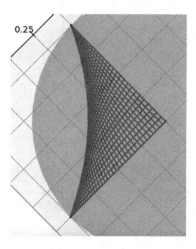

Fig. 3. The splossom

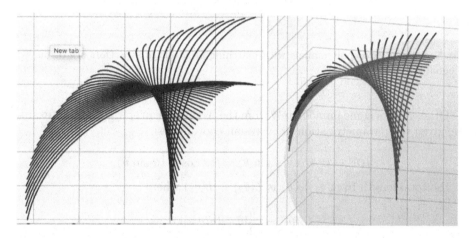

Fig. 4. Two views of the pencil of spirals defining the splossom.

5   Some Implications

The range of implications will be expanded later in a full report, but several consequences are worth noting here. The first is that, as with Bezier curves, Bezier spolynomials can be joined at endpoints if the ending bivector of the first curve has the same orientation as the beginning bivector of the second curve, and they match at end/beginning points. The result of this is the spline in Fig. 5. The proof follows by use of the blossom principles. Other proofs and algorithms are anticipated akin to the blossom for polynomials, such as conversions between bases.

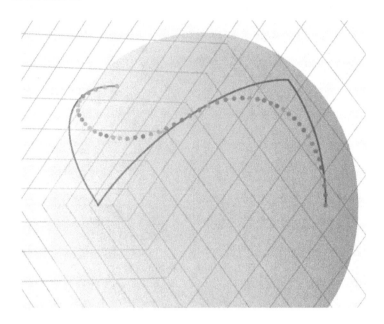

Fig. 5. Splining two spolynomials with matching great circle legs. Dots are displayed at equal parameter steps

Other results come immediately from the Archimedean spiral; thus, for example, given the parametrization in cartesian coordinates:

$$f(\theta) = (r \cos \theta, r \sin \theta) = (b\theta \cos \theta, b\theta \sin \theta),$$

the total length from θ_1 to θ_2 is $L(\theta_2) - L(\theta_1)$ where

$$L(\theta) = \frac{b}{2}[\theta + ln(\theta+)].$$

The curvature is given by

$$\kappa = \frac{\theta^2 + 2}{b \, (\theta^2 + 1)^{\frac{3}{2}}}.$$

In shape design, it is the manifold swept out by the function that is usually important, e.g. two curves that meet with *tangent continuity* (G^1 continuity) may be sufficient. The more restrictive *parameter continuity* (C^1 continuity) is often unneeded. Applications that use orientation paths are, however, notably dependent on parametrization. Following an animation path can be quite distracting if there is a sudden jump in viewpoint speed. Similarly, discontinuous rotational speed of a robot arm is physically impossible to achieve. The SQUAD approach of [9] was an early attempt to achieve C^1 continuity of SLERP splines on the sphere. It required inserting extra control points that had no design purpose and made subsequent modification awkward. A great deal of research has focused on this problem, much of it looking at post-processing optimization approaches (see [8] and its references). The splossom approach offers a new tool for this problem.

Figure 6 shows the dotted sploynomial curve of Fig. 3 from a different view. The boundary curves of its splossom are shown in black and gray. Spiral arcs for one parameter go from the left black curve to the right gray curve. Similarly, the gray/black curves are the boundaries of the arc in the other parameter. Surprisingly, the manifold of the spolynomial is the same regardless of the number chosen for the offset off in (8). Note that the dots are from the same curve which represents the intersection of the splossom arcs with the sphere. It is less mysterious when one thinks of the splossom as measuring distance to the sphere in a linear fashion with respect to angle θ.

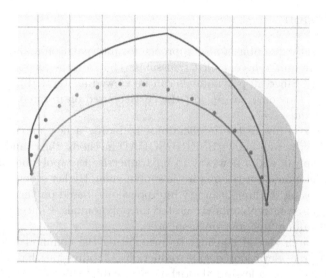

Fig. 6. Dots are spolynomial parameter steps. Splossom boundaries are solid.

Although changing the offset does not change the manifold of the spolynomial, it does change the parameterization. The black and gray pairs of points were produced at the same parameter steps respectively, though they differ in position on the curve in Fig. 7. It shows two instances of differing offsets producing the same spolynomial manifold, but differing parameterizations. This attribute of blossoming can be used to match parametrizations e.g., C^1 continuity, at endpoints among other possibilities.

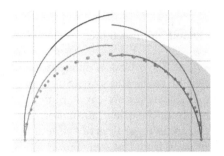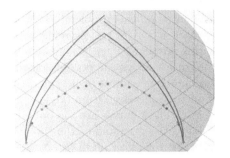

Fig. 7. Two views of the same spolynomial with different parameterizations based on different offsets for the splossom.

6   Conclusion

This report briefly describes a new approach for interpolation and design of orientations on the unit sphere, called *splossoms*. They are the analog to blossoms for polynomials. Since all polynomials can be viewed as iterated linear interpolation based on blossoms, we suggest the curves based on iterated splossoms be called *spolynomials*.

We allude to a few of the implications, including a new and more general way to conceive the well-known SLERP/SQUAD methods, the connection to the Archimedean spiral, and a new way to reparametrize the spolynomial. We have shown the development for the quadratic spolynomial. Higher order spolynomials follow from nesting Archimedean arc interpolations, based on the order, in the same way as linear interpolants are nested for polynomials. Conceptually this is creating multi-affine functions on n-spheres.

Future research should consider re-formulating the common blossom algorithms for degree elevation, degree reductions, subdivision, basis conversion knot insertion, etc. as splossom algorithms. Extending this work to spolynomial splines with controllable parametrizations is of particular interest.

The conformal geometric algebra [5] linearizes conformal space and is, therefore, an obvious candidate to explore the blossoming technique, which might then allow for polynomial-like descriptions of hyper-spherical and hyper-planar curves and splines.

Finally, we note that as the control points get close to each other, i.e., the size of the splossom gets smaller compared to the sphere, the shape of the splossom approaches that of a blossom and the spolynomial approaches the polynomial. There is a Lie group/Lie algebra relationship that should be investigated.

We anticipate a collection of papers that include a rigorous development for all algorithms and degrees, and a broader set of applications.

References

1. Barr, A.H., Currin, B., Gabriel, S., Hughes, J.F.: Smooth interpolation of orientations with angular velocity constraints using quaternions. SIGGRAPH Comput. Graph. **26**(2), 313–320 (1992)
2. Duff, T.: Splines in animation and modeling. State of the Art in Image Synthesis (SIGGRAPH'86 Course Notes No. 15, Dallas, TX) (1986)
3. Hestenes, D.: New Foundations for Classical Mechanics. D. Reidel Publishing (1986)
4. Hughes, J.F., et al.: Computer Graphics: Principles and Practice. The Systems Programming Series. Addison-Wesley (2014)
5. Lasenby, A., Doran, C.: Geometric Algebra for Physicists. Cambridge University Press, Cambridge (2013)
6. Ramshaw, L.: Blossoming: a connect-the-dots approach to splines. Technical report, Digital Research Center, Palo alto, CA (1987)
7. Shoemake, K.: Animating rotation with quaternion curves. SIGGRAPH Comput. Graph. **19**(3), 245–254 (1985)
8. Terzakis, G., Lourakis, M., Ait-Boudaoud, D.: Modified Rodrigues parameters: an efficient representation of orientation in 3D vision and graphics. J. Math. Imaging Vis. **60**, 422–442 (2018). https://doi.org/10.1007/s10851-017-0765-x
9. Dam, E.B., Koch, M., Lillholm, M.: Quaternions, Interpolation and Animation, vol. 2. Citeseer (1998)

A Hybrid Supervised Fusion Deep Learning Framework for Microscope Multi-Focus Images

Qiuhui Yang[1,2], Hao Chen[3], Mingfeng Jiang[4], Mingwei Wang[5], Jiong Zhang[6,7], Yue Sun[1], and Tao Tan[1(✉)]

[1] School of Faculty of Applied Sciences, Macao Polytechnic University, Macao, China
p2209432@mpu.edu.mo, taotanjs@gmail.com

[2] Guangxi Key Laboratory of Machine Vision and Intelligent Control, Wuzhou University, Wuzhou, China

[3] Jiangsu JITRI Sioux Technologies Co., Ltd., Suzhou, China

[4] School of Computer Sciences and Technology, Zhejiang Sci-Tech University, Hangzhou, Zhejiang, China
m.jiang@zstu.edu.cn

[5] Department of Cardiovascular Medicine, Affiliated Hospital of Hangzhou Normal University, Clinical School of Medicine, Hangzhou Normal University, Hangzhou Institute of Cardiovascular Diseases, Hangzhou, China

[6] Cixi Institute of Biomedical Engineering, Ningbo Institute of Materials Technology and Engineering, Chinese Academy of Sciences, Ningbo, China

[7] The Affiliated Ningbo Eye Hospital of Wenzhou Medical University, Ningbo, China

Abstract. The quality of multi-focus microscopic image fusion hinges upon the precision of the image registration technology. However, algorithms for registration tailored specifically for multifocal microscopic images are lacking. Due to the presence of fuzzy regions and weak textures of multi-focus microscope images, the registration of patches is suboptimal. For these problems, this paper formulates a hybrid supervised deep learning model. It can improve the accuracy of registration and fusion. The generalization ability of the model to the actual deformation field enhance by the artificial deformation field. A step of patch movement simulation is employed to blur the multi-focus microscopic images and make synthetic flow, thus emulating distinct fuzzy regions in the two images to be registered, consequently enhancing the model's generalization ability. The experiments demonstrate that our proposed approach is superior to the existing registration algorithms and improves the accuracy of image fusion.

Keywords: Multi-focus microscope images · Supervised registration · Fusion

1 Introduction

In biology and medicine, microscopic analysis often provides sample information. However, conventional optical microscopes possess a limited depth of field, resulting in taking clear images on a single focal plane solely. For slightly larger or three-dimensional samples, achieving distinct single-image imaging or extracting three-dimensional structural

---

Q. Yang and H. Chen—Co-first author.

B. Sheng et al. (Eds.): CGI 2023, LNCS 14498, pp. 210–221, 2024.
https://doi.org/10.1007/978-3-031-50078-7_17

information presents difficulties. Multi-focus image fusion technology synthesizes a range of images with different focal planes to obtain a full-depth image that increases the efficiency of medical personnel.

The accuracy of image registration is closely related to the results of multifocal image fusion. Inefficient registration of image sequences may lead to the introduction of substantial artifacts in fusion results. Currently, most algorithms researching multifocal image fusion assume that the source image sequences are aligned and that the in-focus regions of the source images have the same magnification. However, in practical application scenarios, some surgical microscopes are operated by surgeons, and there may be significant differences in translation, rotation, viewing angle, and magnification between captured images. Therefore, image registration is a necessary step in image fusion. Typically, every pixel must transform into the reference image's spatial coordinate system according to a non-linear mapping relationship for the registration method to function, that is, to construct the deformation field between images. Achieving precise simulation of the practical mapping relationship between image sequences is challenging. For example, microscope images have the characteristics that the texture features are not obvious, which can easily lead to a high mismatch rate.

In order to solve the above problems, this paper advances a comprehensive chain pipeline for fusion based on the registration process utilizing hybrid supervision methods. The main work has the following aspects: (1) In the registration model of the framework, a hybrid supervise method is employed to improve registration accuracy. The artificial deformation field is used as the ground truth in supervised learning to assist the registration model optimization parameters. (2) According to the characteristics of the multi-focus microscopic images, the artificial generation of the deformation field and Gaussian blur data processing methods are carried out to improve the generalization ability of the model. (3) By training and testing the model with various types of microscopic images, the model has a wide range of applications. The model can be applied not only to images of biological cells but also to images of objects such as teeth and small electronic components.

2 Related Work

2.1 Image Registration

Image registration is for imaging sequences of the same object having different environmental contexts, devices, or perspectives in quest of corresponding spatial transformation. Depending on the selection of the feature space, image registration techniques can be potentially categorized into region-based [1–4] or feature-based approaches such as Harris, SIFT, SURF and so on [5–12]. If the image quality is low, or there are many repetitive texture features, there remains the possibility of significant mismatches in the matching results.

Deep learning tackles the constraints of traditional registration techniques. There are various techniques, such as deep iterative registration [13], supervised learning, and unsupervised learning. The supervised learning method directly estimates the deformation field by the model and relies on the actual deformation field to refine the transformation parameters and boost learning speed [14, 15]. However, obtaining authentic label information from manual labeling during practical applications poses a challenge for the supervised learning method. The unsupervised learning methods majorly revolve around feature [17, 18] or similarity learning of image data [16].

2.2 Multi-focus Image Fusion

Multi-focus image fusion can execute in various ways, including spatial domain [19], transform domain, and deep learning [22, 23]. The transform domain method converts the image into another feature domain for effective fusion. The Laplace pyramid decomposition, curvelet transform, contourlet transform, discrete wavelet transform, and other fusion algorithms have been proposed by researchers [20, 21]. The deep learning method can thoroughly leverage the strengths of robust learning capability and generalization. Nonetheless, the network fusion capability is confined since only image blocks or image grayscale information utilize for fusion.

3   Method

A comprehensive framework for registration and fusion of multi-focus microscopic images is presented in this paper. The moving image serves as the image to be registered, while the fixed image acts as the reference image. The moving and fixed image are fed into the hybrid supervised model to realize the registration. And the registered image is eventually fused with the fixed image. The structure of the framework is shown in Fig. 1.

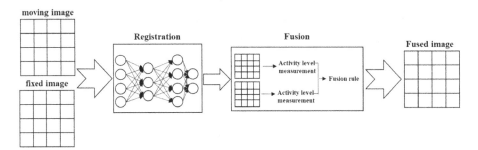

Fig. 1. The structure of the framework

3.1   Dataset and Preprocessing

Dataset. The data presented in this paper are collected using two microscopes, a biological microscope, and a dental surgical microscope. The dataset contains a total of 115 images, 68 of which are acquired using a biological microscope with a magnification of 10–30 times and an image resolution of 1024*768. On the other hand, the remaining images are obtained by the dental surgical microscope, with a magnification of approximately ten times and an image resolution of 1920*1080.

Data Augmentation. In hybrid supervised models, we employ artificially generated deformation fields as labels to help the model parameter optimization. We perform a similarity transformation on the original images to generate their deformation field labels and corresponding fixed images. We randomly generate the translation vector $[t_x, t_y]$ and the rotation angle θ, and use Eq. (1) to transform the image to generate a fixed image.

$$\begin{bmatrix} x' \\ y' \\ 1 \end{bmatrix} = \begin{bmatrix} cos\theta & sin\theta & t_x \\ -sin\theta & cos\theta & t_y \\ 0 & 0 & 1 \end{bmatrix} \begin{bmatrix} x \\ y \\ 1 \end{bmatrix} \tag{1}$$

The deformation vector $[u, v]$ of each pixel is calculated by Eq. (2).

$$\begin{bmatrix} u \\ v \end{bmatrix} = \begin{bmatrix} x' - x \\ y' - y \end{bmatrix} \tag{2}$$

3.2 Deep Learning Registration Algorithm

Dense deformable registration [24] is selected. Consequently, the registration challenge is converted into a pursuit of nonlinear dense deformation field, as explicated by Eq. (3). Herein, f and m respectively denote the fixed and moving image. The function Sim measures the similarity between the fixed image f and the moving image m are transformed by ϕ.

$$arg \; minE(\phi) = \min_{\phi}(Sim(f, m \cdot \phi)) \tag{3}$$

If the deformation field derived through the traditional registration method is used as the ground truth, the model performance is inevitably capped at that of the traditional algorithm. Given that the registration task is an unsupervised task, the establishment of a universally-applicable image similarity measurement standard proves daunting, given the differentiation within different datasets. Thus, in this paper, a hybrid supervision model is posited, maintaining the unsupervised underpinnings characteristic of the registration problem while concurrently providing the network with supplementary information to facilitate superior convergence.

Registration Network. Figure 2 portrays a comprehensive depiction of the proposed methodology. Primarily, in the training stage of the model, in order to better fit the real deformation field, supervised learning needs to preprocess the input image. Subsequently, the CNN module is leveraged to acquire knowledge of the registration function parameter $g_\theta(f, m) = \phi$. The spatial transformation layer [24] prognosticates a deformation field utilizing a grid generator, which is subsequently mapped onto the moving image through interpolation operations through a sampler. This process eventually produces a moved image similar to the fixed image, that is, $m \circ \phi$. The CNN module adopts the structure of the Unet model.

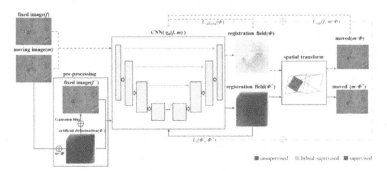

Fig. 2. The registration network of our method

The loss function of the unsupervised network comprises two individual components: the similarity loss (L_{sim}) and the smoothing loss (L_{smooth}), as shown in Eq. (4). The similarity loss gauges the similarity between the moved and fixed image, while the smoothing loss incorporates a regularization loss that serves to optimize the deformation field and ensure the network generates a sufficiently smooth deformation field.

$$L_{us}(f, m, \phi) = L_{sim}(f, m \circ \phi) + \lambda L_{smooth}(\phi) \qquad (4)$$

The similarity loss is related to the local gray level and structural similarity of image. The normalized cross-correlation is utilized in this paper as the similarity loss function.

The smoothing loss of the deformation field is shown in Eq. (5), where, r, c and ch represent the rows, columns and channels of the image.

$$L_{smooth}(\phi) = \sum_{i=1}^{r} \sum_{j=1}^{c} \sum_{k=1}^{ch} \|\nabla\phi(i,j,k)\|^2, \nabla\phi(i,j,k)$$
$$= \left(\frac{\partial\phi(i,j,k)}{\partial x}, \frac{\partial\phi(i,j,k)}{\partial y}, \frac{\partial\phi(i,j,k)}{\partial z} \right), \frac{\partial\phi(i,j,k)}{\partial x} \approx \phi(i+1,j,k) - \phi(i,j,k) \qquad (5)$$

Supervised Learning. We have used the generation of artificial deformation fields in order to simulate the movement of a microscope lens. The fixed image and artificially transformed image by applying a deformation field are used as inputs for supervised learning. In the case of closer object distances, the Gaussian blur is closer to the real blur model, and the variance in the Gaussian blur can represent the depth of field. So we chose to use a Gaussian filter to simulate the blur effect in the multi-focus images.

$$f' = gaussian(m \circ \phi') \qquad (6)$$

The artificial deformation field $\phi\prime$ is obtained by the data augmentation method featured in Sect. 3.1. The more similarity between the deformation field(ϕ'') that is output through the use of supervised learning methods, and the artificial deformation field ($\phi\prime$), the more precise will be the prediction derived via this supervised learning. The similarity between the artificial deformation field ϕ' and the deformation field ϕ'' predicted by the supervised learning serves as the loss function L_s.

$$L_s(\phi', \phi'') = \frac{1}{r \times c \times ch} \sum_{i=1}^{r} \sum_{j=1}^{c} \sum_{k=1}^{ch} (\phi''(i,j,k) - \phi'(i,j,k))^2 \qquad (7)$$

Hybrid Supervised Learning. The deformation field generated by random is usually too simple, which restricts the type of image transforms. Therefore, we use a mixture of unsupervised and supervised learning methods to simulate the actual deformation field better. The moving image and the fixed image, the moving image and the fixed image which is corresponding to the manual transformation of the moving image are the two image pairs as inputs in the hybrid training method. The former is the input of unsupervised learning, and the latter is the input of supervised learning so that the network can better simulate the real deformation field between the moving image and the fixed image.

The hybrid supervised loss function can be expressed as Eq. (8). The employment of the supervised loss function is limited to the model training.

$$L_h(f, m, \phi, \phi', \phi'') = L_{us}(f, m, \phi) + \gamma L_s(\phi', \phi'') \tag{8}$$

3.3 Fusion Method

The wavelet transform enables to decompose of the image into low-frequency and high-frequency information, thereby taking into account the image's details and average information that can be processed through diverse methods. Furthermore, its reconstruction aptitude is excellent, leading to information preservation, and the multi-scale transformation is better aligned with human visual cognition and the characteristics of a multi-focus image.

To preserve more image details in the image fusion process, this paper uses the wavelet-based image fusion technique and subsequently evaluates the fusion efficiency. The Gabor filter delivers good localization competency in frequency and spatial domains. Through the selection of an optimal low-end center frequency, low-pass filtering via the Gabor filter is realized. By filtering the image along diverse directions, the low-frequency components obtainable in different directions facilitate the extraction of characteristics in various orientations. The original image is then subtracted from the low-frequency output in each direction to get the high-frequency component in every direction. The sum of the high frequency energy output from all directions is used as the fusion decision rule.

4 Experiments

The experimental PC platform configuration is: the system is Ubuntu 20.04, the graphics card is NVIDIA RTX A6000, and the memory is 46G.

4.1 Comparison of Unsupervised, Supervised and Hybrid Supervised Models

We have employed a total of 91 out of the available 115 microscopic images for both training and validation, allocating the remaining 24 images for testing purposes. Each group of training images was paired in pairs, thus generating a grand total of 660 moving and fixed image pairs. The model training iteration has been set to 100 rounds with a

Table 1. Deep learning algorithm registration evaluation comparison

Algorithm	Group	EN (mean)		MI(mean)		PSNR(mean)	
		before	after	before	after	before	after
supervised	powder 1	1.576	1.450	0.805	0.121	35.509	18.616
	powder 2	0.663	0.533	1.137	0.311	29.134	16.293
	flower	0.271	0.427	1.591	0.693	24.884	10.732
	teeth	0.181	0.223	0.845	0.67	21.584	12.552
	object	0.91	0.922	1.491	1.124	24.884	10.928
supervised (with Gaussian blur)	powder 1	1.576	1.481	0.816	0.118	35.617	18.586
	powder 2	0.663	0.536	1.142	0.335	30.072	16.414
	flower	0.271	0.431	1.612	0.718	25.12	11.008
	teeth	0.181	0.217	0.854	0.701	21.734	12.824
	object	0.91	0.918	1.503	1.186	24.913	10.928
unsupervised	powder 1	1.576	1.967	0.805	1.542	35.509	35.865
	powder 2	0.663	1.119	1.137	1.554	29.134	35.93
	flower	0.271	0.891	1.591	1.811	24.884	20.461
	teeth	0.181	0.590	0.845	1.512	21.584	19.892
	object	0.91	1.696	1.491	1.518	24.884	20.461
hybrid	powder 1	1.576	2.323	0.805	1.707	35.509	34.956
	powder 2	0.663	1.274	1.137	1.726	29.134	36.595
	flower	0.271	0.907	1.591	1.878	24.884	**21.703**
	teeth	0.181	0.602	0.845	1.742	21.584	**21.885**
	object	0.91	1.778	1.491	1.535	24.884	20.671
hybrid (with Gaussian blur)	powder 1	1.576	**2.379**	0.805	**1.771**	35.509	**35.207**
	powder 2	0.663	**1.331**	1.137	**1.827**	29.134	**36.679**
	flower	0.271	**1.12**	1.591	**1.889**	24.884	20.98
	teeth	0.181	**0.705**	0.845	**1.824**	21.584	21.861
	object	0.91	**1.982**	1.491	**1.572**	24.884	**20.979**

batch of 16. The unsupervised, supervised, and hybrid supervised networks have adopted normalized cross-correlation as their L_{sim}. In the hybrid supervised network, the weight of L_{sim} stands at 1, that of L_{smooth} at 0.1, and that of L_s at 0.01.

In Table 1, we have conducted a comparison of the alterations in image similarity before and after registration. The entropy (EN), mutual information (MI), and peak signal-to-noise ratio (PSNR) of moving and fixed images remain the same across all these algorithms prior to registration. The similarity between images increases with higher values of these three similarity indices. And the average values are separately calculated for each set of different images.

As the image is a micro-multi-focus image, it encompasses a significant amount of fuzzy regions and weak texture areas, rendering its entropy, mutual trust and peak signal-to-noise ratio lower than that of a clear natural image. The supervised network has employed an artificially generated deformation field as its ground truth, a simulation that cannot ideally replicate the deformation field of the actual image, thus, the indices after registration are comparatively lower than those beforehand. That means, the indices after registration of both the unsupervised network and hybrid supervised network stand significantly higher than those before registration. It is worth mentioning that one of the indices recorded by the hybrid supervised network following registration has experienced a significant improvement. The image post application of the Gaussian blur renders superior results in contrast to the one without such filter.

4.2   Comparison of Harris, SIFT, our Registration Algorithm Based on Feature Points and Our Hybrid Supervised Algorithm

For purposes of evaluating the model's effectiveness, we have conducted a comparative analyzing the registration outcomes of the traditional registration algorithm [25] against those attained by our model.

Table 2. Performance of the three traditional registration algorithms on different images

Algorithm	Group	Feature points (mean)	Matching accuracy(mean)	EN (mean)		MI(mean)		PSNR(mean)	
				before	after	before	after	before	after
Harris	powder 1	372	65.23%	1.576	1.662	0.805	1.19	35.509	18.516
	powder 2	388	62.68%	0.663	0.804	1.137	1.337	29.134	16.094
	flower	416	70.37%	0.271	0.75	1.591	1.605	24.884	10.245
	teeth	392	36.08%	0.181	0.418	0.845	0.929	21.584	20.221
	object	387	60%	0.91	1.152	1.491	1.483	24.884	10.245
SIFT	powder 1	272	78.67%	1.576	1.583	0.805	1.276	35.509	17.532
	powder 2	625	89.07%	0.663	0.814	1.137	1.19	29.134	16.496
	flower	1046	91.32%	0.271	0.719	1.591	1.472	24.884	17.274
	teeth	541	72.03%	0.181	0.42	0.845	1.037	21.584	17.103
	object	878	93.29%	0.91	1.667	1.491	1.543	24.884	17.274
Harris-SIFT	powder 1	358	96.02%	1.576	1.740	0.805	1.37	35.509	22.611
	powder 2	429	93.05%	0.663	1.138	1.137	1.422	29.134	16.978
	flower	687	94.11%	0.271	0.763	1.591	1.71	24.884	19.345
	teeth	314	80.77%	0.181	0.507	0.845	1.495	21.584	21.379
	object	357	79.31%	0.91	1.65	1.491	1.605	24.884	19.345

Our Registration Algorithm Based on Feature Points Used for Comparison. Using Harris, SIFT and the Harris-SIFT algorithms, experiment with the test set in the data set. Then, calculate the number of feature points, matching accuracy and other indicators, and take the average value, as shown in Table 2. Due to the texture features of the circuit element images in the last row are richer and closer to natural images, the SIFT algorithm performs better than our algorithm in such images. The improved Harris-SIFT algorithm generally performs better than the Harris algorithm and SIFT algorithm on the three similarity indexes EN, MI and PSNR. However, compared with the data of Table 1 in Sect. 4.1, it is relatively less effective than the hybrid supervised registration algorithm proposed in this paper.

4.3   Evaluation of Fusion Effectiveness

Utilizing a multi-directional Gabor filter to fuse registered images using six algorithms, the results are depicted in Fig. 4. The foremost row showcased in the figure represents the moving and fixed images, whereby moving image is transformed into a moved image to being fused with the fixed image. To better understand the effectiveness of the fusion process, we have selected a group of flower images with obvious differences in displacement and blurred areas to showcase. The second and third rows in Fig. 8 provide a magnified display of the sections targeted by the red box in the moving and fixed images. Observing the resulting image, it becomes obvious that Harris, SIFT, and Harris-SIFT algorithm has obvious artifacts near the edges of petals in the image due to the low accuracy of registration. When relying solely on supervised registration models, discrepancies between the predicted deformation field and real deformation field notably impair fusion accuracy. Conversely, unsupervised and hybrid supervised models yield a superior level of output, reducing the presence of artifacts and enhancing the natural effect of the fused image, with results that indicate the hybrid supervised approach produces the most effective outcomes overall.

Fig. 4. The fusion results of the moved and fixed images from different registration algorithms

Calculate the evaluation indicators after image fusion, the higher the value of these indicators, the result of fusion is better. As shown in Table 3, the Harris-SIFT registration algorithm can improve the quality of the fusion to some extent. The unsupervised learning algorithm can achieve better performance. The best evaluation of image quality is obtained among these algorithms by using the hybrid supervised model.

Table 3. Comparison of these registration algorithms in fusion evaluation indicators

Algorithm	Group	EN	MI	PSNR	AG	NCC	VIF
Harris	powder 1	5.403	3.613	71.768	2.313	0.632	1.125
	powder 2	6.002	2.695	61.391	3.708	0.711	1.488
	flower	5.794	3.209	62.061	3.834	0.730	0.724
	teeth	7.084	3.171	71.326	10.861	0.86	0.657
	object	7.228	4.098	66.419	7.668	0.639	0.685
SIFT	powder 1	5.454	3.218	70.567	2.794	0.599	0.945
	powder 2	6.034	2.595	68.44	4.017	0.506	0.934
	flower	5.697	3.213	61.44	4.915	0.752	0.902
	teeth	7.038	3.18	62.606	12.368	0.903	0.673
	object	7.239	3.58	62.265	7.593	0.69	0.745
Harris-SIFT	powder 1	5.507	4.494	75.463	3.455	0.759	1.548
	powder 2	6.112	3.029	70.48	4.163	0.853	1.736
	flower	5.870	3.635	63.758	6.989	0.821	**1.27**
	teeth	7.323	3.203	72.287	12.838	0.878	0.711
	object	**7.33**	4.32	**72.997**	7.685	0.778	0.708
Supervised (with Gaussian blur)	powder 1	4.208	3.221	61.654	2.558	0.567	0.758
	powder 2	5.314	3.164	59.76	2.657	0.527	0.824
	flower	5.560	3.135	55.873	4.041	0.65	0.717
	teeth	5.013	2.955	58.904	7.352	0.509	0.684
	object	5.855	2.833	54.34	5.926	0.531	0.486
Unsupervised	powder 1	6.056	7.368	84.068	4.456	0.926	1.889
	powder 2	6.127	7.523	83.831	4.728	0.934	1.898
	flower	7.545	9.171	73.297	8.379	0.932	1.059
	teeth	7.744	7.24	70.465	12.206	0.837	0.806
	object	7.124	7.146	72.378	6.624	0.922	0.971
Hybrid (with Gaussian blur)	powder 1	**6.318**	**7.913**	**88.479**	**4.873**	**0.94**	**1.938**
	powder 2	**6.232**	**7.873**	**89.725**	**4.942**	**0.938**	**1.941**
	flower	**7.562**	**9.891**	**75.222**	**8.912**	**0.944**	1.12
	teeth	**7.775**	**8.389**	**74.855**	**18.73**	**0.905**	**1.167**
	object	7.312	**7.787**	72.848	**10.545**	**0.934**	**1.191**

* EN = entropy, MI = mutual information, PSNR = peak signal-to-noise ratio, AG = average gradient, NCC = nonlinear correlation coefficient, VIF = visual fidelity.

5   Conclusion

In this paper, we propose a hybrid supervised deep learning registration and fusion framework for multi-focus images taken through microscopes. The artificial deformation field is introduced as a label in the supervised learning training to help optimize the model parameters. Moreover, the steps of patch movement simulation can better simulate the features of the multi-focus image, so that the model is closer to the real data. Experimental results show that the registration and fusion framework proposed in this paper can improve the accuracy of fused images. The images obtained by this algorithm perform better in terms of mutual information, entropy, signal-to-noise ratio and other indicators, with an average performance improvement of 31.7%, 17.6% and 38.2% respectively compared to our Harris-SIFT registration algorithm. The quality evaluation indicators related to the final fusion image are also improved, and the indicators such as entropy are increased by an average of 10.3%, 130%, 13.2%, 34.1%, 14.4% and 31.5% respectively. Our current framework employs traditional image fusion method, we shall explore the feasibility of using an end-to-end deep-learning-based fusion method. Due to the small number of images in the dataset, we will further collect images and evaluate and optimize the model.

Acknowledgment. The project was supported by the Project of National Natural Science Foundation of China (No.62002268, No.61961036), the Guangxi science and technology major special projects innovation driven major projects (No. AA18118036), Natural Science Foundation of Guangxi (No. 2021JJB170060) and Macao Polytechnic University Grant (No. RP/FCA-15/2022).

References

1. Litjens, G., Kooi, T., Bejnordi, B.E., Setio, A.A.A., Ciompi, F., Ghafoorian, M., et al.: A survey on deep learning in medical image analysis. Med. Image Anal. **42**, 60–88 (2017)
2. Li, Z., Mahapatra, D., Tielbeek, J.A., Stoker, J., van Vliet, L.J., Vos, F.M.: Image registration based on autocorrelation of local structure. IEEE Trans. Image Process. **35**, 63–75 (2015)
3. Cao, S.Y., Shen, H.L., Chen, S.J., Li, C.: Boosting structure consistency for multispectral and multimodal image registration. IEEE Trans. Image Process. **29**, 5147–5162 (2020)
4. Dong, Y., Long, T., Jiao, W., He, G., Zhang, Z.: A novel image registration method based on phase correlation using low-rank matrix factorization with mixture of Gaussian. IEEE Trans. Geosci. Remote Sens. **56**, 446–460 (2017)
5. Harris, C., Stephens, M.: A combined corner and edge detector. In: Alvey Vision Conference, pp. 147–151 (1988)
6. Lowe, D.G.: Object recognition from local scale-invariant features. J. Comput. Vis. **60**, 91–110 (2004)
7. Bay, H., Tuytelaars, T., Gool, L.: Surf: speeded up robust features. In: Leonardis, A., Bischof, H., Pinz, A. (eds.) ECCV 2006. LNCS, vol. 3951, pp. 404–417. Springer, Heidelberg (2006). https://doi.org/10.1007/11744023_32
8. Rosten, E., Drummond, T.: Machine learning for high-speed corner detection. In: Leonardis, A., Bischof, H., Pinz, A. (eds.) ECCV 2006. LNCS, vol. 3951, pp. 430–443. Springer, Heidelberg (2006). https://doi.org/10.1007/11744023_34

9. Alcantarilla, P.F., Bartoli, A., Davison, A.J.: KAZE features. In: Fitzgibbon, A., Lazebnik, S., Perona, P., Sato, Y., Schmid, C. (eds.) ECCV 2012. LNCS, vol. 7577, pp. 214–227. Springer, Heidelberg (2012). https://doi.org/10.1007/978-3-642-33783-3_16

10. Ma, J., Zhou, H., Zhao, J., Gao, Y., Jiang, J., Tian, J.: Robust feature matching for remote sensing image registration via locally linear transforming. IEEE Trans. Geosci. Remote Sens. **53**, 6469–6481 (2015)

11. Ma, J., Zhao, J., Jiang, J., Zhou, H., Guo, X.: Locality preserving matching. Int. J. Comput. Vision **127**, 512–531 (2019)

12. Ma, J., Jiang, J., Zhou, H., Zhao, J., Guo, X.: Guided locality preserving feature matching for remote sensing image registration. IEEE Trans. Geosci. Remote Sens. **56**, 4435–4447 (2018)

13. Wu, G., Kim, M., Wang, Q., Munsell, B.C., Shen, D.: Scalable high-performance image registration framework by unsupervised deep feature representations learning. IEEE Trans. Biomed. Eng. **63**, 1505–1516 (2015)

14. Gao, Y., Dai, M., Zhang, Q.: Cross-modal and multi-level feature refinement network for RGB-D salient object detection. Vis. Comput. **39**, 3979–3994 (2023). https://doi.org/10.1007/s00371-022-02543-w

15. Salehi, S.S.M., Khan, S., Erdogmus, D., Gholipour, A.: Real-time deep pose estimation with geodesic loss for image-to-template rigid registration. IEEE Trans. Med. Imaging **38**, 470–481 (2018)

16. Jaderberg, M., Simonyan, K., Zisserman, A.: Spatial transformer networks. Adv. Neural. Inf. Process. Syst. **28**, 2017–2025 (2015)

17. Zhu, J.Y., Park, T., Isola, P., Efros, A.A.: Unpaired image-to-image translation using cycle-consistent adversarial networks. In: IEEE International Conference on Computer Vision, pp. 2223–2232 (2017)

18. Mahapatra, D., Ge, Z., Sedai, S., Chakravorty, R.: Joint registration and segmentation of xray images using generative adversarial networks. In: Shi, Y., Suk, H.-I., Liu, M. (eds.) MLMI 2018. LNCS, vol. 11046, pp. 73–80. Springer, Cham (2018). https://doi.org/10.1007/978-3-030-00919-9_9

19. Bai, X., Zhang, Y., Zhou, F., Xue, B.: Quadtree-based multi-focus image fusion using a weighted focus-measure. Inf. Fusion **22**, 105–118 (2015)

20. Panguluri, S.K., Mohan, L.: An effective fuzzy logic and particle swarm optimization based thermal and visible-light image fusion framework using curvelet transform. Optik **243**, 167529 (2021)

21. Roy, M., Mukhopadhyay, S.: A DCT-based multiscale framework for 2D greyscale image fusion using morphological differential features. Vis. Comput. (2023). https://doi.org/10.1007/s00371-023-03052-0

22. Liu, Y., Chen, X., Peng, H., Wang, Z.: Multi-focus image fusion with a deep convolutional neural network. Inf. Fusion **36**, 191–207 (2017)

23. Guo, X., Nie, R., Cao, J., Zhou, D., Qian, W.: Fully convolutional network-based multifocus image fusion. Neural Comput. **30**, 1775–1800 (2018)

24. Xie, Z., Zhang, W., Sheng, B., Li, P., Chen, C.P.: BaGFN: broad attentive graph fusion network for high-order feature interactions. IEEE Trans. Neural Netw. Learn. Syst. **34**(8), 4499–4513 (2023)

25. Zhou, Y., Chen, Z., Sheng, B., Li, P., Kim, J., Wu, E.: AFF-Dehazing: attention-based feature fusion network for low-light image Dehazing. Comput. Animat. Virtual Worlds **32**(3–4), e2011 (2021)

ScaleNet: Rethinking Feature Interaction from a Scale-Wise Perspective for Medical Image Segmentation

Yu Feng, Tai Ma, Hao Zeng, Zhengke Xu, Suwei Zhang, and Ying Wen[✉]

East China Normal University, Shanghai, China
ywen@cs.ecnu.edu.cn

Abstract. Recently, vision transformers have become outstanding segmentation structures for their remarkable global modeling capability. In current transformer-based models for medical image segmentation, convolutional layers are often replaced by transformers, or transformers are added to the deepest layer of the encoder to learn the global context. However, for the extracted multi-scale feature information, most existing methods tend to ignore the multi-scale dependencies, which leads to inadequate feature learning and fails to produce rich feature representations. In this paper, we propose ScaleNet from the perspective of feature interaction at different scales that can alleviate mentioned problems. Specifically, our approach consists of two multi-scale feature interaction modules: the spatial scale interaction (SSI) and the channel scale interaction (CSI). SSI uses a transformer to aggregate patches from different scale features to enhance the feature representations at the spatial scale. CSI uses a 1D convolutional layer and a fully connected layer to perform a global fusion of multi-level features at the channel scale. The combination of CSI and SSI enables ScaleNet to emphasize multi-scale dependencies and effectively resolve complex scale variations.

Keywords: medical image segmentation · transformer-based method · multi-scale feature interaction · multi-organ and skin lesion segmentation tasks

1 Introduction

Medical image segmentation is an important task in medical image analysis. Accurate segmentation of lesion size and morphology is helpful for determining the grade of the disease, as well as guiding the pre-surgical analysis and the following treatment plan. As the utilization of medical image analysis continues to increase, the need for highly accurate and reliable medical segmentation becomes even more critical.

This work was supported in part by National Nature Science Foundation of China (62273150), Shanghai Natural Science Foundation (22ZR1421000), Shanghai Outstanding Academic Leaders Plan (21XD1430600), Science and Technology Commission of Shanghai Municipality (22DZ2229004).

B. Sheng et al. (Eds.): CGI 2023, LNCS 14498, pp. 222–236, 2024.
https://doi.org/10.1007/978-3-031-50078-7_18

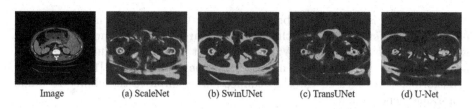

Image   (a) ScaleNet   (b) SwinUNet   (c) TransUNet   (d) U-Net

Fig. 1. Visualization of decoder feature maps from different models, especially for small objects. The CNN-based model U-Net only focuses on some of the targets due to its lack of global modeling capability. Our ScaleNet enhances the learning capability of the transformer-based model by considering multi-scale feature interaction and producing effective feature representations.

For a considerable amount of time, fully convolutional networks (FCNs), as well as convolutional neural networks (CNNs) more broadly, have been the leading approaches in deep learning and have been extensively utilized for medical image segmentation. With their remarkable capability to extract image features, various architectures based on CNNs have been used for image segmentation task. However, these architectures face a huge challenge, important feature information is often lost in the deeper layers of the network. To solve this problem, medical image segmentation architectures use a symmetric top-down encoder-decoder design and develop a U-shaped network family, where the most classical network is U-Net [1]. U-Net innovatively incorporates the horizontal propagation of intermediate signals into the traditional symmetrical top-down encoder-decoder structure. This integration enhances the ability of the decoder to recover the predicted results by supplementing the spatial information lost in the downsampling process. Due to its simplicity and scalability advantages, many improved models are proposed, such as U-Net++ [2] and mU-Net [3]. Andrity et al. [4] used autoencoder regularization for MRI brain tumor segmentation. Oktay et al. [5] combined the skip connection with the attention mechanism for medical image segmentation. However, despite the great success of the CNN-based approaches mentioned above, CNNs fail to model explicit long-range relationships beyond the local region (as shown in Fig. 1(d)), since the effective receptive of the network is severely limited [6].

Recently, motivated by the outstanding achievements of transformers in natural language processing (NLP), vision transformers have been developed to mitigate the shortcomings of CNNs in image processing tasks. Transformers primarily use a multi-head self-attention (MSA) mechanism, which plays a crucial role in constructing long-range dependencies between the sequence of tokens. ViT [7] has better performance compared to CNNs, but requires a large amount of data to generalize and has the problem of quadratic complexity. Several methods have been developed to tackle these limitations. DeiT [8] designs a highly efficient training framework for knowledge extraction, addressing the challenge that vision transformers require large amounts of data to learn. Huimin et al. [9] used multi-level feature aggregation to reduce computational effort while maintaining semantic information. Although vision transformers can model global context, their self-attention mechanism may lead to the neglect of low-level features.

To address this issue, many hybrid transformer-CNN methods have been proposed. TransUNet [10] replaces the deepest feature map in the encoder of U-Net with the feature extracted by ViT. LeVit-UNet [11] uses a lightweight transformer embedded in U-Net to improve efficiency. STM-UNet [12] adds Swin Transformer [13] block to the skip connection to improve the ability to build long-range dependency.

However, the previous works still have the following problems. Firstly, although the transformer blocks in the hierarchical encoder capture global information at various stages, the transformer only processes a single scale feature, and can only learn global context information at a single receptive field. Thus, the multi-scale dependencies are not properly exploited within each stage. TransUnet only adds the transformer to the deepest layer of the encoder, which leads to learning insufficient information to recognize small objects (as shown in Fig. 1(c)). SwinUnet [14] is a pure transformer-based medical image segmentation model that can learn information from multiple scales but has more invalid information (as shown in Fig. 1(b)). Secondly, most models tend to focus only on spatial scale operations when extracting feature information, ignoring the inter-channel interaction. Our main motivation is using multi-scale feature interaction to learn rich feature representations at the spatial scale and channel scale.

In this paper, we propose an encoder-decoder network called ScaleNet that realizes multi-scale feature interaction to explore the application of medical image segmentation. In the encoder, we use CNN and Swin Transformer [13] to effectively leverage the global long-range relationships of transformers and local feature representations of CNNs for an accurate medical image segmentation task. For the acquisition of multi-stage and multi-scale information, feature interaction modules are proposed for spatial and channel scales, dubbed as spatial scale interaction (SSI) and channel scale interaction (CSI). With the help of the modules mentioned above, we can extract more feature information and maintain a competitive segmentation effect. Our main contributions are as follows:

- A new deep neural network (ScaleNet) is proposed. To the best of our knowledge, it is the first model to realize multi-scale feature interaction at the spatial and channel scales.
- We innovatively design the combination of CNN and Swin Transformer, which can effectively fuse the local features and global features of each layer and enhance the modeling ability of long-range dependency.
- Experimental results demonstrate the effectiveness and superiority of the proposed ScaleNet compared to the competing methods on several publicly available medical image segmentation datasets.

2   Related Work

In the most current research, firstly, most hybrid transformer CNN methods often consider the transformer as a complement to the CNN encoder. TransCASCADE [15] is an efficient and simple segmentation framework that can

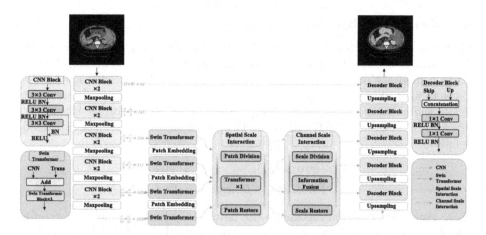

Fig. 2. An overview of our ScaleNet, which consists of two interaction modules, SSI and CSI.

obtain features through a hierarchical transformer encoder. HST-MRF [16] learns dependencies between pixels in a single scale image by adding the transformer into the skip connection structure. The methods mentioned above do not consider the interaction of CNN and transformer. Different from existing methods, we design a novel encoder that couples local CNN blocks and global Swin Transformer [13] blocks at each scale. Secondly, multi-scale features are important for improving image segmentation performance. U-Net3+ [17] uses full-scale skip connection and deep supervision to enhance feature representation. Missformer [18] uses enhanced transformer block and context bridge to learn multi-scale feature dependencies. CASTformer [19] adjusts the multi-head self-attention (MSA) mechanism from the perspective of spatial multi-scale feature extraction. The above networks are designed to extract multi-scale features while ignoring the dependencies and interaction between different scales. Therefore, based on previous studies, this paper proposes a multi-scale feature interaction model for medical image segmentation.

3   Proposed Method

Sufficient feature representations are important for fine-grained medical image segmentation. The core idea of ScaleNet is to enhance the feature representation by interacting multi-scale features. The proposed ScaleNet is shown in Fig. 2, which consists of a proposed encoder and two feature interaction modules, SSI and CSI. In the encoder, we extract global features and local features using Swin Transformer and CNN. Then we implement multi-scale feature interaction using SSI and CSI at the spatial and channel scales. Finally, the reinforced feature maps are fed into the decoder block for the final segmentation. Then, we will elaborate each module of ScaleNet specifically in the following subsections.

3.1   Hierarchical Encoder Module

As shown in Fig. 2, the initial Swin Transformer only receives input from the CNN branch of the same stage, whereas the input of other Swin Transformer blocks combines global information from previous Swin Transformer and CNNs stages to aggregate fine-grained details and coarse semantics information. Let i denote the index of the down-sampling layer along the transformer branch. N indicates the stage of Swin Transformer. The feature map X_{trans}^i can be expressed as follows:

$$X_{trans}^i = \begin{cases} Trans(X_{cnn}^i), & i = 1 \\ Trans([X_{cnn}^i, Down(X_{trans}^{i-1})]), & i = 2, ..N \end{cases} \quad (1)$$

where the $Down$ function represents the patch embedding, which consists of a convolution operation followed by a batch normalization and a ReLU function. $[\cdot]$ is an add operation that can simultaneously keep the local feature information from CNNs. $Trans(\cdot)$ represents the Swin Transformer block, which can efficiently focus on local and global features.

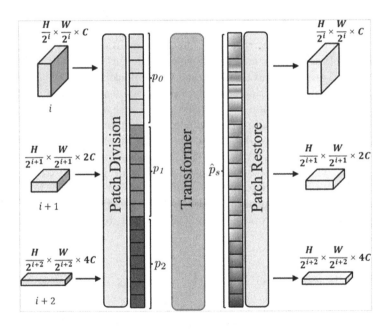

Fig. 3. An overview of the spatial scale interaction (SSI)

3.2   Spatial Scale Interaction

Multi-scale feature information is important for complex vision tasks, especially medical image segmentation. To refine the feature information, we design a novel

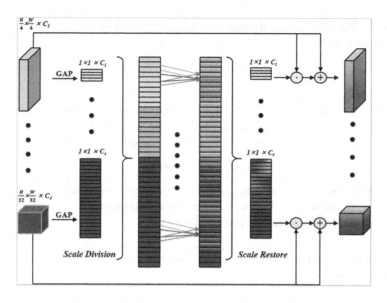

Fig. 4. An overview of the channel scale interaction (CSI)

SSI, a transformer-based block that interacts among different scales, as shown in Fig. 3. The input sequence of SSI is initially reorganized into a 2D lattice. Instead of directly concatenating all tokens of different scale feature maps, the same number of patches are sampled from different scales of feature maps, which is called **Patch Division**. Taking a partial feature map as an example, Fig. 3 illustrates how to generate the same number of spatially-aware patches on three consecutive feature maps from i-th to $(i + 2)$-th scale. Specifically, we obtain the feature map X_i at different scales by the encoder, where $X_i \in \mathbb{R}^{h_i \times w_i \times c_i}$, h_i, w_i, and c_i respectively denote the spatial resolution and the number of channels of the i-th feature map. The size of the tokens p_i that the X_i generates is $(h_i \times w_i, c_i)$. Let L represent the kind of feature map, as in Fig. 3, $L{=}3$. Next, let z_i denote a scale factor which is used to adjust the size of the patch, and $z_i \in 2^{L-i-1}$. Let d_i denote the number factor, and $d_i \in 4^i$, where $i = 0,1,2$. In this way, we make X_i have the same number of patches. The expression of p_i is as follows:

$$p_i = (\tfrac{h_i}{z^i} \times \tfrac{w_i}{z^i}, z^i \times z^i \times d^i, \tfrac{c_i}{d^i}) \tag{2}$$

in this way, we maintain the spatial size and correspondence as well as reduce the redundancy. Then, we concatenate all p_i to obtain p_s, and the expression of p_s is as follows:

$$p_s = (\tfrac{h_i}{z^i} \times \tfrac{w_i}{z^i}, z^i \times z^i \times d^i, \sum_{i=0}^{2} \tfrac{c_i}{d^i}) \tag{3}$$

later, p_s is fed into a transformer to obtain the enhanced sequence $\hat{p}_s$. This process is as follows:

$$p'_s = MSA\big(LN\big(p_s\big)\big) + p_s \tag{4}$$

$$\hat{p}_s = MLP\big(LN\big(p'_s\big)\big) + p'_s \tag{5}$$

where MSA [7], MLP [7], and LN($\cdot$) denote multi-head self-attention, multi-layer perception, and layer normalization. Then we use **Patch Restore** to reverse the enhanced sequence to patches according to the order of concatenation:

$$p_0, p_1, p_2 = Split(\hat{p}_s) \tag{6}$$

where $Split(\cdot)$ is an inverse process of the previous concatenation operation. Contrary to the process of Patch Division, **Patch Restore** combines all patches of the same spatial scale into a feature map.

Table 1. Quantitative results of our segmentation model compared to SOTA on Synapse Dataset.

Method	DSC($\uparrow$)	HD($\downarrow$)	Aorta	Gallbladdr	Kidney(L)	Kidney(R)	Liver	Pancreas	Spleen	Stomach
DARR [21]	69.77	–	74.74	53.77	72.31	73.24	94.08	54.18	89.90	45.96
U-Net [1]	76.85	39.70	89.07	69.72	77.77	68.60	93.43	53.98	86.67	75.58
R50 Att-UNet [22]	75.57	36.97	55.92	63.91	79.20	72.71	93.56	49.37	87.19	74.95
Att-UNet [22]	77.77	36.02	**89.55**	68.88	77.98	71.11	93.57	58.04	87.30	75.75
TransUNet [10]	77.48	31.69	87.23	63.13	81.87	77.02	94.08	55.86	85.08	75.62
SwinUNet [14]	79.12	21.55	85.47	66.53	83.28	79.61	94.29	56.58	90.66	76.60
LeVit-UNet [11]	78.53	16.84	78.53	62.23	84.61	80.25	93.11	59.07	88.86	72.76
MT-UNet [23]	78.59	26.59	87.92	64.99	81.47	77.29	93.06	59.46	87.75	76.81
HiFormer [24]	80.69	19.14	87.03	68.61	84.23	78.37	94.07	60.77	90.44	82.03
MISSFormer [18]	81.96	18.20	86.99	68.65	85.21	82.00	94.41	65.67	**91.92**	80.81
CASTformer [19]	82.55	22.73	89.05	67.48	86.05	82.17	**95.61**	67.49	91.00	81.55
TransCASCADE [15]	82.68	17.34	86.63	68.48	**87.66**	**84.56**	94.43	65.33	90.79	**83.52**
ScaleNet (w/o SSI)	81.42	19.88	88.75	72.93	83.71	78.37	95.12	63.25	89.37	79.87
ScaleNet (w/o CSI)	81.86	19.07	88.56	**73.26**	84.57	79.98	95.14	62.62	89.40	81.37
ScaleNet	**83.26**	**16.24**	88.98	72.97	85.33	80.88	95.43	**69.30**	91.31	82.14

3.3 Channel Scale Interaction

Inspired by CBAM [20], both spatial scale and channel scale are equally important for refining image features. Therefore, we propose a channel scale interaction module, CSI, as shown in Fig. 4. It is used to generate channel attention maps by concatenating features of different scales to better integrate feature information. Let y_i denote the feature maps of different scales extracted in the previous stage. Firstly, we perform a pooling and concatenation operation to fuse channel information from different scale features, and this process is called **Scale Division**:

$$y'_i = GAP(y_i) \tag{7}$$

$$Y = Concat(y'_1, y'_2, \ldots, y'_s) \tag{8}$$

where GAP represents global average pooling, and s denotes the total number of stages. Next, we fuse the feature information by the following operations:

$$Y' = Conv1D(Y) \tag{9}$$

$$Y_i'' = \sigma(FC_i(Y')) \tag{10}$$

where Conv1D denotes 1D convolution operation, and FC_i is the fully connected layer, and σ denotes the sigmoid function. Finally, we use **Scale Restore** to get the enhanced features, and this process is as follows:

$$Out_i = y_i + y_i \odot Y_i'' \tag{11}$$

where $\odot$ denotes the element-wise multiplication. Specifically, we focus on local and global full-scale channel information by performing 1D convolution and fully connected layer operations. Then in the decoder, feature maps are progressively upsampled for the final segmentation.

4   Experiments

4.1   Datasets

Multi-organ CT segmentation (Synapse): Synapse [25] consists of 30 abdominal CT scans, where 13 organs are annotations. Following [10], after pre-processing, we extract 3,779 slices from all CT cases. We split the whole dataset into training (18 scans, 2,211 slices) and test (12 scans, 1,568 slices) sets. We report the Dice Coefficient (DSC) and Hausdorff Distance (HD) on 8 different organs.

Automated cardiac diagnosis (ACDC): The automated cardiac diagnosis challenge [26] contains 100 MRI scans involving three organs: myocardium (MYO), right ventricle (RV), and left ventricle (LV). Consistent with [19], we present the DSC results using a random split of 70 training cases, and 30 testing cases.

Skin Lesion Segmentation: To validate the universality of ScaleNet, we further evaluate its performance using the *ISIC2018* [27] dataset, consisting of 2594 images and corresponding labels. We randomly divide the dataset into 1816, 260, and 518 for training, validation, and testing, respectively. We use the Dice score (DSC), Sensitivity (SE), Specificity (SP), and Accuracy (ACC) as evaluation metrics for the dataset.

4.2   Implementation Details

Our proposed method is implemented using the PyTorch library and is trained on a single Nvidia RTX 3090 GPU without any pre-trained weights. All the images and masks are resized to 224×224, and we set the batch size and learning rate to 8 and 0.003 during training, respectively. The maximum number of training epochs is set to 600. Our model is optimized using the SGD optimizer with a momentum of 0.9 and weight decay of 0.0001. For a fair comparison, we use the same experimental settings and combine dice loss and cross entropy loss for all experiments.

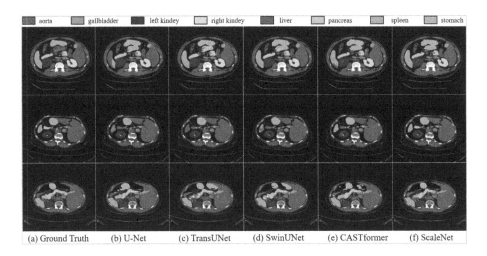

Fig. 5. Visualization results on Synapse dataset. All columns respectively represent: (a) Ground Truth; (b) U-Net; (c) TransUNet; (d) SwinUNet; (e) CASTformer; (f) ScaleNet.

4.3   Results of Multi-organ Segmentation

Table 1 presents the performance of our proposed ScaleNet on Synapse dataset. ScaleNet surpasses the previous state-of-the-art (SOTA) methods in terms of

Table 2. Comparison to SOTA methods on ACDC dataset.

Methods	DSC(↑))	RV	Myo	LV
U-Net [1]	87.55	87.10	80.63	94.92
Att-UNet [22]	86.75	87.58	79.20	93.47
ViT [7]	87.57	86.07	81.88	94.75
TransUNet [10]	89.1	88.86	84.54	95.73
SwinUNet [14]	90.00	88.55	85.62	95.83
MT-UNet [23]	90.43	86.64	89.04	95.62
MISSFormer [18]	90.86	89.55	88.04	94.99
CASTformer [19]	91.18	87.34	88.16	95.03
ScaleNet	**92.03**	**89.97**	**90.17**	**95.95**

DSC score. Compared with CNN-based methods, ScaleNet has a significant improvement in segmentation results. Furthermore, we confirm an increase in the Dice score and HD by 0.58% and 1.1 compared to the previous state-of-the-art method, TransCASCADE [15]. Figure 5 shows the visualization of the segmentation maps. We can observe that the competitive methods fail to accurately predict small organs, such as the pancreas, while our model successfully produces a smooth segmentation for all organs. Table 2 presents the DSC score on the ACDC dataset, and our ScaleNet achieves the best performance, which denotes the superior robustness and generalization of ScaleNet.

4.4   Results of Skin Lesion Segmentation

Table 3. Performance comparison of the proposed method against the SOTA approaches on skin lesion segmentation benchmarks.

Methods	DSC	SE	SP	ACC
U-Net [1]	85.45	88.00	96.97	94.04
Att-UNet [22]	85.66	86.74	**98.63**	93.76
TransUNet [10]	84.99	85.78	96.53	94.52
TransNorm [28]	89.51	87.50	97.90	95.80
MCGU-Net [29]	89.50	84.80	98.60	95.50
TMU-Net [30]	90.59	90.38	97.46	96.03
SwinUNet [14]	89.46	90.56	97.98	96.45
TransCeption [31]	91.24	91.92	97.44	96.28
ScaleNet	**91.36**	**92.28**	97.26	**96.58**

The comparison results of the *ISIC2018* skin segmentation tasks against state-of-the-art methods are presented in Table 3. Our ScaleNet performs better than other competitors in most of the evaluation metrics. Specifically, the superiority of ScaleNet on the skin segmentation dataset demonstrates its excellent generalization ability. Additionally, in Fig. 6, we visually compare the skin lesion segmentation results, demonstrating that our proposed method effectively captures finer structures and produces more accurate contours. Despite the presence of overlapping regions between the background and the skin lesion class, our method still achieves highly accurate segmentation results. ScaleNet outperforms models such as the SwinUNet [14] in terms of boundary precision.

4.5   Ablation Study

In order to understand the different factors on the performance of the proposed ScaleNet, we conduct an ablation study using the Synapse dataset. This study

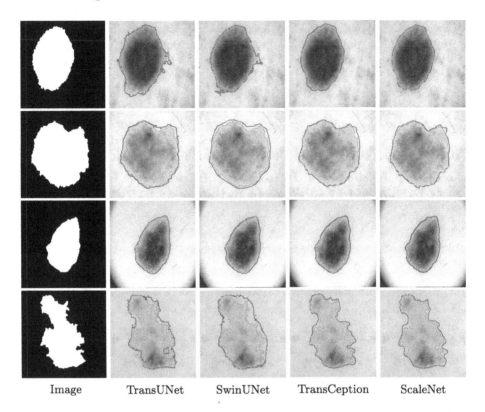

Image   TransUNet   SwinUNet   TransCeption   ScaleNet

Fig. 6. Visual comparisons of different methods on the *ISIC2018* skin lesion medical segmentation dataset, where the ground truth boundaries are shown in green, and the predicted boundaries are shown in blue. (Color figure online)

focuses on examining the effect of the feature interaction modules, SSI and CSI, and the number of multi-scale features, which are discussed in detail below.

Effect of SSI and CSI. The impact of SSI and CSI on the segmentation results is presented in Table 1. The results indicate that both feature interaction modules play a crucial role in improving the segmentation performance significantly. Moreover, we also verify the effect of the sequential order of SSI and CSI on the segmentation performance, and the results are shown in Table 4. We can see that it is better to perform multi-scale feature interaction at the spatial level first than at the channel level. To demonstrate the robustness and generalization of our proposed feature interaction modules SSI and CSI, we embed them into some typical medical segmentation networks, such as U-Net, TransUNet, and Swin-UNet. As shown in Table 5, it is evident that the features interaction modules have good generality over many models and significantly improve segmentation results.

Table 4. Different order of feature interaction modules on Synapse Dataset.

1px Methods	DSC($\uparrow$))	HD($\downarrow$))
ScaleNet (CSI, SSI)	83.04	18.85
ScaleNet (SSI, CSI)	**83.26**	**16.24**

Table 5. Effectiveness and generalization of the feature interaction modules on Synapse Dataset.

Methods	DSC($\uparrow$)	HD($\downarrow$)
U-Net [1]	76.85	39.70
TransUNet [10]	77.48	31.69
SwinUNet [14]	79.12	21.55
U-Net (SSI, CSI)	78.04	25.85
TransUNet (SSI, CSI)	79.26	24.27
SwinUNet (SSI, CSI)	81.25	17.62

Effect of the number of multi-scale features. Based on the architecture of ScaleNet, we perform the ablation of its multi-scale feature in Table 6. The original spatial size of the input image is $H \times W$. The feature maps that are fed into the SSI and CSI are F_1 ($H/4$, $W/4$), F_2 ($H/8$, $W/8$), F_3 ($H/16$, $W/16$), and F_4 ($H/32$, $W/32$). By changing the number of multi-scale features, we verify the influence of different scale features on the segmentation results of our ScaleNet. The results in Table 6 show that the number of multi-scale features has an important effect on the segmentation performance. Our proposed ScaleNet demonstrates an enhanced segmentation effect as the number of multi-scale features increases. ScaleNet achieves superior results when the number of multi-scale features is 4, highlighting the effectiveness of multi-scale interaction in preserving the information from both deep and shallow features.

Table 6. Ablation study on the number of multi-scale features on Synapse Dataset.

multi-scale features	DSC($\uparrow$)	HD($\downarrow$)
None	80.78	19.01
F_4	81.28	18.91
F_3, F_4	81.97	18.36
F_2, F_3, F_4	82.46	17.48
F_1, F_2, F_3, F_4	83.26	16.24

5   Conclusion

In this paper, from the perspective of multi-scale feature interaction, we present ScaleNet, a novel hybrid transformer-CNN method for medical image segmentation. Specifically, we introduce two feature interaction modules named spatial scale interaction (SSI) and channel scale Interaction (CSI) to jointly enhance the feature representations of the model. SSI uses a transformer to aggregate feature information from different scales at the spatial level, and CSI uses pooling and convolution operations to learn global information at the channel level. The combination of SSI and CSI makes ScaleNet effective for segmenting even small-sized objects. Experimental results on several datasets show that our method achieves substantial improvement over many methods in medical image segmentation.

References

1. Ronneberger, O., Fischer, P., Brox, T.: U-Net: convolutional networks for biomedical image segmentation. In: Navab, N., Hornegger, J., Wells, W.M., Frangi, A.F. (eds.) MICCAI 2015. LNCS, vol. 9351, pp. 234–241. Springer, Cham (2015). https://doi.org/10.1007/978-3-319-24574-4_28
2. Zhou, Z., Rahman Siddiquee, M.M., Tajbakhsh, N., Liang, J.: UNet++: a nested U-Net architecture for medical image segmentation. In: Stoyanov, D., et al. (eds.) DLMIA/ML-CDS -2018. LNCS, vol. 11045, pp. 3–11. Springer, Cham (2018). https://doi.org/10.1007/978-3-030-00889-5_1
3. Hyunseok, S., et al.: Modified U-Net (mU-Net) with incorporation of object-dependent high level features for improved liver and liver-tumor segmentation in CT images. IEEE Trans. Med. Imaging $39(5)$, 1316–1325 (2019)
4. Myronenko, A.: 3D MRI brain tumor segmentation using autoencoder regularization. In: Crimi, A., Bakas, S., Kuijf, H., Keyvan, F., Reyes, M., van Walsum, T. (eds.) BrainLes 2018. LNCS, vol. 11384, pp. 311–320. Springer, Cham (2019). https://doi.org/10.1007/978-3-030-11726-9_28
5. Oktay, O., Schlemper, J., Folgoc, L.L.: Attention U-Net: learning where to look for the pancreas. ArXiv preprint arXiv:1804.03999 (2018)
6. Luo, W., Li, Y., Urtasun, R., Zemel, R.: Understanding the effective receptive field in deep convolutional neural networks. In: Advances in Neural Information Processing Systems, vol. 29 (2016)
7. Dosovitskiy, A., et al.: An image is worth 16x16 words: transformers for image recognition at scale. ArXiv preprint arXiv:2010.11929 (2020)
8. Touvron, H., Cord, M., Douze, M., et al.: Training data-efficient image transformers distillation through attention. In: International Conference on Machine Learning, PMLR, pp. 10347–10357 (2021)
9. Huang, H., et al.: ScaleFormer: revisiting the transformer-based backbones from a scale-wise perspective for medical image segmentation. ArXiv preprint arXiv:2207.14552 (2022)
10. Chen, J., et al.: TransUNet: transformers make strong encoders for medical image segmentation. ArXiv preprint arXiv:2102.04306 (2021)

11. Xu, G., Wu, X., Zhang, X., He, X.: LeViT-UNet: make faster encoders with transformer for medical image segmentation. ArXiv preprint arXiv:2107.08623 (2021)

12. Shi, L., et al.: STM-UNet: an efficient U-shaped architecture based on Swin transformer and multi-scale MLP for medical image segmentation. ArXiv preprint arXiv:2304.12615 (2023)

13. Liu, Z., et al.: Swin transformer: hierarchical vision transformer using shifted windows. In: Proceedings of the IEEE/CVF International Conference on Computer Vision (ICCV), pp. 10012–10022 (2021)

14. Cao, H., et al.: Swin-UNet: UNet-like pure transformer for medical image segmentation. In: Karlinsky, L., Michaeli, T., Nishino, K. (eds.) ECCV 2022. LNCS, vol. 13803, pp. 205–218. Springer, Cham (2022). https://doi.org/10.1007/978-3-031-25066-8_9

15. Rahman, M.M., Marculescu, R.: Medical image segmentation via cascaded attention decoding. In: Proceedings of the IEEE/CVF Winter Conference on Applications of Computer Vision, pp. 6222–6231 (2023)

16. Huang, X., Gong, H., Zhang, J.: HST-MRF: heterogeneous Swin transformer with multi-receptive field for medical image segmentation. ArXiv preprint arXiv:2304.04614 (2023)

17. Huang, H., et al.: UNet3+: a full-scale connected UNet for medical image segmentation. In: IEEE International Conference on Acoustics, Speech and Signal Processing (ICASSP), pp. 1055–1059 (2020)

18. Huang, X., Deng, Z., Li, D., Yuan, X: MISSFormer: an effective medical image segmentation transformer. ArXiv preprint arXiv:2109.07162 (2021)

19. You, C., Zhao, R., Liu, F.: Class-aware adversarial transformers for medical image segmentation. In: Advances in Neural Information Processing Systems, vol. 35, pp. 29582–29596 (2022)

20. Woo, S., Park, J., Lee, J.Y., Kweon, I.S.: CBAM: convolutional block attention module. In: Proceedings of the European Conference on Computer Vision (ECCV), pp. 3–19 (2018)

21. Fu, S., et al.: Domain adaptive relational reasoning for 3D multi-organ segmentation. In: Martel, A.L., et al. (eds.) MICCAI 2020. LNCS, vol. 12261, pp. 656–666. Springer, Cham (2020). https://doi.org/10.1007/978-3-030-59710-8_64

22. Schlemper, J., Oktay, O., Schaap, M.: Attention gated networks: learning to leverage salient regions in medical images. Med. Image Anal. 53, 197–207 (2019)

23. Wang, H., Xie, S., Lin, L.: Mixed transformer U-Net for medical image segmentation. In: Proceedings of the ICASSP, pp. 2390–2394 (2022)

24. Heidari, M., et al.: HiFormer: hierarchical multi-scale representations using transformers for medical image segmentation. In: Proceedings of the IEEE/CVF Winter Conference on Applications of Computer Vision, pp. 6202–6212 (2023)

25. Ben, L., et al.: Segmentation outside the cranial vault challenge. In: MICCAI: Multi Atlas Labeling Beyond Cranial Vault-Workshop Challenge (2015)

26. Bernard, O., Lalande, A., Zotti, C.: Deep learning techniques for automatic MRI cardiac multi-structures segmentation and diagnosis: is the problem solved. IEEE Trans. Med. Imaging 37(11), 2514–2525 (2018)

27. Codella, N., et al.: Skin lesion analysis toward melanoma detection, a challenge hosted by the international skin imaging collaboration (ISIC). ArXiv preprint arXiv:1902.03368 (2019)

28. Azad, R., Heidari, M., Merhof, D.: TransNorm: transformer provides a strong spatial normalization mechanism for a deep segmentation model. IEEE Access 10, 108205–108215 (2022)

29. Azad, R., Bozorgpour, A., Asadi-Aghbolaghi, M., Merhof, D., Escalera, S.: Deep frequency re-calibration U-Net for medical image segmentation. In: Proceedings of the IEEE/CVF International Conference on Computer Vision, pp. 3274–3283 (2021)
30. Azad, R., Heidari, M., Wu, Y.: Contextual attention network: transformer meets U-Net. ArXiv preprint arXiv:2203.01932 (2022)
31. Azad, R., Jia, Y., Aghdam, E.K., Cohen-Adad, J., Merhof, D.: Enhancing medical image segmentation with TransCeption: a multi-scale feature fusion approach. ArXiv preprint arXiv:2301.10847 (2023)
32. Zongwei, W., Guillaume, A., Fabrice, M.: HiDAnet: RGB-D salient object detection via hierarchical depth awareness. IEEE Trans. Image Process. **32**, 2160–2173 (2023)
33. Zhou, T., Fu, H., Chen, G.: Specificity-preserving RGB-D saliency detection. In: Proceedings of the IEEE/CVF International Conference on Computer Vision, pp. 4681–4691 (2021)

Large Language Model for Geometric Algebra: A Preliminary Attempt

Jian Wang[1,2], Ziqiang Wang[1,2], Han Wang[1,2], Wen Luo[1,2], Linwang Yuan[1,2], Guonian Lü[1,2], and Zhaoyuan Yu[1,2(✉)]

[1] Key Laboratory of Virtual Geographic Environment, Ministry of Education, Nanjing Normal University, Nanjing 210023, China
yuzhaoyuan@njnu.edu.cn
[2] Jiangsu Center for Collaborative Innovation in Geographical Information Resource Development and Application, Nanjing 210023, China

Abstract. Geometric algebra serves as the unified language of mathematics, physics, and engineering in the 21st century. Coinciding with the era of artificial intelligence, the utilization of a Large Language Model (LLM) can significantly benefit the learning and application of geometric algebra. This study develops a representative application called PrivateGPT, based on the ggml-ggml-nous-gpt4-vicuna-13b model, to explore the integration of geometric algebra and LLM by building a knowledge base of geometric algebra expertise. The Geometric Algebra Knowledge Base was created by collecting 20,711 papers and data, categorizing them by topics. This application possesses the capability of iterative refinement, enhancing its understanding and reasoning of geometric algebra knowledge. It accomplishes the textual summarization of research content, methods, innovations, and conclusions. It facilitates the development of tailored learning plans for students from diverse fields to acquire knowledge of geometric algebra in their specific domains. Additionally, we compared the performance of PrivateGPT and ChatGPT in providing personalized learning paths for the same group of learners and evaluated their responses through a questionnaire survey. The results showed that PrivateGPT has an advantage in devising tailored learning plans for learners from various disciplines.

Keywords: Large Language Model · Geometric Algebra · Geometric Algebra Learning

1 Introduction

Geometric algebra serves as the unified language of mathematics, physics, and engineering in the 21st century [1]. Geometric algebra is a versatile mathematical tool that encompasses highly specialized mathematical abstractions, rigorous logical thinking, and intricate symbol systems. However, the lack of standardization in terminology and

Supported by the National Natural Science Foundation of China (No. 42130103, 42230406 and 41930404).

B. Sheng et al. (Eds.): CGI 2023, LNCS 14498, pp. 237–249, 2024.
https://doi.org/10.1007/978-3-031-50078-7_19

symbols across different domains within geometric algebra, due to its intricate disciplinary branches, presents challenges for effectively integrating geometric algebra knowledge [2]. Proficiently mastering geometric algebra requires not only learning a vast amount of knowledge and formulas but also developing one's mathematical abstraction and logical thinking abilities. This process incurs significant learning costs. Existing educational methods, such as specialized classes, textbook studies, online learning, and graphical approaches, offer some assistance to students in their learning journey. However, these methods have limitations in terms of limited audience reach and low generality. The core issue in geometric algebra education lies in constructing a teaching methodology that combines disciplinary expertise with cross-branch universality to address the current challenges in geometric algebra learning.

Large Language Models (LLMs) play a significant role in geometric algebra learning. Especially in the acquisition of domain-specific knowledge and intricate knowledge relationships in geometric algebra. LLM are crucial tools that support artificial intelligence in learning domain-specific knowledge in geometric algebra [3]. The mainstream LLM frameworks include GPT [4], LLaMa [5], and BERT [6]. These language models, composed of neural networks with a vast number of parameters, undergo unsupervised or semi-supervised training on large language datasets to aid machines in understanding and processing human language [7–9]. With the aid of AI, interaction with LLMs, and relevant knowledge documents, users can pose questions to computers and receive the desired knowledge. This approach exhibits considerable generality across diverse fields and yields high-quality responses. Its application has already made significant strides, particularly in the realm of medical education [10]. By leveraging LLM to aid students in learning elementary geometric algebra knowledge, the challenges of learning costs and scattered learning resources in geometric algebra can be addressed. However, General LLM may struggle to comprehend intricate language expressions and lack expertise in relatively specialized domains. Consequently, formulating question templates for LLM and enhancing and supplementing the knowledge base of LLMs with rule constraints become pivotal in further integrating artificial intelligence and geometric algebra education [11, 12].

This paper aims to address the complexity of learning geometric algebra, the limited applicability of traditional teaching methods, and the challenges posed by the shortcomings of general artificial intelligence in specialized fields. It does so by constructing a localized knowledge repository for geometric algebra vectorization, utilizing geometric algebra literature, books, formulas, and code. Through the interaction between the LLM and the knowledge repository, users can receive question-and-answer assistance based on their specific needs. Furthermore, user data and feedback are collected to enable the self-refinement of the model, thereby strengthening the understanding and reasoning abilities of PrivateGPT. The feasibility of this approach is demonstrated through case studies on geometric algebra paper interpretation and the development of Geometric Algebra Learning Routes in different fields within the paper.

2 PrivateGPT Construction Based on GA Knowledge

2.1 Geometric Algebra

Geometric algebra serves as an algebraic language used to describe and compute geometrical problems. Geometric algebra is formed based on the Hamilton quaternion and Grassmann's extended algebra, utilizing dimensional operations. Geometric algebra's key fundamental elements are multivector and geometric products, combining multidimensional objects into a single structure and incorporating the notions of orthogonality and collinearity into one operation. GA can be used for multidimension-unified expression and analysis in a coordinate-free way. The compactness of expression of GA and the multidimension-unified operations is conveyed, which greatly reduces the computation complexity and improves the analysis abilities. Geometric algebra has already become an important tool in various fields, including mathematical analysis, theoretical physics, geometry, mechanical theorem proving, computer graphics, Geographic Information Systems (GIS), robotics, and physics. Many study materials such as books exist for Geometric Algebra, however, these study materials cover different fields and the lack of standardization of terms and notation for Geometric Algebra in different fields makes it difficult to learn Geometric Algebra. Therefore, there is a need to develop learning programs that are more appropriate for different learners in terms of their disciplinary backgrounds and fields of application.

2.2 Construction of PrivateGPT and GA Knowledge

The limited representation of geometric algebra disciplines in general language models' training datasets can lead to responses that seem plausible but are ultimately incorrect or nonsensical when faced with such specialized inquiries. Geometric algebra, as a highly specialized field with multiple branches and concepts prone to ambiguity, and having a complex symbol system, necessitates constraints on the localized knowledge repository. PrivateGPT is an application capable of local private deployment. With the help of LLM, PrivateGPT can interact with the professional knowledge base using natural language. The localized nature of PrivateGPT fulfills this requirement. The localized version of PrivateGPT primarily includes three key aspects: establishing a localized knowledge repository, question answering constrained by the localized knowledge repository, and self-iterative refinement of the model. The construction process is illustrated in Fig. 1.

The constraints on the geometric algebra knowledge base primarily lie in the construction of the knowledge base itself. A knowledge base of geometric algebra is constructed by collecting 20,711 papers and books from sources such as arXiv and AACA and categorizing them based on research area, research space, and other relevant factors. This knowledge base is specifically designed to extract specialized geometric algebra knowledge. The clustering results based on the keywords from the knowledge base are illustrated in Fig. 2.

Utilizing the aforementioned data sources, establish a localized knowledge repository focused on geometric algebra, requiring the vectorization of geometric algebra documents. Due to the considerable scale of the documents and the complexity of semantic relationships, it is crucial to begin by segmenting the documents. This enables the

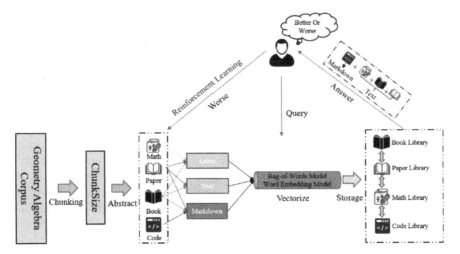

Fig. 1. Knowledge base data processing process and model self-iteration.

model to comprehend the context of each unit more effectively and capture more nuanced semantics. After completing the processing, block data and corresponding metadata (e.g., file names, types, and page numbers) can be obtained. As geometric algebra involves numerous mathematical symbols, equations, and operators, which may not be effectively extracted and learned from PDF and similar files, perform data extraction from the segmented text after segmenting the documents. Extract code snippets and mathematical formulas from papers and books, categorizing the data into four categories: Paper, Book, Code, and Math.

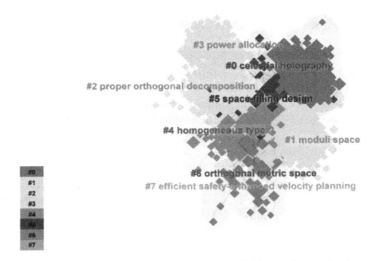

Fig. 2. Geometric Algebra Paper Key Words K-Means Cluster Graph.

Figure 1 illustrates the construction of the knowledge base constraints. Text containing mathematical symbols and formulas can be converted into LaTeX representation using conversion operators. This process translates mathematical language into a specific textual format. For documents such as PDFs that cannot directly interpret formulas, OCR can be utilized to identify the mathematical language and convert it into corresponding LaTeX code, facilitating the vectorization of mathematical language. For example, when considering the scaling operator $I(x_e) = \frac{\rho^2(x_e - C_e)}{x_e - C_e} + C_e$, convert it to Latex format \[I(\{x_e\}) = \frac\{\{\{\rho ^2\}(\{x_e\} - \{c_e\})\}\}\{\{\{\{\{((\{x_i\} - \{c_e\})\}^2\}\}\}\} + \{c_e\}\], this formula represents scaling based on a ball or circle, where C_e is the circle and ρ is the radius. Code vectorization involves dividing the code into different units, such as functions, statements, or lines, based on its structure and syntax. The structural information of the code, such as indentation, spaces, and line breaks, remains preserved. Code parsing tools, like abstract syntax trees, are employed to extract the structural information of the code and transform it into markdown code blocks for further processing. Consequently, the original data, including papers and books, is transformed into Text+Latex+markdown, formulas into LaTeX, and code into markdown. Next, employing techniques like a bag of words models, word embeddings, or pre-trained language models, the text is transformed into vector representations. Finally, leveraging rich representations of text vectors, such as LangChain[13] and Chroma[14], provides additional linguistic features and semantic information about the text. This process leads to the construction of a geometric algebra vectorized knowledge base, which includes paper knowledge, book knowledge, code knowledge, and formula knowledge.

Besides converting the external knowledge repository into vectors, the user's query is also vectorized. The user's inquiry is transformed into a vector representation and subsequently compared and matched with the text vectors in the knowledge repository. By utilizing similarity calculation methods like cosine similarity, the similarity between the query-generated vector and the text vectors in the knowledge repository is assessed. The top sentences that exhibit the highest similarity to the query vector are selected and sorted based on their similarity scores. The highest scoring k texts are selected as the matching results and presented as the answer generated in response to the user's query.

The constraints of the geometric algebra knowledge base are evident in the model's fine-tuning [15, 16], driven by user feedback on generated answers, which indicates their quality as "better" or "worse". If users are dissatisfied or identify errors in the model's feedback, such as incorrect mathematical symbols, operators, or code, the answer is directly categorized as "worse," prompting the model to make corrections. The correction process may involve users providing more accurate information, such as supplying the correct answer or pointing out errors in the model's response. These user-provided inputs serve as training data, which includes the question, the original answer, and the user's perceived correct answer or error indication. Repeating these steps, continuously collecting user feedback, and making corrections facilitate an iterative reinforcement learning process, gradually enhancing the model's understanding and inference capabilities in geometric algebra knowledge.

3 PrivateGPT Application Based on GA Knowledge

3.1 LLM Assisted Geometric Algebra Learning

The role of the Prompt [17] can be understood as how we engage in dialogue with the model. Similar to how we pose questions or provide contextual information when communicating with others, the Prompt offers guiding clues that assist the model in understanding our intentions and generating corresponding responses. Thus, this paper aims to enhance the relevance and accuracy of the model's outputs by designing a Prompt template tailored to geometric algebra education. Taking into consideration the depth of students' desired learning, the language of instruction, the language of instruction, communication methods, language style, research domain, research space, students' disciplinary background, and learning approaches, the template aims to facilitate PrivateGPT in addressing instructional inquiries about geometric algebra. as shown in Table 1 and 2.

Table 1. Geometric Algebra Learning Prompt.

Geometric Algebra Learning Prompt Template	xx
I hope you will play a teacher in the field of {Field of Study} in the {Research Space} of geometric algebra. You will use {Learning Styles} learning methods and {Communication} like communication methods for teaching. Your reasoning framework is {Reasoning Frameworks} and I hope your tonal style is {Tone Styles}. Your students want to delve deeper into {Depth} studies, and their academic background is {Students' Academic Background}. I will play your student, I hope to learn in {Method of Study}, and I hope you can assist me in my studies, your student's native language is {Language}, next is the student's first question:	xx

3.2 Geometric Algebra Paper Automation Summary

Considering the various areas of specialization and intricate notation systems in geometric algebra across different fields, a concise review of papers covering diverse fields and notation systems benefits researchers in exploring applications and learning geometric algebra. Thus, utilizing LLM for automated summarization of scientific papers can significantly aid scholars in efficiently exploring various domains in geometric algebra. Firstly, the paper should be automatically divided into four sections: abstract, introduction, method, and conclusion. As the abstract does not provide a comprehensive description of the research content, it is necessary to summarize the paper's research content in the Abstract and Introduction sections. Next, use the Method section to summarize the methods and innovations of the thesis. Lastly, summarize the conclusion based on the preceding content from the output and conclusion sections. The keywords represent the paper's key terms, and the content of each section is retrieved from the knowledge base. The template is presented in Table 3.

Table 2. Geometric Algebra Learning Prompt Option.

Configuration	Options
Depth	Elementary (Grade 1-6), Middle School (Grade 7-9), ..., Undergraduate, Graduate, Master's, Doctoral Candidate, Postdoc, Ph.D.
Learning Styles	Sensing, ..., Verbal, Deductive, Reflective
Reasoning Frameworks	Deductive method, ..., causal method
Language	English (support for other languages)
Communication	Stochastic, Formal, Textbook, ..., Storytelling
Tone Styles	Encouraging, ..., Neutral, Informative, Friendly
Field of Study	GIS, Computer animation and video processing, ..., GA for artificial intelligence
Research Space	Conformal Space, Homogeneous Space, ..., Projective Space
Students' Academic Background	GIS, ..., Geometric mathematics
Method of Study	Computing machines, code, ..., formulas

Table 3. GA Paper Summary Prompt.

GA Paper Summary Prompt Template
As a researcher proficient in the field of {Key Word}, your expertise lies in crafting succinct summaries of academic papers. I kindly request you to utilize the {Abstract} and {Introduction} sections of the {Paper Name} to summarize the research content of the paper. Additionally, please use the {Methodology} section to outline the methods and innovative aspects of the paper. Finally, based on the previous outputs and the {Results} section of the paper, please provide a comprehensive conclusion in the specified format.   1. Research Contents: XXX/n   2. Methods: XXX/n   3. Innovation points: XXX/n   4. Results:- XXX /n - XXX /n - XXX /n - XXX /n

4 Assisting in GA Research and Learning

4.1 Assisted Learning

Using a learning plan formulation for introducing conformal GA into Geographic Information Systems (GIS) as an exemplar, this paper employed the provided prompt from Tables 1 and 2. This paper showcases the responses from both ChatGPT and PrivateGPT, utilizing the identical prompt, in Table 4. Both sources provide valuable guidance on devising a learning plan for incorporating conformal GA in GIS, covering aspects like utilizing conformal GA for spatial data representation. Compared to ChatGPT, the privateGPT developed in this study demonstrates the ability to provide reasoning behind its responses, thereby assisting students in retracing their learning through scholarly papers, code, and other resources.

This paper conducts a questionnaire survey to compare the two learning routes based on 5 aspects. Each question is rated on a scale of 1 to 10, where 1 indicates dissatisfaction, and 10 indicates satisfaction. The survey yielded 12 pieces of valid data, and the average score of the two learning routes for the 5 questions is calculated. Based on the average score, PrivateGPT outperforms ChatGPT in responding to professional questions by 1.75 points, which can be attributed to its reliance on a professional knowledge base. Moreover, PrivateGPT provides reference resources when answering questions, making it beneficial for beginners to learn Geometric Algebra, as evidenced by the fourth and fifth items in Table 5.

4.2 Analysis and Summary of Geometric Algebra Papers

This paper experimented with evaluating PrivateGPT's capability to comprehend and summarize research content, research methods, innovation, and conclusions. The experiment used the paper titled "Multilevel Declassification Method for Geographic Vector Field Data: A Geometric Algebra Approach" by Luo et al. [23]. Based on the given prompt, PrivateGPT accurately summarized the aforementioned aspects of the paper, as shown in Fig. 3 [24, 25]. In general, this method effectively captures the essence of Luo's paper, which introduces a multilevel decryption method for geographic vector field data based on geometric algebra, which can progressively hide detailed information while retaining general geospatial features.

Table 4. GIS Learning Plan under Conformal GA.

PrivateGPT	ChatGPT
PrivateGPT Prompt: I hope you will play a teacher in the field of geographic information systems in the conformal space of geometric algebra. You will use inductive learning methods and textbook-like communication methods for teaching. Your reasoning framework is deductive and I hope your tonal style is encouraging. Your students want to delve deeper into undergraduate studies, and their academic background in computer science. I will play your student, I hope to learn in computer science, and I hope you can assist me in my studies, your student's native language is English, next is the student's first question: Please help me discuss a learning outline in detail, and its output format is as follows: 1. XXX\n a): XXX; \n b): XXX; \n c): XXX; \n 2. XXX\n a): XXX; \n b): XXX; \n c): XXX; \n	

(continued)

Table 4. (*continued*)

PrivateGPT	ChatGPT
Response:	**Response:**
1. Introduction to GIS and its applications	**1. Introduction to Geographic Information Systems**
a): Definition of GIS and its importance in various fields	**(GIS)**
b): Types of data used in GIS	a) Definition and fundamental concepts of GIS
c): Applications of GIS in urban planning, natural	b) Applications of GIS in various domains (e.g.,
resource management, and other fields	environmental science, urban planning,
2. Basic concepts of GA	transportation)
a): Definition and introduction to GA	c) Overview of the conformal space of GA and its
b): Vectors and bivectors in GA	relevance to GIS
c): Geometric product and wedge product	**2. Basics of GA**
d): Introduction to conformal space and its	a) Introduction to GA and its mathematical foundations
representation in GA	b) Geometric interpretation of GA elements (e.g.,
3. Representation of spatial data using GA	points, lines, planes)
a): Introduction to spatial data and its representation in	c) Geometric operations in conformal GA (e.g.,
GIS	intersection, projection, duality)
b): Repression of spatial data using GA	**3. Geospatial Data Representation**
c): Example problems and solutions using GA	a) Representation of spatial data using geometric
4. Computing with GA in GIS	algebra
a): Introduction to computing with GA	b) Conformal representation of points, lines, polygons,
b): Implementation of geometric algebra in GIS	and other spatial objects
software	c) Transformation and manipulation of geospatial data
c): Examples of computational problems and their	using GA operations
solutions using geometric algebra	**4. Geometric Analysis in GIS**
5. Spatial analysis and modeling using geometric	a) Spatial analysis techniques using GA
algebra	b) Geometric relationships and operations (e.g.,
a): Introduction to spatial analysis and modeling	distance, area, buffering)
b): Application of geometric algebra in spatial analysis	c) Topological analysis and spatial queries in
and modeling	conformal GA
c): Example problems and solutions using geometric	**5. Spatial Data Visualization**
algebra	a) Visualization techniques for geospatial data b)
6. Advanced topics in GIS and geometric algebra	Cartographic principles and map design
a): Introduction to advanced topics in GIS and	c) Visualization of conformal GA objects and
geometric algebra	operations
b): Current research and trends in GIS and geometric	**6. GIS Data Management**
algebra	a) Data acquisition and preprocessing
c): Example problems and solutions using advanced	b) Data models and database design for GIS
topics in GIS and geometric algebra	c) Conformal geometric algebra-based data storage
7. Project work on real-world GIS problems using	and retrieval
geometric algebra	**7. GIS Algorithms and Applications**
a): Introduction to project work	a) Advanced algorithms in GIS (e.g., spatial
b): Selection of real-world GIS problems for a solution	interpolation, network analysis)
using geometric algebra	b) Applications of GIS in computer science domains
c): Implementation of geometric algebra in solving the	(e.g., machine learning, computer vision)
selected problem I hope this helps! Let me know if you	c) Case studies and practical examples illustrating the
have any questions or need further clarification on any	use of conformal geometric algebra in GIS
of these topics.	**8. Project Work and Practical Applications**
	a) Hands-on projects to reinforce learning and apply
	GIS concepts
	b) Developing geospatial applications using geometric
	algebra libraries
	c) Presenting and discussing project outcomes for
	feedback and improvement

(*continued*)

Table 4. (*continued*)

PrivateGPT	ChatGPT

ChatGPT Source: null
PrivateGPT Source:
1. Guide to Geometric Algebra in Practice[18]**(Book):**
PhD projects in this direction!
To conclude this introduction, some sobering thoughts. Geometric algebra has been with us in application form for about 15 to 20 years now, with general application software available for the last 10 years. There have been tutorial books written for increasingly applied audiences, migrating the results from mathematics to physics, to engineering and to computer science. Still, a conference on applications.
2. Articulating Space: Geometric Algebra for Parametric Design —Symmetry, Kinematics, and Curvature. [19]**(Book):**
ability to communicate form. Each synthesis technique has relied heavily on the previous work of others, both inside and outside the geometric algebra community, and by sheer necessity we have built upon known algorithms by unearthing details critical to their use in construction. Throughout we have consistently returned to the groundbreaking textbook by Dorst, Mann, and Fontijne [45](References in the original literature[20]), which provides much of the syntax of geometric relationships
3. Introducing Geometric Algebra to Geometric Computing Software Developers A Computational Thinking Approach[21] **(Paper):**
implementable by a digital or human computing device. CT relies on using abstraction and decomposition when attacking a large complex task or designing a large complex system; it requires thinking at multiple levels of abstraction [42] (References in the original literature[22]). Geometric Algebra can be a valuable mathematical language to acquire and develop such CT skills for handling Geometric Computing problems. As illustrated in Fig. 1.1, a Geometric Algebra is an abstract, elegant, and

Table 5. GIS Learning Plan under Conformal Geometric Algebra.

Questionnaire contents	PrivateGPT	ChatGPT
Is the teaching objective of the learning routes clear?	8.75	8.75
Are the learning routes effectively integrating geometric algebra with Geographic Information Systems for study?	8.67	8.25
Can a specialized knowledge base improve the credibility of LLM output?	8.42	6.67
For beginners, what kind of learning routes would you prefer to follow to learn the integration between GA and GIS?	7.83	7.33
Can learning routes be an aid to geometric algebra?	*9.08*	8.33

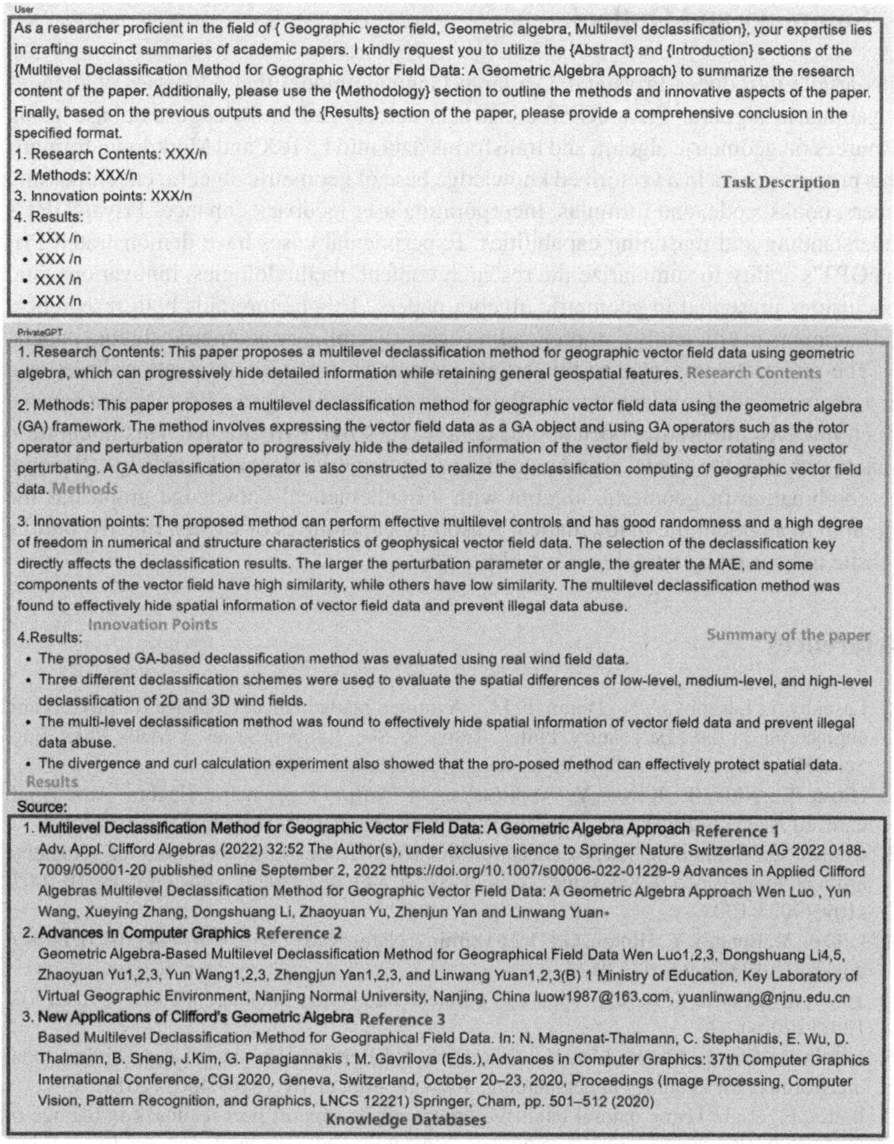

As a researcher proficient in the field of { Geographic vector field, Geometric algebra, Multilevel declassification}, your expertise lies in crafting succinct summaries of academic papers. I kindly request you to utilize the {Abstract} and {Introduction} sections of the {Multilevel Declassification Method for Geographic Vector Field Data: A Geometric Algebra Approach} to summarize the research content of the paper. Additionally, please use the {Methodology} section to outline the methods and innovative aspects of the paper. Finally, based on the previous outputs and the {Results} section of the paper, please provide a comprehensive conclusion in the specified format.

1. Research Contents: XXX/n

2. Methods: XXX/n

3. Innovation points: XXX/n   **Task Description**

4. Results:

- XXX /n
- XXX /n
- XXX /n
- XXX /n

1. Research Contents: This paper proposes a multilevel declassification method for geographic vector field data using geometric algebra, which can progressively hide detailed information while retaining general geospatial features. Research Contents

2. Methods: This paper proposes a multilevel declassification method for geographic vector field data using the geometric algebra (GA) framework. The method involves expressing the vector field data as a GA object and using GA operators such as the rotor operator and perturbation operator to progressively hide the detailed information of the vector field by vector rotating and vector perturbating. A GA declassification operator is also constructed to realize the declassification computing of geographic vector field data. Methods

3. Innovation points: The proposed method can perform effective multilevel controls and has good randomness and a high degree of freedom in numerical and structure characteristics of geophysical vector field data. The selection of the declassification key directly affects the declassification results. The larger the perturbation parameter or angle, the greater the MAE, and some components of the vector field have high similarity, while others have low similarity. The multilevel declassification method was found to effectively hide spatial information of vector field data and prevent illegal data abuse.

    Innovation Points

4. Results: Summary of the paper

- The proposed GA-based declassification method was evaluated using real wind field data.
- Three different declassification schemes were used to evaluate the spatial differences of low-level, medium-level, and high-level declassification of 2D and 3D wind fields.
- The multi-level declassification method was found to effectively hide spatial information of vector field data and prevent illegal data abuse.
- The divergence and curl calculation experiment also showed that the pro-posed method can effectively protect spatial data.

Results

1. **Multilevel Declassification Method for Geographic Vector Field Data: A Geometric Algebra Approach** Reference 1
    Adv. Appl. Clifford Algebras (2022) 32:52 The Author(s), under exclusive licence to Springer Nature Switzerland AG 2022 0188-7009/050001-20 published online September 2, 2022 https://doi.org/10.1007/s00006-022-01229-9 Advances in Applied Clifford Algebras Multilevel Declassification Method for Geographic Vector Field Data: A Geometric Algebra Approach Wen Luo , Yun Wang, Xueying Zhang, Dongshuang Li, Zhaoyuan Yu, Zhenjun Yan and Linwang Yuan﹡

2. **Advances in Computer Graphics** Reference 2
    Geometric Algebra-Based Multilevel Declassification Method for Geographical Field Data Wen Luo1,2,3, Dongshuang Li4,5, Zhaoyuan Yu1,2,3, Yun Wang1,2,3, Zhengjun Yan1,2,3, and Linwang Yuan1,2,3(B) 1 Ministry of Education, Key Laboratory of Virtual Geographic Environment, Nanjing Normal University, Nanjing, China luow1987@163.com, yuanlinwang@njnu.edu.cn

3. **New Applications of Clifford's Geometric Algebra** Reference 3
    Based Multilevel Declassification Method for Geographical Field Data. In: N. Magnenat-Thalmann, C. Stephanidis, E. Wu, D. Thalmann, B. Sheng, J.Kim, G. Papagiannakis , M. Gavrilova (Eds.), Advances in Computer Graphics: 37th Computer Graphics International Conference, CGI 2020, Geneva, Switzerland, October 20–23, 2020, Proceedings (Image Processing, Computer Vision, Pattern Recognition, and Graphics, LNCS 12221) Springer, Cham, pp. 501–512 (2020)
    Knowledge Databases

Fig. 3. Paper Summary System Demonstration Diagram.

5 Summary and Outlook

This article introduces PrivateGPT, a large language model that addresses challenges in geometric algebra. PrivateGPT constructs a localized knowledge database using resources on geometric algebra and transforms data into LaTeX and Markdown formats. This process results in a vectorized knowledge base of geometric algebra, encompassing papers, books, code, and formulas. Incorporating user feedback enhances PrivateGPT's understanding and reasoning capabilities. Experimental cases have demonstrated PrivateGPT's ability to summarize the research content, methodologies, innovations, and conclusions presented in geometric algebra papers. This feature aids both researchers and beginners in efficiently comprehending cross-disciplinary geometric algebra papers.

The prospects presented in this article encompass several optimization directions. First, there is a need to construct an efficient and standardized geometric algebra dataset, which involves integrating open-source data sources like Bivector.net. This integration aims to enhance the model's understanding of geometric algebra knowledge. Second, the combination of geometric algebra with a mathematical knowledge graph has the potential to augment the mathematical reasoning capabilities of LLMs. Finally, build a website to be used by a total number of people.

References

1. Lasenby, J., Lasenby, A.N., Doran, C.J.L.: A unified mathematical language for physics and engineering in the 21st century. Philos. Trans. R. Soc. London Series A-Math. Phys. Eng. Sci. **358**(1765), 21–39 (2000). https://doi.org/10.1098/rsta.2000.0517
2. Hitzer, E., Nitta, T., Kuroe, Y.: Applications of Clifford's geometric algebra. Adv. Appl. Clifford Algebras **23**(2), 377–404 (2013). https://doi.org/10.1007/s00006-013-0378-4
3. Cooper, G.: Examining science education in ChatGPT: an exploratory study of generative artificial intelligence. J. Sci. Educ. Technol. **32**(3), 444–452 (2023). https://doi.org/10.1007/s10956-023-10039-y
4. LeCun, Y., Bengio, Y., Hinton, G.: Deep learning. Nature **521**(7553), 436–444 (2015). https://doi.org/10.1038/nature14539
5. Touvron, H., et al.: LLaMA: open and efficient foundation language models. arXiv:2302.13971 (2023)
6. Devlin, J., Chang, M. W., Lee, K., Toutanova, K.: Bert: pre-training of deep bidirectional transformers for language understanding. arXiv preprint arXiv:1810.04805 (2018)
7. Bauer, E., et al.: Using natural language processing to support peer-feedback in the age of artificial intelligence: a cross-disciplinary framework and a research agenda. Br. J. Educ. Technol. 107–125 (2023). https://doi.org/10.1111/bjet.13336
8. Sorin, V., Barash, Y., Konen, E., Klang, E.: Large language models for oncological applications. J. Cancer Res. Clin. Oncol. **363**, 1287–1289 (2023). https://doi.org/10.1007/s00432-023-04824-w
9. Brants, T., Popat, A. C., Xu, P., Och, F. J., Dean, J.: Large Language Models in Machine Translation. 2007
10. Kung, T.H., et al.: Performance of ChatGPT on USMLE: potential for AI-assisted medical education using large language models. PLOS Digit. Health **2**(2), e0000198 (2023). https://doi.org/10.1371/journal.pdig.0000198

11. Oh, N., Choi, G.-S., Lee, W.Y.: ChatGPT goes to the operating room: Evaluating GPT-4 performance and its potential in surgical education and training in the era of large language models. Ann. Surg. Treat. Res. **104**(5), 269–273 (2023)
12. Lee, H.: The rise of CHATGPT: exploring its potential in medical education. Anat. Sci. Educ. (2023)
13. Kraus, M., et al.: Enhancing large language models with climate resources arXiv preprint arXiv:2304.00116 (2023)
14. Chroma. https://www.trychroma.com/
15. Hu, E.J., et al.: Lora: low-rank adaptation of large language models. arXiv preprint arXiv: 2106.09685 (2021)
16. Lester, B., Al-Rfou, R., Constant, N.: The power of scale for parameter-efficient prompt tuning. arXiv preprint arXiv:2104.08691 (2021)
17. Hu, S., et al.: Knowledgeable prompt-tuning: incorporating knowledge into prompt verbalizer for text classification. arXiv preprint arXiv:2108.02035 (2021)
18. Lasenby, J.: Guide to Geometric Algebra in Practice, 1st edn. Springer, New York (2011). https://doi.org/10.1007/978-0-85729-811-9
19. Colapinto, P.: Articulating space: geometric algebra for parametric design-symmetry, kinematics, and curvature. Ph.D. University of California, Santa Barbara (2016)
20. Dorst, L., Daniel, F., Stephen, M.: Geometric Algebra for Computer Science: An Object-Oriented Approach to Geometry, 1st edn. Elsevier, San Francisco (2009)
21. Hosny Eid, A.: Introducing geometric algebra to geometric computing software developers: a computational thinking approach. arXiv:1705.06668 (2017)
22. Jeannette, M.W.: Computational thinking. Commun. ACM **49**(3), 33–35 (2006)
23. Luo, W., et al.: Multilevel declassification method for geographic vector field data: a geometric algebra approach. Adv. Appl. Clifford Algebras **32**(5), 52–72 (2022)
24. Magnenat-Thalmann, N., et al.: Advances in Computer Graphics, 1st edn. Springer, Cham (2020). https://doi.org/10.1007/978-3-030-89029-2
25. Breuils, S., Tachibana, K., Hitzer, E.: New applications of Clifford's geometric algebra. Adv. Appl. Clifford Algebras **32**(2), 17–56 (2022)

Game Physics Engine Using Optimised Geometric Algebra RISC-V Vector Extensions Code Using Fourier Series Data

Ed Saribatir[1]([✉]), Niko Zurstraßen[2], Dietmar Hildenbrand[3], Florian Stock[3], Atilio Morillo Piña[4], Frederic von Wegner[5], Zheng Yan[6], Shiping Wen[6], and Matthew Arnold[1]

[1] School of Mathematical and Physical Sciences, University of Technology Sydney, Ultimo, Australia
`ed.saribatir@student.uts.edu.au`
[2] RWTH Aachen University, Aachen, Germany
[3] Technische Universitaet Darmstadt, Darmstadt, Germany
[4] Applied Math Research Center (CIMA), Engineering School, The University of Zulia, Maracaibo, Venezuela
[5] School of Biomedical Sciences, The University of New South Wales, Sydney, Australia
[6] Intelligent Computing and Systems Lab, Australian Artificial Intelligence Institute, University of Technology Sydney, Ultimo, Australia
`https://www.gaalop.de/`

Abstract. We describe an example of using a Geometric Algebra algorithm to compute motion in a game physics engine, we optimise the Geometric Algebra algorithm using GAALOP and utilise RISC-V Vector Extensions (RVV) to perform computations on vectors, we combine this with vectors used to represent a number of Fourier series to model x, y and z components of gravity, wind and surface friction. When RISC-V Vector Extension devices become available, we anticipate this method will lead to performance improvements over alternative approaches.

Keywords: Geometric Algebra algorithm · GAALOP · RISC-V Vector Extension (RVV) · Fourier series · Game physics engine

1 Introduction

Computer games perform many calculations in real-time to model game physics. Improving performance of software algorithms by using optimisation and new hardware designs to take advantage of vector operations will allow for more realistic game physics and allow game developers to design more complex games.

In this paper we introduce related work on game physics engines (Sect. 2.1), Geometric Algebra and Geometric Algebra algorithms (Sect. 2.2), GAALOP

© The Author(s), under exclusive license to Springer Nature Switzerland AG 2024
B. Sheng et al. (Eds.): CGI 2023, LNCS 14498, pp. 250–261, 2024.
https://doi.org/10.1007/978-3-031-50078-7_20

(Sect. 2.3), the RISC-V Instruction Set Architecture and RISC-V Vector Extension (RVV) (Sect. 2.4), and Fourier series (Sect. 2.5).

We demonstrate how Geometric Algebra algorithms can be used to compute the forces acting on a particle in a game physics engine (Sect. 3) as well as show optimised code that can be generated by GAALOP, which uses vector operations on hardware that supports RISC-V Vector Extensions (RVV) (Sect. 4), we provide an example of code that uses a bitmask to select data in a Fourier series (Sect. 5). Future work is described in Sect. 6. Code examples are available at the repository [1], for quick reference relevant source code has also been listed in the Appendix (Sect. A).

2   Related Work

2.1   Game Physics Engines

Computer games and simulation software use physics engines to perform real-time calculations using mathematical models to provide a realistic approximation for the motion of objects and effects of forces and collisions [2–4]. These calculations need to be performed with low latency using the hardware computing resources available on game consoles and gaming computers.

2.2   Geometric Algebra

Geometric algebra is a powerful mathematical framework that has applications in all areas of physics and engineering [5]. It is well suited for game physics engine development [2–4]. Geometric Algebra algorithms use the mathematical objects in Geometric Algebra for computational tasks. For the examples in this paper, we will be using 3D Projective Geometric Algebra which has a signature of (3, 0, 1).

2.3   GAALOP

GAALOP (Geometric Algebra ALgorithms OPtimizer) [6] is an open-source software to optimize geometric algebra algorithms [7–9]. Geometric Algebra algorithms can be described using GAALOPScript[1], and code can be generated for C/C++, Python, Java and many other languages. In 2009, a Geometric Algebra robotics grasping algorithm optimised by GAALOP running on CUDA hardware saw a speed-up by 44 times compared to conventional math running on a CPU [10]. We anticipate performance improvements with hardware such as RISC-V Vector Extensions that allow vector operations to be computed efficiently.

---

[1] See Sect. 3.2 of [7].

2.4 RISC-V and RISC-V Vector Extension (RVV) Instructions

RISC-V is an open-source instruction set architecture (ISA). RISC-V stands for Reduced Instruction Set Computing - Version 5. RISC-V is an open standard, its specifications are freely available for anyone to use, modify, and implement [11].

RISC-V Vector Extension (RVV) [12,13] is an extension to the RISC-V instruction set architecture that introduces vector instructions. Vector instructions allow processors to perform operations on multiple data elements simultaneously, which can accelerate certain types of computations, such as signal processing, scientific simulations, and machine learning.

2.5 Fourier Series

A Fourier series is an expansion of a periodic function into a sum of trigonometric functions [14]. There are many applications of the Fourier series [15], and a Fourier series in 1-D, 2-D, or 3-D can be used to describe a wave, surface or shapes of objects [16].

Related work is the use of 3D Fourier Descriptors with Conformal Geometric Algebra which has been described in [17] and Chap. 7 of [18].

In a game physics engine, a vector (an array of floating-point numbers) can be used to represent a 3D Fourier Descriptor [19], tracing the surface of an object (See Fig. 4. in [16]), it is possible to compute interactions with the environment e.g. collision detection with other objects, forces acting on object points touching the ground or ray-tracing using mathematical computations such as linear algebra, although these will not be discussed in this paper.

To illustrate how Fourier Descriptors can be used to model terrain in a computer game, a simple script generated using ChatGPT [20] to create 1,000,000 random points in a 1,000 × 1,000 × 1,000 pixel 3D volume to represent mountains. The terrain data was compressed using a Fast Fourier Transform and the coefficients of the Fourier Descriptor were reduced to 10,000, 5,000, 2,000, 1,000, 500, 200, 100 and 50 coefficients, to illustrate how 3D shapes and surfaces can be modelled using Fourier Descriptors with a level of resolution that is appropriate for the design of the game. The Python code used to generate the data and high resolution images of the charts are available at [21].

While there are methods to generate more realistic terrain or have the terrain data imported from computer graphics software, this is outside the scope of this paper.

The normal at each point on the mesh can be used to calculate a multi-dimensional vector field that represents the x, y and z components of the force of gravity at each point, as well as store the coefficient of friction due to the material properties at that point of the surface.

The pre-computed values in the vector field can be used to speed up game physics engine calculations, with the accuracy and level of approximations adjusted depending on game needs, with trade-offs between processing power required, time of computation for each object and frame rate requirements taken into consideration (Fig. 1).

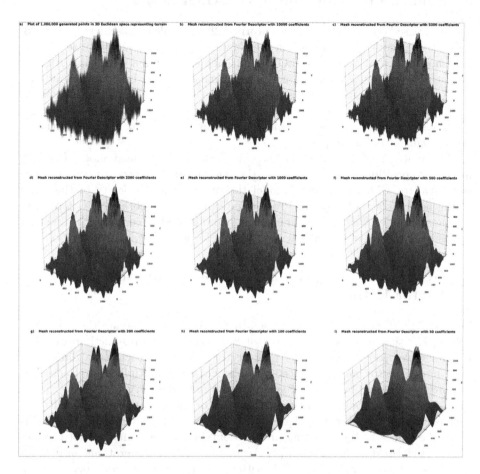

Fig. 1.
a) Plot of 1,000,000 generated points in 3D Euclidean space representing terrain,
b) Mesh reconstructed from Fourier Descriptor with 10,000 coefficients,
c) Mesh reconstructed from Fourier Descriptor with 5,000 coefficients,
d) Mesh reconstructed from Fourier Descriptor with 2,000 coefficients,
e) Mesh reconstructed from Fourier Descriptor with 1,000 coefficients,
f) Mesh reconstructed from Fourier Descriptor with 500 coefficients,
g) Mesh reconstructed from Fourier Descriptor with 200 coefficients,
h) Mesh reconstructed from Fourier Descriptor with 100 coefficients,
i) Mesh reconstructed from Fourier Descriptor with 50 coefficients.
Compression errors can be seen as the resolution of the terrain is reduced due to
the reduction of coefficients in the Fourier Descriptor used to reconstruct the mesh.
Features in the terrain are smoothed out as the number of coefficients used are reduced.
Higher resolution images and the Python script used to generate charts are available
[21].

3   Simulation Algorithm in GAALOPScript

We have based our example on the tutorial [22] available on the bivector.net [23] website, with code [24] available on the Ganja.js CoffeeShop [25] website. Listing 1. 2 shows an example of GAALOPScript code describing a Geometric Algebra algorithm to compute the motion of a point mass affected by gravity, wind and friction. A macro named Line is used to create a bivector which can model the forces for gravity, wind, friction and a component for a motor (motion operator) which can describe the position and orientation of the point (the orientation is not relevant in this example).

The macro nextM is used for the computation of the next motor (used to model the position and orientation), the macro nextB is used to compute the next bivector which is used to model the direction and velocity of the point at the next instant of time, in Projective Geometric Algebra (PGA) force and torque are unified with a force line, the F macro is used to compute the line that represents the sum of the effects of the forces for gravity, wind and friction.

4   Generation of Optimized RISC-V Code that Utilises Vector Extensions

The GAALOPScript code is optimised by GAALOP to generate the C code in Listing 1. 3 that utilises RISC-V Vector Extension (RVV) instructions called in the assembler code in Listing 1. 4 for vector operations such as loading array data into a vector memory (vle32.v) element-wise multiplication/Hadamard product (vfmul.vv) and sum of vector values (vfredusum.vs).

A vector dot-product operation takes two or more vector values, multiplies each element in the vector(s) element-wise (Hadamard product), and then sums all of the values in the resulting array to obtain a scalar value. A dot-product can be performed by using Multiply Accumulate (MAC) operations on individual elements. GAALOP reduces algorithms to simple arithmetic operations on values of dot-products. This can be seen in Listing 1. 3, with functions named dot_product_2 and dot_product_3 that are called in the C program which are implemented in the assembler code in Listing 1. 4 with the same function names.

5   Fourier Series to Represent X, Y and Z Components of Forces in a Game Physics Engine

Fourier series are useful in a game physics engine to represent computed values of the x, y and z components of forces such as gravity, wind and surface friction.

The coefficients used in the Fourier series can be stored in a single vector, with design decisions for constants such as the length of the vector, range of output values and level of resolution being set as per requirements of the game and the target hardware.

In the example of a golf game, once a terrain is generated, the normal at each point on the surface of the ground can be used to generate a vector field for the x, y and z components of the force of gravity. A Fourier transform can be used on the vector field data to compute a Fourier series for the x, y and z components. In games where the terrain doesn't change this can be computed as soon as the terrain is generated, or an in-game computation thread can update the vector values of the Fourier series, when events such as collisions with the ground change the terrain surface.

Similarly, for dynamic forces such as wind, a Fourier series can be computed for the x, y, z components. An in-game thread can update vector values for wind using an algorithm, e.g., taking account air pressure and fluid mechanics for wind.

The surface friction can be modelled in the same way, i.e., a Fourier series can be computed for the x, y, z components, and once again the values of the vector can be updated as the surface changes or substances, such as water, change the surface friction. For realism, the surface friction value at a point can be multiplied with a factor or a computation that takes into account the velocity of the object at that point.

Compressing all of the data for a terrain or wind and friction forces into a single vector can be beneficial when performing many computations in real-time on many different objects as required in a computer game physics engine. The number of computations increases exponentially when the configuration parameters such as number of objects, the number of surfaces on a terrain and the resolution of the effects of wind are increased. Memory utilisation can be reduced substantially when using a Fourier series representing vectors in a 3D space such as required for modelling the wind.

When computing the value for a force component, the bits of the three floating point numbers x, y, z representing position can be used as a mask to include/exclude Fourier series vector values. The RISC-V Vector Extension vector load assembler instruction has an optional parameter (vm) that is a vector mask that includes/excludes values depending on if the vector mask element is 0. The vfmerge.vfm instruction can also be used for this process.

Listing 1. 1. RISC-V Vector Extension vector load and vector merge instructions.

```
1  vle32.v      vd, (rs1), vm
2  vfmerge.vfm  vd, vs2, rs1, v0
3  # vd[i] = v0.mask[i] ? f[rs1] : vs2[i]
```

Once the vector is loaded, it can be multiplied with another vector containing base elements that correspond with the magnitude of the vector element, that is an exponentially increasing value for the vector elements, which give a range of the minimum and maximum values for a 32-bit floating point number.

Listing 1. 6 shows an example of a C program making use of RISC-V Vector Intrinsics [27], this program uses an unsigned integer as a bitmask to filter values from a vector.

We have included the Makefiles we have used in Listing 1. 5 and Listing 1. 7 to assist researchers as there is limited documentation, tutorials or examples available online. The RISC-V GNU Compiler Toolchain has been used in compilation [28].

This C code can be combined with the function generated with GAALOP to compute forces acting on an object efficiently, by taking advantage of Geometric Algebra algorithms and data in Fourier series.

Hardware emulators such as the open-source QEMU emulator [26], or MachineWare [29] SIM-V simulator [30] can emulate RISC-V devices that support RISC-V Vector Extensions, allowing testing of code before hardware is available.

We anticipate that the first RISC-V devices that ratify the RISC-V Vector Extensions v1.0 will be available this year, allowing us to benchmark performance of software on hardware that supports vector operations.

6   Future Work

Potential directions of future work are:
Development of example computer game using Geometric Algebra algorithms, with code optimised by GAALOP to use RISC-V Vector Extensions running on simulated RISC-V hardware.

When RISC-V Vector Extension hardware devices are available, benchmarking performance of software algorithms and comparing with other hardware.

Coding a more complete physics engine using Geometric Algebra, for example, modelling the physics required to make a realistic car racing game, taking into account physical properties of components in a race car, e.g. size of wheels, weight distribution of car, engine power, car aerodynamic profile, forces acting on car such as gravity, centripetal forces, tire friction, effects of race track banking.

7   Conclusion

We have described an example of using a Geometric Algebra algorithm to compute motion in a game physics engine, we optimised the Geometric Algebra algorithm code using GAALOP and utilised RISC-V Vector Extensions (RVV) to perform computations on vectors, we combined this with vectors used to represent a number of Fourier series to model x, y and z components of gravity, wind and surface friction.

Once RISC-V devices that provide vector operation functionality are available, we anticipate performance improvements of computations required for a game physics engine over existing software/hardware systems.

Acknowledgements. This research is partly supported by an Australian Government Research Training Program Scholarship.

A Appendix

A Code Listing for GAALOPScript Code

Listing 1. 2. GAALOPScript code calculating motion of object affected by gravity, wind and friction.

```
 1  Line = {
 2      x = _P(1); y = _P(2); z = _P(3);
 3      x * (e0 ^ e1) + y * (e0 ^ e2) + z * (e0 ^ e3);
 4  }
 5
 6  Point = {
 7      px = _P(1); py = _P(2); pz = _P(3);
 8      e0 + px * e1 + py * e2 + pz * e3;
 9  }
10
11  F = {
12      M = _P(1);
13      gx = _P(2); gy = _P(3); gz = _P(4);
14      wx = _P(5); wy = _P(6); wz = _P(7),
15      fx = _P(8); fy = _P(9); fz = _P(10);
16
17      gravity    = Line(gx, gy, gz);
18      wind       = Line(wx, wy, wz);
19      friction   = Line(fx, fy, fz);
20
21      dG = *(~M * gravity * M);
22      dW = *(~M * wind * M);
23      dF = *(~M * friction * M);
24      dG + dW + dF
25  }
26
27  nextM = {
28      M = _P(1);
29      B = _P(2);
30      dM = -0.5 * M * B;
31      M + dM
32  }
33
34  nextB = {
35      M = _P(1);
36      B = _P(2);
37      gx = _P(3); gy = _P(4); gz = _P(5);
38      wx = _P(6); wy = _P(7); wz = _P(8);
39      fx = _P(9); fy = _P(10); fz = _P(11);
40
41      B_dual = *B;
42      forque = F(M,gx,gy,gz,wx,wy,wz,fx,fy,fz);
43      dB = *(forque -0.5 * (B_dual * B - B * B_dual));
44      B + dB
45  }
46
47  M = m0 + Line(mx, my, mz);
48  B = Line(bx, by, bz);
49  P = Point(px, py, pz);
50
51  ?MNew = nextM(M,B);
52  ?BNew = nextB(M,B,gx,gy,gz,wx,wy,wz,fx,fy,fz);
53  ?PNew = MNew * P * ~MNew;
```

B   Code Listings for C Code Generated by GAALOP Making Use of RISC-V Vector Extension Instructions, Assembler Code Calling RISC-V Vector Extension Instructions for Vector Multiplication and Sum, and Makefile

Listing 1. 3. C code generated by GAALOP making use of RISC-V Vector Extension instructions.

```
1   #include <stdio.h>
2   #include <stdlib.h>
3   #include <string.h>
4   #include <math.h>
5
6   float vector_sum(float *v1, int size);
7   float dot_product_2(float *v1, float *v2, int size);
8   float dot_product_3(float *v1, float *v2, float *v3, int size);
9
10  float MNew[16] = {0,0,0,0,0,0,0,0,0,0,0,0,0,0,0,0};
11  float BNew[16] = {0,0,0,0,0,0,0,0,0,0,0,0,0,0,0,0};
12  float PNew[16] = {0,0,0,0,0,0,0,0,0,0,0,0,0,0,0,0};
13
14  void script(float bx,float by,float bz,
15              float fx,float fy,float fz,
16              float gx,float gy,float gz,
17              float m0,
18              float mx,float my,float mz,
19              float px,float py,float pz,
20              float vx,float vy,float vz){
21
22      MNew[0] = m0;
23      // MNew[0] = m0
24
25      float ve0[2] = {mx,-0.5};
26      float ve1[2] = {1.0,bx};
27      float ve2[2] = {1.0,m0};
28      MNew[5] = dot_product_3(ve0,ve1,ve2,2);
29      // MNew[5] = mx - ((0.5 * bx) * m0)
30
31      float ve3[2] = {my,-0.5};
32      float ve4[2] = {1.0,by};
33      float ve5[2] = {1.0,m0};
34      MNew[6] = dot_product_3(ve3,ve4,ve5,2);
35      // MNew[6] = my - ((0.5 * by) * m0)
36
37      // much of the code is repeated with the
38      // same structure and has not been included
39  }
40
41  int main(int argc, char *argv[]){
42
43      float bx = 5.0, by = 0.0, bz = 10.0;
44      float fx = 0.0, fy = 0.0, fz = 0.0;
45      float gx = 0.0, gy = 0.0, gz = -9.8;
46
47      float m0 = 1.0;
48      float mx = 0.0, my = 0.0, mz = 0.0;
49      float px = 0.0, py = 0.0, pz = 20.0;
50      float vx = 0.0, vy = 5.0, vz = 0.0;
51
52      script(bx, by, bz, fx, fy, fz, gx, gy, gz, m0,
53             mx, my, mz, px, py, pz, vx, vy, vz);
54  }
```

Listing 1. 4. Assembler code calling RISC-V Vector Extension instructions for vector multiplication and sum.

```
1        .text
2        .align 2
3
4        .globl vector_sum
5    vector_sum:
6        vsetvli t0, a1, e32
7        fmv.w.x fa0, zero
8        vfmv.s.f v1, fa0
9        vle32.v v0, (a0)
10       vfredusum.vs v1, v0, v1
11       vfmv.f.s fa0, v1
12       ret
13
14       .globl dot_product_2
15   dot_product_2:
16       vsetvli t0, a2, e32
17       fmv.w.x fa0, zero
18       vfmv.s.f v3, fa0
19       vle32.v v0, (a0)
20       vle32.v v1, (a1)
21       vfmul.vv   v2, v1, v0
22       vfredusum.vs v3, v2, v3
23       vfmv.f.s fa0, v3
24       ret
25
26       .globl dot_product_3
27   dot_product_3:
28       vsetvli t0, a3, e32
29       fmv.w.x fa0, zero
30       vfmv.s.f v5, fa0
31       vle32.v v0, (a0)
32       vle32.v v1, (a1)
33       vle32.v v2, (a2)
34       vfmul.vv   v3, v1, v0
35       vfmul.vv   v4, v3, v2
36       vfredusum.vs v5, v4, v5
37       vfmv.f.s fa0, v5
38       ret
```

Listing 1. 5. Makefile using the RISC-V GNU Compiler Toolchain, compiling C code with assembler code file making use of RISC-V Vector Extension instructions, the executable is run in the QEMU emulator.

```
1   go: main
2     qemu-riscv64 -cpu rv64,v=true,zba=true,vlen=128 ./main
3
4   main: main.c vec.S makefile
5     riscv64-unknown-elf-gcc -ggdb -O main.c vec.S -o main -march=rv64gcv_zba -lm
```

C   Code Listing for C Code Using a Bitmask to Mask Vector Values and Makefile

Listing 1. 6. C Code using a bitmask to mask vector values

```
1   #include <stdio.h>
2   #include <riscv_vector.h>
3
4   #define NUM_VALUES 32
5
6   void merge(uint32_t bitmask, float* result) {
7     asm volatile("vsetvli␣zero,␣%0,␣e32,␣m1,␣ta,␣mu" : : "r"(1));
8     // load 32-bit bitmask
9     asm volatile("vle32.v␣v0,␣(%0)" : : "r"(&bitmask) );
10    size_t l = 0;
11    for (size_t avl = NUM_VALUES; avl > 0; avl -= 1) {
12      asm volatile("vfmv.v.f␣v1,␣%0" : : "f"(0.0f));
13      asm volatile("vsetvli␣%0,␣zero,␣e32,␣m1,␣ta,␣mu" : "=r"(1) : );
14      asm volatile("vfmerge.vfm␣v3,␣v1,␣%0,␣v0" : : "f"(1.0f));
15      size_t index = NUM_VALUES - avl;
16      asm volatile("vse32.v␣v3,␣(%0)" : : "r"(&result[index])  );
17      bitmask >>= 1;
18      // load shift 32-bit bitmask
19      asm volatile("vle32.v␣v0,␣(%0)" : : "r"(&bitmask) );
20    }
21  }
22
23  int main() {
24    float values[NUM_VALUES] = {0.5};
25    uint32_t bitmask = 0b11110101;
26    merge(bitmask, values);
27    for (size_t i = 0; i < NUM_VALUES; ++i) {
28      printf("%f␣", values[i]);
29      if (!((i + 1) % 4))
30        printf("\n");
31    }
32    return 0;
33  }
```

Listing 1. 7. Makefile using clang compiler and GNU linker for the RISC-V 64-bit architecture when targeting a Linux environment.

```
1  clang    -I/usr/riscv64-linux-gnu/include/ \
2           -I/usr/riscv64-linux-gnu/include/c++/11/ \
3           --target=riscv64 -march=rv64gcv main.c -c -o main.o
4  riscv64-linux-gnu-ld -o main -dynamic-linker \
5      /usr/riscv64-linux-gnu/lib/ld-linux-riscv64-lp64d.so.1 \
6      /usr/riscv64-linux-gnu/lib/crt1.o \
7      /usr/riscv64-linux-gnu/lib/crti.o \
8      -lc main.o /usr/riscv64-linux-gnu/lib/crtn.o
```

References

1. GitHub repository for code examples for the paper Game Physics Engine Using Optimised Geometric Algebra RISC-V Vector Extensions Code Using Fourier Series Data. https://github.com/ed-uts/GA-Game-Physics-Engine. Accessed 05 Aug 2023
2. Lengyel, E.: Foundations of game engine development. Terathon Software LLC (2016). https://books.google.com.au/books?id=9
3. Dorst, L.: The representation of rigid body motions in the conformal model of geometric algebra (2008)

4. Selig, J., Bayro-Corrochano, E.: Rigid body dynamics using Clifford algebra. Adv. Appl. Clifford Algebras **20**, 141–154 (2010)
5. Hitzer, E., Lavor, C., Hildenbrand, D.: Current survey of Clifford geometric algebra applications. Math. Meth. Appl. Sci. (2022)
6. GAALOP Website. https://www.gaalop.de. Accessed 05 Aug 2023
7. Hildenbrand, D.: The power of geometric algebra computing: for engineering and quantum computing (2021)
8. Hildenbrand, D.: Introduction to geometric algebra computing (2020)
9. Hildenbrand, D.: Foundations of geometric algebra computing (2012)
10. Wörsdörfer, F., Stock, F., Bayro-Corrochano, E., Hildenbrand, D.: Optimizations and performance of a robotics grasping algorithm described in geometric algebra (2009)
11. About RISC-V - RISC-V International RISC-V is a free and open ISA enabling a new era of processor innovation through open standard collaboration. https://riscv.org/about. Accessed 05 Aug 2023
12. RISC-V V Vector Extension Specification GitHub repository. https://github.com/riscv/riscv-v-spec. Accessed 05 Aug 2023
13. RISC-V V Vector Extension Specification v1.0. https://github.com/riscv/riscv-v-spec/releases/download/v1.0/riscv-v-spec-1.0.pdf. Accessed 05 Aug 2023
14. Marks II, R.: Handbook of Fourier Analysis and Its Applications. Oxford University Press, Oxford (2009). https://doi.org/10.1093/oso/9780195335927.001.0001
15. Hollingsworth, M.: Applications of the Fourier series (2008)
16. Schmitt, R., Fritz, P.: OP5 - A 3D-Fourier-descriptor approach to compress and classify 3D imaging data (2009)
17. Rosenhahn, B., Perwass, C., Sommer, G.: Pose estimation of 3D free-form contours. Int. J. Comput. Vis. **62**, 267–289 (2005). https://doi.org/10.1007/s11263-005-4883-3
18. Rosenhahn, B.: Pose estimation revisited. Christian-Albrechts-Universitat, Kiel (2003)
19. Li, H., Hartley, R.: New 3D Fourier descriptors for genus-zero mesh objects (2006)
20. ChatGPT. https://chat.openai.com. Accessed 05 Aug 2023
21. https://github.com/ed-uts/GA-Game-Physics-Engine/tree/main/terrain   . Accessed 05 Aug 2023
22. May The Forque Be With You. https://bivector.net/PGADYN.html. Accessed 05 Aug 2023
23. Bivector.Net. https://bivector.net. Accessed 05 Aug 2023
24. Ganja.js.   https://enki.ws/ganja.js/examples/coffeeshop.html#irAoiHVhn. Accessed 05 Aug 2023
25. De Keninck, S.: ganja.js. (Zenodo 2020). https://zenodo.org/record/3635774
26. QEMU A generic and open source machine emulator and virtualizer. https://www.qemu.org. Accessed 05 Aug 2023
27. RISC-V Vector Extension Intrinsic Document. https://github.com/riscv-non-isa/rvv-intrinsic-doc. Accessed 05 Aug 2023
28. RISC-V GNU Compiler Toolchain. https://github.com/riscv-collab/riscv-gnu-toolchain. Accessed 05 Aug 2023
29. MachineWare GmbH. https://www.machineware.de. Access 05 Aug 2023
30. MachineWare   SIM-V.   https://www.machineware.de/pages/products.html. Accessed 05 Aug 2023

Quadratic Phase Quaternion Domain Fourier Transform

Eckhard Hitzer$^{(\boxtimes)}$ ⓘ

International Christian University, Mitaka, Tokyo 181-8585, Japan
hitzer@icu.ac.jp
https://geometricalgebrajp.wordpress.com/

Abstract. Based on the quaternion domain Fourier transform (QDFT) of 2016 and the quadratic-phase Fourier transform of 2018, we introduce the quadratic-phase quaternion domain Fourier transform (QPQDFT) and study some of its properties, like its representation in terms of the QDFT, linearity, Riemann-Lebesgue lemma, shift and modulation, scaling, inversion, Parseval type identity, Plancherel theorem, directional uncertainty principle, and the (direction-independent) uncertainty principle. The generalization thus achieved includes the special cases of QDFT, a quaternion domain (QD) fractional Fourier transform, and a QD linear canonical transform.

Keywords: Fourier transforms · quaternion algebra · quaternion domain functions · linear canonical transform · fractional Fourier transform · uncertainty

1 Introduction

Quaternions were introduced in the 19th century [10] and soon applied in physics, e.g. by J.C. Maxwell to electro-magnetism [17]. Nowadays, in theory and applications they are widely known and applied, e.g. in aero-space engineering [16], color image and signal processing [6], crystallography and material science [2,18], and machine learning [20]. Quaternion analysis for holomorphic functions in the plane and space may be found in [9]. Quaternion based Fourier transforms are reviewed in [4] and [14]. In particular we refer to the quaternion domain Fourier transform (QDFT) introduced in 2016 [13] also described in Sect. 4.3.3 of [14]. A generalization to a special affine quaternion domain Fourier transform (SAQDFT) was undertaken in [15]. Independently, in 2018 the classical Fourier transform has been generalized to the quadratic-phase Fourier transform [5], with favorable new convolution identities. Most recently, the quadratic-phase Fourier transform (QPFT) has been extended to a new quaternion quadratic-phase Fourier transform (Q-QPFT) [3] for two-dimensional quaternionic signals in $L^2(\mathbb{R}^2; \mathbb{H})$, with the well-known QFT [6,11] as a special case. Following up on these recent

---

I dedicate this paper to the late Ms. Aslaug Langaasdalen, missionary from Rjukan (Norway) to Fukui in Japan, for her true Christian practice of agape. The use of this paper is subject to the *Creative Peace License* [12].

B. Sheng et al. (Eds.): CGI 2023, LNCS 14498, pp. 262–273, 2024.
https://doi.org/10.1007/978-3-031-50078-7_21

developments we extend in our current work the QPFT to quaternion domain function signals in $L^1(\mathbb{H}; \mathbb{H})$ resulting in a quadratic-phase QDFT (QPQDFT).

The paper is organized as follows. Section 2 gives a brief introduction to quaternions and the QDFT, introducing some of its properties needed later in this work. Then Sect. 3 defines the QPQDFT and studies its basic properties, including its representation in terms of the QDFT, linearity, Riemann-Lebesgue lemma, shift and modulation, scaling, inversion, Parseval type identity and Plancherel theorem. Next, Sect. 4 investigates uncertainty relationships for (directed) effective spatial- and spectral (obtained from the QPQDFT) width of a quaternion domain signal. The paper concludes with Sect. 5, acknowledgments and references. Some proofs are given explicitly while others are only outlined.

2 Quaternions and the Quaternion Domain Fourier Transform

Gauss, Rodrigues and Hamilton's four-dimensional (4D) *quaternion algebra* $\mathbb{H}$ is defined over $\mathbb{R}$ with three imaginary units:

$$ij = -ji = k, \; jk = -kj = i, \; ki = -ik = j,$$
$$i^2 = j^2 = k^2 = ijk = -1. \tag{1}$$

Every quaternion can be written explicitly as

$$q = q_r + q_i i + q_j j + q_k k \in \mathbb{H}, \quad q_r, q_i, q_j, q_k \in \mathbb{R}, \tag{2}$$

and has a *quaternion conjugate*

$$\tilde{q} = q_r - q_i i - q_j j - q_k k, \qquad \widetilde{pq} = \tilde{q}\tilde{p}. \tag{3}$$

This leads to the *norm* of $q \in \mathbb{H}$

$$|q| = \sqrt{q\tilde{q}} = \sqrt{q_r^2 + q_i^2 + q_j^2 + q_k^2}, \qquad |pq| = |p||q|. \tag{4}$$

The *inverse* of a non-zero quaternion $q \in \mathbb{H}$ is

$$q^{-1} = \frac{\tilde{q}}{|q|^2}. \tag{5}$$

The *(symmetric) scalar part* of a quaternion is defined as

$$\langle q \rangle_0 = Sc(q) = q_r = \frac{1}{2}(q + \tilde{q}), \qquad Sc(pq) = Sc(qp) = Sc(\tilde{p}\tilde{q}), \tag{6}$$
$$Sc(pqr) = Sc(qrp) = Sc(rpq). \tag{7}$$

Every quaternion $a \in \mathbb{H}$, $a \neq 0$, can be written as scalar part plus *(pure) vector part*

$$a = a_r + a_i i + a_j j + a_k k = a_r + \mathbf{a} = |a|(\cos\alpha + \frac{\mathbf{a}}{|a|}\sin\alpha) = |a|e^{\hat{\mathbf{a}}\alpha}, \tag{8}$$

with $\hat{\mathbf{a}} = \mathbf{a}/|a|$, $\cos\alpha = a_r/|a|$, $\alpha \in [0, \pi)$.

A *scalar product* of quaternions can be defined for $x, y \in \mathbb{H}$ as

$$x \cdot y = Sc(\tilde{x}y) = x_r y_r + x_i y_i + x_j y_j + x_k y_k, \qquad x \cdot x = \tilde{x}x = |x|^2. \qquad (9)$$

Every *quaternion valued quaternion domain function* f maps $\mathbb{H} \to \mathbb{H}$, and its four coefficient functions f_r, f_i, f_j, f_k, are in turn real valued quaternion domain functions:

$$f : x \mapsto f(x) = f_r(x) + f_i(x)\boldsymbol{i} + f_j(x)\boldsymbol{j} + f_k(x)\boldsymbol{k} \in \mathbb{H}. \qquad (10)$$

Quaternion valued quaternion domain functions have been historically studied in [8,19,21,22], and applications are described in [9].

We define for two functions $f, g : \mathbb{H} \to \mathbb{H}$ the following *quaternion valued inner product*[1]

$$(f, g) = \int_{\mathbb{H}} f(x)\tilde{g}(x)d^4x \qquad (11)$$

with $d^4x = dx_r dx_i dx_j dx_k \in \mathbb{R}$.

Let S be the Schwartz space, and $C_0(\mathbb{H})$ the Banach space of all continuous quaternion domain functions that vanish at infinity, with the supremum norm $||\cdot||_\infty$. In $L^1(\mathbb{H};\mathbb{H})$ we use the norm defined by

$$||f||_1 := \frac{1}{(2\pi)^2} \int_{\mathbb{H}} |f(x)|d^4x, \qquad (12)$$

where $1/(2\pi)^2$ is for convenience later on. For $1 < p < \infty$ the space $L^p(\mathbb{H};\mathbb{H})$ has the norm

$$||f||_p = \left(\int_{\mathbb{H}} |f(x)|^p d^4x \right)^{\frac{1}{p}}. \qquad (13)$$

Definition 1 (Quaternion Domain Fourier Transform (QDFT) [13]).
The quaternion domain Fourier transform[2] (QDFT) for $h \in L^2(\mathbb{H};\mathbb{H})$ is defined as

$$\mathcal{F}_{QDFT}\{h\}(\omega) = \hat{h}(\omega) = \frac{1}{(2\pi)^2} \int_{\mathbb{H}} h(x)e^{-Ix\cdot\omega} d^4x, \qquad (14)$$

with $x, \omega \in \mathbb{H}$, and some constant pure unit quaternion[3] $I \in \mathbb{H}$, $I^2 = -1$.

---

[1] We note that (11) is quaternion valued, but by construction $(f, f) = ||f||_2^2$ is real valued and positive for $f \neq 0$.

[2] We also assume always that $\int_{\mathbb{H}} |h(x)|d^4x$ exists as well. But we do not explicitly write this condition again in the rest of the paper. Strictly speaking, the integral definition of Definition 1 only works for $h \in L^1(\mathbb{H};\mathbb{H})$. But one can first define the QDFT on the dense subset $L^1(\mathbb{H};\mathbb{H}) \bigcap L^2(\mathbb{H};\mathbb{H})$, and then use the continuity of the Fourier transform on $L^1(\mathbb{H};\mathbb{H}) \bigcap L^2(\mathbb{H};\mathbb{H})$, due to Plancherel's theorem for the QDFT, see equations (4.19) to (4.201) in [13], to define the QDFT on $L^2(\mathbb{H};\mathbb{H})$, see e.g. [7]. .

[3] The QPQDFT of Definition 2 inherits this choice of constant pure unit quaternion $I \in \mathbb{H}$, $I^2 = -1$. We thank one of the reviewers to draw our attention to [1], which appears to allow for another use of pure quaternions in the kernel factor of (14).

The QDFT has the following inverse transform [13].

Lemma 1 (Inverse QDFT). *For $h, \mathcal{F}_{QDFT} \in L^2(\mathbb{H}; \mathbb{H})$, we obtain the inverse transform as*

$$h(x) = \frac{1}{(2\pi)^2} \int_{\mathbb{H}} \mathcal{F}_{QDFT}\{h\}(\omega) e^{+Ix\cdot\omega} d^4\omega, \quad d^4\omega = d\omega_r d\omega_i d\omega_j d\omega_k. \quad (15)$$

We will also need the *directional uncertainty principle* for the QDFT of (4.24) in [13].

Theorem 1 (Directional QDFT Uncertainty Principle). *For unit norm signals $f \in L^2(\mathbb{H}; \mathbb{H})$, $||f|| = 1$, and constant quaternions $a, b \in \mathbb{H}$, we have*

$$\Delta x_a \Delta \omega_b \geq \frac{|a \cdot b|}{2}, \quad (16)$$

with (directed) effective spatial and spectral widths

$$\Delta x_a = ||(x \cdot a)f||_2 = \sqrt{\int_{\mathbb{H}} (x \cdot a)^2 |f(x)|^2 d^4 x,}$$

$$\Delta \omega_b = ||(\omega \cdot b)\mathcal{F}_{QDFT}\{f\}||_2 = \sqrt{\int_{\mathbb{H}} (\omega \cdot b)^2 |\mathcal{F}_{QDFT}\{f\}(\omega)|^2 d^4\omega.} \quad (17)$$

3   The Quadratic-Phase Quaternion Domain Fourier Transform

Generalizing (1.1) of [5] to quaternionic variables, for parameters $a, b, c \in \mathbb{R}$ (with $b \neq 0$) and $d, e \in \mathbb{H}$, we define the quadratic phase function for $x, \omega \in \mathbb{H}$,

$$Q(x, \omega) := a|x|^2 + bx \cdot \omega + c|\omega|^2 + d \cdot x + e \cdot \omega. \quad (18)$$

Remark 1. Note that in (18) the entities d, e need to be quaternions and not scalars in order to construct a scalar phase function $Q(x, \omega)$. This means the parameter dimension of $Q(x, \omega)$ consists of three real and two quaternionic degrees of freedom corresponding to a total of 11 real degrees of freedom.

Definition 2. *The quadratic-phase quaternion domain Fourier transform[4] (QPQDFT) for $h \in L^2(\mathbb{H}; \mathbb{H})$ is defined as*

$$\mathcal{F}\{h\}(\omega) = \hat{h}(\omega) = \frac{1}{(2\pi)^2} \int_{\mathbb{H}} h(x) e^{-IQ(x,\omega)} d^4 x, \quad (19)$$

with $x, \omega \in \mathbb{H}$, some constant pure unit quaternion $I \in \mathbb{H}$, $I^2 = -1$, and phase $Q(x, \omega)$ of (18).

---

[4] We refer the reader to footnote 2 for the density argument that also applies for the QPQDFT, where we note also the computation of the QPDFT in terms of the QDFT according to Lemma 2.

Remark 2 (**Special QPQDFT Cases**).

(i) For the parameter values $a = c = d = e = 0$ and $b = \pm 1$ we obtain the QDFT and its inverse transform.
(ii) For parameters $d = e = 0$, the QPQDFT includes linear canonical transforms and fractional Fourier transforms for quaternion domain functions, up to constant factors, like $\sqrt{-i}$ for the linear canonical transform, and $\sqrt{(1 - i \cot(\alpha)/2\pi}$ for the fractional Fourier transform.

Defining the function

$$g(x) := h(x)e^{-I(a|x|^2 + d \cdot x)}, \tag{20}$$

it is possible to compute the QPQDFT of $h \in L^1(\mathbb{H}; \mathbb{H})$ in terms of the QDFT of g.

Lemma 2.

$$\mathcal{F}\{h\}(\omega) = \mathcal{F}_{QDFT}\{g\}(b\omega)e^{-I(c|\omega|^2 + e \cdot \omega)}. \tag{21}$$

Then we obtain the following lemmata.

Lemma 3. *The L^2-norms of $\mathcal{F}\{h\}$ and $\mathcal{F}_{QDFT}\{h\}$ are related by*

$$||\mathcal{F}\{h\}||_2 = \frac{1}{b^2}||\mathcal{F}_{QDFT}\{h\}||_2. \tag{22}$$

Proof.

$$\begin{aligned}
||\mathcal{F}\{h\}||_2 &= \left[\int_{\mathbb{H}} |\mathcal{F}\{h\}(\omega)|^2 d^4\omega\right]^{\frac{1}{2}} \\
&= \left[\int_{\mathbb{H}} |\mathcal{F}_{QDFT}\{h\}(b\omega)|^2 d^4\omega\right]^{\frac{1}{2}} \\
&= \left[\int_{\mathbb{H}} \frac{1}{b^4} |\mathcal{F}_{QDFT}\{h\}(\omega')|^2 d^4\omega'\right]^{\frac{1}{2}} \\
&= \frac{1}{b^2}\left[\int_{\mathbb{H}} |\mathcal{F}_{QDFT}\{h\}(\omega)|^2 d^4\omega\right]^{\frac{1}{2}} \\
&= \frac{1}{|b|^2}||\mathcal{F}_{QDFT}\{h\}||_2, \tag{23}
\end{aligned}$$

Lemma 4 (Riemann-Lebesgue lemma). *If $h \in L^1(\mathbb{H}; \mathbb{H})$ then $\mathcal{F}\{h\} \in C_0(\mathbb{H})$, and $||\mathcal{F}\{h\}|| \leq ||h||_1$.*

Proof. Because $|e^{-IQ(x,\omega)}| = 1$, we have

$$\begin{aligned}
||\mathcal{F}\{h\}||_\infty &= \sup_{\omega \in \mathbb{H}} |\mathcal{F}\{h\}(\omega)| = \sup_{\omega \in \mathbb{H}} \frac{1}{(2\pi)^2}\left|\int_{\mathbb{H}} h(x)e^{-IQ(x,\omega)} d^4\omega\right| \\
&\leq \sup_{\omega \in \mathbb{H}} \frac{1}{(2\pi)^2}\left|\int_{\mathbb{H}} |h(x)||e^{-IQ(x,\omega)}| d^4\omega\right| = ||h||_1. \tag{24}
\end{aligned}$$

Furthermore, the function $g(x)$ of (20) is in $L^1(\mathbb{H};\mathbb{H})$ if and only if $h \in L^1(\mathbb{H};\mathbb{H})$. Hence the classic Riemann-Lebesgue lemma results in

$$|\mathcal{F}\{h\}(\omega)| = \frac{|e^{-I(c|\omega|^2+e\cdot\omega)}|}{(2\pi)^2}\left|\int_{\mathbb{H}} e^{-Ibx\cdot\omega}g(x)d^4x\right| = \frac{1}{(2\pi)^2}\left|\int_{\mathbb{H}} e^{-Ibx\cdot\omega}g(x)d^4x\right| \to 0,$$
(25)

as $|\omega| \to \infty$, completing the sketch of the proof.

The QPQDFT has the following linearity properties.

Theorem 2 (Linearity). *The QPQDFT is left linear with respect to coefficients* $\alpha_1, \alpha_2 \in \mathbb{H}$ *for* $h_1, h_2 \in L^1(\mathbb{H};\mathbb{H})$

$$\mathcal{F}\{\alpha_1 h_1 + \alpha_2 h_2\}(\omega) = \alpha_1\mathcal{F}\{h_1\}(\omega) + \alpha_2\mathcal{F}\{h_2\}(\omega).$$
(26)

It is right linear for coefficients $\beta_1, \beta_2 \in \mathbb{H}$ *that commute with the unit pure quaternion* I *of Definition 19.*

$$\mathcal{F}\{h_1\beta_1 + h_2\beta_2\}(\omega) = \mathcal{F}\{h_1\}(\omega)\beta_1 + \mathcal{F}\{h_2\}(\omega)\beta_2,$$
$$\forall \beta_1, \beta_2 \in \mathbb{H}: \quad \beta_1 I = I\beta_1, \beta_2 I = I\beta_2.$$
(27)

The QPQDFT has the following shift-, modulation-, and scaling properties obtained by straightforward computation.

Theorem 3 (Shift). *For* $h \in L^1(\mathbb{H};\mathbb{H})$, $x,\omega \in \mathbb{H}$ *and constant quaternion* $s \in \mathbb{H}$ *we have*

$$\mathcal{F}\{h(x-s)\}(\omega) = \mathcal{F}\{h(x)\}(\omega - \frac{2a}{b}s)e^{-I(\frac{4ac}{b}\omega\cdot s - \frac{4a^2c}{b^2}|s|^2 + \frac{2a}{b}e\cdot s)}.$$
(28)

Remark 3. Alternative ways of expressing the shift property are

$$\mathcal{F}\{h(x-s)\}(\omega) = \mathcal{F}\{h(x)e^{-2Iax\cdot s}\}(\omega)\,e^{-I(bs\cdot\omega + a|s|^2 + d\cdot s)}$$
(29)

or

$$\mathcal{F}\{h(x-s)\}(\omega) = \frac{1}{(2\pi)^2}\int_{\mathbb{H}} h(x)\,e^{-IQ'(x,\omega)}d^4x e^{-I(a|s|^2 + d\cdot s)},$$
(30)

with

$$Q'(x,\omega) := a|x|^2 + bx\cdot\omega + c|\omega|^2 + d'\cdot x + e'\cdot\omega, \quad d' = d + 2as, \quad e' = e + bs. \quad (31)$$

Theorem 4 (Modulation). *For* $h \in L^1(\mathbb{H};\mathbb{H})$, $x,\omega \in \mathbb{H}$ *and constant quaternionic frequency* $\mu \in \mathbb{H}$ *we have*

$$\mathcal{F}\{h(x)e^{Ix\cdot\mu}\}(\omega) = \mathcal{F}\{h(\mathbf{x})\}(\omega - \frac{\mu}{b})e^{-I\left(2\frac{c}{b}\omega\cdot\mu + \frac{1}{b}e\cdot\mu - \frac{c}{b^2}|\mu|^2\right)}.$$
(32)

Theorem 5 (Quaternionic Scaling). *For* $h \in L^1(\mathbb{H};\mathbb{H})$, $x,\omega \in \mathbb{H}$ *and constant quaternionic scaling factor* $p \in \mathbb{H}$, $h_p(x) = h(px)$, *we have*

$$\mathcal{F}\{h_p(x)\}(\omega) = \frac{1}{(2\pi)^2|p|^4}\int_{\mathbb{H}} h(x)e^{-I\frac{1}{|p|^2}Q'(x,p\omega)}d^4x,$$
(33)

with

$$Q'(x,\omega) = a|x|^2 + bx\cdot\omega + c|\omega|^2 + d'\cdot x + e'\cdot\omega, \quad d' = pd, \quad e' = pe. \quad (34)$$

Corollary 1 (Real Scaling). *For $h \in L^1(\mathbb{H}; \mathbb{H})$, $x, \omega \in \mathbb{H}$ and constant real scaling factor $r \in \mathbb{R}$, $h_r(x) = h(rx)$, we have*

$$\mathcal{F}\{h_r(x)\}(\omega) = \frac{1}{(2\pi)^2 r^4} \int_{\mathbb{H}} h(x) e^{-I \frac{1}{r^2} Q'(x, r\omega)} d^4 x, \tag{35}$$

with

$$Q'(x, \omega) = a|x|^2 + bx \cdot \omega + c|\omega|^2 + d' \cdot x + e' \cdot \omega, \quad d' = rd, \quad e' = re. \tag{36}$$

The QPQDFT has the following inverse.

Theorem 6 (Inverse QPQDFT). *For $h, \mathcal{F} \in L^2(\mathbb{H}; \mathbb{H})$, we obtain the inverse QPQDFT transform as*

$$h(x) = \frac{b^4}{(2\pi)^2} \int_{\mathbb{H}} \mathcal{F}\{h\}(\omega) e^{+IQ(x, \omega)} d^4 \omega. \tag{37}$$

Proof.

$$\frac{b^4}{(2\pi)^2} \int_{\mathbb{H}} \mathcal{F}\{h\}(\omega) e^{+IQ(x, \omega)} d^4 \omega$$

$$= \frac{b^4}{(2\pi)^2} \int_{\mathbb{H}} \mathcal{F}_{QDFT}\{g\}(b\omega) e^{-I(c|\omega|^2 + e \cdot \omega)} e^{+I(c|\omega|^2 + e \cdot \omega)} e^{I(a|x|^2 + bx \cdot \omega + d \cdot x)} d^4 x$$

$$= \frac{b^4}{(2\pi)^2} \int_{\mathbb{H}} \mathcal{F}_{QDFT}\{g\}(b\omega) e^{Ibx \cdot \omega} d^4 \omega e^{I(a|x|^2 + d \cdot x)}$$

$$= \frac{b^4}{(2\pi)^2 b^4} \int_{\mathbb{H}} \mathcal{F}_{QDFT}\{g\}(\mu) e^{Ix \cdot \mu} d^4 \mu e^{I(a|x|^2 + d \cdot x)}$$

$$= h(x) e^{-I(a|x|^2 + d \cdot x)} e^{I(a|x|^2 + d \cdot x)} = h(x), \tag{38}$$

where in the first equality we used Lemma 2 with g given by (20), and for the third we substituted $\mu := b\omega$, $d^4 \mu = b^4 d^4 \omega$, and in the fourth we used the inverse QDFT of Lemma 1 and (20).

Theorem 7 (Parseval-Type Identity, Plancherel Theorem). *(i) For any $f, h \in L^2(\mathbb{H}; \mathbb{H})$, the following identity holds*

$$(\mathcal{F}\{f\}, \mathcal{F}\{h\}) = \frac{1}{b^4}(f, h). \tag{39}$$

In the special case of $f = h$, we have

$$\|\mathcal{F}\{f\}\|_2^2 = \frac{1}{b^4} \|f\|_2^2. \tag{40}$$

(ii) Plancherel Theorem. If $b = \pm 1$, then $\mathcal{F}$ defines a unitary operator in $L^2(\mathbb{H}; \mathbb{H})$.

Proof. By simple computations we have

$$(\mathcal{F}\{f\}, \mathcal{F}\{h\})$$

$$= \frac{1}{(2\pi)^4} \int_{\mathbb{H}} \int_{\mathbb{H}} \int_{\mathbb{H}} f(x) e^{-IQ(x,\omega)} e^{+IQ(y,\omega)} \widetilde{g}(y) d^4x d^4y d^4\omega$$

$$= \frac{1}{(2\pi)^4} \int_{\mathbb{H}} \int_{\mathbb{H}} \int_{\mathbb{H}} f(x) e^{-I(c|\omega|^2 + e\cdot\omega)} e^{I(c|\omega|^2 + e\cdot\omega)} e^{-Ibx\cdot\omega} e^{+Iby\cdot\omega} d^4\omega$$

$$e^{-I(a|x|^2 - d\cdot x)} e^{+I(a|y|^2 - d\cdot y)} \widetilde{g}(y) d^4x d^4y$$

$$= \frac{1}{b^4} \int_{\mathbb{H}} \int_{\mathbb{H}} f(x) \delta(x-y) e^{-I(a|x|^2 - d\cdot x)} e^{+I(a|y|^2 - d\cdot y)} \widetilde{g}(y) d^4y d^4x$$

$$= \frac{1}{b^4} \int_{\mathbb{H}} f(x) \widetilde{g}(x) d^4x = \frac{1}{b^4}(f, g), \tag{41}$$

where we have applied that (see Appendix A for more details)

$$\frac{1}{(2\pi)^4} \int_{\mathbb{H}} e^{-Ibx\cdot\omega} e^{+Iby\cdot\omega} d^4\omega = \delta(b(x-y)) = \frac{1}{b^4} \delta(x-y). \tag{42}$$

This proves proposition (i). For $f = g$ we have (40), and for $b = \pm 1$ we obtain proposition (ii). $\qquad\blacksquare$

4   QPQDFT and Uncertainty

Theorem 8 (Directional Uncertainty). *Let $h \in L^2(\mathbb{H}; \mathbb{H})$ with QPQFT $\mathcal{F}\{h\}$. Assume that $||h||_2 < \infty$, then the following inequality holds for arbitrary constant quaternions $v, w \in \mathbb{H}$:*

$$||(x \cdot v)h||_2 \, ||(\omega \cdot w)\mathcal{F}\{h\}||_2 \geq \frac{1}{|b|} \frac{|v \cdot w|}{2} ||h||_2 \, ||\mathcal{F}\{h\}||_2. \tag{43}$$

Proof. By direct computation we obtain

$$||(\omega \cdot w)\mathcal{F}\{h\}||_2 = \left[\int_{\mathbb{H}} (\omega \cdot w)^2 |\mathcal{F}\{h\}(\omega)|^2 d^4\omega \right]^{\frac{1}{2}}$$

$$= \left[\int_{\mathbb{H}} (\omega \cdot w)^2 |\mathcal{F}_{QDFT}\{h\}(b\omega)|^2 d^4\omega \right]^{\frac{1}{2}}$$

$$= \left[\int_{\mathbb{H}} \frac{1}{b^4} (\omega' \cdot w)^2 |\mathcal{F}_{QDFT}\{h\}(\omega')|^2 d^4\omega' \right]^{\frac{1}{2}}$$

$$= \frac{1}{b^2} \left[\int_{\mathbb{H}} (\omega \cdot w')^2 |\mathcal{F}_{QDFT}\{h\}(\omega)|^2 d^4\omega \right]^{\frac{1}{2}}$$

$$= \frac{1}{|b|^3} \left[\int_{\mathbb{H}} (\omega \cdot w)^2 |\mathcal{F}_{QDFT}\{h\}(\omega)|^2 d^4\omega \right]^{\frac{1}{2}}$$

$$= \frac{1}{|b|^3} ||(\omega \cdot w)\mathcal{F}_{QDFT}\{h\}||_2, \tag{44}$$

where for the second equality we applied Lemma 2, for the third we substituted $\omega' = b\omega$, $d^4\omega' = b^4 d^4\omega$, $w' = \frac{1}{b}w$ (then $\omega \cdot w = \omega' \cdot w'$), for the fourth equality we renamed $\omega' \rightarrow \omega$, for the fifth we inserted $w' = bw$ again, and the last equality applied the definition of $|| \cdot ||_2$ of (13) for $p = 2$. According to the directional uncertainty principle for the QDFT of Theorem 1 we have (not assuming unit norm signals)

$$||(x \cdot v)h||_2 \, ||(\omega \cdot w)\mathcal{F}_{QDFT}\{h\}||_2 \geq \frac{v \cdot w}{2}||h||_2 \, ||\mathcal{F}_{QDFT}\{h\}||_2, \qquad (45)$$

and with the norm relation of Lemma 3 we finally obtain

$$||(x \cdot v)h||_2 \, ||(\omega \cdot w)\mathcal{F}\{h\}||_2 \geq \frac{1}{|b|}\frac{|v \cdot w|}{2}||h||_2 \, ||\mathcal{F}\{h\}||_2. \qquad (46)$$

Remark 4. For $b = \pm 1$ and unit norm signals, i.e., $||h||_2 = ||\mathcal{F}\{h\}||_2 = 1$, we obtain the familiar form of the directional uncertainty principle, relating the (directed) effective spatial and spectral widths by

$$\Delta x_v \Delta \omega_w \geq \frac{|v \cdot w|}{2}, \qquad (47)$$

where

$$\Delta x_v = ||(x \cdot a)h||_2 = \sqrt{\int_{\mathbb{H}} (x \cdot v)^2 \, h(x)|^2 d^4 x},$$

$$\Delta \omega_w = ||(\omega \cdot a)\mathcal{F}\{h\}||_2 = \sqrt{\int_{\mathbb{H}} (\omega \cdot w)^2 |\mathcal{F}\{h\}(\omega)|^2 d^4 \omega}. \qquad (48)$$

Corollary 2 (Uni-directional Uncertainty Principle). *For the single direction $w = \pm v$, $|v| = 1$, we get the following uni-directional uncertainty principle*

$$||(x \cdot v)h||_2 \, ||(\omega \cdot v)\mathcal{F}\{h\}||_2 \geq \frac{1}{2|b|}||h||_2 \, ||\mathcal{F}\{h\}||_2. \qquad (49)$$

Remark 5. In (49) equality holds for Gaussian wave packets

$$G(x) = Ae^{-k|x|^2}, \qquad (50)$$

with $x \in \mathbb{H}$, and constants $A \in \mathbb{H}$, $k \in \mathbb{R}$, $k > 0$.

Corollary 3 (Uncertainty and Orthogonal Directions). *For orthogonal v and w, i.e., $v \cdot w = 0$, the uncertainty can be zero*

$$||(x \cdot v)h||_2 \, ||(\omega \cdot w)\mathcal{F}\{h\}||_2 \geq 0. \qquad (51)$$

Finally, we can extend the directional uncertainty principle to the direction-independent QPQDFT uncertainty principle

Theorem 9 (QPQDFT Uncertainty Principle). *Let $h \in L^2(\mathbb{H}; \mathbb{H})$ with QPQFT $\mathcal{F}\{h\}$. Assume that $||h||_2 < \infty$, then the following inequality holds:*

$$||xh||_2 \, ||\omega\mathcal{F}\{h\}||_2 \geq \frac{1}{|b|}||h||_2 \, ||\mathcal{F}\{h\}||_2. \qquad (52)$$

5   Conclusion

This paper first gave a brief introduction to quaternions and the quaternion domain Fourier transform (QDFT). Then the quadratic-phase QDFT (QPQDFT) was defined and its basic properties established, including its representation in terms of the QDFT, linearity, Riemann-Lebesgue lemma, shift and modulation, scaling, inversion, Parseval type identity and Plancherel theorem. Finally, the uncertainty relationships for (directed) effective spatial- and spectral (obtained from the QPQDFT) width of a quaternion domain signal were investigated.

Following [5], it may be interesting to see how far the favorable convolution properties of the scalar quadratic-phase Fourier transform can be extended to the quaternion domain function case, to study related Young type inequalities, the asymptotic behavior of quaternionic oscillatory integrals and solvability of quaternionic convolution integral equations. Future research should also look into establishing quadratic-phase quaternion domain wavelets and their application in science and technology. Rich applications are expected in fields like physics, electro-magnetism, aero-space engineering, color image and signal processing, crystallography and material science, machine learning, and quaternion analysis for holomorphic functions in the plane and space, etc.

Acknowledgement. I thank God for his wonderful creation: *When I look at thy heavens, the work of thy fingers, the moon and the stars which thou hast established; what is man that thou art mindful of him, and the son of man that thou dost care for him?* [Bible, Psalm 8:3+4, Revised Standard Version]. I thank my dear family and people from whom I have learned: M.Y. Bhat, B. Mawardi, T.L. Saaty, S. Sangwine, L. Waseem, and all ENGAGE 2023 and CGI 2023 organizers. We thank the anonymous reviewers for carefully reviewing our paper and suggesting important improvements.

A   Quaternion Domain Intergration and Dirac Delta Function

We want to look at Eq. (42) in some more detail:

$$\frac{1}{(2\pi)^4} \int_{\mathbb{H}} e^{-Ibx\cdot\omega} e^{+Iby\cdot\omega} d^4\omega = \delta(b(x-y)) = \frac{1}{b^4}\delta(x-y). \tag{53}$$

We do have the variables $b \in \mathbb{R}$, $b \neq 0$, and the three quaternion variables $x, y, \omega \in \mathbb{H}$. But they only appear in the scalar product, i.e.

$$x \cdot \omega = Sc(\tilde{x}\omega) = x_r\omega_r + x_i\omega_i + x_j\omega_j + x_k\omega_k \in \mathbb{R}, \tag{54}$$

$$y \cdot \omega = Sc(\tilde{y}\omega) = y_r\omega_r + y_i\omega_i + y_j\omega_j + y_k\omega_k \in \mathbb{R}. \tag{55}$$

Furthermore we have the pure unit quaternion $I \in \mathbb{H}$, $I^2 = -1$. This means that the arguments of the exponential functions commute and therefore we can rewrite the product of the two exponential factors as

$$e^{-Ibx\cdot\omega}e^{+Iby\cdot\omega} = e^{-Ib[(x-y)\cdot\omega]}$$
$$= e^{-Ib(x_r-y_r)\omega_r}e^{-Ib(x_i-y_i)\omega_i}e^{-Ib(x_j-y_j)\omega_j}e^{-Ib(x_k-y_k)\omega_k}. \quad (56)$$

We further note that

$$d^4\omega = d\omega_r d\omega_i d\omega_j d\omega_k. \quad (57)$$

Therefore the integral has simplified to

$$\frac{1}{(2\pi)^4}\int_{\mathbb{H}} e^{-Ibx\cdot\omega}e^{+Iby\cdot\omega}d^4\omega$$
$$= \frac{1}{(2\pi)^4}\int_{\mathbb{H}} e^{-Ib(x_r-y_r)\omega_r}e^{-Ib(x_i-y_i)\omega_i}e^{-Ib(x_j-y_j)\omega_j}e^{-Ib(x_k-y_k)\omega_k}d\omega_r d\omega_i d\omega_j d\omega_k$$
$$= \left(\frac{1}{2\pi}\int_{\mathbb{R}} e^{-Ib(x_r-y_r)\omega_r}d\omega_r\right)\left(\frac{1}{2\pi}\int_{\mathbb{R}} e^{-Ib(x_i-y_i)\omega_i}d\omega_i\right)$$
$$\times \left(\frac{1}{2\pi}\int_{\mathbb{R}} e^{-Ib(x_j-y_j)\omega_j}d\omega_j\right)\left(\frac{1}{2\pi}\int_{\mathbb{R}} e^{-Ib(x_k-y_k)\omega_k}d\omega_k\right)$$
$$= \delta(b(x_r-y_r))\,\delta(b(x_i-y_i))\,\delta(b(x_j-y_j))\,\delta(b(x_k-y_k)). \quad (58)$$

References

1. Adler, S.L.: Quaternionic quantum field theory. Commun. Math. Phys. **104**, 611–656 (1986)
2. Altmann, S.A.: Rotations, Quaternions and Double Groups. Clarendon Press, Oxford (1986)
3. Bhat, M.Y., Dar, A.H.: Towards quaternion quadratic-phase Fourier transform. Math. Meth. Appl. Sci. 1–20 (2023)
4. Brackx F., Hitzer, E., Sangwine S.J.: History of quaternion and Clifford-Fourier transforms. In: Hitzer, E., Sangwine, S.J. (eds.) Quaternion and Clifford Fourier Transforms and Wavelets, Trends in Mathematics (TIM), vol. 27, pp. xi-xxvii. Birkhäuser, Basel (2013). http://link.springer.com/content/pdf/bfm%3A978-3-0348-0603-9%2F1.pdf
5. Castro, L.P., Minh, L.T., Tuan, N.M.: New convolutions for quadratic-phase Fourier integral operators and their applications. Mediterr. J. Math. **15**, 13 (2018)
6. Ell, T.A.: Quaternionic-Fourier transform for analysis of two-dimensional linear time-invariant partial differential systems. In: Proceedings of the 32nd IEEE Conference on Decision and Control, 15–17 December, pp. 1830–1841 (1993)
7. Friesecke, G.: Course Material Fourier analysis, Lecture 13: The Fourier Transform on L^2 (2013). https://www-m7.ma.tum.de/foswiki/pub/M7/Analysis/Fourier13/lecture13.pdf. Accessed 08 Jan 2021
8. Fueter, R.: Die Funktionentheorie der Differentialgleichungen $\Delta u = 0$ und $\Delta\Delta u = 0$ mit vier reellen Variablen. Comment. Math. Helv. **7**(1), 307–330 (1935)
9. Gürlebeck, K., Habetha, K., Sprössig, W.: Holomorphic Functions in the Plane and n-Dimensional Space. Birkhäuser, Basel (2008). https://doi.org/10.1007/978-3-7643-8272-8
10. Hamilton, W.R.: On quaternions, or on a new system of imaginaries in algebra. Phil. Mag. **25**(3), 489–495 (1844)

11. Hitzer, E.: Quaternion Fourier transform on quaternion fields and generalizations. Adv. Appl. Clifford Algebras **17**, 497–517 (2007)
12. Hitzer, E.: Creative Peace License. http://gaupdate.wordpress.com/2011/12/14/the-creative-peace-license-14-dec-2011/
13. Hitzer, E.: The quaternion domain Fourier transform and its properties. Adv. Appl. Clifford Algebras **26**, 969–984 (2016)
14. Hitzer, E.: Quaternion and Clifford Fourier Transforms. Chapman and Hall/CRC, London (2021)
15. Hitzer, E.: Special affine quaternion domain Fourier transform, In: García, H.M.C., de Jesús Cruz Guzmán, J., Kauffman, L.H., Makaruk, H. (eds.) Scientific Legacy of Professor Zbigniew Oziewicz, Series on Knots and Everything (SKAE), vol. 75, pp. 537–552. World Scientific, Singapore (2023). https://doi.org/10.1142/13275
16. Kuipers, J.: Quaternions and Rotation Sequences: A Primer With Applications to Orbits, Aerospace, and Virtual Reality (reprint edition), Princeton University Press, Princeton (2002)
17. Maxwell. J.C.: A treatise on Electricity and Magnetism. Clarendon Press, Oxford (1873)
18. Meister, L., Schaeben, H.: A concise quaternion geometry of rotations. Math. Meth. Appl. Sci. **28**, 101–126 (2005)
19. Nono, K.: Hyperholomorphic functions of a quaternion variable. Bull. Fukuoka Univ. Educ. **32**, 21–37 (1982)
20. Parcollet, T., Morchid, M., Linarès, G.: A survey of quaternion neural networks. Artif. Intell. Rev. **53**, 2957–2982 (2020)
21. Schuler, B.: Zur Theorie der regulären Funktionen einer Quaternionen-Variablen. Commun. Math. Helv. **10**, 327–342 (1937/1938)
22. Sudbery, E.: Quaternionic analysis. Math. Proc. Camb. Philos. Soc. **85**(2), 199–225 (1979)

MSINET: Multi-scale Interconnection Network for Medical Image Segmentation

Zhengke Xu, Xinxin Shan, and Ying Wen[✉]

East China Normal University, Shanghai, China
ywen@cs.ecnu.edu.cn

Abstract. In this work, an improved end-to-end U-Net structure, a hierarchical multi-scale interconnection network (HMINet), is proposed to make full use of the information contained in different feature maps in encoders and decoders to improve the accuracy of medical image segmentation. The network consists of two main components: a multi-scale fusion unit (MSF) and a multi-head feature enhancement unit (MFE). In the encoder part, the multi-scale fusion unit is used to fuse the information between the feature maps of different scales. By using convolution at different levels, a wider range of context information can be captured and fused into a more comprehensive representation of features. In the decoder part, multiple feature enhancement units can fully pay attention to the coordinates and channel information between feature maps, and then splice the encoded feature maps step by step to maximize the use of information from different feature maps. These feature maps are joined by a well-designed skip connection mechanism to retain more feature information and minimize information loss. The proposed method is tested on four public medical datasets and compared with other classical image segmentation models. The results show that HMINet can significantly improve the accuracy of medical image segmentation tasks and exceed the performance of other models in most cases.

Keywords: Transformer-based method · Multi-scale fusion · Feature enhancement · Encoder-decoder network · Medical image segmentation

1 Introduction

Convolutional neural networks (CNNs) have revolutionized medical image segmentation, playing a vital role in advancing the field of medical image segmentation. U-Net [1], a widely recognized and influential architecture, has demonstrated exceptional performance in segmenting medical images. However, as the demand for more accurate and efficient segmentation models grows, researchers have developed various U-Net variants [2,3] that leverage the benefits of CNNs.

This work was supported in part by National Nature Science Foundation of China (62273150), Shanghai Nature Science Foundation (22ZR1421000), Shanghai Outstanding Academic Leaders Plan (21XD1430600), Science and Technology Commission of Shanghai Municipality (22DZ2229004).

B. Sheng et al. (Eds.): CGI 2023, LNCS 14498, pp. 274–286, 2024.
https://doi.org/10.1007/978-3-031-50078-7_22

One such variant is U-Net3+ [4], which uses several layers of depth adjustable submodules in the encoder to capture more context information and enhance feature representation consistency. In the decoder, U-Net3+ introduces an attention gating mechanism to adaptively focus on the region of interest and suppress irrelevant information. It also uses atrous convolution and inversion convolution to increase the receptive field size and improve feature recovery ability. These improvements make U-Net3+ perform better in medical image datasets, especially in processing high-resolution images. Similarly, Azad et al. [5] combined bi-directional ConvLSTM with skip connection for medical image segmentation. Gu et al. [6] integrated dense atrous convolution blocks and residual multi-kernel pooling blocks into U-Net to capture more advanced feature information. By leveraging these advanced feature extraction techniques, the model can capture more detailed and informative representations, ultimately enhancing segmentation performance. Xie et al. [7] used CNNs to extract MRI image features and feed these features into a recurrent neural network with memory modules for processing in order to effectively capture spatial relationships and contextual information in MRI images. Oktay et al. [8] combined jump connection with gating mechanisms, This approach allows the network to focus more on areas of interest, resulting in more accurate segmentation results. SegNet [9] uses a hierarchical CNN to extract features and pairs them with deconvolution layers in the decoder to generate masks. In encoders and decoders, SegNet uses the max pooling operation to reduce the size of the feature map, which is conducive to increasing the computational efficiency and memory utilization of the model. SFNet [10] combines two different types of convolutional neural networks: the fully convolutional network and the spatio-temporal convolutional network. In this way, Semantic Flow can make use of multi-scale information and spatio-temporal information at the same time to improve the effect of scene analysis. DFM [11] uses directional convolution and directional pooling operations on the basis of CNN to capture richer local spatial information and to segment hearts of different sizes and shapes using feature maps with multiple resolutions.

While CNN-based methods have made significant strides in medical image segmentation, they still face inherent limitations. One such limitation is the restricted receptive field of convolutional operations. Convolutional filters are localized and can only capture information within a limited neighborhood, which restricts the model's ability to capture long-range dependencies and global context. To overcome this limitation, researchers have turned to Transformer models, which have demonstrated exceptional performance in capturing global features and dependencies.

Transformers [12] have gained attention in natural language processing tasks, where they excel in modeling relationships between distant words in a sentence. One notable example is TransUNet [13], which transforms medical images into sequences and leverages the Transformer's attention mechanism to encode global information. By encoding the images as sequences, TransUNet enabled the model to capture contextual dependencies across the entire image, enhancing segmentation accuracy.

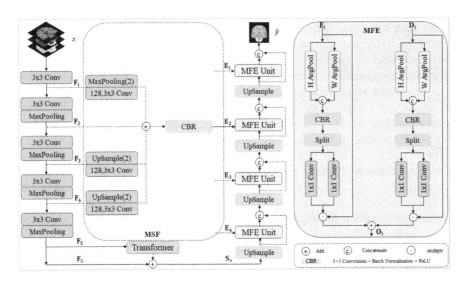

Fig. 1. Overview of the proposed HMINet.

Another approach is UTNet [14], which combines self-attention with relative location coding. By incorporating spatial relationships between pixels, the model can capture remote dependencies of different sizes, further improving segmentation performance. Levit-UNet [15] takes a different approach by incorporating LeViT transformer modules into the U-Net architecture. This integration enables fast and accurate medical image segmentation by leveraging the benefits of both CNNs and Transformers. TCRNet [16] uses CNN module to extract local features from input sequences, RNN module to capture global context information, and Transformer module to integrate both local features and global information. SwinUNet [17] uses Swin Transformer [18] to extract features from the input image in the encoder stage, and uses UNet-like structure to gradually reduce the size of the feature map. In the decoder stage, a structure similar to UNet was adopted, the feature map output from the encoder was gradually upsampled, and the low-level information was combined with the high-level information by cross-layer connection.

Despite these advancements, CNN-Transformer hybrid methods face two primary challenges. Firstly, effectively utilize the information contained within feature maps of different scales remains a challenge. Large-scale feature maps capture fine-grained details [19], while small-scale feature maps provide crucial semantic information for accurate segmentation [20]. Current methods struggle to fully exploit the complementary nature of these scales. Secondly, existing methods primarily focus on channel-wise information in skip connections and overlook the long-distance positional dependencies between feature maps. These positional dependencies carry essential spatial information that can aid in accurate segmentation.

To address these challenges, we propose a novel encoder-decoder network called HMINet, which effectively leverages multi-scale feature maps in both the encoder and decoder stages. In the encoder, we introduce a multi-scale fusion unit (MSF) designed to fuse information from feature maps of different scales. The MSF facilitates the combination of fine-grained and semantic information, ensuring that the full potential of feature maps at different scales is harnessed.

In the decoder, we introduce a multi-head feature enhancement unit (MFE) to encode both the coordinate and channel information of the feature maps. While existing methods mainly focus on channel-wise information, we recognize the importance of positional dependencies and incorporate coordinate information into the segmentation process. HMINet can capture long-distance positional dependencies and enhance the overall information content of the feature maps, leading to improved segmentation accuracy. The MFE module in HMINet utilizes multiple heads to capture different aspects of the feature maps. By encoding both the coordinate and channel information, the model can effectively exploit the rich spatial and semantic information within the feature maps.

2 Methodology

2.1 Overview of the Proposed HMINet

The structure of HMINet is shown in Fig. 1, where the encoder contains CNN, Transformer, and MSF, the decoder contains MFE. In the encoder, MSF is used to complete information fusion, Transformer is used to complete global feature extraction, and then MFE is used in the decoder for further information fusion to obtain segmentation results.

2.2 Hybrid Encoder Combining CNN and Transformer

In the encoder of HMINet, as illustrated in the left part of Fig. 1, the process begins with an input image, denoted as $x \in \mathbb{R}^{C \times H \times W}$, where C, H, and W represent the number of channels, height, and width of the image, respectively. If the input consists of multiple modalities, they are concatenated along the channel dimension for joint processing.

Initially, the image undergoes convolutional operations in a CNN to generate feature maps at different scales. These feature maps are denoted as $\{\mathbf{F}_i\}_{i=1,2,\ldots,5}$, where the subscript i represents the scale, ranging from 1 to 5, c_i, h_i, and w_i denote the number of channels, height, and width of $\mathbf{F}_i$, respectively.

As the encoder progresses, the number of channels in the feature maps doubles while their height and width are halved compared to the previous scale. This hierarchical structure captures increasingly abstract and high-level information as the encoder deepens.

However, CNNs have limitation in capturing global contextual information due to their localized receptive fields. To overcome this limitation, a Transformer unit is incorporated at the bottom of the CNN. The Transformer unit is applied to the feature map $\mathbf{F}_5$ since it has the largest receptive field and contains the richest semantic information. Before feeding $\mathbf{F}_5$ into the Transformer unit, it is resized to $\hat{\mathbf{F}}_5 \in \mathbb{R}^{c_5 \times r \times r}$ to match the input requirements of the Transformer, where c_5 is the number of channels in $\mathbf{F}_5$, and r represents the length of the longer side in $\mathbf{F}_5$.

The Transformer unit processes $\hat{\mathbf{F}}_5$ and generates a global feature representation denoted as $\mathbf{F}'_5 \in \mathbb{R}^{c_5 \times r \times r}$. This global feature incorporates long-range dependencies and captures the contextual information across the entire feature map. To fully leverage the semantic information from both local and global perspectives, the resized feature map $\hat{\mathbf{F}}_5$ and the Transformer output $\mathbf{F}'_5$ are added together:

$$\mathbf{S}_5 = \hat{\mathbf{F}}_5 + \mathbf{F}'_5 \tag{1}$$

Here, $\mathbf{S}_5 \in \mathbb{R}^{c_5 \times r \times r}$ represents a feature map that combines complementary local and global features. By fusing these features, HMINet benefits from both the detailed local information captured by the CNN and the global contextual information captured by the Transformer. This fusion process enhances the representation power of the feature map and contributes to improved segmentation accuracy.

To sum up, the encoder in HMINet applies a CNN to generate multi-scale feature maps, with the largest-scale feature map undergoing additional processing in a Transformer unit to capture global contextual information. The resized feature map and the Transformer output are then combined to create a feature map that integrates both local and global features. This fusion process enables HMINet to effectively leverage information from different scales and enhance the segmentation performance.

2.3   Multi-scale Fusion Unit

Considering that the existing U-Net structures do not make full use of the semantic information between feature maps of different scales, we design a MSF in the decoder to fuse feature maps on the first four feature maps of different scales generated by CNN. Each decoder layer of MSINet contains feature maps of the same scale, smaller scale and larger scale from the encoder to capture feature maps of fine-grained details and coarse-grained semantics at full scales. Figure 1 illustrates the construction process of feature map $\mathbf{E}_2$. The process of MSF is as follows:

$$\mathbf{E}_i = \begin{cases} \text{CBR}\left(\sum_{k=2}^{4} \text{B}\left(X_k\right) + X_1\right), \text{if} \quad i = 1 \\ \text{CBR}\left(\sum_{k=1}^{i-1} \text{M}\left(X_k\right) + X_i + \sum_{k=i+1}^{4} \text{B}\left(X_k\right)\right), \text{else} \\ \text{CBR}\left(\sum_{k=1}^{3} \text{M}\left(X_k\right) + X_4\right), \text{if} \quad i = 4 \end{cases} \tag{2}$$

where $\{\mathbf{E}_i\}_{i=1,2,\ldots,4}$ denote the fused feature maps obtained from the feature maps of different scales through MSF. B $(\cdot)$ represents bilinear interpolation; M $(\cdot)$ represents maximum pooling. CBR$(\cdot)$ represents convolution, batch normalization and ReLU activation.

2.4   Multi-head Feature Enhancement Unit

To obtain accurate segmentation results, it is necessary to better fuse the four feature maps $\{\mathbf{E}_i\}_{i=1,2,\ldots,4}$ generated by MSF and $\mathbf{S}_5$. Therefore, we propose a MSF to encode channel information and coordinate information of feature maps in the encoder and decoder. As the right part of Fig. 1, the input of MFE consists of two parts, one is the fusion feature maps $\{\mathbf{E}_i\}_{i=1,2,\ldots,4}$ generated in the encoder, and the other is the feature maps $\{\mathbf{D}_i\}_{i=1,2,3}$ generated in the decoder. $\mathbf{D}_4$ is obtained by bilinear interpolation of $\mathbf{S}_5$. After concatenating the output of MFE $\{\mathbf{O}_i\}_{i=1,2,\ldots,4}$ with $\{\mathbf{D}_i\}_{i=1,2,\ldots,4}$, the upsampling operation is performed to obtain $\{\mathbf{D}_i\}_{i=1,2,3}$.

As shown in Fig. 1, given the inputs $\mathbf{E}_i$ and $\mathbf{D}_i$, for each input, we use the average pooling operation to encode each channel along the horizontal and vertical directions, the step can be formulated as follows:

$$e_c(h) = \frac{1}{W} \sum_{0 \le i < W} E_c(h, i) \tag{3}$$

$$e_c(w) = \frac{1}{H} \sum_{0 \le j < H} E_c(j, w) \tag{4}$$

$$d_c(h) = \frac{1}{W} \sum_{0 \le i < W} D_c(h, i) \tag{5}$$

$$d_c(w) = \frac{1}{H} \sum_{0 \le j < H} D_c(j, w) \tag{6}$$

where $e_i(\cdot)$ denotes the output obtained by encoding $\mathbf{E}_i$ in both horizontal and vertical directions, and $d_i(\cdot)$ denotes the output obtained by encoding $\mathbf{D}_i$ in both horizontal and vertical directions.

After obtaining the outputs, we concatenate the outputs of the corresponding stages along the channel, followed by a CBR operation to produce the intermediate variables, represented as:

$$\hat{e}_i = \mathrm{CBR}\left(\mathrm{c}\left[e_i(h), e_i(w)\right]\right) \tag{7}$$

$$\hat{d}_i = \mathrm{CBR}\left(\mathrm{c}\left[d_i(h), d_i(w)\right]\right) \tag{8}$$

To reduce the model complexity, we consider an appropriate compression of the number of channels of the intermediate variables, and the compression ratio is set to σ. Then, $\hat{e}_i$ and $\hat{d}_i$ are split to obtain the intermediate variables $e_i'(h) \in \mathbb{R}^{C/\sigma \times H}$, $e_i'(w) \in \mathbb{R}^{C/\sigma \times W}$, $d_i'(h) \in \mathbb{R}^{C/\sigma \times H}$, $d_i'(w) \in \mathbb{R}^{C/\sigma \times W}$ and the number of channels, width and height of the intermediate variables are adjusted to be be consistent with $\{\mathbf{E}_i\}_{i=1,2,\ldots,4}$ and $\{\mathbf{D}_i\}_{i=1,2,\ldots,4}$ using 1×1 convolutional transformations T_h and T_w. To fully capture the channel dependency, the intermediate variables and the corresponding initial inputs are multiplied to obtain the corresponding outputs, and the outputs of the two processes are added to obtain the output of each stage of the MFE. The process can be expressed as follows:

$$\hat{\mathbf{E}}_i = \delta \left(T_h \left(e_i'(h)\right)\right) \odot \delta \left(T_w \left(e_i'(w)\right)\right) \odot \mathbf{E}_i \tag{9}$$

$$\hat{\mathbf{D}}_i = \delta \left(T_h \left(d_i'(h)\right)\right) \odot \delta \left(T_w \left(d_i'(w)\right)\right) \odot \mathbf{D}_i \tag{10}$$

$$\mathbf{O}_i = \hat{\mathbf{E}}_i + \hat{\mathbf{D}}_i \tag{11}$$

where $\delta(\cdot)$ is the ReLU activation function, $\odot$ denotes multiply operation. Finally, we make full use of the coordinate information and channel information of the feature maps in the MFE and obtain the prediction result $\hat{y} \in \mathbb{R}^{C \times H \times W}$.

3   Experiment

3.1   Datasets and Implementation

The proposed method is evaluated on four different datasets: Choledoch [21], HVSMR [22], MRBrainS [23], and BrainWeb [24]. Each dataset serves a specific segmentation goal and consists of a varying number of images. Sample images are shown in Fig. 2, and Table 1 displays the specific information of the four datasets.

Table 1. The specific information of BrainWeb, MRBrainS, HVSMR and Choledoch.

Name	Num	Resolution	Modality	Segmented regions
BrainWeb	399	181×181	T1, T2, PD	WM, GM
		217×181		CSF, BG
		181×217		
MRBrainS	174	240×240	T1, T1ir, Flair	WM, GM
				CSF, BG
HVSMR	3341	100×300	–	Blood pool,
				Myocardium, BG
Choledoch	514	1280×1024	–	Cancerous,
				Normal Areas

The Choledoch dataset comprises hyperspectral images focusing on the bile duct. It is divided into cancerous and normal areas, providing a basis for differentiating between the two. The dataset consists of 514 high-resolution images with dimensions of 1280×1024 pixels. The HVSMR dataset focuses on cardiovascular magnetic resonance imaging (MRI) and aims to segment blood pools and myocardium. It contains 3341 slices from 10 MRI volumes. The MRBrainS dataset is a widely recognized resource for brain MRI segmentation. It consists of 174 images, each with a size of 240×240 pixels. The dataset includes cerebrospinal fluid (CSF), white matter (WM), gray matter (GM), and background classes. The BrainWeb dataset is another well-known resource for brain MRI segmentation. It comprises 399 images with three different sizes: 181×181, 181×217, and 217×181 pixels. Similar to MRBrainS, BrainWeb includes CSF, WM, GM, and background classes. The dataset provides images with different dimensions, enabling the evaluation of the proposed method's scalability and adaptability.

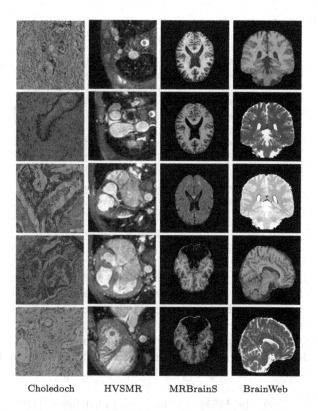

Choledoch   HVSMR   MRBrainS   BrainWeb

Fig. 2. Sample images from Choledoch, HVSMR, MRBrainS and BrainWeb.

For the experimental setup, all experiments are conducted on an Intel®Xeon®Gold 6230 CPU @ 2.10 GHz machine with a total of 40 CPU cores. The implementation is based on PyTorch 1.6.0.

The joint loss function used in the experiments is a combination of cross-entropy loss and generalized Dice loss. The SGD optimizer is employed with an initial learning rate of 0.003, a momentum of 0.9, and a weight decay of 0.0001. The batch size is set to 1, and a total of 30,000 iterations are performed during training.

For evaluating the performance of the proposed method, two metrics are selected: pixel accuracy (PA) and dice similarity coefficient (DSC). These metrics provide quantitative measures of segmentation accuracy.

3.2   Ablation Study

To assess the individual contributions of each proposed module, we perform ablation experiments on the four datasets by removing each module. The results of these experiments are presented in Fig. 3.

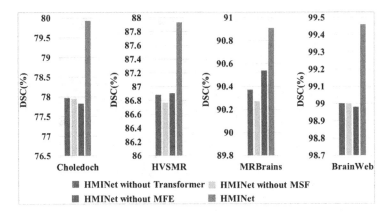

Fig. 3. Experimental results of ablation study.

From Fig. 3, we observe that HMINet without the Transformer module fails to effectively extract global feature maps and essentially reduces to a pure CNN model. This demonstrates the importance of the Transformer module in achieving global feature extraction.

Similarly, HMINet without the MSF module struggles to fuse information from multi-scale feature maps, resulting in a significant performance degradation. This highlights the crucial role of the MSF module in information fusion across different scales.

Additionally, when the MFE module is excluded from HMINet, the model loses the ability to capture channel information and coordinate information of the feature maps. Consequently, the segmentation performance is significantly compromised. This emphasizes the necessity of the MFE module.

In conclusion, HMINet outperforms the ablated versions by effectively leveraging feature map information, capturing channel information, and incorporating coordinate information. These findings highlight the significance of the proposed modules and demonstrate the superior segmentation performance of HMINet.

3.3   Comparison with State-of-the-Art Methods

To evaluate the performance of HMINet, we compare it with leading medical image segmentation methods and present the results in Table 2. To ensure a fair comparison, all images are adjusted to a resolution of 256 × 256. The top part of Table 2 includes methods that use either a pure CNN architecture or a pure

Table 2. Segmentation results of comparison on Choledoch, HVSMR, MRBrainS and BrainWeb datasets.

Method	Metrics on Choledoch		Metrics on HVSMR		Metrics on MRBrainS		Metrics on BrainWeb	
	PA(%)	DSC(%)	PA(%)	DSC(%)	PA(%)	DSC(%)	PA(%)	DSC(%)
U-Net [1]	65.57	62.10	92.51	83.67	91.83	74.02	93.26	80.89
U-Net3+ [4]	71.09	67.36	93.42	86.37	96.73	89.19	99.05	98.12
FCN-8s [25]	66.35	61.84	91.79	82.93	92.61	75.70	90.30	78.89
Attn-UNet [8]	68.20	64.98	93.72	87.90	97.09	89.33	99.71	99.42
SFNet [10]	69.02	64.20	92.98	86.24	97.02	90.07	99.48	99.02
SegNet [9]	65.66	61.46	90.27	80.99	92.44	75.60	93.36	86.13
SwinUNet [17]	77.47	73.15	93.58	86.73	97.28	90.83	99.59	99.34
CRDN [7]	72.50	66.83	93.36	87.00	97.18	90.38	99.64	99.32
UTNet [14]	70.63	67.57	92.54	86.53	96.83	89.60	99.05	98.13
TransUNet [13]	71.15	68.36	92.06	85.78	92.87	79.68	94.40	88.97
LeVit-UNet [15]	74.67	71.93	93.26	86.54	95.98	88.84	99.41	99.24
TCRNet [16]	76.38	72.80	93.49	86.66	97.23	90.81	99.70	99.40
HMINet	**81.60**	**79.93**	**94.33**	**87.93**	**97.38**	**90.91**	**99.74**	**99.46**

Transformer architecture, such as FCN [25], U-Net [1], SegNet [9], and SwinUNet [17]. The bottom part includes methods that combine CNN and Transformer, such as TransUNet [13] and LeVit-UNet [15].

Existing methods that focus on multi-scale fusion, such as U-Net3+ [4], only consider feature fusion in the encoder using CNN, thus lacking global feature information. Other methods, like UCTransNet [26], only consider channel information while disregarding coordinate information, resulting in underutilization of feature map information. In contrast, HMINet integrates both channel information and coordinate information in the decoder, making full use of feature map information.

Comparing HMINet with representative CNN-based methods such as U-Net [1], U-Net3+ [4], and SegNet [9], we observe significant improvements across all four datasets. When compared to methods combining CNN and Transformer, such as TransUNet [13], HMINet achieves an increase of 11.57%, 2.15%, 11.23%, and 10.49% in performance on the respective datasets. These comparisons clearly demonstrate the effectiveness of HMINet in medical image segmentation.

In Fig. 4, we provide a visual comparison of the segmentation maps from various models. We can see that HMINet identifies the details of Blood Pool and CSF in HVSMR and BrainWeb, respectively, which indicates that our method obtains sufficient feature representations.

Therefore, the results presented in Table 1 highlight the superior performance of HMINet compared to state-of-the-art methods. HMINet surpasses existing CNN-based approaches and outperforms methods that combine CNN and Transformer, showcasing its effectiveness in medical image segmentation tasks.

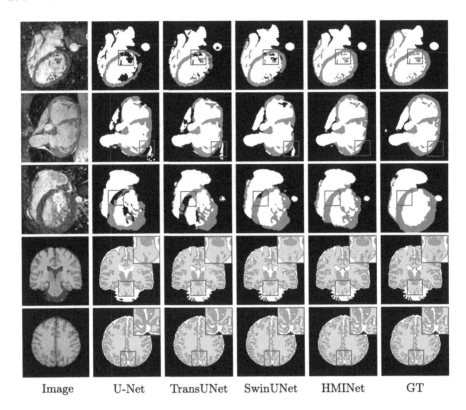

Image   U-Net   TransUNet   SwinUNet   HMINet   GT

Fig. 4. Some visualization results of the proposed HMINet and other encoding-decoding methods, i.e., U-Net, TransUNet and SwinUNet. The top three rows are samples from HVSMR(Myocardium in white, Blood Pool in gray), the fourth and the last rows are samples from MRBrainS and BrainWeb (CSF in white, GM in green, WM in yellow) (Color figure online)

4   Conclusion

In this paper, from multi-scale fusion and information capture, we propose a novel medical segmentation network based on CNN and Transformer called HMINet. Specifically, we introduce two new modules named multi-scale fusion unit (MSF) and multi-head feature enhancement unit (MFE). In the encoder, MSF is used to carry out multi-scale feature fusion for feature maps of different scales generated by CNN, and Transformer is used to supplement global information. In the decoder, MFE is used to capture the coordinate information and channel information of feature maps. Experimental results on four datasets validate the effectiveness of HMINet.

References

1. Ronneberger, O., Fischer, P., Brox, T.: U-Net: convolutional networks for biomedical image segmentation. In: Navab, N., Hornegger, J., Wells, W.M., Frangi, A.F. (eds.) MICCAI 2015. LNCS, vol. 9351, pp. 234–241. Springer, Cham (2015). https://doi.org/10.1007/978-3-319-24574-4_28

2. Zhou, Z., Siddiquee, M.M.R., Tajbakhsh, N., Liang, J.: UNet++: redesigning skip connections to exploit multiscale features in image segmentation. IEEE Trans. Med. Imaging **39**, 1856–1867 (2019)

3. Zhang, Y., Wu, J., Liu, Y., Chen, Y., Wu, E.X., Tang, X.: MI-UNet: multi-inputs UNet incorporating brain parcellation for stroke lesion segmentation from T1-weighted magnetic resonance images. IEEE J. Biomed. Health Inform. **25**, 526–535 (2020)

4. Huang, H, et al.: UNet 3+: a full-scale connected UNet for medical image segmentation. In: ICASSP 2020 IEEE International Conference on Acoustics, pp. 1055–1059 (2020)

5. Azad, R., Asadi-Aghbolaghi, M., Fathy, M., Escalera, S.: Bi-directional ConvLSTM U-Net with densley connected convolutions. In: Proceedings of the IEEE/CVF International Conference on Computer Vision Workshops (2019)

6. Gu, Z., et al.: CE-Net: context encoder network for 2d medical image segmentation. IEEE Trans. Med. Imaging **10**, 2281–2292 (2019)

7. Wen, Y., Xie, K., He, L.: Segmenting medical MRI via recurrent decoding cell. In: Proceedings of the AAAI Conference on Artificial Intelligence, pp. 12452–12459 (2020)

8. Oktay, O., et al., Attention U-Net: learning where to look for the pancreas. arXiv preprint arXiv:1804.03999 (2018)

9. Badrinarayanan, V., Kendall, A., Cipolla, R.: SegNet: a deep convolutional encoder-decoder architecture for image segmentation. IEEE Trans. Pattern Analysis Mach. Intell. **39**, 2481–2495 (2017)

10. Li, X.: Semantic flow for fast and accurate scene parsing. In: Vedaldi, A., Bischof, H., Brox, T., Frahm, J.-M. (eds.) ECCV 2020. LNCS, vol. 12346, pp. 775–793. Springer, Cham (2020). https://doi.org/10.1007/978-3-030-58452-8_45

11. Cheng, F., et al.: Learning directional feature maps for cardiac MRI segmentation. In: Martel, A.L., et al. (eds.) MICCAI 2020. LNCS, vol. 12264, pp. 108–117. Springer, Cham (2020). https://doi.org/10.1007/978-3-030-59719-1_11

12. Vaswani, A., et al.: Attention is all you need. In: Advances in Neural Information Processing Systems, vol. 30 (2017)

13. Chen, J., et al.: TransUNet: transformers make strong encoders for medical image segmentation. arXiv preprint arXiv:2102.04306 (2021)

14. Gao, Y., Zhou, M., Metaxas, D.N.: UTNet: a hybrid transformer architecture for medical image segmentation. In: de Bruijne, M., et al. (eds.) MICCAI 2021. LNCS, vol. 12903, pp. 61–71. Springer, Cham (2021). https://doi.org/10.1007/978-3-030-87199-4_6

15. Xu, G., Wu, X., Zhang, X., He, X.: LeViT-Unet: make faster encoders with transformer for medical image segmentation. arXiv preprint arXiv:2107.08623 (2021)

16. Shan, X., Ma, T., Gu, A., Cai, H., Wen, Y.: TCRNet: make transformer, CNN and RNN complement each other. In: ICASSP 2022 IEEE International Conference on Acoustics, Speech and Signal Processing (2022)

17. Cao, H., et al.: Swin-UNet: UNet-like pure transformer for medical image segmentation. In: Karlinsky, L., Michaeli, T., Nishino, K. (eds.) ECCV 2022. LNCS, vol.

13803, pp. 205–218. Springer, Cham (2023). https://doi.org/10.1007/978-3-031-25066-8_9

18. Liu, Z., et al.: Swin transformer: hierarchical vision transformer using shifted windows. In: Proceedings of the IEEE/CVF International Conference on Computer Vision, pp. 10012–10022 (2021)

19. Peng, Z., et al.: Conformer: local features coupling global representations for visual recognition. In: Proceedings of the IEEE International Conference on Computer Vision, pp. 1–13 (2021)

20. Dosovitskiy, A., et al.: An image is worth 16x16 words: transformers for image recognition at scale. In: International Conference on Learning Representations, pp. 1–22 (2021)

21. Zhang, Q., Li, Q., Yu, G., Sun, L., Zhou, M., Chu, J.: A multidimensional Choledoch database and benchmarks for cholangiocarcinoma diagnosis. IEEE Access **7**, 149414–149421 (2019)

22. Pace, D.F., Dalca, A.V., Geva, T., Powell, A.J., Moghari, M.H., Golland, P.: Interactive whole-heart segmentation in congenital heart disease. In: Navab, N., Hornegger, J., Wells, W.M., Frangi, A.F. (eds.) MICCAI 2015. LNCS, vol. 9351, pp. 80–88. Springer, Cham (2015). https://doi.org/10.1007/978-3-319-24574-4_10

23. Mendrik, A.M., et al.: MRBrainS challenge: online evaluation framework for brain image segmentation in 3T MRI scans. In: Computational Intelligence and Neuroscience (2015)

24. Kwan, R.K.-S., Evans, A.C., Pike, G.B.: An extensible MRI simulator for postprocessing evaluation. In: Höhne, K.H., Kikinis, R. (eds.) VBC 1996. LNCS, vol. 1131, pp. 135–140. Springer, Heidelberg (1996). https://doi.org/10.1007/BFb0046947

25. Zhang, Y., Qiu, Z., Yao, T., Liu, D., Mei, T.: Fully convolutional adaptation networks for semantic segmentation. In: Proceedings of the IEEE Computer Society Conference on Computer Vision and Pattern Recognition, pp. 6810–6818 (2015)

26. Wang, H., Cao, P., Wang, J., Zaiane, O.R.: UCTransNet: rethinking the skip connections in U-Net from a channel-wise perspective with transformer. In: Proceedings of the AAAI Conference on Artificial Intelligence, pp. 2441–2449 (2022)

CASCO: A Contactless Cough Screening System Based on Audio Signal Processing

Xinxin Zhang[1], Hang Liu[1], Xinru Chen[1], Rui Qin[1], Yan Zhu[2], Wenfang Li[2], Menghan Hu[1(✉)], and Jian Zhang[1]

[1] Shanghai Key Laboratory of Multidimensional Information Processing, East China Normal University, Shanghai, China
mhhu@ce.ecnu.edu.cn

[2] Department of Emergency and Critical Care, Shanghai Changzheng Hospital, Shanghai, China

Abstract. Cough is a common symptom of respiratory disease, which produces a specific sound. Cough detection has great significance to prevent, assess, and control epidemics. This paper proposes CASCO (Cough Analysis System using Short-Time Fourier Transform (STFT) and Convolutional Neural Networks (CNN) in the WeChat mini Program), a cough detection system capable of quantifying the number of coughs through an audio division algorithm. This system combines STFT with CNN, achieving accuracy, precision, recall, and F1-score with 97.0%, 95.6%, 98.7%, and 0.97 respectively in cough detection. The model is embedded into the WeChat mini program to make it feasible to apply cough detection on smartphones and realize large-scale and contactless cough screening. Future research can combine audio and video signals to further improve the accuracy of large-scale cough screening.

Keywords: Cough detection · Deep neural network · Audio Signal Processing

1 Introduction

Cough is a common symptom associated with various respiratory diseases such as bronchitis, and asthma. It serves as a powerful mechanism of the human body to expel foreign particles and clear secretions from the upper respiratory tract, resulting in a specific sound that plays a significant role in disease diagnosis [1].

Respiratory diseases pose a significant threat to human health worldwide [2]. As the details about the cough frequency, intensity, and sound help physicians in their diagnostics of respiratory diseases, the field of automatic cough sensor research has been established with various systems achieving high precision and sensitivity. The Leicester cough monitor consists of an audio recorder and a microphone and detects the time-varying spectral features of cough sound based on hidden Markov models [3]. Costa et al. [4] applied a mechanomyography sensor on the abdominal region to detect cough events. Doddabasappla et al. [5]

X. Zhang and H. Liu—These authors contributed equally to this work.

© The Author(s), under exclusive license to Springer Nature Switzerland AG 2024
B. Sheng et al. (Eds.): CGI 2023, LNCS 14498, pp. 287–300, 2024.
https://doi.org/10.1007/978-3-031-50078-7_23

achieved cough detection using the multiband spectral summation features of acceleration signal measured by a portable accelerometer. Most of these automatic cough sensors are considered to be uncomfortable to wear during daily activities, and their expensive cost hindered the application of large-scale cough screening.

Large-scale cough detection plays a pivotal role in epidemiological research, disease screening, and epidemic control efforts. The global impact of the COVID-19 pandemic, which primarily affects the respiratory system, has resulted in a significant number of confirmed cases worldwide, as reported by the World Health Organization (WHO) by March 2, 2022 [6]. The emergence and dominance of the Omicron variant, along with other COVID-19 variants, have further exacerbated the health crisis and posed immense challenges to human health and the global economy [7]. Given that cough is a prominent symptom of COVID-19, there has been a growing focus on developing large-scale and contactless cough detection systems in research initiatives. These systems hold immense potential in facilitating early detection, monitoring, and effective control of infectious diseases. By enabling non-invasive and convenient screening, they can contribute significantly to mitigating disease transmission, informing public health strategies, and supporting timely interventions. The development and implementation of such systems are crucial steps toward safeguarding public health and minimizing the impact of future epidemics and pandemics.

In response to the distinct acoustic characteristics associated with cough events, several studies have made significant strides in developing models that utilize cough audio features for remote and contactless detection of cough events. For instance, Islam et al. proposed an algorithm that leverages acoustic features extracted from cough sound samples, combined with a deep neural network, for automated and noninvasive diagnosis of COVID-19 [8]. Tena et al. focused on extracting time-frequency cough features from audio signals and applied a supervised machine-learning algorithm to identify the most relevant features for COVID-19 diagnosis [9]. Another notable study by Monge-Álvarez et al. involved the construction of a machine hearing system specifically designed for robust cough detection, incorporating short-term spectral features and the standard deviation of short-term descriptors [10]. These advancements demonstrate the potential of using cough audio analysis in developing efficient and accurate diagnostic tools, providing valuable insights for the detection and management of respiratory diseases.

The widespread use of smartphones has made large-scale cough detection possible. Patients and medical professionals now have the convenience of capturing cough audio signals using the built-in microphone and voice recorder on their smartphones, eliminating the need for additional specialized cough assessment devices. Notably, Hoyos-Barcelo et al. proposed a cough detector on smartphones that leverages local Hu moments as robust features, combined with an optimized k-NN classifier [11]. Imran et al. built a COVID-19 diagnosis app analyzing cough sound by an Artificial Intelligence (AI)-based engine [12]. Most of the aforementioned studies utilizing AI algorithms failed to accurately measure cough frequency and intensity.

One significant challenge in utilizing smartphones for cough detection is the limited battery consumption of these devices. Executing complex machine learning or deep learning algorithms directly on smartphones can quickly drain the battery and hinder their practicality. Consequently, alternative approaches are necessary to overcome this limitation and enable efficient cough analysis [13,14]. One feasible solution is to leverage the capabilities of external servers for audio signal processing. With the widespread application of 5G technology, it becomes increasingly feasible to use smartphones solely for audio collection while offloading computationally intensive tasks to remote servers [2]. The high-speed and low-latency characteristics of 5G networks facilitate seamless and efficient transmission of cough audio signals from smartphones to external servers.

In this paper, we propose a novel cough detection system called CASCO, which can calculate the number of coughs by an audio division algorithm. This system combines STFT with CNN, achieving an impressive accuracy rate of 97.0% in classifying cough sounds and non-cough sounds. The integration of this system into the WeChat mini program enables the deployment of cough detection on smartphones, enabling widespread and contactless screening for coughs at a large scale. Furthermore, by processing the audio recorded on smartphones in an external server, we alleviate the issue of high battery consumption associated with complex algorithms, ensuring a smoother user experience. The subsequent sections of this paper are organized as follows: In Sect. 2, we outline the methodology and the specific procedure of cough detection system. In Sect. 3, we explain the dataset we used and the training process, compare the experimental results in terms of performance metrics, and discuss the potential and limitations of the study. We conclude the paper by summarizing the key findings and contributions of the research.

2 Cough Detection System

The overall system architecture is shown in Fig. 1. The WeChat mini program in a smartphone records sound when the "Start recording" and "Finish recording" buttons are pressed. When the "Detect cough" button is pressed, the recorded sounds are transmitted to the server for further processing. At the server, the audio division algorithm extracts the high parts above the threshold from a long piece of audio. This process divides the long audio into shorter segments, each containing only a single suspicious sound. Then STFT is applied to the short audio to generate a spectrogram that serves as the feature of the audio. Subsequently, the spectrogram is forwarded to CNN, classifying cough samples and non-cough samples. The server performs cough detection and counts the number of coughs in the long audio. Finally, the output results are displayed in the WeChat mini program for user accessibility.

The details of detection and diagnosis classifiers are presented below.

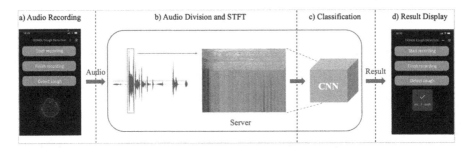

| a) Audio Recording | b) Audio Division and STFT | c) Classification | d) Result Display |

Fig. 1. Pipeline of the CASCO cough detection system: a) record a long piece of audio to be detected via the WeChat mini program; b) divide the long audio into several short sounds and extract features using STFT; c) classify cough sounds and non-cough sounds through CNN; d) display the result and the number of coughs on the WeChat mini program.

2.1   Audio Division

To select a suitable threshold for extracting a single suspicious sound, we use Otsu's thresholding method in the audio division algorithm. Otsu's method is a global thresholding algorithm, which can automatically generate the optimal segmentation threshold based on the input signal [15]. For the input audio signal, we suppose the number of points is denoted as N, which are dichotomized into two classes: the low part C_0 and the high part C_1, using a threshold at level T. The proportion of points belonging to the low part in the whole audio is denoted by ω_0 and its average amplitude level is μ_0. Similarly, the proportion of points belonging to the high part in the whole audio is denoted by ω_1 and its average amplitude level is μ_1. Then the total average amplitude level of the audio is given by:

$$\mu_T = \omega_0\mu_0 + \omega_1\mu_1 \tag{1}$$

We can easily verify the following relation for any choice of T:

$$\omega_0 + \omega_1 = 1 \tag{2}$$

To evaluate the class separability of the threshold at level T, we introduce the following between-class variance used in the discriminant analysis:

$$\begin{aligned}\sigma_B^2 &= \omega_0\left(\mu_0 - \mu_T\right)^2 + \omega_1\left(\mu_1 - \mu_T\right)^2 \\ &= \omega_0\omega_1\left(\mu_1 - \mu_0\right)^2\end{aligned} \tag{3}$$

In Eq. (3), it can be observed that the farther the two means μ_0 and μ_1 are from each other, the larger the between-class variance is, which indicates that the between-class variance serves as an effective measure of differentiability between classes. To determine the optimal threshold T^* that maximizes the between-class variance, we employ the following equation:

$$\sigma_B^2\left(T^*\right) = \max \sigma_B^2(T) \tag{4}$$

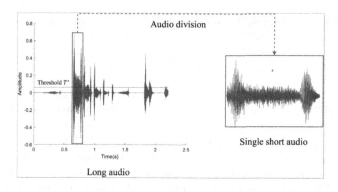

Fig. 2. Processing steps of the audio division algorithm.

After selecting a suitable threshold, we extract the high parts above the threshold from a long piece of audio. This process involves splitting the long audio into shorter segments, each containing only a single suspicious sound. The length of the short segments is not fixed but adaptively determined based on the threshold and characteristics of the audio signal. It is expected to implement the function of counting the number of coughs. The processing steps of the audio division algorithm can be seen in Fig. 2.

2.2 Feature Extraction

For automatic speech recognition, STFT has been considered to be an effective feature extraction method. The spectrogram generated by STFT can show the relationship of time and frequency of audio signals, thus extracting features of audio and then differentiating different audio signals [16]. The process of STFT is illustrated in Fig. 3. The STFT form of signal $x(t)$ can be defined by the following equation:

$$\text{STFT}(t, f) = \int_{-\infty}^{\infty} x(\tau)h(\tau - t)e^{-j2\pi f\tau}\mathrm{d}\tau \tag{5}$$

where $h(\tau - t)$ means window function.

The audio signal is first pre-emphasized by a first-order high-pass filter to improve the signal-to-noise ratio in the high-frequency portion of the signal. After the audio signal is framed and windowed, Fast Fourier Transform (FFT) is applied to all the frames and generates spectrums. The amplitude values of the spectra are quantified and mapped to different colors, providing a visual representation of the frequency content. Finally, the transformed multi-frame spectrums are stitched together in the time dimension to form a final spectrogram of the audio signal.

We apply the STFT to the short audio to generate a spectrogram with time on the horizontal axis, frequency on the vertical axis and color indicating amplitude as the feature of the audio. The spectrogram generated through STFT enables visual representation and facilitates accurate differentiation of cough sounds.

2.3   Classification

Mapping the time-frequency spectrogram into a color representation as the input to a CNN serves two main purposes: 1) Channel dimensions: By converting the time-frequency spectrogram to a color image with three channels (R, G, B), it aligns with the common CNN input format, such as RGB images. This allows the CNN to process the spectrogram as image-like input, with height, width, and three color channels, enabling the use of standard image-based CNN architectures. CNNs excel in learning hierarchical features, progressing from local patterns to global representations. 2) Feature representation: The STFT output consists of the real and imaginary parts (or magnitude and phase), representing different aspects of the audio signal. By mapping it to a color spectrogram, the CNN can potentially learn distinct features from different parts of the spectrogram. For instance, the CNN can capture spatial patterns, temporal changes, and frequency content from the color representation, leading to a more comprehensive and distinctive feature representation for cough detection.

The generated spectrogram is then fed into the CNN to decide whether the audio corresponds to a cough or not. An overview of the used CNN structure is illustrated in Fig. 4. The CNN consists of eight layers: 5 convolutional layers, 2 fully connected layers, and a softmax classification layer. In each convolutional layer, the Rectified Linear Unit (ReLU) is utilized as the activation function. The first, second, and fifth convolutional layers are connected to a 3×3 max-pooling layer, which is performed with a stride of 2. The first convolutional layer takes in the $224\times224\times3$ spectrogram as inputs and consists of 96 filters of kernel size 11×11, a stride of 4, and padding of 2. It is followed by a 5×5 convolutional layer with a padding of 2. The last three convolutional layers all have filters of size 3×3 and padding of 1. The features are then passed to two fully connected layers with 4,096 neurons each, which also employ 0.5 dropout regularization to avoid overfitting. Finally, the last layer, comprising two neurons, takes the outputs from the second fully connected layer and employs the softmax function to classify the spectrograms as either cough or non-cough. By utilizing this CNN architecture, we aim to capture and learn the distinguishing patterns and characteristics of cough events, enabling accurate classification of cough and non-cough spectrograms. The combination of convolutional layers, max-pooling layers, fully connected layers, and the softmax classification layer provides the necessary capacity for CNN to effectively differentiate between cough and non-cough audio samples.

3   Experiments

3.1   Dataset Explanation

To train and build the proposed system, we create a dataset consisting of cough samples and non-cough samples. The dataset of cough samples comprises

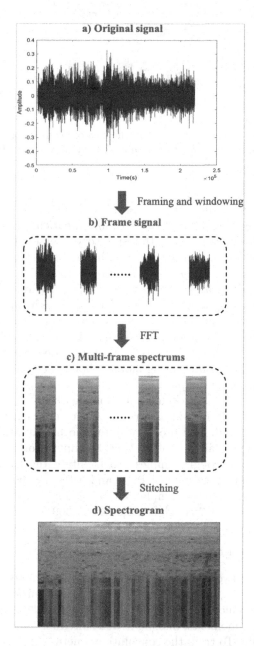

Fig. 3. Processing steps of generating spectrogram by STFT: a) the amplitude-time graph of the original signal; b) the separated signals after framing and windowing; c) multi-frame spectrums with amplitude values mapped into colors; d) the final spectrogram.

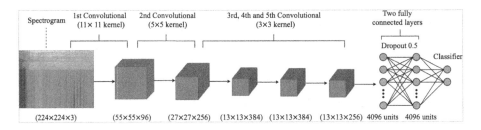

Fig. 4. Structure of the used CNN classifier: the network consists of eight layers, including five convolutional layers, two fully connected layers and a softmax classification layer.

self-recorded coughing audio, cough recordings sourced from the Environmental Sound Classification (ESC-50) dataset [17], and inpatient cough recordings collected from individuals diagnosed with respiratory diseases. The inpatient cough recordings were collected from 24 patients, including 15 males and 9 females, in the respiratory disease department at Ruijin Hospital [18]. The inpatient's cough samples ranged in age from 48 to 85 years old and suffered from respiratory diseases with symptoms of cough. The non-cough samples contain self-recorded environmental audio and labeled environmental recordings from the ESC-50 dataset, including interior sounds, exterior noises, natural sounds, and human (non-speech) sounds [17]. Both the self-recorded samples and inpatient cough recordings were recorded using mobile phone microphones, incorporating background noise in these samples.

Before training, we apply the audio division algorithm to split the long audio from the previously collected dataset into shorter audio clips, each containing a single suspicious sound. The preprocessed audio has durations ranging from 230 ms to 670 ms. In total, we obtain 13,529 samples, comprising 6,985 cough samples and 6,544 non-cough samples. To facilitate the training process, we divide the dataset into a training dataset and a testing dataset. The training dataset consists of 5,588 cough samples and 5,235 non-cough samples, while the test dataset comprises 1,397 cough samples and 1,309 non-cough samples.

3.2   Network Training

The convolutional network employed in this study is trained using the Adam optimizer, which is a first-order gradient-based optimization algorithm for stochastic objective functions [19]. The Adam optimizer leverages adaptive estimates of lower-order moments, making it well-suited for handling large datasets and sparse gradients. To train the convolutional network, the cross entropy loss function is utilized. This loss function is commonly employed in classification tasks and measures the dissimilarity between the predicted probabilities and the true labels. An initial learning rate of 0.0002 is set, allowing the network to gradually adjust its weights based on the optimization process.

During the training process, a batch size of 32 is utilized. The batch size determines the number of samples processed in each iteration, allowing for efficient utilization of computational resources and improved generalization performance. By carefully selecting these hyperparameters and leveraging the capabilities of the Adam optimizer, we optimize the performance of the convolutional network and enhance its ability to accurately classify cough and non-cough samples.

3.3 Experimental Results

To evaluate and compare the performance of the system in cough detection, two experiments are undertaken.

In the initial experiment, we assess the system's performance using True Positive (TP), False Negative (FN), False Positive (FP), and True Negative (TN) values obtained from the confusion matrix presented in Table 1. From this matrix, we derive several performance metrics including accuracy, precision, sensitivity/recall, and F1-score. These metrics provide valuable insights into the effectiveness and reliability of the model when applied to the test dataset. The calculation of these metrics is as follows:

$$\text{accuracy} = \frac{TP + TN}{TP + TN + FP + FN} \tag{6}$$

$$\text{precision} = \frac{TP}{TP + FP} \tag{7}$$

$$\text{sensitivity/recall} = \frac{TP}{TP + FN} \tag{8}$$

$$\text{F1-score} = 2 * \left(\frac{\text{precision} \times \text{recall}}{\text{precision} + \text{recall}} \right) \tag{9}$$

Table 1. Confusion matrix for cough detection.

True Class	Predicted Class	
	Cough	Non-cough
Cough	TP: 1379	FN: 18
Non-cough	FP: 63	TN: 1246

Based on the classification results presented in Table 2, the cough detection model demonstrates excellent performance in distinguishing between cough events and non-cough samples. The accuracy of the model is measured at 97.0%, indicating a high level of overall correct classification. Additionally, the recall (also known as sensitivity) is calculated at 98.7%, which signifies the model's ability to correctly identify the majority of actual cough events. The precision of the model stands at 95.6%, indicating the proportion of correctly identified cough events among the total number of predicted cough events. Moreover, the F1-score, which combines both precision and recall, is calculated as 0.97. The F1-score is a measure that balances the trade-off between precision and recall, providing an overall assessment of the model's performance. These results demonstrate its potential as a reliable tool for large-scale and contactless cough screenings.

Table 2. Comparison of SM, SVM, CNN, ResNet, and VGG for cough classification.

Model	Accuracy (%)	Sensitivity/Recall (%)	Precision (%)	F1-Score
MFCC+SM	85.7	87.4	83.9	0.86
MFCC+SVM	94.9	97.1	93.1	0.95
STFT+CNN	**97.0**	**98.7**	**95.6**	**0.97**
STFT+ResNet	94.2	95.6	92.9	0.94
STFT+VGG16	95.4	97.8	94.1	0.95

In the second experiment, we conduct a comprehensive comparative analysis to assess the effectiveness of the cough detection model in comparison to machine learning and other deep learning algorithms for cough classification. Considering the widely-used Mel-Frequency Cepstral Coefficients (MFCC) as classical speech recognition features, we construct a Support Vector Machine (SVM) model using MFCC features to examine how a more complex machine learning classifier performs in comparison to the CNN-based model. Additionally, we train a model using the softmax (SM) function on the MFCC features to directly compare with CNN's classification layer. Furthermore, we build comparative deep learning models utilizing ResNet [20] and VGG16 [21] architectures.

The performance metrics of these comparative models are summarized in Table 2, providing insights into their respective accuracy, recall, precision, and F1-score. The results clearly demonstrate that the cough detection model outperforms the SVM model employing MFCC features, exhibiting a remarkable improvement of 2.1% in terms of accuracy.

The main reasons for the superiority of STFT+CNN over other combinations lie in its feature representation, deep learning architecture, and data representation. STFT extraction captures rich time-frequency information, providing a comprehensive description of cough sounds, whereas MFCC only considers Mel frequency information, and SM and VGG16 may not effectively utilize time-frequency information. CNN, designed for image processing, excels in handling color spectrograms and can learn spatial, temporal, and frequency features, facilitating accurate cough sound classification and detection. The color spectrogram leverages the three channels to enhance feature diversity, while other combinations might not fully exploit audio data characteristics. This comparative experiment highlights the superiority of the CNN-based approach over traditional machine learning algorithms and other deep learning architectures in accurately detecting and classifying cough sounds.

3.4 Discussion

The remarkable accuracy achieved by the cough detection model, surpassing that of the comparative models, clearly demonstrates the immense potential of the system. However, the system's capabilities extend beyond accurate detection. It also offers the ability to count the number of coughs through the implementation of the audio division algorithm, providing valuable information such as cough frequency and intensity. This has various applications, including respiratory health monitoring, identifying cough outbreaks, and tracking medical interventions. For instance, in a healthcare setting, the system could be deployed in hospitals or clinics to monitor the cough frequency and intensity of patients with respiratory conditions, enabling healthcare professionals to gain insights into the severity and progression of their conditions. One of the key advantages of the system is its integration with a WeChat mini program, enabling the implementation of cough detection on smartphones and facilitating large-scale, contactless cough screenings.

By processing the audio recordings on an external server, the issue of high battery consumption typically associated with continuous audio processing on mobile devices is mitigated. This opens up a wide range of possibilities for deploying the system in various public settings, including hospital wards, subway stations, and classrooms, where monitoring the frequency of coughs is essential. With the ability to accurately assess coughing incidents, the system can contribute to proactive measures in maintaining public health and safety. Furthermore, the non-intrusive nature of the system, coupled with its ease of deployment, allows for efficient monitoring and analysis of coughing patterns in real time. This information can aid in identifying potential outbreaks, tracking the effectiveness of preventive measures, and providing early warnings in situations where the spread of respiratory illnesses is a concern.

The performance of the cough detection model is subject to certain limitations, which we acknowledge and aim to address in future improvements. Two key factors affecting model performance are given below:

Feature Extraction Method: In real-world environments, noise poses a challenge to system accuracy, especially in cases of confusion between cough and speech sounds. Low-amplitude cough signals may be masked or overlooked by high-amplitude background noise, affecting threshold selection and segmentation. To overcome these limitations, future research can employ novel noise suppression techniques to reduce the impact of background noise on threshold selection. Utilizing multiple Otsu's thresholds for multi-scale analysis can detect cough signals with different amplitudes, reducing the likelihood of missing low-amplitude cough signals [22]. Data augmentation by adding various noise and low-amplitude cough signals can enhance the model's adaptability to different audio conditions and improve cough signal detection accuracy. Moreover, considering the fusion of other signals, such as video or sensor data, can provide comprehensive information about cough events, aiding in more accurate cough signal detection and enhancing the model's robustness to various types of background noise.

Furthermore, the distance between the smartphone and the user during cough sound recording can affect the volume of the recorded signal. If users are at a considerable distance from the smartphone while recording cough sounds, the cough volume may be lower, resulting in the potential masking or reduced detectability of cough signals, especially in environments with higher background noise. To address this issue, multiple microphones or microphone arrays can be employed to capture sound from different angles, and adaptive volume control or dynamic gain adjustment techniques can be introduced in the system. These measures ensure that cough sounds can be effectively captured under various distances and environmental noise conditions, thereby enhancing the reliability and robustness of cough signal detection.

Additionally, we will continue to refine the models by incorporating new feature extraction methods and exploring advanced deep learning architectures. By combining multiple feature extraction techniques, such as MFCCs and other spectral or temporal features, we can capture a broader range of characteristics related to cough events. This will help us improve the discrimination between coughing and other sounds, further enhancing the precision and reliability of the system.

Limited Types of Signals Collected: The current system solely relies on audio signals for cough detection. However, in certain situations where cough waveforms densely overlap, distinguishing individual cough events becomes challenging, leading to inaccurate cough counting. To enhance system performance, it is crucial to incorporate additional signals. Coughing is often accompanied by specific movements and physical cues, which can be valuable in understanding coughing events comprehensively. By incorporating additional signals, we can gain a more comprehensive understanding of coughing events. The integration of motion or video data can provide valuable insights into the physical manifestations of coughing, such as body movements, hand gestures, or facial expressions. These cues can contribute to more accurate and reliable detection of cough events, reducing both false negatives and false positives.

In future research, we will explore the fusion of audio and image sequence data to develop a more robust and comprehensive cough detection system. By leveraging the complementary nature of these modalities, we aim to achieve even higher accuracy and reliability in detecting and analyzing cough events, contributing to the advancement of large-scale and contactless cough screenings in various fields.

4   Conclusion

Cough detection plays a vital role in epidemiological research, disease screening, and epidemic control. In this paper, we present CASCO, an advanced cough detection system that combines CNN with a WeChat mini program. The system accurately detects cough events in real time and provides an automated count of the number of coughs. To train the robust cough detection model, we construct a comprehensive dataset comprising self-recorded audio samples, labeled environmental recordings from the ESC-50 dataset, and inpatient cough recordings from respiratory disease patients.

The WeChat mini program integrated into smartphones serves as the primary interface for the system, allowing users to record audio and view the cough detection results. The recorded audio is then processed on an external server using the sophisticated cough detection model. An audio division algorithm is employed to extract high-intensity segments from the audio, isolating individual cough events. The extracted segments are subsequently converted into spectrograms using STFT, capturing the distinctive time-frequency patterns of cough sounds. These spectrograms are then fed into the CNN model, which categorizes them as either cough or non-cough samples.

Extensive evaluations demonstrate the outstanding performance of the cough detection model, achieving an accuracy, recall, precision, and F1-score of 97.0%, 98.7%, 95.6%, and 0.97, respectively. The integration of the system with the WeChat mini program allows for large-scale and contactless cough screenings, overcoming the limitations of traditional detection methods. Additionally, processing audio on an external server reduces battery consumption while leveraging the server's computational power for faster and more accurate detection.

In future work, we will focus on improving the noise robustness of the model and exploring new application scenarios for the CASCO cough detection system. The goal is to develop a versatile and user-friendly solution that enhances public health monitoring through reliable and scalable cough detection.

References

1. McCool, F.D.: Global physiology and pathophysiology of cough: ACCP evidence-based clinical practice guidelines. Chest **129**(1), 48S–53S (2006)
2. Alqudaihi, K.S., et al.: Cough sound detection and diagnosis using artificial intelligence techniques: challenges and opportunities. IEEE Access **9**, 102327–102344 (2021)
3. Matos, S., Birring, S.S., Pavord, I.D., Evans, D.H.: An automated system for 24-h monitoring of cough frequency: the Leicester cough monitor. IEEE Trans. Biomed. Eng. **54**(8), 1472–1479 (2007)
4. Costa, T.D., Nogueira-Neto, G.N., Nohama, P.: Cough detection through mechanomyographic signal in synchronized respiratory electrical stimulation systems. In: 2015 37th Annual International Conference of the IEEE Engineering in Medicine and Biology Society (EMBC) (2015)
5. Doddabasappla, K., Vyas, R.: Spectral summation with machine learning analysis of tri-axial acceleration from multiple wearable points on human body for better cough detection. IEEE Sens. Lett. **5**(9), 1–4 (2021)
6. WHO Coronavirus (COVID-19) Dashboard. https://covid19.who.int/
7. Weekly epidemiological update on COVID-19 - 1 March 2022. https://www.who.int/publications/m/item/weeklyepidemiological-update-on-covid-19--1-march-2022
8. Islam, R., Abdel-Raheem, E., Tarique, M.: A study of using cough sounds and deep neural networks for the early detection of COVID-19. Biomed. Eng. Adv. **3**, 100025 (2022)

9. Tena, A., Clariá, F., Solsona, F.: Automated detection of COVID-19 cough. Biomed. Signal Process. Control **71**, 103175 (2022)
10. Monge-Álvarez, J., Hoyos-Barceló, C., San-José-Revuelta, L.M., Casaseca-de-la-Higuera, P.: A machine hearing system for robust cough detection based on a high-level representation of band-specific audio features. IEEE Trans. Biomed. Eng. **66**(8), 2319–2330 (2019)
11. Hoyos-Barceló, C., Monge-Álvarez, J., Shakir, M.Z., Alcaraz-Calero, J.M., Casaseca-de-La-Higuera, P.: Efficient k-NN implementation for real-time detection of cough events in smartphones. IEEE J. Biomed. Health Inform. **22**(5), 1662–1671 (2018)
12. Imran, A., Posokhova, I., Qureshi, H.N., et al.: AI4COVID-19: AI enabled preliminary diagnosis for COVID-19 from cough samples via an app. Inform. Med. Unlocked **20**, 100378 (2020)
13. Agu, E., et al.: The smartphone as a medical device: assessing enablers, benefits and challenges. In: 2013 IEEE International Conference on Sensing, Communications and Networking (SECON) (2013)
14. Chen, X., Hu, M., Zhai, G.: Cough detection using selected informative features from audio signals. In: 2021 14th International Congress on Image and Signal Processing, BioMedical Engineering and Informatics (CISP-BMEI) (2021)
15. Otsu, N.: A threshold selection method from gray level histograms. IEEE Trans. Syst. Man Cybern. **9**, 62–66 (1979)
16. Griffin, D., Lim, J.: Signal estimation from modified short-time Fourier transform. IEEE Trans. Acoust. Speech Signal Process. **32**(2), 236–243 (1984)
17. Piczak, K.J.: ESC: dataset for environmental sound classification. In: Proceedings of the 23rd ACM International Conference on Multimedia (2015)
18. Jiang Zheng, H., Menghan, G.Z.: Detection of respiratory infections using RGB-infrared sensors on portable device. IEEE Sens. J. **20**(22), 13674–13681 (2020)
19. Kingma, D.P., Ba, J.: Adam: a method for stochastic optimization. In: International Conference on Learning Representations (2015)
20. He, K., Zhang, X., Ren, S., Sun, J.: Deep residual learning for image recognition. In: 2016 IEEE Conference on Computer Vision and Pattern Recognition (CVPR) (2016)
21. Simonyan, K., Zisserman, A.: Very deep convolutional networks for large-scale image recognition. CoRR, arXiv: 1409.1556 (2015)
22. Wu, Z., Allibert, G., Meriaudeau, F., Ma, C., Demonceaux, H.: RGB-D salient object detection via hierarchical depth awareness. IEEE Trans. Image Process. **32**, 2160–2173 (2023)

A Novel Neighbor Aggregation Function for Medical Point Cloud Analysis

Fan Wu[1], Yumeng Qian[1], Haozhun Zheng[2], Yan Zhang[1], and Xiawu Zheng[3(✉)]

[1] Key Laboratory of Multimedia Trusted Perception and Efficient Computing,
Ministry of Education of China, Xiamen University, Xiamen, China
wfanstory@stu.xmu.edu.cn
[2] Tsinghua University, Beijing, China
[3] Peng Cheng Laboratory, Shenzhen, China
zhengxw01@pcl.ac.cn

Abstract. Point cloud analysis is a technique that performs analysis and processing of point cloud data. In the medical field, point cloud analysis has been widely used. However, the existing common neighbor aggregation module in point cloud analysis networks can only aggregate some of the neighbor features, which will lead to the omission of valid information and affect the performance of point cloud analysis, which may lead to serious consequences in the medical diagnosis process. In this paper, we improve the ability of point cloud analysis networks to extract complex biological structures by improving the neighbor aggregation module in point cloud analysis. Specifically, we enable the module to efficiently extract more adequate information by softening the max pooling function commonly used in the neighbor aggregation module. In particular, we improve 2.18% IoU on the IntrA dataset compared to the previous state-of-the-art method, and we also surpass the previous state-of-the-art method on the S3DIS dataset. Code is available at https://github.com/wfan1203/PointSWT.

Keywords: Point Cloud · Aneurysm · Neighbor Aggregation Function

1 Introduction

Compared to 2D medical images, 3D medical images can carry more information to help medical professionals make the right judgment [1,10,36]. As a 3D representation of data, point cloud can show the patient's organs and lesions very visually, so they are also widely used in tasks such as medical image processing and medical diagnosis. The classification, segmentation, and detection of medical point cloud data can effectively assist medical personnel in more accurately identifying lesion areas, measuring lesion size, and locating structures. Point cloud technology can also be used for surgical planning, where medical personnel can use pre-surgical data to model and simulate surgical procedures in order to avoid accidents.

In recent years, point-based point cloud processing methods [14,22,25,26, 28,41] are attracting more and more researchers' attention. In previous study

B. Sheng et al. (Eds.): CGI 2023, LNCS 14498, pp. 301–312, 2024.
https://doi.org/10.1007/978-3-031-50078-7_24

[15], several typical and excellent models of point-based point cloud processing methods have been analyzed by researchers. They found that the encoder part of many models can be unified into a meta-architecture. This meta-architecture consists of four main parts: neighbor update module, neighbor aggregation module, point update module, and position embedding module. Although the design and details of each model are different, they can be divided into these four main parts. In many point-based point cloud processing methods, max pooling function [25], Vector Self-attention (VSA) [41], or other similar operators are usually specified as the neighbor aggregation module. However, there are some drawbacks to using max pooling function as a neighbor aggregation module. First, max pooling function does not work well when dealing with sparse point cloud data. Second, since max pooling function can only retain the maximum value of the neighbor point information vector, it can lead to the loss of some important information, which also affects the accuracy of the analysis and thus has a negative impact on medical diagnosis. So exploring a more effective and robust way of neighbor aggregation is an important issue for research in the field of point cloud.

According to our analysis, max pooling function can be regarded as an attention mechanism with sparsity, which applies all the attention to the information with the highest intensity in the neighbor aggregation process while ignoring other valid information, which is unacceptable in the field of medical image processing. In order to capture the information in medical point cloud data more accurately and efficiently, we propose a new neighbor aggregation function: SWT, which is instantiated as a softmax operator with temperature in the point cloud network, where the temperature is a parameter that can be learned during the training process. We can use this parameter to dynamically adjust the information aggregation ratio of each point in the point cloud for different neighbors, so as to obtain the optimal information aggregation method. Our method has the advantage of low computational performance consumption compared to VSA. Compared with max pooling function, it can significantly improve the performance of point cloud analysis. Our method improves PointMetaBase [15] to make it more suitable for processing point cloud data, and provides a more high-performance solution for medical point cloud data processing. Our contributions are summarized as follows:

- We analyze the advantages and disadvantages of the classical, computationally efficient max pooling function and the high-performance VSA (Vector Self-attention) module as a neighbor aggregation module in point cloud processing networks. We argue that max pooling function should be considered as a binary attention mechanism for neighbor point information, which can lead to performance loss in medical point cloud data processing.
- According to our analysis, in order to overcome the shortcomings of max pooling function as a neighbor aggregation module, we propose a new neighbor aggregation function, called SWT, based on soft attention mechanism, which is computationally friendly compared to VSA and performs better in medical point cloud processing tasks compared to the max pooling function.

2   Related Work

2.1   Point Cloud

The applications of deep learning [12] are widespread, including image classification [5] and image quality assessment [7,16–20], among others. As deep learning continues to advance, researchers have proposed some methods for point cloud analysis by combining deep learning techniques with point cloud.

Point cloud is a discrete data structure consisting of a large number of 3D coordinate points representing the geometry of an object or scene surface [4]. Point cloud alignment, classification, segmentation [24] and reconstruction are all common tasks in point cloud processing. The point cloud classification and segmentation task also has some applications in the field of medical image processing.

Unlike traditional two-dimensional data, point cloud data are located in higher dimensions and are very irregular, which makes handling such data very challenging and requires special methods. So far, the mainstream approaches for point cloud processing can be categorized into three types: projection-based [11,30,35], voxel-based [23,47] and point-based [14,22,25,26,28,41] methods. The point-based method is a common approach for point cloud processing with better performance at present. This method has a good ability to deal with the irregularity of point cloud data, and its basic idea is to analyze the interaction of each point in point cloud data with its neighboring points, and analyze the properties and categories of the point cloud by processing the features and attributes of these neighboring points.

The neighbor aggregation module is an important part of the model used in this series of methods, which determines how each point in the point cloud obtains information from its neighbors. Pointnet [25] uses max pooling function to aggregate the information of neighboring points. Point transformer [41] introduces a self-attention mechanism, and proposes Vector Self-attention. Pospool [21] has analyzed the neighbor aggregation module in point cloud analysis.

Designing effective neural network architectures is crucial for obtaining high-performance neural networks. To automate the process, some researchers have proposed Neural Architecture Search (NAS) techniques for designing neural network architectures [42–44,46]. Although NAS has been combined with point clouds [31], such methods require significant computational resources and, in practice, manual design of the network architecture is still necessary.

2.2   3D Medical Image Processing

Deep learning is widely used in the field of medical image processing, which provides doctors with a traversal in medical diagnosis [37,40]. 3D medical imaging is a rapidly growing field that provides doctors and researchers with more accurate and comprehensive information compared to ordinary 2D medical imaging medical image data. The most common imaging technologies are Computed Tomography (CT), Magnetic Resonance Imaging (MRI) and Positron Emission

Tomography, (PET), which produce high-quality 3D images of the human body. In the same way as 2D image processing, 3D medical image data can be classified, segmented, and detected.

The 3D U-NET [3] series is an excellent method for 3D medical image segmentation. 3D U-Net is the pioneer of this series and uses 3D convolutional neural network to compose the model. DUNet [9] uses deformable convolution to replace each 3×3 convolutional layer in the original UNet, which can adapt to different shapes of input. to improve performance.

The nnFormer [45] combines transformer [34] and nn-UNet [8], using different attention mechanisms in the shallow and deep layers of the model, and also achieves good performance in 3D medical image processing tasks.

It is also possible to convert 3D medical image data into point cloud data for processing, which can be processed using traditional point cloud analysis networks, and the attention module included in 3DMedPT [39] can better capture global information.

3   Method

3.1   Preliminary

Some researchers [15] have analyzed the structure of different point-based point cloud analysis models in detail and found that the core modules of different point cloud analysis networks can be defined as a unified building block, and the building block can be defined as a combination of four sub-modules.

- Neighbor update module: This sub-module contains the operations to obtain and update the neighboring points of each point in the point cloud. The common group method is usually K-Nearest query or ball query, and the MLP is often used to update the features of each point in order to make the neighbor update function with permutation equivariance.
- Neighbor aggregation module: This sub-module aggregates the features of each group of points grouped and updated in the Neighbor update sub-module, and generally uses the max pooling operator to satisfy the permutation invariance.
- Point update module: This sub-module, usually in the form of MLP, is usually used for further extraction of the assembled features.
- Position embedding module: Each building block in the point cloud analysis needs to obtain the position information of each point in the point cloud to help the point cloud model to better analyze the point cloud data.

Each sub-module can be represented using a formula. The forward pass of the whole building block can be expressed as:

$$f_{\mathcal{N}(i)} = \phi^n \circ \phi^e(f_i, p_i) \tag{1}$$

$$f_i^{(1)} = \phi^a \circ \phi^e(f_i, p_i, f_{\mathcal{N}(i)}, p_{\mathcal{N}(i)}) \tag{2}$$

$$f_i^{(2)} = \phi^p(f_i^{(1)}, p_i) \qquad (3)$$

where ϕ^n, ϕ^a, ϕ^p, ϕ^e denote the neighbor update function, neighbor aggregation function, point update function and position embedding function in the building block. f_i and p_i represent the feature and the coordinate of point i respectively. The neighbors of point i are denoted by $\mathcal{N}(i)$.

The above four sub-modules can be instantiated as different components combined into different point cloud analysis models, of which many existing classical as well as recent models such as PointNet++ [26], PointCNN [14], PointNeXt [28], etc.

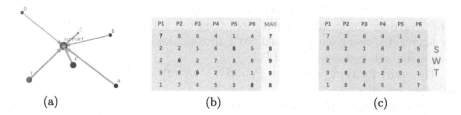

(a)   (b)   (c)

Fig. 1. The process of neighbor aggregation: (b) Using max pooling function as the neighbor aggregation function, it will only select the largest value to participate in the aggregation process, and smaller values will be directly ignored. (c) Using SWT in the neighbor aggregation phase, it aggregates the information of all neighbor nodes to reduce the information loss.

$$f_i^{(1)} = \text{Max}(f_{\mathcal{N}(i)}) \qquad (4)$$

Figure 1 visualizes the neighbor point aggregation process using the max pooling function and using SWT as the neighbor aggregation function. In fact, we can intuitively find that when max pooling function is used as the neighbor aggregation function in point cloud analysis, it only aggregates to the maximum value of each dimension of all points and ignores all other features, and these ignored features often contain a lot of important information as well. In medical diagnosis, such a loss is not tolerated.

Recently, there are many approaches to introduce attentional mechanisms into the neighbor aggregation process of point cloud analysis to selectively obtain the information of neighbor points. But in fact, max pooling function is also an atypical, binary and sparse attention mechanism from the attention point of view. So is there a way of neighbor aggregation that is adaptive in obtaining information about neighbor points and does not consume as much computational resources as ordinary attention? We find that, from the same perspective, the softmax operator is also a special attention mechanism that fits the requirements as a function of the neighbor aggregation module. At the same time, we can define a learnable parameter to be added to the softmax operator to adaptively select the information aggregation ratio and refer to this learnable parameter as temperature. The new softmax with temperature function we use can be considered as a max pooling function with soft, learnable properties, which improves performance at the cost of a small increase in computational effort. It can be expressed using the following equation:

$$f_i^{(1)} = \text{Softmax}_T(\boldsymbol{f}_{\mathcal{N}(i)}) \tag{5}$$

In this subsection we present the building block that we ended up using, which is a simple modification of the neighbor aggregation module of PointMetaBase [15], which uses max pooling function as the neighbor aggregation function. The building block is also a combination of four sub-modules, specifically, the building block of PointSWT uses explicit position embedding. The points in the point cloud are first grouped by ball query, then the grouped features are updated using MLP to reduce the model computation, then the updated neighboring features are aggregated using our proposed SWT module, and finally the InvResMLP is passed through two layers of MLP.

The entire forward pass of our PointSWT module can be expressed using the following equation:

The neighbor update is described as:

$$f_i' = \text{MLP}_1(f_i) \tag{6}$$

$$\boldsymbol{f}_{\mathcal{N}(i)}, \boldsymbol{p}_{\mathcal{N}(i)} = \text{Group}(f_i, p_i). \tag{7}$$

The neighbor Aggregation module is an SWT that uses our proposed:

$$f_i^{(1)} = \text{Softmax}_T(\boldsymbol{f}_{\mathcal{N}(i)}) \tag{8}$$

Finally, a two-layer MLP is used for Point update:

$$f_i^{(2)} = \text{MLP}_{inv}\left(f_i^{(1)}\right) + f_i \tag{9}$$

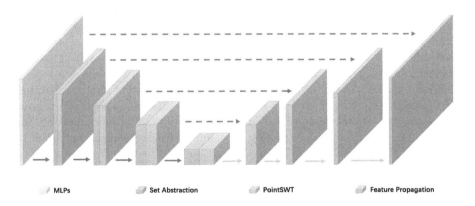

MLPs   Set Abstraction   PointSWT   Feature Propagation

Fig. 2. The overall architecture of our proposed model.

3.2 PointSWT

The overall architecture of our model is shown in Fig. 2. The model can be divided into three components: PointSWT block, Set Abstraction block and Feature Propagation block, where PointSWT block is the main module, Set Abstraction block can be regarded as a kind of PointSWT-like module that implements the downsampling function, and the Feature Propagation block is responsible for decoding the features into the final result.

We construct our PointSWT family:

$$\text{PointSWT-S} : C = 32, B = (0,0)$$

$$\text{PointSWT-L} : C = 32, B = (2,4,2,2)$$

$$\text{PointSWT-XL} : C = 64, B = (3,6,3,3)$$

The notations used in our proposed model are as follows: C represents the channel size of the stem MLP, while B denotes the number of PointSWT blocks in each stage. It is noteworthy that when $B = 0$, only one Set Abstraction block is employed in each stage without PointSWT blocks.

4 Experiments

4.1 IntrA

Table 1. Segmentation results on IntrA dataset.

Method	PointConv	PointNet++	3DMedPT	PointMetaBase	**PointSWT-S**
IoU (%)	79.53	76.21	80.13	84.37	**86.55**

IntrA [38] dataset is a 3D point cloud dataset containing 116 divisible vascular segment samples, each of which is divided into aneurysm segment and normal vessel segment, which can be used as the standard dataset for binary segmentation task to verify the performance of our proposed point cloud model. We used four-fifths of the data as the training set, the rest as the test set, and the IoU as the evaluation metric. In the experiment, we use cross entropy as the loss function and Adam optimizer to optimize the model. The initial learning rate is set to 0.001, the number of input points is set to 2048, and the batch size of each iteration is set to 16. A total of 400 epochs were trained on the PointSWT-S model on an NVIDIA Tesla V100 GPU and a 12-core Intel Xeon @ 2.40 GHz CPU.

As shown in the Table 1, compared to other point cloud models, our PointSWT-S achieves higher performance in the point cloud segmentation task on the IntrA dataset, and the increase in performance is mainly attributed to our superior neighbor aggregation function compared to other models.

We set the initial temperature parameter in the SWT module to 0 and collected the changes in the mean values of all temperature parameters in the PointSWT-S model throughout the training process. As shown in the Fig. 3a, it can be observed that the mean values of the temperature parameters show an increasing trend as the model is optimized. The characteristic of our proposed SWT module is that the closer its temperature parameter is to 0, the closer the SWT module acts with the max pooling function, and when the temperature parameter is equal to 0, the SWT module becomes a pure max pooling function. The rise of the temperature parameter with the training process indicates that during the training process of the point cloud analysis network, the model will be biased to utilize more comprehensive information, i.e., it is necessary to use SWT as the function of the neighbor aggregation module.

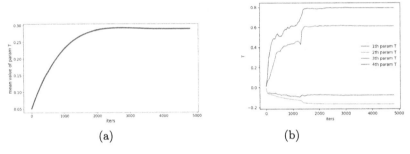

(a)   (b)

Fig. 3. (a) The change in the mean value of the temperature parameters included in the model throughout the training process. (b) The change of temperature parameters in all SWT modules in the model during training, where *xth param T* denotes the temperature parameter in the *xth* temperature SWT module from shallow to deep in the model.

In addition to this, as shown in the Fig. 3b, we also collected the changes of each temperature parameter included in the model during the training process separately in order to analyze the effectiveness of the SWT module from a spatial perspective. We used PointSWT-S which contains a total of four temperature parameters distributed in four Set Abstraction modules. According to the data we collected, there are regular differences in the values of the temperature parameters depending on the depth. Specifically, as the depth increases, the temperature parameter of the model becomes larger, where the temperature parameter of the shallowest layer tends to be close to 0 even at the end of training, indicating that the shallow layers of the model requires less information, while the temperature parameter of the deeper layer has steadily increased at the beginning of training, and its dependence on the SWT module is stronger. The functions used by the neighbor aggregation module can be selected more rationally according to the characteristics of the model at different layer depths in order to weigh the cost and performance, which will be the focus of our next work.

4.2 S3DIS

S3DIS [2] is a widely used dataset for 3D semantic segmentation, comprising a total of 6 large-scale indoor areas with a total of 271 rooms, which are classified into 13 semantic categories.

In our experiments, we use mIoU and overall accuracy (OA) as evaluation metrics, use cross-entropy as loss function, optimize the model using Adamw optimizer, set the initial learning rate to 0.01 and the batch size of each iteration to 8. As shown in the Table 2, our model outperforms existing SOTA methods in terms of performance due to our use of a better neighbor aggregation function. We also collected the temperature parameters of the model and found similar phenomena as in the experiments conducted on the IntrA dataset.

Table 2. Semantic segmentation results on the S3DIS Area 5 dataset.

Method	S3DIS Area-5		Params.	FLOPs	Throughput
	mIoU (%)	OA (%)	M	G	(ins./sec.)
PointNet++ [26]	53.5	83.0	1.0	7.2	237
PointCNN [14]	57.3	85.9	0.6	-	-
DeepGCN [13]	52.5	-	3.6	-	-
KPConv [33]	67.1	-	15.0	-	-
RandLA-Net [6]	-	-	1.3	5.8	-
BAAF-Net [29]	65.4	88.9	5.0	-	-
Point Transformer [41]	70.4	90.8	7.8	5.6	-
CBL [32]	69.4	90.6	18.6	-	-
ASSANet [27]	65.8	88.9	2.4	2.5	300
ASSANet-L [27]	68.0	89.7	115.6	36.2	136
PointNeXt-L [28]	69.0 ± 0.5	90.0 ± 0.1	7.1	15.2	109
PointMetaBase-L[15]	69.5 ± 0.3	90.5 ± 0.1	2.7	2.0	187
PointSWT-L	**70.1 ± 0.2**	**90.9 ± 0.1**	2.7	≥2.0	136

5   Conclusion

In this paper, we first present a brief analysis of the point cloud analysis model, focusing on the advantages and disadvantages of existing neighbor aggregation functions. In order to solve the disadvantage of max pooling function as a neighbor aggregation function, which is difficult to aggregate all the valid information, we propose a new neighbor aggregation function: SWT, which can take into account all the neighbor point information and thus improve the model performance. Our experiments demonstrate the effectiveness of this improvement, which provides a new idea for future point cloud analysis studies in the medical field.

Acknowledgements. This work was supported by National Key R&D Program of China (No. 2022ZD0118202), the National Science Fund for Distinguished Young Scholars (No. 62025603), the National Natural Science Foundation of China (No. U21B2037, No. U22B2051, No. 62176222, No. 62176223, No. 62176226, No. 62072386, No. 62072387, No. 62072389, No. 62002305 and No. 62272401), and the Natural Science Foundation of Fujian Province of China (No. 2021J01002, No. 2022J06001).

References

1. Ali, S.G., et al.: Cost-effective broad learning-based ultrasound biomicroscopy with 3d reconstruction for ocular anterior segmentation. Multimed. Tools Appl. **80**, 35105–35122 (2020). https://api.semanticscholar.org/CorpusID:221110873
2. Armeni, I., Sax, S., Zamir, A.R., Savarese, S.: Joint 2d–3d-semantic data for indoor scene understanding. CoRR abs/1702.01105 (2017)
3. Çiçek, Ö., Abdulkadir, A., Lienkamp, S.S., Brox, T., Ronneberger, O.: 3D U-Net: learning dense volumetric segmentation from sparse annotation. In: Ourselin, S., Joskowicz, L., Sabuncu, M.R., Unal, G., Wells, W. (eds.) MICCAI 2016. LNCS, vol. 9901, pp. 424–432. Springer, Cham (2016). https://doi.org/10.1007/978-3-319-46723-8_49
4. Guo, Y., Wang, H., Hu, Q., Liu, H., Liu, L., Bennamoun, M.: Deep learning for 3d point clouds: a survey. IEEE Trans. Pattern Anal. Mach. Intell. **43**, 4338–4364 (2019)
5. He, K., Zhang, X., Ren, S., Sun, J.: Deep residual learning for image recognition. In: Proceedings of the IEEE Conference on Computer Vision and Pattern Recognition, pp. 770–778 (2016)
6. Hu, Q., et al.: RandLA-Net: efficient semantic segmentation of large-scale point clouds. In: CVPR, pp. 11105–11114 (2020)
7. Hu, R., Liu, Y., Gu, K., Min, X., Zhai, G.: Toward a no-reference quality metric for camera-captured images. IEEE Trans. Cybern. (2021)
8. Isensee, F., Jaeger, P.F., Kohl, S.A., Petersen, J., Maier-Hein, K.H.: nnU-Net: a self-configuring method for deep learning-based biomedical image segmentation. Nat. Methods **18**(2), 203–211 (2021)
9. Jin, Q., Meng, Z., Pham, T.D., Chen, Q., Wei, L., Su, R.: DUNet: a deformable network for retinal vessel segmentation. Knowl.-Based Syst. **178**, 149–162 (2019)
10. Kamel, A., Sheng, B., Li, P., Kim, J., Feng, D.D.: Efficient body motion quantification and similarity evaluation using 3-d joints skeleton coordinates. IEEE Trans. Syst. Man Cybern.: Syst. **51**, 2774–2788 (2021). https://api.semanticscholar.org/CorpusID:189977703
11. Lang, A.H., Vora, S., Caesar, H., Zhou, L., Yang, J., Beijbom, O.: Pointpillars: fast encoders for object detection from point clouds. In: Proceedings of the IEEE/CVF Conference on Computer Vision and Pattern Recognition, pp. 12697–12705 (2019)
12. LeCun, Y., Bengio, Y., Hinton, G.: Deep learning. Nature **521**(7553), 436–444 (2015)

13. Li, G., Müller, M., Thabet, A.K., Ghanem, B.: DeepGCNs: can GCNs go as deep as CNNs? In: ICCV, pp. 9266–9275 (2019)
14. Li, Y., Bu, R., Sun, M., Wu, W., Di, X., Chen, B.: PointCNN: convolution on x-transformed points. In: NeurIPS, pp. 828–838 (2018)
15. Lin, H., et al.: Meta architecure for point cloud analysis. ArXiv: abs/2211.14462 (2022)
16. Liu, Y., Gu, K., Li, X., Zhang, Y.: Blind image quality assessment by natural scene statistics and perceptual characteristics. ACM Trans. Multimed. Comput. Commun. Appl. (TOMM) **16**(3), 1–91 (2020)
17. Liu, Y., Gu, K., Wang, S., Zhao, D., Gao, W.: Blind quality assessment of camera images based on low-level and high-level statistical features. IEEE Trans. Multimed. **21**(1), 135–146 (2018)
18. Liu, Y., Gu, K., Zhai, G., Liu, X., Zhao, D., Gao, W.: Quality assessment for real out-of-focus blurred images. J. Vis. Commun. Image Represent. **46**, 70–80 (2017)
19. Liu, Y., et al.: Unsupervised blind image quality evaluation via statistical measurements of structure, naturalness, and perception. IEEE Trans. Circuits Syst. Video Technol. **30**(4), 929–943 (2019)
20. Liu, Y., Zhai, G., Gu, K., Liu, X., Zhao, D., Gao, W.: Reduced-reference image quality assessment in free-energy principle and sparse representation. IEEE Trans. Multimed. **20**(2), 379–391 (2017)
21. Liu, Z., Hu, H., Cao, Y., Zhang, Z., Tong, X.: A closer look at local aggregation operators in point cloud analysis. In: Vedaldi, A., Bischof, H., Brox, T., Frahm, J.-M. (eds.) ECCV 2020. LNCS, vol. 12368, pp. 326–342. Springer, Cham (2020). https://doi.org/10.1007/978-3-030-58592-1_20
22. Ma, X., Qin, C., You, H., Ran, H., Fu, Y.: Rethinking network design and local geometry in point cloud: a simple residual MLP framework. In: ICLR (2022)
23. Maturana, D., Scherer, S.: Voxnet: A 3d convolutional neural network for real-time object recognition. In: 2015 IEEE/RSJ International Conference on Intelligent Robots and Systems (IROS), pp. 922–928. IEEE (2015)
24. Morel, J., Bac, A., Kanai, T.: Segmentation of unbalanced and in-homogeneous point clouds and its application to 3d scanned trees. Vis. Comput. **36**, 2419–2431 (2020). https://api.semanticscholar.org/CorpusID:222094240
25. Qi, C.R., Su, H., Mo, K., Guibas, L.J.: PointNet: deep learning on point sets for 3d classification and segmentation. In: CVPR, pp. 77–85 (2017)
26. Qi, C.R., Yi, L., Su, H., Guibas, L.J.: Pointnet++: deep hierarchical feature learning on point sets in a metric space. In: NeurIPS, pp. 5099–5108 (2017)
27. Qian, G., Hammoud, H., Li, G., Thabet, A.K., Ghanem, B.: ASSANet: an anisotropic separable set abstraction for efficient point cloud representation learning. In: NeurIPS, pp. 28119–28130 (2021)
28. Qian, G., et al.: PoiNtneXt: revisiting PointNet++ with improved training and scaling strategies. In: NeurIPS (2022)
29. Qiu, S., Anwar, S., Barnes, N.: Semantic segmentation for real point cloud scenes via bilateral augmentation and adaptive fusion. In: CVPR, pp. 1757–1767 (2021)
30. Su, H., Maji, S., Kalogerakis, E., Learned-Miller, E.: Multi-view convolutional neural networks for 3d shape recognition. In: Proceedings of the IEEE International Conference on Computer Vision, pp. 945–953 (2015)
31. Tang, H., et al.: Searching efficient 3D architectures with sparse point-voxel convolution. In: Vedaldi, A., Bischof, H., Brox, T., Frahm, J.-M. (eds.) ECCV 2020. LNCS, vol. 12373, pp. 685–702. Springer, Cham (2020). https://doi.org/10.1007/978-3-030-58604-1_41

32. Tang, L., Zhan, Y., Chen, Z., Yu, B., Tao, D.: Contrastive boundary learning for point cloud segmentation. In: CVPR, pp. 8479–8489 (2022)

33. Thomas, H., Qi, C.R., Deschaud, J., Marcotegui, B., Goulette, F., Guibas, L.J.: KPConv: flexible and deformable convolution for point clouds. In: ICCV, pp. 6410–6419 (2019)

34. Vaswani, A., et al.: Attention is all you need. In: Advances in Neural Information Processing Systems, vol. 30 (2017)

35. Wu, B., Wan, A., Yue, X., Keutzer, K.: SqueezeSeg: convolutional neural nets with recurrent CRF for real-time road-object segmentation from 3d LiDAR point cloud. In: 2018 IEEE International Conference on Robotics and Automation (ICRA), pp. 1887–1893. IEEE (2018)

36. Xiang, N., Liang, H.N., Yu, L., Yang, X., Zhang, J.J.: A mixed reality framework for microsurgery simulation with visual-tactile perception. Vis. Comput. **39**, 3661–3673 (2023). https://api.semanticscholar.org/CorpusID:259765573

37. Yang, M., Yuan, Y., Liu, G.: SDUNet: road extraction via spatial enhanced and densely connected UNet. Pattern Recogn. **126**, 108549 (2022)

38. Yang, X., Xia, D., Kin, T., Igarashi, T.: Intra: 3d intracranial aneurysm dataset for deep learning. In: Proceedings of the IEEE/CVF Conference on Computer Vision and Pattern Recognition, pp. 2656–2666 (2020)

39. Yu, J., et al.: 3d medical point transformer: introducing convolution to attention networks for medical point cloud analysis. arXiv preprint arXiv:2112.04863 (2021)

40. Zhan, B., et al.: Multi-constraint generative adversarial network for dose prediction in radiotherapy. Med. Image Anal. **77**, 102339 (2022)

41. Zhao, H., Jiang, L., Jia, J., Torr, P.H.S., Koltun, V.: Point transformer. In: ICCV, pp. 16239–16248 (2021)

42. Zheng, X., et al.: MIGO-NAS: towards fast and generalizable neural architecture search. IEEE Trans. Pattern Anal. Mach. Intell. **43**(9), 2936–2952 (2021)

43. Zheng, X., Ji, R., Tang, L., Zhang, B., Liu, J., Tian, Q.: Multinomial distribution learning for effective neural architecture search. In: Proceedings of the IEEE/CVF International Conference on Computer Vision, pp. 1304–1313 (2019)

44. Zheng, X., et al.: Rethinking performance estimation in neural architecture search. In: Proceedings of the IEEE/CVF Conference on Computer Vision and Pattern Recognition, pp. 11356–11365 (2020)

45. Zhou, H.Y., Guo, J., Zhang, Y., Yu, L., Wang, L., Yu, Y.: nnFormer: interleaved transformer for volumetric segmentation. arXiv preprint arXiv:2109.03201 (2021)

46. Zhou, Q., et al.: EC-DARTS: inducing equalized and consistent optimization into darts. In: Proceedings of the IEEE/CVF International Conference on Computer Vision, pp. 11986–11995 (2021)

47. Zhou, Y., Tuzel, O.: VoxelNet: end-to-end learning for point cloud based 3d object detection. In: Proceedings of the IEEE Conference on Computer Vision and Pattern Recognition, pp. 4490–4499 (2018)

Cup-Disk Ratio Segmentation Joint with Key Retinal Vascular Information Under Diagnostic and Screening Scenarios

Kuo Yang[1], Wenhao Jiang[1], Yiqiao Shi[1], Rui Qin[1], Wanli Bai[1], Duo Li[2], Yue Wu[3(✉)], and Menghan Hu[1(✉)]

[1] Shanghai Key Laboratory of Multidimensional Information Processing, East China Normal University, Shanghai, China
mhhu@ce.ecnu.edu.cn
[2] DiDi Chuxing, Beijing, China
[3] Department of Ophthalmology, Ninth People's Hospital Affiliated to Shanghai Jiao Tong University School of Medicine, Shanghai, China
wuyue@shsmu.edu.cn

Abstract. Glaucoma is one of the leading causes of irreversible blindness worldwide. Numerous studies have shown that a larger vertical Cup-to-Disc Ratio (CDR) is closely associated with the glaucoma diagnosis. CDR is highly useful in the clinical practice and evaluation of glaucoma. However, the determination of CDR varies among clinicians and is highly dependent on the doctor's subjectivity. Existing methods only segment the cup and disc features without considering the nearby vascular information. Based on guidance and criteria from experienced clinicians in diagnosing glaucoma, we incorporate segmented essential vascular information to constrain CDR segmentation. We add key vessel information to the network as the prior knowledge to better guide the model to distinguish the boundary of the optic cup. The effectiveness of incorporating essential vascular information has been demonstrated through experiments conducted on the public dataset REFUGE as well as the home-made dataset. The home-made dataset consists of high-quality CDR images and remade CDR images, corresponding to the diagnosis scenario and the screening scenario in which the patient needs to upload the fundus image by taking photos. The model is deployed on the Wechat mini-program for practical glaucoma diagnostic and screening applications.

Keywords: Cup-disk ratio segmentation · Retinal vascular · Glaucoma diagnostic and screening

1 Introduction

Glaucoma is currently the leading cause of irreversible blindness worldwide [2], and it is one of the major causes of irreversible vision loss in the world. It

Supported by the GHfund B (Grant No. 202302028692).
K. Yang and W. Jiang—These authors contributed equally to this work.

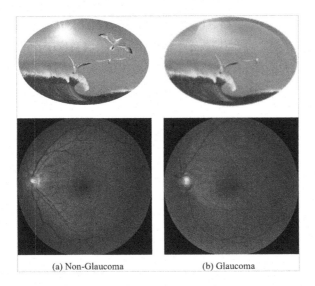

(a) Non-Glaucoma   (b) Glaucoma

Fig. 1. Top image illustrates the difference in visual fields between non-glaucoma and glaucoma patients [1]. Glaucoma patients often experience blurry vision and visual field loss. The images below are from the REFUGE dataset, with the left showing a non-glaucomatous retinal image and the right showing a glaucomatous retinal image.

has a high prevalence and blindness rate. According to estimates by the World Health Organization, the number of glaucoma patients worldwide exceeded 88 million in 2020 [3]. The progression of glaucoma is initially asymptomatic and gradually leads to vision loss, which can only be observed in the late stage. Once diagnosed, it results in permanent visual impairment. Early detection and timely treatment of glaucoma can further control disease progression, making it an important means of preventing glaucoma [4,5]. It is usually caused by elevated intraocular pressure (IOP), which leads to mechanical strain and torsion of the optic nerve, as well as loss of retinal nerve fibers. Glaucoma alters the morphology of the optic nerve head (ONH), typically manifesting as a larger CDR, pale optic disc, disc hemorrhage, etc. Digital fundus imaging is an important medical tool that assists doctors in diagnosing and analyzing glaucoma [6,7]. Fundus images include various features of the fundus area, such as the optic disc, cup, arterioles, and venules. As shown in Fig. 1, the visual field of a normal individual and that observed by glaucoma patients differ [8].

In digital fundus images, the optic disc (OD) appears as a pale yellow region, and within the OD, there is a relatively bright elliptical or circular area called the optic cup (OC). The CDR, which represents the ratio of the size of the central depression to the size of the OD, is an important auxiliary parameter for glaucoma diagnosis. Clinicians identify the specific boundaries of the OD and OC and calculate the corresponding ratio to assist in determining whether it is glaucoma. Although both the OC and disc exist in normal individuals, the area or diameter ratio of the OD and OC in glaucoma patients' fundus images is higher than that of normal individuals. Due to elevated IOP, the size of the OC is larger than that of normal individuals. Therefore, when the vertical CDR ratio exceeds 0.65 [9], the patient is classified as having glaucoma according to clinical standards.

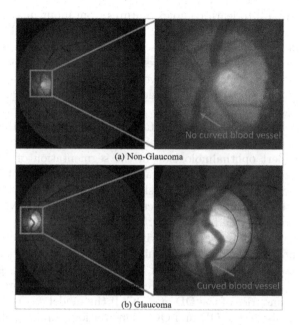

Fig. 2. Fundus images of non-glaucoma and glaucoma. (a) depicts a glaucomatous retinal image where VC, primarily concentrated at the OD and OC boundaries, is caused by glaucoma. In non-glaucoma fundus images as (b), the blood vessels at the boundary are not curved.

Since doctors need to manually segment the OD and OC regions in fundus images and estimate the approximate CDR value for classification, this glaucoma diagnosis method requires a considerable amount of manual effort, is time-consuming, and inefficient. Moreover, it depends to some extent on the expertise of ophthalmologists, and the information extracted manually from fundus images is limited. Therefore, computer-assisted medical diagnosis is of paramount importance.

In recent years, there have been numerous efforts to utilize computer-aided medical diagnosis, broadly categorized into traditional methods and deep learning methods. Traditional methods include approaches based on color, contrast thresholds, and morphological operations on the OD. These traditional methods are sensitive to image quality and pathological variations, resulting in low accuracy. Studies have employed edge detection methods to segment the OD and OC, assuming clear boundaries between them. Nevertheless, in certain cases, the boundaries may be indistinct, leading to inaccurate segmentation. Machine learning algorithms have also been applied to the OD and OC segmentation, relying on manual feature extraction and lacking the ability to automatically learn complex features.

Significant progress has been made in OD and OC segmentation using deep learning methods [10–12]. These approaches employ convolutional neural networks (CNNs) [13,14] to learn complex features from input images. Studies use CNNs with encoder-decoder structures, such as U-Net [15] and Mask R-CNN [16], for OD and OC segmentation. These methods have achieved high accuracy, but they still face challenges in accurately segmenting the boundaries between the OD and OC. This is because blood vessels near the fundus can influence the OD and OC segmentation, causing the models to struggle with precise boundary delineation.

Existing methods for CDR segmentation do not consider the information from blood vessels in the segmentation of the OD and OC. Based on the clinical experience of expert ophthalmologists, in the segmentation of CDR for glaucoma, doctors pay attention to the curvature of blood vessels within the OC to determine the boundary of the OC. As shown in the Fig. 2, there is a curvature in the blood vessels of glaucoma, and doctors use the location of vessel curvature to assist in determining the boundary of the OC.

Motivated by this observation, we incorporate the information of retinal blood vessels into the network for learning. By learning the prior information about blood vessels through the network, we aim to assist in the segmentation of the OD and OC. We introduce the concept of Vascular Curvature (VC), as VC can affect the boundaries of the OD and OC. If the model can utilize this vessel information to assist in the OD and OC segmentation, similar to how clinicians do, the performance of CDR segmentation can be improved. Therefore, we define how blood vessels in retinal images impact the OD and OC segmentation, as well as the VC degree. We incorporate the VC information into the model to enable it to learn the vessel information that affects the boundaries of the disc, thereby assisting in the OD and OC segmentation.

2   Related Work

Lalonde et al. initially proposed a template matching-based approach to obtain the boundary of the OD [17]. Since the shape of the OD and OC [18] is generally elliptical or circular, the method segments the OD and OC by extracting the edges of the retinal image and matching them with a template [19–21]. Due to the heavy reliance on template matching, the method suffers from poor performance when the shape of the boundary is affected by the surrounding blood vessels. Mendels et al. employed a contour model to detect the boundary of the OD based on image gradients [22–24]. To suppress the influence of blood vessels on the boundary, an active contour model based on Gradient Vector Flow (GVF) was used for disc boundary detection, followed by minimizing the high gradients caused by vessel locations to reduce the impact [25,26]. Lowell et al. employed circular transform techniques to obtain the boundary of the OD [27,28]. The segmentation of the OC, which is located within the disc and has low contrast, poses a greater challenge. Li et al. proposed a variational level set-based algorithm for OD segmentation, utilizing ellipse fitting operations for smoothing to obtain the segmentation result of the disc [29]. Li et al. represented features for OC segmentation based on visual characteristics such as color histograms [30]. Relying on manually extracted features, the method heavily depends on image quality and the position of pathological regions, resulting in poor robustness. Wong et al. first discovered the usefulness of vessel tortuosity for OC segmentation [20], but did not consider the influence of natural vessel curvature around the OC. There are also some methods [27,31,32] combining vascular information that do not solve the OD and OC segmentation problem. Sevastopolsky et al. proposed a modified U-Net for OD and OC segmentation [33], but did not perform joint OD and OC segmentation, instead separating them in a sequential manner. Zilly et al. proposed an integrated learning method based on CNN for OC and OD extraction [34].

3   Methods

3.1   Background

Our goal is to address the CDR measurement in real glaucoma diagnosis and screening scenarios. Directly applying models trained on public datasets to real-world applications results in poorer performance due to the inherent blurriness of images in screening scenarios compared to the original fundus images. To better align with real-world application scenarios, we not only require the original fundus images as data for glaucoma diagnosis, but also incorporate user-uploaded fundus images taken manually during the screening process into the training set. We collect 400 images captured by users from different angles using mobile phones during the glaucoma screening phase, which are included as part of the training set. Additionally, we performed joint training using the REFUGE dataset, which represents the diagnostic scenario.

3.2   Data Preprocessing

For semantic segmentation using deep learning methods, data plays a crucial role. Previous studies have utilized retinal datasets such as REFUGE [21], ORIGA [35], Drishti [36], and others. These datasets consist of images captured using professional equipment and annotated by experts, ensuring high data quality and relieving the pressure on neural networks to learn from them. To address the issues of model overfitting and poor generalization caused by limited data, researchers employ various data augmentation techniques to enhance model performance. In real-world scenarios, acquiring high-quality datasets is challenging, making data preprocessing even more important.

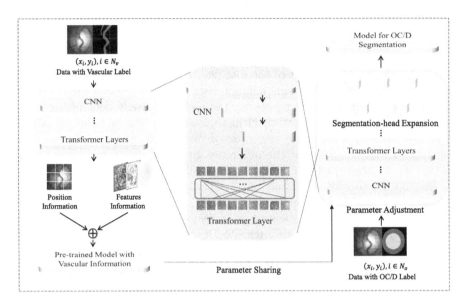

Fig. 3. Overall framework for CDR segmentation. In this diagram, we describe the entire process of the model. We first pre-train the model using vascular data, then transfer learning on OC and OD data, and expand the classification head for new tasks.

The ultimate goal is to apply this model to real clinical diagnostics and screenings. Existing methods perform well on publicly available datasets such as REFUGE, but they often struggle with generalization in real-world diagnostic and screening scenarios. Various factors and conditions can impact the performance of existing algorithms in practical applications. To enhance the model's generalization, we include images collected during actual diagnostic processes as part of the dataset and perform joint training with the REFUGE dataset. This approach better aligns with the requirements and scenarios encountered in real-world applications.

In this work, we employ object detection algorithms to locate the OD region in retinal images and crop fixed-size regions to reduce interference from complex backgrounds and noise. Since we emphasize the learning of vascular information and useful VC information is primarily present within the OD region, cropping the region of interest may aid in learning vessel information and the OD and OC segmentation. Additionally, some retinal datasets provide only annotations for the OD and OC without corresponding vessel information. To strengthen the influence of vessels, two approaches can be adopted: explicit intervention and implicit intervention.

In this task, explicit intervention refers to directly utilizing the position information of VC as the criterion for OC segmentation. For example, we employ feature point detection or curvature calculation to obtain VC information and use it as the boundary for the OC. Such an approach overlooks the impact of other important information in retinal images on OC segmentation. In complex vessel scenarios, this judgment method poses a significant challenge to the model robustness. The impressive performance demonstrated by neural networks leads us to believe that they are capable of learning hierarchical feature information from retinal images and considering it comprehensively. Therefore, we adopt an implicit intervention approach, providing label information for vessels that influence the boundary of the OC in retinal images, thereby enhancing the network's ability to discriminate vessels and making VC information one of the key factors improving the final segmentation results.

3.3   Blood Vessel Feature Extraction and Information Fusion

After implicitly introducing VC information, we divide the entire training process into two parts. In the first step, the network learns vessel information from retinal images. Convolutional neural network based methods have achieved remarkable results for vessel segmentation. The label information provides for retinal images contains only a portion of vessels that may affect the OC boundary, which may lead to fragmented vessel states and higher requirements for positional information. While CNN demonstrates powerful feature extraction capabilities and can handle most vessel segmentation tasks, it falls short compared to Transformers in capturing contextual information and extracting global information. To enable the network to better learn crucial vessel information, we adopt a network that combines CNN and Transformers, as shown in Fig. 3. The original image undergoes CNN to obtain feature distribution data, which is then combined with positional information and fed into the Transformer. This combination leverages the strengths of both CNN and Transformers to enhance the acquisition of specific vessel information. Notably, the incorporation of vascular information fundamentally serves as prior knowledge for model learning. The selection of different network architectures leads to variations in the final results, which can be categorized as horizontal comparisons. The vertical enhancement brings by vascular information proves effective for CNNs as well, providing a novel perspective primarily aims at improving the OD and OC segmentation performance.

After fully learning vessel information from retinal images, a key challenge is how to incorporate it into the OD and OC segmentation task. As mentioned earlier, the implicit intervention approach embeds vessel information in the model, allowing us to utilize this knowledge as prior information for guiding the model in learning OD and OC segmentation. Previous work has demonstrated the effectiveness of transfer learning using pre-trained models. The challenges we face are similar yet distinct. Transfer learning primarily involves pre-training on large-scale datasets to obtain powerful feature extraction models and achieve excellent performance on downstream tasks. In contrast, the data we train on the

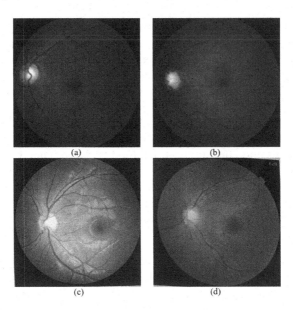

Fig. 4. Typical examples in GSD dataset. (a) represents the original retinal image, (b) displays the retinal image with added noise, (c) shows screen-captured images, and (d) exhibits retinal images uploaded by portable devices such as mobile phones or tablets.

pre-training and fine-tuning stages lack such features, and thus, factors improving the final performance mainly stem from the prior knowledge provided by vessels. We use the vessel information learning model as a pre-trained model and fine-tune it on the new OD and OC segmentation task. Given the significant differences between the two tasks, to preserve the guiding function of vessel information, we need to consider retaining information from the old task while adjusting to the new task. We transfer the feature extraction component from the existing vascular model to a new model, while incorporating a novel classification head for the new model. Moreover, we adopt a lower learning rate to ensure a smooth transition from old knowledge to new knowledge.

4   Experiment

4.1   Dataset

GSD: GSD dataset is collected for Glaucoma Screening and Diagnosis. We collect a dataset consisting of images specifically acquired for glaucoma screening and diagnosis. The real screening scenario comprises 400 images captured during actual clinical procedures. Images taken toward a screen may exhibit variations in clarity and angles due to differences in shooting angles and imaging devices. The dataset collects under various conditions aligns with real-world scenarios encountered in clinical practice. In addition to the data presented above, we have

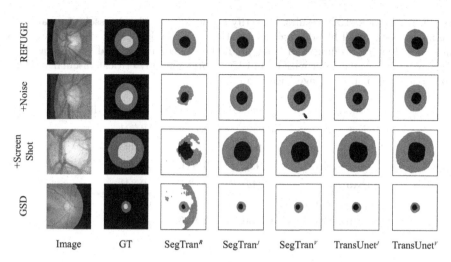

Image   GT   SegTran^R   SegTran^J   SegTran^V   TransUnet^J   TransUnet^V

Fig. 5. Comparison of model performance. Input consists of fundus photos from four different scenes; GT refers to the pre-annotated ground truth; The rest is the result of Segtran [35] prediction visualization under different dataset and different conditions. R represents the model trained on REFUGE dataset, J represents the model jointly trained on REFUGE and GSD dataset, and V represents the model obtained by adding key blood vessel information and jointly trained.

collected some additional processed data. Among them, 400 images are captured from the screen with reference to the REFUGE dataset, and 200 images are artificially augmented with noise on the REFUGE dataset, including Gaussian noise, contrast adjustment, brightness conversion and other operations. Some typical examples of the GSD dataset are shown in Fig. 4.

Table 1. Experimental results. We conduct joint training on the REFUGE dataset and the GSD dataset separately using the U-Net [15], TransU-Net [37], Segtran [38] architecture. This process yields models that are subsequently utilized to make predictions on both the REFUGE dataset and the GSD dataset. VC represents only critical vascular information.

	REFUGE			GSD		
	Dice (OD)	Dice (OC)	Average dice	Dice (OD)	Dice (OC)	Average dice
U-Net [15]	0.873	0.805	0.839	0.490	0.715	0.603
U-Net with VC	**0.927**	**0.819**	**0.873**	**0.872**	**0.813**	**0.843**
TransU-Net [37]	0.958	0.900	0.929	0.899	0.801	0.850
TransU-Net with VC	0.956	**0.901**	0.929	**0.913**	**0.819**	**0.859**
Segtran [38]	0.870	0.835	0.853	0.917	0.849	0.883
Segtran with VC	**0.895**	**0.841**	**0.868**	**0.942**	0.845	**0.894**

Table 2. Ablation study results. To verify the validity of blood vessel information on the model, we add all blood vessel information and only key blood vessel information into the model for training, and make predictions on REFUGE and GSD datasets. V represents all vascular information, and VC represents only critical vascular information. The result is the average Dice of all data.

Methods	Dice (OD)	Dice (OC)	Average dice
U-Net [15]	0.682	0.760	0.721
U-Net with all V	0.490	0.715	0.603
U-Net with VC	**0.900**	**0.816**	**0.858**
Segtran [38]	0.848	0.834	0.841
Segtran with all V	0.820	0.811	0.816
Segtran with VC	**0.936**	**0.846**	**0.891**

REFUGE: It consists of a dataset of 400 images for OD and OC segmentation, including 40 images of glaucomatous fundus and 360 images of non-glaucomatous fundus with different sizes and resolutions.

4.2 Experimental Setting

To assess the impact of data quantity in different scenarios on the model, we add 200 noisy images created by introducing noise to the original images in the dataset. Using an initial model as the pre-training model, we select 75% of the retinal fundus photographs from each respective scenario as the training set and performed joint training on retinal fundus photographs from different scenarios, resulting in the current model. To enhance user experience, we incorporate functionalities for retinal photograph localization and automatic classification of left and right eyes. The experimental results are shown in Fig. 5.

To evaluate the performance of the model, we use the remaining 25% of the dataset as the test set, including 100 original images from REFUGE dataset, 50 images with added noise, 100 images captured from screens, and 100 actual diagnostic images. We conduct separate tests on the initial model trained on REFUGE dataset and the existing model trained on retinal fundus photographs from multiple scenarios. The test results are presented in Table 1, and a subset of actual segmentation results is shown in Fig. 5. The dice coefficient serves as an evaluation metric for image segmentation.

4.3 Ablation Study

We evaluate the usefulness of the newly introduced VC information for CDR segmentation, we utilize the PyTorch framework with identical hyperparameters. We employ SegTran as the baseline model and compared its performance with the addition of key vessel information. Furthermore, to demonstrate the efficacy of glaucoma-induced VC, we incorporate all vessel information learned by the model. The ablation results, depicted in Table 2, indicate that only the glaucoma-induced VC information is beneficial for CDR segmentation.

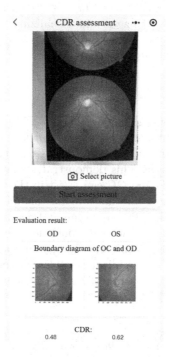

Fig. 6. Interface of our designed WeChat mini-program. Users can choose to upload images from their photo album or capture images using portable devices such as mobile phones or tablets. The lower section displays the segmentation of the OD and OC, as well as the calculation of the CDR after evaluation by the intelligent model. In response to practical requirements from patients, the user interface of our system is designed in Chinese. For the sake of convenience in presentation, we have chosen to display the interface in English.

4.4   Intelligent Diagnostic System

We develop a WeChat mini-program to deploy the model, allowing users to upload their original retinal fundus images or directly capture images of their own cases using the built-in camera. The system diagram is shown in Fig. 6. Upon completion of the upload, the intelligent model deployed in the backend automatically performs CDR segmentation and visualizes the results on the user interface, along with the automatic calculation of the CDR. To enhance user experience, we introduce functionalities for retinal photograph localization and automatic classification of left and right eyes. Retinal photograph localization is implemented to accommodate various scenarios. Users may upload retinal fundus images captured under different conditions, which may not be the original images. In such cases, we localize the retinal photographs to the most suitable central regions within the images. Since the positions of the left and right retinal fundus images differ, we facilitate identification by automatically classifying the user-uploaded retinal fundus images and visualizing them as left or right eye images. The user interface of the system is illustrated in Fig. 6. The system is used for the screening and diagnosis of glaucoma.

5   Conclusion

In this paper, we incorporate glaucoma-affected VC information into CDR segmentation based on recommendations from clinically experienced doctors. We create the GSD dataset and achieve promising results on both the REFUGE dataset and the GSD dataset. This demonstrates that the curved vessel information surrounding the OD and OC can assist in the segmentation process. By focusing solely on key vessel information, the model reduces the influence of other retinal vessels. Additionally, we design and deploy an intelligent glaucoma diagnosis system. In the future, we will continue to collaborate with hospitals and patients to collect diverse datasets, encompassing various scenarios and more data, to enhance the model's generalization and robustness. We will also optimize and improve the intelligent glaucoma diagnosis system based on user feedback.

References

1. https://mp.weixin.qq.com/s/vcA_9izdwLwHvC8aL33oBQ
2. World health organization programme for the prevention of blindness and deafness-global initiative for the elimination of avoidable blindness World health organization, Geneva, Switzerland, WHO/PBL/97.61 Rev. 1 (1997)
3. Tham, Y.-C., et al.: Global prevalence of glaucoma and projections of glaucoma burden through 2040: a systematic review and meta-analysis. Ophthalmology **121**(11), 2081–2090 (2014)
4. Garway-Heath, D.F., Hitchings, R.A.: Quantitative evaluation of the optic nerve head in early glaucoma. Brit. J. Ophthalmol. **82**(4), 352–361 (1998)
5. Jonas, J.B., Bergua, A., Schmitz-Valckenberg, P., Papastathopoulos, K.I., Budde, W.M.: Ranking of optic disc variables for detection of glaucomatous optic nerve damage. Invest. Ophthalmol. Vis. Sci. **41**(7), 1764–1773 (2000)
6. Almazroa, A., Burman, R., Raahemifar, K., Lakshminarayanan, V.: Optic disc and optic cup segmentation methodologies for glaucoma image detection: a survey. J. Ophthalmol. 2015, 180972 (2015)
7. Gulshan, V., et al.: Development and validation of a deep learning algorithm for detection of diabetic retinopathy in retinal fundus pho- tographs. J. Amer. Med. Assoc. **316**(22), 2402–2410 (2016)
8. Michael, D., Hancox, O.D.: Optic disc size, an important consideration in the glaucoma evaluation. Clin. Eye Vis. Care **11**(2), 59–62 (1999)
9. Wu, M., Leng, T., de Sisternes, L., Rubin, D.L., Chen, Q.: Automated segmentation of optic disc in SD-OCT images and cup-to-disc ratios quantification by patch searching-based neural canal opening detection. Opt. Exp. **23**(24), 31216–31229 (2015)

10. Lee, K., Niemeijer, M., Garvin, M.K., Kwon, Y.H., Sonka, M., Abrámoff, M.D.: Segmentation of the optic disc in 3-D OCT scans of the optic nerve head. IEEE Trans. Med. Imag. **29**(1), 159–168 (2010)

11. Fu, H., Xu, D., Lin, S., Wong, D.W.K., Liu, J.: Automatic optic disc detection in OCT slices via low-rank reconstruction. IEEE Trans. Biomed. Eng. **62**(4), 1151–1158 (2015)

12. Fu, H., et al.: Segmentation and quantification for angle-closure glaucoma assessment in anterior segment OCT. IEEE Trans. Med. Imaging **36**(9), 1930–1938 (2017)

13. Krizhevsky, A., Sutskever, I., Hinton, G.E.: ImageNet classification with deep convolutional neural networks. In: Proceedings of the NIPS, pp. 1097–1105 (2012)

14. Shelhamer, E., Long, J., Darrell, T.: Fully convolutional networks for semantic segmentation. IEEE Trans. Pattern Anal. Mach. Intell. **39**(4), 640–651 (2017)

15. Ronneberger, O., Fischer, P., Brox, T.: U-Net: convolutional networks for biomedical image segmentation. In: Navab, N., Hornegger, J., Wells, W.M., Frangi, A.F. (eds.) MICCAI 2015. LNCS, vol. 9351, pp. 234–241. Springer, Cham (2015). https://doi.org/10.1007/978-3-319-24574-4_28

16. He, K., Gkioxari, G., Dollár, P., et al.: Mask r-cnn. In: Proceedings of the IEEE International Conference on Computer Vision, pp. 2961–2969 (2017)

17. Lalonde, M., Beaulieu, M., Gagnon, L.: Fast and robust optic disc detection using pyramidal decomposition and Hausdorff-based template matching. IEEE Trans. Med. Imaging **20**(11), 1193–1200 (2001)

18. Patton, N., et al.: Retinal image analysis: concepts, applications and potential. Prog. Retinal Eye Res. **25**(1), 99–127 (2006)

19. Pallawala, P.M.D.S., Hsu, W., Lee, M.L., Eong, K.-G.A.: Automated optic disc localization and contour detection using ellipse fitting and wavelet transform. In: Pajdla, T., Matas, J. (eds.) ECCV 2004. LNCS, vol. 3022, pp. 139–151. Springer, Heidelberg (2004). https://doi.org/10.1007/978-3-540-24671-8_11

20. Wong, D.W.K., Liu, J., Lim, J.H., et al.: Automated detection of kinks from blood vessels for optic cup segmentation in retinal images. In: Medical Imaging 2009: Computer-Aided Diagnosis, vol. 7260, pp. 459–466. SPIE (2009)

21. Orlando, J.I., Fu, H., Breda, J.B., et al.: Refuge challenge: a unified framework for evaluating automated methods for glaucoma assessment from fundus photographs. Med. Image Anal. **59**, 101570 (2020)

22. Mendels, F., Heneghan, C., Thiran, J.: Identification of the optic disc boundary in retinal images using active contours. In Proceedings of the IMVIP (1999)

23. Osareh, A., Mirmehdi, M., Thomas, B., Markham, R.: Colour morphology and snakes for optic disc localization. In: Proceedings of the MIUA, pp. 21–24 (2002)

24. Chan, T.F., Vese, L.A.: Active contours without edges. IEEE Trans. Image Process. **10**(2), 266–277 (2001)

25. Lee, S., Brady, M.: Optic disk boundary detection. In: Proceedings of the BMVC, pp. 359–362 (1991)

26. Mumford, D., Shah, J.: Optimal approximation by piecewise smooth functions and associated variational problems. Commun. Pure Appl. Math. **42**, 577–685 (1989)

27. Lowell, J., et al.: Optic nerve head segmentation. IEEE Trans. Med. Imag. **23**(2), 256–264 (2004)

28. Novo, J., Penedo, M., Santos, J.: Localisation of the optic disc by means of GA-optimised topological active nets. Image Vis. Comput. **27**(10), 1572–1584 (2009)

29. Li, H., Chutatape, O.: Boundary detection of optic disk by a modified ASM method. Pattern Recogn. **36**(9), 2093–2104 (2003)

30. Li, H., Chutatape, O.: A model based approach for automated feature extraction in fundus images. IEEE Trans. Biomed. Eng. **51**(2), 246–254 (2004)
31. Joshi, G.D., Sivaswamy, J., Krishnadas, S.R.: Optic disk and cup segmentation from monocular color retinal images for glaucoma assessment. IEEE Trans. Med. Imaging **30**(6), 1192–1205 (2011)
32. Fu, H., Cheng, J., Xu, Y., et al.: Joint optic disc and cup segmentation based on multi-label deep network and polar transformation. IEEE Trans. Med. Imaging **37**(7), 1597–1605 (2018)
33. Sevastopolsky, A.: Optic disc and cup segmentation methods for glaucoma detection with modification of U-Net convolutional neural network. Pattern Recogn. Image Anal. **27**(3), 618–624 (2017)
34. Zilly, J., Buhmann, J.M., Mahapatra, D.: Glaucoma detection using entropy sampling and ensemble learning for automatic optic cup and disc segmentation. Comput. Med. Imag. Graph. **55**, 28–41 (2017)
35. Zhang, Z., Yin, F.S., Liu, J., et al.: Origa-light: an online retinal fundus image database for glaucoma analysis and research. In: 2010 Annual International Conference of the IEEE Engineering in Medicine and Biology, pp. 3065–3068. IEEE (2010)
36. Sivaswamy, J., Krishnadas, S.R., Joshi, G.D., et al.: Drishti-GS: retinal image dataset for optic nerve head (onh) segmentation. In: 2014 IEEE 11th International Symposium on Biomedical Imaging (ISBI), pp. 53–56. IEEE (2014)
37. Chen, J., Lu, Y., Yu, Q., et al.: Transunet: transformers make strong encoders for medical image segmentation. arXiv preprint arXiv:2102.04306 (2021)
38. Li, S., Sui, X., Luo, X., et al.: Medical image segmentation using squeeze-and-expansion transformers. arXiv preprint arXiv:2105.09511 (2021)

FLAME-Based Multi-view 3D Face Reconstruction

Wenzhuo Zheng, Junhao Zhao, Xiaohong Liu[✉], Yongyang Pan,
Zhenghao Gan, Haozhe Han, and Ning Liu[✉]

Shanghai Jiao Tong University, Shanghai, China
{darkcorvus,200217zjh,xiaohongliu,panyongyang,
ganzhenghao,h2411522561,ningliu}@sjtu.edu.cn

Abstract. At present, face 3D reconstruction has broad application prospects in various fields, but the research on it is still in the development stage. In this paper, we hope to achieve better face 3D reconstruction quality by combining a multi-view training framework with face parametric model FLAME, and propose a multi-view training and testing model **MFNet** (Multi-view FLAME Network). We build a self-supervised training framework and implement constraints such as multi-view optical flow loss function and face landmark loss, and finally obtain a complete MFNet. We propose innovative implementations of multi-view optical flow loss and the covisible mask. We test our model on AFLW and facescape datasets and also take pictures of our faces to reconstruct 3D faces while simulating actual scenarios as much as possible, which achieves good results. Our work mainly addresses the problem of combining parametric models of faces with multi-view face 3D reconstruction and explores the implementation of a FLAME-based multi-view training and testing framework for contributing to the field of face 3D reconstruction.

Keywords: 3D face reconstruction · Multi-view · Parametric model

1 Introduction

Face 3D reconstruction [13] mainly focuses on the reconstruction of human facial regions, and broadly speaking, also includes hair, ear, neck, and other regions. The human face is a special 3D object that has not only more complex shape and texture features, but also strong prior constraints. This poses a great challenge to face 3D reconstruction on one hand, and on the other hand, it also provides feasible technical approaches to reconstruct the face 3D structure from

W. Zheng and J. Zhao—Contribute equally to this work.

Supported in part by Shanghai Pujiang Program under Grant 22PJ1406800 and Shanghai Jiao Tong University under U1908210.

2D information, and the face parametric model is one of them. The face parametric model is a statistical model based on a large number of faces, and its core idea is that faces can be matched one-to-one in the 3D feature space and can be obtained by weighted linear summation of orthogonal bases for a large number of other faces. The most widely used model is 3DMM [1,2], but it has two core problems: (1) 3DMM is in a low-dimensional space and thus the face detail characterization is weak; (2) 3DMM only reconstruct the front face region without neck or hindbrain. Therefore, we choose FLAME [11], which has a better characterization of details and more complete reconstruction. FLAME has three parameters: shape, pose, and expression, which can more accurately classify faces into more dimensions, and the face reconstructed by FLAME includes the whole head. However, there is not much research work on FLAME so far, and there is a gap in the field of multi-view training using FLAME. Our work fills this gap and makes an exploratory contribution to FLAME-based multi-view training.

In the past decade, deep learning technologies have become a dominant trend in face 3D reconstruction. Some works [7,15] use neural networks to regress end-to-end to compute the inputs needed for face parameterization models, but are limited to single-view, while our proposed MFNet can utilize features from multiple views and fuse them to obtain more complete face information. In this paper, we use FLAME as a powerful tool to reconstruct fine-grained 3D face models with low cost and only 2D RGB images.

Our main contributions are listed as follows:

- We innovatively combine multi-view training with FLAME, propose a multi-view self-supervised framework, and implement a complete multi-view training and testing process. Our proposed model MFNet achieves good results on both test datasets and actual captured images.
- We propose a multi-view optical flow loss for our multi-view training framework and propose a novel implementation of the technical details such as covisible mask.

2   Related Work

2.1   Parametric Model

In 1999, Blanz and Vetter et al. [1,2] proposed the 3D Morphable Model (3DMM) for the human face, which is the most widely used 3D face reconstruction model. Subsequent studies related to 3DMM have been published in the next decade, either by adding coefficients to the original model, such as Pascal Paysan et al. [9] updated the expression coefficients of the 3DMM model for BFM (Basel Face Model) model in 2017, or build larger datasets, such as James Booth et al. [4] built a dataset of 9663 faces, or propose better ways to optimize the solution coefficients, such as adding deep learning ideas to the coefficient solution in recent years to achieve better results [3,19], or make nonlinear adjustments to the model, such as the nonlinear 3DMM model proposed by Luan Tran et al. [18], but none of them have departed from the original framework of 3DMM. This also leads to the fact that these changes do not solve the two core problems of 3DMM mentioned above. Therefore, we choose FLAME [11] as our face parametric model.

FLAME was proposed by Li Tianye et al., referring to the expression of the body model SMPL [12], combining linear blend skinning (LBS) and the corresponding corrected blendshape. Not many researches have been done on FLAME [7,15], and they are all limited to single-view. We want to utilize the features and data from multiple perspectives, so we propose a self-supervised multi-view training framework and achieve better reconstruction results.

2.2   Multi-view Reconstruction

There are many works based on face parametric models, but very few of them [16,21] are trained using multi-view data, and the only ones are based on 3DMM. MVFNet [21] is the first work that proposed the idea of multi-view parametric model training, but it is based on 3DMM and the implementation is very rough, which leads to poor results. MGCNet [16] makes some improvements on its basis, proposing novel multi-view loss functions, using multi-view training, but only using a single image for testing. It does improve the quality of the face reconstruction, but the reconstructed faces were still rough and incomplete. The field of FLAME-based multi-view training remains a gap. To the best of our knowledge, MFNet is the first work on 3D face reconstruction using multi-view training and testing framework based on the face parametric model FLAME.

3   Method

3.1   Overall Architecture

The overall architecture for our proposed is show in Fig. 1. Resnet is a highly mature technology that has performed well in numerous image recognition and classification. So we extract features from each input image by a shared weight Resnet50, and then concatenate the features together and put them into a fully connected layer to regress a set of flame parameters for the person. Also, we separate a pose and texture feature from Resnet50 for each perspective for subsequent reconstruction work and calculate loss.

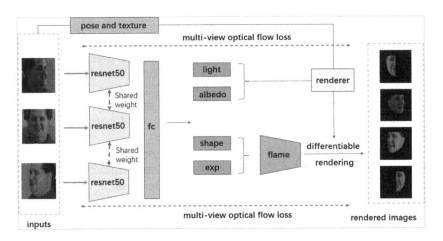

Fig. 1. Architecture of MFNet.

3.2   FLAME

After extracting features from the multi view images in the input batch through Resnet50 and converting them into fully connected layers, we can obtain the desired FLAME model input vectors β, pose θ, expression ψ. Next, the FLAME model acts as a decoder to convert these hidden layer vectors into three-dimensional facial information. These three-dimensional information mainly consists of two parts, the first is the information of each vertex, such as coordinate T_P, Normal vector N_{uv} and faces F, and the second is landmark coordinates of the face. The equation of the FLAME model is as follows:

$$M(\beta, \theta, \psi) = W(T_P(\beta, \theta, \psi), \mathbf{J}(\beta), \theta, \mathcal{W}) \tag{1}$$

3.3   Feature Extraction

We use part of DECA [7] as the pretrained model of Resnet50 for better feature extractoin and finetune it. In order to obtain better feature information, we use a fully connected layer to fuse the features extracted by Resnet50 from three perspectives together for consideration, thereby obtaining a more accurate model.

3.4   Differentiable Renderer

After getting the 3D information of the face through FLAME model, we need to use 3D rendering to get the 2D image. Our shadow facial image $B(alpha, l, N_{UV})$ is calculated based on the following equation:

$$B(\alpha, l, N_{uv})_{i,j} = A(\alpha)_{i,j} \odot \sum_{k=1}^{9} l_k H_k(N_{i,j}) \tag{2}$$

In the Eq. 2, $A(\alpha)$ represents UV albedo map, N_{UV} is the normal vector of the face surface output by FLAME. $B_{i,j} \in R^3$, $A_{i,j} \in R^3$, $N_{i,j} \in R^3$ represents the various attributes of pixel (i,j) in the UV coordinate system. $\odot$ represents Hadamard product.

In addition, we also need to extract texture from the original input image and obtain vertex coordinates T_P and faces F to calculate the correspondence between points in the 3D mesh and the 2D texture map U_V. Then, the texture map I'_{uv} is obtained from the original input image by using this correspondence U_V, and the missing part in the middle is supplemented by bilinear interpolation. We extract the texture of multi views and perform simple fusion to obtain I'_{uv}, which contains information from multi views. Finally, we use facial mask M_{face} to get UV texture map I_{uv}:

$$I_{uv} = M_{face} \odot I'_{uv} \tag{3}$$

Given the geometric parameters (β, θ, ψ), albedo α, lighting condition l, and camera parameter c of the mesh, we can render different two-dimensional face images I_r from various perspectives:

$$I_r = \mathcal{R}(M, B, c, I_{uv}) \tag{4}$$

3.5   Loss Function

Multiview Optical Loss. The optical flow loss [22] calculates the optical flow between the rendered facial image and the original image. The design of the optical flow loss is based on an intuitive fact. That is, the coordinates of a point on a correct 3D model projected onto a 2D plane should be the same as the original image. We hope that these two points can coincide, so the distance should be as close to zero as possible. And that's exactly what the optical flow loss does (Fig. 2).

Fig. 2. Optical flow estimation. From left to right are original image, rendered image and the optical flow. We use RAFT [17] to extract optical flow.

However, due to the occlusion of the face, the reconstruction of the invisible part of the image view becomes very blurry. So we proposed an implementation method for a covisible mask. It can mask the blurry parts, so that these parts do not participate in the calculation of the optical flow loss. For the input face image, we first generate a projected two-dimensional face mask MF according to the position of the three-dimensional face model. Then we use face landmarks to roughly extract the parts that can be seen from two viewpoints and get MB. The bounding box MB composed of keypoints and the face mask MF can be combined to obtain a better covisible mask MC:

$$MC_{a,b} = MB_{a,b} \odot MF_b \tag{5}$$

Here we show the usage of the covisible mask (Fig. 3). In order to reduce the estimation error of the optical flow for the uninterested region, we also mask the complex regions such as the mouth, so that the covisible mask basically achieves our expected goal.

Fig. 3. Covisible mask. From left to right are original images, rendered images and covisible masked images.

Given the image I_b and the rendered image $I_{a \to b}$, the optical flow estimator **F**, the covisible mask $MC_{a,b}$, we can calculate the multi-view optical flow loss function $L_{multiop}$:

$$L_{multiop}(I_b, I_{a \to b}) = |\mathbf{F}(MC_{a,b} \odot I_b, MC_{a,b} \odot I_{a \to b})| \tag{6}$$

Single View Keypoint Loss. We project the 3D face keypoints to the 2D image and re-projecte them back to compared them. We hope that this can provide stronger face constraints for the model and prevent it from ignoring the constraints of the face itself:

$$L_{singlelmk}(k_a, k_{a \to a}) = \sum_{i \in MF_a} \|k_a(i) - k_{a \to a}(i)\|_1 \tag{7}$$

Eye and Lip Keypoint Loss. Since the eye and lip area of the face is relatively complex, we implemented an eye keypoint loss and a lip keypoint loss to achieve better face reconstruction results. We compute the relative offset between the keypoints $k_a(i)$ and $k_a(j)$ of the upper and lower eyelids and lips on a certain view a, and measure the difference between their offset and the offset between the corresponding re-projected keypoints $k_{a \to a}(i)$ and $k_{a \to a}(j)$ of the 3D model:

$$L_{eye}(k_a, k_{a\to a}) =$$
$$\sum_{(i,j)\in E_a} \|k_a(i) - k_a(j) - (k_{a\to a}(i) - k_{a\to a}(j))\|_1 \tag{8}$$

$$L_{lip}(k_a, k_{a\to a}) =$$
$$\sum_{(i,j)\in P_a} \|k_a(i) - k_a(j) - (k_{a\to a}(i) - k_{a\to a}(j))\|_1 \tag{9}$$

Regularized Loss. We need to regularize some vectors to prevent overfitting, including shape vector $\boldsymbol{\beta}$ regularization, expression vector $\boldsymbol{\psi}$ regularization and albedo α regularization:

$$L_{reg} = \|\boldsymbol{\beta}\|_2 + \|\boldsymbol{\psi}\|_2 + \|\alpha\|_2 \tag{10}$$

Total Loss. The total loss function is shown below:

$$L_{total} = \lambda_1 L_{multiop} + \lambda_2 L_{singlelmk} + \lambda_3 L_{eye} + \lambda_4 L_{lip} + \lambda_5 L_{reg} \tag{11}$$

4 Experiments

In this section, we first introduce our implementation details for conducting the experiments, including the datasets and evaluation metrics (Sect. 4.1). Then we make qualitative and quantitative comparisons to other 3D face reconstruction methods (Sect. 4.2 and Sect. 4.3). Finally, we demonstrate the effectiveness of the proposed method with extensive ablation studies in Sect. 4.4.

4.1 Implementation Details

Training Datasets. Our training is performed on Multi-PIE dataset, which contains over 750,000 images recorded from 337 subjects using 15 cameras in different directions 963 under various lighting conditions. We take frontal-view images as anchorsand randomly select side-view images (left and right) to form a three view triplet which is the input of our model. In this way, we take 36k training triplets.

Evaluation Datasets. We mainly perform quantitative and qualitative evaluations on the facescape benchmark containing in-the-wild and in-the-lab data. 14 recent methods are evaluated on the dimensions of camera pose and focal length, which provides a comprehensive evaluation.

Hyper-parameters Setting. In actual training, we set the hyper-parameters in Eq. (11) to $\lambda_1 = 1$, $\lambda_2 = 1$, $\lambda_3 = 1$, $\lambda_4 = 0.5$, $\lambda_5 = 1e - 04$. learning rate $= 1e - 3$. Train epochs on multi-PIE are 10.

4.2   Qualitative Results

We first present our reconstruction results, as shown in Fig. 4. It can be seen that MFNet's reconstructed facial model performs well in various perspectives.

Fig. 4. MFNet reconstruction. From left to right are input images, MFNet reconstruction.

Next, we compared the reconstruction results of DECA and MFNet. We used DECA and our model to reconstruct 2000 images from AFLW2000-3D respectively. Some of them are shown in Fig. 5. Through observation, it can be found that DECA has problems in predicting facial edges in certain situations, but MFNet can reconstruct more accurately due to the involvement of multiple perspectives.

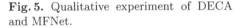

Fig. 5. Qualitative experiment of DECA and MFNet.

Fig. 6. MFNet reconstruction.

We also set up three-viewed cameras on site to take images of the people around us, obtaining multi-view images that are close to the real environment. We tested the reconstruction effect of MFNet on these images and added texture, as shown in the Fig. 6.

Table 1. Comparison with other single-view methods.

methods	0–5			5–30			30–60			60–90		
	CD	MNE	CR	CD	MNE	CR	CD	MNE	CR	CD	MNE	CR
extreme3dface [20]	5.02	0.16	0.62	5.512	0.18	0.56	7.91	0.20	0.40	25.3	0.26	0.27
PRNet [8]	2.61	0.12	0.83	3.11	0.11	0.83	4.25	0.11	0.78	3.88	0.14	0.75
Deep3DFaceRec [6]	2.30	**0.07**	0.83	**2.50**	**0.07**	0.83	3.56	0.08	0.77	6.81	0.14	0.62
RingNet [15]	2.40	0.08	**0.99**	2.99	0.09	**0.99**	4.78	0.10	0.98	10.7	0.18	0.97
DFDN [24]	3.67	0.09	0.87	3.27	0.09	0.86	7.29	0.12	0.84	27.4	0.30	0.57
DF2Net [24]	2.92	0.12	0.57	4.21	0.13	0.56	6.54	0.15	0.46	19.7	0.30	0.30
UDL [5]	**2.27**	0.09	0.69	2.59	0.09	0.68	3.45	0.10	0.64	6.32	0.17	0.49
facescape_opti [23]	2.81	0.09	0.84	3.17	0.09	0.82	4.08	0.10	0.78	6.57	0.16	0.67
facescape_deep [23]	2.70	0.08	0.87	3.69	0.09	0.86	4.22	0.09	0.85	9.09	0.15	0.70
MGCNet [16]	2.97	**0.07**	0.84	2.94	**0.07**	0.85	**2.78**	**0.07**	0.81	4.20	**0.09**	0.74
3DDFA_V2 [10]	2.49	**0.07**	0.86	2.66	**0.07**	0.86	3.17	**0.07**	0.83	**3.67**	**0.09**	0.79
SADRNet [14]	6.60	0.11	0.90	6.87	0.11	0.89	6.39	0.10	0.84	8.62	0.16	0.82
LAP [25]	4.19	0.11	0.94	4.47	0.12	0.93	6.15	0.14	0.87	13.7	0.20	0.68
DECA [7]	2.88	0.08	**0.99**	2.64	**0.07**	**0.99**	2.88	0.08	**0.99**	4.83	0.11	**0.99**
MFNet	3.98	0.11	**0.99**	4.07	0.11	**0.99**	3.60	0.10	**0.99**	5.25	0.12	**0.99**

4.3 Quantitative Results

At present, there are few benchmarks suitable for multi-view reconstruction test for face parametric models. Therefore, in order to conduct a broader comparison, we test our model on a single view setting and compare it with other algorithms. Due to the original intention of designing MFNet for multi view input methods, this testing method inevitably reduces the reconstruction effect of MFNet. As shown in Table 1, MFNet can not perform best on a single-view testing, but it has already surpassed most models.

To demonstrate the complete performance of MFNet, we also compared it with other models on facescape-lab dataset, which is a multi-view dataset. MFNet used inputs from three views, and others randomly selected one view as input. As can be seen in Table 2, the performance of the complete MFNet model is comprehensively ahead of other models.

It can be seen that on the facescape-lab dataset, when MFNet was tested with a complete multi-view input, its various indicators showed significant improvement compared to DECA and also other single-view models, indicating that our multi-view training gives MFNet better reconstruction ability and achieves our expected goals.

Table 2. comparison of MFNet and other single-view models.

method	facescape-lab		
	CD	MNE	CR
DECA [7]	5.25	0.16	0.97
LAP [25]	9.76	0.20	0.85
SADRNet [14]	7.21	0.18	0.89
DFDN [24]	14.10	0.32	0.93
Deep3DFaceRec [6]	5.28	0.15	0.80
extreme3dface [20]	15.38	0.26	0.66
PRNet [8]	4.97	0.15	0.85
facescape_opti [23]	5.14	0.16	0.76
DF2Net [24]	7.39	0.17	0.67
MFNet	**4.89**	**0.14**	**0.99**

4.4 Ablation Study

In this section, we conduct an ablation study on the mentioned loss function. In the ablation experiment, we remove one Loss function, keep other Loss function unchanged, and train the same epochs on the same training set. Testing is performed on the fasescape-wild dataset. The results are shown in Table 3. We can see that the whole MFNet has the best performance.

Table 3. Ablation study of loss function.

methods	0–5			5–30			30–60			60–90		
	CD	MNE	CR	CD	MNE	CR	CD	MNE	CR	CD	MNE	CR
- multiop	4.29	0.12	0.98	4.43	0.12	**0.99**	3.62	**0.09**	0.99	**5.12**	0.12	0.99
- singlelmk	6.54	0.14	**0.99**	5.85	0.13	**0.99**	12.2	0.18	0.97	38.6	0.25	0.93
- eye	140	0.33	**0.99**	423	0.38	0.98	61.8	0.24	0.96	5.91	0.14	**0.99**
- lip	6.95	0.13	**0.99**	11.2	0.15	0.98	13.7	0.17	0.94	13.6	0.18	0.95
- reg	23.3	0.19	**0.99**	32.3	0.19	**0.99**	7.39	0.12	**0.99**	8.75	0.16	**0.99**
MFNet	**3.98**	**0.11**	0.98	**4.06**	**0.11**	0.98	**3.60**	0.10	**0.99**	5.25	**0.12**	**0.99**

We also reconstruct each ablation model on the alfw dataset as shown in Fig. 7. In general, the ablation experiment shows that the performance of the model has declined after the removal of some loss function, which shows that the design of our loss function is reasonable.

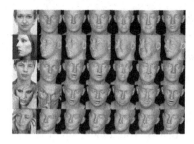

Fig. 7. Ablation study of loss function. From left to right are the images with reg, lip, lmk, eye, multiop removed respectively, and the last column is the reconstruction of MNFet.

5 Conclusion

In this paper, we innovatively combine multi-view training with FLAME, propose a multi-view self-supervised framework and implement a complete multi-view training and testing process. Our proposed model MFNet achieve good results on both test datasets and actual captured images. For the implementation of MFNet, we propose a multi-view optical flow loss for our multi-view training framework and propose a novel implementation of the technical details such as covisible mask. Experiments show that our model outperforms other methods in face reconstruction and detail capture, which indicates that the combination of multi-view and FLAME is reasonable.

References

1. Blanz, V., Vetter, T.: A morphable model for the synthesis of 3d faces. In: Proceedings of the 26th Annual Conference on Computer Graphics and Interactive Techniques, pp. 187–194 (1999)
2. Blanz, V., Vetter, T.: Face recognition based on fitting a 3d morphable model. IEEE Trans. Pattern Anal. Mach. Intell. **25**(9), 1063–1074 (2003)
3. Booth, J., Antonakos, E., Ploumpis, S., Trigeorgis, G., Panagakis, Y., Zafeiriou, S.: 3d face morphable models "in-the-wild". In: Proceedings of the IEEE Conference on Computer Vision and Pattern Recognition, pp. 48–57 (2017)
4. Booth, J., Roussos, A., Zafeiriou, S., Ponniah, A., Dunaway, D.: A 3d morphable model learnt from 10,000 faces. In: Proceedings of the IEEE Conference on Computer Vision and Pattern Recognition, pp. 5543–5552 (2016)
5. Chen, Y., Wu, F., Wang, Z., Song, Y., Ling, Y., Bao, L.: Self-supervised learning of detailed 3d face reconstruction. IEEE Trans. Image Process. **29**, 8696–8705 (2020)
6. Deng, Y., Yang, J., Xu, S., Chen, D., Jia, Y., Tong, X.: Accurate 3d face reconstruction with weakly-supervised learning: from single image to image set. In: Proceedings of the IEEE/CVF Conference on Computer Vision and Pattern Recognition Workshops (2019)
7. Feng, Y., Feng, H., Black, M.J., Bolkart, T.: Learning an animatable detailed 3d face model from in-the-wild images. ACM Trans. Graph. (ToG) **40**(4), 1–13 (2021)

8. Feng, Y., Wu, F., Shao, X., Wang, Y., Zhou, X.: Joint 3d face reconstruction and dense alignment with position map regression network. In: Proceedings of the European Conference on Computer Vision (ECCV), pp. 534–551 (2018)

9. Gerig, T., et al.: Morphable face models-an open framework. In: 2018 13th IEEE International Conference on Automatic Face & Gesture Recognition (FG 2018), pp. 75–82. IEEE (2018)

10. Guo, J., Zhu, X., Yang, Y., Yang, F., Lei, Z., Li, S.Z.: Towards fast, accurate and stable 3D dense face alignment. In: Vedaldi, A., Bischof, H., Brox, T., Frahm, J.-M. (eds.) ECCV 2020. LNCS, vol. 12364, pp. 152–168. Springer, Cham (2020). https://doi.org/10.1007/978-3-030-58529-7_10

11. Li, T., Bolkart, T., Black, M.J., Li, H., Romero, J.: Learning a model of facial shape and expression from 4d scans. ACM Trans. Graph. 36(6), 194–201 (2017)

12. Loper, M., Mahmood, N., Romero, J., Pons-Moll, G., Black, M.J.: SMPL: a skinned multi-person linear model. ACM Trans. Graph. (TOG) 34(6), 1–16 (2015)

13. Roberts, L.G.: Machine perception of three-dimensional solids. Ph.D. thesis, Massachusetts Institute of Technology (1963)

14. Ruan, Z., Zou, C., Wu, L., Wu, G., Wang, L.: SADRnet: self-aligned dual face regression networks for robust 3d dense face alignment and reconstruction. IEEE Trans. Image Process. 30, 5793–5806 (2021)

15. Sanyal, S., Bolkart, T., Feng, H., Black, M.J.: Learning to regress 3d face shape and expression from an image without 3d supervision. In: Proceedings of the IEEE/CVF Conference on Computer Vision and Pattern Recognition, pp. 7763–7772 (2019)

16. Shang, J., et al.: Self-supervised monocular 3D face reconstruction by occlusion-aware multi-view geometry consistency. In: Vedaldi, A., Bischof, H., Brox, T., Frahm, J.-M. (eds.) ECCV 2020. LNCS, vol. 12360, pp. 53–70. Springer, Cham (2020). https://doi.org/10.1007/978-3-030-58555-6_4

17. Teed, Z., Deng, J.: RAFT: recurrent all-pairs field transforms for optical flow. In: Vedaldi, A., Bischof, H., Brox, T., Frahm, J.-M. (eds.) ECCV 2020. LNCS, vol. 12347, pp. 402–419. Springer, Cham (2020). https://doi.org/10.1007/978-3-030-58536-5_24

18. Tran, L., Liu, X.: Nonlinear 3d face morphable model. In: Proceedings of the IEEE Conference on Computer Vision and Pattern Recognition, pp. 7346–7355 (2018)

19. Tran, L., Liu, X.: On learning 3d face morphable model from in-the-wild images. IEEE Trans. Pattern Anal. Mach. Intell. 43(1), 157–171 (2019)

20. Trn, A.T., Hassner, T., Masi, I., Paz, E., Nirkin, Y., Medioni, G.: Extreme 3d face reconstruction: seeing through occlusions. In: Proceedings of the IEEE Conference on Computer Vision and Pattern Recognition, pp. 3935–3944 (2018)

21. Wu, F., et al.: MVF-Net: multi-view 3d face morphable model regression. In: Proceedings of the IEEE/CVF Conference on Computer Vision and Pattern Recognition, pp. 959–968 (2019)

22. Wu, G., et al.: AccFlow: backward accumulation for long-range optical flow. In: International Conference on Computer Vision (2023)

23. Yang, H., et al.: Facescape: A large-scale high quality 3d face dataset and detailed riggable 3d face prediction. In: IEEE/CVF Conference on Computer Vision and Pattern Recognition (CVPR) (2020)

24. Zeng, X., Peng, X., Qiao, Y.: DF2Net: a dense-fine-finer network for detailed 3d face reconstruction. In: Proceedings of the IEEE/CVF International Conference on Computer Vision, pp. 2315–2324 (2019)
25. Zhang, Z., et al.: Learning to aggregate and personalize 3d face from in-the-wild photo collection. In: Proceedings of the IEEE/CVF Conference on Computer Vision and Pattern Recognition, pp. 14214–14224 (2021)

Paraxial Geometric Optics in 3D Through Point-Based Geometric Algebra

Leo Dorst[(✉)]

Computer Vision Group Informatics Institute, University of Amsterdam, Amsterdam, The Netherlands
l.dorst@uva.nl

Abstract. The versors of a homogeneous-point-based geometric algebra $\mathbb{R}_{d,0,1}$ (dubbed HGA) are related to the basic operations in geometric paraxial optics. Odd versors represent reflections in spherical mirrors (be they concave or convex) and even versors implement the lens equation. We extend the results to arbitrarily positioned optical elements by embedding $\mathbb{R}_{d,0,1}$ into CGA $\mathbb{R}_{d+1,1}$. The total transformation through a paraxial optical system now consists of successive teleportation (by CGA dot and outer product) to the next optical center, and then applying its local HGA versors.

The result is a straightforward sequence of operations which implements a total system of arbitrarily placed paraxial lenses and mirrors in 3D (or any dimension), parameterized by their CGA tangent vectors (from each optical center to the corresponding focal point) for each optical component. This can be used to compile the homogeneous transformation matrices of a total paraxial system in terms of those geometric parameters.

Keywords: paraxial geometric optics · geometric algebra · homogeneous coordinates

1 HGA: The Geometric Algebra of Homogeneous Coordinates

Ray transfer matrices have traditionally been used to compute with planar paraxial optical systems, but in a height/slope parametrization of rays that includes a needless linearizing approximation. Recently, [1] showed that by using homogeneous coordinates in 2D, the ray matrices can be exact, and matrices for point imaging also be included. The homogeneous matrices of rigid body transformations can then be employed to process optical systems with different optical axes, still on the 2D optical table. In the present paper, we demonstrate how the geometric algebra HGA of homogeneous coordinates affords a natural parametrization to unify the imaging of geometric primitives by a generally placed system of paraxial optical elements in 3D space (with 2D still included,

© The Author(s), under exclusive license to Springer Nature Switzerland AG 2024
B. Sheng et al. (Eds.): CGI 2023, LNCS 14498, pp. 340–354, 2024.
https://doi.org/10.1007/978-3-031-50078-7_27

of course). It can then be used to generate the corresponding 4×4 homogeneous matrices, if desired.

The homogeneous coordinates of a point at location $\mathbf{x} = [x_1, \cdots, x_d]^\top$ in a Euclidean space $\mathbb{R}^d$ are obtained by adding one extra representational dimension; they are $[1, x_1, \cdots, x_d]^\top$. In geometric algebra, we introduce a basis vector e_0 for the extra dimension, and we need to decide the metric relationships for all vectors. The metric for the Euclidean part remains Euclidean (so $\mathbf{e}_i \cdot \mathbf{e}_j = \delta_{ij}$ for an orthonormal basis). Relative to the Euclidean basis vectors $\mathbf{e}_i$, we set $e_0 \cdot \mathbf{e}_i = 0$; the extra representational dimension is orthogonal to the Euclidean spatial aspects. But we will explicitly choose e_0 to be a *null vector* (i.e., $e_0^2 = 0$), so that our algebra is of signature $\mathbb{R}_{d,0,1}$; let us call it HGA, for *homogeneous geometric algebra*.

This signature differs from the 'homogeneous model' in [2] (where $e_0^2 = \pm 1$), but is used in [3] for the point-based algebra of Euclidean space. It should not be confused with the plane-based Euclidean PGA $\mathbb{R}^*_{d,0,1}$ in [4,5] (although they suggest that the Cayley-Klein approach would dually associate the different point-based GA $\mathbb{R}_{1,0,d}$ with that plane-based GA).

A point with homogeneous weight α at location $\mathbf{x}$ is represented by the HGA 1-vector:

$$X = \alpha(e_0 + \mathbf{x}),$$

employing a bold notation for the Euclidean part, and Greek for the real scalars. The null basis vector e_0 of HGA thus represents the point at the origin, where $\mathbf{x} = \mathbf{0}$. Since $X^2 = \alpha^2 \mathbf{x}^2$, the vector e_0 is *the only null point* in the algebra. Thus the origin is special in HGA; and this implies that HGA does not contain translation versors (there is no equivariant way of changing the origin). That will be an issue for using HGA in physical modelling, resolved later in this paper.

We look upon any geometric algebra through the Cartan-Dieudonné perspective: the vectors of the algebra represent reflections, their geometric product generates (as versors) the orthogonal transformations, whose application by sandwiching (aka conjugation) is equivariant for all operations and elements in the algebra. Our approach in interpreting the HGA algebra of points is therefore to determine its elementary motions by applying its vectors in a sandwiching manner; first to its vectors, then to general elements, and interpret the result. We will find that HGA is the *algebra of d-dimensional paraxial geometric optics*, with its versors representing paraxial imaging by lenses, and by spherical and planar mirrors (all with optical center at the origin). It is capable of imaging arbitrary flats (points, lines, planes), also those that are not meridional (in a plane through the optical axis; in contrast to [6], though they do go beyond the paraxial framework). The desire to concatenate the imaging by such elements leads us to extend the use of HGA in a manner that permits arbitrary translations as versors. This will be done by viewing HGA as a subalgebra of CGA $\mathbb{R}_{d+1,1}$ (conformal geometric algebra), by placing a copy of HGA $\mathbb{R}_{d,0,1}$ at each point in space.

This paper is meant to demonstrate the tools that HGA and CGA offer to encode the straightforward geometry of paraxial imaging – it is an algebraic rather than a physics treatise. Our focus is the simple parametrization of the system of paraxial lenses and mirrors that it facilitates (just locations of optical center and focus of each component), and how that immediately generates the composite imaging operators.

1.1 The Paraxial Lens Equation

Let us briefly derive the basic Gaussian lens equation of paraxial geometric optics, so that we may recognize it when it occurs in HGA. We give a derivation in the Euclidean GA $\mathbb{R}_d$ of directions, for the location of a point imaged by a thin convex lens with focal length f in the paraxial approximation of geometric optics, with Fig. 1 as our guide. Here we use a Cartesian sign convention (see e.g. [6]), in which coordinates are chosen such that the focal point is at the positive side of the lens, and the input objects at the negative side.

A point X is characterized by its location vector $\mathbf{x}$ relative to the optical center O, and the lensed result is at $\mathbf{x}' = \lambda\mathbf{x}$. If $\mathbf{x}$ is far enough from the lens, we should find $\lambda < 0$, so $\mathbf{x}'$ is at the opposite side of optical center, see Fig. 1. Algebraically and geometrically, λ is determined from the usual construction: the line from X parallel to the optical axis, which runs in the direction of the focal point vector $\mathbf{f}$, hits the lens in a point; the line from that point through the focal, point intersected with the line from X through the optical center, gives the image point. This leads to the linear equations $\mathbf{x} + \mu\mathbf{f} + \nu(\mathbf{x} + \mu\mathbf{f} - \mathbf{f}) = \lambda\mathbf{x}$ and $\mathbf{f} \cdot (\mathbf{x} + \mu\mathbf{f}) = 0$. Reduce these to scalar equations for the unknowns, by using the operations '$\mathbf{f}\wedge$' and '$\mathbf{x}\wedge$', and solve to find that the imaged point is at location

$$\mathbf{x} \mapsto \frac{\mathbf{x}}{1 + \mathbf{f}^{-1} \cdot \mathbf{x}}, \tag{1}$$

where $\mathbf{f}^{-1} \equiv \mathbf{f}/(\mathbf{f} \cdot \mathbf{f})$ is the reciprocal of $\mathbf{f}$.

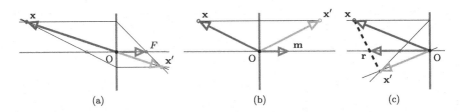

(a)   (b)   (c)

Fig. 1. (a) A convex lens in the paraxial approximation of geometric optics, viewed in a plane containing the optical axis. F and O are focal point and optical center, $\mathbf{x}$ points at the input point, $\mathbf{x}'$ at the output point imaged by the lens. (b) The reflection in a planar mirror represented by a vector $\mathbf{m}$. (c) Paraxial reflection in a spherical mirror with radial center at $\mathbf{r}$ is represented as versor sandwiching by the homogeneous point at $\mathbf{r}$. It transforms directly along the dotted line, or by the classical ray construction using a focal point halfway.

1.2   The Vectors of HGA $\mathbb{R}_{d,0,1}$

HGA $\mathbb{R}_{d,0,1}$ is an algebra in which homogeneous points are represented as vectors. We choose a basis $\{e_0, \mathbf{e}_1, \cdots, \mathbf{e}_d\}$ with $(e_0)^2 = 0$ and $\mathbf{e}_i^2 = 1$ for $i \neq 0$, the Euclidean subalgebra. There are three kinds of vectors, differing in their algebraic properties and their geometric semantics:

-   **Directions:** A purely Euclidean vector $\mathbf{m}$ represents a direction in d-dimensional space. Its inverse is $\mathbf{m}^{-1} \equiv \mathbf{m}/(\mathbf{m} \cdot \mathbf{m})$. In terms of homogeneous coordinates, one may view directions as 'ideal points', i.e., points at infinity.
-   **The origin:** The point at the origin is represented by the null vector e_0. Since the square of e_0 equals zero, it is not invertible, and therefore it cannot be used as a versor, or as a versor factor.
-   **Non-origin points:** A general point is of the form $P = \alpha(e_0 + \mathbf{p})$. Geometrically, it represents a point of weight α at the location $\mathbf{p}$. Its inverse is $P^{-1} = P/(P \cdot P) = P/(\alpha^2 \mathbf{p}^2)$, and thus exists iff $\alpha \neq 0$ and $\mathbf{p}^2 \neq 0$. It is unfortunately customary to ignore the weight α in a 'projective geometry' approach to homogeneous coordinates, but both it and its sign contain relevant information, especially for a point constructed from other primitives (such as the intersection of lines [2]). Since sandwiching is insensitive to a non-zero weight α, we will use normalized point vectors for which $\alpha = 1$ for our versor factors (though not for the arguments and results of operators!).

Let us determine the semantics of the versors we can construct from a HGA vector.

1.3   Reflection in a Direction: Planar Mirror

A purely Euclidean vector indicates a 1-dimensional direction. Such a vector versor $\mathbf{m}$ acts on a point $X = e_0 + \mathbf{x}$ by sandwiching, to produce:

$$-\mathbf{m}\,X\mathbf{m}^{-1} = -\mathbf{m}\,(e_0 + \mathbf{x})\,\mathbf{m}^{-1} = e_0 - \mathbf{m}\mathbf{x}\mathbf{m}^{-1},$$

and we recognize in $-\mathbf{m}\mathbf{x}\mathbf{m}^{-1} = (\mathbf{x}\mathbf{m} - 2(\mathbf{m} \cdot \mathbf{x}))\mathbf{m}^{-1} = \mathbf{x} - 2(\mathbf{m} \cdot \mathbf{x})\mathbf{m}^{-1}$ the reflection of the vector $\mathbf{x}$ in a plane with normal $\mathbf{m}$ passing through the origin. Thus X reflects in the origin plane with normal $\mathbf{m}$; the point is seen at the other side of the mirror, at the same perpendicular distance as X (see Fig. 1b).

1.4   Reflection in a Point: Spherical Mirror

A general unit weight vector $R = e_0 + \mathbf{r}$ (geometrically the point at location $\mathbf{r}$) can also be used in sandwiching as a versor to transform points. With $R^{-1} = R/\mathbf{r}^2$ we obtain:

$$-R\,(e_0 + \mathbf{x})/R = -(e_0 + \mathbf{r})\,(e_0 + \mathbf{x})\,(e_0 + \mathbf{r})/\mathbf{r}^2 = -e_0\mathbf{x}\mathbf{r}^{-1} - \mathbf{r}^{-1}\mathbf{x}e_0 - \mathbf{r}e_0\mathbf{r}^{-1} - \mathbf{r}\mathbf{x}\mathbf{r}^{-1}$$

$$= (1 - 2\mathbf{r}^{-1} \cdot \mathbf{x})\,e_0 - \mathbf{r}\mathbf{x}\mathbf{r}^{-1} = (1 - 2\mathbf{r}^{-1} \cdot \mathbf{x})\,\Big(e_0 + \frac{-\mathbf{r}\mathbf{x}\mathbf{r}^{-1}}{1 - 2\mathbf{r}^{-1} \cdot \mathbf{x}}\Big). \quad (2)$$

Note in Eq. 2 how the versor action produces an additional factor for e_0, proportional to the $\mathbf{r}$-component of the input term $\mathbf{x}$. In the final expression, we factored out the 'weight' of the point to expose its Euclidean location. The location is a vector proportional to the reflection of $\mathbf{x}$ in the plane with normal $\mathbf{r}$ by an $\mathbf{x}$-dependent factor $1/(1 - 2\mathbf{r}^{-1} \cdot \mathbf{x})$. If $\mathbf{r}^{-1} \cdot \mathbf{x}$ is sufficiently large, that factor is negative, and the image is a negatively weighted point at the same side of the $\mathbf{r}$-plane as the input point $\mathbf{x}$.

The outcome is almost, but not quite, entirely unlike Eq. 1: the scaling factor of the coordinates seems similar to what happens in the thin lens; but there is a strange reflection in the plane with normal $\mathbf{r}$ included, making the point end up at the wrong side.

In fact, when we take $\mathbf{r}$ on the negative side of the origin on the optical axis (in the Cartesian sign convention), this is the GA form of the formula for *reflection in a concave spherical mirror* with spherical center $R = e_0 + \mathbf{r}$, in the paraxial approximation of geometric optics, see Fig. 1a and 3a. Choosing $\mathbf{r}$ on the positive side gives a *convex spherical mirror*, see Fig. 3b. Thus *a homogeneous point R acts as a spherical mirror versor* in HGA.

1.5   The Lensing Versor $L_{\mathbf{f}}$

It is now natural to consider a lens as the combination of a spherical mirror and a reflection, so to use a versor $L = \mathbf{m}R$ to represent it. Let us see if this works; from the above we suspect that we should take $\mathbf{m} = \mathbf{r}$ and relate R to the desired focal point F.

The post-reflection factor in the plane with normal $\mathbf{r}$ gives the HGA versor:

$$\mathbf{r}\,(e_0 + \mathbf{r}) = \mathbf{r}^2 - e_0\mathbf{r} = \mathbf{r}^2\,(1 - e_0\mathbf{r}^{-1}).$$

We can divide out the factor $\mathbf{r}^2$: scaling is irrelevant since the versor is always applied in a sandwiching with its inverse. We also replace $\mathbf{r}$ by the parameter $\mathbf{f} = -\mathbf{r}/2$ (which will turn out to be the location of the focal point of the lens, in the Cartesian sign convention) so that we effectively use the versor

$$L_{\mathbf{f}} \equiv 1 + \tfrac{1}{2}e_0\mathbf{f}^{-1}.$$

This gives as a result of sandwiching the homogeneous point

$$L_{\mathbf{f}}\,(e_0 + \mathbf{x})\,L_{\mathbf{f}}^{-1} = (1 + \tfrac{1}{2}e_0\mathbf{f}^{-1})\,(e_0 + \mathbf{x})\,(1 - \tfrac{1}{2}e_0\mathbf{f}^{-1}) = e_0 + \mathbf{x} + \tfrac{1}{2}e_0\mathbf{f}^{-1}\mathbf{x} - \tfrac{1}{2}\mathbf{x}e_0\mathbf{f}^{-1}$$

$$= (1 + \mathbf{f}^{-1} \cdot \mathbf{x})\,e_0 + \mathbf{x} = (1 + \mathbf{f}^{-1} \cdot \mathbf{x})\,\Big(e_0 + \frac{\mathbf{x}}{1 + \mathbf{f}^{-1} \cdot \mathbf{x}}\Big). \tag{3}$$

The resulting location indeed corresponds to the Euclidean result of lensing of Eq. 1.

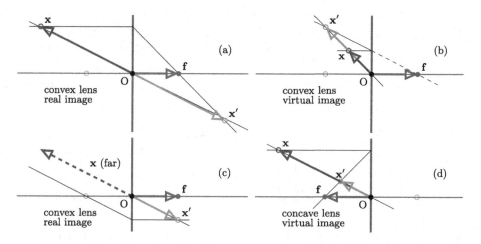

Fig. 2. Imaging a point at **x** by a lens, in the paraxial geometric optics approximation. a) convex lens, real image; b) convex lens, virtual image; c) convex lens, real image of infinite point; d) concave lens, virtual image. All situations are generated by the HGA versor $1 + e_0 \mathbf{f}^{-1}/2$, which gives $\mathbf{x}' = \mathbf{x}/(1 + \mathbf{f}^{-1} \cdot \mathbf{x})$ for the point. The versor moreover applies to lines, planes, etc.

1.6   Convex and Concave Mirrors and Lenses, Virtual Images

We thus found for the convex lens mapping:

$$L_{\mathbf{f}} (e_0 + \mathbf{x}) L_{\mathbf{f}}^{-1} = (1 + \mathbf{f}^{-1} \cdot \mathbf{x}) e_0 + \mathbf{x}, \tag{4}$$

with $L_{\mathbf{f}} = 1 + e_0 \mathbf{f}^{-1}/2$ as the versor for a thin convex lens at the origin, with focal vector $\mathbf{f}$. Like all even versors, it can also be written in an exponential form: $L_{\mathbf{f}} = \exp(e_0 \mathbf{f}^{-1}/2)$. Replacing $\mathbf{f}$ by $-\mathbf{f}$ (or taking $\mathbf{f}$ to be negative) gives the formula for a *concave lens*.

The imaged point is at $\mathbf{x}' = \mathbf{x}/(1 + \mathbf{f}^{-1} \cdot \mathbf{x})$, and corresponds to the usual construction, see Fig. 2a. It is easy to derive the common formula for object and image distances from this, by taking the dot product with the unit vector $\bar{\mathbf{f}} \equiv \mathbf{f}/\|\mathbf{f}\|$:

$$\frac{1}{\bar{\mathbf{f}} \cdot \mathbf{x}'} = \frac{1}{\bar{\mathbf{f}} \cdot \mathbf{x}} + \frac{\mathbf{f}^{-1} \cdot \mathbf{x}}{\bar{\mathbf{f}} \cdot \mathbf{x}} = \frac{1}{\bar{\mathbf{f}} \cdot \mathbf{x}} + \frac{1}{\|\mathbf{f}\|}. \tag{5}$$

Due to our formulation in terms of dot products, the 'distances' along the optical axis are *signed* distances. With the Cartesian sign convention, $\bar{\mathbf{f}} \cdot \mathbf{x}$ is negative for a convex lens, and positive for a concave lens (which has its focal point at the same 'negative' left side as the object point $\mathbf{x}$). For a concave lens, the image point is thus always at the same side as the object point; this is called a 'virtual image', Fig. 2d. For a convex lens, a virtual image happens for object points too close to the lens, namely when $0 > \bar{\mathbf{f}} \cdot \mathbf{x} > -\|\mathbf{f}\|$, see Fig. 2b.

Incidentally, one can also easily retrieve Newton's characterization of imaging by a convex lens, involving the signed distances from object and image point to the focal point at their side of the lens: $((\mathbf{x} + \mathbf{f}) \cdot \bar{\mathbf{f}}) ((\mathbf{x}' - \mathbf{f}) \cdot \bar{\mathbf{f}}) = -\|\mathbf{f}\|^2$.

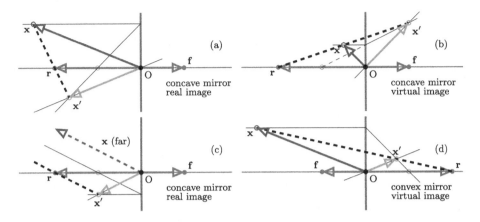

Fig. 3. Imaging a point at **x** by a spherical mirror, in the paraxial geometric optics approximation. a) concave mirror, real image; b) concave mirror, virtual image; c) concave mirror, infinite point; d) convex mirror, virtual image. All situations are captured by the HGA versor $e_0 + \mathbf{r}$, which gives $\mathbf{x}' = -\mathbf{r}\mathbf{x}\mathbf{r}^{-1}/(1 - 2\mathbf{r}^{-1} \cdot \mathbf{x})$ for the point by a special reflection along the dotted line where it intersects the reflected **x**-carrier. The versor moreover applies to lines, planes etc.

From the lens versor expression we can now return to the earlier odd versor R of a single point, simply by reflecting once more in the **f**-plane (i.e., the plane with normal **f** through the optical center). We then get a formula for the spherical mirror characterized by its 'focal point' $\mathbf{f} = -\mathbf{r}/2$ rather than by its center of curvature **r**, as

$$\mathbf{x}' = (-\mathbf{f}\,\mathbf{x}\,\mathbf{f}^{-1})/(1 + \mathbf{f}^{-1} \cdot \mathbf{x}).$$

The image is thus along the reflected ray from the optical center to **x** (reflected in the mirror). All plots of Fig. 3 show this, but also that the imaged point is along the line connecting **x** and the radius center at $\mathbf{r} = -2\mathbf{f}$, as follows from the point-like nature of the mirroring versor $e_0 + \mathbf{r}$. A convex spherical mirror is characterized by a positive $\mathbf{f}^{-1} \cdot \mathbf{x}$, and thus always results in a virtual image (at the other side of the mirror, see Fig. 3d); a concave mirror has a real image when $\mathbf{f}^{-1} \cdot \mathbf{x} < -1$, i.e. $\bar{\mathbf{f}} \cdot \mathbf{x} < -\|\mathbf{f}\|$, the object point is far enough to the left, see Fig. 3b.

Thus multiplication by **f** (normalized to $\bar{\mathbf{f}}$ if you wish) swaps the versor $L_{\mathbf{f}}$ for a *convex lens* into the versor for a *concave mirror*. All is consistent: letting $\|\mathbf{f}\|$ go to infinity (a lens with infinite focal point) shows that $\bar{\mathbf{f}}(1 + e_0\mathbf{f}^{-1})$ becomes a purely directional element $\bar{\mathbf{f}}$, and thus becomes the reflection in a planar 'lens', like the planar mirror versor **m** above.

For the lenses and mirrors, when the weight factor $1 + \mathbf{f}^{-1} \cdot \mathbf{x}$ of e_0 is positive, the point is virtual; when negative, real.

2   Imaging Arbitrary Flats

Once we have specified how points are imaged, we can of course also know how lines and planes are imaged. This is true in any formalism, but in HGA it takes a particularly simple form.

2.1   Equivariance of the Versor Mapping

The versor computation may seem needlessly involved compared to the Euclidean computation of Sect. 1.1, but it has a property that the earlier derivation lacked: it is equivariant under composing points into lines, planes etc. Any element X of the algebra representing an affine subspace (be it point, line or plane) will be imaged by the lens as

$$X \mapsto L_{\mathbf{f}} X / L_{\mathbf{f}} \quad \text{with} \quad L_{\mathbf{f}} = 1 + \tfrac{1}{2} e_0 \mathbf{f}^{-1}. \tag{6}$$

It is the integrated manner in which general flats are represented in HGA (see e.g. [2]) that enables this. A general flat in d dimensions is the element

$$A = (e_0 + \mathbf{p}) \wedge \mathbf{A},$$

with $\mathbf{A}$ its k-dimensional direction blade, and $\mathbf{p}$ a Euclidean location vector. It is formed by the outer product $\wedge$ of the algebra, which can be defined as a specific weighted linear sum of geometric products. And the geometric product of two elements transforms equivariantly under a versor L, due to its associativity:

$$(L X L^{-1})(L Y L^{-1}) = L(XY) L^{-1}.$$

It also transforms linearly:

$$L X L^{-1} + L Y L^{-1} = L(X + Y) L^{-1}.$$

So when we image a line that was constructed as the join of two points X_1 and X_2, there is no need to first image these points and then join the results to obtain the resulting line. HGA allows you to make the geometric line as the algebraic element $\ell = X_1 \wedge X_2$, and this is imaged by the versor $L_{\mathbf{f}}$ to $L_{\mathbf{f}} \ell / L_{\mathbf{f}}$; which is automatically identical to the element $(L_{\mathbf{f}} X_1 / L_{\mathbf{f}}) \wedge (L_{\mathbf{f}} X_2 / L_{\mathbf{f}})$ which would have been obtained by joining the imaged points.

Applying the versor, a general flat with directional part $\mathbf{A}$ and passing through $\mathbf{p}$ lenses to:

$$(e_0 + \mathbf{p}) \wedge \mathbf{A} \overset{L_{\mathbf{f}}}{\mapsto} (e_0 + \mathbf{p}) \wedge \mathbf{A} + e_0 \wedge (\mathbf{f}^{-1} \cdot (\mathbf{p} \wedge \mathbf{A}) = e_0 \wedge (\mathbf{A} + \mathbf{f}^{-1} \cdot (\mathbf{p} \wedge \mathbf{A})) + \mathbf{p} \wedge \mathbf{A}. \tag{7}$$

This uses $\mathbf{x} \wedge \mathbf{A} = \tfrac{1}{2}(\mathbf{x} \mathbf{A} + \widehat{\mathbf{A}} \mathbf{x})$ with $\widehat{\mathbf{A}} \equiv (-1)^{\text{grade}(\mathbf{A})} \mathbf{A}$, with the grade being the dimensionality of a blade, i.e., its number of outer product factors. Note that if $\mathbf{A} = 1$, the flat is a point, and we retrieve the earlier Eq. 4.

2.2   Homogeneous Matrix Representation

If you wish, you could compose a *matrix* for the linear map $X \mapsto L_{\mathbf{f}} X / L_{\mathbf{f}}$, rather than characterize it by a versor. However, this matrix would depend on the type of element X (just like the 2D homogeneous matrices from [1]). If X was a 3D point, you would express it on the 4D basis $\{e_0, \mathbf{e}_1, \mathbf{e}_2, \mathbf{e}_3\}$, by transforming each of the basis vectors and finding the transformed coefficients as columns of a 4×4 matrix. If X was a 3D line, you would express it on the 6D basis $\{\mathbf{e}_{01}, \mathbf{e}_{02}, \mathbf{e}_{03}, \mathbf{e}_{23}, \mathbf{e}_{31}, \mathbf{e}_{12}\}$ of Plücker coordinates, by transforming each of the basis bivectors and finding the transformed coefficients as columns of a 6×6 matrix.

For points, it follows from $L_{\mathbf{f}}(e_0 + \mathbf{p})/L_{\mathbf{f}} = (1 + \mathbf{f}^{-1} \cdot \mathbf{p})e_0 + \mathbf{p}$ that the matrix representation of $\underline{L}_{\mathbf{f}}$ on a homogeneous vector $[\mathbf{p}^{\top}, 1]^{\top}$ is:

$$\begin{bmatrix} \mathbf{p} \\ 1 \end{bmatrix} \overset{L_{\mathbf{f}}}{\mapsto} \begin{bmatrix} [1] & \mathbf{0} \\ [\mathbf{f}^{-1}]^{\top} & 1 \end{bmatrix} \begin{bmatrix} \mathbf{p} \\ 1 \end{bmatrix}.$$

For lines in 3D, we effectively have a Plücker coordinate representation on a bivector basis, but this is usually encoded on a 6D vector basis. We can convert the outer product on a coordinate basis to the classical cross product and its corresponding matrix. We find after some manipulation using $\mathbf{f}^{-1} \cdot (\mathbf{p} \wedge \mathbf{u}) = \mathbf{f}^{-1} \times (\mathbf{p} \times \mathbf{u}) \equiv [\mathbf{f}^{-1}]^{\times}(\mathbf{p} \times \mathbf{u})$:

$$\begin{bmatrix} \mathbf{u} \\ \mathbf{p} \times \mathbf{u} \end{bmatrix} \overset{L_{\mathbf{f}}}{\mapsto} \begin{bmatrix} [1] & \mathbf{0} \\ [\mathbf{f}^{-1}]^{\times} & 1 \end{bmatrix} \begin{bmatrix} \mathbf{u} \\ \mathbf{p} \times \mathbf{u} \end{bmatrix}.$$

Note that the line transformation matrix works on any 3D line, not just those in a plane containing the optical axis.

3D planes in HGA are represented as $(e_0 + \mathbf{p}) \wedge \mathbf{N}$, with $\mathbf{N}$ a Euclidean unit 2-vector. In homogeneous coordinates one uses the unit normal vector $\mathbf{m} = \mathbf{N}\mathbf{e}_3\mathbf{e}_2\mathbf{e}_1$ and the scalar signed distance $\delta = \mathbf{p} \cdot \mathbf{m}$. Re-expressing Eq. 7 in those parameters, the plane transforms as:

$$\begin{bmatrix} \mathbf{m} \\ -\delta \end{bmatrix} \overset{L_{\mathbf{f}}}{\mapsto} \begin{bmatrix} [1] & -[\mathbf{f}^{-1}] \\ \mathbf{0}^{\top} & 1 \end{bmatrix} \begin{bmatrix} \mathbf{m} \\ -\delta \end{bmatrix}.$$

The homogeneous coordinate matrices should look familiar from the literature on imaging in computer graphics. If you need to transform many elements of the same type (points, lines), then these matrices may offer a computational advantage. But note that they lose the explicit connection between the transformations of points and lines (and planes). Explicitly computing the proper matrices is better left to an LA compiler, based on an algebraic specification at the symbolic level of the required computation given by the HGA approach, or more generally by the CGA approach that follows.

3   Paraxial Geometric Optics Anywhere in Space

The null vector e_0 encoding the optical center makes the lensing versor work properly. If we want to move the lens to another location than the origin, we therefore need a null vector at that new location. That is not possible in HGA, where e_0 is the only null point. Rigid body motions are simply not among the versors of HGA, all of which we just exposed.

3.1 Placing a HGA at Any Spatial Location

We move to the larger algebra CGA $\mathbb{R}_{d+1,1}$ (conformal geometric algebra), which has *all* points as null vectors, and construct a copy of HGA at every point. Then locally, we can perform the lens versor construction we had before at any point we like. Concatenation of lenses will then be done by hopping from one optical center to the next, for each choosing the corresponding algebraic embedding.

CGA is the algebra of spheres, and (by their intersections) of circles, point pairs, in general 'rounds'. It does contain planes, lines, points, but those 'flat' elements are based on spheres passing through infinity. Precisely those flat elements correspond to the geometric primitives of HGA. Since in CGA planes can be (dually) represented by vectors, among its versors are multiple reflections in planes, which generate the motions of Euclidean geometry. Therefore CGA allows us to produce Euclidean equivariant constructions, which HGA could not. And because CGA thus has translation versors, we will be able to put lenses anywhere, and construct composite optical systems.

We will use CGA with its null basis elements o and ∞ orthogonal to the Euclidean basis $\mathbf{e}_1, \cdots, \mathbf{e}_d$ [2]. The null basis vector o can be interpreted as the CGA origin point (though any point may be taken as origin, since CGA is translation invariant), and the null basis vector ∞ can be interpreted as the point at infinity. The two are related by $o \cdot \infty = -1$, using the dot product of CGA.

A point at location $\mathbf{p}$ in CGA is represented by the vector $p = o + \mathbf{p} + \frac{1}{2}\mathbf{p}^2 \infty$; this is a null vector. The origin point of HGA denoted by its null vector e_0 seems to correspond naturally to the vector o of CGA; however, the whole purpose of embedding into CGA is our desire to have a HGA at *any* point p of CGA. Since any CGA point is a null vector (a sphere of zero radius), such recasting will not affect the local algebra and geometry of lensing as designed with HGA.

A geometrical point, such as might occur in the intersection of a line and a plane, is a 'flat point' in CGA, of the form $p \wedge \infty$, since those intersecting flat elements always also have the point at infinity ∞ in common. A unit flat point squares to 1: $(p \cdot \infty)^2 = (\infty \cdot p)^2 = 1$. The flat point can be rewritten as $p \wedge \infty = (o + \mathbf{p}) \wedge \infty$, and we recognize in the first factor a natural identification with the point representation $e_0 + \mathbf{p}$ of HGA. With the identification of the origin elements of the two algebras $e_0 = o$, we can write the HGA point $e_0 + \mathbf{p}$ as an element $o + \mathbf{p}$ of CGA,[1] parametrized by CGA point p:

$$e_0 + \mathbf{p} \leftrightarrow o + \mathbf{p} = o \cdot (-\infty \wedge p). \tag{8}$$

---

[1] Considered as an element of CGA, $o \cdot (-\infty \wedge p)$ is geometrically an oriented dual sphere with center p, and passing through o. While that geometric interpretation can be maintained through the subsequent algebra, it is rather distracting, so we will not emphasize it.

This final form of the point representation contains explicitly the point o which we took as the origin of our local HGA. Without changing the algebra, we can now choose any other CGA point as corresponding to the null vector e_0 of HGA; then a HGA point at location $\mathbf{x}$ but viewed from another 'origin' c is represented by the CGA element:

$$x|_c \equiv c \cdot (-\infty \wedge x). \tag{9}$$

where c and x are CGA points. You may pronounce '$|_c$' as 'from c'. This operation considers x in a copy of HGA at the location c. It is structure-preserving: the formation of new elements by the HGA outer product is equivariantly preserved by this construction (it is a *linear outermorphism*):

$$x|_c \wedge y|_c = \big(c \cdot (-\infty \wedge x)\big) \wedge \big(c \cdot (-\infty \wedge y)\big) = \big(x + \infty \wedge (c \cdot x)\big) \wedge \big(y + \infty \wedge (c \cdot y)\big)$$
$$= x \wedge y - \infty \wedge x \wedge (c \cdot y) + \infty \wedge (c \cdot x) \wedge y = x \wedge y + \infty \wedge \big(c \cdot (x \wedge y)\big) = c \cdot (-\infty \wedge x \wedge y)$$
$$= (x \wedge y)|_c. \tag{10}$$

Therefore an arbitrary HGA element X (point, line, plane, direction element) can be embedded into CGA as a 'from c'-element through:

$$X \mapsto X|_c \equiv c \cdot (-\infty \wedge X), \tag{11}$$

(where we substitute HGA's e_0 always by CGA's o before putting X in the 'from c' formula, to make the formula computable within CGA). Note that $c|_c = c$. The original HGA element X can be retrieved from this as:

$$X|_c \mapsto X = o \cdot \big(-\infty \wedge (X|_c)\big), \tag{12}$$

and then substituting $e_0 \mapsto o$ (to formally get out of CGA back to standard HGA). Therefore the re-representation of HGA element X as CGA element $X|_c$ is *invertible*.

A highly useful property is that the 'from c' mapping can be applied multiple times, but that the result only depends on the *last* application (we could call this '*neopotent*', it is more general than 'idempotent'):

$$(X|_{c_1})|_{c_2} = X|_{c_2}. \tag{13}$$

This is easily shown:

$$(X|_{c_1})|_{c_2} = c_2 \cdot (-\infty \wedge (c_1 \cdot (-\infty \wedge X))) = c_2 \cdot (-\infty \wedge (X + \infty \wedge (c_1 \cdot X)) = c_2 \cdot (-\infty \wedge X) = X|_{c_2}.$$

We can therefore always rerepresent a rerepresented element, and in a concatenation of operations there is no need to revert from $X|_c$ to the original X before we can perform the next step. Jumping to a new viewpoint c is not a relative translation, but an absolute teleportation.

3.2   The HGA Lens Versor in CGA

For a lens with optical center c, we should move its lens versor (which was $\exp(\frac{1}{2}e_0 \wedge \mathbf{f}^{-1})$ at the origin) also to that location. With the substitution $e_0 \mapsto o$, the lens versor becomes a versor $\exp(\frac{1}{2}o \wedge \mathbf{f}^{-1})$ in CGA (it is a conformal transformation called a *transversion*, see [2]). It involves the CGA tangent vector $o \wedge \mathbf{f}^{-1}$, and it and its versor can be moved to c by the CGA translation versor $\exp(-\infty \wedge \mathbf{c}/2)$, which transforms that tangent vector into

$$\ell_{c,\mathbf{f}} \equiv c \wedge (\mathbf{f}^{-1} + (\mathbf{f}^{-1} \cdot \mathbf{c})\, \infty). \tag{14}$$

Perhaps more elegantly, we can rewrite the original tangent vector at the origin as:

$$o \wedge \mathbf{f}^{-1} = o/(o \wedge \infty \wedge \mathbf{f}) = o/(o \wedge \infty \wedge f),$$

with f the CGA version of the focal point, and then simply substitute c for o to move it. That gives the same result as the translation versor approach, but in a factorized geometric format (as a point divided by a line through it):[2]

$$\ell_{c,f} = c/(c \wedge \infty \wedge f) = c/(c \wedge \infty \wedge \mathbf{f}), \tag{15}$$

with f the focal point, and $\mathbf{f}$ the relative vector from c to f. Note that in this format, either point f or relative vector $\mathbf{f}$ could be used as input parameter for an identically defined function computing the tangent vector; no conversion is required since $c \wedge \infty \wedge f = c \wedge \infty \wedge \mathbf{f}$. With that tangent vector $\ell_{c,f}$, the lens versor is:

$$L_{c,f} = \exp(\tfrac{1}{2}\ell_{c,f}) = 1 + \tfrac{1}{2}\ell_{c,f}. \tag{16}$$

The full lens mapping cannot simply be this CGA versor applied to a CGA point – that would be a conformal transformation, and lensing is not (it transforms circles to ellipses, not to other circles as a conformal map would).[3] In our local copy of HGA at the point c, the lens versor should act on an element X by first converting that to the 'relative to c' form $X|_c$ and then applying the c-based versor:

$$X \;\mapsto\; X'|_c = L_{c,f}\,(X|_c)\,L_{c,f}^{-1} \equiv \underline{L_{c,f}}[X|_c]. \tag{17}$$

(The underline notation is a common compact way to denote the versor sandwiching/conjugation operation.) The result $X'|_c$ is again a 'from c' type element of CGA. The corresponding flat element is $-\infty \wedge (X'|_c)$, but it is more

---

[2] To show that this is equivalent to Eq. 14, we compute: $c/(c \wedge \infty \wedge f) = c \cdot (c \wedge \infty \wedge f)/(c \wedge \infty \wedge f)^2 = c \cdot (c \wedge \infty \wedge (f-c))/(-2(c \cdot f)^2) = c \cdot (c \wedge \infty \wedge \mathbf{f})/\mathbf{f}^2 = c \cdot (c \wedge \infty \wedge \mathbf{f}^{-1}) = c \wedge (\mathbf{f}^{-1} + (\mathbf{f}^{-1} \cdot \mathbf{c}) \wedge \infty)$.

[3] Actually, in CGA $X|_c$ is a round element (a sphere for a point, a circle for a line, a point pair for a plane), and the versor $L_{c,f}$ maps it to another round element of the same kind, so a conformal transformation does take place; but only on the CGA-embedded version $X|_c$ of X, not on X itself.

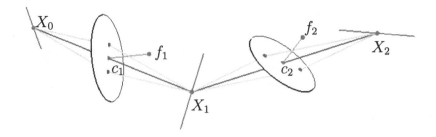

Fig. 4. Propagation of a point on a line through two lenses parametrized by centers and foci in 3D using Eq. 20 implemented in GAviewer [7].

convenient to keep it in the 'from c' form if one wants to apply another lens to it next. We can write Eq. 17 more explicitly, and rewrite slightly, using $\underline{L_{c,f}}[c] = c$:

$$c \cdot (-\infty \wedge X') = \underline{L_{c,f}}[c \cdot (-\infty \wedge X)] = c \cdot \underline{L_{c,f}}[-\infty \wedge X]. \tag{18}$$

The latter shows clearly that the lens versor action is concentrated on the flat elements of CGA, of the form $-\infty \wedge X$. We cannot also pull ∞ out of the versor, since ∞ is not invariant under the action of $L_{c,f}$.[4]

The spherical mirroring versor $R = o - 2\mathbf{f}$ can also be brought into a form in which it may be parametrized by either the relative Euclidean vector $\mathbf{f}$ or by the CGA point f, namely:

spherical mirror versor R at c with focus f: $R = c - 2\,(c \wedge \infty \wedge f)/(c \wedge \infty)$.

Remember from general GA that this odd versor should be applied to an element $X|_c$ as $\underline{R}[X|_c] = R\,\widehat{X}|_c\,R^{-1}$, the grade involution $\widehat{}$ giving a minus sign for odd-grade X. Only then do weight signs in the homogeneous representation maintain their geometric meaning.

3.3   Concatenation of Lenses

With the above, one can compute the paraxial image of an element X in HGA through a succession of n lenses and/or mirrors in d-dimensional space, by the CGA embedding.

1. Let the lenses have optical centers at CGA points c_i, and focal points at CGA points f_i (or have relative focal vectors $\mathbf{f}_i$ from their c_i). Form the *lens versors*

$$L_i \equiv 1 + \tfrac{1}{2}\,c_i/(c_i \wedge \infty \wedge f_i) \tag{19}$$

---

[4] In fact, $L\infty/L = \mathsf{T}_{\mathbf{c}+2\mathbf{f}}[o]/(2\mathbf{f}^2)$, a conformal point at location $\mathbf{c}+2\mathbf{f}$. The 'point at infinity' in HGA is not ∞, but $o+\mathbf{x}$ for large $\|\mathbf{x}\|$; it maps to a point on the parallel plane at $\mathbf{f}$ behind the lens, at location $(\mathbf{f}^{-1} \cdot \mathbf{x})/\mathbf{x})^{-1}$ determined by the direction of $\mathbf{x}$.

or the *spherical mirror versor* $R_i = c_i - 2(c_i \wedge \infty) \cdot (c_i \wedge \infty \wedge f_i)$, or the *planar mirror versor* $M_i = (c_i \wedge \infty) \cdot (c_i \wedge \infty \wedge \mathbf{f}_i)$ (for which $\mathbf{f}_i$ is the mirror normal vector pointing from c_i to f_i).

2. Embed the HGA element X into CGA by replacing its e_0 by o. Then perform the iteration:

$$X_0 = X, \quad X_i = c_i \cdot \underline{L_i}[-\infty \wedge X_{i-1}] \quad \text{for} \quad i = 1, \cdots, n. \tag{20}$$

(or similarly for $\underline{R_i}[]$ and $\underline{M_i}[]$, with the grade involution in both sandwichings).

3. After processing all n optical elements, the result is $X' = o \cdot (-\infty \wedge X_n)$ relative to an origin o; it can be converted back to HGA by replacing o by e_0, if desired.

Figure 4 shows a 3D example of a point and line imaged through two lenses by this method, using GAviewer [7].

3.4   Generating Optical System Matrices

Since any flat geometric primitive can be propagated through the system, it is now easy to find the total homogeneous matrix for a composition of optical elements, for any flat geometric element. For instance, if you need the matrix for the imaging of an arbitrary 3D line, use the Plücker coordinate basis $\{e_{01}, e_{02}, e_{03}, e_{23}, e_{31}, e_{12}\}$ to represent both it and the result. Simply process the i-th basis element by Eq. 20 and denote the resulting components as the i-th column of the transformation matrix. This extends the 2D techniques of [1] to 3D, and conveniently parametrizes the system by the absolute position and focal points of the optical elements.

4   Conclusion

We have shown that by using the geometric algebra HGA $\mathbb{R}_{d,0,1}$ of points, directly related to homogeneous point coordinates, one obtains an extended set of tools to handle paraxial optics. To build composite paraxial systems, one embeds HGA in CGA $\mathbb{R}_{d+1,1}$. The versorial form of the resulting lensing equation means that arbitrary flat elements (points, lines, planes etc.) can be imaged by exactly the same formulas. The parametrization, by merely the location of optical center and focal point of each component of the system, is very easy to use in specifications of composite 3D paraxial optical systems. The versors can be used to generate homogeneous ray tracing matrices in 3D, considerably extending current 2D capabilities.

References

1. Corcovilos, T.: Beyond the ABCDs: a better matrix method for geometric optics by using homogeneous coordinates. Am. J. Phys. **91**, 449–457 (2023)

2. Dorst, L., Fontijne, D., Mann, S.: Geometric Algebra for Computer Science: An Object-oriented Approach to Geometry. Morgan Kaufman, Burlington (2009)
3. Lengyel, E.: (2022). https://projectivegeometricalgebra.org/
4. Gunn, C.: On the homogeneous model of Euclidean geometry. In: Dorst, L., Lasenby, J. (eds.) Guide to Geometric in Practice, pp. 297–327. Springer, London (2011). https://doi.org/10.1007/978-0-85729-811-9_15
5. Gunn, C.: Geometric algebras for Euclidean geometry. Adv. Appl. Clifford Algebras **27**(1), 185–208 (2016). https://doi.org/10.1007/s00006-016-0647-0
6. Sugon, Q., McNamara, D.: Paraxial meridional ray tracing equations from the unified reflection-refraction law via geometric algebra (2008). https://arxiv.org/abs/0810.5224
7. Dorst, L., Fontijne, D.: 3D Euclidean geometry through conformal geometric algebra (a GAViewer tutorial). http://www.science.uva.nl/ga/

Camera Motion Correction with PGA

Danail Brezov[1][(✉)] and Michael Werman[2]

[1] Department of Mathematics UACEG,
1 Hristo Smirnenski Blvd., 1046 Sofia, Bulgaria
`danail.brezov@gmail.com`
[2] The School of Computer Science, The Hebrew University of Jerusalem,
428 Rothberg, Jerusalem, Israel
`michael.werman@mail.huji.ac.il`

Abstract. In this paper we study the geometry and kinematics of stabilizing a moving camera in order to track a stationary scene both in the 2D and 3D setting. This is being done initially in a rather straightforward manner, using the tools of analytic and differential geometry, after which we discuss the advantages of the so-called 'projective geometric algebra' (PGA) approach in this context. In the planar case one can easily get equivalent results with complex numbers, but in 3D it is a convenient substitute for Plücker line geometry and the theory of screws. While a lot can be done using quaternions and differential geometry, PGA is quite handy when there are different rotation or screw axes involved. Its basic constructions and properties are briefly summarized in the appendix.

Keywords: surveillance drones · attitude kinematics · differential geometry · camera motion correction · PGA

1 Introduction

Video stabilization designed to eliminate shakiness or blurriness has three main types: digital, optical, and mechanical [1,2]. Digital stabilization estimates the motion vectors of the successive frames and warps the images to compensate for the motion. Optical stabilization is widely used in smartphones and SLR cameras. This stabilization moves the lens group on a plane perpendicular to the optical axis to offset image vibration. Mechanical stabilization usually employs a gyroscopic stabilizer. One more recent application of these types of problems has been used to control a drone for cinematography [3,4] and of course, there are also new methods based on deep learning [5]. Our analysis is especially relevant to mechanical stabilization where we have some control over the pose of the camera and want to keep it pointed at a static object and preserving the initial orientation. We first derive our results in a classical manner and only then discuss the advantages of the PGA approach. Examples for illustration are given as well.

© The Author(s), under exclusive license to Springer Nature Switzerland AG 2024
B. Sheng et al. (Eds.): CGI 2023, LNCS 14498, pp. 355–367, 2024.
https://doi.org/10.1007/978-3-031-50078-7_28

2   The Planar Setting

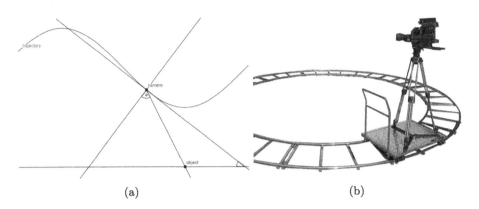

(a)   (b)

Fig. 1. Camera following a smooth plane trajectory while keeping a static object in sight (a) and a primitive version of the 'Dolly' camera-on-rails system (b).

We begin with a simple setting used in cinema: the camera K moves along straight tracks at constant speed v and the object, O, being filmed is static, at non-zero distance d from the tracks. It is convenient to choose a Cartesian coordinate system with O at the origin, in which the camera's path ℓ has the slope-intercept equation $y = kx + n$. Note also that the counter-clockwise orientation angle $\varphi(t)$ added in order keep the camera pointing to O at all times (with $\varphi = 0$ along the normal to ℓ) varies as K follows its path according to

$$\varphi = -\arctan\frac{x}{y} - \arctan k \quad \Rightarrow \quad \dot\varphi = \frac{x\dot y - y\dot x}{x^2 + y^2}. \tag{1}$$

The problem becomes much more interesting if we allow the camera to follow a generic smooth path γ in the plane (Fig. 1a), in this case, the orientation φ is corrected by the angle equal to $\arctan y'$, i.e. the one the tangent makes with O_x

$$\varphi = -\arctan\frac{x}{y} - \arctan y'(x) = -\arctan\frac{x}{y} - \arctan\frac{\dot y}{\dot x} \tag{2}$$

where for the second equality it is convenient to use the time-parametrization for the curve $\gamma : \mathbf{r} = \mathbf{r}(t)$. It allows us to compute the angular velocity via

$$\dot\varphi = \frac{\mathbf{r} \wedge \dot{\mathbf{r}}}{\mathbf{r}^2} - \frac{\dot{\mathbf{r}} \wedge \ddot{\mathbf{r}}}{\dot{\mathbf{r}}^2} = \frac{\mathbf{r} \wedge \mathbf{v}}{\mathbf{r}^2} - |\mathbf{v}|\kappa \tag{3}$$

where $\mathbf{v}(t) = \dot{\mathbf{r}}(t)$ is the linear velocity and $\kappa(t)$ stands for the curvature of γ. On the other had, the orientation angle is easily determined using the wedge and dot products of the radius-vector $\mathbf{r}(t)$ parameterizing γ with the normal $\mathbf{n}(t)$ as

$$\varphi = \arctan\frac{\mathbf{r} \wedge \mathbf{n}}{\mathbf{r} \cdot \mathbf{n}} = \arctan\frac{\langle\mathbf{rn}\rangle_2}{\langle\mathbf{rn}\rangle_0} = \ln(\mathbf{rn}). \tag{4}$$

For example, if γ is introduced as a level curve with the implicit function $F(x,y) = const.$, we use the gradient (∇-operator) to determine the normal $\mathbf{n} = \nabla F$ corresponding to $\varphi = 0$ at any point. In particular, for parameterized $\gamma = \gamma(t)$ and explicitly given curves $\gamma : y = y(x)$ the above provides respectively

$$\varphi = \arctan \frac{x\dot{x} + y\dot{y}}{y\dot{x} - x\dot{y}}, \qquad \varphi = \arctan \frac{x + yy'}{y - xy'}. \tag{5}$$

Apart from being covariant, formula (4) is written in terms of operations in the geometric algebra $\mathrm{Cliff}(\mathbb{R}^2)$, namely the ratio of the bivector and the scalar part of the geometric product $\mathbf{rn}$. But the even subalgebra in this case is $\mathbb{C}$, so we may use the complex representation $\gamma : z = x(t) + iy(t)$ and a few tricks from elementary trigonometry to obtain

$$\varphi = \arctan \frac{\ln' |z|}{\arg' z} = \arg (i\bar{z}\dot{z}). \tag{6}$$

In particular, if we choose a circular trajectory around the object of interest, i.e., $\gamma : z = re^{i\omega_o t}$ $(\omega_o > 0)$, so

$$\dot{z} = ir\omega_o e^{i\omega_o t} \quad \Rightarrow \quad i\bar{z}\dot{z} = -r^2\omega_o \in \mathbb{R}^-$$

which yields $\varphi = \pi$. Similarly, (3) now takes the form[1]

$$\dot{\varphi} = r^{-2}\mathrm{Im}(\bar{z}\dot{z}) - r^{-1}|\dot{z}| = \omega_o - \omega_o = 0$$

since the curvature on the circle is the inverse radius.

Note that the ambiguity in the angle φ has several reasons. Firstly, it is associated with the choice of default orientation ($\varphi = 0$) which we relate to the normal direction, but instead one may use the tangent vector, which in a way is more natural and makes sense also in the 3D setting. Secondly, the orientation of the normal is ambiguous itself until we link the parametrization to a given direction of motion, then we assume $\mathbf{n}$ points to the right with respect to $\mathbf{v}$, i.e., $\mathbf{n} \wedge \mathbf{v} > 0$. Thirdly, the 'arctan' function yields only solutions in half the circle, so one may use the so called 'proper quadrant inverse tangent' $\mathrm{atan}_2(y, x)$ instead as it takes into account the individual signs of x and y, e.g. $\mathrm{atan}_2(1, -1) \neq \mathrm{atan}_2(-1, 1)$ and the two differ by π which remains hidden in the usual inverse tangent. Also, since we use polar angles, there is a coordinate singularity at the origin, resulting in a phase shift by π. However, it is safe to assume that the camera will not move directly through the object which is being observed, due to the laws of physics.

---

[1] the cancellation of the two terms is well known from geostationary satellites and other cases of circular orbits (see Fig. 1b).

3   Cameras Floating in Space

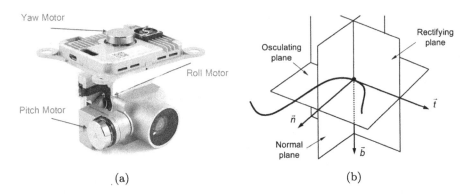

Fig. 2. Camera's gimbal axes (a); the Frenet frame of a smooth spatial curve (b).

As in the previous section, we begin with a simplified version of the problem considering aircraft with the ability to spin around its axis which floats along a straight trajectory ℓ (assuming $O \notin \ell$). Since ℓ and O determine a unique plane α, we simply refer to our previous solution (1) using coordinates in α. However, it is not always convenient to change the coordinate system so we may instead resort to vector covariance and simply write

$$\varphi = \pm \arctan \frac{\mathbf{r} \cdot \dot{\mathbf{r}}}{|\mathbf{r} \times \dot{\mathbf{r}}|}, \qquad \dot{\varphi} = \pm \frac{|\mathbf{r} \times \dot{\mathbf{r}}|}{\mathbf{r}^2} \qquad (7)$$

where the sign depends on the choice or normal to ℓ and the orientation of the plane, according to our previous convention. Every plane trajectory γ may be treated in this manner as long as O belongs to the same plane: the default camera axis at $\varphi = 0$ will then be restricted to α as well. Otherwise, we need spherical coordinates with azimuth $\vartheta \in \left[0, \frac{\pi}{2}\right]$ measuring the deviation from the vertical axis, while φ remains a polar angle measuring the camera rotation in the plane α determined by γ and the above results apply to it if we replace O with its orthogonal projection O' in α. As for ϑ, using the altitude h of α and

$$\rho = \sqrt{x^2 + y^2}$$

as a radial variable measuring the distance to O', one can easily show that

$$\vartheta = \arctan \frac{\rho}{h}, \qquad \dot{\vartheta} = \frac{h\dot{\rho}}{h^2 + \rho^2}. \qquad (8)$$

Although this particular setting is rather specific, plane trajectories are important for the applications, e.g. in the case of surveillance drones at fixed altitude.

Let us briefly discuss the PGA approach in this relatively simple setting. Firstly, we need the construction of α for which it is sufficient to have three points $P_i \in \gamma$ and use the 'join' operator: $\alpha = P_1 \vee P_2 \vee P_3$. The projection of O in α is given as $\Pi_\alpha(O) = (O \cdot \alpha)\alpha^{-1}$ and we define ρ as the magnitude of the projection $\Pi_\alpha(\mathbf{r})$.

Finally, we are going to approach the general 3D setting in the context of relative orientation and parallel transport in the frame bundle (see [6] for more details). The moving Frenet frame $\{K\}$ attached to the camera is spanned by the unit tangent, normal and binormal vectors $\{\mathbf{t}, \mathbf{n}, \mathbf{b}\}$. On the other hand, the aircraft has its local frame $\{K'\}$ determined by the three axes allowing for attitude adjustment, labeled respectively 'roll', 'pitch' and 'yaw' (see Fig. 2a) and at some point we are going to need the relations between the $\{K\}$, $\{K'\}$ and $\{O\}$ frames.

This local frame $\{K\}$ evolves according to the famous Frenet-Serret equations

$$\begin{pmatrix} \dot{\mathbf{t}} \\ \dot{\mathbf{n}} \\ \dot{\mathbf{b}} \end{pmatrix} = |\mathbf{v}| \begin{pmatrix} 0 & \kappa & 0 \\ -\kappa & 0 & \tau \\ 0 & -\tau & 0 \end{pmatrix} \begin{pmatrix} \mathbf{t} \\ \mathbf{n} \\ \mathbf{b} \end{pmatrix} \tag{9}$$

where κ and τ are respectively the curvature and torsion of γ defined as

$$\kappa = \frac{|\dot{\mathbf{r}} \times \ddot{\mathbf{r}}|}{|\dot{\mathbf{r}}|^3}, \qquad \tau = \frac{(\dot{\mathbf{r}} \times \ddot{\mathbf{r}}) \cdot \dddot{\mathbf{r}}}{|\dot{\mathbf{r}} \times \ddot{\mathbf{r}}|^2} \tag{10}$$

and if we consider both the aircraft and the camera as point objects, it has the same center as $\{K'\}$ in aircraft typically the 'roll' axis is collinear with $\mathbf{t}$ at all times due to aerodynamics, so the two frames are calibrated by a simple (typically small) phase shift $\phi \in \mathbb{S}^1$ between $\mathbf{b}$ and the 'yaw' axis in the common normal plane (Fig. 2b). The default orientation of the camera would be downwards when the two axes coincide, so ϕ provides one source of correction to the azimuthal angle ϑ. Another one would be the changing orientation of K with respect to O described by the system of ODE's (9) and a third one: the translational component of this change. We discuss these in the following sections.

At the initial moment of departure, one may choose a common orientation for the three frames, but even then O appears on the screen relative to the distance vector $\mathbf{r}$ connecting it with K. More precisely, the position on the viewing sphere would be given by the spherical coordinates of its normalized reverse $-|\mathbf{r}|^{-1}\mathbf{r}$. As the aircraft travels along $\mathbf{r} = \mathbf{r}(t)$ this point moves on $\mathbb{S}^2$ accordingly and at the same time the unit sphere itself undergoes two rotations: one described by the Frenet equations (9) and another one calibrating the axes of $\{K\}$ and $\{K'\}$ via the phase ϕ. While the latter yields more of an engineering problem, the former one is quite interesting even from a purely mathematical perspective.

4   Parallel Transport and Calibration

In this section we formulate the general 3D problem in more abstract terms in an attempt to provide a covariant solution, similar to (3). To begin with, the geometry and kinematics are modeled on the pull-back $\iota^\star$ of the (orthogonal) frame bundle $\mathcal{F}(\mathbb{E}^3)$ over affine 3-space, given by the inclusion map $\iota : \gamma \to \mathbb{E}^3$, i.e., the curve's parametrization. Since we know that $\mathcal{F}(\mathbb{E}^3)$ is identical with the Euclidean group $E(3)$, the fibre of $\mathcal{F}(\gamma) = \iota^\star \mathcal{F}(\mathbb{E}^3)$ over any given base point $\mathbf{r}_\circ = \mathbf{r}(t_\circ)$ on γ is isomorphic to $SO(3)$. For the Frenet frame $\{K\}$ this fibre is described by the orthogonal matrix $A(t_\circ) = \{\mathbf{t}, \mathbf{n}, \mathbf{b}\}_{\mathbf{r}_\circ}$ whose entries are the coordinates of the unit tangent, normal and binormal vectors at $\mathbf{r}_\circ \in \gamma$ in the standard basis, associated with the fixed frame $\{O\}$. The time-evolution of this matrix is given by (9), which one may also define with its kinematic equation

$$\dot{A} = A\omega \quad \Rightarrow \quad \omega = A^t \dot{A} = \mathbf{\Omega}^\times \in \mathfrak{so}_3 \qquad (11)$$

where $\mathbf{\Omega}(t) = |\mathbf{v}|\,(\tau,\,0,\,\kappa)^t$ is the angular velocity of $\{K\}$ whose adjoint yields the generator $\omega(t)$ in the Lie algebra of the orthogonal group. In particular, for plane curves $\tau = 0$ and the solutions are rotations about the binormal vector with angle given by the line integral

$$\varphi(t) = \int_{t_\circ}^{t} \kappa(t)\,\mathrm{d}s(t), \qquad \mathrm{d}s = |\mathbf{v}|\mathrm{d}t \qquad (12)$$

while for the general case, it is convenient to use quaternion description with $q \in SU(2)$ and kinematic equation

$$\dot{q} = \frac{1}{2}\hat{\omega}q, \qquad \hat{\omega} = i|\mathbf{v}|\begin{pmatrix} \tau & \kappa \\ \kappa & -\tau \end{pmatrix} \in \mathfrak{su}_2. \qquad (13)$$

The latter may easily be integrated in the case of constant curvature or more generally, as long as $\hat{\omega}$ commutes with its integral, the above time-ordered exponent reduces to a regular one (see [7]). The path $q(t)$ on $\mathbb{S}^3$ is then projected to $A(t) \in SO(3)$ and its action on $p(t)$, i.e., the trace of $-\mathbf{r}(t)$ on $\mathbb{S}^2$, yields the camera orientation in $\{K\}$. Finally, to calibrate $\{K\}$ and $\{K'\}$, we perform an additional rotation by an angle ϕ about the tangent $\mathbf{t}$. As already pointed out, this is an engineering problem depending on the particular hardware setting. For some applications it may not be needed to invoke the use of $\{K\}$ at all: the camera's local frame would be determined by the attitude axes and its rotation by the corresponding sequence of adjustments, provided by the board computer. Hence, the path $p(t) \in \mathbb{S}^2$ describing the camera orientation is derived from $\mathbf{r}(t)$ and $A(t)$, i.e., the translational and rotational components of the Euclidean group action on the frame bundle $\mathcal{F}(\gamma)$. Our goal here is to find this connection.

One familiar example

Let us consider as an illustrative example a classical trajectory: the helix given in cylindrical coordinates as $\rho = a$, $\psi = t$, $z = bt$ with $a, b > 0$. Since (10) yields

$$\kappa = \frac{a}{a^2 + b^2}, \qquad \tau = \frac{b}{a^2 + b^2}$$

from (13) we have

$$\hat{\omega} = \frac{i}{\sqrt{a^2 + b^2}} \begin{pmatrix} b & a \\ a & -b \end{pmatrix} \quad \Rightarrow \quad \hat{\omega}^2 = -\mathcal{I}$$

which allows us to use Euler's formula and represent the matrix exponential

$$q(t) = \exp\left(\frac{1}{2}\int_0^t \hat{\omega}\, dt'\right) = \mathcal{I}\cos\frac{t}{2} + \hat{\omega}\sin\frac{t}{2} \tag{14}$$

so the local frame $\{K\}$ gradually rotates by an angle t about the unit vector

$$\mathbf{\Omega} = \frac{1}{\sqrt{a^2 + b^2}}\left(b, 0, a\right)^t$$

and since the parametrization in (10) is arbitrary, for any constant circular frequency $\omega_o > 0$ of the helix $\psi(t) = \omega_o t$ we may simply substitute $a \to a\omega_o$. Next, we denote $b = a\omega_o \tan\varphi_o$ which yields $\mathbf{\Omega} = (\cos\varphi_o, 0, \sin\varphi_o)^t$, thus obtaining from (14) the expression (see [7] for similar examples)

$$q = \begin{pmatrix} \cos\omega_o t + i\sin\varphi_o \sin\omega_o t & i\cos\varphi_o \sin\omega_o t \\ i\cos\varphi_o \sin\omega_o t & \cos\omega_o t - i\sin\varphi_o \sin\omega_o t \end{pmatrix}$$

and to apply the inverse rotation to $-\mathbf{r}$ we express it in quaternion basis as

$$-\mathbf{r} \in \mathbb{E}^3 \;\to\; \xi = \begin{pmatrix} ia\cos\omega_o t & ibt + a\sin\omega_o t \\ ibt - a\sin\omega_o t & -ia\cos\omega_o t \end{pmatrix} \in \mathfrak{su}_2.$$

The inverse adjoint action $\tilde{\xi} = q^\dagger \xi q$ then yields the camera's direction vector in the form $\tilde{\mathbf{r}} = -A^t \mathbf{r}$ with

$$A^t = \begin{pmatrix} 1 + a\kappa\cos\omega_o t & \sqrt{a\kappa}\sin\omega_o t & a\tau\cos\omega_o t \\ -\sqrt{a\kappa}\sin\omega_o t & 1 + \cos\omega_o t & \sqrt{b\tau}\sin\omega_o t \\ a\tau\cos\omega_o t & -\sqrt{b\tau}\sin\omega_o t & 1 + b\tau\cos\omega_o t \end{pmatrix}.$$

The above solution, however, has one major drawback: it ignores the camera's axial rotation needed to stabilize the picture. This problem may be addressed using classical Euler decomposition once we study the overall impact of camera motion - considering both translations and rotations, as we are about to do next.

5   Putting It All Together

In practice, one rarely has the luxury of knowing the time-parameterized path $\gamma = \gamma(t)$, except in the case of pre-calculated trajectories, e.g. interplanetary missions or aircraft put on auto-pilot. What we typically have as initial data instead, are the spatial coordinates of the camera's carrier, given by the GPS and altitude devices, plus the instantaneous linear $\mathbf{v}$ and angular $\hat{\omega}$ velocity or relevant physical quantities from which they may be derived. So, we may use (13) and (9) to retrieve the time-evolution of the Frenet frame at least locally, via simple numerical integration. This step is needed at the final stage to obtain the desired patch of a smooth trajectory on the covering group

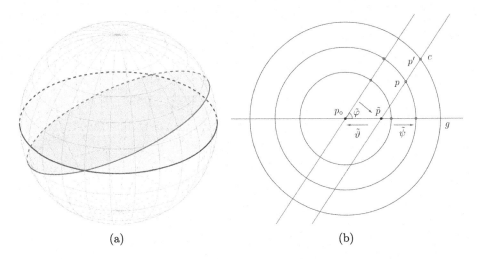

Fig. 3. Planes through the origin in $\{O\}$ represented as great circles on $\mathbb{S}^2$ (a) and the order of the camera's orientation corrections as viewed form $p_\circ$ (b).

$$\tilde{G} \cong \mathrm{SU}(2) \times \mathbb{R}^+ \cong \mathbb{R}^4/\{0\} \cong \mathbb{H}^\times \tag{15}$$

parameterizing the camera orientation and zoom. It is more accurate to take $G \cong \mathrm{SO}(3) \times I$ where I is a finite interval, but it is nicely embedded in $\tilde{G}$ which we may describe using quaternions or PGA, thus avoiding some singularities. Then, the q-solution may easily be expressed in terms of physically relevant parameters for the camera manipulator, such as Euler angles, matrices or axis-angle coordinates (with an additional zoom factor) derived from $q(t)$, namely

$$q \in \mathbb{H}^\times \longrightarrow p \in \mathbb{S}^2, \quad \psi \in \mathbb{S}^1, \quad d \in \mathbb{R}^+ \tag{16}$$

where p is the projection of the observed object's center onto the celestial sphere of the moving camera, given with its polar angle φ and azimuth ϑ, while d is the relative distance, compensated with zoom and focus adjustments; ψ here measures the of the camera's axial spin. The latter is irrelevant if we consider only point objects, in which case the spherical coordinates of the relative radius-vector **r** connecting the two frames are sufficient. Hence, this additional degree of freedom allows us to fix two pixels on the screen (one adjusting p and the other - circling around it), preserving the orientation by keeping the horizontal axis steady at all times. One more thing to consider in real-life scenarios is that the aircraft is not a point object either, but rather a rigid body floating in space. The sensors, the camera, and the geometric center have different trajectories, so one should properly compose the corresponding infinitesimal motions before looking for a solution. Moreover, the typical aircraft axes differ from the Frenet frame, as mentioned above, except for the "roll" which is aligned with the tangent during maneuvering, so additional adjustment is required to determine κ and τ.

T-motion

For clarity, we consider separately pure translations (T-motion) of the camera's local frame $\{K\}$ with respect to the one attached to the observed object $\{O\}$, and rotations (R-motion) of the Frenet basis, described by (9), although they are generally entangled. If the moving camera is considered point object observing a faraway scene for instance, the relative T-motion of $\{O\}$ with respect to $\{K\}$ simply adds to the radius-vectors of all points in the observed object a fixed translation vector $\Delta\mathbf{r}$:

$$\Delta\mathbf{r} = \int_{t_o}^{t} \mathbf{v}(t)\mathrm{d}t, \qquad \mathbf{v}(t) = \dot{\mathbf{r}}(t) \tag{17}$$

where $\mathbf{r}(t)$ represents the origin[2] of $\{O\}$ in the camera's local frame. We choose $\mathbf{r}_o = \mathbf{r}(t_o)$ to be aligned with the z-axis of the camera, or the north pole ($\vartheta = 0$) in spherical coordinates. As the polar angle is arbitrary, we may pick a second reference point $\mathbf{r}$, corresponding to some initial ϑ_o within the viewing angle and $\varphi_o = 0$. Thus, we have a line connecting $\mathbf{r}_o$ and $\mathbf{r}$ that projects onto the Greenwich meridian $\varphi = 0$ of the camera's celestial sphere and may be used for orientation of the observed image, e.g. as the horizontal axis. To keep both the center $\vartheta = 0$ and the orientation $\varphi = 0$ fixed at all times, the camera's manipulator needs to counter the shifts in the spherical angles caused by $\Delta\mathbf{r}$ performing a ϑ-correction followed by a φ-correction. Moreover, to keep the scale of the image consistent, one uses optical or digital zoom compensating for the variable distance between $\{K\}$ and $\{O\}$. Ideally, one knows the pre-calculated time-parameterized trajectory $\gamma(t)$, e.g. for spacecraft and satellites, which means we can easily obtain the corresponding path $\mathbf{r}(t)$ and therefore, its trace $p(t)$ on $\mathbb{S}^2$. To preserve orientation however, one needs to take into account a second point on the object whose radius-vector in the moving frame $\{K\}$ we denote with $\mathbf{r}'$. Then, $\mathbf{r}$ and $\mathbf{r}'$ determine a plane α intersecting the camera's

---

[2] the preferred reference point of the observed object.

viewing sphere at a great circle c (Fig. 3a) which intersects the $\varphi = 0$ meridian $g = \mathbb{S}^2 \cap \{y = 0\}$ at a point $\mathbb{S}^2 \ni \tilde{p} = c \cap g$ easily determined by (see Fig. 3b)

$$\tilde{p}: \begin{vmatrix} 0 & 0 & 0 & 1 \\ x & y & z & 1 \\ x' & y' & z' & 1 \\ \sin\tilde{\vartheta} & 0 & \cos\tilde{\vartheta} & 1 \end{vmatrix} = 0 \Rightarrow \tan\tilde{\vartheta} = \frac{\begin{vmatrix} x & y \\ x' & y' \end{vmatrix}}{\begin{vmatrix} z & y \\ z' & y' \end{vmatrix}}. \tag{18}$$

The next step is to bring $\tilde{p}$ to the north pole $p_\circ$ adjusting the azimuth by an angular correction $\tilde{\vartheta}$ and rotate in the equatorial plane in order to make p and p' incident with g. The corresponding polar angle $\tilde{\varphi} = \measuredangle(c, g)$ equals the one between the normal $\mathbf{n}_c = \mathbf{r} \times \mathbf{r}'$ and the y-axis, for which we obtain (see Fig. 3b)

$$\tilde{\varphi} = \pm\arccos\begin{vmatrix} z & x \\ z' & x' \end{vmatrix} = \pm\arccos\star(\mathbf{r} \wedge \mathbf{r}' \wedge \mathbf{e}_2) \tag{19}$$

with sign depending on the orientation. Finally, we need to bring p back to $p_\circ$ which requires an additional ϑ-adjustment along g by an angle ψ, equal to the spherical distance between $p_\circ$ and p, followed by proper scaling (zoom), keeping the distance between p and p' fixed. For faraway objects it is given by $|\mathbf{r}|^{-1}|\Delta\mathbf{r}|$.

The above conclusions are quite easy to derive using PGA, e.g. in the frame $\{O\}$ the plane $\alpha = O \vee P \vee P' = \mathbf{n}_c$ intersects $\beta = \mathbf{e}_2$ at the line $\ell = \mathbf{e}_2 \wedge \mathbf{n}_c$ whose directional vector $\mathbf{u} = \star(\mathbf{r} \wedge \mathbf{r}' \wedge \mathbf{e}_3, 0, -\mathbf{r} \wedge \mathbf{r}' \wedge \mathbf{e}_1)^t$ can be represented in polar coordinates in the plane β as $\mathbf{u} = |\mathbf{u}|(\mathbf{e}_1 \cos\tilde{\vartheta} + \mathbf{e}_3 \sin\tilde{\vartheta})$, so we end up with (18). The other two rotations, as well as the scale factor, are quite easy to obtain and do not need special treatment. Note, however, the relation to spherical geometry.

R-motion and Euler angles

One cannot help but notice that the rotation scheme proposed above invokes the classical YZY Euler decomposition in the camera reference frame. We refer to a method used in [8], providing the decomposition parameters in the simple form

$$\tau_1 = \frac{r_{23}}{r_{23} \pm \sqrt{1 - r_{22}^2}}, \qquad \tau_2 = \pm\sqrt{\frac{1 - r_{22}}{1 + r_{22}}} \qquad \tau_3 = \frac{r_{32}}{-r_{12} \pm \sqrt{1 - r_{22}^2}} \tag{20}$$

where r_{ij} denote the compound rotation's matrix entries in the local camera frame and the Euler angles are given respectively as $\phi_k = 2\arctan\tau_k$. Next, we need to add the motion due to internal rotations, not related to the Frenet equations (9). The composition of rotations is an easy task, but since they do not commute, the issue of order becomes relevant. The same refers to the composition of rotations with translations, so the screw interpretation comes handy as both components commute according to the famous Mozzi-Chasles' theorem. Any rotation $R(t)$ of the frame $\{K\}$, whether due to the curvature and torsion of the camera's trajectory or due to maneuvering, corresponds to a rotation R^{-1} of the object with respect to that frame, can be effectively compensated by a proper rotation of the camera itself. In general, we need to deal with both types of motions simultaneously and trajectories are not always predetermined but often depend on various conditions and thus calculated in real time using data from the sensors. Moreover, the camera's coordinate frame $\{K\}$ and the one of the aircraft are generally different $\{K'\}$, as mentioned before, which needs to be taken into account prior to any calculations. One major advantage of the PGA approach in this context is that it deals with these issues almost automatically.

Final remarks

The present paper suggests a straightforward analytic approach to the problem of camera motion correction in the case of a stationary scene and discusses some advantages of the PGA representation in this context. Exact solutions may not always more efficient, but they are at least a valuable aid to the numerical algorithms and especially in the study of theoretical aspects, such as singularities, or possible generalizations, some of which we leave for a future research projects.

Appendix: PGA in a Nutshell

Here we provide a brief idea how projective geometric algebra (PGA) works in this setting. The classical Clifford's geometric algebra is often introduced as a factorization of the tensor algebra or an extension to the Grassmann exterior algebra. However, it is easier to understand starting with a vector space $V \cong \mathbb{R}^n$ with additional structure, called geometric multiplication, which for vectors is just the sum of the familiar'dot' (interior) and'wedge' (exterior) products, i.e.,

$$\xi\eta = \xi \cdot \eta + \xi \wedge \eta, \qquad \xi, \eta \in V. \tag{21}$$

This yields a scalar and a bivector component, referred to as grade zero and grade two elements, respectively. Using grade projectors we may write $\langle \xi\eta \rangle_0 = \xi \cdot \eta$ and $\langle \xi\eta \rangle_2 = \xi \wedge \eta$. The maximal possible grade equals n and is one-dimensional, spanned by the so-called pseudo-scalar I. It yields the Hodge operator $\star$ switching from k to $n-k$ grades by sending each element to its orthogonal complement. This convenient duality is extensively used in all of geometry, and PGA in particular. Allowing hyperbolic or parabolic signatures we model different isometry groups, e.g. Lorenz transformations via the space-time algebra $\mathrm{Cliff}(\mathbb{R}^{3,1})$ or 3D Euclidean motions via PGA: $\mathrm{Cliff}(\mathbb{R}^{3,0,1})$. They are contained in the subalgebra of even grade elements, justified by the $\mathbb{Z}_2$-grading of $\mathrm{Cliff}(V)$, and generated by bivectors. One simple example is the algebra of complex numbers $\mathbb{C} \cong \mathrm{Cliff}_\circ(\mathbb{R}^2)$

$$\mathbf{e}_1^2 = \mathbf{e}_2^2 = 1, \qquad \mathbf{e}_1 \cdot \mathbf{e}_2 = 0, \qquad \mathbf{e}_1 \wedge \mathbf{e}_2 = \mathbf{e}_1\mathbf{e}_2 = I$$

spanned by mutually commuting scalars and bivectors, where we also have

$$I^2 = (\mathbf{e}_1\mathbf{e}_2)^2 = -\mathbf{e}_1^2\mathbf{e}_2^2 = -1 \;\Rightarrow\; \mathrm{Cliff}_\circ(\mathbb{R}^2) \cong \mathbb{R}[i] \cong \mathbb{C}.$$

Restriction to elements of unit norm yields the orthogonal group in the plane $O(2) \cong U(1)$. Similarly, the even part of $\mathrm{Cliff}(\mathbb{R}^3)$ gives rise to the quaternion algebra $\mathbb{H}$ spanned by the scalars in $\mathbb{R}$ and the three basic bi-vectors

$$\mathbf{i} = \mathbf{e}_2\mathbf{e}_3, \qquad \mathbf{j} = \mathbf{e}_3\mathbf{e}_1, \qquad \mathbf{k} = \mathbf{e}_1\mathbf{e}_2$$

carved on that famous Dublin bridge by Hamilton, while $\mathrm{Cliff}(\mathbb{R}^3) \cong \mathrm{Cliff}_\circ(\mathbb{R}^{3,1})$ includes also reflections, interpreted as boosts from the relativistic perspective. In order to extend to the Galilean group of rigid transformations in $\mathbb{E}^n$, however, one needs to add one more dimension spanned by $\mathbf{e}_\circ$ with $\mathbf{e}_\circ^2 = 0$. Then, it is convenient to use the $\star$-duality and represent points as n-vectors, lines as $(n-1)$-vectors etc., with actual vectors corresponding to their orthogonal hyper-planes. In the 3D setting for instance, points are given by their homogeneous coordinates $\{p_i\}$ in the basis of three-vectors as

$$P = p_\circ I_3 - \mathbf{e}_\circ(p_1\mathbf{i} + p_2\mathbf{j} + p_3\mathbf{k}), \quad I_3 = \mathbf{e}_1\mathbf{e}_2\mathbf{e}_3$$

and the Euclidean projection is in the plane $p_\circ = 1$, i.e., $\mathbf{r}_p$ has coordinates $p_i/p_\circ$, while $p_\circ = 0$ corresponds to a 'point at infinity' and cannot be normalized in this way. Similarly, lines are presented by their Plücker coordinates

$$\ell = u_1\mathbf{i} + u_2\mathbf{j} + u_3\mathbf{k} - \mathbf{e}_\circ(m_1\mathbf{e}_1 + m_2\mathbf{e}_2 + m_3\mathbf{e}_3)$$

with $\mathbf{u}$ and $\mathbf{m}$ denoting the so-called *displacement* and *moment* vector, respectively. Finally, planes are given by vectors in $\mathrm{Cliff}(\mathbb{R}^{3,0,1})$, namely as:

$$\alpha = n_1\mathbf{e}_1 + n_2\mathbf{e}_2 + n_3\mathbf{e}_3 - \delta\mathbf{e}_\circ$$

and the incidence relation $P \in \alpha$ is now written as $P \cdot \alpha = 0$ instead of the usual $\mathbf{n} \cdot \mathbf{r}_p = \delta$. If we denote bivectors with $\hat{\mathbf{v}} = \mathbf{v}I_3$, the so-called 'flats' are given as

$$P = p_\circ I_3 - \mathbf{e}_\circ\hat{\mathbf{p}}, \qquad \ell = \hat{\mathbf{u}} - \mathbf{e}_\circ\mathbf{m}, \qquad \alpha = \mathbf{n} - \delta\mathbf{e}_\circ \qquad (22)$$

and we can use the wedge product as a 'meet' operator to find intersections, e.g.

$$\ell \wedge \alpha = (\hat{\mathbf{u}} - \mathbf{e}_\circ\mathbf{m}) \wedge (\mathbf{n} - \delta\mathbf{e}_\circ) = \mathbf{u} \cdot \mathbf{n}I_3 - \mathbf{e}_\circ(\delta\hat{\mathbf{u}} - \mathbf{n} \wedge \mathbf{m})$$

which seems more handy that resolving linear algebraic systems. Note that if $\mathbf{u} \perp \mathbf{n}$, the two flats are parallel and we end up with a point at infinity ($p_\circ = 0$). Likewise, two parallel lines meet at infinity unless their moments are equal. We interpret $\mathbf{e}_\circ$ as the normal vector to the plane at infinity (and to all $\mathbb{E}^3$) but should resist the temptation to replace it with the hypercomplex unit ε used in dual numbers $\mathbb{D} \cong \mathbb{R}[\varepsilon]$ as it does not commute with all elements of our algebra. The interior product on the other hand, is used for projections, e.g. $(\ell \cdot \alpha)\alpha^{-1}$ yields the α-'shadow' of ℓ. Using the Hodge duality, we define the 'join' operator

$$A \vee B = \star^{-1}(\star A \wedge \star B), \quad \star A = AI_3^{-1} = -AI_3 \qquad (23)$$

via the famous De Morgan's law and due to its symmetry, we also have

$$A \wedge B = \star^{-1}(\star A \vee \star B).$$

In particular, one may use $\vee$ to represent the line $\ell = P \vee Q$ through points P and Q, or the plane $\alpha = \ell \vee P$ determined by the line ℓ and a point $P \notin \ell$, i.e. $\ell \wedge R = 0$, etc. Finally, let us see how these geometric objects produce transformations. We begin with plane reflections as they generate all isometries in 3D due to the famous Catrtan-Dieudonne theorem, and in PGA they act as

$$\alpha : \ P \ \rightarrow \ \tilde{P} = \mathcal{M}_\alpha(P) = -\alpha P \alpha^{-1}. \tag{24}$$

They are interpreted as Lie elements generation motion via the exponential map

$$\mathcal{T}_\ell : \ P \ \rightarrow \ \tilde{P} = e^{-\ell} P e^{\ell} \tag{25}$$

which corresponds to either a rotation ($\ell^2 < 0$), translation ($\ell^2 = 0$) or a screw displacement if ℓ is not a blade[3]. The magnitude of ℓ is proportional to the rotation angle, as we know from the examples of quaternions and complex numbers. For a more elaborate introduction to PGA we refer the reader to [9] and [10].

References

1. e Souza, M.R., de Almeida Maia, H., Pedrini, H.: Survey on digital video stabilization: concepts, methods, and challenges. ACM Comput. Surv. **55**(3) (2023). Article 47
2. Wang, Y., Huang, Q., Jiang, C., Liu, J., Shang, M., Miao, Z.: Video stabilization: a comprehensive survey. Neurocomputing **516**, 205–230 (2023)
3. Pueyo, P., Montijano, E., Murillo, A.C., Schwager M.: CineMPC: controlling camera intrinsics and extrinsics for autonomous cinematography. In: 2022 International Conference on Robotics and Automation (ICRA), pp 4058–4064. IEEE Press (2022). https://doi.org/10.1109/ICRA46639.2022.9811827
4. Wu, X., Wang, H., Katsaggelos, A.K.: The secret of immersion: actor driven camera movement generation for auto-cinematography (preprint, 2023). arXiv:2303.17041 [cs.MM]
5. Kang, X., Herrera, A., Lema, H., Valencia, E., Vandewalle, P.: Adaptive sampling-based particle filter for visual-inertial gimbal in the wild. In: 2023 IEEE International Conference on Robotics and Automation (ICRA), London, United Kingdom, pp. 2738–2744 (2023). https://doi.org/10.1109/ICRA48891.2023.10160395
6. Clelland, J.: From Frenet to Cartan: The Method of Moving Frames. American Mathematical Society, Providence (2017)
7. Brezov, D., Mladenova, C., Mladenov, I.: From the kinematics of precession motion to generalized Rabi cycles. Adv. Math. Phys. (2018). Article ID 9256320
8. Brezov, D.: Optimization and gimbal lock control via shifted decomposition of rotations. J. Appl. Comput. Math. **7**, 410 (2018)
9. Dorst, L., De Keninck, S.: A guided tour to the plane-based geometric algebra PGA (preprint, 2022). https://bivector.net/PGA4CS.html
10. Hrdina, J., Návrat, A., Vašik, P., Dorst L.: Projective geometric algebra as a subalgebra of conformal geometric algebra. Adv. Appl. Clifford Algebras **31**(18) (2021)

---

[3] k-blades in $\mathrm{Cliff}(V)$ are products of k vectors and correspond to k-dimensional linear subspaces; in particular 2-blades represent (projectively) planes and satisfy $b \wedge b = 0$.

Weyl Calculus Perspective
on the Discrete Stokes' Formula
in Octonions

Rolf Sören Kraußhar and Dmitrii Legatiuk[(✉)]

University of Erfurt, Chair of Mathematics, Nordhäuser Str. 63, 99089 Erfurt,
Germany
`dmitrii.legatiuk@uni-erfurt.de`

Abstract. Octonions are 8-dimensional hypercomplex numbers which
form the biggest normed division algebras over the real numbers. Motivated by applications in theoretical physics, continuous octonionic analysis has become an area of active research in recent year. Looking at
possible practical applications, it is beneficial to work directly with discrete structures, rather than approximate continuous objects. Therefore,
in previous papers, we have proposed some ideas towards the discrete
octonionic analysis. It is well known, that there are several possibilities
to discretise the continuous setting, and the Weyl calculus approach,
which is typically used in the discrete Clifford analysis, to octonions
has not been studied yet. Therefore, in this paper, we close this gap by
presenting the discretisation of octonionic analysis based on the Weyl
calculus.

Keywords: Octonions · Discrete Dirac operator · Weyl calculus ·
Discrete octonionic function theory

1 Introduction

Generalisations of complex analysis have been area of active research for many
years. Similar to the classical complex analysis, its higher-dimensional generalisations aim to develop tools of function theory and operator calculus for solving
boundary value problems in higher dimensions. Typically, engineering applications have focus mainly on three-dimensional settings and, thus, requiring
tools of quaternionic analysis, see for example [14,16]. Applications in theoretical physics however require consideration of dimensions $n > 3$: for example, Ein-
stein's relativity theory implies consideration of a four-dimensional case. Modern
results on models of a generalised standard model, e.g. [4,13,22], indicate that
an eight-dimensional setting should be considered. Hence, octonions, which are
exactly 8-dimensional hypercomplex numbers, are suitable candidates to address
this generalised standard model.

Broadly speaking, complex numbers and complex analysis can be extended
to higher dimensions in two general ways: (i) constructing associative Clifford

B. Sheng et al. (Eds.): CGI 2023, LNCS 14498, pp. 368–378, 2024.
https://doi.org/10.1007/978-3-031-50078-7_29

algebras leading to several function theories that consider functions defined on open subsets of an arbitrary dimensional vector space $\mathbb{R}^{n+1}$ that take values in a 2^n-dimensional Clifford algebra $\mathcal{C}\ell_n$; or, (ii) the Cayley-Dickson duplication process can be applied to the complex numbers leading first to the four-dimensional Hamiltonian quaternions (which is a Clifford algebra), and after the second application, we obtain a new algebra, namely the octonions, see [1]. The Clifford algebra approach gave rise to the function theory known as *Clifford analysis*, e.g. [2], and provides a complete toolbox of generalised function theory including a Cauchy integral formula, Taylor and Laurent series expansions, a residue theory and a toolkit to study operators of Calderon-Zygmund type on strongly Lipschitz surfaces, and many more. In contrast to Clifford algebras, octonions are not any more associative, and, therefore, they are neither a Clifford algebra nor representable with matrices in general. It is important to remark that in [21] it has been shown, that octonions can be embedded into geometric algebra of space time, which itself can be represented by matrices. Therefore, because of this connection between octonionc and geometric algebra, a matrix embedding of low dimensions is nonetheless possible. Despite of non-associativity, it is nonetheless possible to construct octonionic generalisation of the classical complex analysis, see for example works [9,12,17,18,23–25] and references therein.

Looking at practical applications of function theory, it is necessary to approximate the tools of continuous theories, because explicit calculations of integral formulae can only be done for some canonical domains. An alternative approach to the approximation of continuous structures, is to work directly at the discrete level, implying that a discrete counterparts of continuous theories need to be constructed. In the context of Clifford analysis, a lot of results addressing bounded and unbounded settings have been presented in recent years, see [3,5–8,10,11,15] among others. However, in octonionic setting, the situation is different, since only recently first ideas related to discrete octonionic analysis have been presented in [19,20].

It is known that there are several ways to introduce a discrete counterpart of a continuous theory, which will affect the structure of the discrete setting. In [19,20] discrete octonionic analysis has been discretised by help of a direct discretisation of the continuous Cauchy-Riemann operators by help of finite difference operators. In particular, *discrete forward Cauchy-Riemann operator* $D^+ : l^p(\Omega_h, \mathbb{O}) \to l^p(\Omega_h, \mathbb{O})$ and a *discrete backward Cauchy-Riemann operators* $D^- : l^p(\Omega_h, \mathbb{O}) \to l^p(\Omega_h, \mathbb{O})$ have been introduced as follows

$$D_h^+ := \sum_{j=0}^{7} \mathbf{e}_j \partial_h^{+j}, \quad D_h^- := \sum_{j=0}^{7} \mathbf{e}_j \partial_h^{-j}.$$

Factorisation of the star-Laplacian Δ_h by help f these operators has a more complicated form compared to the continuous setting:

$$\Delta_h = \frac{1}{2} \left(D_h^+ \overline{D_h^-} + D_h^- \overline{D_h^+} \right) \text{ with } \Delta_h := \sum_{j=0}^{7} \partial_h^{+j} \partial_h^{-j},$$

where $\overline{D_h^+}$ and $\overline{D_h^-}$ are the discrete conjugated forward and backward Cauchy-Riemann operators, respectively. In [20], discrete Cauchy formula, discrete Borel-Pompeiu formula, as well as discrete Hardy spaces have been introduced for the operators D_h^+ and D_h^-. However, if it is desired to preserve the classical factorisation of the discrete Laplace operator, it is necessary to consider another setting. In the discrete Clifford analysis, this problem is overcome by considering the *Weyl calculus approach* consisting in splitting basis elements $\mathbf{e}_i$ into positive and negative parts. Further, this splitting is required to satisfy specific relations for non-commutativity. In this paper, we present ideas of using the Weyl calculus approach to discretise octonionic analysis. As we will see, the splitting of basis elements must satisfy also non-associativity conditions for preserving the non-associative structure of octonions.

2   Preliminaries and Notations

Let us now briefly recall some basic facts about octonions and continuous octonionic analysis. Let us consider 8-dimensional Euclidean space $\mathbb{R}^8$ with the basis unit vectors $\mathbf{e}_k$, $k = 0, 1, \ldots, 7$ and points $\mathbf{x} = (x_0, x_1, \ldots, x_7)$. Now an element of $\mathbb{R}^8$ can be expressed as follows

$$x = x_0\mathbf{e}_0 + x_1\mathbf{e}_1 + x_2\mathbf{e}_2 + x_3\mathbf{e}_3 + x_4\mathbf{e}_4 + x_5\mathbf{e}_5 + x_6\mathbf{e}_6 + x_7\mathbf{e}_7,$$

where the basis elements satisfy $\mathbf{e}_4 = \mathbf{e}_1\mathbf{e}_2$, $\mathbf{e}_5 = \mathbf{e}_1\mathbf{e}_3$, $\mathbf{e}_6 = \mathbf{e}_2\mathbf{e}_3$ and $\mathbf{e}_7 = \mathbf{e}_4\mathbf{e}_3 = (\mathbf{e}_1\mathbf{e}_2)\mathbf{e}_3$. Moreover, we have $\mathbf{e}_i^2 = -1$ and $\mathbf{e}_0\mathbf{e}_i = \mathbf{e}_i\mathbf{e}_0$ for all $i = 1, \ldots, 7$, and $\mathbf{e}_i\mathbf{e}_j = -\mathbf{e}_j\mathbf{e}_i$ for all mutual distinct $i, j \in \{1, \ldots, 7\}$, as well as $\mathbf{e}_0$ is the neutral element and, therefore, often will be omitted. Multiplication rules for real octonions are shown in Table 1. In particular, it can be clearly seen from this table that the octonionic multiplication actually is closed but not associative, because we have $(\mathbf{e}_i\mathbf{e}_j)\mathbf{e}_k = -\mathbf{e}_i(\mathbf{e}_j\mathbf{e}_k)$.

Table 1. Multiplication table for real octonions $\mathbb{O}$

$\cdot$	$\mathbf{e}_0$	$\mathbf{e}_1$	$\mathbf{e}_2$	$\mathbf{e}_3$	$\mathbf{e}_4$	$\mathbf{e}_5$	$\mathbf{e}_6$	$\mathbf{e}_7$
$\mathbf{e}_0$	1	$\mathbf{e}_1$	$\mathbf{e}_2$	$\mathbf{e}_3$	$\mathbf{e}_4$	$\mathbf{e}_5$	$\mathbf{e}_6$	$\mathbf{e}_7$
$\mathbf{e}_1$	$\mathbf{e}_1$	-1	$\mathbf{e}_4$	$\mathbf{e}_5$	$-\mathbf{e}_2$	$-\mathbf{e}_3$	$-\mathbf{e}_7$	$\mathbf{e}_6$
$\mathbf{e}_2$	$\mathbf{e}_2$	$-\mathbf{e}_4$	-1	$\mathbf{e}_6$	$\mathbf{e}_1$	$\mathbf{e}_7$	$-\mathbf{e}_3$	$-\mathbf{e}_5$
$\mathbf{e}_3$	$\mathbf{e}_3$	$-\mathbf{e}_5$	$-\mathbf{e}_6$	-1	$-\mathbf{e}_7$	$\mathbf{e}_1$	$\mathbf{e}_2$	$\mathbf{e}_4$
$\mathbf{e}_4$	$\mathbf{e}_4$	$\mathbf{e}_2$	$-\mathbf{e}_1$	$\mathbf{e}_7$	-1	$-\mathbf{e}_6$	$\mathbf{e}_5$	$-\mathbf{e}_3$
$\mathbf{e}_5$	$\mathbf{e}_5$	$\mathbf{e}_3$	$-\mathbf{e}_7$	$-\mathbf{e}_1$	$\mathbf{e}_6$	-1	$-\mathbf{e}_4$	$\mathbf{e}_2$
$\mathbf{e}_6$	$\mathbf{e}_6$	$\mathbf{e}_7$	$\mathbf{e}_3$	$-\mathbf{e}_2$	$-\mathbf{e}_5$	$\mathbf{e}_4$	-1	$-\mathbf{e}_1$
$\mathbf{e}_7$	$\mathbf{e}_7$	$-\mathbf{e}_6$	$\mathbf{e}_5$	$-\mathbf{e}_4$	$\mathbf{e}_3$	$-\mathbf{e}_2$	$\mathbf{e}_1$	-1

As it has been already mentioned in the introduction, octonions are different to classical Clifford analysis. Firstly, octonionic analysis addresses functions from

$\mathbb{R}^8$ to $\mathbb{R}^8$, while the Clifford algebra $\mathcal{C}\ell_7$ is actually isomorphic to $\mathbb{R}^{128}$ and not to $\mathbb{R}^8$. Secondly, left or right octonionic monogenic functions do neither form a right nor a left $\mathbb{O}$-module, see [18] for concrete examples. Nonetheless, it is still possible to construct a consistent function theory and the theory of generalised Hilbert function spaces in octonionic settings, see [9] and references therein.

Another distinct feature of the octonionic analysis is presence of the *associator* in some of construction, which appears because of the lack of associativity. For example, the octonionic Stokes' formula [25] has the form:

$$\int_{\partial G} g(x)\,(d\sigma(x)f(x)) =$$
$$\int_{G} \left(g(x)(\mathcal{D}f(x)) + (g(x)\mathcal{D})f(x) - \sum_{j=0}^{7}[e_j, \mathcal{D}g_j(x), f(x)] \right) dV, \tag{1}$$

where the associator is given by the expression $[a, b, c] := (ab)c - a(bc)$. It was expected that the associator appears also in the discrete setting. However, the results presented in [19, 20] show that the associator surprisingly disappear from the constructions. Studying of different discrete Cauchy-Riemann operators, namely discrete forward, backward, and central operators, indicated that the disappearance of the associator is a particularity of the discrete setting. Nonetheless, it is interesting to study if the associator also disappears in the case of Weyl calculus approach to the discrete octonionic analysis.

For introducing discrete setting, let us consider at first the unbounded uniform lattice $h\mathbb{Z}^8$ with the lattice constant $h > 0$:

$$h\mathbb{Z}^8 := \left\{ \mathbf{x} \in \mathbb{R}^8 \,|\, \mathbf{x} = (m_0 h, m_1 h, \ldots, m_7 h), m_j \in \mathbb{Z}, j = 0, 1, \ldots, 7 \right\}.$$

Classical forward and backward differences $\partial_h^{\pm j}$ are defined in the classical way as follows:
$$\partial_h^{+j} f(mh) := h^{-1}(f(mh + \mathbf{e}_j h) - f(mh)),$$
$$\partial_h^{-j} f(mh) := h^{-1}(f(mh) - f(mh - \mathbf{e}_j h)), \tag{2}$$

with $mh \in h\mathbb{Z}^8$ and for discrete functions $f(mh)$, which are defined on $\Omega_h \subset h\mathbb{Z}^8$ and taking values in octonions $\mathbb{O}$.

Because our goal is to study the Weyl calculus approach to the discretisation of octonionic analysis, we follow the ideas from [3, 11], and split each basis element $\mathbf{e}_k$, $k = 0, 1, \ldots, 7$, into positive and negative directions $\mathbf{e}_k^+$ and $\mathbf{e}_k^-$, $k = 0, 1, \ldots, 7$, i.e., $\mathbf{e}_k = \mathbf{e}_k^+ + \mathbf{e}_k^-$. Further, the splitting of basis elements must satisfy the following relations:

$$\begin{cases} \mathbf{e}_j^- \mathbf{e}_k^- + \mathbf{e}_k^- \mathbf{e}_j^- = 0, \\ \mathbf{e}_j^+ \mathbf{e}_k^+ + \mathbf{e}_k^+ \mathbf{e}_j^+ = 0, \\ \mathbf{e}_j^+ \mathbf{e}_k^- + \mathbf{e}_k^- \mathbf{e}_j^+ = -\delta_{jk}, \end{cases} \tag{3}$$

where δ_{jk} is the Kronecker delta. The main advantage of this approach is that it leads to a canonical factorisation of a star-Laplacian Δ_h by a pair of discrete

Cauchy-Riemann operators, which are defined by help of the splitting of basis elements and finite difference operators as follows

$$D_h^{+-} := \sum_{j=0}^{7} \mathbf{e}_j^+ \partial_h^{+j} + \mathbf{e}_j^- \partial_h^{-j}, \quad D_h^{-+} := \sum_{j=0}^{7} \mathbf{e}_j^+ \partial_h^{-j} + \mathbf{e}_j^- \partial_h^{+j}.$$

Hence, the following factorisation of the star-Laplacian is obtained

$$(D_h^{+-})^2 = (D_h^{-+})^2 = -\Delta_h,$$

with

$$\Delta_h := \sum_{j=0}^{7} \partial_h^{+j} \partial_h^{-j}.$$

While working with splitting of basis elements, it is important to address the non-associativity of octonionic multiplication. Therefore, later on, during the proof of discrete octonionic Stokes's formula, we will introduce relations similar to (3) for addressing the non-associativity in Weyl calculus setting.

3   The Discrete Octonionic Stokes' Formula

In this section, we introduce the discrete Stokes' formula in octonionic setting based on the Weyl calculus approach. Since previous results presented in [19, 20] have shown the surprising effect of the associator disappearing in the discrete setting, the main interest here is to study if the approach based on the Weyl calculus leads to structurally another form of the discrete Stokes' formula in comparison to the results presented in [19, 20]. Precisely, we would like to understand, if the associator will appear in this case. In particular, the proof of the discrete Stokes' formula is the main part of this study, while the discrete formulae for the upper and the lower half-lattices will be obtained immediately by using the same ideas as in [19]. In this regard, the main point is to study, if the associator could be obtained under the splitting of the basis elements respecting the non-associativity.

The following theorem presents the discrete octonionic Stokes' formula for the whole space:

Theorem 1. *The discrete Stokes' formula for the whole space with the lattice* $h\mathbb{Z}^8$ *is given by*

$$\sum_{m \in \mathbb{Z}^8} \left\{ \left[g(mh) D_h^{-+} \right] f(mh) - g(mh) \left[D_h^{+-} f(mh) \right] \right\} h^8 = 0 \qquad (4)$$

for all discrete functions f *and* g *such that the series converge.*

Proof. For providing a clear picture of how Weyl calculus setting can be brought together with the non-associativity of octonionic multiplication, we will present the proof of Stokes' formula with all explicit calculations. Additionally, for shortening the notations, the lattice constant h will be omitted in the argument of discrete functions from now on and we will write simply $f(m)$ or $f(m_0, \ldots, m_7)$ instead of $f(mh)$ or $f(m_0h, \ldots, m_0h)$, respectively.

At first, we start the first term on the left-hand side in (4):

$$\sum_{m \in \mathbb{Z}^8} \left[g(m) D_h^{-+} \right] f(m) h^8 = \sum_{m \in \mathbb{Z}} \sum_{j=0}^{7} \left[\partial_h^{-j} g(m) e_j^+ + \partial_h^{+j} g(m) e_j^- \right] f(m) h^8$$

$$= \sum_{m \in \mathbb{Z}} \sum_{j=0}^{7} \sum_{i=0}^{7} \left[\partial_h^{-j} g_i(m) \left(e_i^+ + e_i^- \right) e_j^+ + \partial_h^{+j} g_i(m) \left(e_i^+ + e_i^- \right) e_j^- \right] f(m) h^8.$$

Splitting similarly the unit vectors of function f and finite difference operators, and multiplying the result, we obtain the following expression:

$$\sum_{m \in \mathbb{Z}} \sum_{j=0}^{7} \sum_{i=0}^{7} \sum_{k=0}^{7} \left[\partial_h^{-j} g_i(m) f_k(m) \left(e_i^+ e_j^+ \right) e_k^+ + \partial_h^{-j} g_i(m) f_k(m) \left(e_i^+ e_j^+ \right) e_k^- \right.$$

$$+ \partial_h^{-j} g_i(m) f_k(m) \left(e_i^- e_j^+ \right) e_k^+ + \partial_h^{-j} g_i(m) f_k(m) \left(e_i^- e_j^+ \right) e_k^-$$

$$+ \partial_h^{+j} g_i(m) f_k(m) \left(e_i^+ e_j^- \right) e_k^+ + \partial_h^{+j} g_i(m) f_k(m) \left(e_i^+ e_j^- \right) e_k^-$$

$$\left. + \partial_h^{+j} g_i(m) f_k(m) \left(e_i^- e_j^- \right) e_k^+ + \partial_h^{+j} g_i(m) f_k(m) \left(e_i^- e_j^- \right) e_k^- \right] h^8.$$

For preserving the anti-associativity of octonionic multiplication, the splitting of basis elements $\mathbf{e}$ must satisfy also the following anti-associative relations:

$$\left(e_i^+ e_j^+ \right) e_k^+ = -e_i^+ \left(e_j^+ e_k^+ \right), \quad \left(e_i^+ e_j^+ \right) e_k^- = -e_i^+ \left(e_j^+ e_k^- \right),$$

$$\left(e_i^- e_j^+ \right) e_k^+ = -e_i^- \left(e_j^+ e_k^+ \right), \quad \left(e_i^- e_j^+ \right) e_k^- = -e_i^- \left(e_j^+ e_k^- \right),$$

$$\left(e_i^+ e_j^- \right) e_k^+ = -e_i^+ \left(e_j^- e_k^+ \right), \quad \left(e_i^+ e_j^- \right) e_k^- = -e_i^+ \left(e_j^- e_k^- \right),$$

$$\left(e_i^- e_j^- \right) e_k^+ = -e_i^- \left(e_j^- e_k^+ \right), \quad \left(e_i^- e_j^- \right) e_k^- = -e_i^- \left(e_j^- e_k^- \right).$$

Taking into account these relations and the definition of finite difference operators leads to the following expression

$$
\sum_{m\in\mathbb{Z}}\sum_{j=0}^{7}\sum_{i=0}^{7}\sum_{k=0}^{7}\left[g_i(m-\mathbf{e}_j)f_k(m)\mathbf{e}_i^+\left(\mathbf{e}_j^+\mathbf{e}_k^+\right)-g_i(m)f_k(m)\mathbf{e}_i^+\left(\mathbf{e}_j^+\mathbf{e}_k^+\right)\right.
$$

$$
+g_i(m-\mathbf{e}_j)f_k(m)\mathbf{e}_i^+\left(\mathbf{e}_j^+\mathbf{e}_k^-\right)-g_i(m)f_k(m)\mathbf{e}_i^+\left(\mathbf{e}_j^+\mathbf{e}_k^-\right)
$$

$$
+g_i(m-\mathbf{e}_j)f_k(m)\mathbf{e}_i^-\left(\mathbf{e}_j^+\mathbf{e}_k^+\right)-g_i(m)f_k(m)\mathbf{e}_i^-\left(\mathbf{e}_j^+\mathbf{e}_k^+\right)
$$

$$
+g_i(m-\mathbf{e}_j)f_k(m)\mathbf{e}_i^-\left(\mathbf{e}_j^+\mathbf{e}_k^-\right)-g_i(m)f_k(m)\mathbf{e}_i^-\left(\mathbf{e}_j^+\mathbf{e}_k^-\right)
$$

$$
-g_i(m+\mathbf{e}_j)f_k(m)\mathbf{e}_i^+\left(\mathbf{e}_j^-\mathbf{e}_k^-\right)+g_i(m)f_k(m)\mathbf{e}_i^+\left(\mathbf{e}_j^-\mathbf{e}_k^-\right)
$$

$$
-g_i(m+\mathbf{e}_j)f_k(m)\mathbf{e}_i^+\left(\mathbf{e}_j^-\mathbf{e}_k^+\right)+g_i(m)f_k(m)\mathbf{e}_i^+\left(\mathbf{e}_j^-\mathbf{e}_k^+\right)
$$

$$
-g_i(m+\mathbf{e}_j)f_k(m)\mathbf{e}_i^-\left(\mathbf{e}_j^-\mathbf{e}_k^+\right)+g_i(m)f_k(m)\mathbf{e}_i^-\left(\mathbf{e}_j^-\mathbf{e}_k^+\right)
$$

$$
\left.-g_i(m+\mathbf{e}_j)f_k(m)\mathbf{e}_i^-\left(\mathbf{e}_j^-\mathbf{e}_k^-\right)+g_i(m)f_k(m)\mathbf{e}_i^-\left(\mathbf{e}_j^-\mathbf{e}_k^-\right)\right]h^8.
$$

Performing change of variables in the last expression and bringing together common terms, we get

$$
\sum_{m\in\mathbb{Z}}\sum_{j=0}^{7}\sum_{i=0}^{7}\sum_{k=0}^{7}\left[g_i(m)\mathbf{e}_i^+\left(f_k(m+\mathbf{e}_j)-f_k(m)\right)\left(\mathbf{e}_j^+\mathbf{e}_k^+\right)\right.
$$

$$
+g_i(m)\mathbf{e}_i^+\left(f_k(m+\mathbf{e}_j)-f_k(m)\right)\left(\mathbf{e}_j^+\mathbf{e}_k^-\right)+g_i(m)\mathbf{e}_i^-\left(f_k(m+\mathbf{e}_j)-f_k(m)\right)\left(\mathbf{e}_j^+\mathbf{e}_k^+\right)
$$

$$
+g_i(m)\mathbf{e}_i^-\left(f_k(m+\mathbf{e}_j)-f_k(m)\right)\left(\mathbf{e}_j^+\mathbf{e}_k^-\right)+g_i(m)\mathbf{e}_i^+\left(f_k(m)-f_k(m-\mathbf{e}_j)\right)\left(\mathbf{e}_j^-\mathbf{e}_k^-\right)
$$

$$
+g_i(m)\mathbf{e}_i^+\left(f_k(m)-f_k(m-\mathbf{e}_j)\right)\left(\mathbf{e}_j^-\mathbf{e}_k^+\right)+g_i(m)\mathbf{e}_i^-\left(f_k(m)-f_k(m-\mathbf{e}_j)\right)\left(\mathbf{e}_j^-\mathbf{e}_k^+\right)
$$

$$
\left.+g_i(m)\mathbf{e}_i^-\left(f_k(m)-f_k(m-\mathbf{e}_j)\right)\left(\mathbf{e}_j^-\mathbf{e}_k^-\right)\right]h^8,
$$

which is by using difference operators and definition of the splitting of basis elements further simplified to

$$\sum_{m\in\mathbb{Z}}\sum_{j=0}^{7}\sum_{i=0}^{7}\sum_{k=0}^{7}\Big[g_i(m)\mathbf{e}_i^+\partial_h^{+j}f_k(m)\left(\mathbf{e}_j^+\mathbf{e}_k^+\right)+g_i(m)\mathbf{e}_i^+\partial_h^{+j}f_k(m)\left(\mathbf{e}_j^+\mathbf{e}_k^-\right)$$

$$+g_i(m)\mathbf{e}_i^-\partial_h^{+j}f_k(m)\left(\mathbf{e}_j^+\mathbf{e}_k^+\right)+g_i(m)\mathbf{e}_i^-\partial_h^{+j}f_k(m)\left(\mathbf{e}_j^+\mathbf{e}_k^-\right)$$

$$+g_i(m)\mathbf{e}_i^+\partial_h^{-j}f_k(m)\left(\mathbf{e}_j^-\mathbf{e}_k^-\right)+g_i(m)\mathbf{e}_i^+\partial_h^{-j}f_k(m)\left(\mathbf{e}_j^-\mathbf{e}_k^+\right)$$

$$+g_i(m)\mathbf{e}_i^-\partial_h^{-j}f_k(m)\left(\mathbf{e}_j^-\mathbf{e}_k^+\right)+g_i(m)\mathbf{e}_i^-\partial_h^{-j}f_k(m)\left(\mathbf{e}_j^-\mathbf{e}_k^-\right)\Big]h^8$$

$$=\sum_{m\in\mathbb{Z}}\sum_{j=0}^{7}\sum_{i=0}^{7}\sum_{k=0}^{7}\Big[g_i(m)\mathbf{e}_i^+\partial_h^{+j}\mathbf{e}_j^+f_k(m)\mathbf{e}_k+g_i(m)\mathbf{e}_i^-\partial_h^{+j}\mathbf{e}_j^+f_k(m)\mathbf{e}_k$$

$$+g_i(m)\mathbf{e}_i^+\partial_h^{-j}\mathbf{e}_j^-f_k(m)\mathbf{e}_k+g_i(m)\mathbf{e}_i^-\partial_h^{-j}\mathbf{e}_j^-f_k(m)\mathbf{e}_k\Big]h^8$$

$$=\sum_{m\in\mathbb{Z}}\sum_{j=0}^{7}\Big[g(m)\partial_h^{+j}\mathbf{e}_j^+f(m)+g(m)\partial_h^{-j}\mathbf{e}_j^-f(m)\Big]h^8$$

$$=\sum_{m\in\mathbb{Z}}g(m)\left[D_h^{+-}f(m)\right]h^8.$$

Thus, the statement of the theorem is proven.

Evidently, the discrete octonionic Stokes' formula (4) does not contain the associator, similar to the results based on forward, backward, and central Cauchy-Riemann operators presented in [19,20]. This fact confirms a possible reason for this behaviour hypothesised in [20], that this is the effect of a discretisation. Further, again we have that the non-associativity is reflected in the change of the sign of the second summand in (4) in comparison to the discrete Clifford analysis case [6,8].

To complete the discussion of discrete Stokes' formula, let us present now this formula for two cases of interest: upper and lower half-spaces (or half-lattices). The half-lattices are defined as follows

$$h\mathbb{Z}_+^8:=\left\{(h\underline{m},hm_7)\colon\underline{m}\in\mathbb{Z}^7,m_7\in\mathbb{Z}_+\right\},$$
$$h\mathbb{Z}_-^8:=\left\{(h\underline{m},hm_7)\colon\underline{m}\in\mathbb{Z}^7,m_7\in\mathbb{Z}_-\right\}.$$

Next, we present two theorems providing discrete octonionic Stokes' formulae for $h\mathbb{Z}_+^8$ and $h\mathbb{Z}_-^8$, respectively. The proofs of these theorems will be omitted, since they follow the general strategy of the proofs presented in [19] while considering also non-associativity relations for splitting of basis elements presented in the proof of Theorem 1.

Theorem 2. *The discrete Stokes' formula for the upper half-lattice $h\mathbb{Z}_+^8$ is given by*

$$\sum_{m \in \mathbb{Z}_+^8} \left\{ \left[g(mh) D_h^{-+} \right] f(mh) - g(mh) \left[D_h^{+-} f(mh) \right] \right\} h^8$$

$$= \sum_{\underline{m} \in \mathbb{Z}^7} \left[\mathbf{e}_7^+ \left(g(\underline{m}, 0) f_k(\underline{m}, 1) \right) + \mathbf{e}_7^- \left(g(\underline{m}, 1) f_k(\underline{m}, 0) \right) \right] h^8 \tag{5}$$

for all discrete functions f and g such that the series converge.

Theorem 3. *The discrete Stokes' formula for the lower half-lattice $h\mathbb{Z}_-^8$ is given by*

$$\sum_{m \in \mathbb{Z}_-^8} \left\{ \left[g(mh) D_h^{-+} \right] f(mh) - g(mh) \left[D_h^{+-} f(mh) \right] \right\} h^8$$

$$= -\sum_{\underline{m} \in \mathbb{Z}^7} \left[\mathbf{e}_7^+ \left(g(\underline{m}, -1) f_k(\underline{m}, 0) \right) + \mathbf{e}_7^- \left(g(\underline{m}, 0) f_k(\underline{m}, -1) \right) \right] h^8 \tag{6}$$

for all discrete functions f and g such that the series converge.

4   Summary

First results in the discrete octonionic analysis, which are based discrete forward and discrete backward Cauchy-Riemann operators, have been presented recently. Looking at the results in the discrete Clifford analysis, the typical approach there is use the Weyl calculus approach, since it preserves the canonical factorisation of the discrete Laplace operator. Therefore, in this short paper, we discussed the Weyl calculus approach to the discrete octonionic analysis, since it is of particular interest to see how the non-associativity of octonionic multiplication will affect the constructions, as well as if the associator appears in this case.

The results presented in this paper show, that the Weyl calculus approach follows the same steps as previous results meaning that the discrete octonionic Stokes's formula has structurally the same form (different in sign to the case of discrete Clifford analysis) as in the previous works and the associator does not appear. Hence, it is safe to assume that the disappearance of the associator is a distinct feature of the discrete setting. It is particularly interesting to study in future work the approximation properties of discrete structures, because if we take the limit $h \to 0$, then the associator must appear, because it is present in the continuous case. This topic will be addressed in the future works.

References

1. Baez, J.: The octonions. Bull. Am. Math. Soc. **39**, 145–205 (2002)
2. Brackx, F., Delanghe, R., Sommen, F.: Clifford analysis. In: Pitman Research Notes in Mathematics, vol. 76. Boston (1982)

3. Brackx, F., De Schepper, H., Sommen, F., Van de Voorde, L.: Discrete Clifford analysis: a germ of function theory. In: Hypercomplex Analysis, Birkhäuser Basel, pp. 37–53 (2009)
4. Burdik, C., Catto, S., Gürcan, Y., Khalfan, A., Kurt, L., La Kato, V.: $SO(9,1)$ group and examples of analytic functions. J. Phys.: Conf. Ser. **1194**, 012016 (2019)
5. Cerejeiras, P., Faustino, N., Vieira, N.: Numerical Clifford analysis for nonlinear Schrödinger problem. Numer. Methods Partial Differ. Eq. **24**(4), 1181–1202 (2008)
6. Cerejeiras, P., Kähler, U., Ku, M., Sommen, F.: Discrete Hardy spaces. J. Fourier Anal. Appl. **20**(4), 715–750 (2014)
7. Cerejeiras, P., Kähler, U., Legatiuk, A., Legatiuk, D.: Boundary values of discrete monogenic functions over bounded domains in $\mathbb{R}^3$. In: Alpay, D., Vajiac, M. (eds.) Linear Systems, Signal Processing and Hypercomplex Analysis. Operator Theory: Advances and Applications, vol. 275, pp. 149–165. Birkhäuser (2020)
8. Cerejeiras, P., Kähler, U., Legatiuk, A., Legatiuk, D.: Discrete Hardy spaces for bounded domains in $\mathbb{R}^n$. Complex Anal. Oper. Theory **15**, 4 (2021)
9. Constales, D., Kraußhar, R.S.: Octonionic Kerzman-Stein operators. Complex Anal. Oper. Theory **15**, 104 (2021)
10. Faustino, N., Kähler, U.: Fischer decomposition for difference Dirac operators. Adv. Appl. Clifford Algebras **17**, 37–58 (2007)
11. Faustino, N., Kähler, U., Sommen, F.: Discrete Dirac operators in Clifford analysis. Adv. Appl. Clifford Algebras **17**(3), 451–467 (2007)
12. Frenod, E., Ludkowski, S.V.: Integral operator approach over octonions to solution of nonlinear PDE. Far East J. Math. Sci. (2017)
13. Gogberashvili, M.: Octonionic geometry and conformal transformations. Int. J. Geomet. Methods Mod. Phys. **13**(7), 1650092 (2016)
14. Gürlebeck, K., Sprößig, W.: Quaternionic and Clifford Calculus for Physicists and Engineers. John Wiley & Sons, Chichester, New York (1997)
15. Gürlebeck, K., Hommel, A.: On finite difference Dirac operators and their fundamental solutions. Adv. Appl. Clifford Algebras **11**, 89–106 (2001)
16. Gürlebeck, K., Habetha, K., Sprößig, W.: Application of Holomorphic Functions in Two and Higher Dimensions. Birkhäuser, Basel (2016)
17. Kauhanen, J., Orelma, H.: Cauchy-Riemann operators in octonionic analysis. Adv. Appl. Clifford Algebras **28**, 1 (2018)
18. Kauhanen, J., Orelma, H.: On the structure of octonion regular functions. Adv. Appl. Clifford Algebras **29**, 77 (2019)
19. Kraußhar, S., Legatiuk, A., Legatiuk, D.: Towards discrete octonionic analysis. In: Vasilyev, V. (eds.) Differential Equations, Mathematical Modeling and Computational Algorithms. DEMMCA 2021. Springer Proceedings in Mathematics and Statistics, vol. 423, pp. 51–63. Springer, Cham (2023). https://doi.org/10.1007/978-3-031-28505-9_4
20. Kraußhar, S., Legatiuk, D.: Cauchy formulae and Hardy spaces in discrete octonionic analysis. In: Complex Analysis and Operator Theory (2023). (Accepted for Publication)
21. Lasenby, A.N.: Some recent GA results in mathematical physics and the GA approach to the fundamental forces of nature. Presentation at AGACSE 2021, YouTube Video (2021). https://www.youtube.com/watch?v=fFj4E7q4hbY
22. Najarbashi, G., Seifi, B., Mirzaei, S.: Two- and three-qubit geometry, quaternionic and octonionic conformal maps, and intertwining stereographic projection. Quant. Inf. Process. **15**, 509–528 (2016)

23. Huo, Q., Ren, Q.: Structure of octonionic Hilbert spaces with applications in the Parseval equality and Cayley-Dickson algebras. J. Math. Phys. **63**(4), 042101 (2022)
24. Li, X.-M., Peng, L.-Z.: Three-line theorems on the octonions. Acta Math. Sinica **20**(3), 483–490 (2004)
25. Li, X.-M., Peng, L.-Z., Qian, T.: Cauchy integrals on Lipschitz surfaces in octonionic space. J. Math. Anal. Appl. **343**, 763–777 (2008)

Algorithmic Computation of Multivector Inverses and Characteristic Polynomials in Non-degenerate Clifford Algebras

Dimiter Prodanov[1,2]([⊠]) [iD]

[1] PAML-LN, IICT, Bulgarian Academy of Sciences, Sofia, Bulgaria
[2] Neuroelectronics Research Flanders and EHS, IMEC, Leuven, Belgium
`dimiter.prodanov@imec.be`

Abstract. The power of Clifford or, geometric, algebra lies in its ability to represent geometric operations in a concise and elegant manner. Clifford algebras provide the natural generalizations of complex, dual numbers and quaternions into non-commutative multivectors. The paper demonstrates an algorithm for the computation of inverses of such numbers in a non-degenerate Clifford algebra of an arbitrary dimension. The algorithm is a variation of the Faddeev-LeVerrier-Souriau algorithm and is implemented in the open-source Computer Algebra System Maxima. Symbolic and numerical examples in different Clifford algebras are presented.

Keywords: multivector · Clifford algebra · computer algebra

1 Introduction

Clifford algebras provide the natural generalizations of complex, dual and split-complex (or hyperbolic) numbers into the concept of *Clifford numbers*, i.e. general multivectors. The power of Clifford or, geometric, algebra lies in its ability to represent geometric operations in a concise and elegant manner. The development of Clifford algebras is based on the insights of Hamilton, Grassmann, and Clifford from the 19$^\text{th}$ century. After a hiatus lasting many decades, the Clifford geometric algebra experienced a renaissance with the advent of contemporary computer algebra systems. Clifford algebras can be implemented in a variety of general-purpose computer languages and computational platforms. Recent years have seen renewed interest in Clifford algebra platforms: notably, for Maple, Matlab, Mathematica, Maxima, *Ganja.js* for JavaScript, *GaLua* for Lua, *Galgebra* for Python, *Grassmann* for Julia.

Computation of inverses of multivectors has drawn continuos attention in the literature as the problem was only gradually solved [1,4,5,9]. The present contribution demonstrates an algorithm for multivector inversion, which involves only multiplications and subtractions and has a variable number of steps, depending on the spanning subspace of the multivector. The algorithm is implemented in Maxima using the Clifford package [6,8].

B. Sheng et al. (Eds.): CGI 2023, LNCS 14498, pp. 379–390, 2024.
https://doi.org/10.1007/978-3-031-50078-7_30

In order to compute an inverse of a multivector, previous contributions use series of automorphisms of special types. This allows one to write basis-free formulas with increasing complexity. On the other hand, the present algorithm is based on Faddeev–LeVerrier–Souriau (FVS) algorithm for characteristic polynomial and matrix inverse computation. The correctness of the algorithm is proven using an algorithmic, constructive representation of a multivector in the matrix algebra over the reals, but it by no means depends on such a representation. The present FVS algorithm is in fact a proof certificate for the existence of an inverse. To the present author's knowledge the FVS algorithm has not been used systematically to exhibit multivector inverses.

2 Notation and Preliminaries

$C\ell_n$ will denote a Clifford algebra of order n but with unspecified signature. Clifford multiplication is denoted by simple juxtaposition of symbols. Algebra generators will be indexed by Latin letters. Multi-indices will be considered as index **lists** and not as sets and will be denoted with capital letters. The operation of taking k-grade part of an expression will be denoted by $\langle . \rangle_k$ and in particular the scalar part will be denoted by $\langle . \rangle_0$. Set difference is denoted by $\triangle$. Matrices will be indicated with bold capital letters, while matrix entries will be indicated by lowercase letters. The *scalar product* of the blades will be denoted by $*$; t in superscript will denote the grade negation operation, while $\sim$ – the Clifford product reversion.

Definition 1. *The generators of the Clifford algebra will be denoted by indexed symbol e. It will be assumed that there is an ordering relation $\prec$, such that for two natural numbers $i < j \implies e_i \prec e_j$. The **extended basis** set of the algebra will be defined as the ordered power set $\mathbf{B} := \{P(E), \prec\}$ of all generators $E = \{e_1, \ldots, e_n\}$ and their irreducible products.*

Definition 2. *Define the diagonal scalar product matrix as $\mathbf{G} := \{\sigma_{IJ} = e_I * e_J | e_I, e_J \in \mathbf{B}, I \prec J\}$.*

A multivector will be written as $A = a_1 + \sum_{k=1}^r \langle A \rangle_k = a_1 + \sum_J a_J e_J$. The maximal grade of A will be denoted by $\mathrm{gr}[A]$. The pseudoscalar will be denoted by I.

3 Clifford Algebra Real Matrix Representation Map

In the present we will focus on non-degenerate Clifford algebras, therefore the non-zero elements of $\mathbf{G}$ are valued in $\{-1, 1\}$. Supporting results are presented in Appendix A.

Definition 3 (Clifford coefficient map). *Define the linear map acting element-wise $C_a : C\ell_n \mapsto \mathbb{R}$ by the action $C_a(ax + b) = x$ for $x \in \mathbb{R}, a, b \in \mathbf{B}$.*

*Define the Clifford **coefficient map** indexed by e_S as $\mathbf{A}_S := C_S(\mathbf{M})$, where $\mathbf{M}$ is the multiplication table of the extended basis $\mathbf{M} = \{\mathcal{R}(e_M e_N) \mid e_M, e_N \in \mathbf{B}\}$, and $\mathbf{A}_S$ action of the map.*

Definition 4 (Canonical matrix map). *Define the map* $\pi : \mathbf{B} \mapsto \mathbf{Mat}_{\mathbb{R}}(2^n \times 2^n)$, $n = p + q + r$ *as* $\pi : e_S \mapsto \mathbf{E}_s := \mathbf{GA}_s$ *where s is the ordinal of $e_S \in \mathbf{B}$ and* $\mathbf{A}_S$ *is computed as in Definition 3.*

Proposition 1. *The π-map is linear.*

The proposition follows from the linearity of the coefficient map and matrix multiplication with a scalar.

Theorem 1 (Semigroup property). *Let e_s and e_t be generators of $C\ell_{p,q}$. Then the following statements hold*

1. *The map π is a homomorphism with regard to the Clifford product (i.e. π distributes over the Clifford products):* $\pi(e_s e_t) = \pi(e_s)\pi(e_t)$.
2. *The set of all matrices $\mathbf{E}_s$ forms a multiplicative semigroup.*

Proof. Let $\mathbf{E}_s = \pi(e_s), \mathbf{E}_t = \pi(e_t), \mathbf{E}_{st} = \pi(e_s e_t)$. We specialize the result of Lemma 2 for $S = \{s\}$ and $T = \{t\}$ and observe that $m_{\lambda\lambda'} e_{st} = m_{\lambda\mu}\sigma_\mu m_{\mu\lambda'} e_{st}$ for $\lambda, \lambda', \mu \leq n$ and $\sigma_\lambda m_{\lambda\lambda'} = \sigma_\lambda m_{\lambda\mu}\sigma_\mu m_{\mu\lambda'}$. In summary, the map π acts on $C\ell_{p,q}$ according to the following diagram:

Therefore, $\mathbf{E}_{st} = \mathbf{E}_s \mathbf{E}_t$. Moreover, we observe that $\pi(e_s e_t) = \mathbf{E}_{st} = \mathbf{E}_s \mathbf{E}_t = \pi(e_s)\pi(e_t)$.

For the semi-group property observe that since π is linear it is invertible. Since π distributes over Clifford product its inverse π^{-1} distributes over matrix multiplication:

$$\pi^{-1}(\mathbf{E}_s \mathbf{E}_t) \equiv \pi^{-1}(\mathbf{E}_{st}) = e_{st} \equiv e_s e_t = \pi^{-1}(\mathbf{E}_s)\,\pi^{-1}(\mathbf{E}_t)$$

However, $C\ell_{p,q}$ is closed by construction, therefore, the set $\{\mathbf{E}\}_s$ is closed under matrix multiplication.

Proposition 2. *Let $\mathbf{L} := \{l_i | l_i \in \mathbf{B}\}$ be a column vector and $\mathbf{R}_s$ be the first row of $\mathbf{E}_s$. Then $\pi^{-1} : \mathbf{E}_s \mapsto \mathbf{R}_s \mathbf{L}$.*

Proof. We observe that by the Proposition 4 the only non-zero element in the first row of $\mathbf{E}_s$ is $\sigma_1 m_{1s} = 1$. Therefore, $\mathbf{R}_s \mathbf{L} = e_s$.

Theorem 2 (Complete Real Matrix Representation). *Define the map $g : \mathbf{A} \mapsto \mathbf{GA}$ as matrix multiplication with $\mathbf{G}$. Then for a fixed multiindex s $\pi = C_s \circ g = g \circ C_s$. Further, π is an isomorphism inducing a Clifford algebra representation in the real matrix algebra:*

$$Cl_{p,q}(\mathbb{R}) \underset{\pi^{-1}}{\overset{\pi}{\rightleftarrows}} \mathbf{Mat}_{\mathbb{R}}(2^n \times 2^n)$$

Proof. The π-map is a linear isomorphism. The set $\{\mathbf{E}_s\}$ forms a multiplicative group, which is a subset of the matrix algebra $\mathbf{Mat}_{\mathbb{R}}(N \times N), N = 2^n$. Let $\pi(e_s) = \mathbf{E}_s$ and $\pi(e_t) = \mathbf{E}_t$. It is claimed that

1. $\mathbf{E}_s\mathbf{E}_t \neq \mathbf{0}$ by the Sparsity Lemma 1.
2. $\mathbf{E}_s\mathbf{E}_t = -\mathbf{E}_t\mathbf{E}_s$ by Proposition 5.
3. $\mathbf{E}_s\mathbf{E}_s = \sigma_s\mathbf{I}$ by Proposition 6.

Therefore, the set $\{\mathbf{E}_S\}_{S=\{1\}}^{P(n)}$ is an image of the extended basis $\mathbf{B}$. Here $P(n)$ denotes the power set of the indices of the algebra generators.

What is special about the above representation is the relationship

$$\mathrm{tr}\mathbf{A} = 2^n \langle A \rangle_0 \tag{1}$$

for the image $\pi(A) = \mathbf{A}$ of a general multivector element A and it will be used further in the proof of FVS algorithm.

Remark 1. The above construction works if instead of the entire algebra $Cl_{p,q}$ we restrict a multivector to a sub-algebra of a smaller grade max $\mathrm{gr}[A] = r$. In this case, we form grade-restricted multiplication matrices $\mathbf{G}_r$ and $\mathbf{M}_r$.

4   FVS Multivector Inversion Algorithm

Multivector inverses can be computed using the matrix representation and the characteristic polynomial. The matrix inverse is $\mathbf{A}^{-1} = \hat{\mathbf{A}}/\det \mathbf{A}$, where $\hat{\ }$ denotes the adjunct operation and $\det \mathbf{A}$ is the determinant. The formula is not practical, because it requires the computation of $n^2 + 1$ determinants. By Cayley-Hamilton's Theorem, the inverse of $\mathbf{A}$ is a polynomial in $\mathbf{A}$, which can be computed as the last step of the FVS algorithm [3]. The algorithm has a direct representation in terms of Clifford multiplications as follows:

Theorem 3 (Reduced-grade FVS algorithm). *Suppose that $A \in Cl_{p,q}$ is a multivector of maximal grade $r \leq s$ and $A \subseteq \mathrm{span}[e_1,\ldots,e_s]$. The Clifford inverse, if it exists, can be computed in $k = 2^{\lceil s/2 \rceil}$ steps as*

$$
\begin{array}{ll|ll}
m_1 = A & & c_1 = -kA * 1, & t_1 := -c_1 \\
m_2 = Am_2 - t_1 & & c_2 = -\frac{k}{2}A * m_1, & t_2 := -c_2 \\
\ldots & & \ldots & \\
m_k = Am_{k-1} - t_k & & c_k = -A * m_{k-1}, & t_k := -c_k
\end{array}
$$

until the step where $m_k = 0$ so that

$$A^{-1} = -m_{k-1}/c_k. \tag{2}$$

The inverse does not exist if $c_k = -\det A = 0$.

The (reduced) characteristic polynomial of A of maximal grade r is

$$p_A(\lambda) = \lambda^k + c_1\lambda^{k-1} + \ldots c_{k-1}\lambda + c_k. \qquad (3)$$

Proof. The proof follows from the homomorphism of the π map. We recall the statement of FVS algorithm:

$$p_A(\lambda) = \det(\lambda\mathbf{I}_n - \mathbf{A}) = \lambda^n + c_1\lambda^{n-1} + \ldots c_{n-1}\lambda + c_n, \quad n = \dim(\mathbf{A}),$$

where

$$
\begin{array}{lll}
\mathbf{M}_1 = \mathbf{A}, & t_1 = \text{tr}[\mathbf{M}_1], & c_1 = -t_1 \\
\mathbf{M}_2 = \mathbf{A}\mathbf{M}_1 - t_1\mathbf{I}_n, & t_2 = \frac{1}{2}\text{tr}[\mathbf{A}\mathbf{M}_1], & c_2 = -t_2 \\
\ldots & \ldots & \ldots \\
\mathbf{M}_n = \mathbf{A}\mathbf{M}_{n-1} - t_n\mathbf{I}_n, & t_n = \frac{1}{n}\text{tr}[\mathbf{A}\mathbf{M}_{n-1}], & c_n = -t_n.
\end{array}
$$

The matrix inverse can be computed from the last step of the algorithm as $\mathbf{A}^{-1} = \mathbf{M}_{n-1}/t_n$ under the obvious restriction $t_n \neq 0$.

Therefore, for the kth step of the algorithm application of π^{-1} leads to

$$\pi^{-1} : \mathbf{M}_k = \mathbf{A}\mathbf{M}_{k-1} - t_k\mathbf{I} \mapsto m_k = Am_{k-1} - t_k.$$

Furthermore, $\text{tr}[\mathbf{M}_k] = n\langle m_k\rangle_0 = t_k$ by Eq. 1. Moreover, the FVS algorithm terminates with $\mathbf{M}_n = \mathbf{0}$, which corresponds to the limiting case $n = 2^{p+q}$ wherever A contains all grades.

On the other hand, examining the matrix representations of different Clifford algebras, Acus and Dargys [2] make the observation that according to the Bott periodicity the number of steps can be reduced to $2^{\lceil n/2 \rceil}$. This can be proven as follows. Consider the isomorphism $C\ell_{p,q} \supset C\ell^+_{p,q} \cong C\ell_{q-1,p-1}$. Therefore, if a property holds for an algebra of dimension n it will hold also for the algebra of dimension $n-2$. Therefore, suppose that for n even the characteristic polynomial is square free: $p_A(v) \neq q(v)^2$ for some polynomial. We proceed by reduction. For $n = 2$ in $C\ell_{2,0}$ and $A = a_1 + e_1a_2 + e_2a_3 + e_{12}a_4$ we compute $p_A(v) = \left(a_1^2 - a_2^2 - a_3^2 + a_4^2 - 2a_1v + v^2\right)^2$ and a similar result holds also for the other signatures of $C\ell_2$. Therefore, we have a contradiction and the dimension can be reduced to $k = n/2$.

In the same way, suppose that n is odd and the characteristic polynomial is square-free. However, for $n = 3$ in $C\ell_{3,0}$ and $A = a_1 + e_1a_2 + e_2a_3 + e_3a_4 + a_5e_{12} + a_6e_{13} + a_7e_{23} + a_8e_{123}$ it is established that $p_A(v) = q(v)^2$ for $q(v) =$

$$(a_1^2 - a_2^2 - a_3^2 - a_4^2 + a_5^2 + a_6^2 + a_7^2 - a_8^2 + 2i(a_3a_6 - a_4a_5 - a_2a_7 + a_1a_8) - 2(a_1 + ia_8)v + v^2)$$
$$(a_1^2 - a_2^2 - a_3^2 - a_4^2 + a_5^2 + a_6^2 + a_7^2 - a_8^2 + 2i(a_4a_5 - a_3a_6 + a_2a_7 - a_1a_8) - 2(a_1 - ia_8)v + v^2).$$

The above polynomial is factored due to space limitations. Similar results hold also for the other signatures of $C\ell_3$. Therefore, we have a contradiction and the dimension can be reduced to $k = (n+1)/2$. Therefore, overall, one can reduce the number of steps to $k = 2^{\lceil n/2 \rceil}$.

As a second case, suppose that $\mathrm{gr}[A] = r$. Let $E_r = \mathrm{span}[A]$ be the set of all generators, represented in A and s their number. We compute the restricted multiplication tables $\mathbf{M}(E_r)$ and respectively $\mathbf{G}(E_r)$ and form the restricted map π_r. Then

$$\pi_r(AA^{-1}) = \pi_r(A)\pi_r(A^{-1}) = \mathbf{AA}^{-1} = \mathbf{I}_n, \quad n = 2^s.$$

Therefore, the FVS algorithm terminates in $k = 2^s$ steps. Observe that π^{-1} : $\mathbf{AM}_k \mapsto Am_k$. Therefore, $\mathrm{tr}[\mathbf{AM}_k]$ will map to $nA * m_k$ by Eq. 1. Now, suppose that $t_k \neq 0$; then for the last step of the algorithm we obtain:

$$Am_{k-1} - t_k = 0 \Rightarrow Am_{k-1}/t_k = 1 \Rightarrow A^{-1} = m_{k-1}/t_k.$$

Therefore, by the argument of the previous case, the number of steps can be reduced to $k = 2^{\lceil s/2 \rceil}$.

5   Implementation

Computations are performed using the *Clifford* package in Maxima, which was first demonstrated in [8]. The present version of the package is 2.5 and it is available for download from a Zenodo repository [6]. The function fadlevicg2cp returns the inverse (if it exists) and the reduced characteristic polynomial $p_A(v)$ of a multivector A (Appendix B).

6   Experiments

Experiments were performed on a Dell 64-bit Microsoft Windows 10 Enterprise machine with configuration – Intel® Core™ i5-8350U CPU @ 1.70 GHz, 1.90 GHz and 16 GB RAM. The computations were performed using the Clifford package version 2.5 on Maxima version 5.46.0 using Steel Bank Common Lisp version 2.2.2.

6.1   Symbolical Experiments

Example 1. For $C\ell_{2,0}$ and a multivector $A = a_0 + a_1 e_1 + a_2 e_2 + a_3 e_{12}$ the reduced grade algorithm produces

$$t_1 = -2a_1, \; m_1 = a_1 + e_1 a_2 + e_2 a_3 + a_4 e_{12},$$

resulting in $A^{-1} = (a_1 - e_1 a_2 - e_2 a_3 - a_4 e_{12})/(a_1^2 - a_2^2 - a_3^2 + a_4^2)$ and the characteristic polynomial is $p_A(v) = a_1^2 - a_2^2 - a_3^2 + a_4^2 - 2a_1 v + v^2$.

Example 2. For $C\ell_{1,1}$ and a multivector $A = a_0 + a_1 e_1 + a_2 e_2 + a_3 e_{12}$ the reduced grade algorithm produces

$$t_1 = -2a_1, \; m_1 = a_1 + e_1 a_2 + e_2 a_3 + a_4 e_{12},$$

resulting in $A^{-1} = (-a_1 + e_1 a_2 + e_2 a_3 + a_4 e_{12})/(-a_1^2 + a_2^2 - a_3^2 + a_4^2)$ and the characteristic polynomial is $p_A(v) = a_1^2 - a_2^2 + a_3^2 - a_4^2 - 2a_1 v + v^2$.

Example 3. For $C\ell_{0,2}$ and a multivector $A = a_0 + a_1 e_1 + a_2 e_2 + a_3 e_{12}$ the reduced grade algorithm produces

$$t_1 = -2a_1, \, m_1 = a_1 + e_1 a_2 + e_2 a_3 + a_4 e_{12},$$

resulting in $A^{-1} = (a_1 - e_1 a_2 - e_2 a_3 - a_4 e_{12})/(a_1^2 + a_2^2 + a_3^2 + a_4^2)$ and the characteristic polynomial is $p_A(v) = a_1^2 + a_2^2 + a_3^2 + a_4^2 - 2a_1 v + v^2$.

Bespoke computations are practically instantaneous on the testing hardware configuration. Higher-dimensional symbolic examples produce very long expressions and are not particularly instructive.

6.2   Numerical Experiments

Note that the trivial last steps will be omitted because of space limitations. To demonstrate the utility of FVS algorithm here follow some high-dimensional numerical examples.

Example 4. Let us compute a rational example in $C\ell_{2,5}$. Let $A = 1 - 2B + 5C$, where $B := e_{15}$ and $C := e_1 e_3 e_4$. Then $\text{span}[A] = \{e_1, e_3, e_4, e_5\}$ and for the maximal representation we have $k = 2^4 = 16$ steps:

$$
\begin{aligned}
&t_1 = -16, &&m_1 = -15 + 5C - 2B; \\
&t_2 = 288, &&m_2 = 252 - 70C + 28B; \\
&t_3 = -2912, &&m_3 = -2366 + 1190C - 476B; \\
&t_4 = 29456, &&m_4 = 22092 - 10640C + 4256B; \\
&t_5 = -213696, &&m_5 = -146916 + 99820C - 39928B; \\
&t_6 = 1509760, &&m_6 = 943600 - 634760C + 253904B; \\
&t_7 = -8250496, &&m_7 = -4640904 + 4083240C - 1633296B; \\
&t_8 = 43581024, &&m_8 = 21790512 - 19121280C + 7648512B; \\
&t_9 = -181510912, &&m_9 = -79411024 + 89831280C - 35932512B; \\
&t_{10} = 730723840, &&m_{10} = 274021440 - 307223840C + 122889536B; \\
&t_{11} = -2275435008, &&m_{11} = -711073440 + 1062883360C - 425153344B; \\
&t_{12} = 6900244736, &&m_{12} = 1725061184 - 2492483840C + 996993536B; \\
&t_{13} = -15007376384, &&m_{13} = -2813883072 + 6132822080C - 2453128832B; \\
&t_{14} = 32653412352, &&m_{14} = 4081676544 - 7936593280C + 3174637312B; \\
&t_{15} = -39909726208, &&m_{15} = -2494357888 + 12471789440C - 4988715776B.
\end{aligned}
$$

Therefore, $A^{-1} = (1 - 5C + 2B)/22$ and $p_A(v) = (22 - 2v + v^2)^8$. Evaluation took $0.0469\,\text{s}$ using $12.029\,\text{MB}$ memory on Maxima. On the other hand, the reduced algorithm will run in $k = 2^{\lceil 4/2 \rceil} = 4$ steps:

$$
\begin{aligned}
&t_1 = -4, \quad m_1 = 1 + 5C - 2B; \\
&t_2 = 48, \quad m_2 = -24 - 10C + 4B; \\
&t_3 = -88, \quad m_3 = 66 + 110C - 44B;
\end{aligned}
$$

and $p_A(v) = 484 - 88v + 48v^2 - 4v^3 + v^4 = (22 - 2v + v^2)^2$. Evaluation took $0.0156\,\text{s}$ using $2.512\,\text{MB}$ memory on Maxima. Note, that in this case $\det A = AA^\sim = 22$. Therefore, in accordance with Shirokov's approach $A^{-1} = A^\sim/22$.

Example 5. Consider $C\ell_{5,2}$ and let $A = 1 - e_2 + I$. The full-grade algorithm takes 128 steps and will not be illustrated due to space limitation. The reduced grade algorithm can be illustrated as follows. Let $C = e_{134567}$. Then

$$
\begin{aligned}
t_1 &= -16, & m_1 &= 1 - e_2 + I; \\
t_2 &= 120, & m_2 &= -15 + 14e_2 - 14I + 2C; \\
t_3 &= -560, & m_3 &= 105 - 89e_2 + 93I - 26C; \\
t_4 &= 1836, & m_4 &= -459 + 340e_2 - 388I + 156C; \\
t_5 &= -4560, & m_5 &= 1425 - 881e_2 + 1145I - 572C; \\
t_6 &= 9064, & m_6 &= -3399 + 1682e_2 - 2562I + 1454C; \\
t_7 &= -14960, & m_7 &= 6545 - 2529e_2 + 4557I - 2790C; \\
t_8 &= 20886, & m_8 &= -10443 + 3096e_2 - 6648I + 4296C; \\
t_9 &= -24880, & m_9 &= 13995 - 3051e_2 + 8091I - 5448C; \\
t_{10} &= 25480, & m_{10} &= -15925 + 2386e_2 - 8242I + 5694C; \\
t_{11} &= -22416, & m_{11} &= 15411 - 1475e_2 + 7007I - 4934C; \\
t_{12} &= 16716, & m_{12} &= -12537 + 596e_2 - 4932I + 3548C; \\
t_{13} &= -10480, & m_{13} &= 8515 - 35e_2 + 2795I - 1980C; \\
t_{14} &= 5400, & m_{14} &= -4725 - 50e_2 - 1150I + 850C; \\
t_{15} &= -2000, & m_{15} &= 1875 + 125e_2 + 375I - 250C,
\end{aligned}
$$

resulting in $A^{-1} = (1 - e_2 - 3I + 2C)/5..$ The characteristic polynomial can factorize as $p_A(v) = (1 + v^2)^4(5 - 4v + v^2)^4$.

It should be noted that in this case, the determinant $\det A$ can be computed by the sequence of operations $B = AA^t = 1 - 2I$, followed by $\det A = BB^\sim = 5$. This allows for writing the formula

$$
A^{-1} = A^t(AA^t)^\sim/5
$$

in accordance with Shirokov's approach.

7 Concluding Remarks

The maximal matrix algebra construction exhibited in the present paper allows for systematic translation of matrix-based algorithms to Clifford algebra simultaneously allowing for their direct verification.

The advantage of the multivector FVS algorithm is its simplicity of implementation. This can be beneficial for purely numerical applications as it involves only Clifford multiplication, and taking scalar parts of multivectors, which can be encoded as the first member of an array. The Clifford multiplication computation can be reduced to $\mathcal{O}(N \log N)$ operations, since it involves sorting of a joined list of algebra generators. On the other hand, the present algorithm does not ensure optimality of the computation but only provides a certificate of existence of an inverse. Therefore, optimized algorithms can be introduced for particular applications, i.e. Space-Time Algebra $C\ell_{1,4}$, Projective Geometric Algebra $C\ell_{3,0,1}$, Conformal Geometric Algebra $C\ell_{4,1}$, etc. As a side product, the algorithm can compute the characteristic polynomial of a general multivector and, hence, its determinant also without any resort to a matrix representation. This could be used, for example, for computation of a multivector resolvent or some other analytical functions.

One of the main applications of the present algorithms could be in Finite Element Modelling where the Geometric algebra can improve the efficiency and accuracy of calculations by providing a more compact representation of vectors, tensors, and geometric operations. This can lead to faster and more accurate simulations of elastic deformations.

Acknowledgment. The present work is funded in part by the European Union's Horizon Europe program under grant agreement VIBraTE, grant agreement 101086815.

A   Supporting results

Definition 5 (Sparsity property). *A matrix has the sparsity property if it has exactly one non-zero element per column and exactly one non-zero element per row. Such a matrix we call sparse.*

Lemma 1 (Sparsity lemma). *If the matrices* **A** *and* **B** *are sparse then so is* **C** $=$ **AB**. *Moreover,*

$$c_{ij} = \begin{cases} 0 \\ a_{iq}b_{qj} \end{cases}$$

(no summation!) for some index q.

Proof. Consider two sparse square matrices **A** and **B** of dimension n. Let $c_{ij} = \sum_{\mu} a_{i\mu}b_{\mu j}$. Then as we vary the row index i then there is only one index $q \leq n$, such that $a_{iq} \neq 0$. As we vary the column index j then there is only one index $q \leq n$, such that $b_{qj} \neq 0$. Therefore, $c_{ij} = (0; a_{iq}b_{qj})$ for some q by the sparsity of **A** and **B**. As we vary the row index i then $c_{qj} = 0$ for $i \neq q$ for the column j by the sparsity of **A**. As we vary the column index j then $c_{iq} = 0$ for $j \neq q$ for the row i by the sparsity of **B**. Therefore, **AB** is sparse.

Lemma 2 (Multiplication Matrix Structure). *For the multi-index disjoint sets* $S \prec T$ *the following implications hold for the elements of* **M** *:*

$$
\begin{array}{ccc}
m_{\mu\lambda}\, e_S & \xrightarrow{\exists\lambda' > \lambda} & m_{\mu\lambda'} e_T \\
\Big\downarrow{\exists} & & \Big\downarrow \\
m_{\lambda\mu}e_S & \xrightarrow{\exists} m_{\lambda\mu}m_{\mu\lambda'}e_{S\triangle T} & \xrightarrow{\exists\lambda'' = \lambda'} m_{\lambda\lambda''}e_{S\triangle T}
\end{array}
$$

so that $m_{\lambda\lambda'} = m_{\lambda\mu}\sigma_{\mu}m_{\mu\lambda'}$ *for some index* μ.

Proof. Suppose that the ordering of elements is given in the construction of $C\ell_{p,q,r}$. To simplify presentation, without loss of generality, suppose that e_s and e_t are some generators. By the properties of $\mathbf{M}$ there exists an index $\lambda' > \lambda$, such that $e_M e_{L'} = m_{\mu\lambda'}\, e_t$, $L'\backslash M = T$ for $L \prec L'$. Choose M, s.d. $L \prec M \prec L'$. Then for $L \prec M \prec L'$ and $S \prec T$

$$e_M e_L = m_{\mu\lambda}\, e_s, \quad L\triangle M = S \Leftrightarrow e_L e_M = m_{\lambda\mu}\, e_s$$
$$e_M e_{L'} = m_{\mu\lambda'}\, e_t, \quad L'\triangle M = T$$

Suppose that $e_s e_t = e_{st}$, $st = S \cup T = S\triangle T$. Multiply together the diagonal nodes in the matrix

$$e_L \underbrace{e_M e_M}_{\sigma_\mu} e_{L'} = m_{\lambda\mu} m_{\mu\lambda'}\, e_{st}$$

Therefore, $s \in L$ and $t \in L'$. We observe that there is at least one element (the algebra unity) with the desired property $\sigma_\mu \neq 0$.

Further, we observe that there exists unique index λ'' such that $m_{\lambda\lambda''} e_{st}$. Since λ is fixed. This implies that $L'' = L' \Rightarrow \lambda'' = \lambda'$. Therefore,

$$e_L e_{L'} = m_{\lambda\lambda'} e_{st}, \quad L'\triangle L = \{s,t\}$$

which implies the identity $m_{\lambda\lambda'}\, e_{st} = m_{\lambda\mu}\sigma_\mu m_{\mu\lambda'}\, e_{st}$. For higher graded elements e_S and e_T we should write $e_{S\triangle T}$ instead of e_{st}.

Proposition 3. *Consider the multiplication table $\mathbf{M}$. All elements m_{kj} are different for a fixed row k. All elements m_{iq} are different for a fixed column q.*

Proof. Fix k. Then for $e_K, e_J \in \mathbf{B}$ we have $e_K e_J = m_{kj} e_S$, $S = K\triangle J$. Suppose that we have equality for 2 indices j, j'. Then $K\triangle J' = K\triangle J = S$. Let $\delta = J \cap J'$; then

$$K\triangle (J \cup \delta) = K\triangle J = S \Rightarrow K\triangle\delta = S \Rightarrow \delta = \emptyset$$

Therefore, $j = j'$. By symmetry, the same reasoning applies to a fixed column q.

Proposition 4. *For $e_s \in \mathbf{E}$ the matrix $\mathbf{A}_s = C_s(\mathbf{M})$ is sparse.*

Proof. Fix an element $e_s \in \mathbf{E}$. Consider a row k. By Proposition 3 there is a j, such $e_{kj} = e_s$. Then $a_{kj} = m_{kj}$, while for $i \neq j$ $a_{ki} = 0$.

Consider a column l By Proposition 3 there is a j, such $e_{jl} = e_s$. Then $a_{jl} = m_{jl}$, while for $i \neq j$ $a_{il} = 0$. Therefore, $\mathbf{A}_s$ has the sparsity property.

Proposition 5. *For generator elements e_s and e_t $\mathbf{E}_s\mathbf{E}_t + \mathbf{E}_t\mathbf{E}_s = 0$.*

Proof. Consider the basis elements e_s and e_t. By linearity and homomorphism of the π map (Theorem 1): $\pi : e_s e_t + e_t e_s = 0 \mapsto \pi(e_s e_t) + \pi(e_t e_s) = \mathbf{0}$. Therefore, for two vector elements $\mathbf{E}_s\mathbf{E}_t + \mathbf{E}_t\mathbf{E}_s = \mathbf{0}$.

Proposition 6. $\mathbf{E_s E_s} = \sigma_s \mathbf{I}$

Proof. Consider the matrix $\mathbf{W} = \mathbf{GA_s GA_s}$. Then $w_{\mu\nu} = \sum_\lambda \sigma_\mu \sigma_\lambda a_{\mu\lambda} a_{\lambda\nu}$ element-wise. By Lemma 1 $\mathbf{W}$ is sparse so that $w_{\mu\nu} = (0; \sigma_\mu \sigma_q a_{\mu q} a_{q\nu})$.

From the structure of $\mathbf{M}$ for the entries containing the element e_S we have the equivalence

$$\begin{cases} e_M e_Q = a^s_{\mu q} e_S, & S = M \triangle Q \\ e_Q e_M = a^s_{q\mu} e_S, \end{cases}$$

After multiplication of the equations we obtain $e_M e_Q e_Q e_M = a^s_{\mu q} e_S a^s_{q\mu} e_S$, which simplifies to the *First fundamental identity*:

$$\sigma_q \sigma_\mu = a^s_{\mu q} a^s_{q\mu} \sigma_s \tag{4}$$

We observe that if $\sigma_\mu = 0$ or $\sigma_q = 0$ the result follows trivially. In this case also $\sigma_s = 0$. Therefore, let's suppose that $\sigma_s \sigma_q \sigma_\mu \neq 0$. We multiply both sides by $\sigma_s \sigma_q \sigma_\mu$ to obtain $\sigma_s = \sigma_q \sigma_\mu a^s_{\mu q} a^s_{q\mu}$. However, the RHS is a diagonal element of $\mathbf{W}$, therefore by the sparsity it is the only non-zero element for a given row/column so that $\mathbf{W} = \mathbf{E_s^2} = \sigma_s \mathbf{I}$.

B   Program code

The Clifford package can be downloaded from a Zenodo repository [6]. The examples can be downloaded from a Zenodo repository and it includes the file climatrep.mac, which implements different instances of the FVS algorithm [7].

Listing 1.1. FVS Maxima code based on the Clifford package

```
1    fadlevicg2cp (A, v):=block(
     [M:1, K, i:1, n, k:length(clv(A)), cq, c, ss],
        n:2^(ceiling(k/2)),
        array(c,n+1),   for r:0 thru n+1 do c[r]:1,
        A:rat(A),
6       ss:c[1]*v^^n,
        while i<n and K#0 do (
            K:dotsimpc(expand (A.M)),
            cq:-n/i*scalarpart(K),
            if _debug1=all then print("t_{",i,"}=",cq,"
               m_{",i,"}=",K,"\\\\"),
11          if K#0 then
                M: rat(K + cq),
                c[i+1]:cq, ss:ss+c[i+1]*v^^(n-i),
                i:i+1
            ),
16       K:dotsimpc(expand(A.M)),
         cq:-n/i*scalarpart(K),
         if _debug1=all then print("t_{",i,"}=",cq," m_{",
            i,"}=",K,"\\\\"),
         ss:ss+cq,
         if cq=0 then cq:1, M:factor(-(M)/cq),
21       [M, ss]
     );
```

References

1. Acus, A., Dargys, A.: The inverse of a multivector: beyond the threshold $p + q = 5$. Adv. Appl. Clifford Algebras **28**(3), 1–20 (2018). https://doi.org/10.1007/s00006-018-0885-4

2. Acus, A., Dargys, A.: The characteristic polynomial in calculation of exponential and elementary functions in Clifford algebras. Math. Methods Appl. Sci. (2022). https://doi.org/10.22541/au.167101043.33855504/v1

3. Faddeev, D.K., Sominskij, I.S.: Sbornik Zadatch po Vyshej Algebre. Nauka, Moscow-Leningrad (1949)

4. Hitzer, E., Sangwine, S.J.: Construction of multivector inverse for Clifford algebras over $2m + 1$ - dimensional vector spaces from multivector inverse for clifford algebras over 2m-dimensional vector spaces. Adv. Appl. Clifford Algebras **29**(2), 1–22 (2019). https://doi.org/10.1007/s00006-019-0942-7

5. Hitzer, E., Sangwine, S.: Multivector and multivector matrix inverses in real Clifford algebras. Appl. Math. Comput. **311**, 375–389 (2017). https://doi.org/10.1016/j.amc.2017.05.027

6. Prodanov, D.: Clifford Maxima package v 2.5.4. https://doi.org/10.5281/ZENODO.8205828, https://zenodo.org/record/8205828

7. Prodanov, D.: Examples for CGI2023. https://doi.org/10.5281/ZENODO.8207889

8. Prodanov, D., Toth, V.T.: Sparse representations of Clifford and tensor algebras in Maxima. Adv. Appl. Clifford Algebras **27**, 1–23 (2016). https://doi.org/10.1007/s00006-016-0682-x

9. Shirokov, D.S.: On computing the determinant, other characteristic polynomial coefficients, and inverse in Clifford algebras of arbitrary dimension. Comp. Appl. Math. **40**(5), 173 (2021). https://doi.org/10.1007/s40314-021-01536-0

On Singular Value Decomposition and Polar Decomposition in Geometric Algebras

Dmitry Shirokov[1,2]([⊠]) [iD]

[1] HSE University, 101000 Moscow, Russia
dshirokov@hse.ru
[2] Institute for Information Transmission Problems of the Russian Academy of Sciences, 127051 Moscow, Russia
shirokov@iitp.ru

Abstract. This paper is a brief note on the natural implementation of singular value decomposition (SVD) and polar decomposition of an arbitrary multivector in nondegenerate real (Clifford) geometric algebras of arbitrary dimension and signature. We naturally define these and other related structures (operation of Hermitian conjugation, Euclidean space, and Lie groups) in geometric algebras. The results can be used in various applications of geometric algebras in computer graphics, computer vision, data analysis, computer science, engineering, physics, big data, machine learning, etc.

Keywords: Clifford algebra · geometric algebra · orthogonal group · polar decomposition · singular value decomposition · SVD · symplectic group · unitary group

1 Introduction

This paper is a brief note on the natural implementation of singular value decomposition (SVD) and polar decomposition of an arbitrary multivector in nondegenerate real (Clifford) geometric algebras of arbitrary dimension and signature. We naturally define these and other related structures (operation of Hermitian conjugation, Euclidean space, and Lie groups) in geometric algebras. "Natural" means that our definitions and statements involve only operations in geometric algebra and do not involve the corresponding matrix representations. Detailed proofs and examples will be in the extended version of this paper.

The method of singular value decomposition for matrices was discovered independently by E. Beltrami in 1873 [3] and C. Jordan in 1874 [7,8]. Nowadays it is very important because of various applications in computer science, engineering, physics, big data, machine learning, etc. Applications of quaternion singular value decomposition in image processing are considered in [12]. Polar decomposition of complexified quaternions and octonions is discussed in [13]. In the present paper, we present the natural implementation of SVD and polar decomposition in geometric algebras. Theorems 4 and 8 are new.

© The Author(s), under exclusive license to Springer Nature Switzerland AG 2024
B. Sheng et al. (Eds.): CGI 2023, LNCS 14498, pp. 391–401, 2024.
https://doi.org/10.1007/978-3-031-50078-7_31

2   Geometric Algebra (GA)

Let us consider the real Clifford geometric algebra (GA) $\mathcal{G}_{p,q}$ [4, 9, 10, 20] with the identity element $e \equiv 1$ and the generators e_a, $a = 1, 2, \ldots, n$, where $n = p+q \geq 1$. The generators satisfy the conditions

$$e_a e_b + e_b e_a = 2\eta_{ab} e, \qquad \eta = (\eta_{ab}) = \mathrm{diag}(\underbrace{1, \ldots, 1}_{p}, \underbrace{-1, \ldots, -1}_{q}).$$

Consider the subspaces $\mathcal{G}_{p,q}^k$ of grades $k = 0, 1, \ldots, n$, which elements are linear combinations of the basis elements $e_A = e_{a_1 a_2 \ldots a_k} = e_{a_1} e_{a_2} \cdots e_{a_k}$, $1 \leq a_1 < a_2 < \cdots < a_k \leq n$, with ordered multi-indices of length k. An arbitrary element (multivector) $M \in \mathcal{G}_{p,q}$ has the form

$$M = \sum_A m_A e_A \in \mathcal{G}_{p,q}, \qquad m_A \in \mathbb{R},$$

where we have a sum over arbitrary multi-index A of length from 0 to n. The projection of M onto the subspace $\mathcal{G}_{p,q}^k$ is denoted by $\langle M \rangle_k$.

The grade involution and reversion of a multivector $M \in \mathcal{G}_{p,q}$ are denoted by

$$\widehat{M} = \sum_{k=0}^{n} (-1)^k \langle M \rangle_k, \qquad \widetilde{M} = \sum_{k=0}^{n} (-1)^{\frac{k(k-1)}{2}} \langle M \rangle_k \qquad (1)$$

and have the properties

$$\widehat{M_1 M_2} = \widehat{M_1}\widehat{M_2}, \qquad \widetilde{M_1 M_2} = \widetilde{M_2}\widetilde{M_1}, \qquad \forall M_1, M_2 \in \mathcal{G}_{p,q}. \qquad (2)$$

3   Euclidean Space on GA

Let us consider an operation of Hermitian conjugation † in $\mathcal{G}_{p,q}$ (see [11, 20]):

$$M^\dagger := M|_{e_A \to (e_A)^{-1}} = \sum_A m_A (e_A)^{-1}. \qquad (3)$$

We have the following two other equivalent definitions of this operation:

$$M^\dagger = \begin{cases} e_{1 \ldots p} \widetilde{M} e_{1 \ldots p}^{-1}, & \text{if } p \text{ is odd}, \\ e_{1 \ldots p} \widehat{\widetilde{M}} e_{1 \ldots p}^{-1}, & \text{if } p \text{ is even}, \end{cases} \qquad (4)$$

$$M^\dagger = \begin{cases} e_{p+1 \ldots n} \widetilde{M} e_{p+1 \ldots n}^{-1}, & \text{if } q \text{ is even}, \\ e_{p+1 \ldots n} \widehat{\widetilde{M}} e_{p+1 \ldots n}^{-1}, & \text{if } q \text{ is odd}. \end{cases} \qquad (5)$$

The operation[1]

$$(M_1, M_2) := \langle M_1^\dagger M_2 \rangle_0$$

---

[1] Compare with the well-known operation $M_1 * M_2 := \langle \widetilde{M_1} M_2 \rangle_0$ in the real geometric algebra $\mathcal{G}_{p,q}$, which is positive definite only in the case of signature $(p, q) = (n, 0)$.

is a (positive definite) scalar product with the properties

$$(M_1, M_2) = (M_2, M_1), \tag{6}$$
$$(M_1 + M_2, M_3) = (M_1, M_3) + (M_2, M_3), \quad (M_1, \lambda M_2) = \lambda(M_1, M_2), \tag{7}$$
$$(M, M) \geq 0, \quad \forall M \in \mathcal{G}_{p,q}; \quad (M, M) = 0 \Leftrightarrow M = 0 \tag{8}$$

for arbitrary multivectors $M_1, M_2, M_3 \in \mathcal{G}_{p,q}$ and $\lambda \in \mathbb{R}$.

Using this scalar product we introduce inner product space over the field of real numbers (euclidean space) in $\mathcal{G}_{p,q}$. We have a norm

$$||M|| := \sqrt{(M, M)} = \sqrt{\langle M^\dagger M \rangle_0} \tag{9}$$

with the properties

$$||M|| \geq 0, \quad \forall M \in \mathcal{G}_{p,q}; \quad ||M|| = 0 \Leftrightarrow M = 0, \tag{10}$$
$$||M_1 + M_2|| \leq ||M_1|| + ||M_2||, \quad \forall M_1, M_2 \in \mathcal{G}_{p,q}, \tag{11}$$
$$||\lambda M|| = |\lambda| ||M||, \quad \forall M \in \mathcal{G}_{p,q}, \quad \forall \lambda \in \mathbb{R}. \tag{12}$$

4   Matrix Representation of $\mathcal{G}_{p,q}$ and Lie Groups

Let us consider the following faithful representation (isomorphism) of the real geometric algebra $\mathcal{G}_{p,q}$

$$\beta : \mathcal{G}_{p,q} \rightarrow \begin{cases} \mathrm{Mat}(2^{\frac{n}{2}}, \mathbb{R}), & \text{if } p - q = 0, 2 \mod 8, \\ \mathrm{Mat}(2^{\frac{n-1}{2}}, \mathbb{R}) \oplus \mathrm{Mat}(2^{\frac{n-1}{2}}, \mathbb{R}), & \text{if } p - q = 1 \mod 8, \\ \mathrm{Mat}(2^{\frac{n-1}{2}}, \mathbb{C}), & \text{if } p - q = 3, 7 \mod 8, \\ \mathrm{Mat}(2^{\frac{n-2}{2}}, \mathbb{H}), & \text{if } p - q = 4, 6 \mod 8, \\ \mathrm{Mat}(2^{\frac{n-3}{2}}, \mathbb{H}) \oplus \mathrm{Mat}(2^{\frac{n-3}{2}}, \mathbb{H}), & \text{if } p - q = 5 \mod 8. \end{cases} \tag{13}$$

These isomorphisms are known as Cartan–Bott 8-periodicity.

Let us denote the size of the corresponding matrices by

$$d := \begin{cases} 2^{\frac{n}{2}}, & \text{if } p - q = 0, 2 \mod 8, \\ 2^{\frac{n+1}{2}}, & \text{if } p - q = 1 \mod 8, \\ 2^{\frac{n-1}{2}}, & \text{if } p - q = 3, 5, 7 \mod 8, \\ 2^{\frac{n-2}{2}}, & \text{if } p - q = 4, 6 \mod 8. \end{cases} \tag{14}$$

Note that we use block-diagonal matrices in the cases $p - q = 1, 5 \mod 8$.

Let us present an explicit form of one of these representations of $\mathcal{G}_{p,q}$ (see also [15, 21–23]). We denote this fixed representation by β'. For the identity element, we always use the identity matrix $\beta'(e) = I$ of the corresponding size d. We always take $\beta'(e_{a_1 a_2 \ldots a_k}) = \beta'(e_{a_1})\beta'(e_{a_2}) \cdots \beta'(e_{a_k})$.

In some particular cases, we construct β' in the following way:

– In the case $\mathcal{G}_{0,1}$: $e_1 \rightarrow i$.

- In the case $\mathcal{G}_{1,0}$: $e_1 \to \mathrm{diag}(1,-1)$.
- In the case $\mathcal{G}_{0,2}$: $e_1 \to i$, $e_2 \to j$.
- In the case $\mathcal{G}_{0,3}$: $e_1 \to \mathrm{diag}(i,-i)$, $e_2 \to \mathrm{diag}(j,-j)$, $e_3 \to \mathrm{diag}(k,-k)$.

Suppose we know $\beta'_a := \beta'(e_a)$, $a = 1,\ldots,n$ for some fixed $\mathcal{G}_{p,q}$, $p+q=n$. Then we construct explicit matrix representation of $\mathcal{G}_{p+1,q+1}$, $\mathcal{G}_{q+1,p-1}$, $\mathcal{G}_{p-4,q-4}$ in the following way using the matrices β'_a, $a = 1,\ldots,n$.

- In the case $\mathcal{G}_{p+1,q+1}$: $e_a \to \mathrm{diag}(\beta'_a, -\beta'_a)$, $a = 1,\ldots,p, p+2,\ldots,p+q+1$. In the subcase $p - q \neq 1 \mod 4$, we have

$$e_{p+1} \to \begin{pmatrix} 0 & I \\ I & 0 \end{pmatrix}, \qquad e_{p+q+2} \to \begin{pmatrix} 0 & -I \\ I & 0 \end{pmatrix}.$$

In the subcase $p - q = 1 \mod 4$, we have

$$e_{p+1} \to \mathrm{diag}(\beta_1 \cdots \beta_n \Omega, -\beta_1 \cdots \beta_n \Omega), \qquad e_{p+q+2} \to \mathrm{diag}(\Omega, -\Omega),$$

where

$$\Omega = \begin{pmatrix} 0 & -I \\ I & 0 \end{pmatrix}. \tag{15}$$

- In the case $\mathcal{G}_{q+1,p-1}$: $e_1 \to \beta'_1$, $e_i \to \beta'_i \beta'_1$, $i = 2,\ldots,n$.
- In the case $\mathcal{G}_{p-4,q+4}$: $e_i \to \beta'_i \beta'_1 \beta'_2 \beta'_3 \beta'_4$, $i = 1,2,3,4$, $e_j \to \beta'_j$, $j = 5,\ldots,n$.

Using these recurrences and the Cartan–Bott 8-periodicity, we obtain explicit matrix representation β' of all $\mathcal{G}_{p,q}$.

It can be directly verified that for this matrix representation we have

$$\eta_{aa}\beta'(e_a) = \begin{cases} (\beta'(e_a))^{\mathrm{T}}, & \text{if } p - q = 0,1,2 \mod 8, \\ (\beta'(e_a))^{\mathrm{H}}, & \text{if } p - q = 3,7 \mod 8, \\ (\beta'(e_a))^{*}, & \text{if } p - q = 4,5,6 \mod 8, \end{cases} \qquad a = 1,\ldots,n, \tag{16}$$

where T is transpose of a (real) matrix, H is the Hermitian transpose of a (complex) matrix, $*$ is the conjugate transpose of a matrix over quaternions. Using the linearity, we get that these matrix conjugations are consistent with Hermitian conjugation of corresponding multivector:

$$\beta'(M^{\dagger}) = \begin{cases} (\beta'(M))^{\mathrm{T}}, & \text{if } p - q = 0,1,2 \mod 8, \\ (\beta'(M))^{\mathrm{H}}, & \text{if } p - q = 3,7 \mod 8, \\ (\beta'(M))^{*}, & \text{if } p - q = 4,5,6 \mod 8, \end{cases} \qquad M \in \mathcal{G}_{p,q}. \tag{17}$$

Note that the formulas like (17) are not valid for an arbitrary matrix representation β of the form (13). They are true for the matrix representations $\gamma = T^{-1}\beta' T$ obtained from β' by the matrix T such that

- $T^{\mathrm{T}}T = I$ in the cases $p - q = 0,1,2 \mod 8$,
- $T^{\mathrm{H}}T = I$ in the cases $p - q = 3,7 \mod 8$,

– $T^*T = I$ in the cases $p - q = 4, 5, 6 \mod 8$.

Let us consider the following Lie group in $\mathcal{G}_{p,q}$

$$G\mathcal{G}_{p,q} = \{M \in \mathcal{G}_{p,q} : M^\dagger M = e\}, \tag{18}$$

where $\dagger$ is (3). Note that all the basis elements e_A of $\mathcal{G}_{p,q}$ belong to this group by the definition.

Using (13) and (17), we get the following isomorphisms of this group to the classical matrix Lie groups:

$$G\mathcal{G}_{p,q} \simeq \begin{cases} O(2^{\frac{n}{2}}), & \text{if } p - q = 0, 2 \mod 8, \\ O(2^{\frac{n-1}{2}}) \times O(2^{\frac{n-1}{2}}), & \text{if } p - q = 1 \mod 8, \\ U(2^{\frac{n-1}{2}}), & \text{if } p - q = 3, 7 \mod 8, \\ Sp(2^{\frac{n-2}{2}}), & \text{if } p - q = 4, 6 \mod 8, \\ Sp(2^{\frac{n-3}{2}}) \times Sp(2^{\frac{n-3}{2}}), & \text{if } p - q = 5 \mod 8, \end{cases} \tag{19}$$

where we have the following notation for (orthogonal, unitary, and symplectic correspondingly) classical matrix Lie groups

$$O(k) = \{A \in \text{Mat}(k, \mathbb{R}) : \quad A^T A = I\}, \tag{20}$$
$$U(k) = \{A \in \text{Mat}(k, \mathbb{C}) : \quad A^H A = I\}, \tag{21}$$
$$Sp(k) = \{A \in \text{Mat}(k, \mathbb{H}) : \quad A^* A = I\}. \tag{22}$$

The group $Sp(k)$ sometimes is called quaternionic unitary group or hyperunitary group. Note that this group also has the following realization in terms of complex matrices:

$$Sp(k) \simeq \{A \in \text{Mat}(2k, \mathbb{C}) : \quad A^T \Omega A = \Omega, \quad A^H A = I\},$$

where Ω is (15).

5   On the Classical SVD of Real, Complex, and Quaternion Matrices

We have the following well-known theorems on singular value decomposition of an arbitrary real, complex, and quaternion matrices (see, for example, [5,6,24]).

Theorem 1. *For an arbitrary $A \in \mathbb{R}^{n \times m}$, there exist matrices $U \in O(n)$ and $V \in O(m)$ such that*

$$A = U \Sigma V^T, \tag{23}$$

where

$$\Sigma = \text{diag}(\lambda_1, \lambda_2, \ldots, \lambda_k), \quad k = \min(n, m), \quad \mathbb{R} \ni \lambda_1, \lambda_2, \ldots, \lambda_k \geq 0.$$

Note that choosing matrices $U \in O(n)$ and $V \in O(m)$, we can always arrange diagonal elements of the matrix Σ in decreasing order $\lambda_1 \geq \lambda_2 \geq \cdots \geq \lambda_k \geq 0$.

Diagonal elements of the matrix Σ are called singular values, they are square roots of eigenvalues of the matrices AA^{T} or $A^{\mathrm{T}}A$. Columns of the matrices U and V are eigenvectors of the matrices AA^{T} and $A^{\mathrm{T}}A$ respectively.

Theorem 2. *For an arbitrary $A \in \mathbb{C}^{n \times m}$, there exist matrices $U \in \mathrm{U}(n)$ and $V \in \mathrm{U}(m)$ such that*

$$A = U\Sigma V^{\mathrm{H}}, \tag{24}$$

where

$$\Sigma = \mathrm{diag}(\lambda_1, \lambda_2, \ldots, \lambda_k), \qquad k = \min(n, m), \qquad \mathbb{R} \ni \lambda_1, \lambda_2, \ldots, \lambda_k \geq 0.$$

Note that choosing matrices $U \in \mathrm{U}(n)$ and $V \in \mathrm{U}(m)$, we can always arrange diagonal elements of the matrix Σ in decreasing order $\lambda_1 \geq \lambda_2 \geq \cdots \geq \lambda_k \geq 0$.

Diagonal elements of the matrix Σ are called singular values, they are square roots of eigenvalues of the matrices AA^{H} or $A^{\mathrm{H}}A$. Columns of the matrices U and V are eigenvectors of the matrices AA^{H} and $A^{\mathrm{H}}A$ respectively.

Theorem 3. *For an arbitrary $A \in \mathbb{H}^{n \times m}$, there exist matrices $U \in \mathrm{Sp}(n)$ and $V \in \mathrm{Sp}(m)$ such that*

$$A = U\Sigma V^{*}, \tag{25}$$

where

$$\Sigma = \mathrm{diag}(\lambda_1, \lambda_2, \ldots, \lambda_k), \qquad k = \min(n, m), \qquad \mathbb{R} \ni \lambda_1, \lambda_2, \ldots, \lambda_k \geq 0.$$

Diagonal elements of the matrix Σ are called singular values.

6   SVD in GA

In the following theorem, we present singular value decomposition of an arbitrary multivector in geometric algebra $\mathcal{G}_{p,q}$. Note that the statement involves only operations in $\mathcal{G}_{p,q}$.

Theorem 4 (SVD in GA). *For an arbitrary multivector $M \in \mathcal{G}_{p,q}$, there exist multivectors $U, V \in \mathrm{G}\mathcal{G}_{p,q}$, where*

$$\mathrm{G}\mathcal{G}_{p,q} = \{U \in \mathcal{G}_{p,q} : U^{\dagger}U = e\}, \quad U^{\dagger} := \sum_A u_A(e_A)^{-1},$$

such that

$$M = U\Sigma V^{\dagger}, \tag{26}$$

where multivector Σ belongs to the subset K of $\mathcal{G}_{p,q}$, which is real span of a set of d (14) fixed basis elements (always including the identity element e):

$$\Sigma \in K := \mathrm{span}(\{e_{B_i}, i = 1, \ldots, d\}) = \{\sum_{i=1}^{d} \lambda_i e_{B_i}, \quad \lambda_i \in \mathbb{R}\}. \tag{27}$$

Proof. Let us use the matrix representation β' of $\mathcal{G}_{p,q}$ from Sect. 4. Then we use the isomorphisms (19) and SVD of matrices (see Sect. 5). In the cases $p - q = 1, 5$ mod 8, the matrix representation is block-diagonal and we use SVD for each of two blocks. The singular values are always real and we get a real span of d basis elements of $\mathcal{G}_{p,q}$ with real diagonal matrix representation. $\qquad\square$

Thus the meaning of SVD in geometric algebra is the following: after multiplication on the left and on the right by elements of the group $G\mathcal{G}_{p,q}$ (18), any multivector $M \in \mathcal{G}_{p,q}$ can be placed in a d-dimensional subspace K of $\mathcal{G}_{p,q}$, where d is (14).

Example 1. In the case $\mathcal{G}_{2,0}$, we have

$$\beta'(e) = \begin{pmatrix} 1 & 0 \\ 0 & 1 \end{pmatrix}, \quad \beta'(e_1) = \begin{pmatrix} 0 & 1 \\ 1 & 0 \end{pmatrix}, \quad \beta'(e_2) = \begin{pmatrix} -1 & 0 \\ 0 & 1 \end{pmatrix}, \quad \beta'(e_{12}) = \begin{pmatrix} 0 & 1 \\ -1 & 0 \end{pmatrix}.$$

The matrices $\beta'(e)$ and $\beta'(e_2)$ are real and diagonal, we get the 2-dimensional subspace

$$K = \mathrm{span}(e, e_2).$$

Example 2. In the case $\mathcal{G}_{2,1}$, the matrices $\beta'(e)$, $\beta'(e_1)$, $\beta'(e_{23})$, and $\beta'(e_{123})$ are real and diagonal. We get the 4-dimensional subspace

$$K = \mathrm{span}(e, e_1, e_{23}, e_{123}).$$

Example 3. In the case $\mathcal{G}_{1,3}$, the matrices $\beta'(e)$, $\beta'(e_{14})$ are real and diagonal. We get the 2-dimensional subspace

$$K = \mathrm{span}(e, e_{14}).$$

7   On the Classical Polar Decomposition of Real, Complex, and Quaternion Matrices

Let us consider a classical polar decomposition (right and left) of arbitrary square real, complex, and quaternion matrices (for quaternion case, see [24]).

Theorem 5. *For an arbitrary $A \in \mathbb{R}^{n \times n}$, there exist positive semi-definite symmetric matrices P and $S \in \mathbb{R}^{n \times n}$ (i.e. $P^{\mathrm{T}} = P$ and $z^{\mathrm{T}} P z \geq 0$, $\forall z \in \mathbb{R}^n$; $S^{\mathrm{T}} = S$ and $z^{\mathrm{T}} S z \geq 0$, $\forall z \in \mathbb{R}^n$) and matrix $W \in \mathrm{O}(n)$ such that*

$$A = WP = SW. \tag{28}$$

Given a real symmetric matrix P, the following statements are equivalent:

- P is positive semi-definite,
- all the eigenvalues of P are non-negative,
- there exists a matrix B such that $P = B^{\mathrm{T}} B$.

If we have SVD of the real matrix $A = U\Sigma V^{\mathrm{T}}$, then we can take $W = UV^{\mathrm{T}}$, $P = V\Sigma V^{\mathrm{T}}$, and $S = U\Sigma U^{\mathrm{T}}$. Note that $P = \sqrt{A^{\mathrm{T}}A}$ and $S = WPW^{\mathrm{T}} = \sqrt{AA^{\mathrm{T}}}$.

Theorem 6. *For an arbitrary* $A \in \mathbb{C}^{n \times n}$, *there exist positive semi-definite Hermitian matrices* P *and* $S \in \mathbb{C}^{n \times n}$ *(i.e.* $P^{\mathrm{H}} = P$ *and* $z^{\mathrm{H}}Pz \geq 0, \forall z \in \mathbb{C}^n; S^{\mathrm{H}} = S$ *and* $z^{\mathrm{H}}Sz \geq 0, \forall z \in \mathbb{C}^n$) *and matrix* $W \in \mathrm{U}(n)$ *such that*

$$A = WP = SW. \tag{29}$$

Given a complex Hermitian matrix P, the following statements are equivalent:

– P is positive semi-definite,
– all the eigenvalues of P are non-negative,
– there exists a matrix B such that $P = B^{\mathrm{H}}B$.

If we have SVD of the complex matrix $A = U\Sigma V^{\mathrm{H}}$, then we can take $W = UV^{\mathrm{H}}$, $P = V\Sigma V^{\mathrm{H}}$, and $S = U\Sigma U^{\mathrm{H}}$. Note that $P = \sqrt{A^{\mathrm{H}}A}$ and $S = WPW^{\mathrm{H}} = \sqrt{AA^{\mathrm{H}}}$.

Theorem 7. *For an arbitrary* $A \in \mathbb{H}^{n \times n}$, *there exist quaternion positive semi-definite Hermitian matrices* P *and* $S \in \mathbb{H}^{n \times n}$ *(i.e.* $P^* = P$ *and* $z^*Pz \geq 0$, $\forall z \in \mathbb{H}^n; S^* = S$ *and* $z^*Sz \geq 0, \forall z \in \mathbb{H}^n$) *and matrix* $W \in \mathrm{Sp}(n)$ *such that*

$$A = WP = SW. \tag{30}$$

Given a quaternion Hermitian matrix P, the following statements are equivalent:

– P is positive semi-definite,
– all the eigenvalues of P are non-negative,
– there exists a matrix B such that $P = B^*B$.

If we have SVD of the quaternion matrix $A = U\Sigma V^*$, then we can take $W = UV^*$, $P = V\Sigma V^*$, and $S = U\Sigma U^*$. Note that $P = \sqrt{A^*A}$ and $S = WPW^* = \sqrt{AA^*}$.

8   Polar Decomposition in GA

In the following theorem, we present polar decomposition of an arbitrary multivector in geometric algebra $\mathcal{G}_{p,q}$. Note that the statement involves only operations in $\mathcal{G}_{p,q}$.

Theorem 8 (Left and right polar decomposition in GA). *For an arbitrary multivector* $M \in \mathcal{G}_{p,q}$, *there exist multivectors* $P, S \in \mathcal{G}_{p,q}$ *such that*

$$P^\dagger = P, \qquad S^\dagger = S, \qquad U^\dagger := \sum_A u_A(e_A)^{-1}, \tag{31}$$

$$P = B^\dagger B, \qquad S = C^\dagger C \qquad \textit{for some multivectors } B, C \in \mathcal{G}_{p,q}, \tag{32}$$

and multivector

$$W \in \mathrm{G}\mathcal{G}_{p,q} = \{U \in \mathcal{G}_{p,q} : U^\dagger U = e\}$$

such that

$$M = WP = SW.$$

Proof. The statement follows from the results of the previous sections of this paper. Namely, we use the matrix representation β' of $\mathcal{G}_{p,q}$ from Sect. 4, the relation (17) between matrix operations and Hermitian conjugation in geometric algebras, and the classical polar decomposition of matrices discussed in Sect. 7. $\square$

Note that

$$P = \sqrt{M^\dagger M}, \qquad S = WPW^\dagger = \sqrt{MM^\dagger}. \tag{33}$$

If we have the SVD of multivector $M = U\Sigma V^\dagger$ (26), then

$$W = UV^\dagger, \qquad P = V\Sigma V^\dagger, \qquad S = U\Sigma U^\dagger. \tag{34}$$

9   Conclusions

In this paper, we naturally implement SVD and polar decomposition in real Clifford geometric algebras without using the corresponding matrix representations. Note that we use matrix representations in the proofs, namely, we use the classical SVD and polar decomposition of real, complex, and quaternion matrices. The new Theorems 4 and 8 involve only operations in geometric algebras. The theorem on SVD in geometric algebras states that after left and right multiplication by elements of the group $\mathrm{G}\mathcal{G}_{p,q}$ (18), any multivector $M \in \mathcal{G}_{p,q}$ can be placed in d-dimensional subspace of $\mathcal{G}_{p,q}$, where d is equal to (14). The polar decomposition is a consequence of the SVD. We expect the use of these theorems in different applications of geometric algebra in computer science, engineering, physics, big data, machine learning, etc. This paper continues our previous research [1, 2, 14–19] on the extension of matrix methods to geometric algebras, presented at previous ENGAGE workshops within the CGI 2020–2022 conferences.

As noted by one of the reviewers, despite the statements of Theorems 4 and 8 involve only operations in a geometric algebra, their proofs use matrix representation; it could be interesting to investigate, in a future work, alternative and more direct proofs involving only operations in the corresponding geometric algebra. Also note that we do not present a method (algorithm) to find the SVD in this paper. We present an existing theorem. How to find elements Σ, U, and V in (26) using only the methods of geometric algebra and without using the corresponding matrix representations is a good task for further research. The problems of numerical accuracy and computation speed can also be considered.

Acknowledgements. This work is supported by the Russian Science Foundation (project 23-71-10028), https://rscf.ru/en/project/23-71-10028/.

The author is grateful to five anonymous reviewers for their careful reading of the paper and helpful comments on how to improve the presentation.

References

1. Abdulkhaev, K., Shirokov, D.: On explicit formulas for characteristic polynomial coefficients in geometric algebras. In: Magnenat-Thalmann, N., et al. (eds.) CGI 2021. LNCS, vol. 13002, pp. 670–681. Springer, Cham (2021). https://doi.org/10.1007/978-3-030-89029-2_50

2. Abdulkhaev, K., Shirokov, D.: Basis-free formulas for characteristic polynomial coefficients in geometric algebras. Adv. Appl. Clifford Algebras **32**, 57 (2022). https://doi.org/10.1007/s00006-022-01232-0

3. Beltrami, E.: Sulle funzioni bilineari. Giornale di Matematiche ad Uso degli Studenti Delle Universita **11**, 98–106 (1873)

4. Doran, C., Lasenby, A.: Geometric Algebra for Physicists. Cambridge University Press, Cambridge (2003)

5. Forsythe, G., Malcolm, M., Moler, C.: Computer Methods for Mathematical Computations. Prentice Hall, Upper Saddle River (1977)

6. Golub, G., Van Loan, C.: Matrix Computations. JHU Press, Baltimore (1989)

7. Jordan, C.: Memoire sur lesformes bilineaires, J. Math. Pures Appl., 2e serie. **19**, 35–54 (1874)

8. Jordan, C.: Sur la reduction desformes bilineaires. Comptes Rendus de l'Academie Sciences, Paris. **78** (1874)

9. Hestenes, D., Sobczyk, G.: Clifford Algebra to Geometric Calculus - A Unified Language for Mathematical Physics. Reidel Publishing Company, Dordrecht Holland (1984)

10. Lounesto, P.: Clifford Algebras and Spinors. Cambridge University Press, Cambridge (1997)

11. Marchuk, N., Shirokov, D.: Unitary spaces on Clifford algebras. Adv. Appl. Clifford Algebras **18**(2), 237–254 (2008). https://doi.org/10.1007/s00006-008-0066-y

12. Pei, S.-C., Chang, J.-H., Ding, J.-J.: Quaternion matrix singular value decomposition and its applications for color image processing. In: Proceedings 2003 International Conference on Image Processing (Cat. No.03CH37429), Barcelona, Spain, pp. I-805 (2003). https://doi.org/10.1109/ICIP.2003.1247084

13. Sangwine, S.J., Hitzer, E.: Polar decomposition of complexified quaternions and octonions. Adv. Appl. Clifford Algebras **30**, 23 (2020). https://doi.org/10.1007/s00006-020-1048-y

14. Shirokov, D.: Concepts of trace, determinant and inverse of Clifford algebra elements. In: Progress in Analysis. Proceedings of the 8th Congress of ISAAC, vol. 1, Peoples' Friendship University of Russia (ISBN 978-5-209-04582-3/hbk), 2012, pp. 187-194. arXiv:1108.5447 (2011)

15. Shirokov, D.: On computing the determinant, other characteristic polynomial coefficients, and inverse in Clifford algebras of arbitrary dimension. Comput. Appl. Math. **40**, 173 (2021). https://doi.org/10.1007/s40314-021-01536-0

16. Shirokov, D.: On basis-free solution to Sylvester equation in geometric algebra. In: Magnenat-Thalmann, N., et al. (eds.) CGI 2020. LNCS, vol. 12221, pp. 541–548. Springer, Cham (2020). https://doi.org/10.1007/978-3-030-61864-3_46

17. Shirokov, D.: Basis-free solution to Sylvester equation in Clifford algebra of arbitrary dimension. Adv. Appl. Clifford Algebras **31**, 70 (2021). https://doi.org/10.1007/s00006-021-01173-0

18. Shirokov, D.: On Noncommutative Vieta theorem in geometric algebras. In: Hitzer, E., Papagiannakis, G., Vasik, P. (eds.) ENGAGE 2022. LNCS, vol. 13862, pp. 28–37. Springer, Cham (2023). https://doi.org/10.1007/978-3-031-30923-6_3

19. Shirokov, D.: Noncommutative Vieta theorem in Clifford geometric algebras. Math. Methods Appl. Sci. 16 p (2023). https://doi.org/10.1002/mma.9221
20. Shirokov, D.: Clifford algebras and their applications to Lie groups and spinors. In: Mladenov, I., Yoshioka, A., Prima, A. (eds.) Proceedings of the Nineteenth International Conference on Geometry, Integrability and Quantization (Varna, Bulgaria, 2–7, June 2017), Sofia, Bulgaria, pp. 11–53 (2018). https://doi.org/10.7546/giq-19-2018-11-53
21. Shirokov, D.: Symplectic, orthogonal and linear Lie groups in Clifford algebra. Adv. Appl. Clifford Algebras **25**(3), 707–718 (2015). https://doi.org/10.1007/s00006-014-0520-y
22. Shirokov, D.: On some Lie groups containing spin group in Clifford algebra. J. Geom. Symmetry Phys. **42**, 73–94 (2016). https://doi.org/10.7546/jgsp-42-2016-73-94
23. Shirokov, D.: Classification of Lie algebras of specific type in complexified Clifford algebras. Linear Multilinear Algebra **66**(9), 1870–1887 (2018). https://doi.org/10.1080/03081087.2017.1376612
24. Zhang, F.: Quaternions and matrices of quaternions. Linear Algebra Appl. **251**, 21–57 (1997). https://doi.org/10.1016/0024-3795(95)00543-9

Author Index

B. Sheng et al. (Eds.): CGI 2023, LNCS 14498, pp. 403–404, 2024.
https://doi.org/10.1007/978-3-031-50078-7